FROM KARGIL TO THE COUP

EVENTS THAT SHOOK PAKISTAN

NASIM ZEHRA

SANG-E-MEEL PUBLICATIONS
25, SHAHRAH-E-PAKISTAN (LOWER MALL) LAHORE.

954.91 Zehra, Nasim
From Kargil to the Coup/ Nasim Zehra.-
Lahore: Sang-e-Meel Publications, 2018.
532pp. with Maps
1. History - Kargil - Pakistan. I. Title.

2018
Published by:
Afzaal Ahmad
Sang-e-Meel Publications,
Lahore.

ISBN-10: 969-35-3137-X
ISBN-13: 978-969-35-3137-4

Sang-e-Meel Publications
25 Shahrah-e-Pakistan (Lower Mall), Lahore-54000 PAKISTAN
Phones: 92-423-722-0100 / 92-423-722-8143 Fax: 92-423-724-5101
http://www.sangemeel.com e-mail: smp@sangemeel.com
PRINTED AT: HAJI HANIF & SONS PRINTERS, LAHORE.

DEDICATION

My Beloved Mother
(Late Begum Akhtar Akhlaque Hussain)
& my Beloved Motherland

CONTENTS

ACKNOWLEDGEMENTS

Book writing is seldom a solo effort; a book always flows from a web of support, interactions and relationships. Acknowledgments often sketch the web.

Here is the web from which From Kargil to the Coup, was produced.

My appreciation to all those civil and military officers, ministers and politicians in Pakistan, and also in India and in the US (listed in the book) who took time out and were willing to be interviewed.

At the core of this undertaking are the many courageous and conscientious officers of the Pakistan Army without whose cooperation the story of Operation Koh Paima could not have been reconstructed. It included, among others the former army Chief General Parvez Musharraf, Lt. General (retd) Nadeem Ahmad, Lt. General (retd) Gulzar Kiani, Lt. General (retd) Javed Hassan, Lt. General (retd) Amjad Shuaib, Brigadier (retd) Syed Azhar Raza, Brigadier (retd) Khalid Nazir. While some officers have been named many opted to remain anonymous. Some even reached out to me to tell the incredible story that they were part of.

Other central figures including Foreign Minister Sartaj Aziz, Foreign Secretary Shamshad Ahmad, Additional Foreign Secretary Tariq Fatemi, Secretary Defense retired general Iftikhar Ali Khan, Minister of Petroleum Chaudhry Nisar , Chief Minister Shahbaz Sharif, involved in formulating

Pakistan's policy response to Operation Koh Paima, generously shared their experience and understanding of critical events during May to October.

I am grateful to each and every one of them for their trust and confidence.

I am indebted to Professor Rifaat Hussain, Professor Ayesha Jalal, Professor Hassan Abbas and Riaz Mohammad Khan who were particularly generous with their time. At various occasions they acceded to my request and reviewed my work. Jalil Abbas Jillani and Akbar Zeb among others also patiently went through many chapters giving me candid and critical feedback. On occasions friends including Mushahid Hussain Sayed, Dr. Moeed Yusuf, Hamid Haroon, Kathy Gannon, Aga Imran Hameed, Dr. Maleeha Lodhi, Zahid Hussain and Sherry Rehman also took time out to review sections of my work. Dr. Shireen Mazari, throughout remained a dependable friend.

My group of close friends, Shazreh Hussain, Fatima Hameed and Humaira Sheikh helped along the way...they often prodded me to hurry and cross the finishing line!

And to my family: my deepest gratitude to all of them for they believed in me as their unstinted support throughout this long drawn out book writing process. My late mother's 'never give up and never grumble' philosophy helped as did my family's consistent interest in my work, to soldier on and complete what at times seemed to be an impossible task. When my attention was often captured by the more immediate, my siblings - sisters Anjum Zehra, Shamim Zehra, Sharaf Zehra , Qudssia Akhlaque, Asya Akhlaque , Ghazala Kazim and brother Khurshid Kazim- kept me on track by caringly nudging me to carry on, by insisting my effort was worthwhile. A warm thank you to my brothers-in-law, Sadiq Bhai, Jamshed, William , Mahmood, Humair and to my nieces Shahbano, Noor Zehras (senior and junior), Juggun, Sukaina, and nephews Zeeshan, Farhan, Jaffer, Mehdi, Wali, Hussain, Zain and Raza for their affection and encouragement through this journey. Manizeh, both friend and family too had many wise words to share through this long journey.

My late father Mianjan's tough work discipline and brother Abbas's intensely chaotic energy still stay afloat within the family zone…and I benefitted from that too.

In what was so often also a lonely and tedious effort, it was my Mustapha's delightful energy, first as a little boy and then as a teenager, that helped me bounce back.

For their guidance, in especially my down and confusing moments, special gratitude goes to Suhail Bhai, late Shah sahib and to Mian sahib.

Beyond primary sources my research was mainly dependent on newspaper and journals. Nasir Zaidi, the star researcher at the Institute of Regional Studies in Islamabad provided me the gold mine of Indian and Pakistani newspapers, critical to reconstructing the events from Kargil to the coup. Faheem Z. Khan also helped with this project. At the Harvard University libraries, many unnamed individuals also pulled out microfiche copies of newspaper reports and journal articles. Their 'giving' attitudes made my research task truly gratifying.

Without Adil Abbasi's support on the multiple demands I simultaneously worked on, this project would have been an arduous task.

Special appreciation also for Shehrbano Kazim, who remained steadfast in her support especially in the last few years of this undertaking.

A big thank you finally also to all those individuals in the various libraries and coffee shops in Pakistan and abroad, where I intermittently 'resided' over the years for very long hours to work on my manuscript. Whether it was the management and tea-providers at the library of the Institute of Strategic Studies or the program officer Jorge Espada and Holly Angell at the Harvard University's Asia Center, their friendly demeanors energized me to work untiringly in solitude.

There was then the proofing work of the outstanding professional Saman Ghani Khan without which this manuscript would not have arrived at the publishers! My gratitude also to the management and publishing team at Sang-e-Meel, without whose interest and effort this work would not have found its way to you.

Introduction

WHY KARGIL?

In recent years, across the Pakistan-India border and the Line of Control(LOC), guns have tended to converse more often than policy-makers. While the relationship between these two nuclear-armed states, Pakistan and India, influence the lives of almost one fifth of humanity, yet unfortunately hostility appears to be the only real durable factor in this inter-state relationship. This hostility rules out genuine cooperation while minimizing the possibility of resolving outstanding issues ranging from Siachen, Sir Creek, Kashmir, to water and trade disputes. Against the backdrop of this abiding antagonism South Asia remains the world's least economically integrated region. Regional trade in South Asia accounts for only 5% of overall trade. The people of South Asia are confronted with grave environmental threats including global warming, rising water levels leading to water and food scarcity, displacement of large populations, and a rise in infectious disease epidemics.

South Asia, the world's most potent nuclear flash point, is a region in desperate need of peace and security.

Yet why is Pakistan-India peace ellusive?

The 1999 Kargil battle, code-named Koh Paima (Operation KP), explains this well. Its events weave the story of repeated blunders, involving national and regional players that prevent genuine peace efforts from succeeding.

My work on Operation Koh Paima (Operation KP) began as a chapter in a book I started writing in 2002 on Pakistan-India relations during the period after the May 1998 nuclear tests. When the chapter on Kargil had crossed ninety typewritten pages, various friends who read it, insisted that the book should be exclusively on Operation KP.

Operation KP had suddenly surfaced in the news only weeks after the Nawaz-Vajpayee Lahore Summit, which had ended with the Lahore Declaration, in which both governments had decided to open discussions on the perennial and intractable Kashmir dispute. Initial news of heightened fighting along the LOC (Line of Control) had taken Pakistanis by surprise. It raised endless questions regarding the operation: Why was it conducted? Who gave the go-ahead for it? Who participated in it? What was its outcome? What should have been publicly known facts had turned into deep mysteries because the operation itself was a covert undertaking. For example: Who was actually fighting? Was Operation KP government approved? Was it across the LOC in Indian Occupied Kashmir (IOK) or in Azad Jammu and Kashmir (AJK)? Was the operation proving difficult and costly for Pakistan? Had it hurt India in any way? In retrospect, it became evident that there was a deep split over Operation KP between the civilian and military leaderships.

The end phase of Operation KP proved traumatic for Pakistan. The prime minister suddenly left in the early hours of 4 July 1999 for Washington DC where the Clinton-Sharif meeting produced the Pakistan-US statement calling for the 'withdrawal' of troops. At home the fierce—if subdued—contestation began in civil, military, and public circles as to whether Pakistan had 'gained' or 'lost' from the operation. In this highly toxic environment, despite efforts at keeping civil-military trust intact, the proverbial 'man on horseback' did ride in. Pakistan had twice before experienced *coups d'état*. This time, however, it happened with the military chief in the air and key operation planners leading the coup! My chapter had covered Kargil from various angles, including civil-military relations, decision-making processes, comparisons between Operation KP and the 1965 Operation Gibraltar, the triangular Pakistan-US-India relations during the Op, and the impact of the nuclear factor on this kind of limited operation.

In my original chapter on Operation KP, there was some new information on most of these issues. I had written on the operation in real time with access to key Pakistani decision-makers. Later, in 2002, I also met key Indian decision-makers. However, it was not until the end-phase of the operation that I had begun to grasp the facts about it. Until then, I had believed the official narrative that the Mujahideen were the ones doing the fighting in Kargil. After it ended, I occasionally wrote about the facts of the operation, but nothing comprehensive.

Significance of Op KP

However, given the broad canvas over which Operation KP was spread—ranging from Pakistan-India relations to civil-military relations and the decision-making process—I was convinced that a fuller account of the dynamics and implications of Operation KP was needed. The operation had not only brought down an elected government but had replaced it with the longest military regime in Pakistan's coup-studded political history. There had to be a comprehensive narration, one that would weave in critical dimensions of statecraft and policy-making while unraveling the mystery of a military adventure planned for the world's highest and toughest battle ground. Other themes that would emerge within the operation's narrative include civil-military relations, Pakistan-India relations, big power-small power dynamics, and the nuclear factor.

The facts of a controversial operation also needed to be revealed to a people who, in the past too, have had to pay heavily for serious policy blunders of Pakistan's policy-makers, including the ultimate price of the country's breakup.

In 2003, I began writing my book on Kargil. This was, at first, a part-time undertaking; family and professional obligations were preventing me from taking it up full time. I was able to take only a few months out every few years to exclusively focus on writing. As a fellow at the Harvard University Asia Center, I was able to work in an undisturbed space and access excellent research facilities. In 2006, I was asked to teach a course at the School of Advanced International Studies at Johns Hopkins University

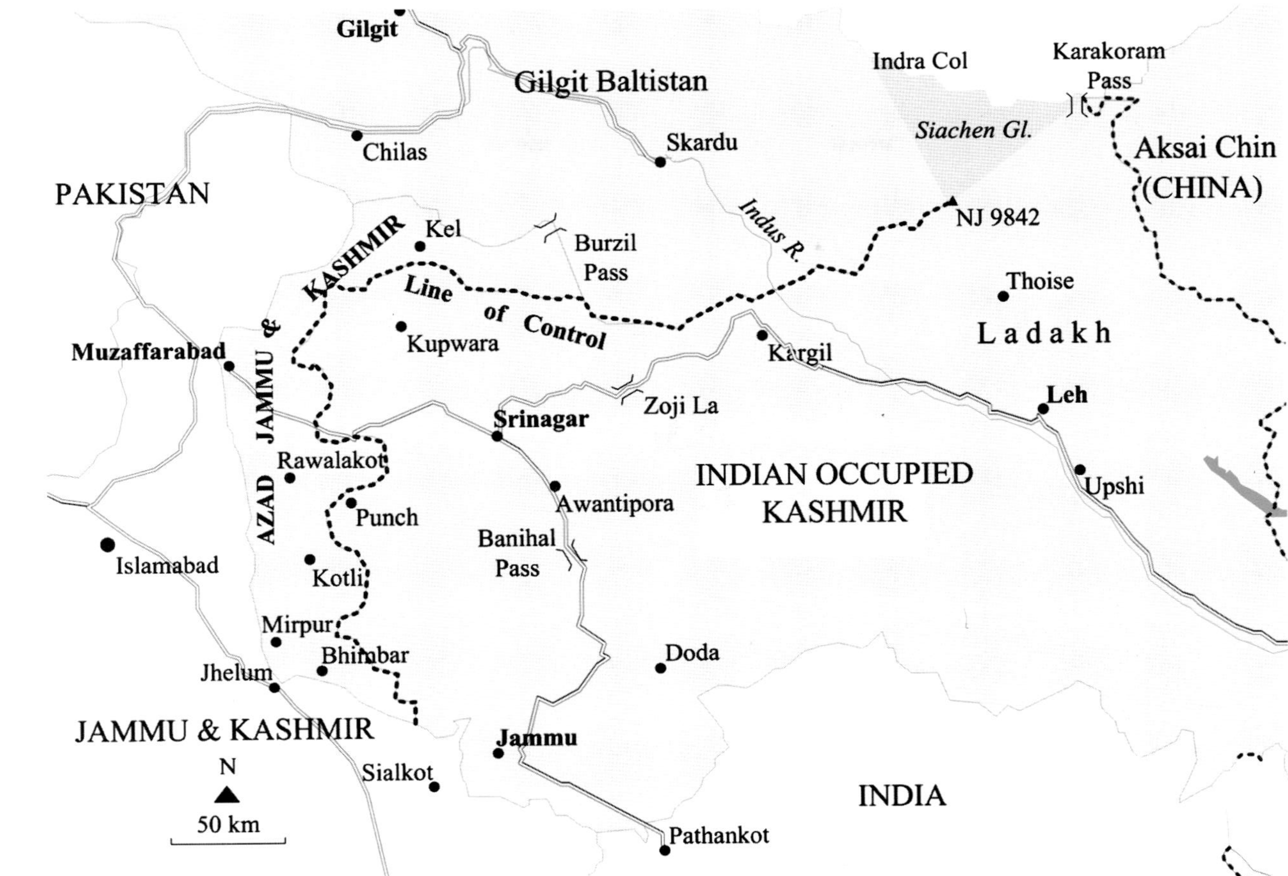

Map of Jammu & Kashmir

in Washington DC. All this meant time away from working on Operation KP.

Deviations and Information Collection

The silver lining to these detours and writing spread over many years was that new information kept trickling in, especially about Operation KP. Information about the military aspect of the operation was especially a boon since initially hardly any first-hand accounts from field fighters were available. The key planner of the operation, General Javed Hassan, had talked about it in two extensive sittings and so did a senior officer from the Directorate of Military Operations (DMO) during multiple meetings. Over the years, moreover, several key field commanders were willing to share critical, field-level information regarding the operational aspects and progress of the operation. There was also open debate between recently retired generals on the merits and demerits of Operation KP. For example, responding to General Pervez Musharraf's defense of Operation KP, the former Chief of General Staff (CGS), General Ali Kuli Khan, attacked the army chief for launching the operation. Similarly Lt. General Shahid Aziz, Musharraf's once blue-eyed boy, wrote extensively about it. Another book by a then serving officer, Colonel (retd) Ashfaq Hussain, *Witness to Blunder: Kargil Story Unfolds* (Idara Matbuat-e-Sulemani, 2008), also deviated from the dominant narrative. This book had a different perspective from that of Dr Shireen Mazari's book, *The Kargil Conflict, 1999: Separating Fact from Fiction* (Institute of Strategic Studies, 2003). Dr Mazari's book details specific Indian military and diplomatic actions arguing that 'Pakistan got sucked into an ever-widening conflict as a result of (these) pre-planned Indian actions'. All this published information and the facts collected first-hand from active field commanders were especially valuable, given the army's super-secrecy syndrome. The illustration of this was my failure to get a copy of the pre and post-op curriculum of strategy courses taught at the Command and Staff College, Quetta. I wanted them because former Chief of Army Staff General Pervez Ashfaq Kayani had said in an interview that as a result of the lessons from Operation KP, the strategy courses taught to military officers at the Command and Staff College were changed. Repeated requests at the highest level bore no fruit.

Beyond Pakistan's Binary Debate

Interestingly, much of Pakistan's political and security debate has veered towards the civilian versus military binary. Pakistan's political journey, with military rule spanning more than half its history, lends itself to such an approach. In the mainstream debate, this promotes a flawed reading of decision-making, policies, and policy impacts. States and societies with a flawed understanding of policy matters can rarely become effective advocates for policy change. Acquiring consensus on Pakistan's India policy has been especially difficult, as official and public debate has tended to follow the civil-military binary path. Acquiring consensus from a deeply divided narrative is often challenging, if not impossible. For example, on wars, the critical landmarks in Pakistan-India relations, the narratives have been influenced by this civil-military binary approach and are deeply divided on who started which war, which political and diplomatic environment were the wars initiated in, what was achieved or lost, etc. In some cases, distance in time has allowed a review of the original text on the wars. For example, the 1948 and 1965 wars now have a revisionist historiography written even by military generals. But this has not been the case with Operation KP, the most recent—albeit limited—Pakistan-India military encounter. As of now, very little comprehensive work on Kargil has been produced. The common narrations either eulogize the army while critiquing the civilians or extol the civilians while critiquing the army. The Paucity of information from both civilian and military perspectives has also fed this situation.

The Historical Context of Operation KP

The significance of Operation KP also flows from what triggered it: the Kashmir issue, around which a never-ending confrontation simmers between the two South Asian neighbors.

In June 1947, the Muslim League leader Mohammad Ali Jinnah had concluded that the 527 princely states, including Jammu and Kashmir, could remain independent while his Congress counterpart, Jawaharlal Nehru, had insisted that they could not be 'allowed to claim independence'.[1] Jinnah had anticipated a far less complex challenge at

Independence. Closer to Partition, mindful perhaps only of the sentiment in the State including the anti-maharaja developments in Poonch, Jinnah predicted that 'Kashmir will fall into our lap like a ripe fruit'.[2] Nevertheless, Jinnah had not registered Nehru's political machinations over Kashmir. India's historian-lawyer, A. G. Noorani, writes in his seminal essay *Bilateral Negotiations on Kashmir: Unlearnt Lesson*,[3] 'Nehru and Vallabhai Patel, the deputy prime minister and the one appointed by Nehru to formulate the strategy to deal with the princely states, were fast sewing up arrangements for Kashmir's accession to India even before Sheikh Abdullah's release from prison on 29 September 1947 and well before the tribesmen from Pakistan entered Kashmir on 21 October.' Elaborating this point, Noorani writes that earlier, on 28 May 1947, Patel had said, 'Kashmir remains within the Indian Union even if a division of India and partition of Punjab takes place.'[4] Subsequently, on 3 July 1947, he wrote to the Jammu and Kashmir Prime Minister, Ram Chandra Kak, 'I realize the peculiar difficulties of Kashmir, but looking to its history and traditions it has, in my opinion, no other choice but to accede to India.'[5]

Nehru, too, was single-minded on accession of Kashmir to India. Even to his friend and India's High Commissioner to Pakistan, Sri Prakash, Nehru had admitted on 25 December 1947, 'The fact is that Kashmir is of the most vital significance to India as well as to Pakistan. There lies the rub.' He added: 'Kashmir is going to be a drain on our resources but it is going to be a greater drain on Pakistan. In a military sense, we are stronger.'[6] Equally, Nehru's 21 November 1947 exchange with Sheikh Abdullah lays bare the Indian prime minister's true thinking on the accession issue: 'Referendum and plebiscite are ill-advised but must only tactically be supported to avoid world criticism; that referendum is merely an academic issue and that after all for the Kashmiris, likely to be defeated in their "little war" against the State and the Indian forces, it would be absurd to want a referendum.'[7]

As early as 1951, Nehru was slipping away from the plebiscite option and from international mediation and calling for merely negotiating adjustments to the ceasefire line. At the 9 January 1951 informal Commonwealth Prime Ministers' Conference plebiscite, Nehru argued, was tantamount to 'upsetting of the somewhat unstable equilibrium'.[8] The

July 1952 Delhi Agreement did not help Nehru with the integration of Kashmir into the Union. In August 1953, by removing and arresting Sheikh Abdullah for not taking rapid enough steps to integrate the state into the Indian Union, Nehru's olive branch of the plebiscite was gone. Abdullah, his pro-India 'winning card', charge-sheeted Nehru for interference by Delhi in the state's internal affairs and for not viewing the Instrument of Accession as a temporary arrangement before a permanent solution through plebiscite could be found.[9]

Throughout the 1950s, India fudged on its own promise of plebiscite in Kashmir while also refusing Pakistan's offer for a settlement on Kashmir. The maximum that Nehru offered Pakistan was to convert the ceasefire line with 'minor modifications'.[10] Significantly, while taking unconstitutional and unpopular steps in Jammu and Kashmir to fully integrate the disputed State into the Indian Union, to deflect international attention from his actions, Nehru amplified his criticism of Pakistan's entry into the Western security bloc. Simultaneously, Nehru also engaged with Pakistan in bad faith. After his July 1953 Karachi meeting with the newly appointed Prime Minister Mohammad Ali Bogra, whom Governor General Ghulam Mohammad had hurriedly recalled from Washington after dismissing Prime Minister Khawaja Nizamuddin, a joint communiqué was issued stating that 'the Kashmir dispute … was examined in all its various aspects'. Two days later Nehru recalled the Pakistanis' 'plaintive and almost pathetic' appeals on Kashmir but nevertheless refusing to accept the Nehru-proposed status quo solution. Nehru began banking on Pakistan as the safety valve, the pressure-releaser. The quid pro quo was an empty promise of a plebiscite. Soon, after the valley erupted in flames against Abdullah's arrest, the Nehru-Bogra Summit issued an agreement to hold a plebiscite. To his Kashmiri collaborators, the 'stunned' president and the newly appointed Kashmir Prime Minister Bakhshi Ghulam Mohammad, Nehru explained that 'a lessening of tension between India and Pakistan will inevitably lessen tension internally in Kashmir and give you that chance of working which you must have.'[11]

With Nehru's velvet gloves off and his full-throttle effort to integrate the disputed territory into the Indian Union, he used engagement with Pakistan as a dampener for the angry and agitated Kashmiris in IOK and to ward off UN concern and involvement in the Kashmir dispute. Confiding in Bakshi, Nehru acknowledged, 'Recent events in Kashmir have had a very powerful reaction in other countries. This is against us completely. I am not referring to Pakistan, which has grown madly hysterical. If this hysteria continues, it would inevitably produce reactions in Kashmir among the pro-Pakistani elements and their sympathizers. The result would be no period of quiet at all and constant trouble.' The advantage of engaging with Pakistan, Nehru explained thus: 'But for some kind of an agreement between us and Pakistan, the matter would inevitably have been raised in the UN immediately and they might well have sent down their representative to Kashmir. All this, again, would have kept the agitation alive and made it grow. In the circumstances, this is a good statement and helps us in trying to get a quieter atmosphere.'[12]

Clearly, of the many challenges that came with the partition of India—that in capacity, manpower, and experience two vastly unequal parties, the Indian National Congress (INC) and the All India Muslim League (AML), had to face—Kashmir was a critical one. While the Congress was well equipped in capacity and experience, the Muslim League, with paucity of experienced personnel, was largely a Jinnah-dependent party. Hence, despite the strong resistance by the majority in Jammu and Kashmir to accession to India, Pakistan was not in a position to outplay Nehru and Patel. Militarily, too, they had calculated that Indian forces could not be defeated by the Kashmiris and Pakistani forces.

Fast forward seventy years, with two wars and many crises in between, one may ask: Was Operation KP in a position to outmaneuver the Indians? It is against this yardstick, amongst others, that this book assesses the operation. If at Partition Jinnah misread India's intentions, how much better is Pakistan doing seventy years later, both in comprehending and responding to the challenge of India?

Structure of the Book

The chapters of this book have endeavored to document a non-binary, comprehensive account of Operation KP, from its planning, through the implementation, and finally, to its impact.

Operation KP can be divided broadly into the following six, somewhat overlapping phases:

First, the euphoria phase in which the Kargil clique, with ominously a euphoric mindset, planned Operation KP in complete secrecy. This euphoria of the Kargil clique emanated from several factors. First and foremost was the belief that Pakistan's nuclear leverage has driven a full-scale confrontation out of the realm of possibilities. This thought, combined with the fantasy of blocking NH-1, India's lifeline to its troops in Leh, was expected to result in the Indian armed forces' withdrawal from the disputed territory of Siachen which Delhi had occupied in 1984. The secondary factors were that with their buddy, General Musharraf, as Chief of Army Staff (COAS), they could plan a surreptitious operation across the LOC—the belief was that the Indians would never fight back based on these 'supposedly irrefutable facts'. It was concluded that the military and diplomatic success of Operation KP was guaranteed.

Second, the excitement phase, when its planners and its participants (soldiers) initiated the operation with no resistance from the adversary. The war theatre was almost empty and the only 'adversary' the Northern Light Infantry (NLI) troops encountered was the inhospitable terrain and harsh weather. Yet, as they trudged ahead with great physical difficulty, they found these uncontested vacant spaces very alluring. In fact, Pakistan's courageous men on a dare-devil mission interpreted this winter drawdown of Indian troops as a virtual walk-over opportunity. Weak aerial surveillance of the Kargil-Drass area was an added advantage. Back at the General Headquarters (GHQ) meetings, the Kargil clique, led by the operational commander Javed Hassan, boasted of complete success.

Third, the expansion phase, in which due to the absence of Indian resistance in the war theatre, the Commanding Officers (COs) and their troops went beyond the original lines drawn for setting up of posts. In fact, for the first eight months on the move, Pakistani troops did not encounter a single Indian soldier despite the audacious setting up of 116 posts.

Fourth, the encounter phase, which began in early May with limited and indirect hostilities between Pakistani-Indian troops. These initial encounters had left both sides confused. Kargil planners were unclear about the type and scale of the Indian military response to be expected.

Meanwhile, within Pakistan the secret of Operation KP, hitherto the secret of the clique of five generals, was now revealed to the wider military command and also to Pakistan's Prime Minister Nawaz Sharif and to his cabinet. In India, the military command was divided about the scale and intent of the Pakistani presence and also did not consider it significant enough to inform Delhi about it. By early June, however, the Pakistan-India encounter had snowballed into a battle in the mountains. Operation KP, planned as a smooth, unhindered military operation in IOK, had turned into a Pakistan-India mountain battle of attrition. The die had been cast. Op Kargil had turned into the Battle of Kargil.

Once there was clarity in Delhi on the scale and depth of Pakistani intrusion in the Indian border, the Vajpayee government decided to hit back with overwhelming military and diplomatic might and political resolve. Combined with aggressive military retaliation, including heavy artillery and aerial attacks, Delhi stonewalled every Pakistani effort to extract some strategic advantage from Operation KP. By early-June, though still holding on to the heights, Pakistani troops had come under tremendous physical and psychological pressure from both the Indian military offensive and from mostly disrupted supply routes. These iconic combatants——on hostile peaks in vicious weather with depleting supplies, deafening sorties, and unending mortar fire—were lodged in imperilled zones, but with no victory formula. As stories from the war theatre trickled into the hallowed halls occupied by Kargil planners, concern, confusion, and even some bravado was their response. Their euphoria and excitement was no more. The spectrum of India-Pakistan encounters had extended to the diplomatic and political level. Delhi overuled every Pakistani effort for a bilateral political dialogue. On 12 June, the Indian foreign minister had categorically told his Pakistani counterpart, Sartaj Aziz, that India was willing to sit at the negotiations table only after Pakistani troop withdrawal to pre-Op KP positions. The message for the prime ministers from Beijing and Washington was no different. The reality slowly settled in that Operation KP could accrue no gains to Islamabad.

Fifth, the exit phase, began around mid-June. By then, it had become clear to the prime minister and to his key advisors that, with the depleting supplies of Pakistani troops, mounting Indian attacks, and a unified global demand that Pakistan immediately and unconditionally withdraw its troops from Kargil, Islamabad had to make some hard decisions. Pakistan's valiant soldiers continued to be under a determined and deadly Indian attack, ruling out all chances of any further operational success. At the 12 June meeting in Lahore, attended by all the Defense Committee of the Cabinet (DCC) members, the PM asked his FM to explore ways towards an honorable exit. These included engaging the Chinese and even working on a back-channel settlement attempt with Delhi. Finally, the PM opted to fly to Washington seeking withdrawal under a futile and controversial US cover.

Sixth, the effect-phase, began once the 4 July Washington statement formally announced Pakistan's exit from Kargil. The effect of the withdrawal statement in a battleground littered with peaks, ravines, and waterways was complex and staggered. Skirmishes between Pakistani-Indian troops continued beyond 4 July and withdrawing Pakistani troops under Indian attacks suffered heavy casualties. Within Pakistan's power structure, throughout its duration, Operation KP infused deep distrust, resentment, and latent antagonism between the elected leadership and the Kargil clique, thereby shaking the foundations of the Sharif government. On the political front, the opposition used Operation KP to further bulldoze the Sharif government. Given Pakistan's asymmetrical power structure with the army chief's coup-making proclivities, it was no surprise that the blundering Kargil clique[13] staged a coup against the elected prime minister.

The penultimate chapter is an analysis of Op KP against the backdrop of the prevailing national, regional and international environment plus against the long-established classical military principles. The chapter also proposes some answers to the questions that have persisted since the operation.

Chapter 1

THE ROOTS OF CONFRONTATION

Pakistan's 1999 Kargil Operation, code-named Operation Koh Paima, conformed perfectly to the post-1947 pattern of Pakistani and Indian military activities in the disputed state of Jammu and Kashmir. The mountainous region on both sides of the Line of Control had become an active zone of conflict ever since the first 1948 Pakistan-India war over the territory of Kashmir.

The Instrument of Accession and UN Involvement

Within days of establishment of the state of Pakistan in 1947, the government organized the tribals to force accession of Jammu and Kashmir to Pakistan. Lord Mountbatten, the man responsible for the division of the subcontinent, had made last-minute changes to the original division, laying the foundations for antagonism between two newly created states. In 1948, Pakistan's regular forces went to war against India to undo the 'wrong' of the annexation of the State of Jammu and Kashmir to India. Without reference to the will of the state's predominantly Muslim population, the ruler of Kashmir, Maharaja Hari Singh, unilaterally signed the Instrument of Accession on 26 October 1947 acceding Jammu and Kashmir to the Dominion of India. He justified the move by citing "a grave emergency"[1] that had arisen in his state and acknowledging that the Indian Dominion "cannot send the help asked for" without his state acceding to India.[2]

Kashmiri agitation over the accession, given the history of the maharaja's rule[3], the history of Kashmiri resistance[4] and Delhi's misrule of the state, was inevitable, as was Pakistan's taking advantage of it. Subsequent developments reinforced the disputed status of the state. These included the Indian Governor-General's acceptance of accession on the condition that "as soon as law and order have been restored in Kashmir and its soil cleared of the invader, the question of the state's accession should be settled by a reference to the people,"[5] a joint submission by India and Pakistan on 27 January 1948, of a *draft* proposal to the president of the United Nations Security Council (UNSC) on the appropriate methods of solving the Kashmir dispute,[6] UNSC resolution 47[7], and the August 13, 1948 resolution passed by the United Nations Commission on India and Pakistan (UNCIP)[8].

Two developments around the signing of the Instrument of Accession made it controversial. The first, Lord Mountbatten's letter to the maharaja asserted that the final status had to be settled with reference to the wishes of the Kashmiri people. Subsequently, the Indian government accepted a UN-executed plebiscite as the means to finally determining the status of the Jammu and Kashmir State. Whatever qualifications the India obtaining accession of Kashmir an government subsequently added to its initial acceptance of a UN- held plebiscite, through its initial acceptance it had nullified the very Instrument of Accession it claimed to be the basis of Jammu and Kashmir being a part of the Indian Union.

Secondly, for Pakistan and the pro-Pakistani Kashmiris the validity of the accession instrument, even without Mountbatten's qualification, stood questioned. For them, India had violated the partition plan of British Indian territories, which had made provision for the accession of over 570 of the princely states to either India or Pakistan. While the rulers could themselves decide which country to join, it was envisaged that the religious composition of their populations and their geographical situation would be taken into account in each circumstance.

When the Muslim ruler of the overwhelmingly Hindu Junagadh acceded to Pakistan, the Indian forces invaded the state in September 1947.

The ruler fled. Similarly, in September 1948, Indian troops invaded the State of Hyderabad, although its Muslim ruler the Nizam, had opted for virtual independence.[9] India resorted to the use of force to resolve these two cases. Pakistan also used force, in collaboration with the local Kashmiris, to resolve the Kashmir case by invoking the same principle of majority population to decide accession.

Pakistan's political case in Kashmir was strong. Its 'intervention' and support to the Kashmiris was as much against international law[10] as India's intervention in Hyderabad and Junagadh. Pakistan had already disputed the Boundary Commission's demarcation of the border between India and Pakistan. By granting Gurdaspur, a Muslim majority district in Punjab, to India, Pakistan believed the Boundary Commission had provided India its only road link to Jammu. Pakistanis saw the handing over of Kashmir to India as something pre-planned by Mountbatten.

For Pakistan, the broader question linked to its birth was the unfair attitude of the Indian State, detailed in a 15 January 1948 letter from Pakistani Foreign Minister Sir Zafarullah Khan.[11] Zafarullah Khan complained of India's attempt to paralyze Pakistan; of the genocide of Indian Muslims; of the forcible occupation by India of Junagadh and the adjoining states which had acceded to Pakistan; and of India's refusal that had led to the withholding of Pakistan's apportioned share of the cash balances and military stores vital to its existence. India was accused of obtaining accession of Kashmir by fraud and violence involving large-scale massacre and looting of Kashmiris by the armed forces and other subjects of the maharaja and government of India. Furthermore, Pakistan complained of repeated raids and incursions into its territory by Indian troops and bombings by the Indian Air Force. Finally India was charged with openly threatening Pakistan with direct military attack. Zafarullah's letter had broadened the parameters of complaint much beyond Kashmir. The UNSC factored in Pakistan's complaint in its 20 January 1948 Resolution 39 and mandated the Commisison it set up with a dual responsibility: Kashmir first, but also other matters raised by Pakistan.[12] Following this resolution the item on the agenda on the security council was changed from the "Jammu and Kashmir question" to the "India-Pakistan question."

But in the six months it took the UNCIP to arrive in Kashmir, relations between India and Pakistan had become further strained.

India, sought UN intervention with the only objective of rolling back the ground level military advantages in Jammu and Kashmir accrued to the Kashmiris and Pakistanis. By contrast a fledgling Pakistan sought UN intervention against much stronger India on issues raised in Zafarullah's January 1948 letter.[13] India clearly rejected, as testified by UN records, any UN role in the 'broader' India-Pakistan question. Yet ironically, India itself had unwittingly led Pakistan to the UN, the only forum through which Pakistan could have sought relief from India. After having acquired UN help to contain the fallout of the initial Kashmiri uprising and the Pakistani paramilitary incursion into Jammu and Kashmir, Delhi refused to cooperate with the UN or agree to its suggestions.

Although UN early involvement in the Kashmir dispute could not prevent continuing controversy and confrontation around the status of Kashmir it did prevent a 'complete win' over Kashmir to either India or Pakistan. Both had staked claims to the entire state of Jammu and Kashmir.

The July 1949 Karachi Agreement, brokered by the UN, led to the acceptance of a ceasefire line across the Jammu and Kashmir state which operationally, though not legally, divided its control between the states of Pakistan and India.

The ceasefire line, however, led to more instability and insecurity. There were three problems. One, no prominent and permanent demarcation line was drawn barring the fixing of poles in some areas. Two, in the areas that the poles were fixed, it was done leaving wide gaps in between. Finally, a major gap was left by not drawing the line along the glacier areas. The assumption was that the highest, snow-clad rocky region in the world would be of 'no interest' to either Pakistan or India. Also given that the ceasefire by international law was a temporary divide, neither side considered setting up permanent division structures.

Gradually as India revised its position towards the UN, the UNCIP was unable to ensure that India follows its suggestion. In fact, in a strong indictment of the working of the UNCIP, the US Chargé d'Affaires in Pakistan Charles Lewis Jr. wrote to the US secretary of state, "It is well to bear in mind that the government of India also did not, contrary to the representatives of India and, by implication of the commission, accept the commission's resolution as a whole and without reservations."[14]

Lewis elaborated on the conditionality set by Nehru in his 20 August letter, in response to the commission's resolution of 13 August 1948 illustrating his assertion that "it is perhaps desirable that certain features of the situation be carefully analyzed with a view to determining whether that onus has in fact been well placed." After identifying the list of Nehru's reservations, Lewis reported to his secretary, "This is totally out of line with the United Nations Security Council Resolution of 21 April 1948."[15]

Lewis wrote, "Whatever may have been the intentions of the Commission the onus of rejecting its Resolution has been placed on Pakistan while India is permitted to pass before world opinion as in effect an aggrieved and injured party, which has accepted without reservation the commission's resolution." Seemingly in agreement with Pakistan, he quoted an 24 April 1948 *Dawn* editorial stating, "To persuade Pakistan to surrender to the will of India to whom the Commission most inadvisedly and against specific terms of the Security Council Resolution of 21 April, itself surrendered."

"I know that most, if not all, of the members of the Commission believe that Kashmir, or most of it, should logically fall to Pakistan, but I also know that they are extremely annoyed with Pakistan for not having bowed to their judgment in the matter of the approach to the settlement of the problem and thereby having made the Commission's efforts to achieve a settlement infructuous." Lewis maintained that there were practical reasons why Pakistan "could not bow to the Commission's judgment." His final conclusion, however, was, "Had the Commission bowed less to India's intransigence on the plebiscite issue those practical reasons would largely have disappeared and with them the questions of principle which troubled Pakistan."[16]

Lewis saw in the UNCIP's handling of the Kashmir issue a larger and more ominous danger; the threat to Pakistan's very existence. While he heartily praised Pakistan for its response stating that "when the tide of the Commission's opinion has steadily and obviously been running against

Pakistan the Government of this country and the press have borne, and still bear, themselves with dignity and without any signs of malice," Lewis also raised the issue of the country's cognizance that there was a broader threat. "It had not escaped them that the question has recently become a matter of far more importance than the mere question of the settlement of the Kashmir dispute, for if world opinion is to gain the impression that Pakistan has been the guilty and obstructive party that impression would inevitably and perhaps disastrously , affect the very existence of Pakistan should India avail itself of the presence of Pakistan troops in Kashmir, or avail itself of any other excuse, for waging war on this country. India's press has always been far more effective then has the press of Pakistan. In the final analysis, therefore should India have aspirations in the direction indicated, Pakistan would be functioning not alone at tremendous odds in terms of military potential but also in terms of world opinion."[17]

Soon the principle behind the Kashmir question got subsumed in the more compelling issues of *realpolitik*, Indian power, Cold War considerations, deteriorating Pakistan-India bilateral relations, and war prevention. The question of Kashmir stayed with the UN but India was determined to prevent, under any circumstances, the holding of the UN mandated plebiscite. Equally, India through its continuous and active non-cooperation of UN's Kashmir-related initiative, especially the United Nations Military Observer's Group on India and Pakistan (UNGOMIP), rendered it ineffective. UNGOMIP was designed to prevent military escalation and ease tensions.

In subsequent years the Cold War influenced the response of the UN and other major powers to Kashmir and to the larger Pakistan-India question. Most post-1949 and pre-1997 bilateral engagements over Jammu and Kashmir, often aided by outside powers including the United States and the Soviet Union, resulted from primarily 'crisis-containment' efforts.

By the mid-fifties the question of Jammu and Kashmir's future became caught up in the dynamics of the Cold War. For example, Pakistan's decision to enter into an alliance with the United States in 1953 was used by India as a pretext to renounce the pledge of plebiscite, refusing to explain how Pakistan's relations with another country could prejudice the Kashmiri right of self-determination or absolve India of its international obligations. The Soviet Union followed India. Furious at Pakistan's decision to join US-sponsored alliances, it discarded its neutral stance in Pakistan-India disputes and threw its powerful weight behind India. To spite Pakistan, Nikolai Bulganin and Nikita Khrushchev, during their visit to India in December 1955, referred to Kashmir as "one of the states of India".

Similarly, it was the Sino-Indian border war in 1962 galvanized American and British diplomacy. Seeking to push Pakistan and India into a joint front against China, Washington and London sent Assistant Secretary of State Averell Harriman and Commonwealth Secretary Duncan Sandys to explain to Nehru the need for negotiations to resolve the Kashmir dispute. Harriman told Nehru that unless tensions over Kashmir eased the US could not continue to provide military assistance. Nehru agreed to join Ayub in a statement on 29 November 1962 for "a renewed effort to resolve the outstanding differences . . . on Kashmir and other related matters."

With hopes raised, Pakistan entered into bilateral talks with India. The Pakistan side, led by its Foreign Minister Zulfiqar Ali Bhutto, suggested that the two sides build on the existing foundation of the security council resolutions and reports of the UN mediators. The Indian side, headed by Foreign Minister Swaran Singh, proposed a "political settlement" meaning division of the state. The Pakistan side probed the idea linking it to ascertainment of the wishes of the people of Kashmir. But India opposed any idea of a reference to the people of Kashmir. No progress was achieved. American and British envoys tried to persuade Pakistan and India to agree to a compromise but neither country was prepared to expend influence to promote a just settlement. As the danger of a further flare up on the border with China receded, India had no incentive for a settlement with Pakistan.

Later in 1965 the Soviet Union intervened to facilitate the signing of the Tashkent Agreement. The primary aim of this agreement was to bring to close the Pakistan-India war.

However the 1972 Pakistan-India engagement was the only one in which the question of Kashmir's political future was recognized as an unresolved issue. Although the Simla Agreement followed the 1971 tragic breakup of Pakistan held on to its UN-mandated position on Kashmir.[18] The clause VI-ii of the agreement acknowledged that (ii) In Jammu and Kashmir, the Line Of Control resulting from the ceasefire of December 17, 1971, shall be respected by both sides without prejudice to the recognized position of either side.

For about two decades after the breakup of Pakistan, the Kashmir question remained a relatively muted issue between Pakistan and India. After the Simla summit, of the forty-four meetings held between the two countries during 1972-94, Kashmir dispute was touched upon merely three times.[19] India consistently maintained that since Kashmir was an integral part of India, the only Kashmir-related bilateral issue was Pakistan's instigation of the Kashmiri insurgency through material and political support.

Pakistan and India were therefore unable to break the pattern of military engagement over Kashmir. Deadlocked dialogue over Kashmir continued to yield space for armed conflict.

Use of Force

The unsettled question of Jammu and Kashmir's future with virtually no political routes available for a credible process had injected the use of force, as if , in the very DNA of the relationship of the two adversarial neighbors.

India for several reasons found itself in a more comfortable position. She occupied the bulk of the most valuable part of the territory Jammu and Kashmir and given that possession is nine-tenths of the law the international community exerted virtually no pressure on India to address issue of Jammu and Kashmir's future. Hence for India, the ownership was easy to maintain while for the Kashmiris and for Pakistan ownership was difficult, if not impossible, to enforce.

Battles in the disputed territory peaked during the wars of 1948, 1965 and 1971. While these were well known, less publicized were cross-Line of Control (LOC) military operations by the two armies. Both sought control of strategically advantageous heights in the rugged terrain of the disputed territory along the LOC. Intense border firing became a regular feature, with occasional interludes of the short-lived, unilateral or bilateral, declaratory ceasefire agreements.[20]

India had subverted established 'rules of the game' regarding the accession of the states of Hyderabad, Junagadh, and Jammu and Kashmir. Pakistan first and India subsequently opted to use force as a means to settle disputes. Pakistan's political and military leadership, which remained firmly committed to Kashmiris' right to accede to Pakistan. But they also feared that its 1947 and 1948 gains on Kashmir were vulnerable to India's control of the major part of Jammu and Kashmir state.

These developments rapidly set the terms of engagement between the two asymmetrically constituted neighbors: the territorially larger, militarily stronger emerging hegemon[21] and the fragile, resource-weak, new-born state. Hence it was not the circumstances of Pakistan's birth, as some scholars have argued,[22] that locked the newly independent Indian state and the new-born Pakistani state in a confrontational mode, but rather it was the unresolved issue of Jammu and Kashmir.

From 1965 onwards, as the two countries went to war, both used force to alter the status of the LOC. India succeeded during the 1965 and 1971 wars, occupying peaks around Kargil.[23] Despite the Tashkent and Simla Agreements, in 1971 India managed to retain some of the strategic peaks it captured around Kargil. Subsequently, India crossed the LOC about two to three kilometers into Pakistan territory.

In addition to Kargil, elsewhere too along the LOC India ensured that it held militarily advantageous heights. The "initial unequal distribution of high ground"[24] and subsequent Indian occupation of heights across the LOC enabled India to maintain control of these peaks.

Twenty years into Pakistan's creation, cracks began appearing in the consensus among Pakistan's civil and military elite on how to undo, what even the UNSC resolutions also affirmed, was an unlawful Jammu and Kashmir accession to India. In 1947-48 there was a cross-ideological civil-military consensus on combining force with diplomacy to settle the Jammu and Kashmir issue. Covert and overt forces worked in 1947 and 1948 when invasion by Pakistani troops helped roll-back Indian troops from a sector of Jammu and Kashmir territory.

Pakistan's 1965 Kashmir initiative, codenamed Operation Gibraltar, was planned in secret by a handful of military men encouraged by Foreign Minister Zulfikar Ali Bhutto. The Operation failed to enable Pakistan to take control of Jammu and Kashmir, sparking off the wider 1965 war with India, which ended in the USSR-brokered controversial Tashkent Agreement.

In 1971, after effectively exploiting the alienation and anger of East Pakistanis, India began a war in the eastern wing. Fighting the Indian Army and Indian-trained Pakistani civilians, the Pakistani Army decided to open a western front, resulting in India taking control of the strategic territory of Kargil, located on the Pakistani side of the LOC.

Following the defeat and surrender of the 1971 war, the consensus within Pakistan's ruling elite and the civil-military institutions on how to deal with India, ended. This monumental debacle, combined with India's growing influence on the world stage and changing Cold War alignments, presented a challenging environment for Pakistani policymakers in a country with a string of martial law, ruled interchangeably by elected civilians and uniformed coup-makers.

Post 1971

Pakistani insecurity that flowed from the asymmetrical positioning of the two neighbors was further reinforced after the Indian intervention in 1971 that facilitated the breakup of Pakistan.[25] For India, the 1971 victory against Pakistan was a watershed. Now it could seek a settlement of the Kashmir issue on its own terms. Delhi proposed as a final settlement, the conversion of the existing LOC into a permanent border. When Delhi was unable to obtain its preferred final settlement through the Simla Agreement, Indian Prime Minister Indira Gandhi announced on the floor of the Indian parliament that Delhi would pursue a policy of linkage on release of Pakistan's 90,000 prisoners of war and the final settlement of the Kashmir issue. Islamabad responded by requesting China to link its vote for the newly independent Bangladesh's entry into the UN with release of

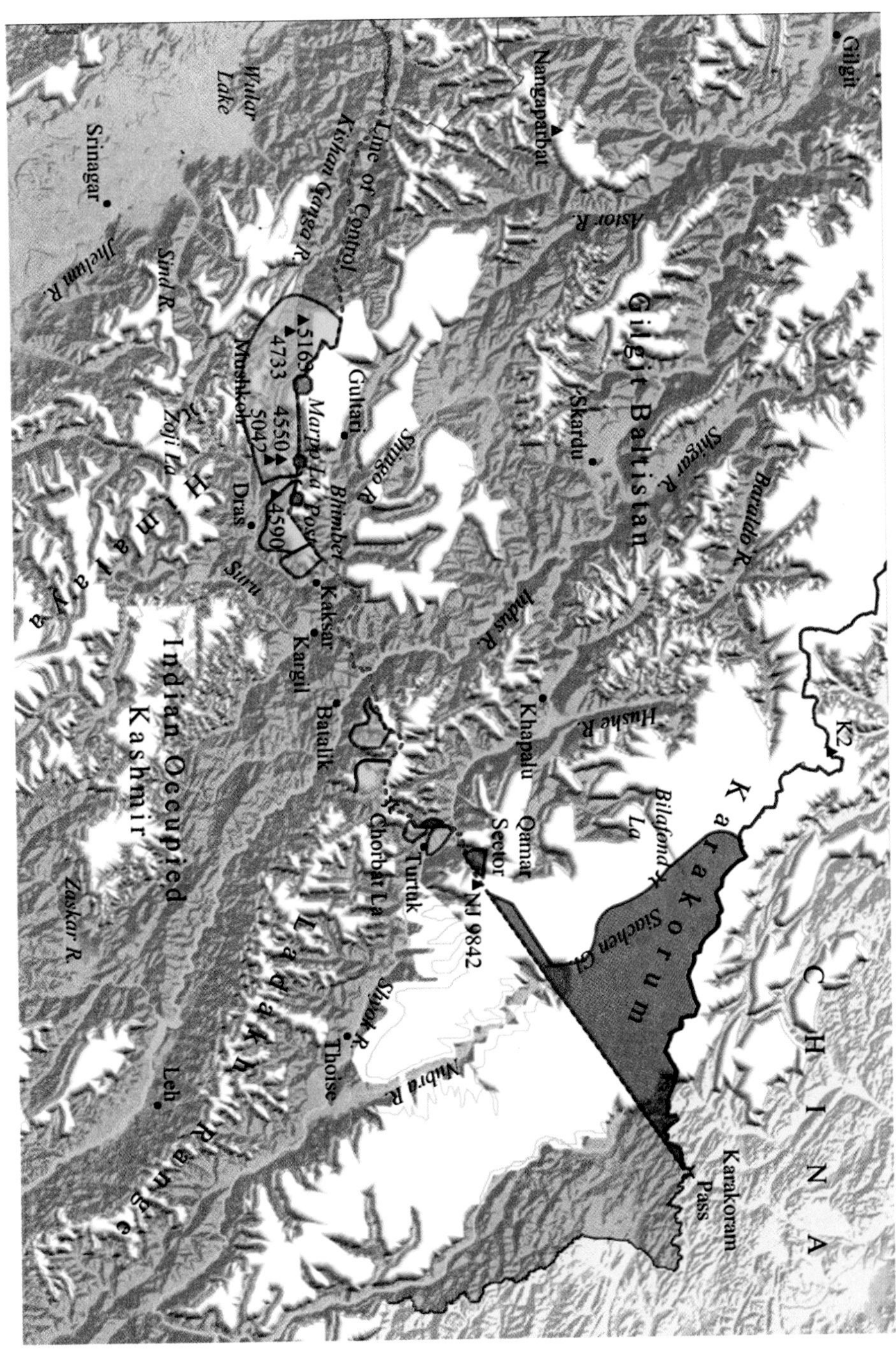

Indian Ingress After 1972 and Indian alleged-Pakistani Incursions

the Pakistani POWs by Delhi. Obliging its friends in Islamabad, Beijing used its veto to turn down Bangladesh's first application for membership of the UN. After Pakistan's POWs were released unconditionally, Bangladesh entered the UN unhindered.

Pakistan was subsequently locked into a classic insecurity dilemma, impacting the behavior and approach of the Pakistani State, its foreign policy, its politics, and its society. There was, however, no consensus on how to deal with the rising Indian threat. This lack of consensus played itself out as one of the key factors in Pakistan's continuing civil-military divide and distrust.

Beginnings of Protracted War for Glaciers and Passes: Roots of Kargil

Recurrent violations of the LOC had essentially turned the LOC into an active war zone. Sporadic firing was the norm with both sides conducting military operations against each other with the express purpose of nibbling away territory along the LOC and positioning their respective armies in strategically advantageous positions. India, militarily stronger than Pakistan, had begun to stake a claim over the entire state of Jammu and Kashmir since the sixties and was triumphant after the 1971 defeat of Pakistan.

Shortly after signing the Simla Agreement, India violated it by occupying the Chorbat La area in 1972. Indian forces crossed the LOC up to a depth of 3 kilometers to establish five Indian posts on the Pakistan-controlled side of the LOC. In 1984 India launched a major military operation to occupy the 2312 square km triangular area lying east of the Saltoro Range between the Karakorum Pass, the Indrakoli Pass, and NJ 9842, the northernmost point on the LOC.[26] This area had not been clearly demarcated in either the July 1949 Karachi Agreement which defined the Cease-Fire Line (CFL) or in the December 1972 Line of Control Agreement signed by the representative armies in accordance with the Simla Agreement of 2 July 1972. Because forces from neither side had ever ventured into the glacier zones that lay beyond point NJ9842, this extremely inhospitable north-eastern terrain had never been disputed.

Both sides therefore found it acceptable that the CFL's definitive end point was NJ9842 located near the base of the Saltoro mountain range near the Shyok River. Beyond NJ9842, vague language identifying the CFL as 'thence north to the glaciers,' was used. Meanwhile this vagueness appeared acceptable to both sides because no human life had ever or was likely to inhabit these glaciers. Yet this area, where Pakistan, India and China rub shoulders subsequently became a mindless bone of contention.

Though the language was vague, Pakistan staked a claim over the area on the basis of having controlled it since 1947. Pakistan maintained that India and the international community both acknowledged its de facto control. India had indeed acknowledged this publicly in the Indian parliament and in its written communications with Pakistan, especially while protesting against the Pakistan-China 1963 Boundary Agreement.[27]

At the international level too, for example within communities like the mountaineering groups, Pakistan's version of the LOC was accepted. They had begun turning to the Karakoram Range which contains four of the fourteen highest mountains in the world. For Pakistan, the indicators of international recognition of Pakistan's control included Pakistan granting permission to foreign mountaineering expeditions visiting the Siachen Glacier[28] and the area to the east accompanied by Pakistanis. Atlases reflecting Pakistan's version of the LOC were produced in the US and UK by *National Geographic* and by *Encyclopedia Britannica* (1979) and in the maps produced in the prestigious *American Alpine Journal* and Hugh Swift's classic *Trekkers Guide to the Himalaya and the Karakoram*.Even US agency maps showed Siachen as part of Pakistan. [29]

India also made somewhat muted counter claims. Indian military launched its first expedition into the area in the late seventies, India opted not to publicly criticize the Pakistani control or express 'fear' of a complete Pakistani take-over of the area. India's rethink on the area and its decision to overturn the status quo began in the late seventies. Until then India had continued with its hands-off policy towards the disputed area of Siachen, believing the ambiguity of the status and control of these remote and inhospitable snow-bound areas would endure. It had ruled out any Pakistani presence or even engagement in these areas. The Indian government had therefore not focused on it. However, when several mountaineering maps caught India's attention, Delhi began focusing on the status of Siachen and its surrounding areas. These international maps, depicting a straight line canting off at a northeasterly angle and terminating on the Chinese border, had placed Siachen inside Pakistan.[30]

Early 1978 the first Indian military reconnaissance mission was sent to Siachen under Colonel Narender Kumar of the High Altitude Warfare School. It was camouflaged as a mountaineering expedition. Lieutenant General M. L. Chibber was then India's Director of Military Operations.The mission scaled Teram Kangri at 24,297 feet. A subsequent expedition in 1980 went to Sia Kangri and Saltoro Kangri (24,500 feet) and to Sia Kangri (24,500 feet).[31] According to Colonel Narender Kumar who led the expedition, "We found labels from tin cans and cigarette packs with Pakistani names, German and Japanese equipment and it is this that convinced the appeared disproportionate to the findings since no evidence of Pakistan's military presence in the area had been found. "There wasn't a soul there," Kumar had recalled.[32] Kumar was the first to scale the uncharted Siachen Glacier and he put the Indian flag at Siachen. Significantly Pakistan had no permanent physical presence in Siachen.

Nevertheless the Indian General Chibber subsequently maintained that he was alarmed to learn that the Pakistanis were accompanying mountaineers to the glacier and that maps printed in the West showed the Siachen area as part of Pakistan.[33] In the summer of 1981 India sent another seventy-man military team posing as a mountaineering expedition, on an eight weeks long mission. It comprehensively surveyed the area, climbing the Saltoro Kangri and the Sia Kangri-I. It hiked to the top of Indira Col and skied Bilafond La. Clearly, India had begun preparations to occupy the area east of the Saltoro Range.

By 1983, Chibber was based in Leh, just east of Kargil, heading India's Northern Command. Chibber was proposing that Indian military power was to be deployed to deny Pakistani presence and control of the area, an action in direct violation of the Simla Agreement. India had, however, already demonstrated, by the 1972 occupation of posts across the LOC at Chorbat La that the Simla Agreement would not be a restraining factor in India's pursuit of its 'national objectives.'

India's preparation was underway to use force to control Siachen, as India argued Pakistan was also gradually doing.[34] Simla agreement did not allow use of force to settle outstanding matters. Significantly despite this and subsequent violation of the Simla Agreement, India faced no diplomatic or military resistance by Pakistan. In fact, there is no record at all of a military or diplomatic reaction by Pakistan to early Indian intrusion, even in Siachen.[35] Pakistan first registered the scale of the Indian engagement in the Siachen area after the Narender Kumar article published in late 1981 in an Indian magazine detailing the occupation. The fact that there is no record of Pakistan's complaint against Indian presence in the Siachen area to UNGOMIP or to India before 1982 indicates Pakistan's ignorance of the earlier Indian engagement. It appeared to have been a major intelligence failure.[36] Meanwhile by now the two neighbors were engaged in controlling the area through force.

Pakistan did not raise the matter adequately at the international or the bilateral levels. Even in October 1983, Pakistan's diplomatic response was restricted to protesting to the Indian government through UNGOMIP and through the Pakistan Foreign Office. Pakistan chose not to raise the matter at the more active and influential forums within the United Nations, to the president of the UNSC, or the secretary general. The complaints came *post facto* after their occupation of Siachen since earlier public recrimination would have provided an early warning for Pakistan, possibly undermining India. Pakistan thus restricted its diplomatic response to India's Siachen engagement to the bilateral forum. Multilateral international diplomacy was missing as was public diplomacy. The matter was missing in the media too.

Indians argued it was a "pre-emptive"[37] take-over, to prevent the "Pakistanis sneaking their way into a place that doesn't belong to them."[38]

India's engagement at Siachen increased Pakistan's already heightened sense of insecurity, made peace ellusive, further undermined trust between the two neighbors, and undermined the mutually endorsed mode of dispute settlement. General Ziaul Haq's government did not effectively flag this. Pakistan's low profile diplomatic response provided India an 'easy' environment.

At the military level too, Pakistan's response was sluggish and inadequate. Its first military expedition to the disputed area was not launched until five years after the Kumar expedition. In 1982, two military patrols were sent from the 10 Corps Headquarters. With limited training and virtually no experience of scaling snow-clad mountains, their climb to the 17,700 feet high Siachen Glacier was impeded. Expedition commander Brigadier Imtiaz Ali Warraich, also the commander Force Command Northern Areas (FCNA) (1982 to 1984), acknowledged, "Beyond this point it was difficult to go because of excessive snow and so we returned." However the expedition, with its base camp at Goma village, crossed Bilafond La at around 14000 feet.[39] They found evidence of the Ladakh Scouts[40] including Indian currency from the villages at Goma.[41] Around this time, Indian preparations to occupy Siachen under General Chibber, were already underway.

In July-August 1983 when a Pakistani Special Services Group (SSG) expedition went to the Siachen Glacier, they encountered Indian presence. The Indian expedition rapidly withdrew but the Pakistanis were convinced that Siachen and the passes had to be militarily occupied.[42] Indians too decided to go beyond their regular intermittent patrols. General Chibber claimed that the 21 August 1983 protest note from Pakistan's northern sector commander was the trigger.[43] He handed over the protest note to his counterpart in Kargil stating that the Line of Control joins with the Karakoram Pass, also that all the area west of this extended line belongs to Pakistan. The Indian Army headquarters upon receiving this written complaint along with information that Pakistan troops had occupied Bilafond Pass, ordered northern command to prepare for military occupation of Siachen. Effectively the two neighbors raced to occupy the unmarked territory.

Delhi deliberately did not publicize it's resentment over what Delhi considered was Pakistan's illegal and presumptuous control. Instead it covertly worked on launching its operation to occupy Siachen. And did so successfully.

Through the winter of 1983, both Pakistan and India began preparations to occupy Siachen by the summer of 1984. Pakistan made ready for a combined SSG and Northern Light Infantry (NLI) mission. By early April, the Indians airlifted two platoons of Ladakh scouts to Siachen. Thus, when on 17 April, two Pakistani reconnaissance helicopters arrived at Siachen, they discovered the Indians.[44] A Pakistani helicopter was fired at. One of the world's highest, most spectacular, and most hostile terrains had turned into a battlefield.

It was not until 1984 that the Indian Army successfully launched Operation Meghdoot[45] to occupy the territory.[46] India controls the forty-three mile long Siachen Glacier, Sia La, Bilafond La and the Gyong La, all three passes of the Saltoro Ridge located on the west of the glacier.[47] This area lay unoccupied before 1984.

Prior to 1984, neither India nor Pakistan had any permanent presence in the area.The conflict began in 1984 with India launching Operation Meghdoot during which it wrested control of the Siachen Glacier from Pakistan and forced the Pakistanis to retreat west of the Saltoro Ridge. India now established control over all of the 70 kilometers long Siachen Glacier and all of its tributary glaciers, as well as the three main passes of the Saltoro Ridge immediately west of the glacier—Sia La, Bilafond La, and Gyong La. Pakistan controlled the glacial valleys immediately west of the Saltoro Ridge.

Pakistan Had Lost the Race to Occupy Siachen.

While senior Pakistani generals, including the military dictator President General Zia, opted for silence as a diplomatic response, there was dismay among some other generals. Kargil, located on the Indian side of the LOC first appeared on the radar screen of Pakistan's senior armed forces command in 1984.[48] Pakistan was then under military rule.[49] Towards the end of May 1984, in a meeting chaired by President General Ziaul Haq at the GHQ, the commander 10 Corps reported that upon the FCNA's return to Siachen in May[50] they discovered Indian occupation. General Ziaul Haq, though publicly dismissive of Indian occupation of the glacier, instructed his forces to reclaim Siachen and met the army's request for military equipment, French-made Lama Helicopters and training to launch a high altitude military operation. The army planned to reclaim Siachen the following year.[51]

However, the army would be forced to report that it had failed to recapture Siachen because India had ensured substantial troop presence there by April 1985.

Another Plan B was also presented at the meeting. According to this, Pakistani troops could go unnoticed across the LOC and set up posts in Kargil sector on the Indian side of the disputed territory of Jammu and Kashmir. Pakistani forces could then block the main artery, the Srinagar to Leh Highway (National Highway-1) from its posts in Kargil. This would force the Indians to negotiate with Pakistan where Pakistan would demand unconditional Indian withdrawal from Kargil. General Ziaul Haq opposed this plan. The Indians, he argued, would opt for all-out war if Pakistan choked their main artery in the North. Zia rejected the B option. He believed India would attack Pakistan at the international border.[52] After 1985, Pakistan did not launch another similar operation to reclaim the Siachen area.

Two incontestable facts have, however, remained integral to the Pakistan-India tussle over Siachen. First, the area was part of the disputed J & K State and therefore neither side could make a rightful ownership claim on the basis of mere control. Second, under paragraph 1(ii) of the Simla Agreement, both States had committed that "neither side shall unilaterally alter the situation" in regard to "any of the problems between the two countries." This commitment clearly covered all unresolved bilateral issues.[53]

The unresolved conflict over the accession question influenced almost all aspects of inter-State relations between Pakistan and India. While diplomatic engagements helped to defuse major crises and also yielded commitments to peacefully resolve all outstanding disputes, the 'ground facts' reflected reality. India's reluctance to diplomatically engage with Pakistan on the Kashmir question was matched only by the resolve of both neighbors to unilaterally change the political and territorial status of the disputed area.

After the 1971 debacle leading to Pakistan's breakup, India was confident it would settle Kashmir on its own terms. Pakistan lost the strategic peaks it had controlled and dominated the Indian lines of communication in the disputed Jammu and Kashmir territory, including the Kargil heights that Pakistan had held at the signing of the 1948 Karachi Agreement. After Pakistan lost Kargil, Shaqma lay at the closest point to Indian supply lines between Srinagar and Leh.

From the fifties onwards, India had changed the constitutional status of Jammu and Kashmir. By the eighties, in the treacherous terrain of the disputed territory India was occupying strategic peaks.

India also had the military, political and psychological might of a rising hegemonic state with the confidence to ignore the pressures of politics, legality, and principles.

Along the LOC, on the Pakistani side, India systematically nibbled away at the disputed territory. India's enhanced military strength, together with men specially trained in snow warfare at the North Pole, enabled India to gain control over additional territory. Pakistan too, through diplomatic and military means, was contesting the Indian control. Significantly from the late seventies onwards, Pakistan had moved to limited and mostly covert military action, a shift in strategy from the launching of major military operations it had employed from the late forties through the early seventies. Overtly and covertly, well-prepared and ill-prepared, with the belief that they were being 'wronged' by India, an anxious Pakistan reciprocated by launching strikes across the LOC.

For example in April 1987, Pakistan launched a successful operation to gain control over some area of the Saltoro Ridge. Armed with ropes and ladders, a dozen commandos climbed a cliff to occupy a position at 21,000 feet, dominating Indian positions at Bilafond La. This post was called the Quaid post. However, within two months, on 25 June, after several attempts, and suffering heavy casualties, to recapture part of the Quaid post. The commandoes at Quaid post had run out of ammunition and they could not be resupplied since their logistics supply base had come under fire.

In September 1987, Pakistan lost the Quaid post, strategically located at considerable height, to the Indians. Subsequently, the Pakistan Army conducted the Dalunang (1988) and Chummik (1989) operations to occupy positions across the LOC. In the Dalunang operation, led by then FCNA commander Brigadier Aziz Khan, 23 posts were established across the LOC, which Pakistan still controls to this day.[54] This was in violation of the CFL agreement. By now neither side was abiding by any agreements. In 1988, India also established 12 posts in the Qamar sector.

Political attempts in the late eighties and early nineties to settle Siachen, a key cause of this war of attrition along the LOC, were unsuccessful. India's political leadership, because of political and military considerations, aborted two near-settlements on Siachen at the eleventh hour.[55] Among Indians, meanwhile, the original triumphalism of Siachen was rethought. An influential group consisting of mostly retired military men and journalists questioned the wisdom of battling over Siachen. This group included even the architect of the Indian occupation General Chibber, who called for settling the Siachen dispute.

This revisionism in limited circles notwithstanding, the problems remained. From 1992 onwards, Indian troops regularly intercepted Pakistani supplies in the Neelum Valley on the Muzzaffarabad–Khel road. In 1992 the Indians established a post across the LOC on Anzbari Feature, which was vacated following negotiations between the Indian and Pakistani Directors-General of Military Operations (DGMO).

Clearly, on the world's highest battlefield, a protracted war over the glaciers and passes had begun. The commanders in khaki reported the shooting and called the shots. Headquartered on the distant plains, the governmental chiefs of Pakistan and India depended on what their commanders from the desolate ice-covered peaks would report. Isolated with their platoons, and weighed under by snowman's gear, these were often daredevil commanders. They were tasked to fly their country's flags on the sequestered Himalayan peaks. Programmed into their DNA were nationalist narratives framing the other as 'the enemy.' Without this mindset, their hardship at such incredible heights would make no sense. From the clash of narratives alone could flow their will to battle their adversary. Institutional training and statist historiography had programmed these men with guns into being willing warriors. Yet, when they accidentally drifted into close proximity, this 'processing' would give way to human connection. With their weather-battered bodies and lonely hearts, quarantined from civilization and set in the harsh and desolate heights, they would share a smoke or a smile with an 'enemy.'[56]

Nevertheless, embattled mindset remained dominant. Among average Pakistani soldiers stationed along the LOC, there was fervor to occupy the heights across the LOC. Their rationale was straightforward: "Siachen must be avenged." Senior generals of the 10Corps commanding the LOC area, especially in the nineties, acknowledged the enthusiasm. One who commanded the 10 Corps in the nineties said, "I know when you find an open space, the temptation to occupy it is very strong."[57] Recalling how he curtailed his soldiers, a former general, "When I took over the command of the 10 Corps I had to put my troops on a leash, because they would say we can move forward since we are on a height."[58]

In addition to occupying each other's vulnerable posts or setting up new posts across the LOC in the adversary-controlled areas, Pakistani and Indian troops would interdict each other's strategic roads. The terrain provided the two sides height advantage at different points. They would fire at vehicles carrying soldiers, ammunition, and logistics to their respective LOC posts. Response strategies included construction of alternate routes and also locally arranged cease-fires. For example, to address the vulnerability of the strategic Neelum Valley road caused by Indian firing on Pakistani military traffic along considerable stretches, passes at Laswa and Kiran were constructed but Indian firing continued. With a professional like General Jehangir Karamat as the army chief, the decision was taken to interdict from the Shaqma sector, India's lifeline, the Kargil-Drass Highway. The possibility of interdiction brought the Indians to the negotiating table. The Pakistani and Indian DGMOs met in 1998 and finalized a two-point agreement. No artillery or mortar fire which would harm civilians could be used and neither side would interdict the other side's roads. In this sector the guns fell silent, however temporarily.

Bilateral diplomacy remained stalemated at the political level. But, on the ground, the repeated interdiction and periodic chipping away at the other's territory close to the LOC persisted. As problems remained unresolved, it was these two abiding, contradictory yet co-dependent realities that best manifested the texture of the troubled relationship in South Asia. Cutting across the many layers of complaints and counter-complaints, at the core lay India's primarily defensive posture. Maneuvers along the LOC notwithstanding, India primarily sought to preserve the status quo on Indian-Occupied Kashmir and the 1984 occupation of Siachen.

Pakistan, as the anti-status quo power, sought the exact opposite. It wanted to end Indian control of Siachen and subsequently of Kashmir. This presented a unique challenge at home for Pakistan. With weak civilian oversight on defense affairs, the frequency of military rule, and the failure to devise institutionalized policy-making, Pakistan's policy tended to vacillate between restraint and aggression. Given the battle-history with India, military men in high positions, with some political support in the initial decades, conducted triumphantly and secretively Operations Venus and Gibraltar, Grand Slam. Military men, trained to think linearly, watching over Pakistan's security undertook, with a sense of responsibility, pride and vengeance ill-conceived Operations. However after the 1977 Zia ul Haq coup and the multifaceted nexus between the Pakistani and US military institutions, Pakistan Army's existing control and authority on Pakistani institutions and policy was further strengthened. For example Subsequently, Pakistan's failed attempts in 1986 to recapture Siachen and the Afghan Mujahideen-partnered 1989 spring offensive to capture Jalalabad were solely military affairs.

The Origins of the Kargil Plan

In 1985, at a Command and Staff conference in Rawalpindi, with Pakistan's military ruler General Ziaul Haq in the chair, discussions began on how to militarily oust India from the Siachen glacier. In April 1984, India had successfully launched Operation Meghdoot to occupy the Siachen glacier. Zia's public nonchalance over Indian occupation of Siachen notwithstanding there was a sense of desperation about Siachen. In the medium-long term, Siachen was also the lifeline for Pakistan. Supply of water the backbone of Pakistan's agrarian economy, was dependent Siachen. Melting water from this highest battleground on earth, the Siachen glacier, also the main source of the Nubra River that falls into the Shyok River, a critical supply line for the Indus River.

Ziaul Haq gave the task to Lt. General Mohammad Safdar, Commander 1 Corps, headquartered at Mangla. Safdar was to war game options for a force to operate behind the enemy lines to expel India from Siachen and report back to the army chief. Following the war-gaming exercise, the army chief attended a debriefing at Mangla.

In 1986, the army chief asked the planning directorate at the GHQ to take the concept developed by 1 Corps during the war-gaming exercise and develop it as an operation. Brigadier Khalid Latif Mughal was put in charge. The planning directorate formulated a plan with three specific inputs. One, Kargil should be the location for the operation. Two, para-drops would be used in the operation, since there were no land routes to Kargil but Skardu airport was close to the planned area of the operation. Three, an entire battalion, approximately 4000 troops, would land in the Kargil area.

Kargil was chosen as the operation area since it was in direct view of and close proximity to NH1, India's main supply route to Siachen. The plan envisaged the battalion of para-drops to cut the NH1 through an undercover Operation. These troops would hold down the enemy and isolate Siachen long enough for the troops to launch a ground attack. The surprise factor in the Operation would feature paramilitary troops, including NLI and SSG commandoes, since radar would not capture their movements. . Deployment of regular troops would kill the surprise factor since Indian radar would pick up their movements.

Planners assessed the international environment from a Cold War prism. They concluded that Pakistan's central role in the Afghan war put Pakistan in a good international position.

Since an air force role was also envisaged, the plan was sent to the Joint Services Headquarters.[59] The Chairman JSC Lt. General Rahimuddin sent the plan to Air chief Jamal A Khan. His Director Air Planning Air Commodore P.Q. Mehdi recommended against air force involvement. Khan declined the requested air support. In a report sent to the Chairman JCSC, the dangerously low flight plan needed for the operation was cited, given the harsh weather and steep and unpredictable terrain.

The chairman agreed with the air force's assessment of its inability to conduct para-drops. He said it was tactically a good plan but strategically bad. He maintained that because the Afghan war meant Pakistan was at the center of global tension, it should keep away from a potentially controversial situation.

Pakistan's army officers seemed to be divided over the plan, among the post and pre-1965 officers. The pre-1965 officers were battle-wisened were cautious about undertaking risky operations. This category included the Director General ISI and the Chairman JS headquarters. Officers including Ali Quli Khan,Asif Nawaz, and Pervez Musharraf were from the post-1965 course and seemed in favor of the plan.

A rejected plan from the JS Headquarters landed with the army chief. He sent the plan for review to the DG ISI, Lt. General Akhtar Abdur Rehman. Rehman was simply asked how to implement the plan.

As the ISI chief from 1979 to 1987, Rehman oversaw the build-up of an elaborate apparatus for the world's most heavily-financed US-funded covert war. As the Soviet pull-out drew closer, he often raised the question of how to use the force, the 'muscle', Pakistan had trained for the Afghan insurgency. The concern also was whether in the post-Afghan war scenario who would these trained and battle-hardened Afghan fighters fight...could it be Pakistan?

Akhtar Abdur Rehman wrote a detailed note arguing that Pakistan should utilize the Mujahideen currently fighting in Afghanistan and also train Kashmiris for the operation in Kargil. Rehman recommended that the ISI lead the recruitment process to ensure no suspects come into the fray. Rehman suggested that as soon as there was a drawdown from the Afghan front of Pakistan's manpower involvement they could be used for this operation. Pakistan had around 15,000 to 20,000 citizens involved in Afghanistan. The plan Rehman proposed was to train the Mujahideen in AJK and launch them in the Kargil sector through the land routes. As locals they would deal well with the environment. The plan was for them to conduct sabotage activities. Pakistan would only be involved in training in AJK, enter undercover in the Mujahideen group as decision-makers and leaders, and conduct the frontal attack in Siachen.

A political crisis, the Ojri Camp explosion, and Prime Minister Muhammad Khan Junejo's dismissal prompted the shelving of the plan.

Zia ul Haq, the army chief and military ruler issued directives to his core team on which his handwritten notes queried why Pakistan was not using its success in Afghanistan and why Pakistan was not taking material advantage of a neutralized India.

In August 1988 a C-130 plane carrying Pakistan's top military command crashed. There were no survivors.

The Kargil Plan was Put in Cold Storage.

Nevertheless, since the capture of Kargil impacted on Siachen and as well as on the routes to Leh, it was often factored in studies conducted by young officers enrolled in military institutions. For example in 1990 a brigade major of 26 Brigade Tariq Khan wrote a cautionary note on Kargil. As part of a routine exercise to examine potential objectives the major had given Kargil a high priority in his study. He argued that on account of it's extreme strategic significance for the Indians would move troops up from the south to clear it and would respond by reinforcing the effort to recapture it. Since these reinforcements would impact on the Indian strike/offensive capability in the south across the international border and since these forces had to pass through defiles along road Madhupur-Samba-Katua-Jammu 80 kilometers long, it was clear that an operation to capture Kargil would only make strategic sense if Pakistan was prepared to mount a supporting offensive across the Working Boundary from Sialkot area.[60]

Dusting off the Kargil Plan

In 1989, Pakistan again turned towards Kashmir. Provoked by Delhi's election rigging in the valley, the rag-a-tag Kashmiri freedom fighters took to urban warfare against Delhi. Pakistan's ISI began deploying its Afghan-trained muscle in the widespread and indigenous insurgency.

Around 1996, a senior General within the ISI retrieved the Kargil plan. Keen to revive it, the General took the plan to his chief General Jehangir Karamat.[61] The chief put the plan on the assessment track within the GHQ, seeking input of its operation feasibility from relevant departments. The paper trail began. First it arrived at the planning directorate, from where it was sent to the director general military operations for his views. ISI too was involved. A little-noticed inter-services to conduct a comprehensive study of the plan. It had representatives from the air force, navy, SSG, and the army. The informally convened team actually traveled to the proposed area of the operation. Using Indian reconnaissance photographs, intelligence information, including intercepts, logistics, hard facts and a visit to the Pakistani side of the proposed operation area, the team conducted a comprehensive assessment of the Indian level of preparedness, intelligence capabilities, and response possibilities.

The team identified problems. To begin with, the idea of training the Mujahideen was not a plausible idea. It was not possible without compromising the surprise factor. It was deemed too difficult to keep a lid on all Mujahideen. The Indian penetration among the Mujahideen could also not be ruled out. The second problem was that regular troops would have to be infused into irregular troops creating unpredictable problems. Finally, the air force could not give 'close' air support to the military field units.

The team underscored the contradiction between the proposed plan and official policy of improving relations with India. Its members feared that once the Mujahideen cover blew, the government would not be able to handle the backlash. A major flaw identified was lack of clarity in the steps that Pakistan would take after the Kargil peaks were occupied. The planners also questioned the assumption that Pakistan would have sufficient time to attain its objectives in Siachen between the time that NH1, India's supply line to Siachen, was blocked and the time that the international community took notice.

Against this backdrop, the report laid out the only two possibilities available to Pakistan; One that included both the blockade of NH-1 and the Siachen offensive and one that limited the operation to a blockade of NH-1. Including the blockade and the offensive would make it difficult for Pakistan to deny involvement in the former. The team ruled out both possibilities suggesting that the plan was not viable. They concluded that while the plan was tactically plausible, strategically it was a nightmare. The sealed report was formally presented to the ISI.

Interestingly one general keen to implement the plan called in a team member that had assessed the environment and timing. Informally he reprimanded him, "You people come from abroad after studying and you think you can teach me strategy." The general trashed the report. However the ISI as an institution did not consider it its mandate to execute this Kargil plan.

While the DG ISI concluded that it was not the ISI's mandate to conduct this operation, the plan was not shelved. For the determined backers of the plan, those keen to settle scores with India on Siachen, those who would point to India's repeated back tracking on the Siachen negotiations and those who insisted that diplomacy alone was not the way forward, the operation remained enticing. Its backers had decided that the Siachen offensive could be dropped from the plan but dropping the operation in total, was out.

Lt. General Aziz Khan was one such man.

Chapter 2

THE KARGIL OPERATION: CONTEXT AND CONTRADICTIONS

India Gifts Pakistan a Good Strategic Space

In May 1998, the world's worst kept nuclear secret was out in the open. India and Pakistan, long known to be clandestine nuclear weapon states, had conducted bomb tests to openly establish their nuclear credentials. If there was a trigger that was needed to push the Pakistan-India relationship, already locked in distrust, constant covert hostility, and periodic open confrontation, further along the hostility path, it was provided by these May 1998 nuclear tests.

To prompt criticism by the global community, which had studiously ignored Pakistan Prime Minister Nawaz Sharif's 2 April letter, warning of India's preparation for such tests, India conducted its nuclear explosions on 11 May and 13 May.[1] The tests, as India's scientists verified were a "culmination of India's weaponization programme." US President Clinton said the tests were unjustified and they clearly created a dangerous new instability in the region.[2] His National Security Advisor Samuel Berger announced that the United States was "deeply disappointed" by the Indian decision to "test nuclear weapons." [3] Germany's Chancellor Helmut Kohl said the tests were "in a way a direct challenge to the neighboring countries."[4] China urged the international community to "adopt a unified stand and strongly demand that India immediately stop development of nuclear weapons." [5]

Another unlikely voice on the Indian nuclear tests was that of Osama bin Laden (OBL). The only one to publicly advocate that Pakistan conduct the nuclear tests, OBL urged "the Muslim nation and Pakistan" to prepare for a *Jihad* which should "include a nuclear force."[6] Even if this OBL advice slipped the attention of the White House and State Department's men at Foggy Bottom, who were focused entirely on South Asia's unfolding nuclear saga, it had grabbed the attention of CIA's Counter-Terrorist Center. Ever since this center's late February alert memo on the OBL threat, it was sharply focused on Osama. They were keen to capture him, either with or without the help of Kabul's Taliban government. In February, the US Ambassador to the UN, Bill Richardson, was in Kabul asking the Taliban to handover Osama, telling them, "Look, bin Laden is in your territory...he's a bad guy.[7] Richardson was aware of the connections that America's oil giant Unocal was developing with the Taliban. After making several trips to Kabul and Kandahar in November 1997 Unocal invited a Taliban delegation to its headquarters. A spokesman for the company, Unocal, said the Taleban were expected to spend several days at the company's headquarters in California.[8] Unocal was competing with the Argentinean firm Bridasfor a multi-billion project to construct a gas pipeline from Turkmenistan across Afghanistan into Pakistan. With the raging civil war in Afghanistan, Unocal remained hopeful of pushing the project forward. In fact, by end 1997,the oil giant had already contracted the University of Nebraska to begin training of around 140 Afghans in the technical skills of pipeline construction. The training, interestingly, was to be held in Kandahar, the ideological headquarter city of the Taliban.

Washington's engagement with Afghanistan proceeded on several not necessarily complementary, commercial, diplomatic, security, intelligence, and counter-terrorism tracks. In spring, the Counter-terrorist center had made plans with its Islamabad-based CIA case officers and Afghan tribals to capture OBL. Since February, OBL, along with the Egyptian physician Ayman al-Zawahiri, was running the World Islamic Front for *Jihad* Against Jews and Crusaders. The front was an international declaration of war against the United States.[9] America was identified as the "distant enemy" and al-Zawahiri advocated "the need to inflict the maximum casualties against the opponent, for this is the language understood by the West, no matter how much time and effort such operations take."[10]Several militants from Egypt, Bangladesh, Kashmir, and Pakistan had signed the Front's manifesto, written by OBL and al-Zawahiri.

Meanwhile, as expected, the international pressure on Pakistan not to respond to India's tests with its own nuclear tests began. At the European Union's Birmingham Summit, the statement urged Pakistan to "exercise maximum restraint in the face of these tests and to adhere to international non-proliferation norms." The US President's personal phone calls were followed by the arrival of his special envoy in Pakistan. A presumptuous Clinton sent off a junior official, deputy secretary of state, to dissuade Sharif from conducting the tests. In his April letter, Sharif had already warned the global community that "Pakistan will be obliged to take cognizance of these alarming developments, and it cannot but exercise its sovereign right to adopt appropriate measures to safeguard its security." Nevertheless, Clinton's message to Sharif was simply: "Don't do it. It's foolhardy."He did not address Pakistan's security concerns.

Clinton's attention was also divided. In Washington, alongside the nuclear issue, red lights were flashing on the OBL issue and the growing threat of terrorism. On both sides of the Potomac, dedicated individuals were bracing America against a threat of a hitherto unprecedented level. On 22 May, Clinton appointed a Counterterrorism Czar at the White House. He signed the Presidential Decision Directive-62 entitled 'Protection Against Unconventional Threat to the Homeland and American Overseas'. A new group, the Counter-Terrorism Security Group,was formed with the heads of the counterterrorism departments of the CIA, FBI,Joint Chiefs of Staff, and Departments of Defense, Justice, and State as core members. Across the Potomac River from Foggy Bottom, the CIA's Counter-Terrorist Center at Langley, in April, had made an elaborate night attack plan to strike OBL's known abode, the Tarnak Farms, located close to Kandahar airport. The area was scouted and satellite photographs taken as Islamabad-based CIA case officers worked on preparing the plan with Afghan assets and with tribal leaders. Finally, the plan was aborted for fear of civilian casualties and lack of legal cover.[11]

Returning to the issue of the nuclear tests, the widespread view in Pakistan was that India's tests went unmonitored in Washington because of the US's benign neglect of its new strategic ally's activities. An agitated Additional Secretary at the Foreign Office had conveyed Pakistan's resentment in undiplomatic words. Around midnight on 11 May, the US deputy chief of mission (DCM) was called and given a demarche. In the demarche Pakistan complained that India and the US were in fact in cahoots with each other. The DCM asked his Pakistani counterpart if he wanted him to send "this shit" to the US? Pakistan did.

Leading British experts indicated that, given the every-thirty-minute coverage of the Indian nuclear site Pokhran by US satellites, their missing the early warnings of the tests was highly unlikely.[12]In Washington, several analysts explained the Clinton Administration's late 1997 decision to strike a strategic alliance with India as a major cause for the Administration's failure to read even the obvious signs pointing to imminent nuclear testing by India, which was "poised to become a new Asian tiger."[13] Reflecting this, a senior State Department official said, "There wasn't a voice in the wilderness…there was nobody anywhere – no voices saying, 'Watch out!'"[14]

For Pakistan, the international call for restraint was meaningless. Pakistan was all set to respond with its own tests. The prime minister was informed of the tests in Kazakhstan where he was attending the ECO summit.[15] Sharif had decided within hours of the Indian tests that Pakistan would conduct its own nuclear tests. Army chief General Jahangir Karamat was given instructions to finalize the arrangements.

On 28 May, Pakistan conducted its tests successfully. After congratulating the Pakistanis, Nawaz Sharif complained that the "international response to the Indian nuclear tests did not factor in the security situation in our region." He complained that from Pakistan the world had sought an "acceptance of the Indian weaponization as a fait-accompli." However, Pakistan's "weapons are to deter aggression, whether nuclear or conventional."

Holding a press conference within hours of Pakistan's tests, the US President declared, "I deplore the decision." In a caricature of reality Clinton complained,"By failing to exercise restraint in response to the Indian test, Pakistan lost a truly priceless opportunity to strengthen its own security [and] improve its political standing in the world."[16] Clinton laid the onus jointly on Pakistan and India. Somewhat unrealistically, he demanded that they "renounce further nuclear and missile testing immediately and take decisive steps to reverse this dangerous arms race."[17] Obviously, India's attempt through the Vajpayee letter, to link its nuclear program to China and delink it from Pakistan, had not worked.

Significantly, within India the news of the tests was received with both surprise and panic. The news landed in the parliament while the BJP government's nuclear policy was under discussion. Indian lawmakers erupted in a shouting bout at the news. The blame game began. Former Prime Ministers I.K. Gujral and H.D. Deve-Gowda said that Pakistan's tests were a reaction to India's tests. Similarly, former Defense Minister and President of the Samajwadi Party, Mulayam Singh Yadav, condemned the BJP-led government for "provoking" Pakistan's tests. Addressing Vajpayee, the leader of the Communist Party of India-(Marxist), Somnath Chatterjee, said: "It is a nuclear arms race that you have started in this region."[18]

As if in support of Islamabad's stance in Islamabad, the Congress pointedly blamed Vajpayee for "using incendiary rhetoric that set off a regional nuclear arms race." In its statement, the Congress party said the tests were a "grave development". Fearing a regional nuclear arms race, they called for restraint by the Hindu nationalist-led government. But Vajpayee denied that India's action had forced Pakistan to respond. He, on the contrary, blamed Pakistan for prompting the Indian tests. Vajpayee said, "In fact, it was Pakistan's clandestine preparation that forced us to take the path of a nuclear deterrent."

India's army chief V.P. Malik was measured in his reaction. "We are no more a soft state and we are not a push-over when it comes to national security concerns." He conceded "a situation of symmetry has finally been established among the country's neighbors now. If there was any ambiguity earlier about Pakistan's nuclear capability, it no longer exists." On a realistic note, the general said, "Now it is known to the world and it is better this way."[19] Ironically, the balance of terror was conceding space to peace initiatives.

Islamabad's official *mantra* for its own May 28 nuclear tests was that Pakistan's tests were "defensive and responsive." The prime minister himself reassured the international community that Pakistan's "nuclear weapon systems are meant only for self-defense."[20] Addressing global disarmament concerns, he said Pakistan would "continue to support the goals of nuclear disarmament and non-proliferation, especially in the Conference on Disarmament."[21] Pakistan also would engage in a "constructive dialogue" with other countries "on ways and means to promoting these goals…"

To the Indian leadership, Sharif's message was clear: "We are prepared to resume Pakistan-India dialogue to address all outstanding issues including the core issue of Jammu and Kashmir, as well as peace and security. These should include urgent steps for mutual restraint and equitable measures for nuclear stabilization." He reiterated Pakistan's earlier offer of a non-aggression pact to India "on the basis of a just settlement of the Jammu and Kashmir dispute."

Seeking to stay clear of ideological and religious blocs, Pakistan had framed the tests solely as a defensive step forced on it by India. Having had its nuclear program labeled as being dedicated to the making of an 'Islamic bomb', Pakistan was wary of linking any cause other than that of its own defense to its nuclear tests. As a testimony to its success in managing this, the Israelis understood to be the first target of any Islamic bomb, did not wave any red flag after Pakistan's tests. Instead, a reassured Israeli Deputy Minister Silvan Shalom said that Israel "did not see the Pakistani nuclear tests as a threat to Israel." In an interview to the Israel Defense Forces Radio, he explained, "We do not view Pakistan as our enemy. Pakistan has never been Israel's enemy, Pakistan has never threatened Israel."[22] There were fears, but only to a negligible extent, of an 'Islamic bomb', or of Pakistan exporting technology to other Muslim countries; indeed, according to Senator Daniel Patrick Moynihan, a former US Ambassador to India, "Pakistan's Ghauri missile demonstrated Pakistan's plan to re-establish Muslim rule over all of India." [23]

After India's 1974 nuclear test, there was never any doubt that, based on clearly calculated security considerations, Pakistan too would become a nuclear weapons state. After 1994 question always was when to test. Clearly there could never have been a better timing than on the heels of the Indian tests. The nuclear club, barring China ,had always given preferential treatment to India for the pursuit of its nuclear program while discriminating against Pakistan by imposing sanctions. But Pakistan testing almost alongside India would have forced it to treat India and Pakistan at par.

Crossing the Rubicon

Pakistan and India had both thus crossed the nuclear Rubicon. The prediction and promise of Pakistan's First Prime Minister ZulfikarAli Bhutto had come true. Three decades earlier, Bhutto, then as a former Foreign Minister, had predicted that India was unlikely to concede nuclear monopoly to others…"It appears that she is determined to proceed with her plans."[24] Pakistan, he foresaw, would "never surrender to a nuclear blackmail by India…The people are willing to do anything, even eat grass, to be at nuclear parity with India." It was no surprise that, taking over as prime minister of a Pakistan soon after losing half the country and being militarily defeated by India, Bhutto took the irreversible decision. In the January 1972 Multan meeting he took specific steps to develop a nuclear option.[25] Clearly, for Bhutto this was the cumulative learning from the 1948 Pakistan-India encounter and the 1965 and 1971 defeats: Nuclear power was now indispensable. "We will eat grass if need be," Bhutto had thundered. Similarly, Bhutto had said "we will fight a thousand years" to resist Indian hegemony.

Pakistan's nuclear tests had also proven the US wrong. In 1979,undeterred by the already clamped in place US sanctions, leading the nuclear talks with a US team led by Secretary of State Cyrus Vance, Pakistan's Foreign Minister Agha Shahihad rejected all American demands. The US wanted Pakistan's signature on the NPT, Kahuta nuclear facilities to be open to IAEA inspection, and a no-test promise. Frustrated, Vance finally took the diminutive, frail-structured Shahi, into the room of a particularly tall and bulky American. Gerard Smith, the veteran US Arms Control negotiator, took one look at Shahi and declared, "As you know you are entering the Valley of Death. The Indians are well in advance of you and they can totally destroy you any time... and you think you are getting security!" Unimpressed by this threatening American bluster, the steel-nerved Shahi retorted, "We understand the psychological and political advantages of our programme."[26]

Regarding India's numerical advantage, the foreign minister reminded the bulky American, was as relevant in the security calculus as the US 3,000 versus the Soviet Union's 300. In 1962, the USSR with its 300 nuclear warheads at that time, had forced Kennedy with his 3,000 to negotiate with the Soviets in the Cuban missile crisis. Shahi also reminded his American hosts that, while the US had imposed sanctions on Pakistan, Carter had asked France to provide enriched Uranium to India for the Trombay nuclear reactor. These debates continued for decades. However, ultimately, served by seasoned gurus like Shahis, twenty years later Pakistan stood vindicated.

Tests, the Indian Harangue and International Response

Meanwhile India went beyond establishing its nuclear status. It also red-flagged the Kashmir issue, one that had for decades bedeviled Pakistan-India relations. India's Home Minister Lal Krishna Advani announced: "India's decisive step to become a nuclear weapon state has brought about a qualitatively new stage in Indo-Pak relations, particularly in finding a lasting solution to the Kashmir problem." Putting Pakistan on notice, Advani added, "Islamabad should realize the change in the geo-strategic situation." Similarly, the BJP spokesman Krishan Lal Sharma warned Pakistan of a heavy price for "fuelling the conflict" and added, "If it continues with its anti-India policy, Pakistan should be prepared for India's wrath." Pakistan was sending trained militants, to keep an already restive Kashmir on the boil. The message from the Indian government's most influential voice, its Home Minister and BJP's former president, was clear: "Any further misadventure on Indian territory shall be dealt with on a proactive basis." This shrillness drowned the sane, more measured voices of the Indian Prime Minster and his foreign minister.

The strategic message from India was unnerving. It was prepared to use its nuclear status to force its way on Kashmir. The entire context was worrying. Pakistan, in the absence of India's willingness to resolve Kashmir through dialogue, remained unrelenting in promoting militancy within Kashmir.

The world could only look on. Interested primarily in fire fighting, it mulled over a viable response. And the response came: The UNSC Resolution 1172. Leading powers from the UNSC platform, in a sharp contrast to India's strategic objective, elevated the Kashmir problem from a bilateral-regional level, to the global stage. Almost four decades after the original UNSC resolutions, the security council again seized itself of the Kashmir problem. Resolution 1172 was passed. This resolution condemned the nuclear tests. Also, in its Operative Para 5 ,both India and Pakistan were urged to resume their dialogue "on all outstanding issues, particularly on all matters pertaining to peace and security, in order to remove the tensions between them, encourages them to find mutually acceptable solutions that address the root causes of those tensions, including Kashmir." Ironically, through its own vitriolic threats India had drawn unprecedented global attention to Kashmir.

Kashmir was now an international issue, no longer a bilateral matterwhich, invoking the 1972 Simla Agreement, India had always insisted it was. In fact, increased violence in Kashmir had further augmented global panic. The political temperatures of South Asia's two newly nuclear-armed states held out little hope for their re-engagement. Kashmir was the reason for the September 1997 breakdown in the bilateral dialogue. Pakistan had called off the talks complaining that, in refusing to set up a separate Working Group on Kashmir, India had reneged on the June 23 Joint Statement.[27]

Yet the heated-up military situation along the LOC required immediate engagement between the two newly revealed nuclear states. In the weeks following the tests, the United Nations, G-8, Japan, EU, and NAM, offered to mediate and host talks between the new nuclear states. Still haunted by the memory of Hiroshima, the Japanese Prime Minister

Keizo Obuchi in his address to the Japanese parliament asked the two countries to accept the Complete Test Ban (CTBT) and Non-Proliferation (NPT) treaties immediately and unconditionally.[28] To the two capitals, the message was: "Tokyo is much worried on the war-like situation at the Line of Control and the tension there could result in a nuclear conflict in South Asia."[29] As the nine-month-old deadlock continued between Pakistan and India, Tokyo offered to host talks to help resolve Kashmir, the Japanese insisted was a "nuclear flashpoint."[30]

Washington took the lead. The rising tensions had confirmed the South Asia specific conclusion of the US Department's 1997 *Proliferation Report: Threat and Response* that "unresolved disagreements, deep animosity and distrust, and the continuing confrontation between their forces in disputed Kashmir make the subcontinent a region with significant risk of nuclear confrontation."

With unusual candor, the daughter of Joseph Korbel, who had presented the best summation of the Kashmir problem in his book *Danger in Kashmir* (Princeton: 1954), addressed the Kashmir problem. On 3 June talking to press reporters, the US Secretary of State Madeleine Albright said of Kashmir, "It is a problem that came about the minute that the partition proposals came about and the princely states chose up which side, which country, they were going to go with. The problem in Kashmir of a primarily Muslim population with a Hindu maharaja that headed it, made it very difficult for them to decide. There have been over the years a number of ways tried...The item has been on the security council agenda."

Within a week on 10 June, dismissing Indian agitation over the P-5 statement on Kashmir, US Assistant Secretary of State Karl Indurfurth said, "Kashmir issue is a fact of life in the region and cannot be wished away. We are absolutely convinced that it is time now for India and Pakistan to meet, to resume the dialogue and address the fundamental issue that had divided the two countries for 50 years." The global limelight on Kashmir was unprecedented. Significantly, the Secretary General of the United Nations Kofi Annan "strongly appealed to both India and Pakistan to make every effort to reduce increasing tensions in the region especially in Kashmir." In fact, Annan took the unprecedented and indeed unpopular step of "recalling the availability of his good offices" to help initiate bilateral dialogue. The European Parliament identified specific steps to help India and Pakistan "establish a framework for reconciliation and cooperation." Specifically, the statement suggested "(co-)sponsoring a regional conference on security and confidence-building measures."[31] In his 31 May statement to the British Parliament, Foreign Secretary Robin Cook said, "There needs to be a meaningful dialogue between India and Pakistan over the issues that at present threaten stability in the region." Collectively, the P-5 foreign ministers undertook the task of "actively encouraging India and Pakistan to find mutually acceptable solutions, through direct dialogue, that address the root causes of the tension, including Kashmir, and to try to build confidence rather than seek confrontation."[32] The communiqué called on India and Pakistan to "avoid threatening military movements, cross-border violations, or other provocative acts."[33]

Committing to an active international effort to proactively focus on creating conditions for a Pakistan-India dialogue, the US ambassador at the UN Bill Richardson, proposed "a multilateral, multinational response to reduce tensions in South Asia."[34] The UN spokesman Fred Eckhard too reiterated his secretary general's offer to mediate between the two countries. In Geneva, the foreign ministers of the G-5 concluded: "The efforts to resolve disputes between India and Pakistan must be pursued with determination."

In linking its nuclear weaponization to forcing through its own version of a resolution on Kashmir, India had clearly committed a diplomatic *faux pas*. Moreover, the Indian President's letter to the US President linking Indian nuclear tests to the Chinese threat did not succeed in disrupting the Pakistan-India equation in global perception and thereby deny Pakistan justification for nuclear tests. Few countries accepted India's original justification that the 'China factor' prompted its nuclear tests. All recognized that Pakistan-India relations were responsible for the beginning of a nuclear arms race in South Asia and the undermining of the non-proliferation regime.

The belligerence at display, by a section of India's Hindu nationalist leadership, immediately after the nuclear tests was in contrast Pakistan's studied statements. Gandhi's India, having consciously crafted its peace image since inception, had now taken to some reckless nuclear brandishing. India's position, even for the US seeking a strategic alliance, was hard to defend. In fact, the US took the lead in pushing India's skeleton in the closet, Kashmir, into the global limelight.

By contrast, Pakistan was in a better diplomatic position. Even if grudgingly, and despite its statements to the contrary, the world was constrained to acknowledge that, after the Indian tests and clearly anti-Pakistan rhetoric, the die had been cast for Pakistan, which was obliged to conduct the tests. Islamabad's simultaneous dialogue offer to India, saying "no" to an arms race, and the renewed commitment to disarmament helped position Pakistan in a comfortable strategic space–of a kind Pakistan had seldom experienced. India's own follies had helped create this space.

The world seemed to be where Pakistan wanted. It acknowledged the unresolved issue of Jammu and Kashmir as the root cause of India-Pakistan problems, acknowledged that the international community had a role in resolving the problem, and offered to do so. Hence, several events conspired to position Pakistan in a better strategic space than it had been in a long time.

Nevertheless, the May tests brought the Pakistan-India conflict squarely onto the center-stage of global security concerns. The international community viewed the tests as directly undermining regional and global peace, security and stability. It believed that the unresolved Kashmir dispute blocked possibilities of peace between the two nuclear-armed neighbors. Such was the anxiety over the direction in which the two antagonistic nuclear states were headed that the P-5 opted for diplomatic micro-management. In their communiqué, they urged India and Pakistan to "halt provocative statements, refrain from any military movements that could be construed as threatening, and increase transparency in their actions. Direct communications between the parties could help to build confidence."

The Peace-Makers

It was clear that until the two nuclear neighbors engaged in a dialogue with Kashmir as a key focus, ending the nine-month Pakistan-India deadlock, the international community would remain actively engaged with South Asia –just what India was keen to avoid. At Simla in 1972, from a defeated and broken Pakistan, India had obtained an agreement that Kashmir would only be discussed within a bilateral forum. Nevertheless, Pakistan intermittently sought international intervention on Kashmir. Through bilateral diplomacy there had been negligible progress on Kashmir, Pakistan would argue. Also, Kashmir as an unresolved issue, drew its raison d'être from the 1953 UNSC Resolution. Thus in June 1998 the entire international community stood exactly where Pakistan would have wanted and India would not.

Delhi was keen to move the Kashmir problem back onto the bilateral track. India offered to revive dialogue, but based on the "Dhaka formula." According to this, a separate Working Group on Kashmir, as agreed upon in the 23 June Joint Agreement of 1997, would not be convened. Pakistan declined. The Working Group on Kashmir was the make-or-break issue for Pakistan. After 50 years of vacillation, finally, in May 1997, on the sidelines of the Male SAARC summit, India had finally accepted Pakistan's position that without resolving the Kashmir dispute normalization was not possible. Sharif's refrain was that exploring possibilities for addressing the Kashmir problem was the only way forward. Hence, discussion was crucial. And Gujral, who would often narrate his favorite Urdu couplet "*guftago bund na ho/Baat sai baat chalay*", essentially in the same vein as Sharif's rationale, did agree.[35] The two Foreign Secretaries announced this agreement between the prime ministers in June. But soon, at home the Indian prime minister came under heavy political fire for agreeing to establish the Working Group on Kashmir. Leading a weak coalition, Gujral, a man without a solid constituency, could not afford to be viewed as a 'soft-liner' on Pakistan. He retracted from the agreement. In a telling comment to the correspondent of an Indian daily, *The Telegraph,* Gujral had said, "Do you think I will give away anything to Pakistan? I am as much a nationalist as anyone else." In November 1997, I. K. Gujral's government fell.

Subsequently, the first dialogue initiative taken by Delhi under the new Prime Minister Vajpayee also did not factor in the 24 June Agreement. Significantly, even under unprecedented international pressure to engage, especially on Kashmir, Delhi's dialogue proposal to Islamabad only cursorily addressed the Kashmir dispute. Such were the ways of Delhi's South Block men. In the first three months, the dialogue offers flew across the divide freely. Most were non-starters since Islamabad and Delhi seemed working at cross purposes. Beyond their common cause of warding off international sanctions and censures, the bureaucrats found no meeting points.

The nuclear tests had proven to be the trigger for revival of the dialogue but leaders were needed to actually take it forward. It was finally left to the two prime ministers, with their known penchant for bilateral peace, to work the bureaucracies for the peace agenda. The Pakistani Prime Minister Nawaz Sharif and the Indian Prime Minister Atal Bihari Vajpayee, the two men now leading the world's most hostile nuclearized neighboring states, were committed to untying the Gordian knot: the Kashmir dispute. The two men were quite far apart in age and ideology. Nawaz Sharif, a businessman from Punjab, home to Pakistan's belligerent ruling class, had had the military dictator General Ziaul Haq for his political mentor. Vajpayee, a man of letters, had launched his political carrier in the lap of the RSS, a Hindu extremist party avowedly committed to the destruction of Pakistan. Whatever their political origins, their respective experiential learnings had wisened the two men to the imperatives of a Pakistan-India peace.

Nawaz Sharif, second time prime minister, had committed to peace with India in an election campaign that had swept him into power with a straight majority. He was convinced that peace with India had a strong constituency among the people. Having followed the conventional India policy in his first round as Prime Minister, Sharif decided to do it differently in his second round. It was in August 1996 that Sharif first raised some fundamental questions about Pakistan-India relations. Preparing to receive the US ambassador to India, Frank Wisner, Sharif asked his party Secretary General Sartaj Aziz if the two neighbors were destined to fight forever since a perfect solution "will never be" possible.[36]

Sharif was equally clear that the status quo too was not acceptable and that "some solution must be found." Aziz agreed but was clear that "giving up on their maximum positions by both sides" was a pre-requisite for a solution. Flexibility was required by both Pakistan and India. Subsequently, Sharif queried his American visitor from Delhi as to whether India would ever negotiate on Kashmir. Wisner was candid. An apparent national consensus by both sides around their respective "maximalist positions" ruled out the flexibility factor necessary for negotiations. Meanwhile Sharif, having pursued Pakistan's traditional policy towards India, was now a convert to sketching pathways to peace with this long-time adversary.

A few months later, on the hustings, this new convert stayed with his theme of resolving the Kashmir issue. He promised his voters, in interviews and speeches, that his "priorities will be to hold intensive serious negotiations with India on Kashmir and try to improve(sic) normalization with India."[37] Sharif's convictions that his peace with India theme was politically viable and that, as a Punjabi, he could pull it off politically without being labeled traitor[38], were proved correct. Sharif came to power with a thumping two-thirds majority. Once in power, he was quick to act. In response to Indian Prime Minister H.D. Deve-Gowda's congratulatory letter, Sharif suggested that foreign secretary talks should be revived within weeks.[39] Indians reciprocated. After a break of three years[40], talks began on 28 March.[41] Nawaz Sharif personally piloted the stalling dialogue process at prime minister level, first with Deve-Gowda and then with I. K. Gujral. No great visionary, only a businessman committed to Pakistan's development, Sharif was convinced that without replacing enmity with cooperation Pakistan's development was not possible. But to alter the dynamics of the relationship, Sharif knew he needed a strong partner in Delhi. Deve-Gowda was short-lived partner and Gujral proved politically weak.

In Vajpayee, Sharif had a serious partner for peace. Senior to Sharif in age and political experience, Vajpayee was a certified peace veteran. A realist on Pakistan-India relations, he understood that normalizing relations between the two neighbors was essential. As Foreign Minister in the Janata government under PM Morarji Desai, Vajpayee had on occasion intervened to salvage collapsing Pakistan-India negotiations. In 1978, for example, Pakistan's Foreign Secretary Aga Shahi arrived in India to resume talks on the Salal Dam. Under the Indus Basin Water Treaty, India could use the water but was not allowed to control the water supply. Shahi had worked out an agreement with his Indian counterpart Jagat Mehta during their 1976 meeting, but domestic political considerations prevented Pakistan from finalizing the agreement. In 1978, when Shahi returned to finalize the agreement, Mehta recanted, perhaps because of political considerations. Shahi, deciding to break protocol, called Foreign Minister Vajpayee to tell him that his delegation was going back on the treaty the two delegations had agreed upon. Vajpayee was informed that, because the negotiations had reached a deadlock, Shahi was returning home with his delegation. Vajpayee told Shahi he would get back to him in a couple of hours, which he did, to tell Shahi that the agreement would be signed. Vajpayee, the unlikely RSS man, who had credentials that made him acceptable at home to a diverse coalition of liberals, conservatives, and Hindu extremists, was acknowledged across India's western borders as a reasonable-minded realist by a wide spectrum of career diplomats.

As a prime minister leading a hard-line Hindu nationalist party, Vajpayee had spent his first eight months in office executing the tough BJP line. This included toughening India's stance on Kashmir, conducting the nuclear tests, seeing his deputy Advani roll off unprecedented threats to Pakistan with the declaration to "unilaterally and proactively" resolve the Kashmir dispute. But the international response to India's nuclear tests and the threats required a more reasonable policy towards Pakistan, and especially on Kashmir.

Delhi made its initial dialogue offer on the basis of the Dhaka formula, offering no separate Working Group on Kashmir. Islamabad rejected it, and variously labeled the offer as "political gimmickry", a "non-starter", and "totally unrealistic." India persisted with its position. However, Delhi also proposed holding foreign secretary-level talks under the rubric of peace and security, as earlier suggested by Pakistan, on items including a ban on nuclear tests, measures for avoidance of conflict, and promotion of nuclear and conventional restraint and stabilization measures.

Vajpayee knew he needed to go beyond the South Block's formulation on dialogue to ward off international pressure as well as genuinely engaging Pakistan. He realized that in Nawaz Sharif he had a willing dialogue partner. The Sharif-Vajpayee 29 July meeting in Colombo, on the sidelines of the SAARC summit, was finalized. Ahead of this meeting a preliminary political back channel was established. Nawaz Sharif deputed a PML Senator and former Secretary General of the Ministry of Foreign Affairs, AkramZaki, to meet with Vajpayee's point man on National Security, the astute former diplomat-turned politician Brajesh Mishra in London. [42] Neither the Mishra-Zaki channel nor the foreign secretaries meeting helped bridge the gap at Colombo. The Indian military's mood too was evident from the Indian defense minister's 18 July declaration that India "needs to hold on to Siachen, both for strategic reasons and wider security in the region."[43] The defense minister's statement subverted the basic principle on which the earlier six rounds of Siachen talks had taken place: disengagement from Siachen on the basis of mutual withdrawal.[44] Fernandes wanted to please the army and the hardliners in the Bharatiya Janata Party (BJP).

Unsuccessful at Colombo

Just before the Colombo meeting, Indian External Affairs Minister Jaswant Singh had met with his American counterpart Madeleine Albright. Albright was clear about the need for addressing Kashmir. During her private meeting with Jaswant Singh, the US secretary of state criticized the Indian nuclear tests as "disastrous." Her deputy Strobe Talbot later recalled that his boss "bore down on Kashmir and why now, more than ever, India and Pakistan had to get serious about finding a settlement–and so did the international community." [45]

On addressing the Kashmir quandary, Jaswant Singh knew it was work in progress. When required to perform a skit or a song as part of a bonding exercise at the ASEAN meeting in Manila, he wrote and sang this song...to no amusement of Madeline Albright.

"Why such a fuss over a few crackers in the Thar?

They weren't as loud as Nevada and Lop Nor.

Sharif took his ones and joined the fun.

Evita lost some sleep. Jiang proliferated in sun."

The 29 July meeting between the two prime ministers in Colombo ended with continuing differences over the dialogue framework.[46] Setting the tone for his bilateral meeting with Vajpayee, Nawaz Sharif had proposed in his opening statement at SAARC that Pakistan and India should engage in a sustained dialogue. "Pakistan," he said, "Is ready for an immediate resumption of bilateral foreign secretaries'- level talks on the basis of understanding reached between Pakistan and India on 23 June 1997."[47] Sharif projected himself as a man of peace. "Pakistan has never coveted nuclear arsenals…I am personally, a man of peace… wars, aggression or power projection have never been on my agenda for Pakistan."[48]

The two prime ministers first held a one-on-one meeting[49] at the Taj Samutra hotel followed by a delegation level meeting.[50] Vajpayee was keen for a joint statement on commitment to peace. Sharif told Vajpayee that the June 1997 dialogue framework was a substantive achievement and no forward movement without reference to that agreement was possible.[51]The Indian prime minister wanted bilateral dialogue. He also suggested that the two neighbors enter into trade with one another.

Yet, on Kashmir, Vajpayee maintained that the primary issue was "Pakistan-supported cross-border terrorism." The Pakistani team unsuccessfully urged the Indians that the unresolved Kashmir dispute be reflected as a central issue in the joint statement. The 90- minute Sharif-Vajpayee meetings in Colombo failed to produce a road map for further dialogue. Ultimately after the first-ever meeting between the two prime ministers no joint statement was issued.

Despite differences on how to move forward and the firm position taken by his bureaucrats[52], Sharif did not want to rule out future summit meetings. [53] After their meeting, Nawaz Sharif announced to over 250 South Asian journalists, "We have decided to continue the dialogue at the next available opportunity….We have understood each others' concerns. We have familiarized ourselves with our pre-occupations." Vajpayee conveyed a similar message to the Indian reporters. He said his meeting with Nawaz had "started the process of resumption of dialogue...the two belligerent neighbors are talking again."

But Pakistan's prime minister also had a blunt message to convey. "We accomplished zero.... Yes, it is a stalemate. We are not here to waste each other's time," Nawaz Sharif told the Sri Lankan daily *The Island*. He was firm on Pakistan's position that resumption of dialogue would be conditional upon India agreeing to talk on the basis of the agreement of 23 June 1997. By backing off from this agreement, Sharif said, India had prompted the collapse of the dialogue. India was dragging its feet "over the core issue of Kashmir", Sharif complained. Underscoring the need to engage on Kashmir, Sharif insisted, "Let us resolve the issue of Kashmir in a serious and substantive manner so that we would be able to make progress" or else "there was no point in meeting and wasting our time."[54]

Harsher words came from the bureaucrats on both sides. Pakistani officials declared that there would be no more talks between senior members of the two governments in the near future. They declared that they had no basis for resuming dialogue. They maintained that India was "rigid and inflexible."

India blamed Pakistan for remaining obsessively focused on the Kashmir issue and refusing to discuss the broader terms of the relationship. An Indian spokesman accused Pakistan of being "obsessive" and "neurotic" about Kashmir.[55] India linked dialogue on Kashmir with Pakistan ending support to Kashmiri freedom fighters.

Subsequent statements by Indian officials suggested the possibility of Indian attacks on "terrorist sanctuaries across the LOC." Vajpayee warned Pakistan that his government will "fully back" the Indian Army to "repulse the nefarious designs."[56] India accused Kashmiri freedom fighters from Azad Jammu and Kashmir of attacking civilians in IOK. Pakistan claimed large-scale deaths by Indian firing.[57] Meanwhile Human Rights organizations reported that Indian troops were responsible for raping, torturing, and executing Kashmiri people.[58]

The Colombo deadlock and grand declarations of self-praise by Pakistani and Indian bureaucrats could not alter the disturbing facts for the two prime ministers. Battles between the Indian security forces and the Kashmiris worried Vajpayee. Sharif knew that continued operations by the militants in the Valley, which was infested with Indian security forces, was unlikely to resolve the Kashmir dispute. Indian intransigence continued as clashes led to mounting Kashmir deaths. For Kashmiris, the human rights conditions deteriorated while the solution was further away than even a dream. The LOC again was on fire with civilians dying on both sides.

Against the backdrop of this worsening situation in Indian-Held Kashmir, the international community increased its pressure for the resumption of bilateral dialogue. The United States urged both governments to exercise restraint. Pakistan continued its dual-track policy of seeking dialogue with India while asking for international mediation.

By July, Nawaz Sharif's government was dealing with the growing problem of sectarianism and militancy. To Strobe Talbot, US Deputy Secretary of State [59],Nawaz complained that his 1997 victory was not against Benazir Bhutto alone. He had won against the "right-wing radicals" who he claimed had wanted an Iranian-style revolution in Pakistan.

From Washington, the pressure to go through with signing the CTBT and the NPT, and to support US's position at the Conference on Disarmament (COD) in Geneva, continued. Defense of Islamabad's position by simply tying it to Delhi position, was relatively simple, as it was strategically logical. But then Nawaz Sharif under pressure would find himself incapable of arguing this robustly. Instead during his difficult solo behind-close-door engagements with the Americans, Nawaz would also raise the specter of the threat that was increasingly worrying Washington, the Islamic militant threat.

Just before Sharif left for Colombo, Talbot met him on 22 July to convince him of the need to sign up on the non-proliferation mechanisms. Part of the tool-kit Talbot carried with him, which he naively believed would help him 'fix' Pakistan's position on non-proliferation, was a letter from his President. It did not work. Sharif was irked by Clinton's reference to Pakistan's nuclear test as a "mistake." Sharif's retort was political and convenient, not strategic and straightforward. "If I had not made the mistake, as the President calls it, someone else would be sitting in the Prime Minister's House right now. That someone probably would be a fanatic.

We have no dearth of those."[60] Adding more flair to perhaps his real fear, Pakistan's prime minister added, "Either that, or the country would have gone to the dogs."[61] This kind of talk was clearly 'conduct unbecoming' for a country's prime minister. Although militancy and sectarianism were on the rise in Pakistan, such comments by the country's prime minister to a US official were highly inappropriate. Unsurprisingly recalling the conversation, the US official wrote, "I could not imagine hearing something similar in Delhi."[62]

Emerging stress on the western front: CIA, OBL, Taliban, and the ISI

Militancy as a tool to flag the Kashmir issue was now boomeranging. For Pakistan too, the law of diminishing returns had kicked in. Pakistan generally and the ISI specifically, were being blamed for most militant activities in Indian Held Kashmir. ISI-CIA's principal partnership objective, of avenging the US defeat in Vietnam by defeating the Soviets in Afghanistan, had been achieved, with the monumental additional bonus of the 1991 breakup of the Soviet Union. Essentially, the partnership had run its course. The former partners were now entering a conflict zone. The CIA watched with great apprehension the beginnings of triangular ties between the Taliban, al-Qaeda, and the Kashmiri Mujahedeen. While the Clinton Administration itself engaged with the Taliban, it was the ISI, as principal mentors and patrons of the Taliban and the Kashmiri Mujahedeen, which the CIA viewed as being indirectly responsible for this three-way nexus. Increasingly, the CIA would expect the ISI to leverage its control and good will with the Taliban to rein in Osama bin Laden, the al-Qaeda chief. While Washington was not confrontational with bin Laden's hosts, it was getting weary of them. The CIA's Counter-terrorist Cell was expanding the focus of its operations to Pakistan's borderlands.

In early August, al-Qaeda struck and struck hard. On 7 August, it conducted signature attacks on the US embassies in Nairobi and Dar-es-Salam, leaving dozens dead. The very next day, not in a connected but related development, on 8 August, al-Qaeda's hosts, the Taliban, with support from the pro-Pakistan Mujahedeen group led by Gulbadin

Hikmatyar, managed a decisive victory in Mazar-i-Sharif. US intelligence claimed that intercepts proved that members of a Pakistan-based sectarian group, Sipah-i-Sahaba, and Pakistan military men also participated in the offensive. A Hazara massacre followed the Taliban victory. A Taliban attack on the Iranian Consulate, in which one journalist and seven intelligence officers were killed, prompted Washington's counter-terrorism machinery to zero in on Pakistan for monitoring and countering bin Laden's activities.

Buoyed by their Mazar victory, the Taliban were gaining in self-confidence. Around the same time, Washington would seek their acquiescence in what was becoming the Clinton's Administration immediate and primary security concern. Washington wanted Osama bin Laden, alive or dead. The intelligence chatter was that he had moved in those areas. CIA Counter-terrorist Center planned the August strike. General Ralston visited the Pakistan Army General Jehangir Karamat to inform him of their Tomahawk missiles flying through Pakistan airspace lest he mistakes them for Indian missiles. Accordingly, through the hour of the planned attack, Ralston arranged to have dinner with the Pakistan Army chief to ensure there were no costly misunderstandings.

The Cruise missiles were fired as planned. But it was an unsuccessful attack. Despite intelligence reports of bin Laden's impending arrival, he never came. Eight men in al-Qaeda training camps were killed, probably men from a Pakistani sectarian outfit being trained to kill. For the reported Pakistani civilian deaths along the border, the US President wrote a letter of regret to the Pakistani prime minister. Later, the reports were proven incorrect. In the coming months, Washington intensified its trailing of Osama bin Laden.

The matter of "sanctuaries" was also raised by Washington. Announcing the Cruise missile strikes against several al-Qaeda camps in Afghanistan and an alleged chemical weapons facility in Sudan, Clinton told the Americans, "There will be no sanctuaries for terror. We will defend our people, our interests, and values."[63] The issue of sanctuaries was to haunt Pakistan-US relations for almost two decades.

Breakthrough at Durban

For Pakistan-India relations, the 29 August to 3 September NAM summit in Durban proved the breakthrough event. The two peace-seeking prime ministers had ensured that the groundwork was done by their respective sides. Nawaz Sharif had inducted his Finance Minister Sartaj Aziz as the new Foreign Minister. Aziz replaced the former military Captain (and military ruler Field Marshal Ayub Khan's son) Gohar Ayub. Sartaj Aziz, an economist, a former international bureaucrat, and two-time Finance Minister in Sharif's government, was Nawaz Sharif's trusted man.

Not surprisingly, at Durban, as NAM members met, the earlier Colombo breakdown of dialogue, between Pakistan and India, the two new nuclear powers had emerged as a global concern. Also, for India, Durban was a reminder of the dilemma it faced. The Non Aligned Movement made an unprecedented call for the resolution of the Kashmir dispute.

Taking over as Chairman of the 12th NAM Summit, Nelson Mandela, President of South Africa and globally acknowledged icon of morality and justice, declared, "All of us remain concerned that the issue of Jammu and Kashmir should be solved through peaceful negotiations and we should be willing to lend all the strength we have to the resolution of this matter."

Vajpayee hit back the following day. In his address, India's annoyed Prime Minister Vajpayee warned "third parties" to stay out of the dispute.[64] Vajpayee knew, however, that the absence of a substantive Pakistan-India dialogue on Kashmir would keep the dispute in the international limelight.

Kashmiri political and armed pressure, combined with Islamabad's legal pressure, sought a credible response from Delhi on the question of Kashmiri self-determination. Instead, Delhi's military oppression and propaganda against the Kashmiri struggle continued. International human rights groups and media often cut through Delhi's rhetoric and oppression. Obviously, denial was no policy. With Delhi as the principal culprit, Islamabad too was errant. Islamabad often let Rawalpindi continue to depend on the armed militants to push for a solution. Pakistan's use of militancy to pressurize India and to draw global attention to the Kashmir question often drew criticism. Transferring the Afghan Mujahedeen phenomenon onto the Kashmir context was backfiring. It was proving divisive for the Kashmiri struggle and was also alienating the non-violent movement. At home in Pakistan, its blowback was increased sectarian killings.

To find a way out of this stalemated situation, the two prime ministers were now agreed in favor of re-engagement. Bureaucrats worked the modalities to resume dialogue. Vajpayee prepared the public for re-engagement. By announcing his dialogue offer, with the caveat that "the dialogue must be comprehensive and not just focused on Kashmir"[65], Vajpayee assured the Indians that his offer was conditional on Pakistan's commitment to stop "cross-border terrorism."

A joint statement at Durban announced, "An understanding in principle, to operationalize the mechanism for dialogue on all issues as per the agreed agenda."[66] The agreement that detailed the modalities and dates for resuming the dialogue had explicitly stated in its preamble that this agreement was "pursuant to the agreement set out in Para 4 of the Joint Statement issued at Islamabad on June 23, 1997."

India did ultimately revert to the June 23 1997 Composite Dialogue Agreement that it had reneged on in September 1997. Pakistan's persistence had paid off. India's hard-line government, boxed-in by its own strategy of combining nuclear tests with threats to Pakistan,[67] opted for greater flexibility. It accepted the very framework which it had criticized the Gujral government for devising.[68]

In Durban, at the 120-member NAM meeting, Kashmir was in full play, beyond just in the bilateral dynamics. Mirroring the dilemma the two countries faced, Pakistan and India both agreed to effectively end the eight-month long diplomatic deadlock and open dialogue on Kashmir yet also found it necessary to state their respective contrasting positions on Kashmir. The bilateral dialogue was to resume in accordance with the June 1997 Composite Dialogue formula. Yet the content, contradictions, and compulsions of Pakistan and India's positions on Kashmir were all out in the open. India's agreement to revive the Composite Dialogue framework signaled new content in diplomacy, namely that Delhi understood the need for dialogue. Yet domestic compulsion dictated a fight-back when any third party suggested just what India and Pakistan were in fact doing. For example, Vajpayee responded somewhat harshly to Mandela's call to resolve Kashmir.

Like at Simla, in Durban too both reiterated their divergent positions on Kashmir, India claiming a rightful control over entire Jammu and Kashmir and Pakistan seeking the Kashmiris' right of self-determination through a UN-mandated plebiscite in the entire Jammu and Kashmir. Yet Durban was unlike Simla. There, seeds for greater animosity had been sown, as is always inevitable if the vanquished retains the will to rise swiftly and fight back. By contrast, in Durban, the engagement between two nuclear powers was underway. The nuclear tests and the global reprimand on unresolved Kashmir, both seemed to have put the prime ministers of the two asymmetrical countries on a temporarily equal footing. Sharif and Vajpayee both knew adjustment in maximalist positions on Kashmir would be integral to any viable modus operandi for détente and cooperation. And Kashmiri concerns too had to be factored in.

Bilateralism and terrorism were the two premises through which India had sought to deflect international focus on the Kashmir dispute. Vajpayee raised both at NAM. Rejecting any third party interference on Kashmir, Vajpayee said, "The Simla Agreement, which both India and Pakistan have ratified, provides an agreed mechanism for resolving these differences amicably among ourselves."[69] Vajpayee maintained that bilateralism had received a boost in Colombo, where he had a "cordial" meeting with his Pakistani counterpart. At Durban, he referred to the ongoing bilateral dialogue. Post-Colombo developments related to Islamabad-Delhi relations had proved him right. Kashmir, the Indian prime minister categorically stated, however, "was and would remain an integral part of India." The "real problem" in Kashmir was one of cross-border terrorism.

Almost a decade into India's failure to crush the Kashmiri freedom movement, for the international community Delhi was increasingly framing the movement as a terrorist movement. And with evidence of Pakistani men, munitions and military training aiding the indigenous freedom struggle Delhi believed it could superimpose the 'terrorism' problem upon the political struggle. Additionally, sections of the freedom movement had taken to violent ways, harming civilians and hence aiding Indian propaganda.

Indian strategy was to dovetail cross-border terrorism into the emerging global level concern regarding terrorism. Delhi began equating what it considered "cross-border terrorism" with the terrorism and Taliban problem of Afghanistan. The concern about terrorism was fast spreading. Washington had also attacked Sudan. India had argued that the common factor linking terrorism, the Taliban, and the cross-border terrorism it faced was Pakistan's intelligence agency, the ISI. At Durban, Vajpayee advocated a "concerted international action" against terrorism. In a veiled criticism of the United States ignoring India's concerns, he said "terrorism could not be fought unilaterally or selectively."

In fact, while seeking bilateral dialogue, Pakistan would simultaneously advocate international mediation. The nuclear tests, Islamabad believed, had turned the assumption of "Kashmir a nuclear flash-point" into a palpable reality, one that Islamabad would work to the benefit of Pakistan and of the Kashmiris. India, meanwhile, would insist Kashmir was a bilateral issue but would seek international intervention to tackle the problem of "cross-border-terrorism" that Delhi claimed was the real Kashmir problem.

Having framed the freedom struggle as cross-border terrorism, Vajpayee argued that terrorism was a "scourge which is a plain naked assault on humanity and the values that civilized societies live by."[70] He went on the offensive against those countries that for "reasons of political convenience or worse" failed to agree on a definition of terrorism. In a direct attack on the governments and human rights groups who criticized India for human rights violations in Kashmir, Vajpayee said, "With myopic loftiness, they judged democracies and terrorists who battered open societies on the same scale." [71]

Clearly these existing paradoxical parameters provided no room for accommodation. Therefore, steering the relations forward could not be left to the bureaucrats. Durban yet again established that genuine breakthrough on Kashmir would require statesmanship from both sides; rising above the conflicting realities of Kashmir built on 50 years of history and perceptions among the Pakistanis, Indians, and now increasingly the Kashmiris.

In Durban, Foreign Minister Sartaj Aziz led the delegation as the prime minister could not attend the summit. Aziz called on Vajpayee but the Durban breakthrough was publicized only after the two prime ministers met in New York. Almost the same joint statement, drafted jointly by the two Foreign Secretaries earlier in Durban, was issued in New York on 23 September

New York Bonding

In an interesting twist of events, from the balance of terror that the May nuclear tests had established had emerged the most substantive peace initiative that the two chronically hostile neighbors of South Asia had witnessed since their birth in 1947. However, unknown to these two peace-partners, a sharply contrasting movement in a parallel universe was taking place. From the Himalayan peaks, a clique of senior Pakistani Generals had interpreted the post-May global concern for the settlement of Kashmir as an opportunity to re-invigorate the smoldering Kashmiri movement in IOK and to force Delhi's hand on Kashmir, or at least on Siachen. They had moves and they had ideas for untying this Gordian knot.

By September, the prime ministers of the two countries met in New York, signaling a new beginning between South Asia's new nuclear states. Putting aside much of the global trepidation about strategic instability following the tests, Prime Minister Nawaz Sharif and Prime Minister Vajpayee decided that the stalled composite dialogue would be resumed. The two prime ministers charted preliminary pathways towards peace. It was now India's Hindu nationalist leadership that undertook to take forward the Composite Dialogue framework that theSharif-Gujral equation had agreed upon in June 1997.

Nawaz and Vajpayee, their respective bureaucracies led by their trusted men, now personally conducted the normalization process. There was never any doubt that only top political personalities could lead the process of a genuine normalization process, for they alone had the legitimacy and the confidence to work through the obstinately tangled problem of Kashmir. It would take none less than the prime ministers to put behind them the chronic hostility and distrust that had virtually become part of the DNA of the Pakistan and Indian civil and military bureaucracy. A paradigm shift was essential.

In New York Nawaz Sharif and Vajpayee had positioned themselves to lead their countries back on the negotiation track. Both were satisfied with their decision to initiate dialogue on Kashmir, on other disputes plus movement on some Confidence Building Measures. Essentially at New York it was clear that at the operational level Pakistan had now moved from its "only Kashmir" position and India from its "no Kashmir" position on bilateral dialogue. Whatever the calculations among the bureaucrats on both sides it was evident that such diplomatic movement would help to create an environment of cooperation conducive to negotiations. At the New York meeting Sharif, however, did emphasize that faster progress on normalization would be contingent on progress on the Kashmir dispute.

In New York, Sharif and Vajpayee concluded they could together smoke the hitherto ellusive peace pipe in a nuclearized South Asia. Both agreed that only political leaders, and not foreign secretaries, could conclusively untangle the knotty bilateral issues.[72]The Americans closely watched these important peacemaking moments between the two and the US President met with both prime ministers.[73] While the global flagging of Kashmir and need for bilateral dialogue were factors that contributed to the Vajpayee-Sharif engagement, the two leaders were themselves convinced on the need for active bilateral cooperation.

The two prime ministers also decided to open a back-channel contact for direct and reliable communication. Sharif was, however, clear that, despite the back channel, direct contact between the two prime ministers was also essential. After the New York meeting, names of back-channel envoys were exchanged. India nominated former journalist R.K Misra.[74] Nawaz Sharif's choice was his Principal Secretary Anwar Zahid.[75] However, Zahid died shortly after.[76]Niaz Naik, a former Foreign Secretary, was the second choice.

The seeds for the historic Lahore summit were sown in New York. At the lunch meeting that Sharif hosted for Vajpayee, he invited the Indian prime minister to visit Pakistan. And, when the two Prime Ministers agreed on starting a Delhi-Lahore bus service, Nawaz Sharif invited Vajpayee to travel on that bus. Vajpayee agreed.

In New York, Pakistan also took the lead in assuaging the fears of the international community on the nuclear question.[77] Although the prime minister told the UN General Assembly that, as declared nuclear powers, "neither side has the luxury to contemplate the use of force," [78] Pakistan was conditionally willing to sign the Comprehensive Test Ban Treaty. First, it had to be in conditions "free from coercion and pressure", which meant the international community had to remove the sanctions. Secondly, it was necessary that India also signed the CTBT. Both conditions were unlikely to be fulfilled.

Vajpayee, meanwhile, detailed the nature of bilateral dialogue decided for October. He announced that the two sides had decided to end cross-LOC firing and discuss defense matters, including the question of deploying nuclear missiles, in the October dialogue. "A new era in Indo-Pakistani co-operation is being opened," a satisfied Vajpayee told the press.

This was happening less than a hundred days of having conducted the nuclear tests and watching their bilateral relations take a steep dive. It had surprised the global community, who, following the tests, with bated breath, had predicted apocalyptic times ahead. Yet fear gave way to hope as the two nuclear neighbors began active diplomatic engagement. To many, the otherwise disputed concept of peace dividends emanating from the shadow of a nuclearized balance of terror in South Asia, perhaps appeared plausible. Hence within months of the nuclear tests, new vistas for peace and cooperation had been opened up.

Burdens of Patronage

Important developments were taking place on the other side of Pakistan's north-western borders. The US Vice President Al Gore telephoned the Saudi Intelligence chief Prince Turki Al-Faisal bin Abd Al-Aziz Al-Saud. Gore told Turki it was time to remind Mullah Umar of his June promise and get possession of the man behind the US embassy bombings in Africa. Turki acquiesced to the UN Vice President's request.

He knew though that the Taliban leader had not responded to his several messages about handing over bin Laden. Turki recalled that several times the Taliban leader had agreed on setting up a joint commission of Islamic scholars to decide the Islamic procedure for handing over bin Laden to the Saudis. On his June trip, the Saudi Minister for Religious Affairs, whose ministry's various outfits often made contributions to al-Qaeda, accompanied Turki as he arrived in Kandahar a worried man.

Turki was mindful that Osama bin Laden was fast emerging as the Arab world's Che Guevara. His followers across the entire Arab World would access his interviews and statements to western media via dish antennas and satellites. As early as January 1998, the Saudi authorities were alerted by their own Saudi intelligence outfits to the al-Qaeda threat within the Kingdom. Bin Laden's militant followers, in possession of deadly weapons, were arrested. By March, information on Saudi financiers of bin Laden was also uncovered. Saudi money from charitable organizations with Wahabi leanings was ending up with terrorist organizations, especially in Pakistan and Afghanistan. Turki believed his June trip had been successful. Recalling the trip, he told the prestigious German magazine *Der Spiegel*, "Incidentally, we had a rather friendly conversation in June 1998. I told Mullah Omar that it would be better to give us bin Laden, that is, if he had any interest in continuing his friendly relations with Saudi Arabia. He agreed, at least in principle. We agreed to set up a joint committee to arrange the details of bin Laden's extradition."[79]

Turki was somewhat more apprehensive about his September meeting with Mullah Umar. [80] Osama bin Laden, the shy, young Saudi financier and dedicated anti-Soviet fighter the Prince had first met in 1984 in Peshawar, had now declared war against the US. In August, bin Laden conducted deadly attacks on US embassies. Within days, American missiles had unsuccessfully targeted him on Afghan soil. Mullah Umar had ignored Turki's repeated reminders of working out a mechanism for handing over bin Laden to the Saudis. The Saudi Intel chief knew that getting a helping hand from the Taliban's Pakistani mentors could be a necessary move. He arrived in Islamabad in his special plane. Turki met the Pakistani prime minister. Nawaz Sharif exercised virtually no influence over the Taliban, whose operational mentors were located in the Inter-Services

Intelligence(ISI), Pakistan's key spy agency. As partners of the biggest covert war in US history, the ISI had moved from power to power in numbers, ranks and resources under US patronage.

While the ISI was "sold on the Taliban", Pakistan's elected prime minister was wary of them. Pakistan's Afghan policy was largely in the military and ISI's hands. For example, on 25 May 1997, the decision to recognize the Taliban government in Afghanistan was made by the ISI chief. The PM was traveling on the Islamabad-Lahore motorway, and he was merely informed that Pakistan had recognized the Taliban government! In a hurry to acknowledge Taliban control of Mazar-i-Sharif on Sunday 25 May,[81] Pakistan extended recognition the same day.[82] It was a Sunday but the ISI, in acknowledgement of the Taliban's Mazari-i-Sharif victory, decided recognition could not be delayed. At the Foreign Office, Director-General Afghanistan Iftikhar Murshid, who for nearly a decade had personally witnessed its political vicissitudes, opened shop on Sunday. At the Foreign Office, Murshid, along with Pakistan's ambassador-at-large for Afghanistan, Aziz Khan, explained to selected foreign envoys Islamabad's decision to recognize the Taliban government.

Ever since the Taliban captured Kabul in September 1996, Islamabad's political governments remained keen to advocate reconciliation between the Taliban and the main opposition group, the Northern Alliance. In December 1996, Pakistan made the first reconciliation effort when Pakistan's Foreign Secretary Najmuddin Shaikh visited the Northern alliance in Shibergan and Mullah Umar in Kandahar. Subsequently, Pakistan's experienced hands on Afghanistan held several rounds on reconciliation with the Northern Alliance and the Taliban. Finally, on Nawaz's invitation, the Northern Alliance leader Professor Burhanudin Rabbani came to Islamabad in December 1997 and the Taliban President Mullah Hasan Rabbani in March 1998. Assisted by his Foreign Office team's groundwork, Nawaz Sharif was able to convince the Afghans of the advantages of holding an intra-Afghan political dialogue. Matters progressed under the joint auspices of the UN and the OIC. A Steering Committee was formed, with Taliban and Northern Alliance representation. It met in Islamabad from 26 April to 3 May. But, soon thereafter, the talks collapsed. This is the extent to which Pakistani civilians could exercise influence over the Taliban and broadly over the Afghan situation. Now, four months later, the Osama bin Laden factor had entered the already complex internal Afghan situation. By virtue of Pakistan being in the inner-most circle of influence within the Taliban set-up and the Saudis being aware of it, it was only normal for the Saudi intelligence chief to believe that the ISI chief could be helpful in convincing Mullah Umar. General Rana, the ISI chief, accompanied Turki.

Interestingly, the other Pakistani official nominated by the civilian government to accompany Turki, Pakistan's Ambassador at-large Aziz Khan , found himself boarding Air Force One, the Pakistan air chief's dedicated airplane. Khan was tasked with delivering five Iranians, who had been captured in Mazar Sharif by the Taliban, to the Iranian authorities. After the capture of 20 Iranians, Tehran had condemned the Taliban but held Pakistan responsible. Accordingly, Tehran demanded that Pakistan ensure the release of its prisoners. Tehran's threat to attack Afghanistan if its citizens were not released, combined with Pakistan's intervention, helped to secure their release. Ambassador Aziz was now traveling in the Pakistan air chief's plane to deliver the Iranian prisoners. Clearly, the burdens of patronage were now mounting on Pakistan.

Meanwhile, the Kandahar Mission had failed. Pakistan's ISI chief was unlikely to have convinced Mullah Umar to hand over bin Laden. In Prince Turki's own words, "I had come to pressure him to go ahead with the extradition, and I encountered a completely transformed Omar. He was extremely nervous, perspired, and even screamed at me. He denied that he had promised us he would extradite bin Laden, and wanted nothing to do with a joint committee. He wanted to know what had possessed us to want to arrest such an illustrious holy warrior as Osama bin Laden! And why didn't we prefer to free the world of the infidels? He was furious. I could not help but think that he might have been taking drugs. When he continued to insult Saudi Arabia and the royal family, I ended the meeting."[83] Pakistani diplomat Murshid described it no differently. He recalled how Mullah Umar left his room in a rage and poured water over his head, returned to the room, and in anger continued to blame the Saudis for being American lackeys. [84]

The failed meeting triggered multiple speculations. For the Americans, with the alarm bells ringing in Langley on OBL's next possible targets, the capture of OBL was a high priority. There were questions within Washington as to how sincere the Saudis actually were in convincing the Taliban to hand over OBL. In the Saudi camp, was there in fact sympathy for OBL, after all a Saudi son? Were the Saudis actually only seeking some guarantee for the protection of the Kingdom from OBL? As for the Pakistanis, there was skepticism in Washington over whether the ISI would make genuine efforts to convince the Taliban to hand over OBL to the Americans.

Peace Gets Going

Meanwhile, following the Nawaz-Vajpayee New York meetings, the India-Pakistan peace process steered by the top leadership was effectively underway. In New York, while in principle the revival of the Composite Dialogue, a framework for dialogue between bureaucrats and military men, was revived, the two PMs decided to use non-official channels, principally back-channel contacts between experienced participants of Track-Two diplomacy. By October the Composite Dialogue process was also underway, beginning with talks on the Kashmir dispute and on Peace and Security, including Confidence Building Measures (CBMs). In November, talks on the bilateral disputes were held. It was hardly surprising that the 'dialogue' was in fact a reiteration by both sides of already held positions. Precisely for this reason, the preparation of the Lahore Summit was overseen by the political leaders, the prime minister and the foreign ministers, and was not left to bureaucrats alone.

Significantly, around this time, on 7 October, against the backdrop of continuous political unrest, the prime minister decided to send the Army chief General JehangirKaramat packing. The newspapers had carried front-page headlines that, during his lecture at the Naval War College, the army chief had recommended the setting up of a National Security Council to act as a joint civil-military arbiter of the nation's affairs.[85] A livid Nawaz Sharif, driving on his way to Murree, wanted the defense ministry to simply issue a notification announcing the army chief's dismissal. Sharif's cool-headed Principal Secretary, the seasoned bureaucrat Saeed Mehdi, advised him to meet with General Karamat personally. The General was called in to meet the prime minister. The prime minister let him know he could not work with him. The army chief sent in his resignation. The civilian chatter was that the matter was "amicably settled."

Interestingly, General Karamat been put to the test for his commitment to the Constitution during the prime minister's 1997 confrontation with the judiciary and the President Farooq Leghari. The general was called upon to act by all sides yet he acted strictly within Constitutional parameters. After the departure of the President, General (retd) Iftikhar Ali Khan, the former Chief of General Staff and then Defense Secretary, made a statement on behalf of the government generously complimenting the army's role, stating, "After the removal of the 8th Amendment, the army has taken its orders from the prime minister and not the President... The army's positive (sic) role during the crisis would be remembered forever."[86] Such praise had seemed unnecessary yet not unprecedented.[87] Perhaps deep in trouble and swamped by endless criticism, Nawaz Sharif, like all politicians, was haunted by the fear of some military general lurking on the side planning his exit. His earlier praise for Karamat had now been converted into apprehension, maybe even resentment. Media criticism was particularly sharp. For example, commenting on Army chief Karamat's advice to be patient, an editorial wrote," This is to be welcomed if it means that the military leadership knows the answers, will drum them into the current political leadership and accept responsibility for their implementation. But if it means that the military leadership is seeking to stay aloof, we would beg to disagree. The peoples' patience could run out faster than the military's. And act of omission no less than those of commission can have far-reaching consequences. Indeed, sometimes they are the very stuff of history."[88]

Karamat's dismissal was not the first of a forces chief by Nawaz Sharif. In May 1997, after a probe into the controversial Agosta submarine deal had established the culpability of the Chief of Naval Staff Admiral Mansur ulHaq, the prime minister asked the then Secretary Defense H. R. Pasha to "advise" the naval chief to resign. The naval chief did resign. That earned Sharif praise from the media. A leading independent weekly wrote, "Prime

Minister Nawaz Sharif deserves high praise for relieving Admiral MansoorulHaq of his duties. The navy chief embroiled his service in unbecoming controversy, gave it a bad name and undermined its morale."[89]

After sending General Karamat home, Prime Minister Sharif appointed General Pervez Musharraf, then serving as Corps Commander Mangla, as the new chief. Musharraf, who superseded two generals, was appointed on the recommendation of his key aide and Minister for Petroleum Chaudhary Nisar. Nisar's brother Iftikhar Ali Khan, the Defense Secretary and a retired general, would vouch for Musharraf as a professional non-political general. Elected prime ministers always factored in these considerations, hoping they would prove a safety valve against coup-makers. The widespread chatter on possible reactions from the GHQ to the unprecedented removal of their chief soon died down. It appeared that the men in khaki would remain subservient to the orders of the elected prime minister.

Within days of his appointment the new army chief set about bringing his own men into key posts. In fact, within three days of his appointment, he had changed the commanders of the three strategic corps: the Lahore 4 Corps, Rawalpindi 10 Corps, and Karachi 5 Corps. While in doing so the new chief was exercising his institutional authority, yet this scale and haste in the shuffle drew comment from the media. After all, there was a history of repeated direct and indirect army coups that had overthrown constitutionally elected prime ministers. Some eyebrows were raised in the prime minister's inner circle too.

However, the only appointment in which the prime minister had a say was that of the chief of the ISI. Musharraf wanted to appoint General Aziz, the head of ISI's Research & Analysis Wing, to the top slot at ISI and General Ziauddin Khawaja as the new Chief of General Staff at the GHQ. The prime minister, constitutionally authorized to appoint the country's spy chief, declined the army chief's request to promote General Aziz. Nawaz Sharif interviewed both officers and selected Ziauddin as the DG ISI. Musharraf appointed Aziz as the Chief of General Staff. The prime minister, constitutionally the reporting as well as the appointing authority for the ISI chief, picked Ziauddin for the post. This general was serving as

Adjutant General and before that had commanded the 30 Corps Gujranwala. The military talk was that Ziauddin, with only limited command experience, was not a strong candidate for either of the two positions. However, he was the new army chief's close friend and also known to the prime minister's family with especially close ties to his father.

While Ziauddin held the top slot, the army chief ensured that his own trusted appointees filled all the strategic slots in the ISI. This included the second tier command positions at the ISI headquarters and in key cities, including Lahore, Karachi, and Quetta, Ziauddin, did not resist this. The DG-Internal security was bound by rules to report to the army chief. Also, with eight to nine brigadiers serving under every section head, the ISI was operationally under GHQ control.

Siachen Moves in Reverse

Meanwhile resumption of bilateral talks on Siachen almost coincided with these top-level changes in the army.

At the Siachen talks, the Indians reneged from their own 1994 offer of mutual withdrawal.[90] Instead, India's four-point proposal presented at the talks called for a comprehensive ceasefire based on a freeze of "present ground positions", discussions on the modalities for implementing the ceasefire within an agreed time-frame, a "bilateral monitoring mechanism", and authentication of existing ground positions. It was crafted for failure. It sought a status quo solution, which Pakistan rejected.

The Indian DGMO Lt.-Gen. Inder K. Verma, claimed at the end of the talks on 6 November that the area north and east of grid point NJ 9842, where the LOC ended, had been under India's control even before the Simla Agreement was signed on 3 July, 1972. This was a completely baseless claim. Why would the 1984 Operation Meghdoot have been conducted if India already controlled Siachen area? Also, why, if Verma was correct about controlling Siachen before the 1972 Simla Agreement, would Rajiv Gandhi on 16 November 1989 referring to Operation Meghdoot declare on the hustings in Kolkata that "We have *recovered* about 5,000 square kilometers of area *from occupied Kashmir* in Siachen. We will not forgo one square kilometer of that."

Rajiv's statement countered Verma's 6 November claim and also explained that Rajiv's politics prompted him to reject the significant June 17, 1989 joint statement on Siachen prepared by the two Defense Secretaries. According to the joint statement issued on June 17, 1989, recorded: "There was *agreement* by both sides to work towards a comprehensive settlement, *based on redeployment of forces* to reduce the chances of conflict, avoidance of the use of force and determination of future positions on the ground *soas to conform with the Simla Agreement* and to ensure durable peace in the Siachen area. The army authorities of both sides will determine these positions" (emphasis added, throughout). The fact of an "agreement" was explicitly mentioned, so also the two basic principles on which it was based: "redeployment of forces" (that is, withdrawal) and "determination of future positions on the ground so as to conform with the Simla Agreement". It was potentially a basis of settling the Siachen dispute. Both parties would withdraw to their positions as at the signing of Simla Agreement.

On June 18, the next day, at a joint press conference the two foreign secretaries acknowledged and praised the Defense Secretaries' June 17 statement. Pakistan Foreign Secretary Humayun Khan referred to the Defense Secretaries' meeting. According to the Voice of America's tape, he called it "a significant advance" and spoke of a joint commitment to *"relocation of forces to positions occupied at the time of the Simla Agreement.*[91] The exact location of these positions will be worked out in detail by military authorities of the two countries." Foreign Secretary S.K. Singh said: "I would like to thank the Foreign Secretary, Dr.Humayun Khan, and endorse everything he has said."

The very next day Aftab Seth, Joint Secretary and official spokesman of the Ministry of External Affairs (MEA) in New Delhi, said that no agreement had been reached on troop withdrawals. "There was no indication of any such agreement in the joint press statement issued at the end of the talks." This was factually incorrect.

Indians also complained about Pakistani troops firing on Siachen.[92]It is possible the firing was taking place. The Kargil planners may have sought a way to engage Indian attention away from the Kargil area. Obviously unaware, the Pakistani delegation denied that their troops had carried out any such attack.[93] The talks ended in a fiasco. There was an unraveling of the progress made during the earlier rounds. For the generals' clique, in the Indian reiteration of its recalcitrance over Siachen, lay a sense of vindication.

And ironically, this too when the Pakistani and Indian prime ministers were busy trying to develop an architecture for dialogue to settle outstanding disputes like Siachen. These contradictory moves from Delhi conveyed that, either Vajpayee had not managed to get other players on board in his peace efforts with Pakistan, or India wanted to play 'good-cop, bad-cop' while fundamentally remaining content with the status quo. India as a bigger power had deliberately opted for an arbitrary approach in its relationship. This was obvious for example on the question of the accession of the Muslim-majority princely State Kashmir. Pakistan's response to this had been use of covert force. Larger in size, a confident Delhi did believe, it could violate explicit and implicit legal parameters. It was this approach that was mirrored in India's 6 November reversal on Siachen.

Choices available to Pakistan were clear. Either it tried to engage with India diplomatically, face the issue head-on, and force India to review its arbitrary approach, or use force to get its own way. India, by backing off from its earlier commitment during the Siachen talks, had demonstrated that it believed in the old adage, the dreaded truth that possession amounts to half-ownership. Pakistan had to choose the path, either of diplomacy or of force.

This was the ongoing dimension of Pakistan-India relations. Chronicled in the history of Pakistan-India relations was Pakistan's desire to 'undo' India's illegal and unfair occupation of Kashmir. Until the 1971 debacle and Pakistan's break-up, Pakistan's civil-military bureaucracy and ruling politicians were generally on the same page about India. Led by ZulfikarAli Bhutto, Pakistan's response to the 1971 tragedy was to set out on the nuclear path, strengthening strategic ties with China and throwing open the world west of its borders for economic and security engagement. Contrary to a politician's response, influential sections within the army leadership believed covert use of force against India was an effective way to tackle the adversary. The military coup of the late seventies and the overall Pakistani institutional power balance tilted in the army's favor allowed the military leadership to autonomously conduct policy. Moreover, the army's partnership with the CIA in conducting the covert war against the Soviet Union in Afghanistan further strengthened the Pakistani military as the principal policy-maker.

By November 1998, two policy approaches towards India were in play. The constitutionally elected government had already opted for diplomacy and dialogue. While a small clique of army generals had, however, surreptitiously, set off on the path of covert war. And this clique must have received India's recalcitrance over Siachen with a sense of vindication.

Unknown to many, there was a new major confrontation in the making. Indian backing off at the negotiating table from even the partially agreed upon basis for settlement of the Siachen issue must have justified for the Kargil planners, their own cross –LOC covert operation that was underway.

The Kargil planners' clique had troops crossing the LOC to pay back in kind to India for Siachen. Or so they had believed.

Chapter 3

DIVERGENT TRACKS: DIALOGUE VS. OPERATION KOH PAIMA

By October 1999, Pakistan was moving on a two-track contradictory policy on India, set to inevitably clash. The Kargil clique's calculation was markedly opposed to the dialogue and détente policy with India that Pakistan's elected political leadership was pursuing after the tests. Prime Minister Nawaz Sharif and Prime Minister Vajpayee had met in New York and decided to resume the Composite Dialogue process. Accordingly, Pakistan had decided to reorient Pakistan's Kashmir policy towards primarily providing diplomatic and moral support to the Kashmiris instead of military support. By contrast, a handful of top Pakistani generals had carved a divergent policy track. Anxious about the weakening of the insurgency inside Indian-controlled Kashmir, these generals believed the nuclear card could be exploited. This operation was designed to directly undermine the elected prime minister's agenda of continuing dialogue with India and to reorient Pakistan's Kashmir policy. It was in the intoxicating yet unconstitutional autonomy in security matters that men in khaki enjoyed that lay the undoing of a policy that Pakistan's political leadership sought to pursue with regards to India. As the elected government planned the historic Pakistan-India summit at Lahore, a generals' clique had Pakistani soldiers climbing the hostile peaks of Kargil across the LOC.

Beginnings of Operation KP

Operation KP was launched by mid-October. The army chief had not formally approved the process. The elected chief executive of Pakistan, the prime minister, had no clue that hundreds of Pakistani troops had begun crossing the LOC.

But the Operation was underway.

Soon after General Musharraf took over as the new army chief, a clique of senior generals began contemplating Operation KP. The members of this clique had all served in strategically important areas along the LOC and, within hours of taking over as the army chief on 7 October, 1998, Musharraf had appointed each of them to a key position. He promoted the Vice Chief of General Staff Major General Mohammad Aziz Khan[1] to a Lieutenant General and appointed him the Chief of General Staff (CGS)at the GHQ. The military chief also appointed Lt. General Mahmud Ahmad ,[2] the recently appointed Commandant National Defense College, as Corps Commander 10 Corps replacing Lt. General Saleem Haider. Musharraf's predecessor General Jehangir Karamat had only recently appointed Mahmud as Commandant National Defense College, moving him from the post of Director General Military Intelligence. With these appointments Musharraf installed his men in the top command and staff positions directly dealing with the territory along the LOC including the 10 Corps and the GHQ. The only exception was the Commander, Force Command Northern Areas (FCNA) Major General Javed Hasan. GHQ retained him as commander FCNA.

Headquartered in Gilgit, as FCNA commander, Major General Hasan had the Northern Light Infantry (NLI) units, the 80 Brigade, the 62 Brigade, and the 323 Brigade reporting to him. The three brigades comprised military units while the NLI units,[3] were paramilitary formations.[4] While the NLI was part of the Civil Armed Forces under the Ministry of Interior, operationally it was under the army command. The

Commander FCNA was also the designated Inspector-General Northern Light Infantry. All NLI officers were posted from the regular army[5] while the NLI[6] troops were drawn up from the local population.

Before taking over as Commander FCNA in October 1997[7], he was posted as Defense Attaché at the Embassy in Washington. Earlier, he had commanded a company, a battalion, and a brigade along the LOC. As Director Military Operations in the GHQ and Defense Attaché in Washington, he had also keenly followed the Kashmir insurgency. Interestingly, after his stint in Washington, Hassan would argue with colleagues that the Americans would exercise benign neglect, if not actively support, a Pakistani military operation in Kashmir. The Americans did not believe Pakistan was serious about the Kashmir issue. He recalled they would tell him, "General, you have neither the will nor the wherewithal. Talk to us when you have the will and the wherewithal."[8]

According to Hassan, when he complained against India, the general thrust of what his hosts would say was an identical, "General, you neither have the will nor the wherewithal. Talk to us when you have the will and the wherewithal (military power)."[9] Hassan, especially during Musharraf's period, was widely regarded within the army High Command as the best mind on India. He advocated an aggressive posture towards India and often maintained that "Pakistan's size and power should match, i.e. if Pakistan did not militarily and otherwise expand, they (India) will atrophy you"[10]

Javed Hassan considered himself a geopolitical strategist. He interpreted most developments within Pakistan as an extension of the agenda of major powers. Indian moves in Siachen were also a result of Russia "asking India to do something against Pakistan because Pakistan is giving us trouble in Afghanistan."[11] Likewise, he maintained, "The Americans got the anti-Zia Movement for the Restoration of Democracy (MRD) started to arm-twist general Zia over Afghanistan." [12]

Hassan insisted that India "had run out of options on Kashmir", but the Pakistani political government's stance on Kashmir was weakening the cause. As evidence of the world noticing a change in Pakistan's position, he would recall that the Kashmiri leader Mirwaiz Umar Farooq during his Washington trip had told Javed Hassan that the Pentagon and State department said that Pakistan neither has the will nor the wherewithal so you move away from Pakistan and we will get you the best deal.

As Director Military Operations, Hassan was actively involved in monitoring the Kashmiri insurgency in Indian Occupied Kashmir. In 1992-93, when Pakistan concluded that the "insurgency's spirit was depleting," to give the home-grown insurgency a fillip the army facilitated the induction of 'mehman mujahideen' (guest mujahids) in Indian Occupied Kashmir. Like many of his colleagues, Hasan also followed subsequent Kashmir-related developments . For example, in 1996, the army's assessment was that Kashmiris were "tending to stay away from the insurgency and tending to return to their normal lives." Later in 1998, the "guest" mujahedeen did not possess major weapons which could enable them to undertake spectacular maneuvers.[13]

Hence, with this orientation, soon after taking over as Commander FCNA in October 1997 and completing the reconnaissance of the area around the LOC, Javed Hassan's general refrain to his officers was "get offensive, we have to cross the borders."[14]

Given Hassan's inclinations, this approach was no surprise. This had also been the way of many of his predecessors. Often the FCNA Commander's enthusiasm for aggressive conduct along the LOC translated into issuing aggressive directives, without always getting the requisite Corps Commander clearances, or not maintaining the required confidentiality or suitable discretion and restraint in the display of the enthusiasm on successful conduct of an operation.

For example, soon after taking over, Hassan wanted operations conducted to capture the Indian observation Hindu Observation Post (OP)[15] on the Marpola range. The commander 80 Brigade, responsible for the proposed operation, refused to conduct it as he had not received written instructions. FCNA Commander Javed Hassan hesitated to give written instructions because he had not received written instructions from his line of command, the Corps Commander.[16] Meanwhile, in early 1998, Domel, an LOC post just on the Indian side, was captured. Since the Commander had not got clearance for the operation from the Corps Commander, the Corps Commander ordered an inquiry against the Brigade Commander and ordered that the post is vacated.

Javed Hassan openly exhibited his enthusiasm for undertaking military operations to capture Indian-held posts on and around the LOC. Once, when present at the 19 Gayari sector, he got news that one of his Brigade Commanders had captured a post earlier held by the Indians. He ordered a gathering of his troops present, chanted "*Allah o Akbar*" ("God is Great"), and urged the other Commanders to also mount post-capturing operations. Perhaps the Indian too adopted the same methods.

As he settled in his position, the FCNA commander gave instructions to Commanding Officer (CO) 6 Northern Light Infantry (NLI) Lt Col Mansoor Ahmad Tariq to prepare a plan for the capture of Drass. The CO NLI 6 also received the orders from his immediate commanding officer, Commander 80 Brigade. Clearly even before the new army chief took over, the FCNA Commander was planning cross-LOC operations, deeper into the Indian-Held territory than Pakistani army had planned eversince the Indian occupation of Siachen in 1984.

It was perhaps no coincidence that Lt. General Mahmud Ahmed, whom the new chief had appointed as the Corps Commander, and who Hassan would report to, did share Hassan's views on India. Mahmud had joined the Pakistan Military Academy in 1966, immediately after the 1965 Pakistan-India war. Commissioned the following year in a Mountain Regiment of Artillery deployed in Azad Kashmir, he was a regimental colleague [17] of his later army chief. Mahmud attended the army's premier Command and Staff College in Quetta and subsequently became an instructor for five years. First as a student of the Staff course and later as Directing Staff of the Command and Staff College, Mahmud oversaw a comprehensive research project on the 1965 Pakistan-India war, undertaken at the order of the then army chief General Zia ul Haq. While vastly different in strategy, calculation, and resource-deployment, the 1965 Operation was also launched by Pakistan, as in 1947, to wrest Kashmir from India and, in Pakistan's civil-military leadership's calculation, to right a wrong. The general had also served as Director Military Operations at the GHQ, commanded 23 Division of the 10 Corps, had served under the new army chief Musharraf when he was Corps Commander Mangla, and was also Director-General Military Intelligence before his only two-month long appointment as Commandant of the National Defense College.

Interestingly, Mahmud was replacing General Saleem, a professional soldier, as opposed to the NLI commander's aggressive passion for capturing military posts by hook or by crook!

Significantly, the new Chief of General Staff, Lt. General Aziz Khan, who had successfully launched the important Dalunang Operation across the LOC in 1988 was a strong proponent of Pakistani troops crossing the LOC and occupying heights on the Indian side. During the Dalunang Operation, Pakistan had captured 28 peaks. Emphasizing his familiarity with the area, Aziz would often recall, "I have walked in the gaps along the LOC." His juniors would recall that Aziz had flown across the gaps as a brigade commander. An old and experienced hand on Kashmir as a director in the country's premier spy agency, the Inter-Services Intelligence, Khan was also in charge of the agency's operations in Kashmir and Afghanistan. An enthusiastic Khan had recommended to his chief General Jahangir Karamat that Pakistan occupy the heights that the Indians would vacate during winter. The army chief "did not want to deflate his enthusiasm and always suggested that we talk to other ministries, analyze the Indian response and assess our ability to deal with it before we take it any further."[18] Aziz had also served as Military Secretary to General Ziaul Haq and as Chief of Staff (COS) to the Commander 10 Corps Lt. Gen Ghulam Muhammad Malik. Later, he had commanded an infantry brigade in the Siachen area and had subsequently become Commander FCNA.

And finally, to match Hasan, Mahmud, and Aziz's orientation on Kashmir and the LOC, was the new army chief General Musharraf's own orientation. Identical to the key line-up of commanders overseeing the 10 Corps area, extending to the LOC, he too believed that conventional military force would play the key role in resolving the Kashmir issue. In fact, this group of commanders was dismissive and distrusting of the role of diplomacy in the matter. As Director-General Military Operations, Musharraf had war-gamed a Kargil-like situation in which Pakistan would have militarily taken Kashmir with then Prime Minister Benazir Bhutto.[19] Musharraf himself recalled only that he had told the prime minister, "The time window for the resolution of the Kashmir dispute is short because with the passage of time the India-Pakistan equation, military equation and the economic equation is going against us..."[20]

Soon after taking over as army chief and with his new team in place, Musharraf made a two day trip to the FCNA headquarters. He was accompanied by the new Corps Commander Mahmud and CGS Aziz made a two day trip to the FCNA headquarters in Gilgit. Before their arrival, the FCNA Commander instructed his GI Operations Lt. Colonel Nisar Ahmad Warraich for a forward areas map, with gaps on the LOC highlighted. During the new army chief's visit, the FCNA commander accompanied by his three guests flew over these gaps and entered into Indian airspace to get a good read of them. The Indians did not react to these air intrusions. For these Pakistani generals, their undetected and unhindered flight through the Indian Held-Kashmir airspace, including the unmanned Drass-Kargil areas, established for them the low level of Indian alertness at these points along the LOC.

The Indians had maintained their normal routine and had pulled back from the Drass Kargil area at the end of summer, discounting several intelligence reports submitted by the Intelligence Bureau and by RAW. As early as August, Kargil-based brigade commander Surinder Singh had conveyed "enhanced threat perceptions" but was ignored and the commanders went ahead with the summer pull-back.[21]

The Plan

By mid October, this generals' clique had decided to launch a cross-LOC operation into Indian held areas. Operation Koh Paima (Op KP) differed from the limited peak-capturing operations the two armies had previously undertaken, which would typically involve a maximum of two kilometers of penetration into the other's territory. After the 1984 Indian occupation of Siachen, Pakistani commanders would undertake these limited 'infiltrate and capture' operations more than the Indians. Pakistan's 1971 surrender in East Pakistan had inflicted the deepest of cuts on the Pakistani psyche. For some, the shame and anger had lingered.

With this past, there were individuals within the Pakistan military and civilian leadership who resented and distrusted India, and the catalyst for Operation KP was the convergence of key generals with a shared view on India. It included commanders in charge of the 10 Corps and of the FCNA. The Rawalpindi-based 10 Corps, occupies a strategic position within the Pakistan Army's force structure. Significantly, the 111 Brigade, dedicated for security and law-enforcement duties in the twin cities of Rawalpindi-Islamabad, which shot to fame for its pivotal role in launching two coups against elected governments, is also commanded by the 10 Corps. [22] Musharraf's predecessor had resisted the call of his Corps Commander to mount such an operation while the civilian leadership had initiated a path-breaking dialogue course.

The Rawalpindi-headquartered 10-Corps which planned and executed Operation KP, is the corps responsible for the entire Kashmir area, the Line of Control, plus the Line of Contact, up to Siachen. The area from Maralla to Siachen is the Line of Contact and, at Siachen, the Line of Control begins. The two Divisions and the FCNA units come under Parvez Ashraf 10 Corps, as do the 23 Division headquartered at Jhelum and the 12 Division headquartered at Murree. Major General Taj commanded the 23 Division, Major General Parvez Ashraf Kayani commanded the 12 Division.

The planning and execution of Op KP pivoted around the FCNA – as the main planner as well as the executor. Under its commander, Major General Javed Hasan, were three Brigades: Brigade 80, commanded by Brigadier Masood Aslam, based at Minimarg; Brigade 62 at Skardu, commanded by Brigadier Nusrat Sial; and Brigade 323 at Siachen, commanded by Brigadier Salahuddin Satti.

A key arm of the FCNA was the Northern Light Infantry (NLI), with 11 battalions. The size of each battalion was 750 to 780 soldiers. They could be placed under any one of the three FCNA brigades, 62, 80 or 323. These Northern Areas-based NLI battalions consisted of officers, junior commissioned officers (JCOs) and paramilitary forces. The officers were posted from the army and their services were on loan to the NLI. The JCOs were from the NLI while the paramilitary second-line forces, similar to the Rangers and Scouts, were technically under the Ministry of Interior[23] but operationally under the army. The uniform of NLI forces was khaki, like that of the regular army.

Clearly, the core team commanding the 10 Corps, including its FCNA brigade and the point-man at the GHQ, the chief of general staff, were generals, by virtue of their past postings and orientation, with a personal proclivity for settling scores with India through dare-devil operations. This was markedly opposed to the dialogue and diplomacy agenda adopted by the country's elected prime minister. After the nuclear tests, these generals believed that a successful Operation KP would force the world powers to intervene to resolve the outstanding J & K issue. They were convinced that the global community, especially the United States, would have no tolerance for a confrontation between the two new and hostile nuclear powers. In the mental calculations of these men, there was also a measure of nuclear black-mail.

Anxious about the weakening of the insurgency inside Indian-controlled Kashmir, this clique believed the nuclear card could also be exploited. Operation KP was an attempt to exploit that nuclear card. This Operation was all set to directly undermine the elected prime minister's agenda of continuing dialogue with India and reorienting Pakistan's Kashmir policy. In the intoxicating yet unconstitutional autonomy that the men in khaki enjoyed on security matters, lay the undoing of the policy on India that Pakistan's political leadership wanted to pursue.

The elected government was planning for the Pakistan-India summit in Lahore at the same time as a clique of generals was organizing a covert military operation. These two contradictory policies on India were set for a clash. The military Operation was planned after an unusually long, six-year period of quiet along the LOC. Then, the hastily planned November 1992 attack to get to the ridgeline ended with high casualties and the removal of the GOC commanding the 1992 Operation. On several previous occasions, Pakistan's leadership was presented proposals almost similar to Op KP, all leading back to the original 1985 proposal. Amongst these generals, it was the CGS who had actively pursued this plan with Musharraf's predecessor. While the civilian leadership remained wary of attempts to reclaim Siachen through force, military men intermittently conducted operations in the Siachen Glacier-Saltoro area. [24]

The three-general clique, leading 10 Corps of the Pakistan Army was responsible for protecting the Line of Control and the international border

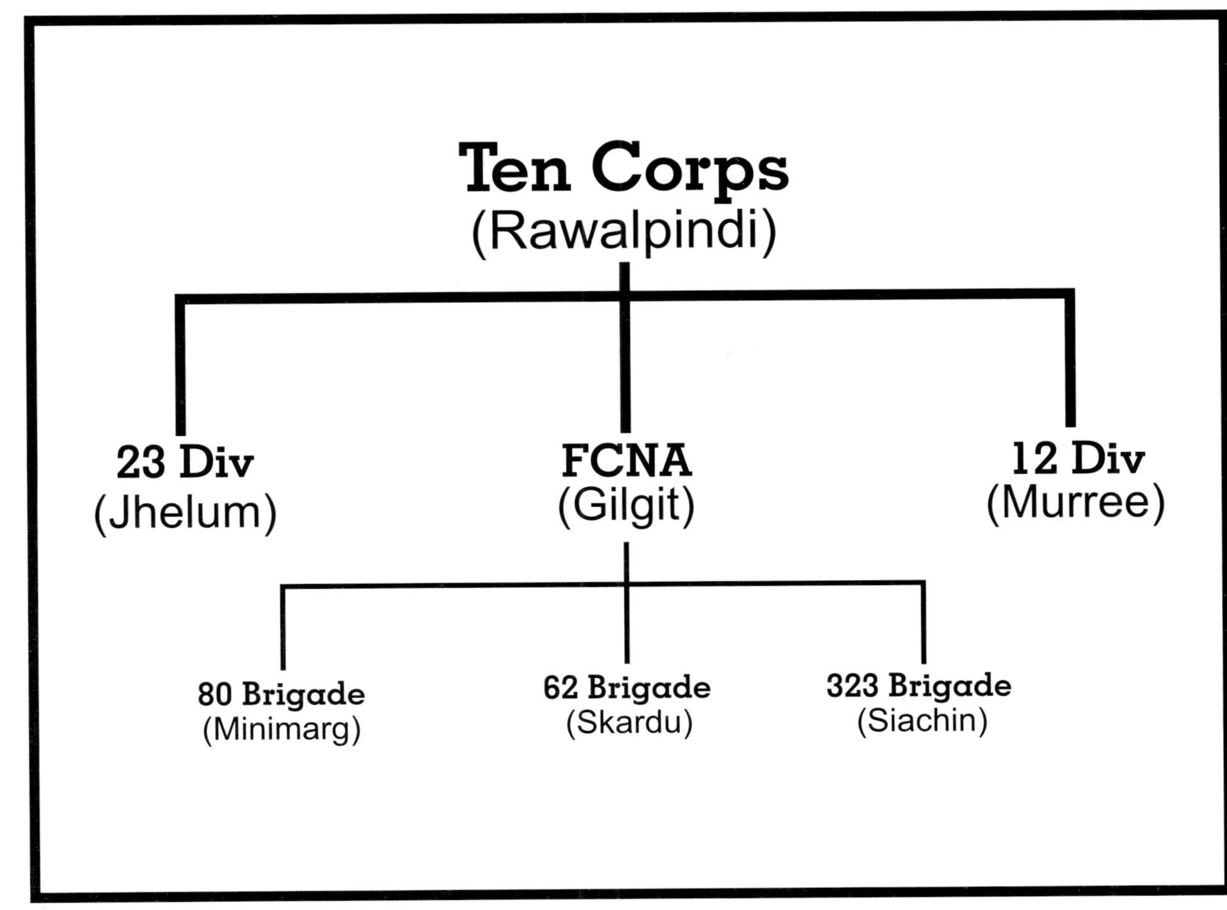

Ten Corps Command

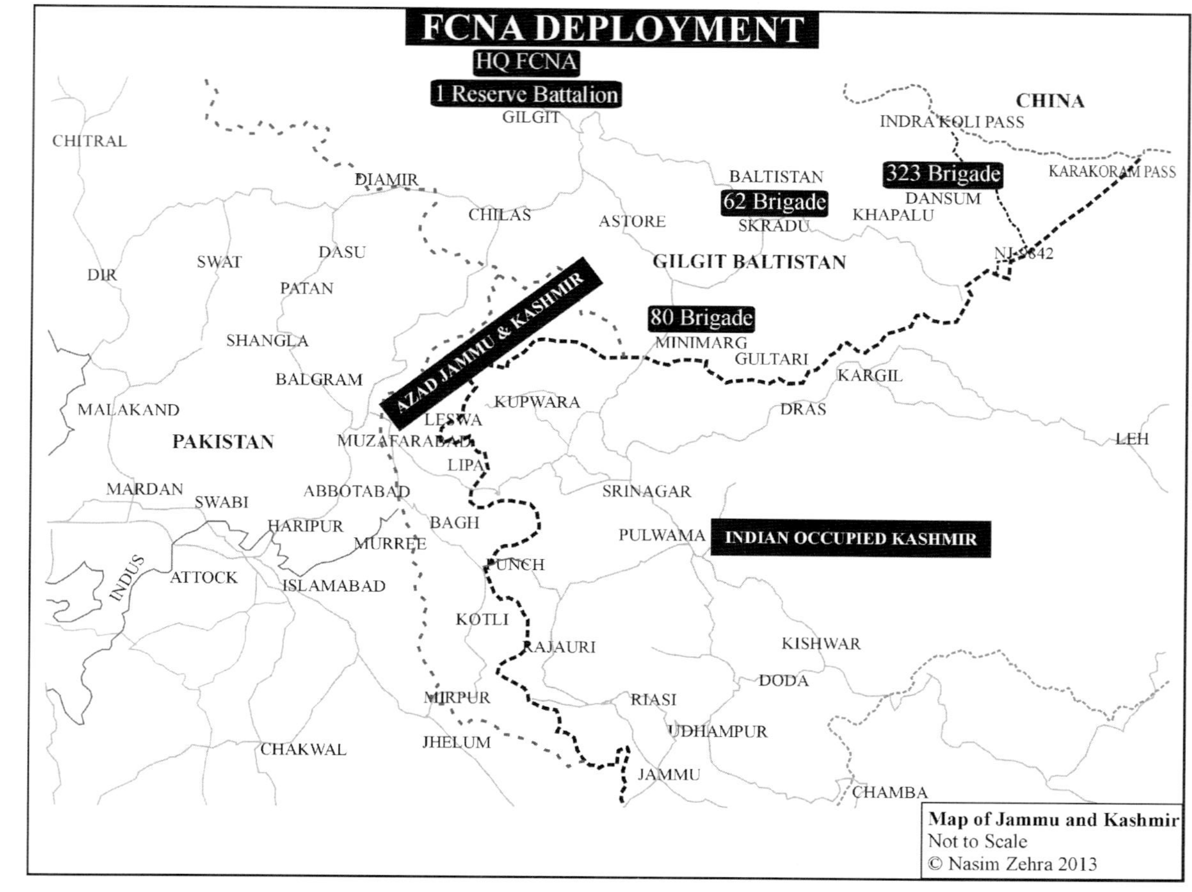

FCNA Deployment

from Mangla to Head Marala.With a nod from the new army chief, but totally unknown to the elected prime minister, now including the army chief this four-general clique began planning a daredevil military adventure. The mid-October aerial reconnaissance of this 'clique of four' was followed by active preparations. From among this clique, it was the man-on-the spot, the FCNA commander Major General Javed Hassan, who was to prepare an operational plan. Hassan had since his arrival signaled his intention to lead his men across the LOC. Like many in the Pakistan Army, his refrain too was that Siachen had to be avenged and military pressure on India would force them to settle Kashmir.

Active planning for the Operation began in early October, when prior to the arrival of the newly appointed 10 Corps Commander, General Mahmud, the FCNA commander instructed his General Staff Officer (GSO)G-1 Operations, Lt Colonel Nisar Ahmad Warraich[25] to prepare an operational plan for conducting a cross-LOC maneuver. The G-1 asked if it was a hypothetical exercise. The plan was for an actual Operation, his commander informed him, and added, "It has been decided they would cross the LOC." Obviously, the clique of senior generals had decided to go back to the Kargil plan, which had been reviewed and rejected by the CJCSC, the former army chief, and indeed by the ISI. The man most keen to implement the plan then, General Aziz, was now in a position to implement it. He shared a special camaraderie with the new chief too. He would get his way and indeed the operational support for the plan.

The G-1[26] staff officer, of course, carried out his commander's orders. Operational plans were prepared within three days, using a three-dimensional (3-D) map, and covered the Gultari area which was under the command of the 6 NLI. (OPERATIONS MAPS ALREADY PROVIDED TO OUP) It was decided that "3-D was important because this was the way we could be accurate yet concealed, with the planning limited to a G-1 familiar with the area."[27] Planning the operation on a single map was not possible without height implications. The author of the map, as a lieutenant in 1981 had been on a six-month attachment with the 13NLI. He was therefore familiar with the entire post's layout along the LOC. This G1 presented his plan in the Ops room of the FCNA headquarters to the FCNA Commander and to the Colonel Staff Brigadier Muhammad Zubair.

According to the plan, around 200 Pakistani troops would cross the LOC to dominate the Indian supply lines leading to the Northern Division of Kashmir,-essentially beginning from the Zojila pass and going up to the China border and from the River Chenab to the Himachal mountains. The troops would occupy the watershed. The map was presented to the Commander 10 Corps. He said, "It's all approved."

By early October, the generals' clique had agreed to go ahead with Op KP. If there was a leading moving spirit behind the plan, this mastermind was the CGS, the administrative head of the GHQ, General Aziz Khan.[28] The GHQ, courtesy the CGS, was therefore aware of the hush-hush operation but in fact institutionally no one among the senior generals beyond the clique knew of its scope and intent. At best, it was being explained as an exercise which involved retaining the manning levels of the summer in the winter months, in some cases to ensure forward movement of the local reserves.[29] Also, the excuse of a possible Indian offensive was used to take steps for occupying the watershed to deny India observation and fields of fire advantage that they were getting for example from the Marpola post.[30] Somewhat quid pro quo, tasking plans, were also prepared indicating specific Indian posts to be attacked in response to Indian attacks on Pakistani posts.

While the field commanders involved in the Operation did initially knew of its scope, that it involved crossing the LOC and ingress into Indian Held territory, the soldiers initially believed they were involved in an exercise. The planners hoped this deliberate fog of confusion would be an effective way to cover up the reality of the Operation. This would also help to evade the issue of not getting clearance from the country's chief executive. Also, projecting it as an exercise or a localized response to a perceived threat, meant that it did not require top political clearance. The number of operations across the LOC had increased significantly in the period after the Indian occupation of Siachen, which coincided with the military regime of General Ziaul Haq.[31]

For the Operation, around 200 troops were to travel for months, mostly on foot, to reach the Drass sector. There, the troops would occupy posts at Toololong, thereby reducing their distance to NH-1 by almost three kilometers. From the Shaqma post on the Pakistani side of the LOC, the distance to NH-1A was about five kilometers. The task was to occupy the watershed. This Operation, using approximately 200 NLI troops, would position them for easy observation of all activities as well as interdiction of the Srinagar-Leh National Highway-1(NH-1A), India's life-line[32] to its troops stationed in the whole of Ladakh region and in Siachen. This 'life-line' was used during the summer months to transport the critical supplies needed by the troops during the locked-in winter months. Indian troop presence in Ladakh and Siachen areas was of critical significance since India had territorial disputes over the two areas with its two largest neighbors, China and Pakistan.

The NH-1 road was already vulnerable to some Pakistani interdiction since at some points the Indian troop movement was visible to Pakistani troops stationed at the Kaksar and Channigund posts in the Shaqma sector. From these posts, the closest points to NH-1, Pakistani troops could rain artillery fire onto NH-1. The alternate route was the barely jeep-able 473-kilometer-long Manali-Leh track, passing over 16,000 feet heights, and open to traffic only from July to September.[33]

The FCNA commander's key partner and supporter at the operational level was Commander 10 Corps Lt. General Mahmud Ahmed. At his Corps headquarters, Mahmud's core team first heard of an across-the LOC Operation.[34] It was after his return from the Northern Areas that Lt. General Mahmud took his core team in confidence. In an informal gathering, he informed them that a decision had been taken to go across the LOC. The talk at the Corp HQ was that the instructions to the troops were to "establish posts and duck down." [35] The objective of the Operation, Mahmud's team was told, was "bringing alive" the Kashmir issue. The Operation would involve Pakistani soldiers going across the LOC and occupying around 7 to 8 posts in the area of Drass and carrying out sabotage activities. Commander 80 Brigade Brigadier Masood Aslam, with about 100 soldiers, including 18 officers, was to execute the reconnaissance mission.

The planned Operation was principally restricted to 80 Brigade; however, 62 Brigade was involved in reconnaissance for supplementary action. Commander 62 Brigade Nusrat Sial, based at Skardu, was asked to identify possible posts for engaging the Indians on a broaderfront, to spread them thin in case they reacted against the Pakistani posts at Kargil. After the reconnaissance, Brigadier Sayal (who died in a later air crash) said he could occupy 6 posts in Chorbatla, including Battalik[36]

According to the plan, the minimum cross-LOC incursion by the Pakistani troops would extend to 9 kilometers into Indian-held areas of Drass and Kargil. This was unusual. Mahmud's core team knew that ever since 1992 there had hardly been any incursions across the LOC. Even when occupying posts along the LOC, especially after Indian control of Siachen, the two neighbors usually ingressed a maximum of two kilometers across the LOC. Now, when even one step across the LOC could amount to a declaration of war, the plan envisaged crossing a minimum of 9 kilometers! "What if our cover gets blown? What if we are caught?" was their refrain. They raised their fears with their commander. "You do the analysis," was the general's response. He was confident the Operation plan was "perfect." His confidantes wondered: in case Indian retaliation meant they had a bigger conflict on their hands, could Pakistan mobilize a Division of troops? Would the economic situation allow such mobilization? Within the corps, some younger officers, fearing that this was "clear suicide", even urged the COS to abort the Operation. But the plan was a 'done deal' and Mahmud's team was expected to buy into their commander's wisdom and follow orders. Steeped in the discipline of obeying the chain of command, they did exactly that.

The commander's team could, however, see that their newly appointed boss was in sharp contrast to their earlier commander, Mahmud's predecessor Lt. General Saleem Haider. Haider had firmly commanded the 10 Corps. Violation of the LOC by the troops was strictly proscribed. In 1997, when Brigadier Sahi, then Commander 80 Brigade 's triumphant message around early evening was conveyed to Lt. General Haider that he had established a post across the LOC , the irate Haider thrice asked the messenger, "I hope you understand what you are saying." Haider ordered Sahi's immediate withdrawal. "Tell him to withdraw from the post and tell everyone that, until he has come back, you and I will not sleep," were the Corps Commander's orders. He slept around 2.30 am,

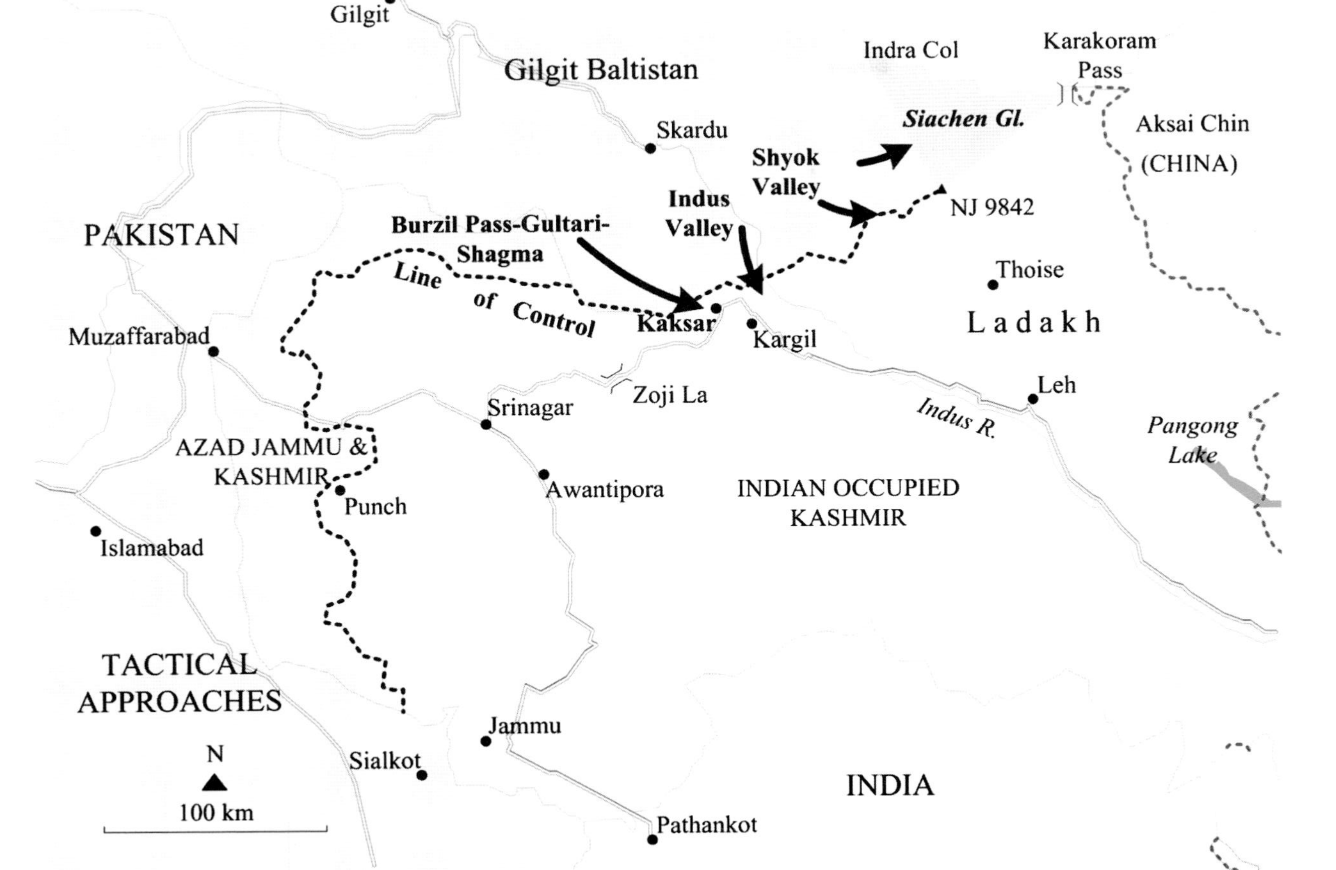

Drass-Kargil Sector

after he was told that the Indian post had been vacated. Summoned by his commander the next morning, Sahi was warned" not a single step across the LOC."

Mahmud's command mode contrasted with that of his predecessor. He was aggressively supporting the crossing of the LOC. His core team members were left as Doubting Thomases with no answers forthcoming. For the planners of OpKP, their questions were not valid. In a more considered environment, drawing upon previous precedents as a guide, however, these questions had clear answers. India's track record was one of an offensive military response whenever Pakistani soldiers violated the LOC. For example, in 1990, when a Brigadier Sher Afghan occupied an Indian post n Forward Kahuta, in the Haji Pir area, the Indians hit back with a bloody offensive. They recaptured the post, leaving 150 people dead. No disciplinary action was taken against the Brigadier. General Asif Nawaz was the army chief. The word in the 10 Corps headquarters was that, while the army chief was aware of the operation, he had not formally cleared it. The prime minister meanwhile, was to be told at "an appropriate time."[37]

Thus, the beginnings of the operation lay in legitimate grievances with India, on the one hand; yet, on the other hand, there were unconstitutional practices, institutional indiscipline, faulty linear outlook, and individualized maverick ways. Even the FCNA Commander Javed Hasan, it was believed, had undertaken reconnaissance of the operational area in mid 1998 without the Corps Commander's explicit approval.

Back at the FCNA, with the initial plan for Operation KP having been approved by the 10 Corps Commander Mahmud and by the Chief of General staff Aziz Khan in October, Pakistani troop movement across the LOC had begun by late-October. Headed for Drass, Brigade Commander Brigadier Masood Aslam was dropped from a helicopter in the Drass are, along with a lieutenant colonel and 10 soldiers, for reconnaissance. They found the Marpola and Tololong areas unoccupied for miles. Lt Col Mansoor, the Commanding Officer of NLI 6, then crossed the LOC and entered the Drass area with his troops to occupy posts vacated by the Indian troops and to set up new ones. A limited logistics operation accompanied the initially limited NLI movement, the troops having merely taken off with basic supplies in their bag packs. The planners were confident they would not be discovered before summer and that their camouflage would carry them unnoticed into winter.[38] Major General Javed Hasan acknowledged, "We were there from October 1998 onwards. We did not know whether we would be discovered in summer or in winter."[39]

Mission Creep

However, within two months of the start of the operation, the FCNA commander believed the opportunity existed to expand the operation. Around the areas where Pakistani troops ingressed, there were vast unoccupied areas across the LOC[40] with no Indian presence. In these areas, either the Indian posts had been vacated during winter or on those steep peaks they simply had no posts.[41] Stashed away in the harsh, remote and forbidding peaks, in the dead of winter, the commanders who were planning to enlarge their operation, foresaw no immediate counter-moves as the Indian forces were altogether absent.

This expansion of the originally one-sector Kargil operation to five sectors was in response to the 'opportunity' that was discovered by the NLI command in the zone of operation. The expanded operation was, therefore neither war-gamed nor comprehensively planned. The planners had thought of occupying 10 or 12 posts but the expanded Operation ended with 140 posts. Hence, an operation that expanded on detection of military opportunity by military men at the planning and implementation stage, precluded comprehensive intra-institutional deliberations on the nature of this 'opportunity' and, more importantly, on the merits and demerits of an expanded operation. Although, within the restricted group of military commanders, questions related to India's military, diplomatic, and political reaction and the international community's diplomatic reaction were raised, the linear experience of that one institution combined with the personal proclivity of the individuals towards the Operation influenced their answers to these questions.

There was excitement about the expansion, about undetected penetration into enemy territory. In fact, as some would recall, this was

Pakistan's own territory that had been lost to India in 1971. So they went into Mission Creep and by December 1998 the troops had begun to cross the LOC from seven directions. This included areas west of river Indus, east of river Shyok, from the top of Shyok Valley and from Shaqma. Primarily, NLI infantry troops were the ones involved in Operation KP. They continued establishing of posts undetected by the Indians and penetrated to approximately 14 kilometers into the Indian side of the LOC. Pakistani troops had ended up establishing 196 posts, which included bases and outposts. The daring men, on a victory prowl on the world's highest battlefield and grasped by excitement and a sense of victory, were unaware of the very critical problems of logistical stretch this operational creep would soon generate. Equally, this deeper penetration into the Indian-controlled territory meant the greater risk of exposure to enemy troops and to the unpredictable enemy reaction.

The FCNA Commander Javed Hassan himself acknowledged that "we were there from October 1998 onwards but we did not know whether we will be discovered in summer or winter."[42]

Illusion of Control – 8 November

Clueless about Op KP, Nawaz Sharif had begun the process of re-orienting Pakistan's foreign policy. With his new and presumably 'safe' army chief in the saddle, Nawaz Sharif, now the prime minister of the only nuclear state in the Muslim world, was keen for a broader re-orientation of Pakistan's foreign policy. By November, Sharif believed he had got a handle on key foreign policy issues. Assisted by his Foreign Office team and his kitchen cabinet, he had arrived at specific conclusions on what he considered was in the best interest of Pakistan.

Six months after the nuclear tests, and after several meetings with the Indians, engaging with pushing the intra-Afghan dialogue, watching the growing OBL problem, and the expanding problem of sectarianism, Nawaz Sharif had now come to some conclusions. Subsequently, in the November 1998 meeting of the Defense Committee of the Cabinet(DCC) chaired by the prime minister, he shared those conclusions with the participants. Sharif took some significant decisions regarding the means

Pakistan would opt for to achieve the goals of Pakistan's foreign policy goals. Especially with the two neighbors, India and Afghanistan, diplomacy was to acquire primacy as a policy tool to achieve policy objectives including resolving bilateral issues. Sharif told the DCC participants including the military generals present, that Pakistan would gradually move towards discontinuing armed support for the Kashmiris. He instructed the foreign minister and the ISI chief to jointly implement the new policy. Their mandate was to facilitate the "broadening and deepening of APHC and to highlight the violations of the human rights and political rights by the Indians." [43]

Ironically shortly before this DCC meeting Delhi had taken a U-turn during Pakistan-India Siachen talks held in Delhi. The Indian delegation had rejected significant ground covered by the two sides in an attempt to resolve the Siachen dispute.

Meanwhile Pakistan's prime minister formerly announced re-orientation of Pakistan's foreign policy. He stressed humanitarian, political and diplomatic support to the Kashmiris would be increased. The prime minister was unaware that a clique of his senior-most generals had opted for unprecedented peace-time use of force against India, naively believing they would force India's hand on Kashmir.

Diplomatically, beyond engaging India, Islamabad's key thrust was to engage the US on Kashmir. The Americans also saw that Kashmir loomed large on Pakistan's wish list. Every time Nawaz Sharif and the Foreign Secretary Shamshad Ahmad met with American officials, they hammered at "the need for American intervention to solve Kashmir once and for all." [44]

Similar decisions on Afghanistan and OBL were taken. But among the men in khaki at this DCC meeting, the prime minister's words had fallen on deaf ear. The implementation of Sharif's decision, that the Taliban be pressurized to stop providing a haven for sectarian killers from Pakistan, was directly dependent on the ISI. On the Afghan policy, Pakistan's seasoned ambassador Aziz Ahmed Khan assisted the government on diplomatic and political matters, the operational policy on all form of security cooperation and support was entirely under the ISI's control. Hence, it was ISI that controlled the levers that Pakistan could use to force

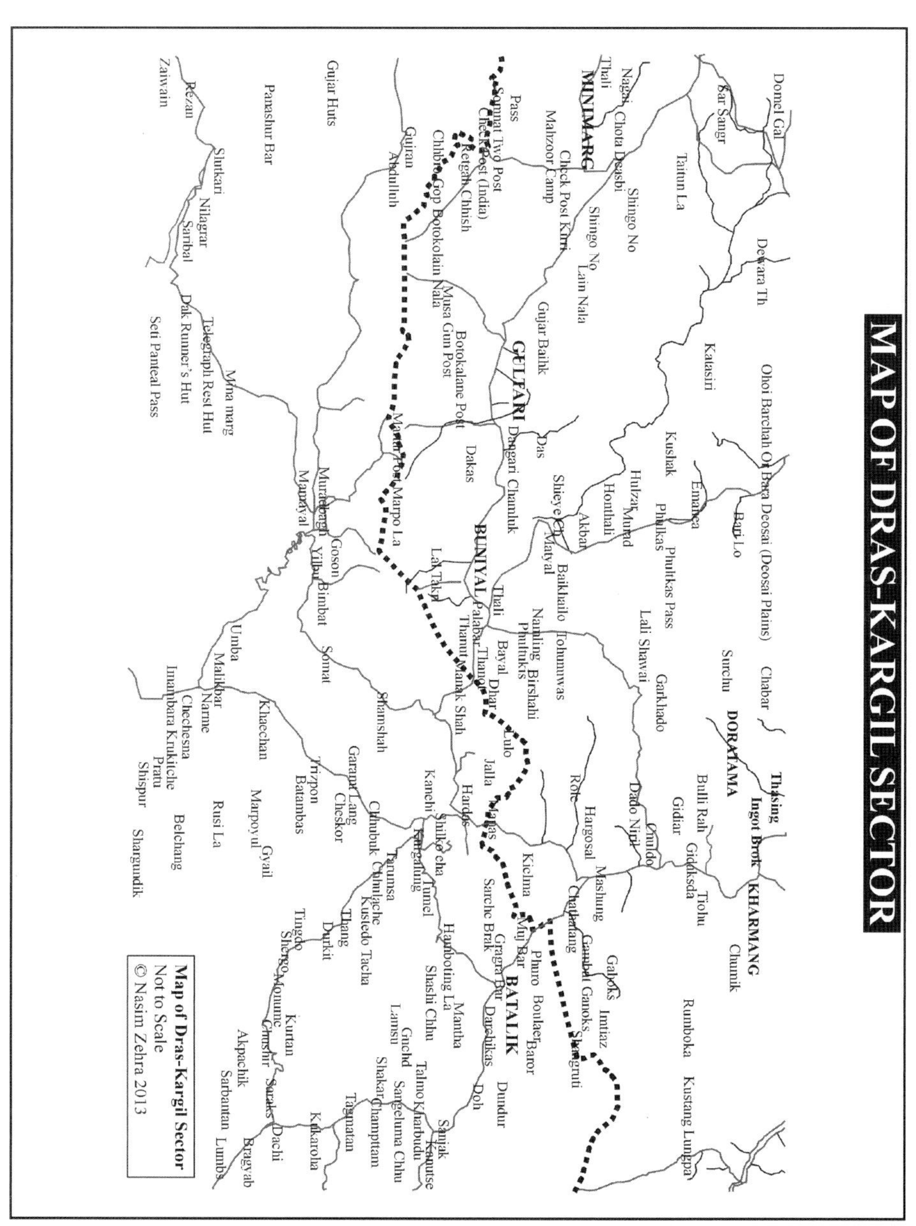

Tactical Approaches Into Op Areas

a change in Kabul's behavior regarding protection of sectarian killers. Similarly, over the OBL question, the ISI alone could forcefully advise the Taliban government. However significantly, Pakistani intelligence was not only not supportive of OBL but, as was documented in the 9/11 Commission Hearings report[45] based on "substantial intelligence of internal arguments,"[46] Pakistan did not exert substantive influence on the Taliban over the OBL issue. For Pakistan, the Afghan Taliban were an ally in Afghanistan, critical for curtailing threats to Pakistan from its western borders. Hence Pakistan's army, Afghan Taliban's main interlocutor was not likely to exert any pressure on the Taliban.

A senior ISI general attending the meeting found the country's elected chief executive, constitutionally the ISI's direct boss, unrealistic and somewhat amusing. For these men, there was no buy-in to Nawaz Sharif's diplomacy-oriented foreign policy. By virtue of their almost unaccountable control of Pakistan's security institutions, they effectively controlled Pakistan's security-dominated India and Afghanistan policies. Military men, trained to see the world in binary terms and accustomed to unaccountably and independently managing Pakistan's security policy, faced with India's stalling of resolution of issues ranging from Kashmir to Siachen and Sir Creek, found little sense in the policy changes that the elected prime minister had announced.

Significantly, until this point, although the army chief was 'in' on the plan, he had given no formal institutional-level approval for Operation KP. More important, no clearance had been sought from the country's elected leadership. The prime minister was unaware of the plan and neither had it been taken to the Cabinet, the highest constitutional body.

With India: Onwards On Peace

Meanwhile, on the non-bureaucratic front, within a fortnight of the New York meeting in early October, Pakistan had suggested that small non-bureaucratic groups from both sides should interact to explore possible ways of resolving bilateral disputes.[47] The group comprised former generals Ghulam Umar and K.M Arif and retired Foreign Secretary Niaz Naik from Pakistan's side and, from India, veteran journalist R.K.Misra and retired Admiral K.K. Nayyar.[48] For several years, they had also been in involved in the Neemrana Dialogue. Pakistani prime minister's mid-October offer to receive the Indian team brought R.K.Mishra and Admiral Nayyar to Islamabad on 2 November. Vajpayee had personally cleared their trip. At the breakfast meeting with Nawaz Sharif, the Indian envoys conveyed Vajpayee's message. India was willing to give one billion rupees in soft loans or three million tons of wheat as a loan to Pakistan.[49] This was Vajpayee's goodwill gesture for an economically troubled Pakistan. Sharif asked his Additional Secretary, Tariq Fatimi, who was also present, to examine the offer. Fatimi told the prime minister that Pakistan had already taken care of its wheat requirements.[50] Given the history of their relationship, it was unthinkable for the Pakistani establishment, or even the political leadership, to let India "bail it out", no matter what its condition.

The other message that Sharif's Indian guests carried from Vajpayee was that "cross-border terrorism" must stop. The prime minister moved three paces, away from Fatemi's hearing, and according to his Indian guest said that Vajpayee should be told that Sharif had his own man in the ISI. And that in two or three months, Sharif will control the LOC situation situation and focus on dialogue."[51] During the breakfast meeting with his Indian guests, Sharif again repeated his idea of Vajpayee traveling to Lahore on the inaugural bus. An optimistic Sharif somewhat lightly said that if Vajpayee sat in the bus and came to Lahore, fifty percent of the problem would be solved and, if he himself went in the bus to India, the remaining fifty percent would also be solved.[52] This non-bureaucratic channel was tasked with examining non-conventional approaches to resolving bilateral disputes. On Kashmir, they had begun discussing the contents of the first report of the Kashmir Study Group and the Chenab formula. The thinking of the political leadership on Kashmir was being influenced by the KSG report. Nawaz Sharif believed it was time to reorient Pakistan's Kashmir policy. He was also getting increasingly uneasy about continuing with Pakistan's pro-Taliban policy.

Nawaz Sharif, was an unlikely candidate for possession of any geostrategic vision; yet, forced by circumstances, guided by a professional team of diplomats in Islamabad and in Washington, and aided his own practical instincts, had focused on security issues critical for peace, stability, and economic progress in Pakistan. Sharif's general policy thrust of seeking peace with neighboring states, engaging in dialogue to work through problems, and remaining neutral between warring factions in Afghanistan had led Pakistan towards the beginning of a course correction. At the November DCC meeting, the prime minister communicated to the civilian bureaucracy and the military leadership the changes he was seeking in Pakistan's foreign policy.

Significantly Sharif was initiating this needed foreign policy reorientation in a hostile domestic environment. His policy blunders were multiplying; the 1997 battle with the judiciary, bulldozing of law through the parliament, gag difference of opinion within the party, passing a less than credible Accountability Bill, failing to control rising sectarian killings, conducting political accountability, accruing financial benefits for family business, 1998 battle with the media and the army.

Pakistan's economy too was in a fairly difficult spot. Contrary to late 1997 when the government through legislative agenda had initiated political and economic reforms to restore the confidence of the business community. Then, despite sectarian and ethnic violence prevailed, especially in the commercial center Karachi, business community's confidence was restored. According to the World Bank, "these reforms paid off and Pakistan judged by its economic indicators through May1998 showed increasing signs of economic growth and stability."[53]Subsequently as the World Bank's report acknowledged that "However events following Pakistan's nuclear testing in May 1998 hampered the reform process and challenged political stability."[54] Given that the fallout of the nuclear tests Pakistan was forced to delay payments owed to FDIs, global confidence in Pakistan's economy continued to take a hit.

Sharif in Washington

Within weeks of the November 1998 DCC meeting, the Nawaz Sharif was in Washington DC on the invitation of US President Clinton. The prime minister of cash-strapped Pakistan led an unusually large delegation, comprising six ministers, a big media contingent, and several family members, wife and children. Contrary to general practice, Sharif had no one from the armed forces on his team.

Clinton hosted Sharif at Blair House and the meetings took place at the White House in the Oval Office. The room was a small one and Pakistan was told the seating would be limited to 1 + 5. However most members of the prime minister's entourage wanted to go to the Oval office. Pakistani Ambassador Riaz Khokhar requested for additional seats on the Pakistani side. Although bin Laden was the key issue for Clinton, he tried to dilute the focus by announcing at a presser just before the meeting began, that they would focus on ending nuclear competition in South Asia, and on working with Pakistan to promote economic growth to support the mutual US-Pakistan concern to fight terrorism, alongside some of the other regional issues."[55] Sharif, told his host in the presence of the global media that it was his "endeavor to remove all the misperceptions which are there in our bilateral relations.[56]

For long, Pakistan had consistently seen its value for the US within the context of Washington's own geostrategic and security policies. Even more significant was the fact that the majority of Pakistan's policy makers viewed the country's own geostrategic policy on its west mostly as an extension of how it fitted in with the US patterns. Zulfikar Ali Bhutto, despite some of his controversial domestic policies, [57] was the only brilliant exception when, as Foreign Minister and then Prime Minister, ZAB opened up with China and the Muslim World. Post-Bhutto Pakistan, under the military ruler Zia ul Haq,was totally immersed in the international jihad tailored to achieve the US objective of destroying the 'Evil Empire' of the USSR. Pakistan's role as the main architect and facilitator of the international jihad led to Islamabad wanting a friendly government in Kabul.

The US had now switched gears, seeking its old partner Pakistan's support against what had mutated into a global anti-US crusade. Standing outside the White House, Sharif was completely obliging. He reassured the US President that Pakistan would be happy to extend all help and assistance…especially on the issue of terrorism."[58] Recalling his government's cooperation, especially on bin Laden, he reminded his host that Pakistan had "been fighting terrorism, and you know that we've been cooperating with the United States of America also." [59]

Clinton and Sharif, two men poles apart in work mode and world outlook, had developed a fondness for each other. Through 1998, several Sharif-Clinton telephone conversations had familiarized the two men with one another. The meeting was at the height of the Monica Lewinsky affair. Sharif, on the advice of a member of his kitchen cabinet, had made a special gesture of support to Clinton. Sharif had called Bill Richardson, a man Clinton had said was the quickest channel to him, to send his special wishes and support to Clinton at this time of personal tribulation. [60]

Clinton was to testify before Congress after the meeting that very day. Nawaz Sharif, despite advice to the contrary from his aides, told Clinton, "Mr President, at this difficult time my and the people of Pakistan's prayers are with you." Clinton had appreciated Nawaz"s sentiment and told his National Security Advisor Sandy Berger, "I was touched by Nawaz's statement." Nawaz had arrived in Washington armed with hugely expensive gifts.[61]

Nawaz and Clinton, aided by their teams, met for two hours at the Oval Office. They discussed non-proliferation, economic sanctions, relations with India, bin Laden, Afghanistan, and the F-16 issue. For Pakistan, the good news was Clinton's commitment to settle the F-16 issue, which had become known in Pakistan as 'highway robbery' by the United States (Pakistan had paid the US $658 million for 28 F-16s. In 1991, after President George H.W. Bush held back non-proliferation certification, Washington unilaterally aborted the sale and held back considerably more than half a billion dollars from cash-strapped Pakistan). while refusing to deliver the F16s.[62] Nawaz Sharif's government decided to inform the Clinton Administration of its decision to take the matter to court. In Islamabad, Foreign Secretary Shamshad had strongly advocated the legal option and an American lawyer had already been engaged. He had already visited Islamabad for discussions. Accordingly, the Pakistan Embassy in Washington sent a *Note Verbale* to the State Department. The US Administration, in possession of Pakistan's $ 658 million and yet cruising along unchallenged by Pakistan, was now somewhat stunned by the contents of this *Note Verbale*. Secretary of State Madeleine Albright asked if they realized the possible implications of such a move on Pakistan-US relations. Her attempt was to discourage Pakistan from taking the court route. The ambassador told her that Pakistan knew the risks involved but had faith in the US judicial system! It was Pakistan's *Note Verbale* that prompted Clinton to personally propose an out-of-court settlement.[63] Pakistan's Foreign Office was opposed to a cash deal but Sharif and Sartaj accepted Clinton's proposal. Sharif sought to have the matter settled by end December. Clinton took Pakistan's deadline seriously and in a later conversation told Nawaz Sharif, "I know you want to complete this by the end of the month and we will do everything we can to meet that deadline." [64]

For Clinton the bin Laden issue topped the agenda. At the meeting, his whereabouts were discussed. Sharif and his team maintained Pakistan could do little since bin Laden was in Afghanistan. None from Clinton's team were convinced. Secretary of State Albright was particularly tough with the Pakistani prime minister. Sharif, to everyone's surprise, at the conclusion of the meeting asked to meet Clinton separately. Clinton agreed. At the meeting, Sharif offered Pakistan's help in abducting bin Laden. Pakistan's prime minister proposed that the US train a Pakistani team to hunt for bin Laden. Clinton, beaten by the Lewinsky scandal, was very keen to achieve a breakthrough on bin Laden. He was tantalized by the offer. After the meeting, a delighted Clinton told US Ambassador to Pakistan Bill Milam and Assistant Secretary of State Karl Inderfurth about Sharif's offer. Milam wondered how significant Sharif's offer if he did not have Pakistan's security apparatus on board. It was unclear if he did. Nonetheless, soon after the offer, the CIA launched their Get-Osama operation. Men from the Special Forces Group arrived in Pakistan to train former Pakistani SSG commandos.

Interestingly, unlike Clinton, who immediately shared Sharif's offer with his team, Sharif did not share his offer with his own team. Even his exceptionally alert and well-plugged-in ambassador to the US was unaware. In fact, the embassy was kept out of the loop. When a senior embassy official turned to the ISI chief for information about bin Laden's whereabouts to vet the curiosity of his American hosts, he was told to tell the Americans that bin Laden was ill and suffering from a disease in which "he was growing taller and taller and would eventually die!" The ISI chief was of course aware of Sharif's offer since his institution was to be the Pakistani executing agency for the Get-Osama plan.

Other than being unhappy about not being able to see the grizzly bears in their habitat at Yosemite Park, Sharif left the US satisfied. He believed Washington's support was critical for him to successfully reorient policy. Some sanctions imposed after the nuclear tests were lifted, the F-16 matter was about to be settled, and World Bank loans had been approved. Clinton also supported Pakistan's peace initiatives towards India and reconciliation between the Taliban and Northern Afghanistan. He also trusted Sharif's commitment to helping the Americans arrest bin Laden. Ambassador Milam, Clinton's man familiar with the civil-military relations in Pakistan, was unsure if Sharif's proposal, unknown to the khakis, could actually be executed.

It was a season of discontent with the Taliban. The international community was running out of patience with the Taliban as manifested by the UNSC resolution 1214 passed on December 8.[65] With escalating conflict causing a threat to international peace, mounting ethnic and religious conflicts, increase in numbers of refugees, the deteriorating human rights situation, and especially discrimination against women and girls, the international community was running out of patience with them. This manifested itself on December 8 when the Security Council passed Resolution UNSC 1214.[66] The Taliban were condemned for the presence of terrorists in areas controlled by them. The Resolution also demanded that "outside interference in the country had to cease immediately." Pakistan, as the mentor and only supporter of the Taliban, clearly came under pressure as a consequence of increasing criticism of the Taliban.

Clinton personally pursued the bin Laden issue with Sharif. The US President had multi-sourced intelligence on bin Laden's very imminent plan to attack American targets. The word was that bin Laden was aiding Saddam Hussain, who was under attack from the Americans. Hence, on 18 December a fortnight after Sharif's Washington visit, Clinton called him. An acutely worried Clinton asked Sharif for his "personal help." He told Sharif that he had "reliable intelligence" and "quite a lot of it that Osama bin Laden intends to strike a US target very soon, perhaps in 48 hours...and that the operations are being orchestrated by bin Laden from within Afghanistan." This coincided with United States and Britain's controversial Operation Desert Fox, a major four-day bombing campaign on Iraqi targets from 16-19 December.[67] The justification for these controversial strikes was Iraq's failure to comply with United Nations Security Council resolutions as well as their interference with United Nations Special Commission inspectors. The US President faced criticism at home and abroad for undertaking military action at a time when he was under fire over his relations with White House intern Monica Lewinsky. Meanwhile, there was an outpouring of Muslim street support for Iraqi President Saddam Hussain. But Clinton assured Sharif, "Now all I can tell you is that this is not a reaction to Iraq: he's been working on this."[68] Clinton was ruling out any linkage.

Clinton told Sharif of his extreme worry regarding the consequences of such an attack by Bin Laden. He asked Sharif, "Do whatever you can to stop this immediately." The Americans were contacting the Saudis for help too. Meanwhile Clinton repeated what he considered the Pakistan-Taliban-bin Laden link. He held the Taliban directly responsible for Bin Laden's actions, given the latter was operating from Afghan territory. Additionally, Clinton reiterated that bin Laden's operations were directly undermining Pakistan's goal of Taliban acceptability within the international community. He told Sharif, "I think Pakistan has a lot of stake in the Taliban being accepted in the international community, and if this (attack) happens it will become virtually impossible."[69] Clinton was also reaching out to the Saudis but wanted Sharif to know "he was very very worried about it and consequences if it (operation) occurs."

An attentive and enthusiastic Sharif was, however, not hopeful. He reminded the US President of their Washington conversation that the "Taliban are very uncooperative people." He also recalled how the Taliban was "very stubborn" over the bin laden issue in the Kandahar meeting between the Pakistanis, Mulla Omar, and Saudi Prince Turki. Sharif assured Clinton of sending his people the following day to meet the Taliban leadership to "tell them this will not be in their interest and serve no purpose, that it will invite retaliation and a world reaction." Clinton wanted Nawaz to explain to the Taliban that "being uncooperative and not giving him (bin Laden) and allowing him to conduct operations are fundamentally different things." Nawaz and Clinton's thoughts fully converged on the bin Laden and Taliban issues but Sharif could hold out little hope for Clinton. The bin Laden-Taliban-ISI axis, even if somewhat unintended, did exist and Sharif had almost no leverage over it.

1998 Draws To A Close In Parallel Universes

In India and Pakistan, the civilian leaderships had decided to go into the high gear of diplomacy, with the objective of creating an environment of trust encouraging candid exchanges. Nawaz Sharif, a straightforward realist, had concluded that this alone was a workable approach for the two leaders, both of whom agreed that maximalist positions could not work and what was needed was a sustained process of engagement, which would factor in Kashmiri rights plus concerns and the positions of both Pakistan and India.

Nawaz Sharif worked closely with the civilian bureaucracy on foreign policy matters. Sharif was not educated in or knowledgeable about international affairs. He was no Zulfikar Ali Bhutto, hence no strategist. Instead, he worked with instincts and a street-sense of what was needed. Beyond that, for policy formulation and policy articulation, the prime minister depended primarily on his team of diplomats. As his core team guided Nawaz Sharif within the parameters of the policy thrust that he himself identified, he rarely overuled their advice.[70] Detailed policy discussions within the Cabinet or even his team of diplomats were not Sharif's mode of operation. That was personalized, cliquish, instinctual, and combined with street-smart calculations. The normal way in foreign policy matters was discussion and decision with his kitchen cabinet: his brother, the CM Punjab; his trusted minister Chaudhary Nisar, and his defense secretary, instead of the Cabinet, his kitchen cabinet which comprised CM Punjab and Chaudhary Nisar. The prime minister's key guide and mentor was Mian Mohammad Sharif, his 83-year-old father, a self-made, Lahore-based businessman dealing in steel, and unfamiliar with the business of the state. The obedient son would follow his father's advice, for example, on the appointment of the President after Leghari's ouster.

Similarly, the prime minister's relationships with top foreign leaders, Indian, American and even Afghan, were guided by straight-forward personal interaction. Some were tutored by his Foreign Office team, and some were the outcome of his discussions with perhaps only his kitchen cabinet and his father. Often, Sharif would seek to have non-institutionalized, one-on-one interactions with foreign dignitaries, including heads of states. This would ensure no documented minutes of the meetings. As for the army, Sharif worked most closely with the ISI chief. Known to the Sharif family, Khawaja Zaheerudin was not well-entrenched within the ISI, the organization involved with the Kashmir and Afghan policies. He had no regular links with the GHQ. None of the generals, except the ISI head, was in Sharif's inner circles.

In the post-nuclear test period, Pakistan's foreign policy formulation was influenced by input from three different outlooks. The outlook of the prime minister, who was simply keen to improve relations with the country's eastern and western neighbors and stay the track with the US. Working closely with the prime minister were his kitchen cabinet, his brother Shehbaz Sharif (Chief Minister of Punjab), and Chaudhri Nisar Ahmed (Minister for Petroleum). Then there was the new Foreign Minister Sartaj Aziz. The third was the Foreign Office bureaucracy. Two parallel chains of commands operated at the FO. The bureaucracy found Aziz a 'dove' on India. While Aziz had indeed questioned the wisdom of conducting the nuclear tests because of the impact on the national economy, as foreign minister he saw flexible conduct of policy vis-a-vis India as necessary to create space for negotiations with India and for improving bilateral relations. The bureaucracy, meanwhile, was completely distrustful of Indian motives and believed that showing flexibility towards India would be tantamount to capitulation. The history of Pakistan-India relations encouraged this distrust.

Significantly, Nawaz Sharif himself ended up having bureaucrats like Shamshad Ahmad and Tariq Fatimi, not his foreign minister, in his inner core of foreign policy-making.

There was, of course, a fourth set of inputs, unknown to the country's elected prime minister: a clique of men in khaki, seemingly with sufficient autonomy and sufficient resources available to them to be unaccountable to the chief executive.

Meanwhile, with the political leadership having determined the outcome of the Lahore Summit, it was left to the bureaucrats to craft a mutually agreeable output. While the political channel was kept open, it took the bureaucrats weeks to jointly prepare the documentation.[71] Pakistan's back-channel point-man also met with the Indian foreign minister to firm up the Lahore Declaration.

It was indeed a measure of the political atmosphere that the Indians even explored the possibility of a Non-Aggression Pact.[72] The bureaucrats went through with discussing the idea, putting their respective versions on paper. The Indians bureaucrats, with the blessing of their political leadership, were "testing the waters"[73] on how far the Pakistanis were willing to cover the friendship road and, more importantly, on what terms.

Nawaz Sharif, now Prime Minister of the only nuclear state in the Muslim world, was on-course implementing his decision to reorient Pakistan's foreign policy. After the nuclear tests, he had decided to make good on his election promise of improving relations with India. Also in his December one-on-one Washington meeting with Bill Clinton, Sharif had assured the US President of finding ways to work together on nabbing OBL, responsible for attacks on US embassies in East Africa.

Hence, as 1998 came to a close, three different strands of activities were underway, all very significant for Pakistan. First, the prime minister was on a course-correction path, generally, and specifically working overtime to normalize relations with India. After 28 years, a Pakistan-India summit in Pakistan had already been scheduled for February. Extensive preparations for the Nawaz-Vajpayee Summit in the historic city of Lahore were already underway. Second, a clique of four Pakistani generals had already dispatched hundreds of Pakistani troops across the LOC to occupy strategic heights in Indian-Held Kashmir. They believed such a covert operation, combined with the global anxiety of Kashmir becoming a possible 'nuclear flashpoint' would force India to resolve the Kashmir issue, or at least pull back from its 1984 occupation of Siachen. Third, Clinton's CIA-led team was testing multiple permutations and combinations for a 'snatch operation' to get United States dreaded enemy bin Laden.

Pakistan's prime minister in his December one-on-one meeting with Clinton had promised that ISI would help in capturing the al-Qaeda leader. While Nawaz had appointed his trusted man general Ziauddin Butt to lead the ISI, the operational tier of generals, including Lt. Generals Aziz Khan, Jamshed Gulzar, and Ghulam Ahmad, were effectively under the GHQ's command and not under the ISI chief's command. Moreover, the quadrangular cooperative setup of the early nineties, which included the ISI, CIA, Taliban, and OBL, were beginning to separate into adversarial groupings. The CIA's sole focus was to capture or kill OBL and they expected nothing less than full cooperation in this from the Taliban and the ISI.

The Taliban, as Mulla Omar's exchange with Saudi Prince Turki had clearly conveyed, were in no mood to handover their benefactor and now comrade to either the Saudis or to the Americans. As for the ISI, it continued to mentor the Taliban as Kabul's rightful and pro-Pakistani government in Kabul. Another dimension of the Taliban-Pakistan link was now the Kashmir factor. Non-Kashmiri militants sent by Pakistan into Indian Held Kashmir[74] were increasingly being trained in Afghanistan and often in bin Laden's training camps.[75] Some of these militants were pursuing a dual agenda. In IOK, they conducted sabotage activities targeting Indian forces and even moderate Kashmiris. Within Pakistan they pursued their own ideological agenda, targeting Pakistan's Shia Muslim population.

In the November 9 DCC meeting, the elected government had already decided that it would take a tougher line with the Taliban, especially with regard to the protection the Taliban regime was providing to sectarian groups responsible for killing ShiaMuslims in Pakistan. Nawaz Sharif, who was personally comfortable with the political leader of the Northern Alliance Professor Burhanuddin Rabbani, also decided that his government would open lines of communications with Ahmad Shah Massoud of the Northern Alliance. This policy decision by the country's chief executive was in opposition to the Pakistan military's operational policy of protecting, supporting, and promoting the Taliban regime. On OBL the military took the position that he was "not Pakistan's headache."

In Washington, the Pakistan military's position did not cut any ice. Based on intercepts, human intelligence and other reporting sources, Washington was convinced of Pakistan's deep links with al-Qaeda's protectors, the Taliban. Hence, even though CIA Counter Terrorist Analysts acknowledged that the ISI had no truck with al-Qaeda's international agenda targeting the Americans, they concluded ISI-Taliban nexus was indirectly protecting, promoting, and also expanding the al-Qaeda network. Another indirect ISI and al-Qaeda link was that the ISI-supported Pakistani sectarian groups, that conducted operations against the Indian force in IOK, were trained in the al-Qaeda camps.

So these parallel and contradictory activities were: peace with India, get OBL, and hit India through a covert Op in Kashmir. For all these clashing activities, Pakistan was the staging ground. Captains of these activities were moving forward on different tracks, all three pursuing their concerns The state of the State of Pakistan was as it would have inevitably been twenty years into the Afghan jihad...disrupted, divided, and debilitated, a far cry from an efficiently run modern State. The former military dictator General Ziaul Haq's policy of the eighties and its conduct had led to the fragmentation of the state. Institutions had been made unaccountable. The military called the shots in foreign policy and natural security. Unprecedented muscle provided by the US to Pakistan's lead spy agency ISI, also ensured its role–expansion in policy formulation and policy conduct.

From Bhutto to Zia, Pakistan had presented a contrasting picture. Bhutto exhibited world-class diplomacy while Zia was of men trained to view the world in a dependent and derivative mode. On the global stage Bhutto had dragged a defeated nation with the power of his vision to impressive levels of self-confidence and expanding influence. Bhutto led the new world opening with South-West Asia, leadership in the strategically important Muslim world, structural bonding with China, engaging the Russian bear, and putting Pakistan on the immutable nuclear path.

Zia, by contrast, had taken Pakistan into a covert war, in a subservient role, believing it to be autonomous. Nevertheless overlooking the damage his policies did to Pakistani State, society and politics, many in the army credited Zia for the hardware he brought to the armed forces, including staying the course on the nuclear program. Zia also abandoned the nuances of diplomacy, he had entirely bought into the threat perceptions of the West. Zia's policy had triggered a dynamic that had begun to atrophy state power and therefore cohesion. Power was proliferating to the groups he patronized. The monopoly of force, symbols of national power, and control of the public space all dissipated and began slipping away. Sectarianism was growing.[76] His sly talk and sham humility may have won some naïve hearts but Pakistan's state power and public peace were being lost. Even worse was the divided picture that Pakistan's institutions presented. For example army chief versus the army, ISI chief versus the rest, etc. Within the very architecture of state and government, there was conflict and contest. The narratives were several and divided. It has resulted in a clash of power and narratives on the foreign policy and national security. Little wonder that often Pakistan did not present a cohesive game plan while engaging interlocutors. Sharif, at the close of 1998, was set to pull all this together.

But it was going to be a tad difficult.

Chapter 4

NECKS ON THE LINE AND THE LOTUS LAKE

The confident clique of Kargil planners was satisfied with the progress of the operation. By the end of December, Pakistani forces had already infiltrated almost seven kilometers from seven directions which included east of Shyok river outflank, from the top of Shyok Valley, from the western side of the river Indus, from Shakma. Pakistan Army troops from 13 NLI, 3 NLI, 5 NLI, 12 NLI and Sindh Regiment directly penetrated the seven areas. Although the army chief had given the nod, formal approval of the Operation was still needed. The revered day of Jumatul Wida, the last Friday of Ramadan, the sacred month of fasting, was picked for a formal approval of Operation Koh Paima. On 16 January, in the operations room of the Military Operations Directorate, Operation KP was approved although the bulk of the plan was already under way.. The meeting, chaired by army chief General Musharraf, was attended by Lt. General Aziz Khan(Chief of General Staff), Lt. General Mahmud Ahmad (Corps Commander 10 Corps), Lt. General Tauqir Zia (Director General Military Operations), Major General Javed Hasan (Commander FCNA), Brigadier Masood Aslam (Commander 323 Brigade), Brigadier Nadeem Ahmad (Director Military Operations) and Colonel Nisar Ahmad (GI

Operations). Colonel Nisar Ahmad formally presented the tactical plan and its execution. The entire plan was spread over 15 pages and included a detailed map with logistics, ammunition, rations, and troops at posts set up across the LOC.

This general's clique, assembled to fulfill a formality, hardly asked any questions. These were upbeat times. In the dead of winter, at more than a 16,000 foot climb, the battlefield was clear and apparently for Pakistan's taking. The brave young men these generals had sent across the LOC to intimidate the Indians, were advancing. The generals were already slipping into class mission creep. Oblivious to whether their indispensable supply lines could match their advancing miles and heights, these dare-devil soldiers charged ahead. Their commanders, equally excited, overlooked the implications of this unplanned expansion. Such was the attitude of these top generals—securely ensconced in their own domains, away from the perilous battle-ground.

Some perfunctory comments and questions followed, then the army chief's approval. Significantly, this approval was a violation of the standard operating procedure (SOP), the preparation of A Note For Consideration (NFC) for the chief. The standard NFC has analysis, options and recommendations. Typically the Military Operations Directorate(MOD) would prepare it and send it to the chief of general staff (CGS), who would endorse it and send it to the chief. The input for the NFC would come from the MI, ISI and the relevant Corps, in this case 10 Corps. The chief's approval would be followed by a series of MO conferences that would thoroughly assess the operational viability of the proposal. For Operation KP, the approval came in a secret huddle, with no input from the intelligence agencies and no assessment by the MOD.

The DG MOD, Tauqir Zia, was brought on at the last minute for the formal approval meeting. Zia was no planner but knew the operation was under way. He demonstrated his near disinterest in the matter by not raising any questions regarding the operation. Zia, whose mandate was to oversee the increasing requirements of troops and all logistics for all military operations, lounging in his chair, barely even moved from his slouching position. He was a new entrant in this clique.[1] Aziz, the lead among the Kargil clique, prompted him to ask some questions. Aziz had keenly watched the disinterested and somewhat baffled Zia during the meeting. Aziz needed him to be involved and interested. He wanted this key general to take ownership.

Perhaps the most poignant moment came when, after approving the operation, General Musharraf made a very prophetic query. "Tell me that the state of this operation will not be similar to that of India's 1962 forward policy against China." He was referring to India's 1962 war against China in which the Indian attack was repulsed with a massive Chinese counter-attack. Javed Hasan was quick to assure the chief that Pakistan's positions were strongly established while the Indians were completely unprepared to respond. He then raised his hands to his throat and said, "If anything goes wrong, my neck is available." His Commander, Mahmud, was quick to take responsibility. "Why yours? My neck will be on the line since I have cleared it." As if taking the cue, in stepped the next man up in the hierarchy, the chief himself. "No, it would not be your neck, it would be my neck."

A three-neck offering had been announced in case of failure but history was to record a different trajectory. These words notwithstanding, for these generals the possibility of being held accountable in case of failure must have seemed distant. There was no precedence; the list of military blunders had not been matched by a corresponding list of penalties for those responsible for blunders.. These men making decisions and giving approvals in hiding knew what they were doing. Their undertaking was hugely risky yet they had convinced themselves it was in the 'national interest.' The operation was baptized and given a name. Commander 10 Corps General Mahmud formally proposed *Operation Koh Paima.* The clique accepted it.[2]

The meeting dispersed as the plan was approved. But, even before this approval, using routes not known to the Indians, the FCNA troops had already crossed the LOC. They had gone several kilometers across and taken up dozens of posts in the Kargil-Drass area at point .5140. These were men who knew of the original Kargil plan that was conceived by their predecessors in the late eighties and the changes made to the original plan. They were also familiar with the criticisms but nursed the desire to punish India, especially for Siachen, by actually implementing the plan.

Musharraf, who led the line to offer his neck, was suppose to have received hardly a fortnight earlier, from a special unit within the ISI, a document about the Kargil Operation[3] The document detailed the strategic disasters that the ongoing Kargil Op may trigger.

The country's chief executive, the prime minister, had neither cleared the operation, nor was he taken in the loop by the army chief. All SOPs had been ignored. On 16 January, when the generals convened to give clearance to the operation (already nearing completion), Musharraf was mindful of the worst, he had images of 'necks on the line' when he gave the approval in the meeting. Perhaps there was a Report from the ISI's special unit after all did get to him and the information and analysis in the Report had left him immensely uncomfortable.

36 Days Apart

The January 16 meeting took place less than five weeks before the Pakistani and Indian prime ministers signed the historic Lahore Declaration on 22 February. This meeting was reminiscent of the 13 May, 1965 meeting that took place between the military President Field Marshal Mohammad Ayub Khan and the GOC 12 Division. The field Marshal was presented with the plan for Operation Gibraltar, which was jointly authored by the ISI and the Foreign Office. Gibraltar called for covert crossing of the Cease Fire Line and was presented around 48 days before the Rann of Kutch Agreement was to be signed. The agreement was signed by India and Pakistan on June 30 and each withdrew their troops from the international border areas. In the backdrop of this Agreement, Pakistan's troops still crossed the then Cease Fire Line between 29 and 30 July. Operation Gibraltar was a grossly miscalculated plan. By September, it had provoked a war. Fifteen years later, Pakistan's determination to stay the blundering course and diligently repeat our mistakes was phenomenal. In 1999, the generals' clique had signed off to a repeat of Operation Gibraltar.

In Pakistan's policy towards its critical neighbour India, an incredible feat was underway. Diametrically opposed advances towards India were being made. Prime Minister Nawaz Sharif had invited the Indian Prime

Minister to Lahore for the 20 February historic Pakistan-India Summit. Musharraf refused to obey the command of the elected prime minister to participate in the welcome ceremony for the Indian prime minister at Wagah border. He and other military men, hidden away from the country's chief executive, were busy planning a comprehensive violation of that section of the Lahore Declaration that stated the two prime ministers "Recognize that the nuclear dimension of the security environment of the two countries adds to their responsibility for avoidance of conflict between them." This was a near identical replay of the 35-year old Operation Gibraltar[4] with the only difference thatin Kargil the civilians and the military were not on the same page. Civilians had moved beyond Gibraltar and had opted for diplomacy by charting new pathways to peace. Operation KP was an attempt by a group within the army to perpetuate the old ways. It was subverting the new. The contrast could not have been starker.

Kargil clique's calculations

The clique of generals was confident about achieving its objectives. Operation KP did not include a direct military offensive on Siachen, as was conceived in the original 1985 plan. Nevertheless, the Kargil clique initially believed that India, under pressure, would be forced to give up Siachen.

The decision to go ahead with the operation was based on several factors. For one, Pakistan's security apparatus had received a major boost after the successful nuclear tests. Also, a section within Pakistan's national security establishment anxiously observed the weakening of the insurgency inside Indian-controlled Kashmir. Another factor was the Pakistan-India dialogue which, led by the two prime ministers, was proceeding ahead rapidly. Certainly, the idea that the civilian leadership should make the decision to overhaul Pakistan's Kashmir policy worried these generals. Finally, there was an erroneous belief within senior military and intelligence ranks that the mention of Kashmir was being omitted from the draft of the Lahore Declaration.[5] Alongside these factors, India's track record of territory-nibbling and the personalities of the FCNA and the

10Corps commanders also influenced how Pakistan planned and conducted Operation KP.

The planners believed that an expanded operation would result in Pakistan's control of a bigger chunk of the strategic heights across the LOC. The bigger the territory, the more diplomatic and political advantage would accrue to Pakistan in negotiations with India. [6]

Their calculation was simple. India would not be able to militarily dislodge the Pakistani forces from the strategic heights they had occupied before the onset of winter. India would be under pressure to enter into negotiations for two reasons. One, the Indians would be desperate to end the near siege of National Highway-1A (NH-1A). Two, the international community has no stomach for military conflict in South Asia, , and would encourage negotiation.

The architects of the operation believed that these factors would put Pakistan in an advantageous position at the negotiating table.[7] In addition to preventing another Indian operation to further occupy territory across the LOC[8], they had calculated a minimum and maximum gain from the operation. The minimum gain would have been India's withdrawal from the Siachen area. The maximum gain would have been an Indian commitment to enter into a "serious dialogue on Kashmir." Also, Pakistan's military operation would reinvigorate the Kashmiri political struggle.

Predicting an Indian Response

The planners calculated a three-stage incremental Indian response to the Kargil operation. First, the Indians would only react locally to what the Pakistani planners saw as a "limited incursion." The Indians would build defensive positions along the ingress areas. Alternatively, Indians might counterattack using local forces[9] to reclaim the Kargil heights.

Pakistan's calculation was that, in the case of a localized Indian response failing to expel the Pakistani forces, "a second tier" Indian response would come into play with India opening additional fronts along the LOC across from the Pakistani towns of Murree and Chamb-Jaurian.[10]

For this, India would require additional forces from outside of Jammu and Kashmir.

Finally, although India could theoretically go for an all-out war across the international border, they believed it would not. They concluded that incremental discovery would largely rule out an all-out Indian war across the international border. Also, according to Pakistan's estimation, India had around 700,000 regular and paramilitary troops in IOK. Of these, there were nine divisions of regular troops. The GHQ was certain that with these forces 'tied down' in Kashmir, the Indians did not have the force structure to execute an all-our offensive against Pakistan elsewhere. The planners moved with a linear calculation of an Indian response. As military men, they only focused on the military dimension.

The Absence of Consensus

Beyond the clique of Kargil planners, the consensus and commitment to the operation varied with what men in uniform knew. Kargil was no regular operation, with no standardized or widely shared script with objectives, maneuvers, and timelines. Generals and commanders met in their homes, not in the Control rooms. They secretly huddled in small groups, in small rooms, maps spread across dinner tables, often away from their headquarters. The majority participating in the operation did what they were trained to do. They were simply following orders. This unusual undertaking in a hostile terrain had triggered a sense of adventure among the mostly the brave and patriotic. For the soldiers of Pakistan, engaging India was fair-game. The recurrent gun-battles along the LOC and the lengthening shadows of unresolved issues found the soldiers always ready to do battle, always heading for the front.

Initially, in what was a heady time for the Kargil clique, when the domain they believed was theirs for the taking, there were only some who questioned them: those who worked within the core teams of the commander 10 Corps and of the FCNA. However, once the operation was under way, all questioning ceased. No one could openly question its logic or feasibility. However, the internal chatter never stopped. There was some hesitation that their troops should participate in the operation among the two and three star generals with whom the core clique shared the plan, especially among some senior field commanders For example, the recently promoted Major-General Ashfaq Pervez Kayani was now posted with GOC 12 Division, commanding the area extending from Forward Kahuta (short of Kotli, Azad Kashmir) to Kel located up in the north. Headquartered at Murree, this Division too was under Lt. General Mahmud, Commander 10 Corps. Before his promotion, Kayani had served under General Mahmud at the National Defense College (NDC), where he was told of Operation Koh Paima.

In a meeting at the Corps Commander's home, where the possible Indian response was being discussed, Kayani's view differed from that of his colleagues. He believed India would not attack where Pakistan's defense was the weakest. Instead Kayani believed India would attack directly at Kargil, which was strategically important for India. In more restricted meetings, Kayani let his seniors know he believed the operation had conceptual flaws. Indian strategic capacity included its existing ammunition dumps, its two airfields, the National Highway, and the large Kargil Valley. On the Pakistani side, there was the smaller Minimarg Valley, the snow-clogged Burzil Pass, and the Deosai Plains. Added to this was the very hostile operation terrain, extending from Minimarg to Drass-Kargil, essentially a pack of formidable mountains, translating into communications barriers for the Pakistani soldiers. [11]

Leading the charge for Operation Koh Paima were simplistic and patriotic mindsets. Commander 10 Corps would tell his team that the aim was to occupy the heights undetected and then inflict heavy casualties on the Indians during summer. The Commander FCNA would say that the Indians would not know what hit them. They only talked of defensive battle and he did not believe they were even capable of that. In response to concerns expressed by other officers about a tough Indian response, Major General Javed Hasan's unprofessional, prejudiced refrain was: "The timid Indian will never fight the battle." Javed Hasan used to go to the battle headquarters but mostly not across the LOC, yet all the posts were established with his clearance.

Lahore Summit: Seeking new pathways

Given the many weeks of preparation, there were no surprise developments at the Lahore summit. Three important bilateral agreements were produced: a Declaration was signed by the two leaders, a Memorandum of Understanding (MOU) was approved by the foreign secretaries, and a Joint Statement was issued. These were comprehensive documents which covered the entire range of bilateral interests, ranging from "commitment to intensify their efforts to resolve all issues, including the issue of Jammu and Kashmir" to "condemnation of terrorism in all its forms and manifestations" and "undertaking national measures to reduce the risks of accidental or unauthorized use of nuclear weapons." Pakistan hoped these Lahore agreements would overrule Simla as the framework for a multi-faceted peace process.

Under international gaze and domestic concern, the two governments admitted that tangible and active bilateral cooperation was indispensable to responsible management of nuclear programmes and arsenals. The MOU outlined a broad commitment to cooperate in specific areas of nuclear restraint, including taking steps to avoid nuclear accidents, and provide each other advance notification of ballistic missile flight tests. However, on the key issues of non-deployment and non-weaponization, no concrete progress was made.

Vajpayee said he was keen to bury the hatchet with Pakistan. At a civic reception hosted at the Governor's House, Vajpayee was clear that, for peacemaking and dispute settlement, "when we are required to take hard decisions, you will find us resolute; you will not find us retreating."

On the hardest question, the Kashmir issue, the Indian PM demonstrated more openness than his predecessors. During the joint press conference with his Pakistani counterpart, he brought up the Kashmir issue at least half a dozen times. Refraining from bracketing it with cross-border terrorism and external interference, Vajpayee stressed that his government would "negotiate with sincerity." In fact, in response to whether India would be willing to concede the right of self-determination to Kashmiris in Indian Held Kashmir, he departed from the standard Indian response. Instead, he said, "Discussion is going on. It's very difficult for me to say what solution will ultimately emerge. Wait for the outcome of the talks." [12]

In an attempt to address the perennial Pakistani complaint that India did not accept the reality of Pakistan, Vajpayee, a member of India's most right-wing party, decided to permanently bury the hatchet. He placed a wreath at the Minar-i-Pakistan where the March 1940 Resolution for the creation of Pakistan was passed. Vajpayee wrote in the visitors' book, "From the Minar-i-Pakistan, I want to assure the people of Pakistan of my country's deep desire for lasting peace and friendship. I have said and I say this again, a stable and prosperous Pakistan is in India's favor. Let there be no doubt about this." Vajpayee also pointedly tackled the question of Akhand Bharat.[13] Speaking at the Governor's House, he said, "Yes, we did not want the break-up of our country; its division created a wound, but the wound has now healed. Yet the scar remains and keeps reminding us of how we should live with each other, in peace and as friends."[14]

The Lahore summit was also an attempt to popularize the peace initiative that the two prime ministers had initiated since Colombo. That explained hosting it in the heart of Pakistan, turning it into a festive occasion, and including huge numbers of civilians and the media in the official events. Nawaz Sharif used the occasion to begin building a constituency in civil society for peace with India.

The Jamaat-i-Islami, Pakistan's right-wing political party, was the principal opponent of Nawaz Sharif's India policy.[15] It organized violent demonstrations in Lahore, especially during the evenings. Young men armed with stones, sticks and batons attacked cars ferrying guests to the historic Lahore Fort for the state banquet. Not angry tough guys, these young fellows, fortified seemingly with deliberated and scripted agitation, were easy to discourage.[16] Hundreds of policemen ordered out by the Chief Minister of Punjab Shehbaz Sharif were handled firmly. Given the army's strong reservations about Pakistan's official India policy, it is not improbable that these scripted protests had input from the intelligence agencies. On India, especially, the Jamaat-i-Islami and the army had an ongoing nexus. This occasion, especially this orchestration of public opposition to the dialogue path, must have been particularly important for the authors of the clandestine Kargil operation.

The absence of the three armed forces chiefs in the reception line at the Wagah border also fuelled the rumours that the armed forces opposed Sharif's policy towards India. They believed that the government's proactive peace offensive with India would weaken diplomatically and politically undermine Pakistan's position on Kashmir. The army's view was that, behind Vajpayee's fig leaf posturing, was the reality of India's inflexible position on Kashmir. The Establishment read Vajpayee as a shrewd leader who would protect Indian interests, including India's claims on Kashmir, at all costs. [17] They were convinced that India would not respond to the language of peace.

Similarly, within the Indian military, there was some disquiet about the usefulness of the Lahore Summit. There was also some concern regarding how effectively Vajpayee would ensure that the Lahore documents reflected India's main concern of "terrorism." At the last minute, the Indian drafting Committee "received word that the Indian army chief, General Ved Malik, had been insistent that the text should carry a reference to terrorism."[18]

At Lahore, during private meetings, Sharif and Vajpayee tried to grapple with the question of Kashmir. Discussions on Kashmir had already started on the non-bureaucratic front. The Neemrana Group was discussing the KSG study. Naik and Mishra had already held several meetings to explore various options.

Sharif was clear that the political leadership on both sides had created a national consensus around their respective maximalist positions on Kashmir. Challenging this consensus, even for those who created it, would not be easy. He urged Vajpayee to come up with a reasonable proposal on Kashmir that he could discuss with his electorate. Sharif was confident that, as a prime minister with a two-thirds majority, and as a Punjabi, his credentials as a peacemaker on Kashmir would be unchallengeable. He insisted that the key to forward the movement was a reasonable proposal by Vajpayee.[19] The drafting committee adhered to the army chief's "advice" after they "agreed to a matching insertion by the Pakistani side."[20]

The time frame for resolving Kashmir was also discussed as being perhaps between twelve to eighteen months from February. Both sides wanted movement before electoral considerations came into play.[21] In another hour-long Vajpayee-Sharif meeting, the Indian prime minister spoke of his dream of normalizing Pakistan-India relations. He told an attentive and agreeable Sharif that at the tail end of his political career he wanted his vision fulfilled.[22]

The atmosphere at the Lahore Summit contrasted sharply with the October-November composite dialogue between the bureaucrats. Then, the two sides had merely restated their respective positions. For sustainable peace, substantive movement on dispute resolution was the key. The next round of the Composite Dialogue was to be held in May. And what would transpire during those negotiations would indicate whether India was truly willing to begin the thousand-mile journey of peacemaking in South Asia. That was the promise of the Lahore Summit.

But the spirit, the substance, and the follow-up of the Lahore Summit were all set for an inevitable clash with the advancing Kargil operation. And more than just the South Asians were to be surprised.

In Washington, the Lahore Summit was predictably applauded as an "encouraging step" for improving Pakistan-India bilateral relations. The outspoken US Secretary of State Madeleine Albright, who in 1998 had spent many frustrating hours trying to calm the political waters in South Asia, was optimistic. At the end of February, addressing the Senate Foreign Relations Committee on the Fiscal Year Budget, she said, "If the past year was a time of disappointment and unfulfilled promise in South Asia, we are working hard to see that the coming year is one of opportunity and progress." Projecting into peaceful days ahead, Albright outlined Washington's 1999 agenda in South Asia. "Throughout the region, we will be working hard to advance our core foreign policy objectives of strengthening democracy, enhancing economic ties, countering terrorism, extending the rule of law, and promoting respect for human rights," the sanguine Secretary said.[23]

Vajpayee's Dogged Ownership

For the Vajpayee government, the month of April became a turbulent one. On 17 April, the Vajpayee government lost a vote of confidence with the narrowest margin in the modern political history of just one vote. Fresh elections were called. The fallen BJP government saw its Pakistan peace initiative as a major winning point in its election campaign. In his first campaign statement on 2 May, BJP's election campaign leader L. K. Advani included the "Bus to Pakistan" as one of the five 'Bs' that would ensure a BJP electoral victory.[24] Earlier, on 16 April, Vajpayee also refuted the Opposition's criticism of the Lahore Summit and his bus trip after the Pokhran nuclear tests, and said that the two events were "the two sides of the same coin."[25]

Around April, the Indian prime minister sent a message across the border to his Pakistani counterpart: please stop the firing, at least while the talks are underway. India used diplomatic channels to alert Pakistan's political leadership about its concern regarding increased firing along the LOC. The Pakistan High Commission in Delhi was asked by the Ministry of External Affairs (MEA) to convey its concerns to Islamabad. Earlier, only 10 days before the Lahore Summit, on 10 February 1999, the Indian Director-General Military Operations (DGMO) had also complained to his Pakistani counterpart about unusual level of firing from across the LOC.

Special Parameters and the Gruelling Wait

Operation KP was initially launched within special parameters. One, only a limited number of NLI paramilitary troops were to be used for the operation.[26] Two, primary and secondary gains had to be made. The primary 'gain' was to choke the Drass-Kargil sector. The secondary yet "auxiliary" gain was to lay siege around Indian troops stationed in the Kaksar and Batalik sector. The Zoji La pass was also snow-bound and would have blocked Indian troop movement along the Pass. [27] The other route, Leh-Manalee, was under construction and at an altitude of around 5000 meters and crossing through five mountain ranges, was not feasible for continual traffic.[28]

The original plan required a crossing of the LOC at Drass to acquire a post at Tololing, thereby acquiring vital proximity to NH1. From Tololing, the distance to NH1 would be only two kilometers whereas Pakistani troops stationed at the LOC were almost six kilometers away from the road. Excited, a member of the Kargil clique explained, "We could have placed an MP [29] on NH1!"

Pakistani troops backed by logistical supplies, including ammunition, pre-fabricated igloos, and dry rations moved towards the 'primary' and 'secondary' sectors. Between March and April they were in position, occupying 140 posts and pickets[30] across five areas. They occupied watersheds in these sectors across the LOC in Mushkoh, Drass, Kaksar, Batalik, and Turtok. (MAP) It was from their posts in the Drass sector that Pakistani troops could access for effective interdiction NH-1A, the life-line to Indian troops in Ladakh and Siachen.

Then began the hard, grueling wait for the troops. With no more than ten to fifteen troops at every post and five to six at pickets, there was virtually no communication with the outside world, as they kept vigil and lay in wait. Because these covert movements spread over several months went completely unnoticed by India, Pakistani troops had uninterrupted time to execute their military plans.

Kargil was an unusual military Op, given the harsh mountainous terrain and weather, the extreme secrecy of the operation, and the Kargil clique's calculation of only limited Indian military response and hence limited combat with the enemy. It combined elements of a guerrilla operation, a holding operation, a covert operation, a mountaineering expedition, and an expedition to test human endurance. The troops in the field, having to negotiate with one of the world's harshest terrains and most vicious climates, were therefore far more in direct and constant combat with nature than with Indian troops.[31]

It was therefore a unique operation, to be conducted in an extremly hostile environment, relying heavily on the sheer courage, outstanding physical fitness, firm willpower and, above all, an unwavering commitment of the troops to the task assigned to them.

For this operation, secrecy was valued above all else. No formal military channels for communication were used. For example, while the FCNA headquarters regularly talked on the telephone with field commanders across the LOC to get updates, this communication was a post-midnight activity. To maintain secrecy, no conversation could take place in the presence of the telephone operators. The GI Operations had to wait for them to leave their post. Despite Operation KP being covert, the practice of maintaining logs and writing reports was not abandoned. But in this covert operation all activities were susceptible to manipulation at many levels. It was planned and fought like a personal war, with ownership of all the critical men in the army's command hierarchy. While it unfolded, with no transparency even institutionally, the operation was not being reviewed for success or viability.

"So, Isn't That What We Want?"

The optimism did not blind the mid-rank officers directly engaged at the operational level. Around five months into Op KP, while the Kargil clique basked in their achievements, confidently declaring the irreversibility of their advances and the virtual invincibility of the posts and pickets, outside of the clique, other officers thought of ways to sustain the momentum. They were more focused on possible Indian responses, less on the near-euphoria of early success that their senior commanders were possessed by. They would often wonder how Indian forces would respond at first contact. But the Kargil clique had concluded, "*Hindustani kadi jang nahi laray ga ... pi ja'ay ga*", ("The Indians will not fight back"), was the Commander FCNA's non-professional retort to questions operation level officers would raise.

By early March, the officers in the thick of events recommended to their seniors that a syndicate be organized on the Indian side, for its response. "We had realized our assessment was faulty," recalled a mid-level officer posted at the FCNA headquarters.

Other potential troubles were also flagged. For example, a colonel of NLI 6 commanding at Tololing warned the FCNA commander, "To go so deep without artillery, logistics support, and without a defense plan would be a disaster." But the advances continued. These advances were without defensive battle plans, a standard SOP for any operations. [32]

One proposal to counter a possible pushback by India was to consider launching a supplementary but aggressive military maneuver by the troops who had already crossed the LOC. The idea, floated by one in the innermost coterie of the Kargil planners, envisioned troops moving across the Zojila pass, descending about 25 kilometers and establishing positions towards the Amarnath cave. The proposal called for them to then deny potential Indian response and capture India's undefended territory, ammunition, and communication controls. It involved positioning Pakistani troops still deeper into Indian-held territory to ensure that, upon India discovering Pakistani troops, even if pushed back they would have penetrated deep enough to threaten India's supply lines.

The lieutenant colonel in charge explained the plan to the corps commander, who rejected it. He agreed that militarily the plan was implementable and India could be under pressure in Kashmir. "So, then, why not?" the enthusiastic colonel asked, "Isn't that what we want?" "Well, what if India opens new fronts on the international border? Then Pakistan would be endangered," was the commander's response. For the colonel, the penny dropped. Stunned, he asked, "Then why did you get us to this point? Why the operation?" Angered, the colonel would later insist, Operation KP floundered because it was "structured in a way to defeat us. We were stopped at a position of weakness…"[33]

Troops and Logistics

By March, additional troops were called in as FCNA troops had ventured deeper. Units were moved from Peshawar. At any given time, Pakistan had 600 to 700 troops across the LOC. One post or picket did not require more than 8 to10 soldiers and the rest were there to support the base, etc. However, with troop rotation, in total around 3000 to 4000 troops participated in the operation,.

Depending on where the troops were positioned, helicopters, human porters, and mule brigades were used for delivering supplies. For the 80 Brigade areas, army helicopters would ferry across supplies daily. For 12 NLI based in the easier terrain in the Mushkoh Valley, human porters were used. About 300 to 400 porters were used.

Supplies for the troops came from the existing forward battalion supplies, dumped especially within the 80 Brigade area. The main logistics base from where supplies were transferred to different battalion headquarters was located at Jaglot, around 40 miles from Gilgit and 250 miles from Skardu. Undetected by the Indians, Lama helicopters were regularly flown across the LOC to drop food and limited medical supplies to feed the forward posts through summer months to last the many snow-bound months.[34]

By April, the brigade commanders gave the FCNA headquarters certificates in writing that promised ration and small arms ammunition until end December 1999.[35] Yet these certificates were no guarantee for a satisfactory logistical supply line for the troops on the ground. Some contingents, including NLI 5, were not supplied. Even those who had food were unable to cook it, either because they were in the igloos or lighting fire raised the possibility of being tracked by the Indians. Troops in Indian-held territory would talk of going hungry for days or surviving only on honey. Home-bound troops would talk of having eaten grass for days.

Deceptive Briefings

Within weeks of the Lahore Summit, and against the backdrop of an expanding Operation KP, General Musharraf organized a briefing for the prime minister on Kashmir. The PM, Foreign Minister Sartaj Aziz, Minister for Kashmir Affairs Lt. General Abdul Majid Malik, the DG ISI, and the Commander 10 Corps were among the attendees. Musharraf was keen to have a say in the diplomatic and political moves Pakistan had made towards India. Within the context of possible options on Kashmir, the options presented in the Report of the Kashmir Study Group were discussed.

On 29 January in Skardu, they told Sharif the general thrust of their intentions while not revealing the plan in full. In order to give a boost to the Kashmir struggle, they said, they needed to become active along the LOC. Sharif was told that local level operations along the LOC were being undertaken. Though he still had no clue that Pakistani troops had already crossed the LOC, Sharif felt that small-scale operations could complement his political and diplomatic efforts to move forward on détente and peace with India. At the Skardu airport, the prime minister was told that, just as the Indians were interdicting our traffic in the Neelum Valley, Pakistan too would set up a couple of posts to interdict the main artery, the Srinagar-Leh NH-1A. The army chief mentioned setting up of a couple of posts across the LOC so that visual rather than the usual blind firing by Pakistan was conducted to interdict NH-IA.[36]

In the second briefing, on 13 March, the then ISI official Major General Jamshed Gulzar, in charge of Afghan and Kashmir policy, gave a presentation on Mujahideen activities. Gulzar's presentation was completely unrelated to Operation KP. In fact, throughout the presentation, the Kargil Operation went unmentioned since neither General Gulzar nor any other official within the ISI were aware of it. The prime minister, the army chief, the DG ISI, and commander 10 Corps were among the attendees.

In his presentation, Gulzar informed the political and military leadership of the limitations within which the Mujahideen operated. They did not have the ability to inflict heavy damage on the Indian Army and make the environment conducive for the Pakistan Army to move in. Infiltration had also increased. The general said the Mujahideen were, however, capable of "imposing caution and casualties" on the Indian troops by laying ambushes, attacking isolated military posts, and blowing up bridges and culverts along the only route available for the movement of weapons, troops and supplies in the Srinagar and Leh area. During the question and answer session, it was suggested to Sharif at the briefing that scaling up the Mujahideen operations would positively impact Pakistan's negotiating position. Musharraf proposed that Pakistan supply Stinger missiles to the Kashmiri Mujahideen, so they could inflict heavier losses on the Indian forces. The great success of the Stinger missiles, first introduced by the US to the Afghan Mujahideen for guerilla warfare against the Soviets, made the Stingers popular weapons among the Pakistan intelligence agencies.

However, with diplomatic engagement now on a relatively positive track, the ministers present opposed delivering Stingers to the Mujahedeen. Former General Majeed Malik strongly objected to such a plan. "The proposal to provide Stinger missiles to the Mujahedeen will be treated by India as an act of war," he argued. Moreover, providing Stingers was also opposed to Pakistan's "basic stand that Kashmiris inside occupied

Kashmir were waging their own struggle for self determination and Pakistan was only providing moral and diplomatic support," [37] Clearly, in proposing handing of missiles to the Mujahedeen, the army chief and his team paid no heed to the government's decision made in the December DCC meeting that only "moral and humanitarian" support would be given the Kashmiri Mujahideen. Foreign Minister Aziz, who was conducting unpublicized back-channel negotiations with his Indian counterpart, warned that giving Stinger missiles could "derail the Lahore process."[38] He explained that, by opening dialogue on Kashmir, "reduction in the cross-border activity in Kashmir" was expected.[39]

However, Musharraf and his Kargil clique were on a different track. As if to justify his clique's stance, Musharraf retorted, "We know the Indians. They will negotiate seriously only under maximum pressure." Deceiving Sharif, he added that he "could not take responsibility for restraining Mujahedeen activity inside Occupied Kashmir." He did, however, agree to "postpone" the plan to supply Stinger missiles.

The prime minister had listened intently. At no point did he reprimand his army chief for proposing Stinger missiles even though it was in clear violation of his policy. The following day, when Sharif's foreign minister recalled the decision taken at the DCC, Sharif instructed him to raise the issue at the next DCC meeting.

While these men in khaki worked on ways to secure their ingress across the LOC and to indirectly justify the clandestine operation to the government at home, the foreign ministers of Pakistan and India were searching unprecedented pathways. Taking forward the results of the Lahore Summit, they were working on ways to resolve the Kashmir issue.

Lotus Lakes and leisurely talks

Barely a month after Lahore, the two foreign ministers continued bilateral discussions on Kashmir. The political track was now proceeding alongside the dialogue between the bureaucracies. It was on 19 March, during the SAARC foreign minister's retreat in Norellia at the Sri Lankan President's summer home, that, after a long walk together in a huge garden with two lotus lakes, Jaswant Singh of India and Sartaj Azz of Pakistan sat down on a bench for a ninety-minute talk. It was about Kashmir. They both acknowledged that their prime minister's had agreed to "discuss Kashmir and to move beyond to their stated positions."

The two foreign ministers agreed that it was not realistic to expect that one party would move ninety percent from its original position and the other only ten percent. It was necessary that a mid-point be found where the two sides could meet.

Singh noted that it was the responsibility of politicians to move to the center. Aziz replied that you have eighteen months and we have two and a half years, referring to the time the respective elected governments had still left in office. Aziz assured his Indian counterpart that if India has a reasonable and just position on Kashmir, Sharif could sell it. Singh agreed that all possible solutions should be explored eliminating what is unacceptable and concentrating on where there is common ground. Aziz said that he could right now do away with the unacceptable ones in my head. Singh reminded him that they were only exploring, emphasizing that official positions remain. Singh was clear that publicizing of even such a conversation would prove counterproductive.[40]

The discussion was more about what was not possible than about concrete proposals. The LOC as permanent border proposed by India was not acceptable to Pakistan. The Pakistani and Kashmiri demand for a plebiscite in entire Jammu and Kashmir according to the UNSC resolution was unacceptable to India. Aziz brought up the aggregated referendum in the Valley and three districts of Jammu[41] as the "most promising proposal." The likely outcome would be that Hindu majority Jammu would favor going to India and the Muslim majority Valley to Pakistan.

For Singh, return to the plebiscite was not an option. He also ruled out an aggregated plebiscite to be conducted in the Valley or the districts of Jammu. Any option involving going back to the concept of Hindu and Muslim majority as a basis for settlement would be a hornet's nest. Aziz believed first an agreement on an approach was required to avoid getting bogged down with details. The Kashmir Study Group's proposal for maximum autonomy without sovereignty was also raised during the discussion.

Behind the scene, on the back-channel (among the Neemrana group and now at the political level) there was a focus on exploring political options. India had passed the post of "denial" and the two had adopted a non-zero sum approach on the dispute. Equally significant was a gradual but joint appreciation of the constraints that Pakistan and India would face in finding a political solution.

Identifying mutually acceptable solutions was still a good way off. At this point, only ideas were being explored. In Pakistan, there was some thinking of framing the solution within the context of the physical features of the area rather than the context of religious identities. The "Chenab formula" was discussed. All majority Muslim areas lay on the west of the river Chenab and the Hindu majority to the east of the Chenab. This formulation would at least convert the negotiations away from a communal discourse. The substance still involved different communities.

Similarly, on the holding of the plebiscite, Owen-Dixon's suggestion to "determine the likely voting pattern of the region and without actual voting..." was quoted to perhaps indicate that a non-plebiscite way forward could be identified. For Singh and Aziz, progress was being made. They had been given the mandate by the Lahore Summit to pursue possibilities on Kashmir. They had a genuinely candid discussion and were clear that no discussion in the glare of TV cameras could succeed.

However, away from the gardens of Norellia, unbeknown to the Pakistani and Indian interlocutors, in the world's highest battleground, the occupation of peaks was underway. "We were not wanting territory, we just wanted to strengthen the hands of the prime minister," was the refrain of the key architect of Kargil, General Aziz. How this linkage would work was anyone's guess.

Opposing and contradictory forces were moving ahead and were bound to collide.

Chapter 5

KARGIL UNCOVERED

'Indians Do Not Fight'

The Kargil plan was based on the belief that, once Pakistani troops would have successfully choked the life-line of the Indian troops based in Leh and Siachen by interdicting NH-1A and by setting up posts and pickets in the Drass-Kargil sectors, the Indian response would not be determined and decisive. In the minds of the Pakistani leadership, Delhi's reaction of anger and panic would attract global attention. In the presence of nuclear overhang in South Asia, world powers would be forced to seek a quick political settlement. Pakistan would have a distinct advantage then, with its troops having cut-off the NH-1A and planted themselves on the strategic peaks of Drass-Kargil, and would be able to dictate its terms for the settlement of Siachen and the Kashmir issue.

This belief of the Operation Koh Paima planners came under test in May.

From Doubts and Suspicions to Zoo Construction

Ever since June 1998, several brigade commanders of India's 15 Chinar Corps[1] had been raising the issue of infiltration from across the LOC with their higher authorities. The Chinar Corps with its headquarters in Srinagar is tasked to keep watch over the Line of Control. Senior commanders, including the Srinagar-based XV Corps Commander Lieutenant General Kishan Pal and XV Corps' 3 Infantry Division

Commander Major-General V. S. Budwar, were on the receiving end of intelligence briefs, observations of field commanders, and conclusions from simulation exercises. All these had only one underlining theme: Pakistan's offensive intents and plans. They also highlighted major weaknesses in the Indian defenses.[2] During June and August 1998, Indian Army High Command received warnings of heightened cross-LOC military activity, including troop deployments, ammunition dumping, and infiltration using "routes through valleys and *nalas* (stream beds)"[3] The top brass lacked the entire perspective of the facts but did have a rough foreshadowing of what was to emanate from across the LOC. In August 1998, during a briefing prepared by the Kargil-based military commanders for the perusal of the Indian Army chief, possible infiltration routes in the Drass-Kargil sectors were identified. These subordinate commanders also warned of "a push by militants across the LOC" with the possibility to "engage National Highway 1A" using air defense weapons.[4] Although this intelligence was spot-on in recognition of the threat, it was on the identity of the intruders that these assessments were off-the-mark. These reports were replete with the terms "Afghan militants," "terrorists," and "Pakistan-backed mujahedeen", while some reports did mention words like arrival of "fresh troops," "irregulars" and "ammunition dumping" across the LOC at forward positions. However, no concrete conclusions were drawn from this scanty information.

A spate of reports on what was viewed as an enhanced threat perception were sent from the Kargil and Leh-based military intelligence. The reports originated from brigade officers and intelligence bureau field officers. However, the top command of the Chinar Corps remained skeptical, if not entirely dismissive, of these reports. In his August 1998 briefing that Brigadier Surinder Singh had prepared for the 3 Infantry Division Commander, he had identified India's specific vulnerabilities at the LOC, including unguarded potential infiltration routes such as Mushkoh Valley, From Doda to Panikar ,Yaldor and through *nalas*.[5] Subsequently, in January 1999, another Indian officer, Colonel Pushpinder Oberoi, had warned in a letter to his commander Budhwar of weak defenses against Pakistani infiltration in the Tiger Hill area. As Pakistani infiltrators had already crossed five to six kilometers in the the Mushkoh, Drass, and Batalik sectors, Oberoi's assessment was correct.

Yet with the Pakistani troops still hidden in the precarious folds of the frozen ridges, the 3 Infantry Commander rejected Oberoi's assessment. The top guns of the Chinar Corps dismissed all assessments that underscored the vulnerability and possible infiltration by Pakistani troops with borderline criminal negligence. In some cases the generals believed there were technical problems in interpreting the data while in other cases the read-out was seen as exaggerated and alarmist. The existence of contrasting priorities between the top-level and mid-level commands was further illustrated in the June memo that went from General Budhwar's office to the field commanders. The general's priority project was building a zoo in Leah and the field commanders were instructed, "that various types of wild animals/birds are procured for zoo at Leah at your earliest."[6]

The irrevocability of the priority was highlighted in the concluding line of the memo "No representation will be entertained."[7]

From gunfire to enemy bunker -- 'Militants, guerrillas and terrorists'

As early as 9 February, Indian troops of the 5 Para Regiment spotted unusual movement in the peaks across the LOC in the region south of Siachen. Later, in March, when Indian troops spotted eight to ten men removing snow from a bunker in the Chorbat La sector, an exchange of fire took place. That was the first actual firing that occurred between Indian and Pakistani troops during the Kargil operation. This did not alert the Indians, who passed it off as a localized militant action.

The local shepherds in the Turtok sector first alerted the Indian military commanders in April about some "unusual movement by unfamiliar faces along the Kargil ridges." However the Indian Army began discovering the intrusion only after it began its summer patrols in May. While weak aerial reconnaissance confirmed some infiltration, India floundered over its nature. The Indian soldiers, barely returned from their routine winter descent to the extremely treacherous and inhospitable terrain, were going to find difficult the task of identifying the infiltrators and getting their count right. Local media reports reflected the confusion of the army commanders.

Similarly, in mid-April, incursions were detected in the Turtok sector after a firing incident on the Indian troops. The retaliatory fire by Indians led to at least two Pakistani deaths. However, the local Indian commanders did not share the incident with anyone among the Indian military hierarchy beyond Batalik.[8] They believed some Mujahedeen had infiltrated across the LOC. On 3 May, one Tashi Namgyal of Gharkhun village and another shepherd, on the payroll of the intelligence unit of India's Kargil-based 121 Brigade, reported unfamiliar faces "digging in" and "building sangars (bunkers)" in the mountainous areas of Batalik-Yaldor in Kargil.[9] It was on 3 May that a section of Pakistani troops occupying peaks in the Tololing area began their offensive. They first attacked an Indian reconnaissance group, then followed this with a major attack on 9 May, destroying huge Indian ammunition dumps in Kargil.[10] Indian retaliated on 4 May, firing from Yaldor in the Batalik sector, and an Indian battalion attacked a Pakistani company. Four died and several were injured. Pakistan also lost five officers in a precision-guided missile attack in the Yaldor area.

The Kargil planners had projected engagement in mid-June; this was several weeks earlier. After the Yaldor firing, the Kargil planners began an operational review. Pakistan Army chief Musharraf arrived in Gilgit, ostensibly on vacation, and on 6 May he was secretly given a comprehensive briefing in cottage number 3 of Skardu's picturesque Shangri La resort hotel. The participants included the FCNA commander Javed Hasan, Commander 10 Corps General Mahmud, commander artillery, brigade commander and GI Operation Lt. Col Nisar.[11]

On 15 May the Delhi-based daily *The Statesman,* quoting "army officers" reported that Indian troops were fighting a heavily-armed posse of Pakistani-backed militants in Jammu and Kashmir's Kargil sector since Tuesday, who "have surrounded the attackers and will pounce on them for final assault next week..."[12] Press reports indicated that the Indian response, which led to "fierce fighting along the LOC in Kargil" had begun on 9 May.[13] The newspaper conveyed the first description of the Kargil operation based on Indian military sources: "The infiltrators, trained terrorists helped by the Pakistan Army, are holed up at an altitude of about 17,000 feet. Army officers said artillery fire was continuing but the terrorists' escape routes were cut off. Currently held up by heavy snow and poor visibility the Indian Army hopes to round up the attackers early next week...The army officers are yet to assess the number of infiltrators in the area but no 'contact' could be established, but it is expected to be substantial. An army brigade of about 3000 troops is stationed in Kargil. The army believes that the infiltrators, perhaps Afghans, are occupying the odd shepherd's hut in the mountains. They are at a tactical advantage as they are occupying heights."[14]

According to the Srinagar-based correspondent of *The Hindu*, "Independent agencies maintained that the number of infiltrators was above 150." The Indian Army by 16 May, based on the information they had collected regarding the mode of the operation of the infiltrators "including some of the intercepts in Pushto language", concluded that "the Pakistani army and Afghan ultras"[15] had a "hand" in it. Another report suggested, "More than 100 Pakistani guerrillas including Pakhtoon and Balti youths, equipped with sophisticated weapons, have infiltrated into the Kargil Sector. Drass which is 46 kilometers from Baltal is strategically important. Once Pakistani troops sneak into Drass it will not be difficult for them to reach Baltal from where they can cross to Ganderbal in Srinagar district and to Pahalgam in eastern Kashmir."[16]

On 16 May *The Tribune*'s correspondent from Jammu also reported that the Indian military had retaliated "to attacks by several hundred militants, some of them said to be trained in Taliban camps in Afghanistan, supported by Pakistani jawans, on Indian positions". The Indians expressed the opinion that the Pakistani objective was "targeting the Drass Kargil highway with the aim of snapping the supply line to Kargil and Leah." In the same report, *The Tribune* claimed, "The Pakistani troops besides having damaged the army's ammunition depot and hitting the television relay center, concentrated on blowing up the Drass-Kargil road in order to cut off Leah and Kargil from the Kashmir Valley."

Quoting Indian military experts, the paper reported that "Pakistan has adopted a strategy in the Kargil-Drass belt similar to one it adopted in the Chamb-Jaurian area of Akhnoor district in 1965. The Pakistani troops had then planned to cut of the Chhamb-Jaurian belt to snap the supply line to the Poonch and Rajouri sectors."[17] The press also drew parallels with the surprise Chinese invasion of the Sum Durong Chu Valley in the Arunachal Pradesh attack in the mid-eighties. The Chinese caught the Indians "napping" and occupied the valley before the snows melted in March-April. By the time the Indian Army arrived, the Chinese had built bunkers all over the valley, which they still occupy.[18]

India's military men claimed through media reports that by 16 May they had "cut off the infiltrators" in the Drass sector of Kargil by forcing them to flee one of the ridges and "had inflicted heavy casualties on them and had Zojila route been made fully functional."[19] They claimed that in Batalik too the "infiltrators" were forced to vacate a ridgeline. Poor visibility owing to bad weather was given as the reason for the initially delayed response to the Pakistani operation._Nevertheless, the report quoted Field Intelligence Units in Kargil which acknowledged that "this was possibly the largest counter-insurgency operation of the army in the past decade in the sensitive northern border state."[20] A Srinagar correspondent of *The Hindu* reported that "11 foreign militants and nine soldiers were killed in fierce fighting on the LOC in Kargil since Sunday."[21] The paper reported use of "gun-ships and paratroopers to push back the infiltrators" was reported. *The Tribune* reported more than 10 Indian troop casualties against 20 across the border."[22]

Reports from Jammu indicated that evacuation of the population in the Drass area of Kargil, 146 kilometers north-east of Srinagar, had been begun by the Indian Army. The Indian authorities explained the evacuation as a response to the "Pakistani troops heavy shelling in Drass area."[23]

In the beginning of May, with the early opening of the Zoji La pass, the Indian Army patrols were also sent to the Drass and Kargil sectors to probe the presence of intruders. Supported by aerial reconnaissance missions, which began on 8 May, the "intruders" were spotted in several areas, on the Tololing Hill, about 5 kilometers from Drass, and a mere 2 kilometers from NHA-1A.[24]

Around 14 May, an Indian Army patrol party sent to the Kaksar area went missing.[25] Beginning 6 May when the Indian Lieutenant Saurabh

Kalia's patrol party disappeared, most of the Indian reconnaissance missions sent into the area also went missing. Most became victims of attacks by Pakistani troops who were occupying the numerous strategic heights.[26]

IAF reconnaissance aircraft also began surveillance of the area. Around May 17th a Pakistani helicopter flying on the Indian side of the LOC was detected. The Indian Army responded to this information by launching an attack on Pakistani troop pickets on Point 5353, the peak overlooking NH-1A. The Indian Army discovered it was not easy to dislodge those attacking from the heights and within a day it called off its attempt. The Indians also only gradually discovered how well armed the intruders were. For example, on May 21 a surface-to-air missile hit an IAF aircraft on a photoreconnaissance mission.[27] The first reports on Kargil in the Indian press appeared on May 15. India had clearly been taken by surprise. Explanations on what had happened were numerous and contradictory.

Problems for Pakistan

Meanwhile, during early May, from their posts and pickets at 16,000 to 18,000ft height, the Pakistani troops launched their offensives. Throughout the month of May, when confronted by relatively unprepared Indian troops, the Pakistani troops were able to resist and hold out against the Indian troops with relative ease.

Despite achieving surprise, all was not encouraging on the Pakistani side. The problems began when by May the Indians began counter-attacking. Following the Indian retaliation in the early days of May, SSG commando battalions were brought in for attachment with or as reserves for existing units now sitting atop posts at 16,000 ft height.

As May drew to a close, both the Indian and the Pakistani troops found themselves in difficult military situations.

Pakistan had inducted three SSG commando battalions in the 80 Brigade, 62 Brigade, and in the 82 Brigade as special support units.

As June approached, India's concerted action against Pakistani soldiers had begun depleting Pakistan's ammunition. To address the issue, Pakistan sent additional NLI units across the LOC carrying ammunition. Having won the initial hand, Pakistan was in a relatively difficult situation where the logistics were failing and the troops holed up on tops were in a precarious situation

India - The reality sinks in

In Delhi, however, the Indian government remained ignorant of the extent to which a napping Indian Army had allowed the Pakistani army a walk-over in the Kargil-Drass area. The army commanders seemingly held back information on the infiltration that would have implicated that the army had been 'napping'. Consequently, the Indian political leadership was initially clueless. India's Defense Minister George Fernandez, known more for his leftist ideological leanings and less for his understanding of military affairs, was unaware of Pakistani troops occupying about 140 plus posts and pickets, as he toured a few outposts around May 11.[28] In fact, Fernandez denied that in Jammu and Kashmir "forward posts had been over-run by infiltrators and claimed, "It is confirmed that no post has been lost on our side, contrary to the incorrect and misleading propaganda by Pakistan."[29] On May 16, at Dhanbad, Fernandez was reported to have claimed that the army "had cordoned off the area entirely" and that India's military objectives in Kargil would be realized "within the next two days."[30] India's defense minister was way off the mark. Pakistan's Kargil planners, who were still keen to keep their operation under wraps, were making no such claims. All reports of Pakistani infiltration had appeared in the Indian press based on Indian Army sources.

Obviously, if the Indian press was kept in the information loop by Indian military sources, India's political government was not. Hence, in contrast with military circles' talk of "Kargil having turned into a battle-field", the Indian diplomatic camp's talk was of dialogue with Pakistan. Addressing a think tank in Karachi on May 17th, Delhi's normally hawkish High Commissioner G. Parthasarthy repeated his country's willingness to hold dialogue with Pakistan over Kashmir.[31]

Professional tensions within Indian troops were a cover-up for institutional weaknesses and incompetence. Indian commanders were finding the going tough. On ground serious shortcomings were revealed in the Indian Army's operational preparedness and logistical support since the lop-sided presentations by India's senior commanders had completely ignored the possible Pakistani threat. India's winter surveillance had also been weak and violated the rule-book. The Pakistani government's ignorance of what its own army had carried out in Kargil was matched by the Indian government's ignorance of the extent to which a napping Indian Army had allowed the Pakistani army a walk-over in the Kargil-Drass area.

For India, Kargil came as a huge and staggered shock. Indians discovered only in stages about the scale of the operation, the number of peaks that had been captured in the Kargil-Drass area, and finally who actually carried out the operation. The immediate crisis that the Kargil operation created for Delhi was that it threatened to cut the Leah- Srinagar National Highway No.1 (NH-1), the life-line to Ladakh, and the road connection between Ladakh region and Kashmir Valley. The peaks captured by Pakistani troops were in sectors west of Leah, Kargil, Drass and Batalik. The location and height of these peaks made the interdiction of NH-1 very easy for the Pakistani troops.

In addition to the military and diplomatic challenge, the Kargil operation posed a major political challenge to the BJP government. Kargil began to unfold only days after Vajpayee's 21-party coalition government had faced a vote of no-confidence in the parliament. At the Lahore Summit in February, the Indian prime minister had posed confidence in his counter-part. For India, the Kargil operation was to turn into an election war

The security situation in Kargil district areas was fast deteriorating. The population was being shifted and schools were being shut down. On May 15, the Works Minister of Indian-held Kashmir. Qamar Ali Akhoon, said, "Kargil has turned into a battlefield due to the heavy shelling in the last few days."[32] The same day, an Indian Lieutenant acknowledged, "Our boys had gone on search operations in the area and were fired upon by the advantageously positioned infiltrators, killing seven of them on the spot."[33]

By now alarm bells had evidently begun ringing in Delhi and in Srinagar, yet it was too early for the Vajpayee government to crystallize its response. If there was talk of "Kargil having turned into a battle-field," there was also talk in the Indian camp of dialogue with Pakistan. On May 17, the Indian High Commissioner in Pakistan G. Parthasarthy repeated his country's willingness to hold dialogue with Pakistan over Kashmir.[34]

Throughout May, the Indian Army remained unclear about the scale, location, and nature of the intrusion. Mid-ranking army officers were feeding guesstimates to the local press while senior generals were reassuring the political leadership that it was not more than a routine intrusion around the LOC and that quick eviction of the intruders was possible. They remained murky on the identity of the intruders. In Delhi, where confusion prevailed on the infiltration, no clear policy on tackling the intruders was forthcoming. The local troops were caught between their own propaganda and their misreading of the accent of wireless traffic involving Pakistan's NLI (soldiers from the Northern Areas) as Afghans. Meanwhile, the Kargil clique could have applauded itself for pulling off the surprise factor in the operation but the actual question was whether as a stand-alone achievement could this surprising feat be exploited to achieve a strategic gain for Pakistan?[35]

By end of May Pakistani masterminds had realized that additional troops were required for Operation KP and its supply lines for logistics crucial for Pakistani troops would become the prime target of Indian artillery.

Throughout May, the Indians battled Pakistani intruders virtually blind-fold, with no clear strategy. The Indian troops attacked whenever they spotted intruders or were under attack by Pakistanis dominating the ridges. Pakistani troops, although they suffered some casualties, had the height advantage and so initially it was the Indian casualty count that mounted. With virtually no knowledge of the location and scale of Pakistani troops in early May, the Indian Army battled blind-folded.

The Indian Army found itself bogged down in a long drawn out, guerrilla war in an extremely inhospitable and treacherous terrain. The Indian commander in Kargil-Drass sector publicly conceded that in any military combat, the Mujahideen had the advantage of height and cover.

Contrary to earlier claims that it would be a quick 'flushing out' job, the Indian military spokesmen stated that "it [could] take the Indian Army up to a few months and also cause heavy Indian casualties." It was war for the Indians. Lt General Hari Mohan Khanna, commander-in-chief of the Northern command declared, "It is more or less war ...I am treating it as near war..."

Reflecting a section of the Indian military's view in late May, India's former Vice Chief of Army Staff Lt. General V K Sood summed up the Indian findings and response. "The present intrusions in strength at four different places stretched across 100-odd km..." wrote Sood.[36] The former general outlined India's response to the intrusion as one which would "soften up positions with sustained heavy artillery fire and air-strikes while closing up to deny getaway, reinforcements and replenishments. India would target the most crucial element of Op KP, which was their supply line. He foresaw a "joint operations with a judicious mix of army and Air Force elements" as a pre-requisite to "physically evicting intruders while minimizing own casualties."[37] Sood was not willing to suggest a time-line for the eviction of infiltrators since "clearing operations are time consuming and cannot be accelerated beyond a certain point."[38] Expulsion of the "intruders" was not going to be straightforward in the extremely hostile glacial terrain at altitudes of between 15000 to 17000 feet, with vertical ice-walls, with exceedingly slow and hazardous movement, and with absolutely no human inhabitants. The general consensus was that the intruders were in fact well- armed Pakistan-backed militants "equipped with a panoply of modern weapons, sophisticated equipment and snow clothing..."[39]

In Delhi, Intrusion Demystified

By the end of May, for India, the pieces of the Operation KP puzzle had begun to fall into place. The Indian Army realized that Pakistan had worked out a well-planned, elaborate intrusion to threaten Indian military's strategic position in Jammu & Kashmir. Caught in the fog of war throughout May, they were now beginning to sense the unusual scale and nature of the Pakistani intrusions. It was a planned Op to 'disrupt and capture' the life-line to the Indian troops based in Leh and Siachen. This was highly unusual. Even after India's 1984 occupation of the Siachen Glacier, Pakistan had not ambushed Indian Army patrols in this part of Jammu & Kashmir. Furthermore, Pakistan's systematic support to the 1989 Uprising in the Kashmir Valley did not include an elaborate siege or sabotage of NH-1A, Jammu and Kashmir's most strategic road. Pakistan's most aggressive peacetime military moves had only included the 1997 and 1998 repeated heavy shelling incidents by Pakistani artillery guns. Those were merely aimed at disrupting the movement of traffic along the strategic highway.

By 26 May, the Indian Air Force had entered the battle and on 27 May Operation Vijay began to take shape. Indian Air Force was to bombard the infiltrators, hit out at their supply routes, and also initiate an unceasing free-fall supply of ammunition to the Indian troops.

Massive casualties in attacks, including the one that killed Colonel Ramakrishnan Vishwanathan of the Grenadiers, had convinced Indian generals that assaults without artillery support would be suicidal. Therefore attacks were stopped on all sectors till enough artillery fire support could be mustered.

Kargil Planners' Miscalculations Exposed

The Pakistani troops, although perched on the sky-high peaks, were faced with problems once Indian's retaliation began. Indian attacks were compromising the relatively low-lying supply lines transporting logistics to the Pakistani troops. Early problem areas identified for Op KP included compromised supply lines and shortage of ammunition. For example, the infantry commander who believed he had two months' worth of artillery to help sustain the position at Tololing in the Dras sector, ran out of artillery 48 hours into the Indian attacks.[40]

The Kargil clique, which had believed that India's military response to Pakistani troop infiltration, if any, would be negligible, had accordingly also projected almost no troop exposure to enemy troops. Normally, in military campaigns, artillery is required to fight back and hence in Op KP ammunition usage was to be based on Indian retaliation. The perceived scenario of minimal Indian retaliation anticipated the very limited use of ammunition. Pakistani troops had accordingly moved with only limited supplies of guns, bullets etc. made available, from ammunition dumps close to the LOC. Limited artillery requirement was also promised on the infiltration originally projected, only close to the LOC. FCNA had not carried out deep contingency planning because, given the terrain and weather conditions, operationally and logistically it could not be supported.

The Pakistani troops had been commanded to cross the LOC with no response strategy in place. After crossing the LOC and climbing the critical heights, they were ordered to "occupy and duck down." The flaws with the linear planning of Op KP, focused exclusively on occupying peaks, were now being exposed. These were signposts to what troubles were in store for Pakistani troops in case of heightened military retaliation.

Islamabad Discovers

In contrast with India, where mid-May press reports provoked growing public concern over developments in Kargil, in Pakistan only a few reports of ostensibly routine activity around the LOC trickled in through the press. The army chief had seen no reason to share information on the Yaldor skirmishes with the elected civilian leadership. The daily *Nation* reported on 6 May about a "provoked Indian attack on Pakistan's forward post in the Shyok sector in the Siachen region (MAP), about 20 kilometers from the delineated point of the LOC." The Pakistani media primarily focused on Indian firing along the LOC. Based on information available, the media was to initially locate the cause of the Kargil crisis in this offensive Indian firing.[41]

Foreign news agencies, reporting from Azad Jammu and Kashmir (AJK) were also reporting heavy Indian mortar shelling from across the LOC.[42] There were reports of the deaths of several villagers from the Athmaqam and Kotli sectors in AJK's Neelam Valley. For the policy-makers, press corps, and the people of Pakistan, these reports framed the unfolding of the Kargil conflict. They believed it was initiated by the Indians.

There were reports that Pakistan's 'response' to ostensible Indian provocations was two-fold. One, the Pakistani army "targeted selected military sites" across the LOC. Two, the government reported the ceasefire violations to the United Nations Military Observer's Group in India and in Pakistan (UNMOGIP).

Pakistan's official version of how Kargil unfolded was that it was "a spillover of an unprovoked Indian attack on 6 May on a Pakistani forward post in Shyok sector in Siachen."[43] On 14 May, a Pakistan Army spokesman claimed that its armed forces had inflicted "many casualties" on the Indian Army in six days of artillery duels.[44] On 15 May, upon his return from Singapore, Pakistan's foreign minister complained at the airport that "Pakistan would lodge a strong protest over the unwarranted Indian aggression during last few days causing loss of lives and property."[45] He said that the firing violated the spirit of the Lahore Declaration and Pakistan's High Commissioner Ashraf Jehangir Qazi in Delhi would "lodge a formal protest" with his host government. By this time, however, the Indian government had already launched a strong complaint against Pakistan's incursions through High Commissioner Ashraf Qazi.

Earlier, before his departure for Pakistan, Sartaj Aziz had suggested resumption of Pakistan-India talks on a Strategic Restraint Regime[46] with India to prevent a nuclear war. The talks had halted in April, following the collapse of the Vajpayee government. He proposed that in the interim period until elections were held in October, "technical discussions could be held though we'd have to wait for the news to have any substantial agreement on that subject." The Neemrana Group had prepared a draft for a strategic restraint regime to assist the government-level talks on nuclear restraint.[47]

Sartaj Aziz spoke from ignorance. Nothing was adding up. For Pakistan's civilian leadership, facts about Kargil still lay undiscovered. Barring the gang of four, even the Pakistan Army's top command was unaware of Operation KP until May 16, when they got their first briefing. A day later, the detailed briefing on the operation was arranged at the Ojhri Camp, where the Air and Naval chiefs were taken into confidence. If the events on the ground had not provoked a near war, all this would have made for a bizarre comedy.

"Cock and Bull Story"

Meanwhile, Washington too entered the fray and called for troop withdrawal. Pakistan was asked to vacate immediately. Within a period of one week, Pakistan's ambassador to the United States, seasoned diplomat Riaz Khokhar, was told four times to convey Washington's concern to Islamabad over Pakistan's violation of the LOC.[48] During his first meeting with the US Under Secretary of State Thomas Pickering at the State Department Club, Khokhar was plainly told that the Clinton administration did not believe Islamabad's "cock and bull story of freedom fighters"[49] fighting in Kargil with no Pakistani involvement. After his first meeting, a puzzled Khokhar called the Foreign Office in Islamabad to convey Washington's message. However, the response to his queries on Kargil was that "all will be well, no need to worry!"

The flip side of Washington's message to Islamabad was the message that the US Secretary of State Madeleine Albright conveyed to the Indians. On May 30, Albright called her Indian counter-part Jaswant Singh. She let him know that she had spoken to the Pakistani prime minister and assured Singh that "the United States knew fully well how the chain of events had started."[50] A worried Albright had also suggested that "things could go out of control...it was important to commence the dialogue."[51] Singh said he was not averse to a dialogue but wanted the "aggressor" to first end aggression against India.

After it was known that Pakistani troops had crossed the LOC into IOK and military tensions had begun to rise, Pakistan earned widespread criticism. The criticism was simple: responsible nuclear states always stay away from |military confrontation. They do not undermine nuclear deterrence. They do not sabotage peace initiatives and especially the ones that they themselves initiate, like the Lahore summit. They do not opt for the confrontation path. Operation KP had landed Pakistan in an isolated space where criticism of the present over-rode all else. No one within the global community appreciated the historical precedents like Siachen or was mindful of the historical context within which the unresolved Kashmir issue had complicated bilateral relations. No one was bothered with what had preceded along the LOC and in the disputed state of Jammu & Kashmir.

Chapter 6

BOLT FROM THE BLUE

Around mid-May, when the Indians detected early signs of Op KP, the five-member Kargil clique in Pakistan was forced to take into confidence the elected government, including the senior civil-military bureaucracy. Hitherto, the army chief had neither discussed nor sought approval from the prime minister for Operation KP, which was not merely a battle for posts on the LOC but had involved ingress by Pakistani troops into IOK territory across the LOC. Only around end-January, when the government was planning the Nawaz-Vajpayee Lahore Summit, had there been some discussion among the five planners on the necessity to inform the prime minister. At that time, the Military Operations (MO) Directorate had prepared detailed maps for the prime minister's briefing. But this briefing did not materialize. Instead, the maps were handed to the chief of general staff who let it be known to the MO officers that he himself would brief the prime minister.[1]

Between January and March, the three Kashmir-related briefings the prime minister had received made no mention of Op KP. The first one took place in Skardu on 29 January 1999, the second one in Khel on 5 February, and the Inter-Services Intelligence gave the third one in Islamabad on 12 March, 1999. The prime minister had even visited the staging area after the operation had begun.[2] On 29 January, the Prime

Minister addressed the troops at a public meeting in Skardu. Contrary to general Musharraf's assertion in his book *In the Line of Fire*,[3] there was no briefing on Kargil. According to a retired general who was present during Sharif's Skardu trip, the visit was "just a face-showing, where not a word on Kargil was uttered." [4] The elected prime minister was informed about the need for Pakistan to become active along the LOC through local operations. No detailed briefing on the proposed local operations was given, nor did the prime minister ask any probing questions. On 5 February, the prime minister visited Khel to make an announcement regarding the Khel road. Similarly, the 12 March meeting at the ISI headquarters was held exclusively to discuss Pakistan's Mujahideen policy. There was concern that the Mujahideen movement was "dying down" and the general in-charge sought permission to "upgrade" the movement. Kargil was not mentioned at this meeting. The general making the presentation was not privy to the Kargil plan. [5]

During none of these briefings was there any mention of Op KP or of any military operation that would involve the crossing of the LOC by Pakistani troops in large numbers. It was business as usual, even though the Lahore summit had signaled the elected leadership's policy decision to engage the Indians diplomatically. Kashmir too had been included in the agenda for the talks.

In fact, until mid-May, even the military high command, including the intelligence chiefs, were kept out of the loop on Op KP.

Even the army's own principal intelligence agencies were not in the loop. For example, in one case, a field officer from the MI conveyed information to the MI chief Lt. General Ehsan-ul-Haq regarding major redeployments taking place from FCNA areas of Gilgit and Skardu, under the 10 Corp. Surprised, the MI chief shared this redeployment information with the army chief. Musharraf did not engage on the issue but instead Lt. General Mahmud, Commander 10 Corps, summoned the MI chief and queried him about what he knew and his sources. Subsequently, the vigilant intelligence officer who had reported the deployments and relocation of troops to the MI chief was summoned and reprimanded by the Commander.[6] The episode alerted the Kargil clique to the need to more tightly cover and camouflage the operation-linked troop movement.

Even as late as April, the Kargil clique was determined to keep the operation a guarded secret from the intelligence services. In April, officers posted at the GHQ noticed unusual happenings at the GHQ. With unusual meetings being held within the GHQ, chaired by the army chief himself, there was a departure from what was a Standard Operating Procedure (SOP) for top command meetings.[7] Not inviting the entire core team that always attended the meetings at the Directorate Military Operations (DMO) was a clear departure from the standard practice where the COAS, the CGS, the VCGS, the DGMO and the DGMI were always invited to participate in all DMO meetings. This violation of the SOPs was inevitable given that key men within the GHQ hierarchy had become LOBs (left out of Battle) by virtue of being excluded from the original Kargil plan. The iron-clad secrecy surrounding Op KP was nearly impossible for even critically located men within the military hierarchy to permeate.

This level of secrecy ruled out the possibility of sound evaluation of Op KP. Lone voices from even within the GHQ's Research and Analysis Wing[8] were easily dismissed. For example, around end-May, when questions of Pakistan's cross-LOC actions began to surface internationally, a brigadier wrote a note recommending that Pakistani troops should vacate Kargil. As a diligent member of the research unit mandated to give input on a regular basis, the brigadier candidly noted that existing problems with the Op were likely to compound further, especially within the international context. His note found its way to the army chief's desk. Written in green ink, the chief's remarks in the margins read "I do not agree."[9]

The SOPs institutionally laid down for undertaking an operation had been circumvented. The Pakistan Army, often identified as Pakistan's most professional institution, had seen this happen before. In 1965, the level of the secrecy was such that General Bakhtiar Rana[10], the Corps commander, who was responsible for looking after the geographical area, was not involved in the war planning. When General Rana came to the then Commander-in-Chief, General Muhammad Musa Khan, and asked him about the operation, the chief said, "No, no, It's a secret," and declined to tell him about the operation. [11] Even the then Pakistan Air Force chief was kept unaware. When he took over as the new chief, he heard from the grapevine that some operation was being planned. He approached the army C-in-C General Musa for information on the operation. Musa said he did not know but the Murree-based General Officer Commanding (GOC) the 12th Division maybe able to help him. The air chief flew in a helicopter to Murree and reminded the GOC of the army's need to keep the air force informed of an operation since "You (the army) will need the Air force for the operation after the first two days." Subsequently, the Air force chief himself flew the first flight inside Indian Occupied Kashmir to drop supplies.

Telling Their Own

In early May, the scheduled meeting of the Army Promotion Board and the Formation Commanders Meeting coincided with early reports in the Indian media about the operation. Predictably, therefore, at this gathering of around seventy top army commanders,[12] everyone was keen to know about the basis of these media reports. Several corps commanders and PSOs cribbed and criticized the top command for keeping them in the dark. In fact, from March onwards, there had also been cross-country cantonment chatter about some unusual heightened activity along the LOC. Although not planned but a briefing to the army's brass on Op KP became unavoidable.

The Commander 10 corps Lt. General Mahmud using military maps, began the briefing.[13] Mahmud explained to the participants that Pakistan wanted to increase military action in IOK and draw international attention to the Kashmir issue. The positions held by Pakistan across the LOC were identified. He recalled India's 1984 clandestine operation to occupy the Siachen glacier. Commander FCNA Major General Javed Hassan shared the operational details of Op KP. Their explanation was simple; there were many "yawning gaps along the LOC" that provided them with the opportunity to go across. Their action,.they thought, would force India to come to the negotiating table.

The majority of participants in the meeting appeared to accept what they were told. Only a few raised questions.[14] Inspector-General Frontier

Corps Baluchistan Lt. General Abdul Qadir Baluch warned the Kargil planners that they had not correctly calculated the Indian reaction. Supporting Baluch, Major General Akram, GOC 35 Division, added that negative international reaction to any military tension between newly nuclear power had also not been factored in. Major General Rafiullah Khan Niazi too was very critical.

General Qadir pointedly asked if the objective was to capture Kashmir or Srinagar or to sever the Indian line of communication from Leh to Srinagar. He was told that the objective was to sever the Indian line of communication. Qadir proceeded to recall his own experience of interdiction while he was posted as GOC 12 division covering Azad Kashmir. In his territorial responsibility lay the Kiran Sector, which connected Ath Muqam and Khel. Thirty-one kilometers of the Kiran sector were perilously close to Indian posts located at dominating heights. Of these, along sixteen kilometers, the Pakistanis were exposes to direct Indian attack from merely eight to nine hundred meters at dominating heights. In 1995, this vulnerability cost Pakistan around seventy to eighty vehicles. Indian soldiers sat at their posts with machine guns locking in Pakistani vehicles as easy targets. The vehicles with passengers, once shot, would fall into the river Jhelum. In 1996, when Qadir was posted at GOC, a six to eight foot high and four to five-foot-thick wall was constructed to protect the Kiran sector, and specifically the vehicles plying on the road, from Indian firing. It took three thousand people and three months to construct the wall. The significant aspect of this Pakistani effort was that the Indians, located merely 800 meters away, fired almost nonstop during the construction period. But the Pakistanis had a group of soldiers placed at the construction site tasked to retaliate against this Indian firing. Qadir asked the presenters at the meeting why the Indians would not be able to protect their vehicles from Pakistani firing from a distance of three kilometers. Qadir recalled that he was able to protect the construction workers from Indian fire from as close as only eight hundred meters.

These objections went largely unanswered. By the end of the meeting it was evident to most that the central figures in the army's operational and intelligence setup, including the DG Military Intelligence, the PSOs, and the logistics commander 10 Corps had been excluded from the planning of an operation with grave implications. The army chief Musharraf also addressed the generals for about half an hour. He informed Pakistan's top military commanders that the Indians were suffering heavy casualties. Pakistani soldiers occupying strategic heights were retaliating to Indian infantry attacks. The chief dismissed the idea that India would react forcefully and open any new fronts on the international border. He was categorical, "our positions were unassailable." "Luck is always on the side of the bolder and hence it was on our side," was the maverick chief's dangerously naïve reassurance to the commanders. With his remarks "it's a win-win situation[15] Musharraf called the meeting to a close. Everyone was asked to pray for the success of Op KP. With unanswered questions still worrying some among the present, all obeyed the chief. They raised their hands and prayed.

Clearly, while India still combed through the inhospitable terrain to determine the scale of Op KP, the element of surprise still worked in Pakistan's favor. Riding on a euphoric wave, the Kargil clique was set to brief the country's elected prime minister.

But, significantly, the morning after the Kargil clique's briefing to their own, the editorial in a leading Pakistan daily wrote that Pakistan's own forces were fighting in Kargil.[16]

"Fatah-i-Kashmir"... "Liberator of Kashmir"

On 17 May, the prime minister was given a detailed operational briefing on Operation Koh Paima. It was held at the ISI's Ojhiri Camp office, only a few miles away from Islamabad[17] held against the backdrop of Indian press reports claiming that Mujahideen under fire cover provided by Pakistani soldiers had infiltrated along the LOC. Reports claimed they were occupying strategic heights in parts of Indian Occupied Kashmir. According to these reports, Pakistani artillery fire could target India's main supply route to Leh, the Srinagar-Leh Highway.[18] These reports had prompted the prime minister, linked in a high-stakes diplomatic engagement with his Indian counterpart, to ask for this briefing.[19] The Kargil planners were in an upbeat mood since Pakistan's artillery shelling had blown up a bridge on India's main supply route.

The Director-General Military Operations (DGMO) Lt. General Tauqir Zia gave the detailed presentation. The entire Kargil clique, including the army chief, the Chief of General Staff Lt. General Aziz Khan, Commander 10 Corps General Mahmud, and Commander FCNA Brigadier Javed Hassan, was present. Key men from the ISI in attendance included the DG ISI Lt Gen Ziauddin Butt, director analysis Major General Shahid Aziz, and ISI's point-man for Afghanistan and Kashmir Major General Jamshed Gulzar. The prime minister, accompanied by the Foreign Minister Sartaj Aziz, the Finance Minister, the Minister for Northern Areas and Kashmir Affairs Lt. General Majeed Malik, the Foreign Secretary Shamshad Ahmad, and his Principal Secretary Saeed Mehdi.

This was the first interface of the prime minister and his cabinet members with the planners and implementers of the Kargil Operation. The briefing took place in an upbeat environment. Shortly before the meeting Pakistan's artillery shelling had blown up a bridge on India's main supply route and set fire to Indian ammunition dumps.

DGMO Zia began the presentation with the words: "Sir, as per your desire we have made a plan to upgrade the freedom movement in Kashmir."[20] It would be a five-phased operation and the first phase had been completed, he explained. He then proceeded to show on the map scores of positions that had already been taken. However military maps, without any text were used for the briefing. Nothing was written and they only had symbols on them. Normally, even military men receiving briefings on such maps, with only symbols, first required orientation to understand what these maps represented. For example, the LOC was not clearly demarcated on the map. Hence, during the presentation, when Pakistani and Indian positions were pointed out to the prime minister, he was unable to fully comprehend the locations of these posts. Instead, for him, the main focus of the briefing was the achievements of Pakistani troops. There were no mention of Pakistani troops crossing the LOC, nor of the Pakistani troop build-up five to ten kilometers beyond the LOC. One of the retired generals present recalled, "I saw scores of positions across the LOC in the Indian area across the LOC in IOK area."

Indian Held Kashmir is spread over three areas, the Jammu sector, Pir Panjal Range to the Valley, and the Leh and Ladakh sector. The entry from Jammu to the Valley is through to the Manihaal Pass and from Leh and Ladakh the entry is through the Zojila Pass. The DGMO explained that, in phase two, "We will infiltrate freedom fighters into Leh and Ladakh, who will start the insurgency in the area." In phase three, the general predicted that, when pressure was applied on the Indian forces from the flanking sectors through the operations of these infiltrating groups, the Indians would start bringing their troops to Ladakh and Jammu leaving the Valley virtually drained of troops. In phase four, the DGMO explained, Pakistan would rush in large numbers of freedom fighters into the Valley and block the Manihal and Zojila passes, thereby isolating the Valley and occupying the area. The general predicted, that in phase five, the final phase, the Indians would be on their knees begging for talks and Pakistan could dictate its own terms.

The DGMO proceeded to share the four assumptions which, according to its planners, guaranteed the success of the five- phase Operation Koh Paima. First, each post being held was impregnable. Second, the Indians did not have the will or the determination to take on Pakistan in a fight and would not make any serious effort to regain the heights. Third, as far as the international context was concerned Pakistan need not worry because there would be no external pressure. Fourth, that the army recognized the economic crunch faced by the country and therefore the government would not be asked for any extra resources for the operation; the army would use its own sources to fulfill the financial requirements.

The main thrust of the presentation was to inform the elected leadership of the army's "achievements" along and across the LOC. The impression given was that the strategic heights lay somewhere in the undemarcated zones. The DGMO informed the participants that Pakistan's troops had occupied strategic heights that Indians would now find almost impossible to reoccupy. The army chief emphasized the irreversibility factor and said that, based on the wisdom and experience of his entire professional career, he could "guarantee the success of the operation."[21]

The thrust of the briefing was to inform the civilian participants that because of the operation the tempo of "jihad" would increase, that only the Mujahideen were conducting the operations, and Pakistan was only providing logistical support, and that militarily the peaks taken by the Mujahideen were impregnable. The architects of Koh Paima were confident that India would first "create noise, then respond militarily, but the fighting to follow would be restricted to the operation's area. Finally, India would be quiet, the participants were told, and tell its public that it had retaken the peaks. This flawed assumption by the Koh Paima architects was in fact a wishful extrapolation from what had mostly been Pakistan's own response pattern to major Indian incursions across the LOC. Especially after India launched a major operation in 1984 to occupy the Siachen glacier, Pakistan under the military general ruler Ziaul Haq had remained mum. No response from India, the architects concluded, would provide Pakistan with bargaining chips over Kashmir.

Clearly, the masterminds of Kargil were not seeking permission for the operation they has already launched. The prime minister was presented with a fait accompli. With the cover of Operation Koh Paima having been nearly blown and diplomatic pressure imminent, the Kargil clique was seeking political and diplomatic cover for the Op. The prime minister was pointedly asked if he and his team could politically and diplomatically leverage their 'unassailable' military achievements to promote and project the Kashmir cause.[22] Following the DGMO, the CGS Lt. General Aziz Khan rose to flatter the prime minister. "Sir, Pakistan was created with the efforts of the Quaid and the Muslim League and they will always be remembered for creating Pakistan and now Allah has given you the opportunity and the chance to get Indian Held Kashmir and your name will be written in golden letters," he declared. The CGS Aziz also invoked the PM's Kashmiri descent and lured him with the possibility that "after Quaid it is a unique opportunity to be remembered as the Fatah-i-Kashmir."[23]

The ISI's point-man for Afghanistan and Kashmir, Lt. General Gulzar, also gave a presentation on the Mujahideen. Gulzar recounted the limitations of the Mujahideen, their inability to inflict heavy damage on the Indian Army, capable only of 'softening' the environment for the

Pakistan Army to move in, and especially that they were not present in the area of the operation. The only route available for the movement of weapons troops and supplies in the Srinagar and Leh area was where they could lay ambushes, attack isolated military posts, blow up bridges and culverts.

Steadfast in their dedication to their institutional ethos all the men in uniform raised no questions at the presentation. As would later transpire, the top commanders in the ISI were all skeptical of, if not totally opposed to, Operation KP. Lt. General Gulzar would subsequently criticize the Op as a "blunder of Himalayan proportions,"[24] born of a temptation that every commander 10 Corps would face upon finding an "open space." Emphasizing the point, the general would later recall, "When I took over the command of 10 Corps I had to put my troops on a leash because they would say we can move forward since we are on a height."[25] Similarly, years later, the then head of the ISI's analysis wing major general Shahid Aziz would write, "An unsound military plan based on invalid assumptions, launched with little preparation and in total disregard to the regional and international environment, was bound to fail. That may well have been the reason for its secrecy. It was a total disaster."[26]

There was a divided response from the civilian participants. The DGMO pointedly asked Foreign Secretary Shamshad Ahmad if the Kargil situation could be utilized to "feed into our effort to project Kashmir."[27] The general was keen to know if diplomatic advantage could be derived from this military operation. Non-committally, the Foreign Secretary indicated that it might be possible.[28] The foreign minister, however, expressed his reservations on two counts: one, that it was incongruent with the spirit of the Lahore summit and, two, that the U.S. would not support the operation. Sartaj Aziz pointedly asked his PM whether the plan the army had made was not contrary to the undertaking in the Lahore Declaration. "Sartaj Aziz Sahib, can we ever take Kashmir through paperwork? We have here an opportunity to take Kashmir," was a relaxed Nawaz Sharif's response. By contrast, his foreign minister was perturbed. He was clear that this operation would not help Pakistan get international support for Kashmir.

The other obviously perturbed man in the room was Sharif's Minister for Kashmir and Northern Areas (KANA) Majeed Malik. A retired general, Malik grilled the commander 10 Corps about the logistics for the forward troops. He interrogated how the supplies would reach the troops under "adverse weather conditions and in a hostile environment." He recalled the hazardous terrain he had personally visited. Mahmud's curt response was that times had changed, that "our troops are fully covered." The retired general also asked the DGMO, "What if the Indians do not remove their troops from the Valley and instead induct air power in the conflict theatre?" Meanwhile, the silent worrier in the room, Sharif's Defense Secretary, also a retired general, opted to not raise any questions. At the conclusion of the formal meeting, he merely whispered to other military officers, "The foreign office will never be able to handle this." [29]

The prime minister only sought his cabinet members' opinion regarding the operation; he asked no tough questions himself. Based on whatever he understood regarding the operation, and factoring in the reservations expressed by his ministers, the elected prime minister opted to go along with the fait accompli presented to him by the military. He wanted a resolution of the Kashmir issue and appeared convinced that Operation Koh Paima would advance that objective. He was perhaps also swayed by the upbeat tone of the DGMO's 'victory-all-the-way' presentation and partly by the notion that he was well on his way to becoming the man "whose name will go down in history in golden words as the man who liberated Kashmir."[30] The prime minister took well to the words of the CGS that for the PM "after the Quaid it is a unique opportunity to be remembered as the Fatah-i-Kashmir."[31]

Flattery was in abundance. The CGS piled on more, "Sir, you will go down in the history of Pakistan as the PM in whose tenure Kashmir was resolved."[32] In response to this, Nawaz responded, "But then you didn't tell me when you will fly the flag of Pakistan in Srinagar."[33] Civilians present registered this as a comment made in jest. Meanwhile, flattery plus the army chief's claim that based on the wisdom and experience of his entire professional life, he could "guarantee the success of the operation,"[34] had won Nawaz Sharif's support for Op Kp. The prime minister had not factored in the clearly stated reservations of his foreign minister and

Minister for Kashmir and Northern Affairs (KANA). He was assured of no military reverses and he chose to believe his military commanders. Interestingly, at no point during the meeting was there any exchange between the PM and the military men signalling Sharif's prior knowledge of the operation. There was a passing reference made in the DGMO's opening comments to the PM's March approval given at the ISI convened meeting to "upgrade the freedom movement in Kashmir.[35]

As the meeting drew to a close, the CGS proposed a joint prayer for the success of Operation Koh Paima. The prime minister asked him to lead the joint prayer. With this, the meeting concluded. Most present at the meeting, including those who subsequently became the harshest critics of the operation, believed it would be a success.

Immediately after the meeting the defense secretary followed the prime minister in his car. It was about 9pm and Sharif was entering the lift in the Prime Minister's House when Lt. General Iftikhar Ali Khan, hurriedly following him, said, "Sir, can I talk to you? It is important." the nation's chief executive asked him if he could wait till the next morning. The defense secretary persisted. He said he wanted to ask two questions. One: Did the military leadership get his permission to cross the LOC? The prime minister asked him whether the army had actually crossed the LOC. "Didn't you note all that about 'hundreds of posts' and that NLI troops, not freedom fighters, have crossed the LOC." Chaudhary continued, "Crossing the LOC, Mian Sahib, has implications for war." In the middle of the night, the rather surprised prime minister said, "Why a war? And who has crossed the LOC?" He was told that about five to six hundred square kilometers of Indian territory and hundreds of posts had been occupied. The prime minister instructed the Defense Secretary to explain the situation to his Minister the next morning.

Sinking In

The next morning, twelve hours after the top military command had briefed him on Op KP, the Prime Minister summoned key cabinet members to the PM House. Sharif chaired the meeting, which was attended by Foreign Minister Sartaj Aziz, Minister for Kashmir and

Northern areas retired General Majeed Malik, Minister for Religious Affairs Raja Zafar ul Haq, Information Minister Mushahid Hussain, and Defense Secretary Iftikhar Ali Khan. The defense secretary registered his concerns, warning that escalation would be inevitable and the "Indians would not take it lying down." Iftikhar complained that, without consulting anyone or taking any one in confidence, a "few paper tigers" had started the Kargil adventure. The foreign minister also reported that his ministry was getting panic calls from their missions abroad. Aziz complained that his Ministry had no clue about this Op. Retired General Majeed Malik, protested that he was Minister for Kashmir Affairs and he was shocked that he had not been taken into confidence. After hearing these outpourings, the prime minister contacted the army chief.

The army chief arrived at the PM House within an hour. [36] There were only three people present at the time of this crucial moment of the Kargil crisis: the PM, the Defense Secretary, and the army chief. The PM asked Musharraf, "Did you cross the LOC?" Musharraf responded, "Yes, sir, I did." "And on whose authority?" queried the prime minister. The army chief was quick to respond, "On my own responsibility and if you now order, sir, I will order the troops' withdrawal." Nawaz Sharif turned to his Defense Secretary and said, "Did you see? He has accepted his responsibility!" Sharif, perhaps visualizing himself as the "liberator" of Kashmir, added, "Since the army is part of the government, from today onwards we will support the army." After this rather brief meeting, the army was to get the complete support of the country's leadership.[37]

The public message at this stage from all stakeholders, in Islamabad, Rawalpindi and abroad, was identical: The international community must rein in India. The same day, the prime minister said Pakistan was committed to dialogue with India. On 19 May, the COAS General Pervez Musharraf said Indian violations of the LOC would be taken seriously. On 20 May, in Baku, at the Council of Ministers Conference, the Minister of State of Foreign Affairs, Siddiq Kanju, asked the world community to help resolve Kashmir. On 21 May, Pakistan's newly appointed ambassador to France, Shahryar Khan, assured his hosts that Pakistan was involved in "serious talks" with India.

Meanwhile, on the policy front, the prime minister, aided by his key advisors, made important decisions. After the 17 May meeting, at an informal huddle between the prime minister and his trusted men, Shehbaz Sharif, Iftikhar Ali Khanand Chaudhry Nisar, the decision was taken to support the army. The four said that Nawaz should institutionalize the issue and bring it to the DCC. Several formal meetings were subsequently held. The informal consultations with his trusted men also continued. On 23 May, a high-level meeting was held between the prime minister, the COAS, and the Chief of General Staff to discuss Kargil. In fact, once the cover blew from Op KP, the government sought regular military updates from the Kargil clique. The Kargil planners too were keen for a political buy-in to Op KP. The GHQ organized briefings for the President, Senators, and parliamentarians, including special prayer sessions for the success of the Op. At one of the prayer sessions at the ISI headquarters, led by the CGS General Aziz, the Minister for the Interior Chaudhary Shujaat Hussain was also present.[38]

Stunned at Hotel Scheherazade

The prime minister sought an assessment of the situation from his senior diplomatic team before the Defense Committee of the Cabinet (DCC) meeting scheduled for the end of May. Accordingly, Foreign Minister Sartaj Aziz convened a high level meeting at the Foreign Office to discuss the military and diplomatic developments. The participants of the 23 May meeting included senior PML leader Raja Zafarul Haq, Minister for Petroleum Chaudhry Nisar, Secretary Defense Lt. General Iftikhar Ali Khan, Minister of State for Foreign Affairs Siddiq Kanju, Foreign Secretary Shamshad Ahmad Khan, Additional Secretary Prime Minister's Secretariat Tariq Fatemi, Additional Secretary UN Riaz Mohammad Khan, army chief General Pervez Musharraf, Chief of General Staff(CGS) Lt. General Aziz, Director-General ISI Lt. General Ziauddin, Commander 10 Corps Lt General Mahmud, deputy Vice Chief of Air Staff Marshal Aliuddin, and Vice Chief of Naval Staff Vice Admiral Abdul Aziz Mirza.

The briefing was giving by General Aziz, CGS. Aziz said we did this to interdict the Siachen road, thereby forcing India to solve the Kashmir issue.

Most of the civilian participants realized the scale of Operation Koh Paima for the first time. They asked probing questions regarding the objectives of the operation.[39] The army chief was asked about the objectives of Op KP and Pakistan military's ability to retain the territory occupied across the LOC. The confident army chief's response was, "We can defend every inch of our own territory and we are firmly entrenched in the positions we are holding in Kargil."[40]

There were many critics of the operation. For example, many questions came from Minister Majeed Malik, who had himself commanded this area as a Corps commander and earlier on as Div. Commander. He said that, if Pakistan had to interdict this road, it could have been done from lower heights instead of taking our troops to the Kargil peaks, where the weather would be their worst enemy. Malik pointed especially to the difficulty of maintaining supply lines for the troops. The worried elderly Minister for Religious Affairs Raja Zafarul Haq nearly reprimanded the Kargil planners for not taking others in the government into confidence if their objective was to highlight the Kashmir issue. All future action must now follow proper consultation, he emphasized.

The consensus among senior navy and air force officers was that opening of new fronts by India could not be ruled out. They asked why they had not been consulted earlier since any defense plan in case of Indian retaliation had to be an integrated armed forces defense plan. Criticism kept piling up. The deputy air chief also wondered, "After all, what will we achieve from all this?" CGS Aziz's response was that, by applying pressure on the main supply artery NH-1, India would be forced to the negotiating table on Kashmir.[41]

Senior Foreign Office officials in the meeting warned that this operation would be indefensible on global forums. Additional Secretary UN Riaz Mohammad Khan categorically stated, "If it comes to the UNSC, our position will be undercut." The Chinese along with other UNSC members would simply ask Pakistan to respect the LOC and vacate the areas occupied across the LOC in Indian Occupied Kashmir. Foreign Secretary Shamshad expressed concern regarding the possible expansion of the conflict and told the participants, "I cannot guarantee that India will not attack on the international borders."[42] The foreign secretary cautioned the army against repeating the miscalculation made prior to the 1965 Operation Gibraltar, when the key military and civilian officials had guaranteed that India would not retaliate on the international border.[43] The confident army chief dispelled these concerns and maintained, "We can defend every inch of our territory." Discussions bordered on being polemical rather than strategic. One of the generals asserted, "Whatever we may say here, our animosity with India is eternal."

Those diplomats with an institutional memory of Kashmir questioned if the Op KP related discussion could actually help to highlight Kashmir at the UN. Seasoned diplomat additional secretary Riaz Mohammad Khan pointedly said, "if it is brought to the UN, our position will be undermined."[44] There was already discussion within the international community of undermining the sanctity of the LOC. In 1965 and in 1971, when the Kashmir case was taken to the UNSC for discussion, the decision on both occasions was on the cease-fire and not on the Kashmir issue. In the case of Kargil too, had the matter been taken to the UNSC, it would have called for withdrawal and led to the further strengthening of the LOC. The army insisted that the line was fuzzy and in some places the Mujahideen were also involved in the fighting. When asked by one of the foreign office officials how the Mujahideen could fight so valiantly against the well-equipped Indian army, the army spokesperson Rashid Qureshi said, "Because the Indians from the plains are not acclimatized and they die!" [45]

At the conclusion of the meeting, the three ministers, Sartaj Aziz, retired General Majeed Malik, and Raja Zafarul Haq held a post-mortem DCC meeting in Sartaj Aziz's office. There prevailed a feeling among these experienced men that the Op was likely to cause serious military and diplomatic problems. Yet sudden withdrawal, leading to high casualties, was not an option. Indeed, with the army already claiming it a success, who would 'bell the cat' of asking the Kargil clique to withdraw? Nevertheless, Minister Haq also believed the deficiencies in the Op KP had to be addressed. The planners would interpret recommendations regarding the Op as a signal to continue.[46] The civilian government may be held responsible in case Op KP failed. What followed could also be army take-over.[47]

The three senior ministers then shared their concerns and conclusions with the prime minister, who agreed with them on the need to take the navy and air force on board in all future discussions on Op KP.

"Kicked & Face Fell"

Around this time, Pakistan's Military Intelligence (MI), also got active. Major General Ehsanul Haq invited the military attachés of Western countries to the GHQ for a briefing on Operation Koh Paima. The DG Military Intelligence and the DG Military Operations (MO) conducted the briefing followed by a question and answer session. The defense attachés left the briefing with the understanding that these senior Pakistani military officials had acknowledged that Pakistani troops were involved and it was not a Mujahideen operation.[48] The western military attachés, including the American and the British, reported back to their embassies and subsequently to their headquarters that fighting was actually taking place on the Indian side of the LOC.[49] Publicly, however, Islamabad still maintained that only the Mujahideen were involved.[50] The media, based on western embassy backgrounders, reported that the DG MI had acknowledged that there were Pakistani troops across in the Indian side of the LOC. Interestingly, at this time Islamabad's own diplomats, stationed even at the headquarters, were groping in the dark for information about the reported flare-up along the LOC.

After the MI briefing, the US military attaché in the embassy informed his ambassador William Milam that fighting was going on the Indian side of LOC. The American information until then was that it was a group of Mujahideen. The military attaché had attended the briefing at the GHQ given by the DG MI and the DG MO.[51] Following the briefing, the attachés snooped around for more information. The military attaché met his counterpart while the political attaché met with retired military officers. With confirmation that Pakistani troops had crossed the LOC, the "really excited US diplomats" told Washington about it. The State Department responded by issuing its first statement, calling upon Pakistan to withdraw its troops. This statement prompted the Additional Secretary of the Foreign Office, Tariq Altaf, to call in Ambassador Milam and ask why Washington had accused Pakistan of fighting across the LOC. The US ambassador informed him that it was the Pakistan Army itself who had given them this information. Upon hearing Milan's response, it seemed that "Altaf had been kicked and his faced fell."[52] Following the Altaf-Milam exchange, Foreign Minister Aziz called the DG MI and complained about the embarrassing faux pas he had committed. The MI chief said he had been misquoted.[53] Nevertheless, the stories of the defense attaché regarding Pakistani troop presence remained in circulation.

Cabinet Clueless

Towards the end of May, the prime minister decided to take his cabinet into confidence on Op KP. He convened a cabinet meeting at which the director-general ISI Lt. General Ziauddin Butt was to present a briefing. Foreign Secretary Shamshad Ahmad and Defense Secretary Iftikhar were also present. Although in his private meetings with the prime minister the DG ISI was critical about Op KP, at this cabinet meeting he presented broad details of the Op. He talked of the freedom fighters and held that the Op was progressing satisfactorily. The intelligence chief, however, opted to not share his own assessment of the Op. Similarly, the foreign secretary, who had expressed some reservations about Op KP at earlier meetings, at this cabinet meeting opted to pick no holes. He gave no hint of the Op being a potential source of any diplomatic disadvantage for Pakistan, and, instead, indicated that some benefit could be derived from it.

A barrage of hard questions followed Butt's briefing. The majority present was pleased with the progress reported on Op KP. The Minister for Water and Power Gohar Ayub praised the army for doing a "great job" and advocated support for the operation. Minister of Culture, Sports, Tourism, and Youth Affairs, Sheikh Rashid Ahmad, also praised the army, while the Minister for Religious Affairs said, "The time is now ripe for jihad." There were also critics of Op KP. These included Minister for Communications Raja Nadir Pervez and Minister for Health Makhdoom Javed Hashmi. The most vocal critic, however, was the secretary of defense. The retired general spoke for about twenty minutes, warning that Op KP would either end in all-out war or as a total military disaster for Pakistan. He alluded to what he believed was less than the whole truth that others before him, had spoken on Kargil. He especially alluded to the Director-General ISI Butt's presentation.

To support his own contention, Iftikhar discussed recent Indian troop movements. Indian divisions deployed at the Chinese borders had moved towards the Pakistani borders. India's defensive formations had also moved to Pakistan's borders in offensive posturing. The Indian navy too was moved from its eastern maritime borders to its western maritime borders, alongside Pakistan's borders. His assessment was that the Op would not be restricted to Kargil but would lead to war. The worried Defense Secretary gave a comparative fact sheet on the two armies, navies and air forces. His assessment was that, in case of an all-out Pakistan-India war, Pakistan would be in a difficult situation. Implying that the army command had launched Op KP without clearance from the government, the Defense Secretary emphasized that the army was not an independent body and had to take orders from the government. He was also critical of placing jihad as a central element in Pakistan's defense structure. He wondered, "Why have we after fifty-two years realized the importance of jihad?"[54] The Defense Secretary's brother Chaudhry Nisar Ali Khan, the Minister for Petroleum, also raised hard questions. The thrust of Nisar's remarks was that, based on his information, Pakistan was heading for a military disaster in Kargil-Drass. "Who had ordered the operation?" the minister rhetorically asked the military presenters. Nevertheless, Nisar's caution was against an Op already underway.

Some altercation among powerful men ensued. Reacting to the defense secretary's presentation, the visibly distraught Minister for Water and Power, Gohar Ayub[55], asked why the defense secretary was opposing the plan of the army chief. Sheikh Rashid also queried why the defense secretary was revealing "secrets." Both had earlier praised the army for doing a "great job" and had advocated support for the operation.

The prime minister called the meeting to an end.[56] He was now facing a divided house within and mounting pressures from the outside. The Kargil planners, meanwhile, saw no reason to pay heed to any concerns expressed in the cabinet meeting.

The Contours of Denial

Throughout May, the army planners of the operation worked with a variety of themes to maintain deniability of the Pakistan Army's involvement. These ranged from contentions that the Mujahideen were conducting the operation, to assertions that the Pakistan Army was not crossing the actual LOC. The decision to attribute the fictitious identity of the Mujahideen to the NLI was largely an unplanned one. It had been triggered by the wireless intercepts of exchanges between the Indian forces, which the ISI and the MI had picked up. The Indians were informing each other that the Afghan Mujahideen had crossed over the LOC. This Indian assessment was based on the wireless exchanges they had picked up between the NLI personnel recruited from Pakistan's Pashto-speaking areas.[57] The Indians mistook them for Afghans.

In fact, there was no Mujahideen participation at all. The Mujahideen, often physically hardy, were "essentially a rag-a-tag force wearing second hand clothes and PT shoes." Incapable of fighting pitched battles, they were certainly not capable of supporting the Kargil operation. At best they could "apply pinpricks" to India using their very weak artillery and ammunition, including AK47 assault rifles, light motors, explosive devices.[58] They were capable of ambushes and of raiding posts. The Mujahideen "could not have operated in the Kargil area where even the eagles do not dare fly."[59]

Nevertheless, to ensure deniability, a decision was taken within the GHQ to "play along" with the Indian version that Afghan Mujahideen had entered the Kargil region.[60] By the third week of May, the FCNA commander got orders from the GHQ that the troops participating in the operation should "go in civvies" and to "remove their identity discs." The FCNA found this order disturbing. The troops were to be identified as Mujahideen. Camouflaging their identity would affect their morale.[61] The broader implications of acquiring the fictitious identity were overlooked by the army generals. The participation of the Afghan Mujahideen in the Kargil area would establish their engagement with the Kashmir freedom struggle. Such a linkage would strengthen the Indian position that, in fact, Pakistan was involved in spreading the Taliban brand of extremism in the region and justify Delhi's framing of the Kashmir movement within the Islamic international terrorism framework and link it to Osama Bin Laden and to al-Qaeda.[62]

Closer to home, the Mujahideen leadership, agitated over Pakistan's decision to project the Op as a Mujahideen operation, sought meetings with the Pakistan leadership. They complained to their ISI interlocutors that linking them to the Kargil Operation gave them "a bad name."[63] In their meetings with the prime minister and the DG ISI they demanded that the projection of this linkage be discontinued. The prime minister pacified them and said their name was included in this national effort to liberate Kashmir and that the success of the operation would mean also the Mujahideen's success.

The planners of Operation Koh Paima continued with this fictitious identity till almost the very end of the Kargil operation. Notwithstanding, of course, the fact that during the mid-May GHQ briefing for the foreign military attachés, the 'cat had been let out of the bag!'[64] By around 26 May, even the Indians publicly confirmed that it was the Pakistan Army and not the Mujahideen who were involved in the operation. Subsequently, international media reports, reflecting the perception of foreign governments, also highlighted army and not Mujahideen involvement. Nevertheless, Pakistan official policy till the end remained to insist throughout the operation that the Afghan and Kashmiri Mujahideen had crossed the LOC.

Beyond identity, on the question of having crossed the LOC, the Kargil clique had believed that, because the "LOC was marked on a quarter inch map and a thick line on the map can actually make the difference of two or three kilometers on the ground", the Op would be "safe" and non-provocative. The commonly heard narration on LOC-crossing, especially by the army spokesperson, simply was that especially in the area of the operation "the LOC was not defined at all."[65] This was also the thrust of the army's briefings to the prime minister.[66] No one from the civilians authoritatively countered this rationale. Pakistan had occupied five areas each around 200 to 300 square kilometers. Indian retaliation was therefore inevitable.

Within the army, any early reservations being expressed regarding the operation were rejected by the high command. For example, towards the end of May, when the international community began blaming Pakistan for the ratcheting up of tensions between the two nuclear-armed neighbors, there were murmurings within the Evaluation, Analysis & Research Cell, which worked directly under the COAS's secretariat in the GHQ. This Cell, formed during general Jahangir Karamat's tenure as army chief, was mandated to provide regular input on the strategic environment.[67] Officers posted in this Cell were anxious. "We kept saying there is something wrong. Our input was that there are problems," recalled one.[68] In fact, a lieutenant colonel serving in the research and analysis wing of the GHQ wrote a note recommending that Pakistani troops pull out of Kargil. The note found its way to the army chief and then back to the brigadier. Musharraf's comments, in green ink, were written in the margin: "I do not agree."[69]

The Illusion of Success

By late May, although some within the military brass were concerned about the outcome, for the architects of Op KP, the month of May was one of self-appreciation. They suffered no trepidations; instead, they were confident of their achievements. They saw themselves in the leadership role in this Op, not only on the military front but also at the diplomatic front. For example, in his telephonic exchanges with Musharraf, who was visiting Beijing, the CGS General Aziz shared the directions GHQ was giving the Foreign Minister and the Foreign Secretary on how to engage Delhi and the international community on the Op.[70]

Throughout May whenever the prime minister 's queries on the risk factor attached with the Operation, were often met with nearly smug responses. During one of his trips to the operation area at Khel,[71] Sharif asked the FCNA Commander if the Indians would not be able to regain control of the area. He was told, "I would be a professional idiot if I say they can't take the position. However, the price they will have to pay will be horrendous."[72] The military planners had also ruled out any possibility of India opening fronts along the international borders. With Pakistani troops in Kargil, the Indians ran the risk of Pakistan cutting off Drass-Kargil, Leh, and Siachen, provoking an uprising in Kashmir, and requiring the movement of additional troops into Indian-held Kashmir.[73]

Through May, the Kargil planners were almost euphoric. They completely ruled out any possibility of reversals. For example, in late May, when major-general Jamshed Gulzar[74] from the ISI while visiting the FCNA headquarters wondered if the Pakistanis could hold on to the strategic heights, he was told that "there was no question of reversals."[75] Typically, this depicted 'a one scenario only' mindset. On the ground, there were no major military reversals and the Op seemed to be moving according to plan. Having taken control of about 140 peaks across the LOC, having managed the surprise and secrecy from the Op KP's launch, Pakistan was now in a commanding position. Through the seven-month period, from October until May, the Op had remained largely undetected by the Indians.

The Indian response had not yet crystallized. The account of Pakistan's military adventurism had not yet travelled beyond the region. In fact, throughout most of May, Pakistan was also in a relatively easy diplomatic space. For the Indians, the military walkover that their napping forces had handed down to the Pakistanis was a slow discovery. Mid-May calls from the US President Bill Clinton and the British Prime Minister Tony Blair urged the Pakistani prime minister to bilaterally tackle the Kargil flare-up. Blaming Pakistan had not yet begun. Internal reservations notwithstanding, Pakistan was not under any significant international pressure. In fact, in Delhi and Islamabad, the need to remain engaged in dialogue was also not lost in the battle of bombs and bullets. On 20 May, an Indian Ministry of External Affairs' statement claimed that Pakistan had pushed a "large number of armed intruders" into Occupied Kashmir. It asked Pakistan to "desist from violating the international boundary and the LoC in Jammu and Kashmir." Twenty-four hours later, the Pakistan Foreign Office retaliated that "the bogey of infiltrators would bode ill for the efforts to improve the atmosphere since February this year." Next spoke Pakistan's High Commissioner Ashraf Jehangir Qazi. He said, "Our perceptions of what has happened in the Kargil area and across the LOC are different from yours." The prime ministers of the two countries were still on telephonic communication terms.

Delhi: From Safe Passage to Pokhran Tests

Meanwhile, in India, after flagging the chronic complaint of Pakistan-aided LOC crossing by the Mujahideen, the Indian Army had virtually held back until late May, even from its own civilian leadership, whatever information they had regarding the extent of Pakistan's penetration into Indian Held territory.[76] An alarmed Indian prime minister offered 'safe passage' to the Pakistan-based Kashmiri Mujahideen, who Vajpayee believed had come from across the LOC. Meanwhile, his flustered government opted for information blackout. "Pakistani propaganda" on the Kargil military operation could not be broadcast in India, asserted India's Information Minister Pramod Mahajan, as he banned Pakistan's official channel Pakistan Television(PTV). It was removed from all dish antennas.[77]

By end May, the Indian prime minister was walking his hard talk. He called Nawaz Sharif on 24 May to complain about the Pakistani military operation. He bluntly told Sharif, "You have betrayed me"[78] and that "no intrusion will be allowed in our territory…all means will be used to clear our territory." Sharif proposed that the two Directors-General Military Operations (DGMOs) talk to each other. On 25 May, the two DGMOs communicated. The Pakistani DGMO, Lt. General Tauqir Zia, decided to call the Indian DGMO again the following day with answers to his questions. But, before the DGMO could make the promised call, Delhi had launched Operation Vijay. At 6.30, am an attack formation of MIGs and MI-25 attack helicopters armed with rockets and laser guided bombs took off from the Srinagar airbase to destroy positions "atop Drass, Batalik, Kargil, and Mashkoh."[79] In fact, hours before the beginning of Operation Vijay, the Indian prime minister publicly provided the justification. On 25 May, Vajpayee had told reporters in Pondicherry, "We are facing a new situation in Kargil. It is not just an intrusion that is taking place when the snow starts. This time the design is to occupy some territory and stay put there. Infiltrators are being helped by armed forces."[80] Vajpayee also signaled the use of airpower to "clear the Kargil area."[81] Interestingly, in emphasizing that India's border were "safer now than any time in the past",[82] the Indian prime minister told the reporters that government had taken steps 'including the nuclear tests in Pokhran and launching of Agni-II.'[83] Within the context of Kargil, it was again the Indian prime minister who first invoked nuclear weapons as a guarantor of security.

By the last week of May, India had begun comprehending the scale of Op KP. However, to keep up public morale, Indian authorities were matching reports of Pakistani infiltration with somewhat exaggerated accounts of their own military achievements. For example, on 25 May, the Indian Additional Director-General Military Operations boasted at a press conference, "Most of the positions have been isolated, the enemy is running out of supplies and ammunition and there is nobody to look after their dead and injured…"[84]

Clearly, the 26 May launch of Operation Vijay had signaled Delhi's evolving response to Op KP. 26 May set the stage for repeated sorties in the Kargil-Drass area by Indian Mirage 2000 jet fighters. The most intense Indian military response to Pakistani incursion came at the point of maximum Indian vulnerability at Drass. The Pakistani posts or pickets at Drass were most dangerous for India because they were near the main artery, the Drass-Kargil highway. The first post reclaimed by the Indians was at the fringe of the watershed[85] in the Mushko sector at point 4540.

The Indian government was making a virtue out of necessity. It knew that evicting the Pakistani troops from Kargil was a tall order.[86] With Indian troops tied down in Kargil and in counter-insurgency operations in Jammu and Kashmir, opening new fronts was risky. Hence, having assessed the overall military situation, Delhi realized the futility of banking on military power alone. Delhi also decided to rally international support in its opening round to reverse the virtual military walkover achieved by Pakistan. Astute diplomacy backed by maximum force deployment on the ground was Delhi's way forward.

The Vajpayee government's calm and calculated statements accusing Pakistan of aggression, demanding its troops withdraw, agreeing for dialogue, calling for reverting back to the Lahore Agreement, deploying the maximum possible Indian military force in Kargil but not allowing its forces to cross the LOC, even after its MIGs were shot down, and simultaneously ruling out both the spread in fighting or the use of nuclear weapons. Assuring the international community that it wanted the conflict to remain localized, made india appear reasonable and earned significant international goodwill and support. [87] Meanwhile, Vajpayee's strict orders to his military command that no cross-LOC military operations were to be carried out, also made the Pakistani planners believe Kargil was unfolding as they had contemplated. They misread Delhi's deliberate tentativeness as disability and fear. This misjudgement by the Kargil clique also contributed to their bluster.

Implausibility

Towards the end of May Pakistan launched its diplomatic maneuver. Largely contra-factual, the content of this maneuver was disjointed and implausible. Pakistan's prime minister argued, "People fighting the Indian Army in the Valley are neither militants nor infiltrators and are freedom fighters."[88] To international criticism, Islamabad's rebuttal that it had not violated the LOC arrangement agreed upon under the Simla Accord[89] was technically correct but grossly mistimed. Pakistan was seeking sympathy from the international community for India's fifteen-year illegal occupation of Siachen in violation of the 1972 Simla Accord.

Pakistan's diplomacy on Kargil cantered around the men at Hotel Scheherazade the political leadership, the army chief, and the Director-General ISPR. Their common objective was to argue for linkage between ending the Kargil crisis and a resolution of the half-century-old Kashmir dispute.[90] Accordingly, their public refrain was three-fold: one, that India had now, as on numerous occasions before, crossed the LOC in violation of the 1972 Simla Accord; two, that the Kargil heights were occupied by Kashmiri freedom fighters demanding an end to the Indian occupation of

Kashmir and not by the Pakistani army; three, that only a resolution of the Kashmir dispute would end the Kargil crisis and ensure a stable peace. [91]

On 24 May, the COAS General Musharraf arrived in Beijing on a week-long visit. In his meetings with his Chinese counterpart, Musharraf criticized "hegemonic India" for violating human rights in Kashmir and warned that Kashmir is a "flash point."[92] The same day, the foreign secretary rejected India's repeated assertion that Pakistani-backed infiltrators had crossed the LOC. He called for neutral experts to "establish the truth." In Islamabad, meanwhile, temperatures rose following Indian deployment of additional brigades and air force squadrons in Kashmir.

While the Nawaz government was still seeking the full picture from the still secretive Kargil clique, Pakistan had also begun its maneuver for external support. But disturbing systemic questions had surfaced: Under whose control is the army? Who checks their operational plans or who are they obliged to get their plans cleared from? At what level does input of the civilian leadership enter into planning? Constitutionally what articles oblige the army to seek civilian clearance, guidance and input? Do rules of business obligate the military to get input from the civilian chief executive? Who is the final decision maker?

Hard Reality

For the Pakistan prime minister, the hard reality was sinking in. Within days of the 17 May meeting and at the speed of lightening, the joy from that meeting's flattery had worn off, the notion of being "the liberator of Kashmir" had evaporated. The first media reports, regarding the responsibility for Kargil surfaced in the Pakistani press. Hard times lay ahead.

Meanwhile India, having been caught napping, had recoiled for review and rapid response.

CHAPTER 7

IN THE FIRING LINE

The battle being fought in Kargil by Pakistani troops may have been confined to a particular area, but the fall-out of this limited war was not that limited. The prime minister, constitutionally obligated to manage the fallout of this ongoing battle, was to find himself swamped by meetings with military commanders, services chiefs, his kitchen cabinet, and his foreign office team. The engagements on the foreign front, especially with his counterparts from the US and India, were few but extremely important. With the international community looking upon Pakistan's action across the LOC as irresponsible, at home the prime minister was searching for reliable information on the actual ground situation. The chronic civil-military distrust had been contained with the prime minister's conviction that this was a Pakistan issue. Nevertheless, with the multi-dimensional challenges that Op KP now posed to the elected government, the competence of the prime minister and his team was to be severely tested…as rarely before.

The prime minister convened a high level meeting with most Defense Cabinet Committee members to discuss Kargil on 25 May. With Sharif in the chair, the meeting was attended by the foreign minister the acting Chief of Army Staff Lt. Gen Saeed-uz-Zafar, the DGMO Major Gen Tauqir Zia, the naval and airforce chiefs. At the meeting, while the army high command's message was 'there was no reason for alarm or panic, the Air Force Chief Marshal Pervez Mehdi, the heads of the intelligence agencies and the defense Secretary, all expressed strong reservations about Kargil.[1] The air force chief opposed the army's request for using air power to counter Indian attacks. At the meeting, naval chief Admiral Fasih Bokhari and the air force chief stated that a naval blockade by India could not be ruled out.. The air force chief said deploying air power for the Op could mean placing squadrons in Azad Kashmir, leaving Lahore and Karachi unprotected. The Pakistan Army Air Defense had already deployed extra radar in the north to observe Indian aircraft movement. According to Chaudhry Nisar, the Party view was not to embarrass but to apportion responsibility. The Pakistani Air Force had only deployed anti-aircraft batteries along the LOC and on 27 May had shot down two Indian MIGs violating Pakistan's airspace.

The internal policy-level differences on the Kargil operation notwithstanding, the steps taken following this meeting reflected the Nawaz Sharif government's decision to go along with the military-authored plan. India was the aggressor, Kashmir and Kargil were linked, and the resolution of the Kashmir dispute would help defuse the crisis.[2] Accordingly, after the meeting, the prime minister, on the advice of the Foreign Office, sent a request to UN Secretary-General Kofi Annan to play an active role in de-escalating the tension between the two nuclear-armed states. Specifically, he requested the Secretary General to increase the number of UNGOMIP monitors along the LOC and to send a UN envoy to the region. Pakistan also requested Moscow to play a mediatory role to de-escalate the crisis. For the home front, the message was: "Now decisions of country's security are made in the country and no NOCs[3] were needed." It was reiterated that Pakistan was committed to both the Simla Accord and the Lahore Declaration, wanted dialogue, but would not tolerate violation of the LOC. Pakistan's potpourri of responses included populism and confidence on the domestic front; pleas, threats and dialogue calls on the external front; and, underlying these a lack of genuine trust and coordination on the internal policy front.

Subsequently, the top military command organized a special briefing at the GHQ exclusively for the two men who would now be on the front-lines for globally framing and domestically financing the now overt operation; the foreign minister and the finance minister.

The briefing, given personally by the army chief, took place in the Operations room at the GHQ in the presence of two members of Kargil clique, the CGS Aziz and the corps commander 10 corps Mahmud, as well as several Principal Staff Officers. The objective of the presentation was to share the current ground situation and the clique's assessment of the possible expansion scenario of the Kargil conflict with the cabinet ministers. The army chief explained that the conflict could move in three possible directions: one, it could stay restricted to the operation area alone; two, it could expand to the territory across the LOC on the Pakistan side; and, finally, the Indians could open fronts along the Pakistan-India international border. Barring the army chief's January comment on a possible replay of the 1962 Chinese-like massive retaliation by the Indians to Op KP[4], the Kargil clique had premised the entire Op on almost no response from the Indians. So was the clique now changing its assessment?

The prime minister and his key men attended several meetings to get briefings on what appeared to be a changing military situation. Meetings were mostly held at the GHQ with the director-general military operations making the presentations. Early on June 2, the prime minister attended a meeting at the 10 corps headquarters. At the briefing, Lt. general Mahmud reported "continued success and holding operations" plus troop pullback from forward positions. The prime minister asked why troops were pulling back from forward positions when they were in a winning situation. Mahmud maintained those were early warning posts meant to inform the Pakistanis of the approaching enemy and were no longer required. Although the commander of the Kargil Operation said the posts were no longer required, in fact his troops had been beaten back by the Indian air force and ground troop's artillery onslaught.

In these initial meetings, the prime minister's enthusiasm about Op KP, triggered in the 17 May meeting, seemed intact. He had then advised the military to go ahead, to "take Allah's name and keep this Operation going, this issue cannot be resolved through buses."[5] The prime minister was alluding to the trip that Indian Prime Minister Vajpayee made by bus from Amritsar to Lahore. At this early June briefing, he remarked, "Mazaay kee baat keh aap Srinagar chalaey ja'ain."[6] The FCNA commander claimed he said that the force ratio was in India's favor.

Weekly meetings were also held at the Joint Services Headquarters, attended mostly by the three services chiefs.

Policy-making in Delhi

Meanwhile, in Delhi, the entire policy-making apparatus worked as a unified unit under civilian command. India's entire policy-making, policy implementation, and policy projection apparatus was engaged in the pursuit of one objective: to evict Pakistan as early as possible from Kargil. All possible means were to be used. The only nuanced difference existed between the political and bureaucratic tracks on the means deployed to evict Pakistan. The Vajpayee-Brajesh-led political track, mindful of Pakistan's military dominance in Kargil and its own vulnerability to the Opposition's criticism of having been hoodwinked by Pakistan, were also keen on exploring the dialogue track. Guided by political pragmatism, Vajpayee's key men in the North Block saw the wisdom in keeping the lines of communication open with Nawaz Sharif and holding the military, not Pakistan's civilian prime minister, responsible for the Kargil crisis.

Accordingly, on 28 May, after a crucial meeting of the Cabinet Committee on Security, the Indian defense minister gave "a virtual clean chit to Nawaz Sharif by seeming to absolve him of all responsibility for the current crisis"[7] Interestingly, in the late afternoon of the same day, Nawaz Sharif called Vajpayee and the two had a twenty minute conversation. Nawaz Sharif offered to send his foreign minister for talks and urged for the settlement of the Kashmir issue. Vajpayee did not reject the dialogue offer but let his counterpart know that the first requirement was that Pakistan undo the violation of the LOC.

Meanwhile, India's bureaucratic track, supported by the Minister for External Affairs Jaswant Singh, treated Pakistan's decision-making apparatus as a monolith. Men in the South Block saw no reason to "reward" Pakistan for aggression by finding a face-saving solution. The MEA spokesman categorically maintained that a stable bilateral relationship between India and Pakistan was not possible as along as Pakistan engaged in "confrontational and hostile activities." [8] The MEA, buoyed by Washington's public censure of Pakistan saw no reason to show any tactical flexibility towards Pakistan. Initial Indian nervousness was gradually turning into anger and confidence.

Indian diplomacy was in high gear. Having signed a strategic cooperation agreement with Russia, Delhi-Moscow ties had been fortified. In Washington, the keenness to engage in a strategic relationship with India was unprecedented. The Jaswant-Talbot nuclear talks had expanded into a platform for evolving a common strategic outlook for the two major powers.[9] Also significantly, the first trip in ten years by an Indian foreign minister to China was in the works. However, Pakistan, by contrast, was in a difficult strategic environment. Its Afghanistan policy was under criticism and it was blamed for facilitating "terrorism" and "Islamic militancy." Following the nuclear tests, it had also come under economic pressure. Perhaps the only silver lining was the beginnings of détente with its eastern neighbour.

Now, however, Pakistan had unraveled that détente, while India appeared to have been trying to salvage it.

With a clear assessment of the scale of Pakistan's incursions into the Kargil-Drass area, Indian diplomacy went into a quiet high gear.[10] In Washington, the Indian ambassador remained in regular contact with State Department officials to update them on the situation.

Indian Foreign Minister Jaswant Singh was in Central Asia when the Indian military apprised their leadership of the scale of the Pakistani intrusion across the LOC.[11] On 25 May, Jaswant Singh travelled to Moscow to discuss the elements of an Indo-Russian Declaration of Strategic Partnership to be signed at the a Russian-Indian summit later in the year.[12] Singh sought Russian censure of Pakistan over the Kargil operation and a public Russian demand for Pakistan's withdrawal from "Indian territory." He also raised the matter in his fifteen minute telephone conversation with Russian President Boris Yeltsin. Significantly, it was in Moscow that the Indians were able to brief the US of their assessment of the Kargil situation and sought US support to force out the Pakistanis. Singh met with his old buddy, the US Deputy Secretary of State Strobe Talbott, who was in Moscow to hold negotiations on the Kosovo crisis with Viktor Chernomyrdin, special envoy of President Yeltsin.[13] On 26

May, in Delhi, the defense minister briefed the US ambassador Richard Celeste and the UK High Commissioner Rob Young.[14]

By end May, the Indian foreign minister had received "unequivocal" assurances from Washington, Moscow, London, and Paris that they accepted the Indian position that the infiltrators had been "pushed in by Pakistan."[15] They were equally clear that Pakistan could neither be rewarded by United Nations mediation nor by any international pressure on India to resolve the Kashmir crisis. The issue was Kargil and the engagement would be bilateral.

"A very, very dumb mistake!"

By end May, several countries, including the US, had come to the conclusion that Pakistan had violated the LOC. Indian reports, information available in Pakistan to the foreign embassies, and the US's own satellite sources had left no doubt in Washington that Pakistan had crossed the LOC. While the LOC was de jure not an international border between Pakistan and India, de facto it was considered a border dividing the state of Jammu and Kashmir between Azad Kashmir and Indian-held Kashmir. Hence, excepting Pakistan's strategic ally China, the international community had concluded that the crossing of the LOC by Pakistani troops amounted to Pakistani aggressing against India. For the Clinton Administration, this was an unacceptable development. This development was in sharp contrast to US Secretary of State Madeleine Albright's earlier upbeat assessment of the security situation in South Asia. Albright's conclusion then, against the backdrop of the Nawaz-Vajpayee Lahore Summit, had been of peace appearing on the horizon of a region tethering at the brink of disaster, as it had seemed following the nuclear tests.

Around end May, Washington began its intensive contacts with Pakistan. By now, US Under-Secretary Pickering's mid-May blunt "cock and bull" retort to Ambassador Khokhar's claim that Kashmiri freedom fighters, not Pakistani troops, were fighting in Kargil, had become US policy.[16] The thinking within Washington's policy-circles was that "Pakistan had made a very, very dumb mistake and it had set things way back, having a serious impact on Pakistan's credibility with reference to India."[17]

Meanwhile, the US Central Command (CENTCOM),[18] responsible for monitoring developments in the region, did not find the initial reports of skirmishes along the LOC alarming. Having routinely followed the ground situation, CENTCOM commanders knew that after the winter thaw either the Indian or Pakistani do get a few kilometers advantage. This winter, CENTCOM believed, "Pakistan had seen the opportunity and had gone for it." To military men like Chief of CENTCOM, General Anthony Zinni, there was "a gentlemen's agreement; unwritten and unstated that Pakistan would go for a typically contained winter engagement."[19] In the State Department, there was concern that this was more than a mere tactical level winter advantage. Nevertheless, by end May, based on subsequent intelligence reports received at CENTCOM headquarters, the US military's read out was that Pakistan had opted for a strategy thrust to cut India's supply lines to Siachen and to Leh. In fact, following the 26 May air incursions by India, alarm bells rang in the CENTCOM headquarters. There was fear that massive Indian mobilization in response to Pakistan would lead to a war situation; Washington needed to intervene before it was too late and the train "would have left the station."[20]

By the end of May, General Zinni called the Pakistani Army chief to assess the ground situation. The CENTCOM chief was no stranger to Musharraf. The two personally knew each other. Not long after General Pervez Musharraf took over as COAS in November 1998,he had hosted General Zinni and his wife on a four day visit to Pakistan, during which, accompanied by Musharraf, Zinni travelled to the LOC, the Siachen Glacier, and the Khyber Pass. In a time of sanctions, this proved to be a 'bonding trip'. Zinni was sympathetic to the bitterness among the service chiefs regarding the F-16 affair. Both wanted the military-to-military institutional relationship to grow. Zinni was keen for the revival of IMET (International Military Education & Training)[21] with Pakistan. Musharraf wanted a greater number of his officers be educated abroad. Together, they worked to keep the military-to-military contact going. Zinni saw that Musharraf "wanted the connection with the West even if it hung on the relationship between us two."[22] Zinni had found Musharraf "very positive, very personable and the chemistry had clicked." Pakistan's newly appointed army chief suggested to Zinni that they ought to become close friends, exchange private numbers, and be able to reach each other at short notice.[23] Both wanted to maintain a personal relationship despite the troubled official relations. Significantly, Zinni's contact with the Pakistan Army pre-dated his taking over as CENTCOM chief. As commander of the US military operations in Somalia, he closely coordinated with General Waheed Kakkar to oversee the withdrawal of US forces.

Diplomatic activity in Washington, especially after the shooting down of the Indian jets, veering across the LOC into Azad Kashmir, gained unprecedented momentum. The US President, the Secretary of State Madeleine Albright, and the Under Secretary of State Karl Inderfurth were all engaged in the Kargil crisis. Their messaging to Pakistan varied; some was more direct, other more diplomatic. After Secretary Albright's 29 May call to Prime Minister Sharif and Foreign Minister Singh, the US State Department explained that the purpose was to express US concern about "the developments and the potential for them spinning out of control." Albright had urged both to "exercise restraint and avoid spreading the fighting beyond the Kargil area."[24] No blame was apportioned but the spokesman was clear: "We obviously have our views as to what has transpired, and the reasons for what has transpired and our views on who is where but we don't think it is wise to engage in public discussion of that at this time."[25] He continued, "The best course of action for our diplomacy and for avoiding the chance of this spinning out of control is to leave our views on subjects like this private," and also that the US was articulating its actual views "strongly in private" to the two countries.

The Under Secretary of State for South Asia Karl Inderfurth's message to Pakistan was blunt: "Clearly, the Indians are not going to cede this territory the militants have taken. They have to depart, and they will depart, either voluntarily or because the Indians take them out."[26] Inderfurth's thinking found its way to the Indian press and his blunt warning angered Islamabad. US ambassador Milam was summoned to the Foreign Office. Tariq Altaf, additional secretary, complained to Milam against Inderfurth's factually incorrect assessment of the situation in Kargil. Milam told Altaf that the US statement was based on information provided in the GHQ briefing. Upon hearing Milam's response it seemed that "Altaf had been kicked and his face fell."[27] Washington's unambiguous message to Islamabad was that the Kargil Op was having a "disastrous impact on the promise of Lahore"[28] and Pakistani troops must be immediately pulled back from across the LOC. No one in Washington was receptive to Islamabad's position that US engage on Kashmir and not just on Kargil.[29]

Meanwhile, Delhi's position of de-linking Kargil from Kashmir was no different from Washington's. While having grudgingly accepted Pakistan's offer to send its envoy to Delhi, the India message was that the one-point dialogue agenda would be Kargil alone.[30] All other issues would have to wait for the resumption of the Composite Dialogue.[31] The Indian prime minister warned, "India faces a war-like situation in Kashmir and it would be better if Pakistan called back the infiltrators. Otherwise, we will force them to go back."[32] A personally peeved Vajpayee said, "They are not just infiltrators, it is a kind of invasion. They are trying to change the boundary, trying to capture our land."[33]

Nuclear play

In Islamabad, meanwhile, temperatures rose following Indian deployment of additional brigades and air force squadrons in Kashmir. Within hours of the Indian MIGs flying across the LOC into Pakistan-controlled territory, raising the possibility of Indian attacks across the LOC, Pakistan issued a tactical strategic warning. The Foreign Secretary Shamshad Ahmad warned, "We will not hesitate to use any weapon in our arsenal to defend our territorial integrity,"[34] implying that Pakistan will defend itself at all costs. Delhi issued its response, but knew the purpose of Shamshad's statement. The *Times of India* captured the Delhi thinking: "Common sense suggested that the remark be discounted. A country resorting to nuclear blackmail is not likely to make its foreign secretary the mouthpiece for the threat."[35] Washington's 'nuclear saints,'[36] however, who were already disposed towards concluding that a Muslim state was unworthy of possessing nuclear weapons, seized the opportunity. Many in Washington therefore concluded that Shamshad's defensive statement alluded to the use of nuclear weapons.[37]

The purpose of the Shamshad Ahmed statement was to deter India from crossing the LOC and also to leverage the international anxiety that the South Asian nuclear states would take the world towards a nuclear Armageddon. Accordingly, from mid-May onwards, Pakistan's diplomatic corps, at home and abroad, advocated to all their foreign counterparts that the Kargil crisis had actually underscored the need to resolve the Kashmir dispute. They maintained that freedom fighters demanding an end to the Indian occupation of Kashmir had occupied the Kargil heights.[38] Clearly there was not even a remote possibility that Pakistan would opt for deployment of nuclear weapons, much less contemplate use of nuclear weapons. The unstated assumption of the Kargil planners was also that this anxiety on the nuclear issue would compel the international community to lean hard on the Indians to resolve Kashmir.

The initial international reaction to Kargil indicated that Kargil planners had miscalculated how the nuclear factor would play out. It in fact made things difficult for Pakistan. Washington had already put the onus of the crisis on this country. In the post-nuclear-test period, the international community seemed to have shared Pakistan's position that resolution of the Kashmir dispute was important to avert the danger of a nuclear war in South Asia. It saw unresolved Kashmir as a nuclear flash-point.[39] The international pressure had contributed bringing India to the negotiating table within the Composite Dialogue framework. Op KP was turning this around.

Not surprisingly, despite the military gains, there was palpable discomfort with the overall situation within sections of the ruling

Party and of the defense forces. Prime Minister Nawaz Sharif's telephone conversations with Vajpayee, Clinton, and Tony Blair had underscored the political and diplomatic costs of the Kargil operation. The three categorically demanded that Pakistan withdraw from Kargil. Although Nawaz Sharif insisted upon the linkage between Kashmir and Kargil and advocated quick resolution of the Kashmir dispute, this increasingly appeared unlikely. Vajpayee was not about to buckle under the initial political and military pressure Op KP had exerted on India. Accordingly, an Indian military buildup was being planned to ensure forcible eviction of Pakistani troops. Vajpayee was clear: no dialogue with Pakistan unless Pakistani troops vacated Kargil.

By end May, strong reservations regarding Kargil were being expressed within Pakistan's civil and military policy-making circles. With confusion and concern marking the overall response within Pakistan to an operation its own army had launched, it was clear that the operation was not conceived as part of a strategic plan. When it did become public, there was not enough unity of purpose in Pakistan's various policy-making and policy influencing institutions to even produce a unified position. Underscoring this, the former American diplomat, Ambassador Robert Oakley, who was also closely following Kargil in Washington, remarked, "Pakistan could have said to India you have Siachen and we have Kargil. Let's trade. Pakistan had no game plan. They had just made a move."[40]

Policy-making hubs

Significantly, as the Kargil operation unfolded, three overlapping policy-making hubs emerged within Pakistan. One was the bureaucratic group. In the post-16 May period, key Foreign Office bureaucrats, who initially appeared to subscribe to the military's view that diplomatic gains could be derived from the military gains in Kargil.[41] Initially they emerged as the prime minister's key advisors. These bureaucrats closely allied themselves with the architects of Kargil, and until the end attempted to convert the military achievements into strategic gains.[42] The second was the prime minister's Kitchen Cabinet group, which in the post-16 May period gradually became the core policy-making group. The third was the constitutionally mandated Defense Committee of the Cabinet (DCC).

The Kitchen Cabinet comprised Sharif's three trusted men, who also were either professionally or personally connected to the army's leadership and had also had connections in Washington: Shehbaz Sharif, the prime minister's brother and Chief Minister of the Punjab province; Chaudhry Nisar, a close friend of the prime minister and Minister of Petroleum; and Iftikhar Ali Khan, the prime minister's trusted defense secretary and Chaudhry Nisar Ali Khan's elder brother. This informal Kitchen Cabinet emerged soon after the army's first detailed 16 May presentation[43] on Kargil, and had indirectly expressed anxiety over the developments. [44] Although critical of the army's operation, which also technically had the prime minister's clearance, it believed that only a collective approach could tide Pakistan through the impending fall-out of Kargil. Pakistan's chronic "civilian-military divide" did not kick in. They were, however, keen to avert what they believed could prove disastrous for Pakistan. In addition, they all had a "soft-corner"[45] for Musharraf and wanted to "protect" him and knew that he had to be brought on board to prevent this operation from proving disastrous for Pakistan.[46] They held several separate meetings with Musharraf to understand the army's thinking and to discuss possible pitfalls of the operation.[47]

The consensus among the Kitchen Cabinet was to institutionalize the handling of the issues that had flowed from Kargil and that the Defense Cabinet Committee (DCC) should be the forum for the meetings. The Nawaz Sharif government had already activated the DCC as a policy-making forum for defense and security matters. Already, the DCC had been used for taking decisions on critical national security issues, including the nuclear tests, the reorientation of Afghan policy, and the re-orientation of the Kashmir policy had already been taken in the DCC. However, bringing policy discussion of an ongoing military operation to the DCC would be a milestone in the civilianization of security policy.

This internal dynamics ran on a parallel track of dealing with the problem in a unified manner while also handling the chronic problem of civil-military relations. Other inevitable questions in Pakistan's power context, rife with civil-military distrust, revolved around the implications on the domestic front. How did the army embark on such a major operation without fully informing the civilian leadership? Were there any other undercurrents that were at work and would the army move towards a take-over? Would the army say Nawaz Sharif is preventing it from settling Kashmir by talking to the Indians while the army is trying to settle it with their blood and sweat?

But, beyond Pakistan's domestic dynamics, the Kargil planners had placed Pakistan in a difficult position.

Chapter 8

FIGHT BACK

The month of June reinforced the military and political trends that had begun emerging in the closing days of May. India, despite heavy reinforcements, was mostly under tremendous military pressure, except at Tololing. But, bit by bit, the Kargil clique's claims of invincibility had begun to be spurned on the ground. In diplomatic terms, the international situation was turning unsympathetic to Pakistan, which was increasingly being viewed as the aggressor against India and also as an irresponsible state that had brought two nuclear powers to the brink of a catastrophic war.

"A damn fool thing to do!"

In the steady correspondence that took place between U.S. President Clinton and the Pakistani prime minister, Clinton's bottom line was: "It's a damn fool thing to do. Get your people out."[1] Pakistan sought support from China, but China was not prepared to give that support. Pakistan's military planners remained unruffled because they continued to dominate the military picture. Confronted with an increasingly hostile diplomatic situation, the Pakistani political leadership was uneasy. Significantly, the first suggestion of Kargil turning into a nuclear conflagration came from US Under-Secretary of State Karl Inderfurth. He warned of "the ingredients for miscalculation and the possibility of events spinning out of control."[2]

Delhi had played its card well. An integrated three-track plan, covering the military, diplomatic, and political fronts, had been astutely developed and executed to expel the Pakistanis from Kargil. While maintaining the unrelenting military force to expel the Pakistani troops, India deployed its main battle armor on the diplomatic front. Through well coordinated and high profile diplomatic moves, India had begun capitalizing on Pakistan's ill-planned, untimely, and technically illegal move in Kargil. Pakistan's mistakes provided Delhi the "enabling environment" to mount an astute diplomatic campaign.

By June India was set to more than make up for its military blunders. In key world capitals Delhi had effectively conveyed the Indian position that Pakistan must vacate Kargil, that Pakistan must not be rewarded for aggression by initiating any bilateral dialogue on Kashmir with Pakistani troops still occupying "Indian territory", and that as a nuclear power India would not be irresponsible and open new fronts by crossing the LOC. A pragmatic India was also moving on another track. Given the difficult military situation and the unpredictability of Pakistan's response to Washington's demand to vacate the Kargil heights, Vajpayee's political team saw wisdom in opening a back-channel with Pakistan. With the scary prospect of the Leh-Srinagar Highway - the supply route for the thousands of Indian troops based in Leh and Siachen - remaining blocked throughout the summer months, the very survival of the troops could be in question. In case Pakistan resisted international pressure to vacate Kargil, the back channel would serve as a 'means of last resort' for settling the conflict in Kargil.

A key plank of India's diplomatic offensive was to obtain US support. India lost no time in reaching out to the US Administration and Congress for help to defuse trouble in the Kargil area. Still unclear of the exact cause of the fighting being reported in the area, Delhi believed Pakistan was involved and accordingly crafted a strategy to generate international pressure on Pakistan to vacate Kargil. Indian politicians and diplomats in Delhi and in Washington worked hard to win over the Clinton Administration. Indian Ambassador Naresh Chandra lobbied at the State department and on Capitol Hill for US support. Delhi sought US involvement, but on its own terms; Delhi wanted direct US involvement to get Pakistan evicted from the Kargil area but would reject any US mediation towards dialogue. This Indian plan helped to frame Kargil as a stand-alone development. All historical underpinning was rejected, whether the LOC's temporary nature, or India's record of violations, or, above all, its 1984 occupation of Siachen. Delhi's efforts were successful. On June 6 the Democratic co-Chairman of the Congressional Caucus Gary Ackerman on India said that if Pakistan did not stop helping "Islamic terrorists in the Kargil and Drass area of Jammu and Kashmir and withdraws its forces from the region, the State Department must add Pakistan to its annual list of state sponsors of terrorism."[3] For the US Executive, the State Department, and the Legislature, the time of discontent with the Taliban and their support for Osama bin Laden had already set in. Accordingly, the co-Chairman pushed the "right buttons." He stated, "A large number of well-trained and heavily armed Afghan mercenaries and fundamentalist Mujahideen terrorists, allegedly with spiritual and other links to the Saudi fugitive Osama bin Laden and Harkat ul Mujahideen, have entered the Indian side of the LOC from Pakistan."[4] Through the cooperative handling of the fall-out of the Kargil conflict, the US-Indian relationship evolved almost like "love in the time of war."[5] These two previously estranged countries grew considerably closer.

At home in India the most knowledgeable and powerful understood the context within which Pakistan had crossed the LOC. For example, India's former Prime Minister V. P. Singh admitted, "Pakistan spotted our weakness and sprang a surprise. Both countries are into elbow nudging and so, yes, Pakistan and India (are) both changing the LOC by force."[6]

Similarly, the then Indian Defense Minister George Fernandez too believed that practice of both sides leaving their LOC positions in winter that had gone on for 25 years, between 1972 and 1999, could only last until one day someone, i.e. Pakistan, decided to cheat against the ground rules ... as India too had done in 1984 when it occupied Siachen.[7]

Disjointed

Meanwhile, in Pakistan, the prime minister and his team were pulling together the military, diplomatic, and political fall-out of Op KP. The prime minister was in regular meetings with the military command, his kitchen cabinet, and the senior diplomats. The news from the battle-field was confusing and the pressures from abroad to withdraw from Kargil were mounting. In private meetings, his cabinet members were worried about the Op snowballing into a full-scale war. At cabinet meetings, the prime minister and some of his ministers expressed their concern and confusion over the military confrontation with India. Few believed it was the Mujahideen. Some suggested that the prime minister ask the US President to intervene to bring an honorable closure to the Operation. The Foreign Office was attempting damage limitation but it could only play a weak hand. On the domestic front, the parliament and the Senate were kept in the loop. On June 3 the foreign minister informed worried members of the Senate that he would soon be visiting Delhi to open negotiations with his counterpart on the need to address the outstanding Kashmir issue and also on ending the Operation.

Everyone hoped something good would come out of what was beginning to appear as an ill-conceived Op. All military decisions rested with the same planners' clique. The prime minister would get briefings in the GHQ or at the PM House. The army generals would bring their maps along for briefings and the meetings. On June 7 the Director Military Operation gave a briefing to the Pakistani Parliament's Standing Committee on Defense. In his 12 June letter to the army chief, the Chairman of the Committee Col Ghulam Sarwar Cheema stated, "Every participant individually and the Committee collectively commended, in very glowing terms, the very high quality of the said presentation." He requested to arrange a visit to "appropriate locations on the LOC and a call on you (the army chief), the CAS, and the CNS by members of the Committee. He assured the chief the nation's eyes are focused on you and through you the total defense machine."[8] This praise was indeed reminiscent of the prime minister's near joy exhibited during the first briefing he had received on OP Kargil. Clearly, between political in fighting, detachment from defense matters, ignorance of facts, and a degree

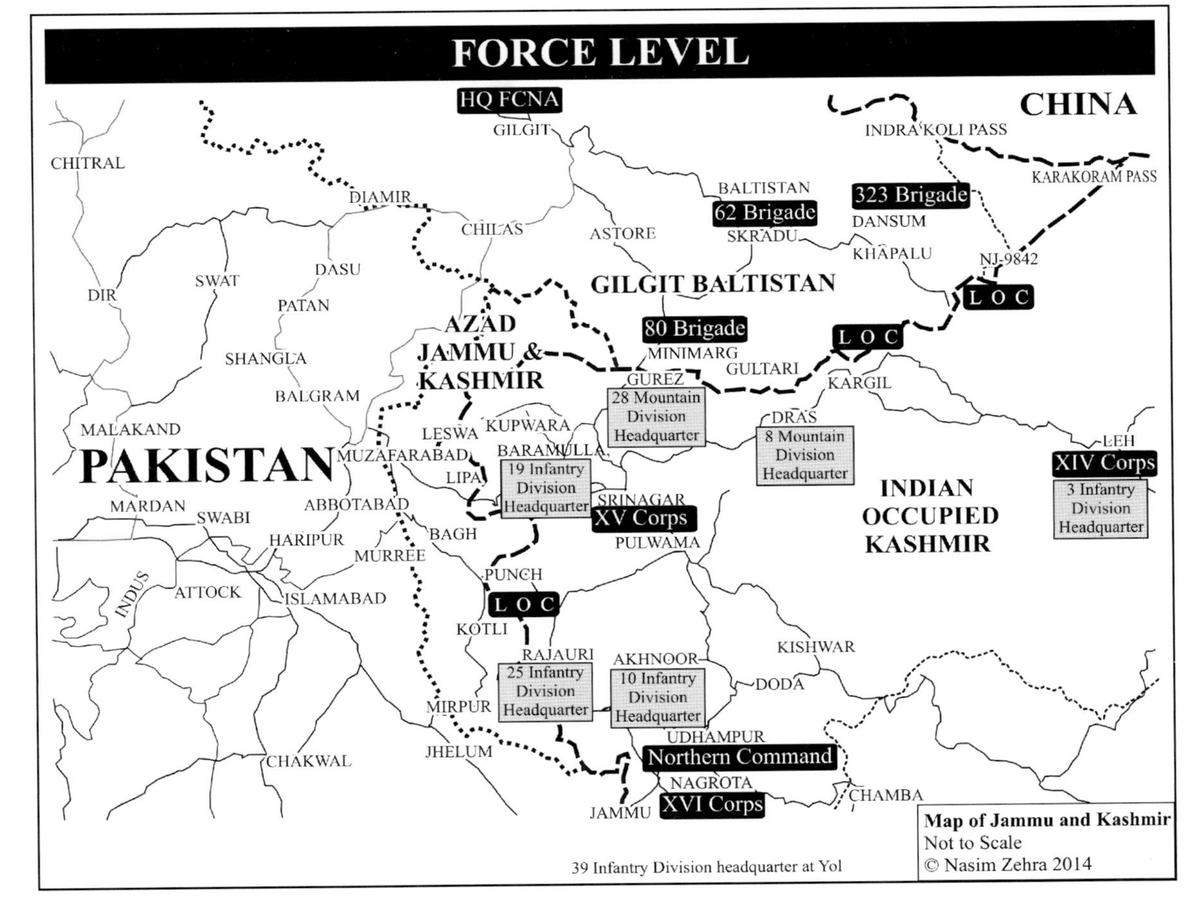

Force Levels

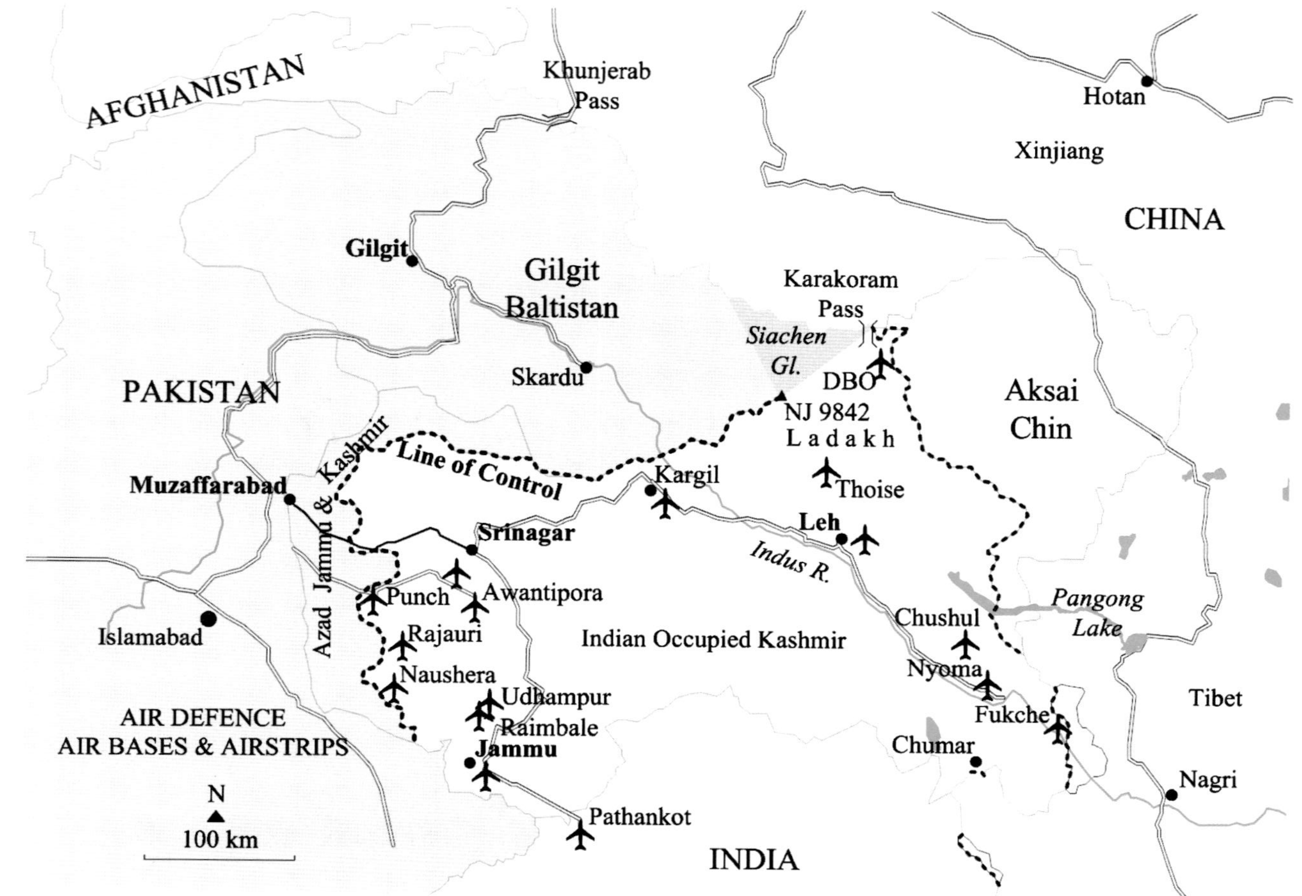
AFGHANISTAN
Khunjerab
Pass
Hotan
Xinjiang
CHINA
Gilgit
Gilgit
Baltistan
Karakoram
Pass
Siachen
Gl.
Skardu
DBO
PAKISTAN
NJ 9842
L a d a k h
Aksai
Chin
Azad Jammu & Kashmir
Line of Control
Muzaffarabad
Kargil
Thoise
Leh
Srinagar
Indus R.
Punch
Awantipora
Pangong
Lake
Islamabad
Chushul
Rajauri
Indian Occupied Kashmir
Nyoma
Naushera
Udhampur
Raimbale
Fukche
Tibet
AIR DEFENCE
AIR BASES & AIRSTRIPS
Jammu
Chumar
Nagri
N
100 km
Pathankot
INDIA

Air Defence

of patriotism, lay the mental space from which this entirely misplaced eulogy flowed from the nation's elected men and women. On the ground, the projected accomplishment of the Kargil clique was turning into an acute crisis.

Military Fight-Back

Against the backdrop of heightened military confrontation there was an eerie calm within the military leadership in the two countries. For example, in Pakistan, a senior general participated in a musical evening at an Islamabad local hotel. Similarly, in India, the 15 Corps commander inaugurated a golf championship some kilometers away from the Srinagar Badami Bagh complex from where the war's dead and wounded were being taken. [9] Yet, by mid-June, adversity struck Pakistan's young warriors perched on mountaintops. The wounded Indians of May had now returned in June with a vengeance and, above all, with a plan. The Pakistanis found themselves in a difficult military environment. The Pakistani posts that previously neither the Indian air force sorties could hit nor the Indian soldiers could scale alive, were now under continuous artillery attack. Their Bofor guns had done the trick for them. [10] Their maximum range of 30 kilometers enabled deep strikes on the enemy's gun positions, administrative installations, ammunition dumps, and headquarters, besides neutralizing forward positions held by the intruders. By moving up these guns, 105 mm field guns, 160 mm and 120 mm mortars and 122 mm GRAD BM 21 Multi Barrel Rocket Launchers (MBRLs) into forward positions, the Indians were capable of 'direct' fire on enemy localities - literally under the nose of the enemy[11] By early June, it became almost impossible to move logistics from the logistic base to the posts and pickets on the forward ridges via *nullahs* and mountains. Intense shelling and bombing destroyed Pakistan's logistics network. If a hundred porters left, only ten could reach their destination.[12] The Indians planned their attacks using a map marking Pakistani deployments that Indian troops had picked up from the Tololing base they had captured around June 6,.

In mid-June, the Indian air force struck at the Badar base, a logistics hub, set up by Pakistan in the Batalik sector, across the LOC, which was heavily stocked with ammunition.[13] The logistics crisis was now mounting for the Pakistanis with no easy or rapid route for replenishment. In the words of the Indian Commander Brigadier Bajwa, the commander of 192 Mountain Brigade, this is what the Pakistani men perched on Tiger Hill and running out of ammunition were confronting: "The sight of over one hundred guns pounding Tiger Hill... The fireballs of the explosions lit up ... We closed in up to 40 meters of the shelling. The accuracy was so great that not one shell strayed from its target ..." [14] The sustained, accurate and close up shooting, using Bofor guns on a vast scale, proved devastating for the Pakistanis.

By June 10th Indian Artillery regiment had amassed a large number of artillery units in extremely difficult terrain. On the military front this Indian artillery fire turned the tables on Pakistan. If the Indian infantry had suffered high casualties until early June, by mid-June it was raining fire and brimstone onto Pakistani troops occupying posts on the Tololing and Tiger Hills. Op KP was facing sharp military reversals and singularly on account of accurate and timely delivery of TNT. The Gunners' fire assaults became the principle battle-winning factor. An Indian account of the intense and lethal use of artillery was thus: "The Indian artillery fired over 250,000 shells, bombs, and rockets during the Kargil conflict. Approximately 5,000 artillery shells, mortar bombs and rockets were fired daily from 300 guns, mortars and MBRLs while 9,000 shells were fired the day Tiger Hill was regained. During the peak period of assaults, on an average, each artillery battery fired over one round per minute for 17 days continuously." [15] This intensive artillery firing sustained through the three weeks was uncommon, almost unparalleled in military history

This intensity of artillery fire devastated both men and mountains. By June 10, India's infantry was provided the solid backing it had lacked during May and early June. The Indian Artillery regiment had amassed a large number of fire units within a short period, in wet weather, and over very hostile terrain at extremely high altitudes. India's point man on the ground GOC in C Southern Command and army chief designate acknowledged that, in Operation Vijay, " (The) devastation caused by extremely accurate and timely fire assaults in most difficult and inhospitable terrain greatly facilitated the capture of key objectives…"[16]

A Handicapped Sartaj

With these facts unknown to him, it was a handicapped Sartaj that was taking off for Delhi. Far from the corridors of power in Islamabad and from the Ops room in the GHQ, where Op KP was still a success story, the Indians with massive firepower were targeting Pakistani troops perched on the peaks and slopes of the Drass and Kargil mountains. For the Pakistani troops, the military situation was turning nasty. Yet the Kargil planners were still heady with the self-created euphoria around Op KP. Reports of heavy Indian attacks were neither easily reaching them nor were being readily received even at the operational headquarters in Skardu. For example, around June 4, the first reports of Pakistani casualties and loss of the Pakistani-held position at Tololing lumbered into the FCNA Operations room, but were received with denial and frustration. In some cases, officers explained away troop injuries caused by Indian attacks as injuries from ricocheting bullets fired by Pakistani troops![17] While his staff collected information on the military situation from officers at different posts, FCNA commander Javed Hasan, the operations point-man within the Kargil clique, often opted to ignore worrying reports. Initially, he was hesitant to send troop reinforcements when requested by the COs occupying posts.[18] It was not until mid-June that troop reinforcements and ammunition replenishments were arranged.[19]

Even as adversity struck, with military pressure mounting on Pakistani troops, the commander FCNA lost his nerve. Although he knew it was not a hopeful position, he tried to paint rosy picture." In a meeting Hasan implored the others, "*Allah kay wasta mujheay ma'af kar do. Bohat ghalti ho ga'ee. Ab dua'aon* [20]*ka waqt hain.*" (For God's sake, forgive me. I have made a big mistake. Now is the time for prayers).[21]

To illustrate the faulty information flow, caused by individual fears and professional incompetence, a key staff officer at the FCNA headquarters recalled: "On June 4 around 3am, a brigade major of artillery called me and said we have lost Tololing. The brigade major had also been informed that Indian troops had mounted a counterattack and our troops had asked for on-site fire. However from the Ops room I contacted CO of 4NLI who assured me everything was OK. However by the morning the CO 4NLI informed Commander FCNA's staff officer that the Tololing post had been lost. But the staff officer forgot to inform the Commander! Meanwhile I asked CO 6NLI if Tololing post had been lost and he confirmed. Subsequently Commander FCNA Javed Hasan called the Brigade Commander Masood Aslam who also confirmed that the post at Tololing had been lost but CO NLI6 continued to deny for at least three days, the loss of the post..."[22]

In fact, it took about 10 days for the FCNA headquarters to convey to the 10 Corps headquarters the news of the fall of the first post at Tololing. The Indians had completely evicted Pakistani troops from the post. Following the fall of this first post, the commander FCNA also decided to sack Lt Col Mansoor Ahmad Tariq CO of NLI 6. The CO, who had been all along been critical of Op KP, had decided to withdraw troops from the Tololing post after the Indians had launched an air, artillery, and land attack on the post. Lt. Col Saleem Mahmud Khan was appointed the new CO of NLI6. Troubles for the Pakistani troops had mounted also because, contrary to Pakistan's expectation that engagement with Indian troops would begin in mid-June, it had begun approximately six weeks earlier, around 5 May. Early opening of the Zojila pass was critical. Normally it would open late summer but in 1999 it opened end-April-early May, facilitating early return of the Indian Army. This early engagement was contrary to Op KP planners' calculation that replenishment of ammunition and ration would be required by mid-June, when it would be managed through the Burzil Pass. However with engagement having started much earlier, and the Burzil Pass still not opened until mid-June, movement of artillery in the forward lines and supply lines replenishment became very difficult.[23] For example, at the 15000 feet high Tashfeen post, the small weapons with the troops had carbonized and could not be used.[24]

The Kargil clique did not share these early military difficulties with the prime minister and his team. The defense secretary, however, had by early June become wary of the military situation. He was being alerted by the battlefield accounts trickling in through junior army officers and by Indian Zee TV reports. By mid-June, it appeared that Pakistani troops were losing hold over several posts in the Batalik sector, at Points 5120 and 5203 in the area of Jabbar complex, plus posts in the Drass sector at 3 Pimple. The Defense Secretary shared this disturbing information with the prime minister's kitchen cabinet. The prime minister too depended on his Defense Secretary for regular updates. For example, barely hours after Sharif had ended the 12 June meeting on Kargil, he was again on the phone with his Defense Secretary. The PM wanted him to check with the army chief if a critical peak on Tololing had fallen. Iftikhar called the DGMO who assured him that Pakistani forces had merely carried out "readjustments in the area." The skeptical Iftikhar informed the PM that Tololing seems to have fallen but the army is not accepting it; instead, it is coining new terms. This misleading flow of information from the Operations room in Skardu confused the ground situation for the prime minister, his cabinet, and the generals.

In Delhi, by contrast, Sartaj Aziz's counterpart had a clear picture of the ground situation. Accordingly, Jaswant Singh's confidence in his meeting with Aziz told the tale of Delhi's growing confidence on the military front complemented by its astute diplomatic strategy. India's growing confidence in being able to resolve Kargil on its own terms was largely derived from the international community's support to the Indian position. Delhi's confidence was distinctly evident in its handling of the Pakistani foreign minister's visit to Delhi. Accordingly in their 12 June meetings with Minister Sartaj Aziz the Indian prime minister and the foreign minister categorically stated that the only one-point formula for resolving Kargil was that "Pakistan vacate Indian territory." [25] The fate of the Pakistan foreign minister's 8-hour Delhi trip was sealed even before the talks began.[26] The body language of the Indian reception team conveyed the tone and tenor of the remaining trip. The Indian foreign minister accompanied by MEA officials and the Indian High Commissioner in Islamabad G. Parthasarthy were present on the airport to receive their unwanted guest from Pakistan.

The 'Shock' Revelation

Waiting inside the airport lounge was the highly disturbed Press Counsellor of the Pakistan High Commission. He was armed with at least half a dozen leading dailies with bold headlines about the situation. The banner headlines were quotes from a telephone conversation between Pakistan's Army chief General Pervez Musharraf, who was visiting Beijing, and the Chief of General Staff (CGS) Lt. General Aziz Khan[27] – a conversation between two leading members of the Kargil clique. The Indian foreign minister, on the eve of Sartaj Aziz's arrival, had held a press conference to release the transcript of this conversation. Their discussion about Op KP was a huge self-indictment. It set the stage for the almost four-hour-long critical Sartaj Aziz visit.[28] The Pakistan Army chief's master-stroke in recklessness, of holding a highly sensitive conversation with his CGS over an open line, made it easy for any interested agency to record the conversation. Most likely recorded by the CIA and shared with the Indians, this conversation publicly affirmed the central role of Pakistan's top army command in the Kargil Op.[29]

Aziz arrived to a hostile Indian environment. His counterpart barely shook hands with him while, earlier in the day, his High Commission in Delhi had been nearly attacked by protestors. The foreign minister was completely stumped. He could only question the veracity of the newspaper reports.[30] Completely baffled, the accompanying Pakistani journalists wondered if it was an Indian ruse to put Pakistan on the defensive. The publication of the Musharraf-Aziz conversation, meanwhile, irrefutably vindicated India's position that Pakistan was involved in the Op KP- a fact that Pakistan had continued to deny. Significantly, the tapes also strengthened the prevailing perception, especially among the Indians, that Pakistan's prime minister did not directly contribute towards the planning and execution of the Kargil conflict and that he had been excluded from the Kargil mischief.

After the first reports of the Kargil Op surfaced, the Indian defense minister and others in the Vajpayee cabinet had believed that the Pakistani prime minister did not know of the Kargil Operation.[31] The Musharraf-Aziz conversation established that the army chief was waiting to see how not only would Delhi react to the Operation but also how Pakistan's elected prime minister would react, and "how would the whole thing really blow up."[32]

Nevertheless the tapes fiasco caused great embarrassment to the visiting foreign minister whose army too was now feeling the heat from the Bofors guns. Sartaj who had already expressed strong reservations against Op KP at the 17 May briefing knew he had landed in Delhi with a weak negotiating position.

Word-Play & Polemics in Delhi

The trip also became the occasion for intense Pakistan-India polemics between the Indian prime minister and the two foreign ministers. Pakistan's foreign minister vigorously defended his government's historically correct but presently flawed position.[33] To Delhi, he carried the categorical position that Pakistan would not unconditionally withdraw from Kargil. However, after his meetings with the Indian prime minister and foreign minister, he was to carry back the equally unambiguous message that India would be unrelenting in the pursuit of its one-point demand that Pakistan must unconditionally vacate the Kargil heights.

Upon arrival in Delhi, the Pakistani foreign minister told his hosts that the three objectives of his visit were "to narrow the gap in perceptions, to determine how to defuse the situation, and determine how to proceed with the dialogue process in accordance with the understanding reached in Lahore to address all issues including Kashmir."[34] The Indians rejected Sartaj's position that violations of the LOC did not begin with the Kargil crisis, that the causal trajectory of Kargil included the unresolved Kashmir problem, the military activity by both armies after the snows melted in an attempt to gain strategic positions along the LOC where there were problems on the ground since the "demarcation pillars were at some distance from each other."[35]

In both his meetings, Sartaj pointed out that India and not Pakistan was the principle violator of the Simla Accord and in fact was in possession of territory on the Pakistani side of the LOC.[36] Significantly, neither the Indian prime minister nor his foreign minister refuted the list of Indian violations. Vajpayee's response was that India was building alternate routes to the Leh-Srinagar highway, which was vulnerable to Pakistani interdiction. Jaswant simply stated that "Pakistan should have raised its objections when the violations occurred."[37] Responding to Sartaj's constant refrain that Pakistan could not overlook violations by India since 1972, Jaswant said "that question could follow later."[38]

The Indian strategy was to treat Pakistan's Kargil operation as a stand-alone problem by isolating it from Kashmir, Siachen, and the post-1972 violations of the LOC. India vehemently pushed this strategy through the Sartaj meetings as the latter sought to locate Kargil within the broader context of the Kashmir crisis. Forcing focus only on Kargil, Jaswant argued that since Simla the LOC running in the Kargil sector was never disputed. He brusquely brushed aside Sartaj's effort at linkage as merely "specious arguments"[39] and as part of Pakistan's attempt to "seek an ex-post ipso facto justification for its Kargil occupation."[40]

The Indian PM also contested Sartaj's position that Kargil fitted in the usual pattern of LOC violations and that India had merely overreacted. "Never before has such an intrusion taken place. You are sitting in our house and killing our people"[41] the distraught Indian prime minister had argued. India's massive violation of the uninhabited Siachen glacier was a decade and a half earlier and so Vajpayee's factually incorrect position could not be politically or diplomatically called into question. The world had no memory for past events if the victims did not care to recall them or, even worse, not condemn them when they occurred.

India out-right rejected Sartaj's proposal that "the right atmosphere to solve the issue must be created" which must include no firing of cross-LOC artillery by India and withholding its air force operations in the Kargil sector." Vajpayee was clear that "the right kind of atmosphere" could only be created" if Pakistan upheld "the sanctity" of the LOC and called back its people. He asked for Pakistan to take the first steps and withdraw from the Kargil sector, since "we are not sitting in your territory nor are we supporting infiltrators."[42] Shooting down Sartaj's proposal for more talks, Vajpayee wondered, "Where was the scope for more talks."[43]

Even Sartaj's hard talk was like water off a duck's back. There were no takers. His attempt to push for shared responsibility, by advocating that "both sides should initiate gradual steps in order to defuse the situation", fell on deaf ears. Alluding to India's demand that Kargil is unilaterally vacated, Sartaj cautioned, "India should not make demands which could not be accepted." He also categorically stated, "It would be difficult to proceed without looking at the sequence of events since 1972." Aziz tried to impress upon his hosts the Pakistani prime minister's peaceful intentions by claiming that "within Pakistan there were strong lobbies against any compromise with India," which even opposed his Delhi trip. However, the Indian position remained unwavering.

India rejected Pakistan's suggestion that after India de-escalates, Jaswant Singh would visit Pakistan to find a "diplomatic solution" to Kargil. Sartaj was told that, only if Pakistan accepted the Indian position that Pakistan vacate Kargil, would Singh visit Pakistan. Sartaj's reiteration of Islamabad's position that the Kashmiris fighting in Kargil were not in Pakistan's control, met with stern rebuttals. Vajpayee maintained they could not have come without Pakistan's blessing and active support and pointedly queried, "Have these people come without your control?" He added, "No one is in any doubt that the LOC in Kargil had been violated by Pakistan Army regulars and infiltrators."[44] Singh asked Aziz to convey to his government that unless the status quo ante was restored in Kargil no bilateral discussions could take place.

When Aziz emphasized Pakistan's commitment to the Lahore process, an agitated Vajpayee wondered why Pakistan "had chosen to alter the situation after Lahore." Vajpayee lamented his inability to counter the domestic charge that while in Lahore he remained unaware of the Kargil situation. He bluntly told the Pakistani prime minister's emissary that the planners of Kargil did not favor the Lahore process. Singh said Pakistan's Kargil operation disrupted the Lahore process which had embodied India's commitment to the principle of peaceful settlement of disputes. He complained that the ink had not dried on the Lahore Declaration and the Pakistani establishment had started making preparations for the Kargil incursions. India, he said had felt "betrayed and disappointed" by this.[45]

Contesting the Pakistani foreign minister's assertion that Kargil was part of the unresolved Kashmir issue, Vajpayee said the Kargil issue was "the result of a well-thought out plan." For the Kashmir issue, he argued, India had already agreed to go to the negotiating table. Meanwhile, Jaswant

Singh insisted that Pakistan could not use the dialogue to give legitimacy to the Kargil intrusion and neither could it be reduced to "your listing our faults and my listing your faults." Knocking out Sartaj Aziz's insistence that expert-level talks must first take place to decide ways to de-escalate tensions, he insisted that first "there has to be an immediate decision to set right a wrong, mechanisms could be worked out later." The Indian message was, "The only one issue was Pakistan's aggression and that could be rectified either physically by India or voluntarily by Pakistan."[46]

Threats and counter-threats also flew across the room during the meeting between the foreign ministers. Jaswant Singh urged Pakistan to end its "aggression" or India would "have the area cleared at all costs." Without enlarging the theatre of conflict, he said, India would "employ all means to clear the aggression that was planned, engineered and launched by the Pakistan Army in the guise of infiltrators."[47] Aziz insisted that Kargil was part of a larger problem and that Pakistan was "capable of an appropriate response in case India felt that the military option was the only solution."[48] Vajpayee's message to his Pakistani counterpart was direct and simple. Kargil was an "attack"; it was not a part of the unresolved Kashmir issue, as the Pakistani foreign minister was arguing. Kargil was a "separate issue, a thought-out plan." and Nawaz Sharif, Vajpayee advised "must take a courageous step otherwise the situation will deteriorate." [49]

The Sartaj Aziz visit was a grand failure. He had made a herculean effort to marshal all possible arguments to support his government's position that India unconditionally open dialogue with Pakistan or at least de-escalate on the military front in Kargil. The two sides had locked horns with no give from either. Both stuck to their negotiating positions. It produced no common ground thereby signalling continued military standoff between the two nuclear neighbors. The threat of a nuclear war emanating from South Asia hung like the sword of Damocles over the world. The global community, mindful of the history of acute hostility between the two neighbors, would not allow this. Only recently had the world marked South Asia as an emerging region of peace and progress. The USA had already welcomed the emerging thaw between India and Pakistan after their nuclear tests. But the Kargil conflict had put the entire peace process in reverse gear. It was therefore to be a matter of time that alignment of forces would terminate the standoff.

And it was now becoming only too obvious in whose favor the stand-off would be terminated.

Chapter 9

MYTH-MAKING AND CRISIS MANAGEMENT

Pakistan was now confronted with mounting challenges. In the world's highest battle-theatre, the Indians rolled in troops, logistics, artillery, and the prized Bofor guns. The men in Delhi's South Block relentlessly sought diplomatic support from the major global powers to evict Pakistan from the Kargil heights. With India gathering its full throttle military response to Op KP, its confident Indian prime minister and Indian foreign minister had conveyed a categorical negative to Pakistan's visiting Foreign Minister: No dialogue with Pakistan would be resumed unless Pakistan withdrew its troops. Their 12 June meeting with Sartaj Aziz, Jaswant Singh had emphasized, was not part of any dialogue but was limited to asking Pakistan to end "aggression."[1] The Vajpayee government was determined to dislodge, at all costs, the Pakistani troops perched on the Kargil heights. The strategic tackiness of Op KP was now taking its toll. Instead of providing, as envisaged by its planners, negotiating leverage for Pakistan, this linearly planned Op was turning into a liability for the Sharif government. At home, anxious cabinet members whispered that the Op must end. Abroad, friends and foes alike, were seeking Pakistan's exit from Kargil. A moment of some despair had set in - even for the hitherto euphoric Kargil clique.

Notably, until 12 June, the prime minister and his team, despite reservations, had gone along with the army's game plan: India's military vulnerability in the Leh and Siachen area after the Kargil operation would be used to pressurize India to enter into serious negotiations to settle the Kashmir dispute. Or at the very least India could be forced to vacate Siachen, which it had occupied in violation of the Simla Agreement.[2] Accordingly, Pakistan adopted the diplomatic and political positions that the Kargil planners had intended: These are not Pakistani troops, but freedom fighters; the LOC is not well-defined[3], we need to sit down and define it better; our troops are on our side of the LOC; the international community must encourage the Indians to resolve the Kashmir dispute; if the Indians agree on dialogue, we can 'influence' the freedom fighters to vacate Kargil. Interestingly the army and the civilian projections of Kargil were often contradictory. This represented more confusion than difference. Yet the army in its background briefings to the press sought to justify Kargil against the backdrop of India's 1984 occupation of Siachen. It expected the international community to be more accepting on Kargil since India too had earlier violated the LOC and occupied an entire glacier with no reaction from the international community.[4]

Pakistan's disjointed ways precluded the possibility of even convincing the international community of the vagueness of the LOC. This vagueness was even acknowledged by the Indian Minister of Defense in a subsequent interview[5] with the author. In a candid recall of the Kargil crisis, the Minister explained, "No one has been able to fix responsibility. There are various theories. I have always believed that, when the line was drawn on a meter-long map, no place was identified on the ground. Each side took the map home, so it was a line which was for the greater part held on the basis of perceptions by both sides, rather than proper delineation on the ground. And otherwise India would have had its defense. After all, if Siachen is defended on both sides, which is more difficult, then the LOC would have been defended - or at least patrolled. So what was happening was that for a brief period in the summer time both sides sat on the perceived LOC and had a dialogue going between the two sides, exchanging cigarettes, etc. And come winter both sides went into the posts up in the mountains and that went on for 25 years between 1972 and 1999."[6] Then, referring to Pakistan's Kargil operation, he said, "And then one day someone decided to cheat against the ground rules." When reminded that India was the first to cheat in conducting Operation Meghdoot to occupy Siachen, George Fernandez laughed and said, "I cannot contradict you." [7]

The world capitals were however following a different trajectory. Pakistan was not successful in acquiring any diplomatic support, not even from its key allies. Sartaj Aziz's June 11 'SOS trip' to Beijing did not produce the expected support for Pakistan's action in Kargil. Instead, Beijing opposed to military action pointedly told the foreign minister not to make Kashmir a "shooting claim."[8] The Chinese categorically told Pakistan that the dispute had to be resolved bilaterally and that Pakistan must vacate Kargil. The Chinese leadership also conveyed to Pakistan that the Chinese had "no influence over India."[9]

Sino-Indian relations were then on the mend. Beijing clearly did not want to support Pakistan's crossing of the LOC and cause a setback to its relations with India.[10] In fact, on the eve of the Pakistani foreign minister's visit the Chinese had publicly conveyed their 'neutral' position on Kargil and their interest in improving relations with India. On the Kargil issue the Chinese position was that "the matter maybe discussed between Chinese foreign minister Tang Jiaxuan and the foreign ministers of India and Pakistan."[11] And regarding the June 14 trip of the Indian foreign minister the Chinese maintained, "We are confident that, through the joint efforts of the two sides, relations between China and India will constantly improve and develop."[12] Upon his return to Islamabad the Pakistan foreign minister's arrival statement stated that two foreign ministers discussed "the need to de-escalate the dangerous situation that has developed along the LOC in Jammu and Kashmir" and both agreed "on the need for a peaceful settlement of the Jammu and Kashmir dispute."[13]

In Delhi, Sartaj Aziz had found no diplomatic opening for dialogue. An unrelenting India, combined with growing international pressure to "uphold the sanctity of the LOC", had begun to unnerve Islamabad. By now the European positions matched that of India and the US. For example, in early June, the Secretary General of the French foreign office.

Mounier Heineken, summoned the Pakistani ambassador to a meeting in which he was polite but firm. He maintained the French reading of Kargil was based on independent French sources and French intelligence from the region. Heinikin said that the status quo disturbed by Pakistan could lead to war. France, he said, "did not believe Pakistan's version that the people gone to war are the Mujahideen." The French maintained that given the strategic knowledge of the area of the men who occupied Kargil and given how they were armed and trained was evidence of the direct involvement by the Pakistan government and the army. Pakistan having upset the status quo was now responsible for reversing it. In case Islamabad failed to do so, Paris threatened to openly declare Pakistan the aggressor.[14]

Washington, too, was making no concessions, accepting no false steps. Washington refused to accept Pakistan's position that it was not involved in Kargil, especially after the Pakistani military had accepted that Pakistani troops were fighting in Kargil. In early June, on a Saturday, the Pakistani foreign minister handed a letter to the US Ambassador for Secretary of State Madeleine Albright from Prime Minister Nawaz Sharif. Milam refused to accept the letter, complaining that it was not a serious communication as it claimed that Pakistan was not involved in Kargil. Subsequently, by that evening, the foreign minister called in the United States Ambassador again and handed him a different letter.[15]

Meanwhile, at home, the fallout of the pressures from Op KP included growing tensions and apparent divergences within the civil and military policy-makers and also between the three armed forces chiefs. Twenty-four hours after Foreign Minister Aziz's unsuccessful Delhi visit, two important meetings were convened. These divergences were underscored at the 12 June meeting called by the army Chief at the Joint Staff Headquarters Rawalpindi and at the 13 June Lahore meeting convened by the prime minister at the Governor's House, Lahore.

"Two Cyclists Flashed Victory"

This meeting, called on short notice, was held at the Joint Staff Headquarters. It was attended by twenty-five to thirty army, air force, and navy officers. The army chief announced at the meeting that two messages from air force centers in Delhi had been intercepted being sent, respectively, to the headquarters at Udhampur (near Jammu) and Bathinda (in Indian Punjab, near Bahawalnagar). The message to the command at the Udhampur base was that it should prepare to use all weapons under its command. Likewise, the message to Bathinda was to carry out air defense of the area. The mood in the room was grim. The participants focused on reading the implication of these intercepts; the army chief was convinced the messages indicated "something big is coming up." The consensus was that the Indians had marked Udhampur base for carrying out air operations in Kargil. Bathinda was given a precautionary message in case air strikes across the international border were required. A worried Musharraf suggested they go and brief the PM, who was in Lahore. It was decided to leave the following day, by when the foreign minister would have returned from Delhi. Musharraf called the PM and conveyed him their decision to come. Meanwhile, the foreign minister upon his return from Delhi was driven straight from the Chaklala airport to the venue of the meeting, the Joint Staff headquarters. He briefed the participants on the outcome of his meeting. Aziz stayed briefly and his bottom line was that he was not welcomed in New Delhi. The meeting carried on with the discussion focusing on whether India would actually start a war along the international border.

Finally, on the army chief's suggestion, the Secretary of Defense, Lt. General Iftikhar Ali Khan, made the closing remarks at the meeting. Iftikhar questioned whether in Pakistan's current economic situation Pakistan go to war and face the consequences. , He quoted the well-known saying that the armed forces fight a battle, but it is the nation that goes to war. In Pakistan's case, the nation was "certainly not prepared." The army chief claimed that many countries, like Saudi Arabia and the UAE, were willing to give money to Pakistan. He was reminded that this would not be possible without US clearance. The meeting concluded around midnight. In their fierce fight-back, the Indians were now taking military, diplomatic and political action. Concern replaced the earlier hype in the Pakistani military camp.

The army chief was equally confident regarding national morale. At the JS Headquarters he insisted, "This nation can be prepared for war in no time. I will tell you that when I was coming from the army house to the JS headquarters that two cyclists flashed victory signs at me. I will request the PM to address two houses of the parliament so I can give points to the parliamentarians and they will spread it in the country side."[16] Such simplistic talk would enter policy-making discussions in the absence of institutionalized decision-making. The simplistic thinking of powerfully placed individuals would raise the probability of flawed decision-making.

Against Pakistan's Security

The June 13 "restricted high level meeting" called by the prime minister was held at the Governor's House in Lahore. All DCC members, including the three services chiefs, attended the meeting. Interestingly traveling in the same aircraft to Lahore, the naval and air chiefs, accompanied by the Defense Secretary, decided to tell the PM "the entire truth". The PM, they believed, was still being misled that Pakistan was doing well, and that the Indians would not escalate and go to war. They were also concerned that the PM fully comprehended the risks involved in the situation.

With the prime minister in the chair, Aziz briefed the participants on his Delhi visit. A candid discussion followed in which differences among the service chiefs surfaced. The naval and air force chiefs criticized the operation and argued that it would compromise Pakistan's overall security. The naval chief maintained that a naval blockade by India could not be ruled out, a position that the army chief contested. Similarly, the air chief opposed the army's advice that air power should be inducted. The army was seeking deployment of air power[17] to not only curtail the damage inflicted on Pakistani troops from the Indian use of heavy artillery and hundreds of air sorties but also to inflict damage on the Indian troops locked up in tight, unprotected spaces." The army ruled out a "full spectrum war" with India and argued that in a limited engagement like

Kargil the Pakistan air force "would not be at a disadvantage."[18] The air chief nevertheless opposed induction of air power, arguing that deploying air power could mean placing squadrons in Azad Kashmir and leaving Lahore and Karachi unprotected. Already, the air force had deployed extra radars in the North to observe Indian aircraft movement.

The thrust of the army's presentation and interventions was that the army could handle the military situation, including war,[19] should such an unlikely development take place.[20] The naval chief, who was especially critical of the Operation, had pointedly asked, "What is the objective of the war and what is Pakistan fighting for?" Fear of an all-our war was also expressed by various participants. Differences over the Kargil Operation were now being openly voiced in the cabinet meetings as well. The ISI chief, who had privately been critical of the operation, had taken a "military army line" during a mid-June cabinet meeting.[21] This prompted the Secretary Defense Iftikhar Ali Khan to raise specific questions regarding the viability of Operation KP. Cabinet Minister Gohar Ayub Khan wondered how the army's views and those of General Iftikhar were at a tangent. At the same meeting, Chaudhry Nisar also asked who had ordered this operation. His thrust was that Pakistan was heading for a disaster in Kargil.[22]

He knew that the news from the battle-zone was not encouraging.

India's Sledge & Hammer

By mid June, India's counter-offensive military plan was in full play. It was comprehensive, yet simple. The air power, raining bombs and shells, psychologically hit the soldiers perched on mountaintops in Kargil-Drass.[23] While air sorties rarely hit soldiers, often hiding in the crevices of mountain ridges or behind boulders, the deafening thunder of pounding shells and bombs and the continuous echoing of their ricocheting sound proved debilitating for the already exhausted soldiers. Artillery was used for targeted attacks. 100 to 120 guns were at times fired in concert. Direct shooting, particularly by the Bofors guns, spread terror amongst the defenders and had a devastating effect in the destruction of enemy bunkers.[24] Its maximum range of 30 kilometers enabled deep strikes on the enemy's gun positions, administrative installations, ammunition dumps, and headquarters, besides neutralizing forward positions held by the intruders. Infantry then followed. Once the Indians were assured of no presence of people at the posts, they would move to occupy the post. The odd Pakistani soldier from among the retreating troops, hidden behind a boulder or around a ridge, would fire upon the approaching Indian troops, at best temporarily halting the Indian advance.[25] Aerial reconnaissance, intel flow, and even possession of Pakistani maps showing Pakistan's deployments, were captured from the fallen post at Tololing.[26]

Posts to Powder

By 10 June, the Indian Artillery regiment had amassed a large number of fire units in extremely difficult terrain. On the military front, this Indian artillery fire turned the tables on Pakistan. The Indian Army lined up the Bofors guns on the NH-1, from where they directly and incessantly hit the Pakistani posts. They succeeded in reducing the posts to "powder"[27] using short and long-range weapons.

Op KP was facing sharp military reversals and singularly on account of accurate and timely delivery of TNT. The Gunners' fire assaults became the principle battle-winning factor.

The intensity of artillery fire devastated both men and mountains. By June 10, India's infantry had the solid backing it had lacked during May and early June. India's point man on the ground Lieutenant General S. Padmanabhan, GOC in C Southern Command and army chief designate, acknowledged that in Operation Vijay that the "Devastation caused by extremely accurate and timely fire assaults in most difficult and inhospitable terrain greatly facilitated the capture of key objectives..."[28]

What were the Indians attacking? In what shape was the 'enemy' that the Indians were drubbing with incessant TNT? Not what the Indian writers claim. They were weather-beaten, very short on rations, facing high casualties, and with almost depleted ammunition and guns that, because of no maintenance, had been reduced to "sticks."[29] A shooter who volunteered to join Op KP actually set about cleaning the guns of his platoon because they would stop working after firing of only one or two rounds. [30]

But the Indians, after hitting on the winning formula of the using the Bofors to reduce to "powder" the bases held by the Pakistanis, were in high morale. "Firing over a hundred guns on a restricted target was like were indeed cracking a nut with a sledgehammer,"[31] as the Indians themselves acknowledged. Following the high Indian casualties when their infantry troops had blindly and tentatively attempted to scale the Kargil-Drass mountains, in June they deliberately opted to use the "sledgehammer" approach "to save valuable lives of one's troops while making the enemy cry out 'Uncle'."[32] The preponderance of firepower now defined the continuing battle in the world's highest war theatre. The Indian "sledgehammer" tactics, literally raining fire onto the exhausted yet still motivated Pakistanis soldiers, worked for the Indians. It incapacitated and killed the troops, already short in numbers, and disrupted supplies, ammunition, and logistics.

June Reversals

After making serious attempts on 3 June to retake the Tololing peak in Drass, Indian troops captured it on June 13. Several important heights in the Batalik sector were captured on 20 and 21 June; on June 23 several heights were captured around point 5203 and on June 30 strategic peaks closer to Tiger Hills.[33] The strategic Tiger Hill came under severe artillery attack. Around June 21, the Operation hit its lowest ebb for Pakistan, when the Indian troops, through fierce, ground, artillery and air attacks, recaptured Tololing complex. After Tololing fell, reports of Indian recapture flowed in daily as the Pakistani-held posts fell like ninepins. [34] The pressure was still on the Indians, given the scale of intrusion by the Pakistani troops.[35]The Indian Army chief himself conceded, "No time-frame could be fixed for vacating the incursions."[36]

The Missing Mujahideen

Significantly, the Mujahideen factor lagged behind at this critical juncture. The mainstay of Pakistan's military strategy, since 1996-1997, was that through guerrilla-type ambushes targeting Indian troops in Indian Held Kashmir, with full artillery support, bridges will be blown up, tracks uprooted, soldiers attacked, to prevent large scale offensive-induction of Indian troops. Yet, keeping the Operation secret from the ISI meant that by the Pakistan Army's own strategic calculations the pivot of such an operation, the Mujahideeen factor, men of the Kashmir Freedom struggle were left out of the calculus. The Kargil planners informed ISI after the Operation was underway, asking for upgrading the struggle in support of the Operation KP. "Too short a notice, we need at least one year to upgrade the movement," was the ISI response. ISI needed presence inside the war zone to plan and execute. Neither was possible.

Logistics

By mid-June, men on the FDL posts required backups. There was a shortage of ammunition and supplies and troops were increasingly suffering from the pressures of a logistical stretch. But with Pakistan's supply lines and the forward posts under attack from Indian artillery-fire and air sorties it was difficult to replenish depleting ammunition and rations, especially for the Forward Defense Lines (FDL) posts. As the snow melted and the Burzil pass opened, mule porters could ferry supplies only till the logistics bases. Base HQ was unable to respond timely to repeated logistics requests from FDLs on Tiger Hill and from other sectors.[37] At several posts, there was food shortage. At others, water too was not easily accessible for miles. In places where there was water, intensely heavy use of artillery had made it undrinkable. Ammunition too was fast depleting. Even the inadequate artillery was rendered ineffective because of wet, freezing weather conditions. Guns with sulphur deposits would stop firing after a thousand rounds. Yet maintenance of artillery in the freezing zones was not always possible.

The soldiers had fought and sustained the Operation against heavy odds. There was no major spike in troop induction. Troop count had only slightly grown with 6 NLIs[38], Brigade 80, and 62 Brigade in the war theatre. As to how long could they hold on to their posts, the odds were heavily against them: terrible weather conditions, low supplies, no reinforcements, and positioned in posts confronted by major Indian numerical superiority in infantry and artillery.

Weapons & Communication

The Pakistani troops were equipped with standard infantry rifles. Typically, in a platoon, jawans had G-3 rifles, officers AK-47 rifles, and rocket launchers, and light machine Guns (LMGs) holder. Air defense units with Hatf battlefield range missiles and restored Stinger missiles were also positioned in several locations. Soldiers from the signals corps managed communications within the Ops area and with the brigade and battalion headquarters. They moved from post to post to keep the communication going using double TT and laying and protecting regular lines and managing the radio wireless communication in the Ops area. Wireless communication that could also help the troops listen in to Indian troop communication through frequency scanning and surfing was rightly dubbed 'shikari det.'

Volunteers & Valor

By mid June, when news spread that there were high casualties, over one hundred officers arrived in FCNA Rear near Rawalpindi and in the FCNA headquarters in Gilgit and volunteered to fight. Many who came without permission from their unit commands were sent back. Those who went forward arrived under India's ferocious artillery fire. Deeds of soldiers' valor and passion surfaced even in this increasingly difficult environment.

For example, one volunteer who arrived at the NLI center took three days to arrive on June 18 at Tashfeen post in the Drass sector. The major recalls, "I arrived at Tashfeen with my commander, also a volunteer from

GHQ. As I set about cleaning and setting the weapons there, I was ordered to reinforce a nearby Observation post .5140 at 16000 feet. For almost four days there was intense and continuous enemy fire leaving behind high casualties."[39] In another example, around 20 June Major Wahab, a volunteer from the intelligence wing in the Wah cantonment, was sent from Gilgit to the Drass sector to join NLI 6 at the Iqbal Post (behind Tashfeen). Soon the post came under heavy enemy attack, leaving Wahab severely injured. Wahab ordered the survivors to withdraw and demanded they fix an LMG such "that I can fire at the approaching enemy." Wahab fell to Indian firing and so did the post.

Even when the odd volunteer got prior warning of what awaited him beyond the LOC in the FDLs, he still marched ahead. The head of logistics at the FCNA HQ, a Lt Colonel rank Assistant Quartermaster General, advised a volunteering officer against going. "Where are you going? I have to send ration and ammunition inside and I haven't sent anything, because what we are sending isn't getting there." Undaunted, the officer joined the Operation.

Despite the Indian onslaught, the Pakistani soldiers, jawans and officers alike, fought on. For these men of discipline, courage, and conviction, it was a time of reckoning. Surrounded by the stark and stony mountains and targeted by Indian artillery, many among them were dealing with contesting compulsions. Many unsung heroes opted to fight back instead of vacating their posts under enemy fire.[40] At Tafsheen post, a major hit by continuous waves of Indian artillery, refused to be evacuated. As his troops moved to a nearby post the injured major stayed back with a loaded rifle firing at the approaching Indians. He was soon martyred. Others, like Captain Karnal Sher Khan, had the determination to 'go all out' against the enemy. Carrying an LMG, Sher dashed alone into the Indian camp. killing several soldiers before embracing shahadat. Many were confronted with tough dilemmas of whether, as lone survivors, to vacate the post or to fight on; to retreat when faced with an Indian artillery onslaught; young commanding officers had to decide whether to abandon the mortally injured on a post or to lug him while risking the lives of others.

Feats of the courageous and the resolute were plenty, even as Indians overran posts. Individuals resisted orders from Headquarters to vacate posts, preferring often to sit behind boulders battling till the end. Retreat for many, was no less than a stigma. These fighting men, having sworn on oath, in the hallowed halls of the Kakul academy and Cadet Colleges, to defend their country at all costs, now atop the 15000-16000ft steep and rugged peaks, were honouring their oath. Even as the miscarriage of Op KP was upon them, the soldiers held on to discipline. But the tables had turned. Only weeks ago, with adrenalin flowing, these daredevils had marched to high command's orders and no less to their own resolve to punish the enemy. Now it was trouble-time. The Kargil clique's calculation of a luke-warm Indian response was proving wrong.

"No…Not Ours"

There were other painful offshoots that Pakistan's policy of denying that Pakistani troops were conducting the Operations meant. Bodies of Pakistani soldiers could not be accepted. From mid-June onwards, Pakistan's Deputy Chief of Mission Jalil Abbas Jillani, whenever asked by his hosts to collect the bodies of Pakistani soldiers, would decline, saying these were not our boys. Resentfully, the Pakistani soldiers would watch the televised Muslim burial of the disowned bodies of their martyred comrades, conducted by the Indians with full honours and bodies wrapped in a Pakistani flag. According to a Brigadier who was witness to all this, "For many of us, the shame and the pain of watching all this happen to our colleagues, was killing."[41]

Clique in Anxiety

Overall, by mid-June, the tables had turned on Pakistan's military fortunes. Pakistani commanders panicked as the posts began falling. The 10 Corps commander lost his balance, became short-tempered, and started throwing around his files as soon as tension mounted, and news of losses started flowing in.[42] His NLI commander Javed Hasan, the man on the ground, appeared confident. His repeated assurances to the dejected commander that reinforcements would work, betrayed his attitude that "nothing was at stake." In a bid to manage growing military pressure, but in a reactive mode, the Commander FCNA moved to change the entire

NLI command and the COs of all the NLIs were removed. The CGS General Aziz, the leading general incharge of the entire army's deployment and also the one who had surreptitiously provided troops for Op KP, now sat in in the Corps HQ firing off instructions for additional troop deployments for the war battle zone. Regular review discussions among the inner circle would take place at the 10 Corps Ops room. Literally minute-by-minute news of the battlefront setbacks was passed to the commanders.[43]

The officers who staffed the corps HQ staff could foresee the impending disaster. In attendance in all the discussions on the KP Operation were the younger officers, who kept "wondering what are they doing." For some it was clear that it was a blundering deviation from the SOPs of planning and executing operations. The offensive operation had been planned with no defensive approach, no defensive layouts, and hence no fallback plans. Delusional thinking dominated the minds of the clique of Kargil planners who had pulled Pakistan into the belly of the beast. Above all, the grim reality was that their dangerous adventure would brook no failure. None of the young officers was convinced this operation could succeed but their doubts were irrelevant to the operation itself.

These generals planned operation KP, less as intelligent and accountable strategists, but as covert, unaccountable campaigners. Their enthusiasm to go ahead with the Operation, in utter disregard of the crucial contextual factors, was akin to the enthusiasm of the brave young soldiers who fought in the operation. Oblivious of the fatal flaws of in the operation, these soldiers, with a sense of obligation combined with an adventurous spirit and high morale, rushed to participate in Op KP.

The army's brave and promising young men were being sent out but would gain nothing from this misadventure.

Lengthening Shadows

By mid-June, the contours of a difficult political and diplomatic situation had surfaced. Internally the very rationale for the Operation was being questioned. Two services chiefs believed that the Operation could undermine Pakistan's security and the foreign office reports were indicating trouble for Pakistan on the diplomatic front. Also, given Indian insistence on no bilateral dialogue without withdrawal from Kargil and the growing international pressure on Pakistan to vacate Kargil, it seemed increasingly unlikely that Pakistan could leverage its military achievements in Kargil for a "just settlement and time-bound settlement" of the Kashmir dispute.[44]

Additionally, another implicit assumption of the Kargil planners that India may not be willing to pay what it would take to recapture the Kargil heights was bring disproved. India not only deployed the requisite manpower and military force to reclaim Kargil but had also deployed a weapon the Kargil planners had not accounted for: the weapon of diplomacy. The Nawaz Sharif government was therefore clear that flexibility and diplomacy was the way forward if Kargil had to be terminated honourably and on a conciliatory note with India.[45] This contrasted with the "no unilateral withdrawal" position taken by Pakistan's foreign minister less than twenty-four hours earlier in Delhi.[46]

By mid June, the opening assumption of the architects of Operation Koh Paima that the military situation heavily favoring Pakistan was irreversible, was beginning to be proven wrong. With a fierce Indian response, on the military front, combined with a forceful diplomatic campaign to frame Pakistan's Kargil operation as an illegal and highly dangerous act, key individuals of the armed forces including the Defense Secretary felt the pressure. They were apprehensive that the Vajpayee government would take the battle to the international borders. In reality, the Indian leadership's strategy to force the Pakistani retreat through focused military pressure in Kargil, accompanied by cohesive diplomatic efforts, was a sound strategy through which to beat back Pakistan from Kargil.

CONCLUSION

In the closing days of June, the young troops occupying ridges and peaks in the Kargil-Drass area were still not allowing a walk-over to the advancing Indian troops. Overwhelmed by uninterrupted artillery and aerial raids and growing numbers of advancing troops, with height and stealth on their side, Pakistani soldiers still launched artillery attacks on the Indian troops. Casualties mounted on both sides but, with numerical superiority, the aerial factor, and with artillery and logistics heavily skewed in favor of the advancing Indian troops, the brave men who had launched the spectacular Op KP, were now facing a dead end. Often marooned on mountain peaks and ridges, confronted with a three-sided advance of Indian troops, the Pakistani troops fought back bravely. Many died in the line of duty, while some were ordered back or brought back injured. The fate of Op KP now squarely confronted the soldiers who had fervently volunteered to fight for their Homeland. The best and the bravest of Pakistan's soldiers fought on.

The Kargil clique had no plans for them when the enemy struck back so ferociously. Instead, the prime minister would have to do something.

Chapter 10

MAPPING EXITS

It fell onto the shoulders of Pakistan's elected prime minister to map an exit route from Kargil. Three countries figured in the end game. Pakistan was engaged with India, the US, and China. Pakistan's bureaucratic channel had become increasingly wary of Washington's "pro-India" stance and was busy working the Mishra-Naik back channel[1], while the politicians believed the US could deliver a "respectable exit."

What gave Pakistan the space to work on mapping exits was that the massive deployment of force by India did not translate into a quick military turn around. The battlefield terrain had proved a leveller for the heavily asymmetrical assemblage of force. A few hundred soldiers on mountain peaks and ridges were aided by the strategic heights and were still targeting those in huge numbers, artillery, and airpower who were trying to scale those heights. No immediate winner was on the cards. There prevailed instead symmetry in desperation, with both sides keen to end the fight. India's overwhelming deployment of infantry, artillery, and air force was not achieving quick results. For Delhi, the casualties kept mounting.

By now most developments from the war zone had signaled that military victory was out. The Kargil clique's objective of leveraging the Kargil, Drass, and Mushkoh peaks, for extracting concessions from India on Siachen or Kashmir, now seemed a pipe dream. These peaks and ridges, hitherto held by Pakistani troops, were slipping out of Pakistan's control. Yet the government's public posture that the Kashmiri Mujahedeen still controlled these peaks remained unchanged. Behind the scenes, Prime Minister Nawaz Sharif began exploring routes for an 'honorable' exit from Kargil. The army command, although also in the loop on the exploring of exit routes[2], still believed that Pakistan could diplomatically leverage the continuously advantageous ground situation in any negotiations. Throughout June, the prime minister held several meetings to remain updated on the military and diplomatic situation in Kargil.

Working the India Option

Although, since the beginning of the Kargil crisis Nawaz Sharif kept the communication channels open with Vajpayee, he called his counterpart only after the failed Jaswant Singh-Sartaj Aziz meeting on 12 June and assured him that Pakistan wanted a peaceful bilateral settlement. Interestingly, with the Pakistan-India diplomatic channels having nearly been shut down after the collapse of the Singh- 12 June talks, a back channel working was set in motion to arrive at a political settlement. In addition to the diplomatic channels of communication, a back-channel exchange led interestingly by political men in India and by diplomatic men in Pakistan was used for seeking an "honorable exit."

In India, Vajpayee himself was involved in the political back channel, along with his National Security Advisor Brajesh Mishra. The interlocutors were R.K.Misra, India's most experienced hand at backchannel negotiations. In Pakistan, the Prime Minister, aided by his core-team at the foreign office, managed this back-channel. The team included Foreign Secretary Shamshad Ahmad, Additional Secretary PM House Tariq Fatemi, and spokesperson Tariq Altaf. A seasoned diplomat Niaz Naik was Pakistan's point man for the back channel.

There were sceptics too. In fact, Additional Secretary Riaz Mohammad Khan the man who had been key in the preparation for the Lahore Summit, and billed as one of the brightest in the Foreign Office, was blunt with his assessment. When he was shown the possible points of an agreement, he told the core team in the foreign office that there was not much to those points and that "India was buying time" while Pakistan was "clutching at straws."[3]

Nawaz Sharif was looking for an "honorable exit" through this Delhi-Islamabad back channel.

Islamabad and Delhi sought different outcomes. Sharif wanted the announcement of talks on Kashmir, to be followed by the withdrawal, so that he could hold up the fig-leaf of talks as Pakistani troops retreated from Kargil. Vajpayee, meanwhile, had made his position clear: vacate Indian territory and talks would follow. Vajpayee needed a Pakistani retreat to wash away the opposition's allegation that a naïve Vajpayee had misread Pakistan,and that while Pakistan talked friendship in Lahore it was planning a war against India.

Imagined secrecy and hopeful men

Nonetheless, back-channel exchanges took place. On June 18, five days after the Vajpayee-Nawaz conversation, India's most adept 'back-channel' man R.K Misra arrived in Pakistan. He flew in with the MEA Additional Secretary Vivak Katju. Nawaz Sharif and the Pakistani bureaucrats remained optimistic of the back-channel negotiations and were hopeful that they would likely deliver a withdrawal agreement.[4] The progress made at the negotiations made them believe that Delhi and Islamabad could arrive at an "arrangement to conclude an agreement on a road map for ending the hostilities and resumption of the Lahore process."[5] This expectation to some extent influenced Islamabad's diplomatic strategy on Kargil. The making of a diplomatic strategy to derive political advantages from an action which was increasingly seen as an illegal action by friends and foes alike, was a near impossible task. From mid-June onwards, Islamabad's exit route from Kargil was through the back-channel dialogue.

The core team believed this route could deliver provided it was conducted in secrecy and involved top leaderships.[6] Accordingly, two key people in the PM's diplomatic team, the Foreign Minister and Pakistan's High Commissioner in Delhi Ashraf Jahangir Qazi were kept outside the loop. They were not privy to the back-channel moves.[7] The military leadership, though not directly involved in the back-channel negotiations, was aware of it. General Musharraf personally knew of the Naik-Misra negotiations and believed that "it was good that something can be worked out."[8]

The Foreign Office core team also believed, though erroneously, that they were conducting back-channel negotiations in secrecy.[9] They principally feared that Washington was using the Kargil crisis to develop closer ties with Delhi. Hence, they believed that Washington would undermine any other exit route that challenged Washington's position as the main interlocutor in the crisis Kargil crisis. Among Sharif's core team, Washington was seen as championing the Indian case. Contrary to these assumptions, Washington was already aware of the back-channel negotiations. According to the US Ambassador, his Political Secretary at the US Embassy, John Schmidt, was told of the back channel by Niaz Naik around early to mid-June.[10] Subsequently, Milam discussed the back-channel developments in a meeting with Tariq Fatemi. After that meeting, he recalled, "I was glad and I was hopeful about it…I thought it might have been the answer, at least some answer."[11] The Islamabad-based US diplomats had pinned more hopes on bilateral Pak-India bilateral diplomacy than the State Department officials in Washington. When the US Ambassador reported the back-channel developments to Washington, no one there attached any significance to them.[12] Inderfurth and Talbott checked with counterparts at the MEA, who told them there was nothing to it.[13]America's key Indian interlocutors were from the MEA team in Delhi and also the Indian Ambassador in Washington, Naresh Chandara. Neither was involved in in the back-channel dialogue. Hence, Washington was aware "of the conversations but didn't have insight into particulars."[14] Neither did they attribute any importance to all this. Because of the Talbott and Inderfurth inclinations Washington went with the Indian view on the back channel."[15]

Triangular Diplomacy

Meanwhile, with a nearly deadlocked bilateral diplomacy, a triangular diplomatic activity surfaced. Washington occupied a critical space, the US emerging as a key factor on the diplomatic front for both India and Pakistan. India moved robustly on the diplomatic track, seeking

Washington's support to force a unilateral withdrawal of the Pakistani forces. India's External Affairs Minister Jaswant Singh led the diplomatic track.

The post-nuclear Jaswant-Talbot dialogues had proved "enormously helpful during Kargil negotiations."[16]

In Pakistan, the diplomats were increasingly less sanguine about the Washington route for exit. Given Washington's public stance about Pakistan's ingress across the LOC, they merely responded to Washington's queries about the Kargil crisis. In Washington, Ambassador Riaz Khokhar had half a dozen meetings with his Washington-based interlocutors. It was Nawaz Sharif's kitchen cabinet[17] that considered Washington an important player for the end game. They believed that Sharif should use his personal rapport with Clinton[18] to manage the Kargil crisis on the domestic, Indian, and international fronts. Thus, through numerous letter exchanges and phone-calls, Nawaz was seeking Clinton's direct involvement in bringing Kargil to a close.[19] Pakistan's army command was also keen to involve the US in Kargil's end game. In fact, the army chief was the first to publicly mention the possibility of a Nawaz-Clinton meeting.[20] Significantly, by end-June, Musharraf himself had talked of positively of US intervention.[21]

In certain quarters, the original view of "nuclear flash-point" working to Pakistan's advantage still held sway.[22] This was at variance with the view that the Pakistan Foreign Office's now held.

Because of the history of the US engagement in successive Pakistan-Indian crisis since 1947, Pakistan and India tipped Washington as a primary candidate for helping in ending the Kargil crisis. Especially since the 1989 Kashmir Uprising and the emergence of the nuclear factor, the US had found itself directly engaged in de-escalating Indo-Pak military tension. In 1990, Washington had dispatched the Gates Mission. Following the 1998 nuclear tests, the US had been more inclined to appreciate the linkage between strategic instability and the unresolved Kashmir conflict.

Initially, the Sharif-Clinton communication culminated in a mutual agreement to meet mid-June in Europe, around the time of the of G-8 summit.[23] Sharif had proposed and Clinton had agreed to the meeting. However, the US Ambassador later conveyed to the Pakistan Foreign Office, the US President's inability to proceed with a Clinton- Sharif meeting.[24]

In Washington, it had been concluded that Pakistan would have erroneously interpreted such a meeting as a sign of US support for Islamabad's position on Kargil.[25] The National Security Council(NSC) and the State Department were sure that an unconditional exit was the only way forward and "unless a meeting would guarantee that outcome it wouldn't be productive." [26] The Talbott-Riedel-Inderfurth team was mindful of the challenge. Washington's clear Kargil policy was not "anything but exercise restrain... Action we wanted out of Pakistan to get Pakistan to back down." Nevertheless, there was a realization that "the Indians were extremely skeptical that we will succeed and suspicious about what we were doing..."[27] Any Pakistan-US meeting therefore that failed to induce a Pakistani withdrawal would have been resented in India and could have undermined Washington's imminent strategic lock with Delhi. [28]

The Clinton administration also believed that Pakistan had not delivered on the earlier commitment that Nawaz Sharif would help in getting the Taliban to expel OBL.[29] Pakistan's Foreign office team saw this as a reason for Clinton to subsequently "wriggle out of the meeting."[30] The US State Department sought a different engagement with Pakistan. In Washington, the nuclear non-proliferation saints and the Indo-philes had also made common cause. They twinned the Kargil aggression with what the non-proliferation saints claimed was Pakistan's plan to use nuclear weapons. They wanted the 'riot act' be read to Pakistan.

For India, no easy victory

Even by end June, the Indians were not in a comfortable military position. Their army had not been able to displace the well-entrenched and strategically located Pakistani troops. Any notion of winding up the war early seemed unrealistic. As the leading *Outlook* reported, "The prospect of the conflict in Kargil dragging on till October or beyond is a cause of great concern to the armed forces. They feel all-out efforts must be made to flush out the infiltrators before then. Three weeks of combat, air strikes and continuous artillery shelling have demonstrated that the infiltrators have locked on to Indian positions and are able to inflict severe damage. Though corresponding harm has been inflicted on the Pakistani-backed aggressors, they still remain at an advantageous position."[31] By end-June, a senior army official acknowledged, "Some of the heights they continue to occupy are impregnable. They occupy strategic posts on the ridge lines in Dras Kaksar Mushkoh Valley, Turtok, and Chorbatla."[32]

The *Outlook* report continued, "As Operation Vijay enters its fourth week, India's armed forces are coming to terms with the difficulty of the task. With the air force and artillery providing fire cover, infantry platoons skilled in mountain warfare have scaled daunting heights averaging 18000 feet to come within striking range of the intruders perched on the strategic ridges. But as some brave soldiers moved in for the kill, they were mowed down by accurate and murderous fire. The death toll had reached 98 by June 11, with over 317 injured. There is little comfort in the army's claim of having killed over 250 intruders. Or that it has been able to push the intruders back by almost 10 kilometers all along the 180-kilometers stretch of the LOC in the Kargil-Leh sector. No doubt the army has been able to wrest control of some key ridges after some hard-fought battles but Pakistan still occupies vital peaks from where it poses a major threat to Indian interests. To dislodge one intruder occupying the high ground it requires as many as 100 Indian fighting men, including infantry and artillery support. As the forces close in the brass is rapidly revisiting its estimates of just how long the battle over Kargil will continue. According to the army there are indicators that the war will not be a brief one."[33]

Despite the food and ammunition shortages, India's nerve-racking air power and loss of Pakistani troops and Pakistani-held posts, an all-out Indian victory was not imminent. The positioning of Pakistan's now ragtag, ill-fed, and ill-supported troops proved to be lethal, as Indian troops tried to scale the mountains. The fight-back was deadly and difficult. In the words of Kargil-based India general staff officer colonel Atvar Singh, "Our men are climbing on all fours, using ropes and special climbing gear, with bayonet rifles fixed at the hip…It's like one of those old Audie Murphy movies."[34] As late as end-June, the Indian press was reflecting the concern of the Indian government regarding whether the Clinton administration was prepared to "add some bite to its bark against Pakistan on Kargil."[35] Almost echoing Delhi's concern, a well-connected commentator wrote, "The general assessment here is that unless the Clinton Administration is prepared to add some real teeth to its attempted persuasion of Pakistan, Islamabad will have no incentive to end its aggression." [36] There was both speculation and suggestion that Washington could impose sanctions in case Pakistan refused to withdraw.[37] This would hardly have been the thrust of a country at the brink of a military victory in Kargil.

While the Indians had recaptured some front-line posts on Tololing and were heading towards the strategically important posts on Tiger Hill facing the NH-1A, the logistical lifeline for Indian troops stationed in Ladakh and Siachen, they had still not managed to achieve any major successes in their operations to recapture their lost posts.[38] In fact, it was not until beginning July that India was able to recapture Tiger hill which was in the farthest reaches, deep inside on the Indian side of the LOC, west of Marpola.

For Pakistan withdrawal inevitable

Although Indian military offensive to drive out the Pakistani troops had generally proceeded along the lines the Kargil planners had envisaged, [39] it was the continuous and intensive deployment of the Indian air factor and the close-up deployment of the Bofors artillery that did come as a total surprise.[40] The Kargil planners had also not anticipated strong opposition from the Pakistani air force chief to deployment of the Pakistani air factor.[41] After the Indian air force was inducted in the theatre, the Pakistan air force opted for only limited engagements. The PAF deployed its aircraft radars and it flew missions of combat air patrols mainly on the Pakistan side of the LOC. Even this was restricted to its 26 May use of surface-to-air missiles to shoot down the two Indian aircrafts that intruded into Pakistani space.

The Indian air force was used for disrupting supply lines rather than directly advancing the prime military objective of the Indian military operation i.e. recapture of the lost territory. But the Indian air power psychologically hit the Pakistani troop morale, making the battle theatre more inhospitable for them.[42] They were continuously exposed to the Indian air and artillery pounding as hundreds of sorties dropped thousands of kilos of bombs.[43] On the ground, the young soldiers wondered why their own airpower was not being deployed. They felt "unnerved by the Indian airpower, in fact terrorized by the sound in the cold weather and those mountains' ungodly heights."[44] This would gradually have impacted their will to fight. A senior military officer complained that the refusal to induct the Pakistan air force had meant that "the Pakistani forces with small arms and light machine guns were braving not only the onslaught of more than two Indian divisions, but the Indians were enjoying total mastery of airspace and artillery was raining on Pakistani forces."[45] Nevertheless, Indian air power was not able to directly target Pakistani troops and posts located 18,000 feet above sea level. The height and concealment advantage still helped the Pakistani soldier, who was otherwise short on supplies, on arms, and on ammunition.

But, notwithstanding that Pakistani troops were fighting back valiantly in the face of heavy artillery, air, and infantry attacks, the question as to how long Pakistan should hold on to these posts Remained. Not only were logistical supplies depleting, injuries and the human cost of fighting on were increasing.

Most importantly, after Tololing, India had begun re-taking the strategically located posts overlooking NH-1A. For Pakistan, holding onto the frontline posts was of actual strategic significance. These were furthermost from the LOC but closest to NH-1, the logistical lifeline for the Indian troops stationed in Ladakh and Siachen. Meanwhile, the mid-zone posts were in Pakistan's control but with no access to India's strategic roads. To what end, then, could or should Pakistan hold on to the mid-posts? Located in the middle of the rugged iced mountain terrain, these had no artillery access to any strategic Indian feature, such as a highway, a cantonment, ammunition dumps etc. Also, Delhi's political resolve of no talks until complete withdrawal appeared ironclad. And the international community fully supported India's position.

Doubts set in

By end-June, the problem of a "logistical stretch"[46] was beginning to surface for the Pakistani troops. In addition to the disruption being caused by air strikes, the Pakistani supply lines and the supplies were becoming increasingly vulnerable to harsh weather and to Indian artillery attacks. The phenomenon of 'Operation Creep'[47] had led to the unplanned increase in the demand for supplies.[48] The increasing demand for supplies in an expanding battle zone, where even maintaining existing bunkers and posts defensively was difficult, had begun to put pressure on the logistics. Launching and sustaining an operation of this scale would have been inconceivable. For example to maintain a force of fourteen hundred people, an additional ten thousand were needed to provide logistical support.

For Pakistan, the operational environment was therefore getting increasingly difficult. The 'logistical stretch' had begun to weaken the military operation from within. Pakistan had no carte blanche on the time factor. Logistics and supply lines were being intercepted by Indian air sorties and artillery attacks. The operation was being compromised. There were also mounting casualties, injuries, and cases of troop fatigue. Several NLI command changes were also ordered by late June.

With June becoming a month of heavy losses, the army chief found himself in a difficult situation. The confidence of the opening days, when the field was open and uncontested for his men, had begun eroding. Doubts had set in. The general had begun conceding in private conversations with members of the prime minister's kitchen cabinet that some 'operation creep' had occurred. The Op had been expanded beyond the originally planned territorial limits. Within his close circles, the army chief was candid. He could see the reasons for his soldiers to return from the war theatre, to end the fighting.[49] But who would bell the cat? The chief, was supposed to have sent one of his friends, also appointed as an envoy in an African country, to convey a suggestion to the prime minister's father. Known to be an exceptionally obedient son to his 'Abbaji', Sharif could never resist his father's 'advice.' Accordingly, Musharraf decided that commanding a retreat in the midst of a hard-fought battle with many sacrifices rendered, could lead to discontent among the soldiers. Also, the army chief feared an Indian offensive on the retreating soldiers. Accordingly, he likely had a message conveyed to Sharif's father that the PM be advised to recall the troops since continued or accelerated fighting could also mean the Indians might open other war fronts. The message was conveyed and the prime minister's father agreed to do as advised. [50]

This difficult military situation was not filtering through in the public arena. Unlike India, where Kargil had turned into a media war, in Pakistan the refrain was that Mujahideen and Kashmiri freedom fighters were fighting Indian forces. Conflicting official statements trickled in. While the army chief was welcoming talks with the Americans, he was also saying that unilateral withdrawal was not on. As news of casualties and perhaps of possible retreat found its way into the chat rooms of influential people, including retired generals, they publicly demanded that pressure on the Indian Army must continue. Retired General Hameed Gul, for example, felt that the Indians should be sucked in in order to get messed up. After mid-June, there were no formal meetings held to consider options, to discuss possibilities, or to build scenarios for exiting from Kargil. Instead, the way out from the Kargil crisis, from this 'symmetry of desperation,' was discussed mostly in informal kitchen cabinet meetings with no sense of a collective decision-making.

Prime Minister Witness to Casualties

The prime minister also witnessed the distressing aspect of warfare: military casualties. This reality of Op Kargil now confronted the prime minister when he was already under pressure on the diplomatic and political fronts. On the army chief's advice, Sharif visited the forward areas. At 8 am on June 24, accompanied by the Minister of State Board of Investment Humayun Akhtar and his acting Principal Secretary Khawaja Zaheer, the prime minister boarded a C-130 for Skardu. The army chief, and other members of the Kargil clique, including CGS generals Aziz and commander 10 Corps, also accompanied him. After a rather turbulent two hour C-130 ride, they landed at the NLI headquarters at Skardu, where a brief presentation on Op Kargil was given by the local commanders. After the presentation, the C-130 team took off, in three helicopters for a 30-

minute ride to the forward areas. From the helipad, they all boarded in jeeps for another 15 minute journey. Finally, they arrived in a valley surrounded by high mountains. The prime minister met the nearly one hundred uniformed soldiers gathered there, handing each one an envelopes with some money in it, and briefly addressed them praising their courage and their commitment to the defense of their homeland. Morale boosting slogans of "Allah-ho-Akbar", "Pakistan Zindabad", and "Pak Fauj Zindabad" reverberated through the valley as the army chief held and raised the prime minister's hand to lead this sloganeering. The prime minister had had a moving encounter with motivated jawans.

The return journey began. The helicopters landed near Skardu's Combined Military Hospital. The army chief led the Sharif into the hospital patients' ward. The medium-sized room, with three-storied bunk-beds, was packed with severely injured soldiers, suffering from the traumas of broken bones, amputated limbs, head injuries, etc. This was a sight the prime minister had not expected. He looked crestfallen and teary-eyed as he walked around and comforted the wounded soldiers. The hospital's commanding officer almost excitedly informed the prime minister that he was daily transporting dozens of battle-front wounded soldiers for treatment to Rawalpindi. The number of the wounded evidently was not small. As Sharif left the CMH, he was met by a crowd of locals who, upon seeing the three helicopters, had gathered outside. Musharraf was keen that the prime minister address the crowd and he helped the PM climb a window-sill from where Sharif briefly praised the sacrifices of the jawans for their homeland. The highly distraught prime minister then boarded the C-130.

Throughout the return journey, the prime minister actively avoided any interaction with the army chief. True to his personal style, the incredulous policy-making ways, and above all the horrors of Op K that were now a fait accompli, he opted to not confront his army chief. The PM engaged with his State Minister on Investment Humayun Akhtar to finalize the government's power investment policy. At one point during the journey, the army chief did manage to sit beside the Prime minister. Much to everyone's shock, he did not ask for additional finances for either the wounded or the battlefront soldiers. Instead he requested that a recently retired general be appointed in a public corporation. The PM acceded to Musharraf's request.

After landing at Chaklala, the prime minister, accompanied by his Principal Secretary Saeed Mehdi and his acting PS Khwaja Zaheer, headed straight to Islamabad. He shared with them his anguish over what he had seen at the Skardu hospital. He was angry with the army chief and recalled Musharraf's repeated, direct and indirect, requests to the prime minister to meet Clinton to plan a retreat from Kargil. Some humour lightened the gloomy atmosphere, as the PM suggested maybe he should send Khwaja Zaheer to meet Clinton. Meanwhile, the PM was scheduled to meet with the CENTCOM chief General Zinni, who had earlier landed at Chaklala.

Depleting Fortunes

As India labored hard to reclaim the lost peaks and ridges, Pakistani troops strenuously fought to retain the peaks. Militarily, there was no easy win for either side. The two elected prime ministers were keen to end what now was a battle on the world's highest war theatre in a difficult situation. On both sides, casualties were mounting and political support was depleting. Sharif and Vajpayee both wanted an early end. Led by the two, a political back channel was at work searching for the impossible, a common exit plan, a win-win for both. Meanwhile, on the diplomatic front, having been widely censured by the international community, Islamabad's political men, as well as the army chief, had faith that Washington could wrest a face-saver for Islamabad.

Kargil for Washington was not merely a Pakistan-India conflict. Kargil was a card that Washington could play in its game of power in South Asia.

Chapter 11

NUCLEAR CARD AND WASHINGTON'S GAINS

By early June, the Clinton administration's ambivalence about Op KP had changed into clarity regarding the facts of the operation. This translated into Washington's support forthe Indian demand that Pakistan unconditionally vacate the Kargil-Drass area. Washington's initial involvement in helping Delhi achieve its demands centerd on telephone conversations, exchanges of letters, and holding of meetings with Pakistani and Indian officials. Washington was largely attempting to respond to Indian concerns by advising Pakistan behind the scenes. The US military was engaging with its counterpart, the Pakistan Army high command, and there were regular exchanges between CENTCOM chief General Anthony Zinni and the Pakistan COAS General Pervez Musharraf. Meanwhile, the State Department was engaged with its Foreign Office counterparts: In Washington, US Under-Secretary of State Thomas Pickering with Pakistan Ambassador Riaz Khokhar and, in Islamabad, Ambassador William Milam with Tariq Fatemi and Shamshad Ahmad, with access to Foreign Minister Sartaj Aziz and prime minister Nawaz Sharif. Interestingly, the Lahore-based US Consul-General would also engage, on need basis, with the prime minister's brother and Chief Minister of Punjab Shehbaz Sharif. This was the less known but nonetheless significant track.

On the Delhi-Washington track, the Indian ambassador Naresh Chandra in Washington and State Department officials, including Assistant Secretary of State for South Asia, Karl Inderfurth, were in regular contact. The Indian External Affairs Minister Jaswant Singh and Deputy Secretary of State Strobe Talbott, having engaged in several rounds of non-proliferation dialogue, were already on direct dial. Vajpayee's closest policy aide, the seasoned diplomat Brajesh Mishra, National Security Advisor, had involved his US counterpart, Under Secretary of State Sandy Berger.

By early June, the senior US and Indian officials, whom policy moves primarily involved, were on the same page. The US President was generally kept in the loop but was not actively involved. By early June, Washington was willing to go public with its view on the Pakistani intrusion. In fact, the first acknowledgment, virtually a tacit approval, of Indian troops crossing the LOC into Azad Kashmir came from Karl Inderfurth. Early in June, as the key official dealing with the Kargil crisis in the State Department, Inderfurth told the *New York Times*, "Indians are not going to cede this territory," and the militants must leave. He added, "They have to depart, either voluntarily or because the Indians take them out." As Indian protagonists, US officials were not hesitant to sound almost threatening on behalf of Delhi. US Secretary of State Madeleine Albright had already called the Pakistani prime minister to urge withdrawal.

Against the backdrop of continuing Indian casualties, for Delhi the question was the extent to which Washington's words alone would weigh-in on Pakistan. By the third week of June, there were no signs of Pakistanis withdrawing under any pressure. Delhi now wondered how far Washington was willing to go in India's support. Delhi's expectation was that Washington would add "sting to its words." Would Washington's straight-talk, through the usual diplomatic channels, pressurize Pakistan to vacate the heights? Pakistan's public postures remained unchanged: that the Mujahideen, with only some support from the Pakistan Army, were determined to fight until India would relent and be willing to engage in dialogue over Kashmir.

Common goal: Pakistani withdrawal

It was towards the middle of June that Washington decided to get involved directly in resolving this Indo-Pak military engagement, which had the potential of turning into a full-scale war.India had by now had mounted a full-fledged military attack on the Pakistani troops. In his June 16 meeting in Geneva with US National Security Advisor Sandy Berger, the Indian NSA Brajesh Mishra handed over Indian Prime Minister Vajpayee's letter for Clinton. The matter had now catapulted directly into the presidential domain. In his letter, Vajpayee had let Clinton know that as caretaker prime minister the public pressure of body bags coming down the Himalayas carrying Indian soldiers was unsustainable. He may therefore be forced to order his troops to strike across the LOC. From Delhi, the message was that Clinton must exert pressure on Pakistan via the G-8 Summit and stop the flow of IFI, including IMF, funding to Pakistan. Vajpayee had spelled out India's bottom line: "India might have to attack Pakistan if Pakistan did not pull back troops who had seized Indian territories in the disputed region of Kashmir." Sandy Berger told Clinton a probable Pak-India war threatened disaster. If India expanded the war, Pakistan would probably lose and inevitably turn to its nuclear arsenal.[1] Although the blunt message came through to the presidential camp in the middle of June, the thrust of Delhi's demands was clear to Clinton's key aides working closely with their Indian counterparts.

The Clinton factor

In Washington, the State Department steered policy during the Kargil crisis. By mid-June, it had two clear objectives. The first objective was to convey a definitive message to Pakistan: vacate the peaks and ridges unconditionally. Key men at the State Department wanted no multi-messaging to Pakistan and would alone control such messaging. US officials even denied the Pakistani prime minister direct access to Clinton. They prevented a tentatively planned Clinton-Sharif June meeting at Cologne. Clinton's NSA Sandy Berger, who knew Clinton better that anyone else, knew that Clinton's "natural inclination was to find a deal." The administration's team which was looking for "an unequivocal

Pakistani climb down"[2] made sure Nawaz had no opportunity to meet Clinton on his own.

The second objective was to ensure President Clinton's direct engagement to help defuse the Kargil crisis. Clinton's involvement would convey to world capitals including Delhi, the importance Washington attached to the crisis and the urgency in resolving it. Clinton's engagement also broadened the scope of policy instruments available to exert pressure on Pakistan. For example, in Cologne, the US President personally lobbied the G-8 leaders for a tough statement holding Pakistan responsible for creating the crisis and demanding that Pakistan defuse the crisis. Similarly, Clinton's involvement, similar to that of the nuclear crisis period, enabled Washington to promptly send off CENTCOM chief General Anthony Zinni and State Department official Gib Lanpher to Pakistan. Delhi was reassured of Washington's complete support for the Indian position on Kargil against Pakistan. Washington used all its available channels of communication with Pakistan to convey only one message: unconditional exit of Pakistani troops. Washington was investing in forging strategic trust with Delhi.

Protecting Sharif

Back in Islamabad, the Pakistan Foreign Office was not keen that Nawaz Sharif meet with Zinni. The pressure from Washington, they feared,was to be a replay of May 1998. Then, it had been overla[[edto prevent Pakistan from conducting nuclear tests. In this difficult time, the Foreign Office was keen to test other than a made-in-Washington mode of settling the Kargil crisis. The Americans were told that Zinni's rank did not qualify him for a meeting with the prime minister. Before Zinni departed the US, the State Department attempted to circumvent the Foreign Office. The US Consul-General in Lahore, Jeffory Pied, went to see the prime minister's younger brother and Chief Minister Shehbaz Sharif and conveyed the Clinton administration's desire that Nawaz Sharif meet with Zinni. Shehbaz Sharif called Nawaz Sharif to convince him to agree to a meeting with Zinni. The prime minister declined.[3]

Washington's pressure on Pakistan overlapped Deli's pressure. It had diversified its sources of pressure on Pakistan. While engaging with Pakistan on the back channel, Delhi's principal reliance was on the US, through whom Delhi relentlessly kept up the pressure. On June 16, the Indian National Security Advisor Brajesh Mishra "air dashed to Paris"[4] and met with his US counterpart Sandy Berger to deliver Vajpayee's letter for Clinton. In fact, India approached all the G-8 countries before the Cologne summit. At the G-8 summit, the US played a crucial role in ensuring that a strong statement was issued against the intruders.

Washington weighs in

The US Department of Defense and CENTCOM were not the first institutions to suggest direct high-level involvement by Washington in resolving the Kargil crisis. The decision to send Zinni to Pakistan was made after the Vajpayee letter was received by the US President in Geneva. This suggestion was the result of a series of face to face meetings involving the United States National Security Council (NSC) and the State Department. No elaborate inter-agency meetings were held. Key individuals who framed United States Kargil policy included Thomas Pickering and Karl Inderfurth from the State Department and Sandy Berger and Bruce Riedel from the National Security Council.

Numerous brain-storming sessions were held, where institutional briefings were provided on the military, political and diplomatic dimensions of the Kargil crisis. After a thorough examination of various response options available to Washington in the face of this growing crises, it was decided in Washington to use the military-to-military channel.

The State Department believed that, given the Pakistan military's predominant role in Pakistan's power structure, direct contact with Pakistan's Chief of Army Staff Pervez Musharraf was critical for ensuring Pakistan's withdrawal from Kargil.[5] Washington believed, "The military was driving Kargil so someone had to talk turkey to the military." And, so, Zinni was sent. A State Department official was to accompany Zinni as per the general practice plus also to signal to the Pakistanis that there was a consensus within the United States administration and the establishment on the policy demanding immediate and unconditional Pakistani withdrawal.

The exchange of letters between Clinton and Nawaz Sharif did not get Clinton any tangible commitment from the latter on withdrawing Pakistani troops from Kargil. A letter from Clinton addressed to the Pakistani prime minister was drafted in the State Department on Saturday on June 19[6] and sent to the White House. Clinton was then traveling in Europe. In the letter, Clinton specifically asked the Pakistani prime minister what steps he would take to get out of Kargil. Clinton wrote in that letter that he wanted the CENTCOM Chief General Anthony Zinni to meet with Sharif as well as with the Pakistani army chief General Musharraf to ensure a Pakistani withdrawal. Gib Lanpher[7] Deputy Assistant Secretary South Asian Affairs at the State Department met Zinni on June 21.

Meanwhile, US Secretary of State Madeleine Albright was attempting to reach Nawaz Sharif to let him know that Clinton was sending Zinni to meet with him and Musharraf. With Zinni's plane on standby to fly them to Pakistan, the two waited for a reply from Islamabad. But no response was received on Monday. When the Zinni team left for Pakistan, they only had a confirmed meeting set with General Pervez Musharraf.[8]

Zinni's departure also signaled that the US bureaucracy had successfully overruled their President's inclination to be accommodating to his friend the Pakistani prime minister. Clinton had suggested to Sharif that, since Clinton was in Europe, they could meet there. However, the State Department believed such a meeting would ease the diplomatic squeeze on Pakistan. The perception within the Pakistani political leadership and the bureaucrats was that the State Department had encouraged Clinton to "wriggle out" out of this suggestion.[9] The White House staff and the State Department officials had shot down what the Pakistanis believed was the possibility of an earlier Clinton-Sharif meeting in Europe.[10] The State Department wanted a Clinton-Sharif meeting be made contingent upon Pakistan first vacating Kargil. [11]

Zinni in Pakistan

Just past midnight, in the early hours of June 24, the plane carrying Anthony Zinni and Edward Lanpher landed at the Chaklala military airbase base in Rawalpindi. They were driven to the Marriott hotel in Islamabad. The following day, at noon, the American team left to meet Musharraf at the General Head Quarters(GHQ). Significantly, before the Zinni meeting, General Musharraf had flown with the prime minister to the forward areas from where the Kargil operation was launched.[12] The prime minister and the army chief visited the injured soldiers and met with the jawans. As the prime minister told the jawans, "The nation's, mine, and General Musharraf's prayers are with you,"[13] he announced an increase in the compensatory allowance for troops serving at high altitudes. It was also a morale booster trip for the soldiers. Yet it was not coincidental that this display of a unified civil-military stance on Kargil was planned for hours before the Zinni-Musharraf meeting.

Meanwhile, the CGS General Aziz and the Director General Inter-Services Intelligence (ISI) General Ziauddin also participated in the meeting. There was no participant from the Pakistan Foreign Office.[14] By contrast, the US General was joined by diplomats including Lanpher, Milam, and political counsellor John Schmidt.

In the meeting, Zinni told Musharraf that he had been specially sent by his President to talk about Kargil. Musharraf was told that the Kargil issue was "dangerously unwise and that Pakistan had no support for its Kargil operation."[15] Clinton's message was simple: "Just get out of there." Musharraf, however, did not acknowledge that there were Pakistani soldiers in Kargil. Throughout the meeting, Musharraf maintained that Pakistan had no control over the Mujahideen who were in Kargil. He insisted that the developments in Kargil had to be seen in the broader Kashmir context. Musharraf discussed all the injustices committed against the Kashmiris in Indian-held Kashmir and referred to the UN resolutions. Zinni was categorical that his President had sent him to discuss Kargil, not Kashmir. Throughout the three-hour-long meeting, held in a cordial atmosphere, [16] the Pakistani army chief remained focused on Kashmir while the US CENTCOM chief focused on Kargil. During the meeting, Zinni attempted to convince Musharraf that withdrawal from Kargil was the only option available to Pakistan. Musharraf, meanwhile, remained focused on the need to resolve Kashmir, while his two generals sat quietly throughout the meeting. Unlike in the Zinni team, there were no civilians in the Musharraf team. No Pakistan Foreign Office officials were present in the meeting.

The meeting ended inconclusively. There was no agreement on the withdrawal of the Pakistan Army since Musharraf refused to acknowledge the presence of Pakistani troops.[17] Towards the end of the meeting a non-committal Musharraf said that perhaps Pakistan would talk to the Mujahideen and see what could be done. Meanwhile, the Pakistani participants of the meeting believed they "had made their point successfully and convinced the Americans that the unresolved dispute of Kashmir and the developments in Kargil were deeply linked." Musharraf's refusal notwithstanding, the American team's reading on whether or not Musharraf wanted to withdraw, was divided.[18]

At the conclusion of the meeting, the US Ambassador told Musharraf that Zinni may well depart that night without having had a chance to meet the prime minister.[19] Musharraf promised to help. As the Zinni team entered their Marriot Hotel rooms, Musharraf had called to say, "You have a meeting with Nawaz Sharif."

The following morning, on June 25, Zinni met with the prime minister. The army chief, DG ISI, and the senior Foreign Office team also participated in the meeting. Zinni's principal message was, "Withdraw from across the LOC and restore its sanctity."[20]Zinni warned Sharif that military escalation could lead to induction of the nuclear factor. With the "use or loose" mentality, Zinni argued, any military escalation could lead to nuclear confrontation. Sharif's position was almost identical to what Musharraf had taken a day earlier. He talked of the linkage between resolving Kargil and settling the Kashmir dispute. Zinni too repeated the argument he had made at the Musharraf meeting. Zinni also carried Clinton's message to Nawaz Sharif that he would not meet the Pakistani prime minister "in the shadow of Kargil." Finally, towards the end of the meeting, the prime minister took a deep breath and said, "What do you want me to do, General Zinni?" Nawaz Sharif then said, "We can talk to these people who are occupying the heights in Kargil and see whether we can do anything."[21]

Interestingly, the Americans and the Pakistanis had different 'takes' on the meeting. The Pakistani camp was clear that the prime minister had been categorical that the "US should take a broader view of the problem - that Kargil was only one aspect of the larger problem of Jammu and Kashmir which must be addressed in it totality in accordance with the wishes of the Kashmiri people."[22] None of the Pakistani participants felt that Sharif had given Zinni a commitment to withdraw.[23] The Americans read almost the opposite. They believed that "not too long into the meeting the prime minister agreed to a withdrawal."[24] They were relieved that they "did not have to wrestle Nawaz Sharif into the ground"[25] and had extracted a verbal agreement from Sharif to withdraw.[26] They also interpreted Musharraf's silence throughout the Nawaz-Zinni meeting as "his body language not showing that he was opposed to withdrawal."[27] However, the Americans differed among themselves on the timing of the withdrawal. Lanpher was more optimistic and believed withdrawal would begin soon. He believed that the Zinni mission had achieved its objective and maintained that the Pakistanis liked Zinni and saw him as "straight shooter." The delay in the response to the Clinton letter was because the letter had provoked a serious debate within the Pakistani government which centerd on the substance of whether or not to pull out of Kargil. Lanpher argued with his colleagues that the Zinni mission got the green signal from Islamabad because the Pakistanis had decided to give him a positive response, not because they wanted to "slam the door in your face." His conclusion was: "The Pakistanis, government officials, army officers and politicians were infinitely polite and these real gentlemen would not want to be rude to people, in contrast to the Indians who enjoyed being rude." Lanpher based his expectation of a Pakistani withdrawal from Kargil on the Pakistani psychology of "wanting to please the Americans." However, Zinni and Milam, both more familiar with the Pakistani working and particularly with Sharif and Musharraf, believed that Musharraf would not easily make his troops vacate Kargil.[28]

Indeed, in his first public statement after Zinni's departure, Musharraf had confirmed the doubts expressed by Milam and Zinni. On

June 26, while responding to a pressman's question if Pakistan would withdraw its forces from Kargil, the army chief said, "It's too early to say (but) it's a government decision. It is the prime minister's decision. We will not withdraw unilaterally."[29] Still clear that nothing less than a "mutually acceptable" settlement would work, Musharraf said, "Obviously, we do not want to reach a solution that is mutually unacceptable to us and to India." [30] Two issues, he argued, needed to be settled:"The tactical military issue of Kargil and Drass and the political dimension of Kashmir, and both have to be tackled altogether."[31] Musharraf's June 26 statement also indicated that a meeting between the Pakistani prime minister and the US president was on the cards.

Lampher later recalled, "We decided we had a success, that they would get them out even if not acknowledging they were Pakistani soldiers. We did not give anything on Kashmir and we did not rub their noses either, we could have insisted that they acknowledge they are Pakistanis but we know they had to save face."[32] Meanwhile, Zinni had left with the 'distinct impression' that Nawaz Sharif had committed to withdrawing the troops.[33] Indian statements also refuted Zinni's assertion that the meeting with Clinton was granted after Pakistan started withdrawing troops. As late as on 4 July, in his briefing, the Indian spokesman said that India had not seen the slightest indication that Islamabad was willing to withdraw its troops. He said, "There is not the slightest sign on the ground that Pakistan is taking the necessary steps that need to be taken for withdrawal and for restoration of the status quo."[34] Upon arrival in Washington, Zinni and his commander-in-chief, the US President, waited for the Pakistanis to begin withdrawing.

In Pakistan, the Zinni visit had left no doubt in the civilian camp, including the Prime Minister, that Washington wanted Pakistan to unconditionally withdraw from Kargil.[35] Zinni had merely reiterated the demand that the US administration had directly and repeatedly made to Islamabad two weeks into the Kargil crisis.[36] For Sharif, personally also, the fear of the possibility of a nuclear engagement was also driven home. Zinni had managed to convince him that a prolonged Kargil crisis could convert into an all-out nuclear war.[37] This further fuelled the uneasiness in Sharif's camp over the Kargil crisis.

Meanwhile, though, there was disappointment in Washington that an immediate Pakistani troop withdrawal did not actually begin, following the Zinni visit, the Zinni-Lanpher trip was viewed as having facilitated achievement of the objectives Washington had set out for itself during Kargil. Recalling the Zinni mission, another senior National Security Council head, Bruce Riedel, said, "He did not get a commitment. When Nawaz Sharif came to the Blair House on 4 July we did not know of the outcome."[38] Referring to Zinni's claim in his book that he had got a commitment from Musharraf, Riedel said, "Zinni is overstating his case…"[39]

Nevertheless, the State Department found the mission helpful on three specific counts. First, the Clinton Administration was satisfied that Zinni had candidly conveyed its concerns to Islamabad and had made it clear to General Musharraf that Pakistan was responsible for the present military flare-up along the LOC and Pakistan had to roll back. Secondly, in the management of the Zinni-Lanpher trip, Washington continued the practice of transparency in its diplomacy initiated during the Kargil crisis. Washington publicized and also shared with the Indians, both privately and publicly, the message conveyed to Islamabad. For example, Lanpher was deputed to inform India of the Zinni meetings in Islamabad. The transparency was more evident in the Washington-Islamabad communication relative to Washington-Delhi communication. On 4 July 4, Clinton made two calls to Vajpayee, one during and one after his meeting with Nawaz Sharif. General Zinni had an opportunity to candidly express the views of the US administration. Thirdly, and perhaps most importantly, "Zinni helped lay the ground work for the successful outcome of the 4 July Clinton-Nawaz meeting,"[40] during which Washington was able to 'deliver' India a unilateral Pakistani withdrawal from Kargil.[41] Musharraf, to the contrary, believed that Pakistan's position on "no unilateral withdrawal" had been conveyed to the Americans. Infact, he found Zinni's "body language positive and sympathetic towards Pakistan's position." The army chief in fact still believed a Clinton-Sharif meeting,[42]to facilitate a negotiated settlement of Kargil and Kashmir, would be possible.

Whatever Sharif said during the Zinni meeting, he was an extremely worried man after what he had heard from Clinton's envoy. The prime minister was convinced that a full-scale Pakistan-India war along the international border was likely and that could mean electronic devices with which India could jam Pakistan's radars and signals. Zinni had also convinced the prime minister that a nuclear war was on the cards and that even his own army, the Pakistan Army, had begun deploying nuclear weapons.[43] He felt that, between electronic and nuclear warfare, it was a doomsday scenario for Pakistan. Hence, it can safely be presumed this was the definitive point at which the Pakistani prime minister had concluded that a war had to be avoided at all costs. The back-channel communications were on but now other avenues for 'exit facilitation' were to be sought: Beijing, Riyadh, and DC. However, Sharif played these cards close to his chest. For example, only his kitchen cabinet knew of his contacts with Washington and Riyadh. The Foreign Office team was working the Delhi and Beijing routes while the Defense Committee and the cabinet knew of neither. The contact with the Saudis was established in the last week of June. Saudi Crown Prince Abdullah, who was close to the Sharif family, was contacted seeking Saudi intervention with Washington for a Clinton-Sharifmeeting.

Lanpher Reports to Delhi

A key component of the Indo-United States engagement throughout the Kargil crises was trust and transparency. Consequently, Washington considered it appropriate that Lanpher be sent off to be the reporter on the CENCOM chief General Zinni's Pakistan meetings in New Delhi. After their meeting with the Pakistani prime minister, the Zinni mission split to travel in opposite directions. Zinni left for Washington and Lanpher left for Delhi. On the evening of June 26, Lanpher arrived in Delhi via Karachi on a commercial flight.

He was a welcome guest. In addition to the difficult military situation, the Ministry of External Affairs in Delhi also feared that Pakistan may raise the Kashmir issue at the UN. There were reports suggesting, "The AtalBihari Vajpayee government is stepping up its diplomatic offensive to ensure that Pakistan does not succeed in raising the issue at the United Nations."[44] Trips to foreign capitals by the Indian foreign minister and the foreign secretary to mobilize international opinion against the raising of Kashmir at the UN were being planned for July and August by the MEA.[45] Delhi also feared escalation of the conflict.[46] The UN General Assembly meeting was scheduled for September and the Ministry of External Affairs had embarked on a mission to ensure that Kargil did not come up for discussion there.

On June 27, Lanpher met with MEA officials and with the Principal Secretary to the Indian Prime Minister, Brajesh Mishra.[47]Lanpher briefed Mishra thoroughly "with a very candid description of those present in the meetings and what they said." He gave Mishra news of a likely withdrawal by the Pakistani forces.[48] Lanpher repeated in detail his conversations with the Pakistanis to assure the Indians that "these guys (Pakistanis) will get out." Still not completely trusting of the United States support for the Indian position, the Indians did not believe "how rough" Zinni had been with the Pakistanis. The Americans saw themselves doing a "front channel thing," Lanpher providing the Indians complete details on the Zinni meeting with the Pakistani prime minister and COAS.[49]

Lanpher found Mishra skeptical about the possibility of a Pakistani withdrawal.[50] "Having been bloodied, totally embarrassed, and caught with their pants down, and suffering heavy casualties,"[51] the Indians tended not to trust Lanpher's reading of the Pakistani intentions. Despite his "honest briefing", the Indians were "very skeptical." Mishra's skepticism was understandable. Only a few hours before the Lanpher meeting, Naik, the Pakistani back-channel interlocutor, had stressed upon the impossibility of a unilateral withdrawal. He had categorically stated that a withdrawal would only follow the joint adoption and declaration of the four points.

In Washington, the Kargil crisis was seen as providing an opportunity to strengthen its relations with India. The Clinton administration had already decided to opt for a paradigm shift in its relations with India, which it viewed as a future strategic partner. It believed that through a transparent and proactive handling of the Kargil crisis Washington could win Delhi's trust and confidence.[52] Hitherto, US engagement in South

Asia had always been episodic and not constant. But, having made the policy decision to opt for a strategic partnership with India, the Clinton administration, unlike past administrations, decided it would remain in South Asia for the long haul. The Clinton administration realized that successive US administrations had walked away after their purpose was served. Washington would now stay to primarily win Indian trust and appreciation, avert a full-scale war, and perhaps to subsequently explore ways to resolve Kashmir. Lanpher carried the message to Delhi that Delhi must show restraint while Washington ensured that the sanctity of the LOC was restored to the pre-Kargil position. Washington's effort was aimed at reviving the spirit of Lahore. It believed its Kargil policy embraced a "straight-forward not convoluted diplomatic strategy." [53]

One of the key objectives of Washington's policy during Kargil was to deny Pakistan any strategic advantage accruing to it from its nuclear status. Washington was determined not to let Pakistan benefit from playing the 'nuclear card.' Hence Pakistan had to undo the violation of the LOC and not derive any political or diplomatic benefit from its Kargil adventure. Allowing any advantage to Pakistan which had banked on, to some degree, deriving advantage from nuclear blackmail, would set off a de-stabilizing precedent between the two nuclear states. Successful deployment of nuclear blackmail as a policy tool would have in fact undermined the only virtue that the deadly weapon possesses, that of deterrence. A nuclear armed South Asia could not have been encouraged to become a theatre for limited wars.

Washington knew it required Delhi's cooperation to bring the Kargil crisis to a peaceful closure. The Vajpayee government and the Clinton administration's views converged on the one point that the Kargil crisis could only be resolved through a total and unconditional withdrawal. In Delhi, Lanpher was convincing his Indian hosts that Washington had played its role in bringing about an imminent Pakistani withdrawal.

Impact on the Back-Channel

Washington was aware of the two exit tracks that a militarily distressed Delhi-Islamabad was pursuing to end the Kargil crisis. One was the straight and open track in which Washington and other powers were involved. The combined global message for the Sharif government, from all the countries, especially India and the US, was that Islamabad must immediately and unconditionally vacate the Kargil heights.

The other exit track, which India worked on, was the relatively concealed back-channel track with Pakistan. Not surprisingly, the External Affairs Minister and India's Pakistan specialists at the South block, who were leading the global campaign against Pakistan's intervention and were calling for punitive action, were not keen on the back channel. The Indian prime minister and his key advisor Brajesh Mishra, however, supported the back channel. They believed it would hasten the end of the bizarre and bleeding military stand-off in the world's highest war zone, reduce the army casualties, prove wrong political critics of his Lahore peace initiative, and return to a diplomatic engagement with Pakistan. However, on June 27, the Vajpayee-Mishra duo changed their view, the day the State department official Lanpher landed in Delhi. His arrival coincided with a crucial back-channel meeting in Delhi. In this last of the series of back-channel meetings, Naik and Indian Prime Minister Vajpayee plus his key team were to finalize the road map out of the Kargil heights, which included the statements which the two prime ministers would issue to defuse the prevailing situation. During the meeting, Naik had raised some doubt about including the line about the withdrawal of Pakistani troops. Nevertheless, in a meeting with his Indian hosts soon after, Lanpher repeated his own and general Zinni's readout of meetings with Pakistan's prime minister and army chief, i.e. that Pakistan had agreed to withdraw its troops from the Kargil-Drass area. This message, conveyed during the Lanpher- Brajesh meeting that had preceded the Vajpayee-Naik meeting by less than an hour, changed Delhi's calculus of the advantages from the Naik-Mishra back-channel. If Washington delivered an immediate and unconditional Pakistani withdrawal, Delhi could then be projected as the winner. The Indo-Pakistan back-channel agreement would meanwhile not deny Delhi the victory card but would also have provided Pakistan with a face-saver. Hence, only a Delhi with its back to the wall would have gone through with the back-channel and conceded a face-saver to Pakistan. Accordingly, when the message for Delhi from Washington of the Zinni-

Lanpher Pakistan meetings was hopeful, the South Bloc men led by the Minister for External Affairs pushed to abandon the back-channel.

What he suppressed from the public was the fact that, contrary to his tall and unwise claims in public, he had secretly sent emissaries to Pakistan on 18 June, six days after Sartaj Aziz trip to Delhi. It is bad form to publicise private exchanges on the phone. I t is worse to deceive the public. On 19 July, Pakistan Foreign Secretary, Shamshad Ahmad revealed that R. K. Mishra had visited Pakistan as India's emissary at least five times during the crisis, while Niaz Naik also kept shuttling between Islamabad and New Delhi (*The Hindu*, 20 July).

The back-channel collapsed and with it seemingly all possibility of the return of Pakistan and Indian relations to the spirit of the February 1999 Lahore Summit.

No Kashmir

Despite heavy deployment of their artillery, infantry, and air force, by all Indian accounts and most estimates of US intelligence, the Indian Army remained under extremely military pressure till end June. However, Washington opted to intervene unconditionally and expended its diplomatic capital to Delhi without seeking any linkage or quid pro quo. No foreign power understood better than the US that at the core of the fifty-year Pakistan-India history of wars and antagonism was the unresolved dispute over the future of the Kashmiri people. Incursion in Kargil was another chapter in the story of Kashmir, as had been the Indian occupation of Siachen. Only thirteen months earlier, the US was one of the sponsors of UNSC 1172, calling for the resolution of the Kashmir issue which was a cause of instability and insecurity in South Asia. But, through the Kargil crisis, its root cause Kashmir was actively delinked from it. Interestingly, if anyone in Washington acknowledged the relevance of the Kashmir issue, during the Kargil crisis, it was General Zinni. The Pakistan Army chief claimed that during their June 26 meeting, Zinni "understood our position on Kashmir and agreed it was needed a quick solution."[54] The army chief's understanding, however, was in complete contrast with how the prime minister's point man, the seasoned diplomat Tariq Fatemi, viewed Zinni's attitude. "Zinni wanted us out immediately,"[55] Fatimi recalled. Zinni repeated the same on arrival in Washington.[56]

In the rush of words, much was said in Delhi and Islamabad about Kashmir. In Delhi, a chorus of Vajpayee critics insisted that by involving the international community to defuse the Kargil crisis Vajpayee had internationalized the Kashmir issue. In Pakistan, conversely, the complaint against Washington and other G-8 members was that Kargil was being delinked from Kashmir.[57]

Gains for Washington: A 'seminal turning point'

Among the negative fall-outs of this ill-conceived operation was the pound of flesh that Washington extricated from Pakistan as a result of the latter's vulnerability. In contrast with its preferred and publicly stated policy of bilateralism as opposed to multilateralism, where it came to the chronically troubled Pakistan and India relationship, during Kargil Washington opted for the multilateral route. The Clinton administration positioned itself as an active interlocutor and weighed in heavily in Delhi's favor.

From Pakistan's Kargil debacle, in cold statistical calculations, the Clinton administration's key South Asian and non-proliferation experts wrested a strategic gain for Washington. The gain was winning Delhi's trust and confidence it's role in South Asia; that no other country's interests, especially Pakistan's, could trump Delhi's interests. It was a classic act of gainful cunning that largely dictates State interaction.

Throughout the Kargil crisis there was coordinated institutionalized decision-making within the various power centres in Washington and Delhi. This helped the two governments to achieve their respective, if overlapping, objectives. Islamabad, by contrast, found itself in a vulnerable and powerless space. The Kargil clique's secret launch of Op KP had inflicted a heavy military and diplomatic cost on the country. Additionally, Washington-Delhi collusion in denying any gains to Islamabad had left Nawaz Sharif with virtually no cards in hand to play.

Meanwhile, Washington earned from Delhi what it was looking for, the foundations for building a strategic relationship. Here is how the Indian External Affairs Minister explains in detail to Deputy Secretary of State Strobe Talbott in the wake of the Kargil crisis: "Something terrible has happened these past several months between us and our neighbors. But something quite new and good has happened . . . between our countries, yours and mine, something related to the matter of trust. My prime minister and I thank your President for that."

Nuclear Card During the Kargil Crisis

It was not until two Indian fighter jets began shelling Pakistan's border areas across the LOC that the nuclear factor came into play. It was Pakistan's Foreign Secretary Shamshad Ahmad who was quick to warn, "We will not hesitate to use any weapon in our arsenal to defend our territorial integrity."[58] In a bind of asymmetry, as the smaller yet nuclear-armed state, Ahmad's statement was logical yet provocative. Along with fears, it triggered a parallel political play around the nuclear factor. This factor had already come alive after the May 1998 nuclear tests by India and later by Pakistan. Hence, Shamshad Ahmad's statement about a recently nuclearized region, with a history of wars, semi-wars, and intensely contested narratives, and now embroiled in conflict, did not go unnoticed.

Washington's old hands on South Asia and non-proliferation were alerted. The State Department's Bureau of South Asia and Bureau of Non-Proliferation were activated. US officials who, as the core group, would handle the nuclear aspect through the Kargil crisis were Assistant Secretary of state for South Asian Affairs Karl Inderfurth, Senior Director on the National Security Council Bruce Reidel, Assistant Secretary of state for Non-proliferation Robert Einhorn, and Deputy Secretary of State Strobe Talbott. Old hands, they had first in May 1998 tried unsuccessfully to dissuade Pakistani officials from conducting the nuclear tests. Post-tests, they had engaged with Islamabad and Delhi to convince them to sign onto Washington's Non-proliferation markers, including the NPT and CTBT.

With Pakistan, the two key departments, the Bureaus of South Asia and of Non-Proliferation, had had important if caustic engagements over such issues as terrorism, Kashmir, Afghanistan, Taliban, OBL, etc. Washington had a longstanding problem with Pakistan over the Non-proliferation question. The problem was both Non-proliferation and a less than even-handed policy towards Pakistan and India. A telling illustration of this approach was a 1979 interaction between Pakistan's legendary Foreign Minister Aga Shahi and Gerard Smith, the veteran American Arms Control negotiator. Shahi had been arguing for complete linkage with India on all matters ranging from opening Kahuta for IAEA inspection and signing of the NPT. Frustrated, the US Secretary of State took the recalcitrant Shahi to Smith. As Shahi entered his room, the tall, bulky American negotiator declared, "As you know, you are entering the Valley of Death. The Indians are well advanced over you and they can totally destroy you any time…You think you are getting security?" Shahi, one not to be easily unnerved, retorted, "We understand the psychological and political advantage of having our programme." On India's numerical advantage, he reminded Smith that the Soviet Union had only 300 nuclear warheads and the US had 3000; yet, in the Cuban Missile Crisis, Kennedy had been forced to negotiate with the Soviets. Shahi reminded his American hosts that the US had imposed sanctions on Pakistan while Carter had asked France to provide enriched uranium to India for the nuclear reactor at the Tarapur Atomic Power station in Trombay, near Mumbai.[59] Nineteen years, later in a replay of this uneven approach, when India had conducted nuclear tests, the Clinton administration had vehemently discouraged Pakistan from conducting tests. Similarly, there was well-documented evidence of Washington's support for or benign neglect of others' support for the Indian weapons programme.

Invisible in India

Now, during Kargil, Washington's uneven policy between the two nuclearized South Asian neighbors again surfaced. The emphasis of the Clinton administration's key men on Pakistan's nuclear activity during Kargil, while completely ignoring what India may have been doing, was a mere continuationof Washington's policy of the seventies. Strobe Talbott, Clinton's personal friend and a journalist-turned diplomat, who documented his failure to convince India's imposing Jaswant Singh to agree to Washington's instruments for non-proliferation, appeared to have made much of very little in the Kargil days.

Meanwhile, by mid-June, India had launched a full-ledged counter-attack. The Indian National Security Advisor delivered Vajpayee's letter to Clinton warning that India might have to attack Pakistan if Pakistan did not pull its troops out. The concern about nuclear conflict was there, but the key question was: how could Washington affect a Pakistani pull-out? In Washington, other than the generic concern regarding military confrontation, the intelligence had its ear to the ground to especially monitor nuclear-related developments. Data flow from several satellite paths, various policy departments, including the Defense Department, the State Department's South Asia section, CENTCOM, the CIA, and the NSC, now focused particularly on nuclear related information. Some intelligence officials claimed that the ground information picked up by US intelligence sources indicated movement of missiles and placement of warheads. The concern, however, about active deployment of nuclear weapons, especially by Pakistan, was not uniformly shared within the Clinton Administration. There was great divergence in interpreting this intelligence data.

Reading Hair-trigger

Only the core group, including Bruce Riedel and Strobe Talbott, viewed it as a potential hair trigger situation. Others in the Administration, including Under Secretary of State Thomas Pickering, the US ambassador in Pakistan, and several officials within the intelligence wing of the South Asian Bureau of the State Department, were less convinced that either side would opt for the use of nuclear weapons. Similarly, CENTCOM and DOD, with their lines of communication open to Pakistan's top military brass, and their own ground-sniffing intelligence assets, did not believe that the conflict could become a full-blown conventional or nuclear war. The nuclear fear of senior experts was based on their calculation that India would be compelled to "open other fronts" since, given the Kargil-Drass battle terrain, "direct assaults would not be successful."[60] In Washington, "there was a particular concern that Pakistan was taking action to make its nuclear weapons capable."[61] Yet, on the question of veracity about intelligence on nuclear preparedness by Pakistan, the refrain was that an "intelligence information cannot be more specific."[62] Interestingly, the Non-proliferation Bureau and the core South Asia team at the State Department stood apart from other officials in reading the tea leaves on Pakistan's deployment of nuclear weapons.[63]

Divergent Read-outs

Hence divergent read-outs of the nuclear-related situation were based only on general intelligence information, since intelligence information could not be more specific.[64] While data interpretation depended on subjectivity, circumstantial evidence, the dynamics of the military situation, and statements by Indian and Pakistani officials too influenced the read-outs. The subjectivity factor, however, trumped all. A senior INS official[65] acknowledged, "The criteria set for checking facts were pretty low. Nuclear saints[66] examine the situation almost subjectively…they are willing to see evil and believe evil. Nuclear was the sacred grail...even a hint of nuclear would get them riled up. On the nuclear issue there was immense room for interpretation so it depends on who the interpreters were." The international intelligence wing of the CIA, following the global nuclear situation, did not pick up any specific intel indicating preparedness of Pakistan's nuclear weapons. There was only a general concern.[67]

The intelligence community's interpretation of data was widely divergent. For example, within the INS section of the South Asia Bureau,a senior official, referring to Riedel's interpretation, maintained, "I did not interpret it the way he did. How solid was the evidence that the missile was being prepared for use as opposed to being dispersed for defensive/protective purposes?"[68] For example, the nuclear alarmists interpreted the Pakistani prime minister's end-June trip as one linked to Pakistan's nuclear preparedness. Core officials claimed an intelligence report came indicating this. However, Sharif had gone to Beijing looking for an honorable exit.

Spun-up on Nuclear

At Kargil, at least the perception among Clinton's core group was that the maximum crossing of the nuclear threshold took place. Even a zero to one percent probability of nuclear engagement would lead to a disastrous outcome, some officials claimed. Nevertheless, information that trickled in from other sources did not corroborate Clinton's core group's assessment that Pakistan was readying nuclear weapons. The US Embassy in Islamabad read the situation differently. It did not at all fear a nuclear conflict. In fact, the embassy officials viewed the State Department's concerns on the nuclear issue as "merely being spun up."[69] The US Ambassador's message to Washington was, "No nuclear, but no one paid attention."[70]

These contrary assessments notwithstanding, from mid-June onwards the administration's core group appears to have been possessed by "nuclear phobia." They directly involved the US President into the Kargil diplomacy. They alerted him to their "concern" regarding Pakistan taking action to make its nuclear weapons capable.[71]

Growing Indo-US strategic interest

The growing Indo-US strategic relations were also at play in producing this nuclear phobia targeting Pakistan. Having discovered that in fact Pakistan regulars and not Mujahedeen were fighting in Kargil, and Pakistan therefore had control over them, the US weighed in heavily on to Pakistan to withdraw the troops. The US President wrote about six letters. The US Ambassador delivered the letters to the foreign minister. He had several meetings with the Pakistani prime minister and spent much of his time at the Prime Minister's Secretariat with Additional Secretary Tariq Fatimi. He visited him almost daily with a constant barrage of escalating pressure on Pakistan to withdraw.

Targeting Nawaz Sharif

There appeared to be politics around the use of even this information on Pakistan, unverified by majority of the US intelligence bodies within the Clinton administration. Why did Washington hold back the information Washington claimed it had on Pakistan's preparedness for the use of nuclear weapons? Why was the information only shared with the prime minister – and that too without his aides? It was used to first target the prime minister behind closed doors. Equally, General Zinni had opted to warn the prime minister in a classified and limited meeting about "electronic" and "finally nuclear warfare." As late as June 26, Zinni decided against raising the risks of a nuclear war with the army chief, the man Washington believed had more control than the prime minister on Pakistan's nuclear trigger. First, the CENTCOM chief sketched a deadly picture for him and subsequently, on 4 July, the information was brought in full throttle at the Clinton-Nawaz meeting. Pakistan's prime minister was instructed to not bring in an aide. Clinton with Riedel, the man riled up about Pakistan's deployment of nuclear weapons, insisted that unknown to the prime minister the Pakistan Army was preparing to use nuclear weapons!

Nuclear Deterrence from Pakistan

Within Pakistan, the Kargil experience prompted excited voices to swing to extremes on what the nuclear issue meant for Pakistan. For example, voices in responsible positions claimed, "If war breaks out, India will surrender within an hour or so because of the superiority of Pakistan's nuclear weaponry"[72] to "How ridiculous that we should think all our security problems have been resolved by the nuclear deterrent that we have."[73] Yet, beyond these debates, clearly at critical junctures during the Kargil crisis, Pakistan worked the deterrence to push back the Indian tendency to heighten military pressure and to open new fronts.

As the military pressures grew and India went full hog deploying air, artillery, and infantry, through press leaks the Pakistan military signaled its nuclear preparedness. On June 24, *The News* reported, "The prime minister has also been told that deployment of short and long range missiles with extremely effective warheads has been completed."[74] Pakistani media reports also focused on Pakistan's nuclear capabilities. For example, one report was headlined, "Pakistan Developing Advanced versions of Ghauri, Shaheen".[75] Other reports were critical of the Indian capability, claiming, for example, "Agni II Test failed."[76] Interestingly, even those in Indian opinion-making circles who argued that Pakistan was using nuclear blackmail to intimidate India, ruled out the possibility of Pakistan's use of nuclear weapons. This thinking was reflected, for example, in General Sharma's comment, "There was no possibility of a so-called nuclear exchange. This was threatened by Pakistan for nuclear blackmail of India and stressed by the USA for restraining India for US strategic interests in the region as perceived by them."[77]

Riedel's disputed assertions

Riedel's subsequent assertions included his loud claim that Pakistan had been ready to drop the nuclear bomb but for Washington's intervention. In an obituary Riedel wrote for Clinton's National Security Advisor Sandy Berger, he claimed, "On the morning of the Fourth, the CIA wrote in its top-secret Daily Brief that Pakistan was preparing its nuclear weapons for deployment and possible use. The intelligence was very compelling."[78] There was no primary evidence to support this assertion. Several individuals from even India contested Bruce Riedel's claim that Pakistan had deployed nuclear weapons during the Kargil crisis. This included the Indian Army chief V.P. Malik,[79] Indian Defense minister George Fernandez,[80] India's lead strategic analyst and also the author of *Kargil Report* K. Subramanian[81]. Perhaps the most emphatic rebuke to Riedel's assertion that Pakistan was preparing nuclear weapons to use in the Kargil conflict and indeed that the CIA had given a definitive report on the morning of the Clinton-Sharif 4 July meeting, came from Pakistan's adversary. Subramanian questions the relevance of even raising the nuclear issue with Sharif once the conflict was drawing to a close and the question of India opening new fronts did not arise.[82]

The factual position was that, of the several factors that prevented the Kargil conflict from expanding into a full-scale war, Pakistan's nuclear weapons were of importance. That nuclear weapons therefore did have a strategic implication for the two protagonists is beyond doubt. The balance of terror created after the 1998 nuclear tests created the space for only a limited war. But for Clinton's South Asia and Non-proliferation teams, the nuclear factor apparently had a strategic relevance of another kind. For Washington, not a direct party to the conflict, the nuclear factor became a useful element in the promotion of US's strategic objectives in South Asia.

Chapter 12

ALL FALLS APART

The last stages of Pakistan's struggle to work out a diplomatic and political face-saver revolved around theback-channel with India and engagement with China.1 Also, alongside the deteriorating situation in the battle-zone, adversity at home was added. The prime minister had to keep the restive military command on board; simultaneously, he had to ward off Opposition attacks directed at him.

The final stages of the back-channel negotiations coincided with Zinni'svisit. While the Americans knew of these developments, it remains unclear if there was any deliberate coordination between Pakistan's Foreign Office and the US State Department to plan the Zinni trip on dates coinciding with acritical stage of the back-channel negotiations. The back-channel negotiations had acquired a momentum of their own.

On 25 June, R. K. Mishra,2 Vajpayee's point-man for the back-channel negotiations, flew in from Delhi on a Pakistan International Airlines (PIA) commercial flight. He met Nawaz Sharif and told him that Pakistan and India were an inch away from war, half an inch because of Vajpayee and half an inch because of Sharif. Mishra pointedly asked Sharif if he knew about Kargil but did not get a clear response. Mishra wanted to meet Nawaz Sharif alone. After ten minutes, Nawaz Sharif called Niaz Naik and wondered what had happened to Mishra, since he could hardly speak. Mishra had been sent by Vajpayee to also ask Nawaz Sharif if he knew about the Kargil operation. Sharif's team had prepared a non-paper to demonstrate to Vajpayee the Pakistani prime minister's commitment to taking the process back on track. According to the non- paper, both the prime ministers would reiterate their commitment to the Lahore process; both sides would respect LOC sanctity and for this purpose ask military officers to meet; India would stop the aerial bombing and shelling; and both prime ministers recommitted to resolving all outstanding issues, including Kashmir, as expeditiously as possible. The two prime ministers had arrived at an understanding that it could be resolved within ten months.

The same day, June 25, Sharif then sent Mishra back on his private plane at 4pm. Mishra was scheduled to meet the Indian prime minister two hours later, at 6 pm. Mishra showed the non-paper to Vajpayee, who was keen to insert as the second paragraph that Pakistan forces would withdraw from the Kargil heights

The next morning at 9 am, India's back-channel negotiator R.K. Mishra called his counterpart, Niaz Naik, saying his government was generally in agreement with the formulation in the non-paper but they also had some input. Naik was told, "Baray Sahib is saying, come immediately." Following this conversation, Naik met with the prime minister and the foreign secretary to review the situation. By 4pm, Naik was dispatched to Delhi in the prime minister's special plane. There, he was received by the MEA official Vivak Katju. Naik stayed at the Imperial Hotel, where Brajesh Mishra and R. K. Mishra both visited him that evening. For around three hours, the three thoroughly discussed the proposed statement. The Indian National Security Advisor was not to be easily convinced of Pakistan's 'good intentions". On the insertion regarding Pakistan's withdrawal from the Kargil heights, Naik indicated that it would create difficulties for Sharif. They had to wait for Vajpayee's return from Patna the same night.

On June 27, Naik met the Indian Prime Minister, Brajesh Mishra, and R. K. Mishra. Vajpayee welcomed Naik by asking him, "We started the journey from Lahore. How did we reach Kargil?" Naik's response was, "We will see how we can come back from Kargil to Lahore." Vajpayee continued, "Very simple. You should just withdraw." He said that Nawaz Sharif should announce the withdrawal before leaving for China that evening and then follow by a meeting of the DGs Military Operations to make arrangements for the withdrawal. Naik said, "Military is not possible; it is completely political." He felt the two prime ministers should meet, saying that the proposed trip to China could be reduced to two days instead of five.

For fifteen minutes, Vajpayee and his two advisors held separate meetings. They then agreed that Nawaz Sharif should issue the statement when flying over Delhi. Naik then left for the airport with R. K. Mishra. Traveling towards the airport, Mishra said that Nawaz Sharif could be invited to Delhi but how would Sharif manage this. Naik proposed that, while overflying Delhi en route to China, Sharif could give a goodwill message to Vajpayee. Mishra suggested the two prime ministers exchange messages indicating that Vajpayee's message in response to Sharif's message would be along the lines that the situation was tense and invite him to come on the way back and land there. R.K Mishra suggested the two prime ministers should talk the same night at 10pm and also exchange fax messages. As Naik was leaving, Vajpayee asked him if he was going to accompany the prime minister to China and, if not, suggested he should come to Delhi on the June 28th to prepare the press statements

Upon his return to Islamabad from Delhi, Naik went to the see the foreign secretary, from whose office, at around 1pm, he spoke to the prime minister in Lahore. Sharif instructed him to complete all the message exchanges with the Indians before coming to Lahore. Till around 7pm, Shamshad and Naik worked from Shamshad's office. At around 7:40pm, Tariq Fatemi reached Chaklala airport. The staff was looking for him, or for Naik, since there were frantic calls from Delhi. R. K. Mishra was on the line. He told Fatemi that news of Naik's visit had been disclosed. Fatemi reassured Mishra and said Naik had friends in India, so his trip could be projected as a personal trip. In Lahore, Shamshad warned the prime minister that the Naik trip was out in the press but, until 10pm, no text of Vajpayee's message had been received. Vajpayee called and Nawaz Sharif said, "I am very happy. It'sgood news." But Vajpayee said, "There is a mistake. I never said that I will invite you. Come, but I will not invite you."

On Nawaz Sharif's instructions, Naik contacted R.K. Mishra, who could not talk then, but called Fatemi around 10.30 pm. Sharif scribbled questions on a piece of paper for Fatemi to ask Mishra. He wanted to know what happened and suggested that Mishra should "come to Dubai, Lahore, Singapore", but he should come, come urgently. Mishra said he would need permission to come. Naik informed him he would be in Lahore till mid day the following day. Mishra did not come.

When Naik, a seasoned diplomat, had arrived from Delhi, he reported, "All on board." An understanding had been reached on the points of an agreement to be signed by Prime Ministers Nawaz Sharif and Atal Bihari Vajpayee in Delhi. Key modalities, including the Pakistan prime minister's flight over, and subsequently into, Delhi; the content of the goodwill messages from Sharif and subsequently from Vajpayee; the duration of Sharif's Delhi stopover; and the content of the joint statement had apparently been worked out and loose ends tied up.

On June 27, at around 5 pm, the implementation of what appeared to be a "done deal" began. The text of the goodwill message from the Pakistani prime minister was faxed from Islamabad to the Indian prime minister's office. The return message was coming in later than expected. The Indians were requested to fax the message to Sharif's Model Town residence.

The message came at around 10 p.m. And it was like a bombshell.

Vajpayee was not inviting Nawaz Sharif to visit Delhi. Instead, he was asking him to "withdraw" the intruders from Kargil so that bilateral dialogue could be resumed. Telephone contacts with the Indians at the highest level did not help. India's principle interlocutor blamed Delhi's going back on a 'done deal' first on some misunderstanding on what had been agreed but subsequently conceded that the hawks in the Indian establishment had won out. There was a sudden panic amongst those who were the principal actors in Pakistan's back-channel diplomacy. The trip to China had still to go ahead. However, a decision was taken to cut it short.

It was June 27, around 10.00 pm, and Prime Minister Nawaz Sharif, along with a top Foreign Office team, was preparing for a historic take-off from Lahore. While, for the world, it was a Beijing-bound take-off, in fact an undisclosed trip to Delhi had been planned. Earlier, around mid-day, Niaz Naik had arrived from New Delhi with what was a revised and finalized plan of action. A former Foreign Secretary, Naik had been picked up as Nawaz Sharif's special envoy, to visit Delhi on June 27. He was to carry the finalized text of the Agreement to Delhi, get a firm concurrence on its wording, and also obtain a first-hand appreciation of the Indian prime minister's degree of commitment.

By the afternoon of June 27, it all appeared to have been finalized. On his way to Beijing, Nawaz Sharif would fly over Indian territory. While doing so, he would send a goodwill message to his Indian counterpart. In response to the Pakistani prime minister's message, Vajpayee would invite him to visit Delhi, to make a "technical stop." Responding to Vajpayee's invitation, Sharif would stop in Delhi on his way back from China. In Delhi, the two prime ministers were to sign the finalized four-point agreement.

Before departing for China, Sharif talked to Vajpayee. The Pakistan prime minister even called R. K. Mishra from China. Sharif had struck a special rapport with the man he had first met in October 1998. During the Kargil crisis, he had called Mishra virtually every day. Mishra claimed that Sharif had told him during one of his visits, "I will within three months punish those responsible for Kargil."3

The veracity of this information is beyond reasonable doubt. Most was collected from primary sources while the back-channel diplomacy was actually taking place, thus ruling out the 'convenient reconstructs' of subsequent recalls. In October 1999, Naik recalled the details of the back-channel at an Asia Society meeting in New York. American diplomat Lanpher confirmed Naik's narration. Also, in the case of Naik, his subsequent recall of events does include discussion of the problem areas, thereby lending credibility to his accounts. No press reports from Delhi and Islamabad doubted that both the Indian and Pakistani leaderships were looking for an agreement from the back-channel negotiations.

Significantly, India did not have a counter-narrative on the back-channel negotiations. The numerous books written on Kargil by Indian authors mostly cover the military aspects of the operation, rarely covering the Mishra-Naik negotiations. In contrast with the Pakistani interlocutor, however, the Indian interlocutor never went public about the back-channel negotiations.4 Only after the negotiations were aborted did the Indian leadership issue sporadic statements contesting that any 'deal' or talks with Pakistan were not being considered until "Islamabad abandoned an armed intrusion in the Kargil sector of occupied Kashmir."5 Untruths were spoken by both sides for differing reasons. On 2 July, in Delhi the MEA spokesman said that he "was not aware if any contact has been established between the two neighbors in recent days."6 A section of the Indian media, however, acknowledged the existence of the Naik-Mishra backchannel. 7

Some facts are undeniable: One, that Naik and Mishra undertook the cross-border trips; two, that the two prime ministers were personally involved in the negotiations; three, that serious discussions on the four points did take place: four, in the late night National Security Council meeting for which Vajpayee had rushed to Delhi, discussions on safe passage did take place; and, five, even in the final moments of the negotiations, the Indians were uncomfortable with the simultaneity of the withdrawal and the Indian agreement to enter time-bound negotiations on Kashmir since this violated the Indian demand of "an unconditional withdrawal." This Indian demand had dovetailed into the US keenness to not let Pakistan be seen as being "rewarded" for its Kargil adventure, which Washington believed was premised on Pakistan's nuclear blackmail calculation. Further, the MEA was not comfortable with the way the back-channel negotiations were progressing and had used the policy tool of a 'press leak' to upset the negotiations.

The Zinni visit had a direct impact on the principle interlocutors of the Pakistan-India back-channel negotiations. To the Indians, who were compelled by the difficult military situation to engage in the negotiations, it gave them hope of the Pakistan military being expelled under US pressure. To the Pakistanis, who were still confident on the ground, the Zinni trip reaffirmed their complete diplomatic isolation. Consequently, while the Indians felt less pressured to continue with the back-channel negotiations the Pakistanis saw them as the only avenue left for their honorable exit from Kargil.

Given these developments, what caused this last minute Indian decision to rollback a peace deal? Three possible explanations can be given.

The first is that Islamabad may have seen an agreement where none in fact existed. It seems, however, unlikely that there was room for such a monumental misunderstanding between two parties who had carried out six rounds of negotiations, the five Mishra and one Naik visits. Also, the June 25 late night meeting of the Cabinet Committee on Security, for which Vajpayee had rushed from Poona, indicated that Delhi was engaged in serious negotiations with Pakistan.

After all, the deal appeared to have been finalized, which is when Islamabad chose to get a first hand reading of Vajpayee's intentions by sending Naik to Delhi. Naik's cautious and understated nature can be vouched for by leading international diplomats with whom he has worked. He could have therefore reported only what had occurred in Delhi. Naik's comments to a BBC correspondent confirmed that an agreement had been reached between India and Pakistan regarding an imminent meeting of the Directors-General Military Operations of the two sides. Above all, the four point agreement that had been worked out was a politically, militarily, and diplomatically logical deal for both sides as it had something in it for both countries.

The second explanation can be that Delhi actually engaged Islamabad in a diplomatic ruse. By engaging in back-channel negotiations, Delhi had in fact planned to deceptively lead on Islamabad, getting it off-guard diplomatically and militarily making it believe that a mutually acceptable peace agreement was around the corner, and, finally,using surprise at the closing moments of the deal (a kind of diplomatic guerrilla warfare), create panic in the enemy ranks.

The third and the most probable explanation for Delhi's last minute decision to roll-back peace is that, at the eleventh hour, the hawks within the Indian establishment prevailed. The Indian hawks in the BJP and in the South block had opposed the deal. Press leaks had been engineered. The news of the secret Naik trip was leaked to the Islamabad-based correspondents of the Press Trust of India and of The Hindu, obviously not by Pakistani sources. Similarly, The Times of India of June 26 carried a story on negotiations on some "deal." Carrying the salient points of the proposal which was finalized during the five Mishra trips, it labelled them as proposals emanating from Islamabad. The South Block's belligerence was evident earlier during the Kargil crisis when, after Vajpayee had personally welcomed Nawaz Sharif' s idea of receiving Sartaj Aziz in Delhi, Islamabad was suddenly informed that Aziz would not be received.

The P-5 and the G-8 policies on Kargil generally, and Washington's policy specifically, gave the Indian hawks "staying" and finally "winning" power. Washington kept up the diplomatic pressure, publicly and privately, on Islamabad, to vacate the Kargil heights throughout the period that the Pakistan-India back-channel was at work. Pressure on Pakistan took various forms, including leaking what Washington claimed was intelligence information on military movement around the LOC and insisting that Pakistan be named in the G-8 statement as being responsible for the Kargil crisis. An indirect threat by the Americans was articulated by the well-connected Michael Krepon around 20 June asserting that the American Administration had decided to make public evidence it had against Pakistan if Pakistan did not withdraw from Kargil-Drass. Interestingly, exactly around the time when the Pak-India agreement was being finalized, an editorial appeared in The Washington Post indicating that Islamabad may face difficulty in getting the next $100 million tranche released. On June 25 the State Department spokesman James Rubin said, "We want to see withdrawal of forces supported by Pakistan from the Indian side of the LOC." All these indications of Washington's clear support of the Indian position indeed provided an enabling environment to the Indian hawks.

It is also no less significant that, after Pakistan's envoy returned to Islamabad and Islamabad began preparing for the 'done deal', the American Assistant Secretary of State Gib Lanpher arrived in Delhi. On June 27, Lanpher met with senior Indian officials to brief them on General Anthony Zinni's talks with the Pakistani prime minister and with the Pakistani army chief. Lanpher's briefing had yet again reaffirmed for the Indians that the objective of US diplomacy was to secure withdrawal of the Pakistani troops. Vajpayee told the Indian press, "The US Assistant

Secretary of State, who was recently in Delhi, briefed us on his and General Zinni's talks with the Pakistani Prime Minister Nawaz Sharif." 8

Later in the day, an MEA statement commenting on the Lanpher visit maintained, "It is imperative that Pakistan heed the advice of the international community and take immediate steps to withdraw the intruders. Once the intruders are withdrawn, it is possible to take steps to resume the dialogue.... "

Inevitably, questions regarding what transpired during the Lanpher-Indian official meetings come to mind. Did the meeting have any impact on India's backing off from what reportedly was a "done deal"? What role were the Americans playing in the back-channel diplomacy when, after all, a deal would have contradicted Washington's public position that no dialogue was possible unless Pakistani backed "intruders" backed off? Would therefore Washington, like the Indian hawks, want the back-channel diplomacy to yield a deal since a deal would have meant Islamabad and Delhi had autonomously reached an agreement? What impact would a diplomatic success earned by a nuclear Pakistan and Kashmiri freedom fighters, in the face of G-8 criticism, have had on western diplomacy? These key questions spell out the built-in risks of the back-channel diplomacy that Islamabad was engaged in. Yet, to a foreign office team wary of the US, this was the best option available for an honorable exit from Kargil-Drass.

Delhi, meanwhile, by backing off from a "done deal" confirmed Pakistan's repeated assertion that Pak-India bilateral dialogues normally fail to lead to any positive conclusions. Islamabad made all the effort required to create an atmosphere of trust in an environment of war. Yet in the final analysis the hawks in the Indian policy-making establishment, aided by Washington, won out. However, weaknesses in Islamabad's own policy-making apparatus were also exposed.

Even by the end of June, India was not markedly close to getting the Kargil heights vacated. Hence, India still worked at multiple levels. It was taking nothing for granted, leaving nothing to chance. The Indian Foreign Secretary K Ragunath had planned early July trips to France and the UK. [9]

Vajpayee's own public statement of June 30 that Kargil had to be resolved immediately by "throwing away the intruders from our land" signaled the failure of back-channel diplomacy.10 According to Vajpayee, he had clearly told Nawaz Sharif's emissary Niaz Naik in their last meeting, "There can be no talks with Pakistan until the latter (Pakistan) withdraws its troops from Kargil."11

Back Channel –The US Knew About It

The US embassy in Islamabad knew about the back-channel dialogue with India. Niaz Naik had informed Political Counsellor John Schmidt about it. In a subsequent meeting with Tariq Fatemi, US Ambassador William Milam was hopeful of its outcome. Milam believed that bilateral dialogue was the answer. However, even Milam was soon to find out that there was little enthusiasm for this back-channel engagement. From Washington, there was already a direct link established to Delhi. And Washington was being told from Delhi that there was nothing to the back-channel diplomacy. The United States diplomats in Islamabad believed that Talbot and Inderfurth's own proclivities went with the Indian view.

On the back-channel, there was a view that, since the Indian thought by late June that they were winning, therefore they backed off from back-channel diplomacy. Washington asked India to not attack elsewhere on the LoC or on the International border. Washington thought they had some hints about nuclear tipped missile movement. The United States Embassy in Islamabad believed that Pakistan's missile movements were routine, undertaken by Pakistan once in a while.

The last attempt: Nawaz Sharif's China trip

Late night on June 27, the prime minister, accompanied by his official team, left for Beijing. The Chinese had invited Nawaz Sharif to come.12 He was leaving, a tired and disappointed man. Minutes before his departure, Vajpayee's back-channel interlocutor, R.K. Mishra had told him that his stop-over in Delhi on his return from Beijing, part of the pull-back plan that NiazNaik had assured the Foreign Office Delhi had agreed to,was not possible. . Frantic phone calls to Delhi were made to salvage the situation. Minutes before leaving for the airport, the Prime Minister met with his Foreign Office team to discuss the fall-out of the now botched up exit plan for Pakistani troop withdrawal from Kargil. Foremost in his mind was the absence of an exit plan for the Pakistan Army.

But in Beijing there was no reprieve for the Pakistani Prime Minister. He met with President Jiang Zemin, Chinese Premier Zhu Rongji, and Chairman of the National People's Congress Li Peng. On June 29 the Chinese Foreign Ministry spokeswoman Zhang Qiyue gave the Chinese account of the meeting between the two Prime Ministers. Zhang said, "China has always followed an independent foreign policy of peace and is committed to the preservation of peace and stability in South Asia…In talks and meetings with the Pakistani side, China has listened to their briefing on relevant issues. The Chinese side is deeply concerned about the situation."13

Nawaz Sharif's host, the Chinese Premier, was "very matter-of fact" with his Pakistani guest.14 Zhu recalled Pakistan's diplomatic isolation over Kargil. He repeated the known Chinese position15 that Pakistan needed to resolve the Kashmir issue bilaterally with India and advised Pakistan to immediately end the Kargil crisis. China, Zhu said, had no influence over India and could not intercede with the Indians. Sharif was also cautioned against involving "other"16 countries in the Kargil affair, urging Sharif to remain mindful of their tendency to exploit the situation to their own advantages.

The Chinese had obliged their Pakistani guests only at the symbolic level,not substantively.17 At the request of the Pakistanis, token "publicized support" was extended. On July 1, the Chinese government issued a statement reaffirming China's interest in the peace and security of South Asia, in the need for de-escalation of the current crisis, and for prevention of a wider war. Similarly, responding to Sharif's request, Beijing called for early resumption of dialogue between India and Pakistan in the spirit of the Lahore Declaration. The China Central Television reported that President Jiang Zemin had told the Pakistani Premier, "China hopes Pakistan and India would jointly ease the current tense situation in Kashmir and settle existing problems through dialogue in the interest of the people of South Asia...As we are close neighbors to South Asia, we are deeply concerned with the conflict in Kashmir....without peace and development in South Asia there will be no real peace and prosperity in Asia."18 These statements did not amount to Chinese support for Pakistan's Kargil position.

Meanwhile, in Islamabad, the Foreign Office spokesman Tariq Altaf informed the press that the meetings in China had been"totally satisfactory."19 The spokesman said the Chinese leadership supported Pakistan's position on Kashmir and agreed with Islamabad's position that Kargil was "essentially an issue arising from the main dispute on Kashmir."20 According to press reports, the spokesman stated that Chinese statement "neither mentioned the Mujahideen role nor suggested any withdrawal of the intruders from Kargil."21 He asserted that India's claim that Pakistan's forces had violated the LOC had also "found no favor with Beijing."22 There was no risk of contradiction from Pakistan's Chinese friends. In fact, the spokesman further emphasized his claim of Chinese support. The Chinese statement, he argued, also supported Pakistan's 12 June offer to India, made during the 12 June Sartaj Aziz-Jaswant Singh talks in New Delhi. Then, Pakistan had proposed to prevent worsening of the situation and to adopt respecting the Line of Control by resuming talks for a fair settlement of all disputes, including Kashmir. He regretted that India had turned down its "peace proposals" and also Islamabad's invitation that Jaswant Singh visit Pakistan.23

Nawaz Sharif had left Beijing a disappointed man. Back-channel negotiations with India had drawn a blank. He had hoped the Chinese would mediate with India to work out an honorable exit for the Pakistani troops.24 The Chinese and the Americans seemed to have been coordinating, even if loosely, on Kargil. Beijing and Washington appear to have been reading from the same page. While the Pakistani prime minister was in China, the State Department announced that Beijing and Washington coordinated their policies on Kargil.

The China visit was curtailed by a day. The sight-seeing programme scheduled for the third day was cancelled. In Islamabad, in off-the-record conversations with journalists, officials explained that the trip had been cut short because "several diplomatic and military initiatives and decisions" related to Kargil required the Prime Minister's personal attention.25 Late at night on June 29, Sharif left for Hong Kong, where he spent the entire day, with the only official engagement being a lunch meeting with Hong Kong's chief executive. In Hong Kong, Sharif waited for a message from Washington regarding a confirmed meeting with Clinton. Instead of returning to Pakistan, he was prepared to fly straight off to Washington from Hong Kong.26 No confirmation came through. The prime minister landed in Islamabad in the early hours of July 1.

Back and beleaguered

Within hours of his return, the Prime Minster convened a high level policy meeting. Two key exit possibilities, the Delhi and the Beijing routes, no longer existed.27 Nawaz Sharif landed back to a troubled domestic environment. The army and the political leaderships were reading the military situation differently. The politicians sought to score points over the government and the difference between fact and fiction was blurred with media reports and comments flowing from half truths. Disseminated through government statements and back-ground briefings, their purpose was to boost government standing and public morale.

The united opposition under the umbrella of the All Parties Conference (APC) had been critical of the government's handling of the Kargil crisis. Its effort to mobilize opinion against the government culminated in holding a conference in the capital on June 30. Representatives of around 35 political and religious parties were critical of the government's "secret diplomacy." The unanimously adopted Islamabad Declaration demanded that an emergency summit of the OIC be held in Islamabad to "muster international support in the face of imminent threat of Indian aggression."28

While the global consensus demanded that Pakistan vacate the Kargil heights, within Pakistan the ill-informed Opposition and the media were harping on a different tune. At the Islamabad Conference, the politicians condemned "Indian aggression on the LOC, violation of Pakistan's airspace and Indian threats of war against Pakistan."29 The Convener, Nawabzada Nasrullah Khan, linked Pakistan's isolation over Kargil to the government's failure to "highlight Kashmir." The Nawabzada said, "It appears that Pakistan had been isolated diplomatically and politically, which is evident from the statements of the US President, the European Union and the G-8 countries."30 The problem identification was correct, but not the diagnosis of the problem.

Predictably, the Opposition was attempting to create new fault-lines within Pakistan's power construct; with the objective of further pressurizing an already beleaguered government. They targeted the prime minister and praised the army chief. The Opposition leader welcomed Musharraf's statement that the Kargil issue could not be seen in isolation from the larger issue of Kashmir. Implicit in such a statement was the Opposition's simultaneous criticism of the Sharif government and its alignment of itself with the army chief. By now, the majority of Sharif's cabinet wanted to get out of Kargil.

Meanwhile, Islamabad's unconsidered response to already problematic developments was compounding problems for the Sharif government. For example, Islamabad's decision to deny that the now collapsed back-channel diplomacy ever took place created yet more trouble at home. The government was already being criticized for not taking the nation or the Parliament into confidence. The government's repeated disowning of Niaz Naik's visit provoked a barrage of criticism from the Opposition.31 The Opposition was asking the obvious questions: Who provided Naik the special plane to travel to Delhi? If the government was not involved in his visit; why would the Indian prime minister decide to meet Naik at this time? An agitated convener of the APC, the veteran politician Nawabzada Nasrullah Khan, told the press, "No man of sound mind would believe that Mr Vajpayee would grant an audience to any ordinary Pakistani in such a tense situation."32 Pakistan's denials were matched only by the Indian leadership's admission that the back-channel negotiations did take place with "Nawaz Sharif's emissary."33 In fact, the emissary himself, Niaz Naik, said on the BBC World Service Radio on June 29 that he had indeed visited India and had met Vajpayee.34

Against the back drop of all this mounting pressure, the Organization of the Islamic Conference (OIC) passed two resolutions on Kashmir; one was a reaffirmation of OIC's traditional stance35 on Kashmir and the second expressed concern over the deteriorating situation along the LOC. India was criticized for this deteriorating condition, the heavy Indian shelling and the cross-LOC air strikes caused by the heavy Indian shelling and the cross-LOC air strikes.36 The OIC foreign ministers also agreed to appoint a "special representative" on Kashmir, to be nominated by the OIC Secretary General. Meanwhile, in Pakistan, the Foreign Office was also informing the media that "a record number of 24 delegations referred to Kashmir in their statements." 37 Of course, OIC resolutions could not translate into any diplomatic leverage for Pakistan. A diplomatically beleaguered Pakistan was clutching at straws.

The Concluding Call

At home upon his return from Beijing, on July 1, the prime minister convened a high level meeting on the Kargil situation. The core team dealing with the military and diplomatic aspects of Kargil attended the meeting, including the Chief of Army Staff General Pervez Musharraf, Director-General ISI General Ziauddin, defense secretary Iftikhar Ali Khan, Foreign Secretary Shamshad Ahmad, and the Prime Minister's Principal Secretary Saeed Mehdi. The Prime Minister debriefed them on his Chinese visit. The military situation was also discussed. Some participants expressed concern about the possibility of Indian moves to expand the war theatre. The army chief ruled out such a possibility.38 Quoting "sources", the press reported, "The army chief also told the PM that all possible measures had been taken to protect Pakistan's borders against any Indian attack. He said that border positions on the LOC and at other places were further being reinforced to meet any challenge."39

The media reported that three decisions were taken at the July 1 meeting. One: the prime minister would contact his Indian counterpart. Two: back-channel diplomacy would be continued. Three: Pakistan-India military-to-military contact should be established to formalize normalization at the border.40 The military buildups of both sides were discussed. The participants were informed, "India had brought its strike aircraft on the forward operating basis, its navy had started exercise in the Arabian Sea, 21 Indian divisions were moved, 13 along the LOC and 8 on the international borders. There was a discussion on the growing panic in the western capitals, as the two neighboring nuclear countries were heading towards a war-like situation."41

Significantly, there was a discussion on the possibility of the two sides withdrawing their troops under a bilateral arrangement. Officials even specified what Indian moves could prompt Pakistan's withdrawal. They specified that, "if India showed signs of de-escalation by withdrawing its jets from Srinagar and Awantipura and lakhs of troops from the forward points along the LOC, Pakistan would respond in the same way…"42 Unilateral withdrawal was ruled out. The prime minister also briefly discussed the possibility of visiting the US "to meet President Bill Clinton and inform him about the latest situation obtaining in the region." 43 At the conclusion of the meeting, the prime minister called a meeting of the Defines Committee of the Cabinet(DCC)44 the following day.

The press reported that the 2 July DCC meeting would "approve the final strategy."45

Chapter 13

THE 2 JULY DCC MEETING

The prime minister chaired the Defense Committee of the Cabinet meeting in the cabinet room of the Prime Minister's House.[1] He had already made the decision to withdraw. He had already begun mapping possible exit routes. The presentations and discussions at this DCC meeting, Sharif had hoped, would validate his withdrawal decision. The atmosphere at the meeting was tense and sober. Reports of India reclaiming the Tololing Hill complex, consisting of several posts, were coming in. Nawaz Sharif's kitchen cabinet, including the director general Inter-Services Intelligence (ISI) and the defense secretary, a retired general, were critical of the military operation. The wisdom in the civilian camp, shared by the naval and air force chiefs, was that Op KP had not been thought through in terms of its strategic consequences. According to one Pakistan cabinet minister, "The army had climbed up a pole without considering how it would get down."[2]

Significantly, through meetings between the Defense Secretary and the Minister for Petroleum, Chaudhry Nisar, the informal communication lines were kept open between the prime minister's camp and the army chief. Yet the issues floating within the formal meetings and through the print waves and Islamabad's power-circles were raising fundamental questions about the Kargil operation. Who cleared the Kargil operation?

What was its objective? How would Pakistan's growing international isolation be handled? Are the Indian forces defeating the Pakistanis in Kargil? According to a key member of the Sharif kitchen cabinet, "The party view was not to embarrass the army leadership but to apportion responsibility."[3] Major differences had surfaced between the services chiefs over Op KP. The naval chief feared an Indian naval blockade. The air chief was also apprehensive about Pakistan's air force being pulled into an all-out war. The army chief believed the air force chief was a "scared man." [4]

Much of this was mirrored in the proceedings of this 2 July DCC meeting, whose participants included the three services chiefs, the Ministers of Interior and of Religious Affairs, the Minister of State for Foreign Affairs,[5] and the Defense and Foreign Secretaries. Presentations began with Foreign Secretary Shamshad Ahmad. He sketched a bleak picture of Pakistan's diplomatic isolation. He recounted the countless diplomatic efforts made by Pakistan in an increasingly hostile environment. Pakistan's position had been projected using every diplomatic and political means possible. This included regular media briefings and contacts with the UNSG, OICSG, OIC members, EU and G-8 countries. Special envoys had been sent, and high level demarches had been made in the form of letters from the prime minister to his G-8 counterparts and from the FM to his EU and OIC counterparts. The world community, especially the G-8 and EU, did not accept Pakistan's position and called for withdrawal. They had managed merely to prevent a condemnation of Pakistan by the G-8 at the Cologne meeting. Also, no OIC country, with the exception of Saudi Arabia, supported Pakistan. Beijing had pointedly stressed upon the need for Pakistan to de-escalate the situation. The US and EU considered the situation as "dangerous", with the potential for eruption into a wider conflict in a nuclear environment.[6]

After the foreign secretary, an army brigadier rose to make a presentation on the military situation. Searching questions by the participants prompted the army chief to take over the presentation. With the help of maps, Musharraf made three specific points. One: India will not take the war beyond Kargil; when pushed by the participants as to what if India did, he said the war would produce a stalemate as India could never achieve a victory. Two: Despite some losses, "our position in Kargil is defensible and we can hold on to our position." Three: Since India had brought its forces north of Kashmir, the army "could take any action it wanted in Kashmir."

Addressing the assumption that Indian airpower was working decisively against Pakistan, the army chief emphasized that, given the extremely hostile terrain, only limited airpower could be deployed by India. What they could deploy would not decisively help the Indian forces.

Musharraf gave a detailed account of the military activity in Kargil. Admiral Fasih Bokhari, who feared a naval blockade, was particularly vocal against the operation. The prime minister even asked the army chief, if the Indians extended the war, what would Pakistan do. He and his cabinet were mindful of the initial briefings which had predicted that India would not be in a position to militarily fight back in Kargil. Privately, when asked how come they were losing the heights, senior military men had conceded, "We never thought that this would happen, that India would play such high human price."[7] Sharif also pointed out that Pakistan's communication lines were being compromised and hence the sustenance for our troops was weakening.

With the army still painting a positive picture, Finance Minister Ishaq Dar asked the army chief if, should they got the required funding, could they get Kashmir. Musharraf reminded Dar that the distance of Kashmir from where they were was a way off. "Will we be able to get Siachen?" Dar then asked.[8] Siachen, he was told, was not "economical" for Pakistan to hold onto. The army chief's general refrain was, "We went in only to flag the issue." Goal-posts set by the Kargil clique were vanishing under the Indian military pressure.

The army chief said that, despite India's intense bombing and capturing around 35 percent of the posts, Pakistani troops were still holding on to the rest.

When he was asked if they would be able to retain what was with them, Musharraf said that, because of weather conditions, by August or September Pakistan would have to vacate all the posts. It was already July!

He explained that, despite the aerial bombing, the Pakistani troops controlling the remaining posts were in a strong position since, sitting at the heights, they could continue to attack the Indian supply lines. The conversation was bordering on the surreal. The dead bodies of young soldiers arriving home had already given lie to the Kargil clique's May claim that "no one can evict us"[9], that "we are invincible." [10]

A cabinet minister, Majeed Malik, also a former army general, said that the Indians would soon wrest away the leverage by creating alternative routes through the mountains.

Musharraf maintained that 95% of the ingressed area was still intact with the Pakistani troops. Of the five main ingress points, the Indians had recaptured only one and a half peaks in the Tololing range. With three main peaks still in Pakistan's control, the army chief was confident that the Indians may be able to regain control of some area but would not be able to remove the Pakistanis from Kargil. Pakistan, he explained, still had the trump card: the ability to block the Srinagar-Leh Highway. Pakistan, he said, had the Indians "by the jugular." The army chief disagreed with the naval chief's assessment regarding the possibility of an Indian naval blockade of Karachi port. Musharraf's conclusion was that even if the Indians went for all-out war, it would merely be a stalemate. The Indians could never be victorious.

Musharraf later recalled his presentation at the DCC meeting. The army chief said that he had made a "complete presentation" that was spread over an hour. According to Musharraf's recollection, "He (Nawaz Sharif) kept asking me should we withdraw and I was avoiding giving an answer. I said it is the leader's job to decide …I will give the military and strategic analysis. I explained whether there would be open war or not, why the military activity would be restricted only to Kashmir and would not go beyond…I gave a complete presentation."[11] Musharraf recalled explaining to the DCC participants how far India could be tied down in Kashmir and said that the civilian leaders "better start talking on Kashmir."[12]

This military assessment made by the architects of Kargil at the DCC meeting was also reflected in the media. For example,the daily *Nation* quoted the Inter-Services Public Relations spokesman, "Pakistan will hold on to its positions on the LOC at all costs."[13] Significantly, only a day before the DCC, the paper reflected the position the army leadership was to take the following day at the DCC. The *Nation*'s editorial emphasized, "India is in a horrible bind. It has nearly two divisions in the Siachen sector, and three divisions in Ladakh against China, all of which are supplied only by the Srinagar–Leh road. If that road is interdicted by the freedom fighters upto mid-September, when it becomes snow bound, then India will not be able to provide Siachen and Ladakh garrisons sufficient supplies to last out the winter. While the troops are unlikely to starve, their combat capability will suffer enough for a Pakistani offensive in Siachen to have good chances of success. The pressure on the Pakistani side is that Kargil will not remain a vital choke point forever. Because of the recent operation, work has been speeded up on alternative road routes to Leh, which have been planned by the Indian government. While there are always construction delays, Pakistan cannot count on there being no alternative route next summer." [14]

At the DCC meeting, there were tense moments. As the military briefing continued, the thrust of the prime minister's question was, "What you are now telling me, you should have told me earlier." At this point, a somewhat agitated Musharraf disputed the assertion that the prime minister had been kept in the dark. He pulled out his diary from his pocket, opened it, and trotted off about seven dates on which he had briefed the prime minister on the military situation. By now, the inevitable blame game had begun.[15] Anticipating this, Musharraf was already prepared. Complete silence followed. The prime minister was quiet. The scales in Pakistan's power construct tilt unmistakably in the army's favor, and this may have accounted for the silence of the country's chief executive. It was at this point that the Minister for the Interior intervened. A seasoned politician who enjoyed Sharif's confidence, he said the need was to "move beyond the technical" and "as political people we needed to be aware of the crisis that had gripped the country." Chaudhry Shujaat referred to the newspaper reports suggesting internal differences over the Kargil operation. He recommended that "a message of unity" must go from the meeting. Shujaat insisted, "Whatever has happened has happened, and is not important any longer." Instead, he suggested that a statement be "jointly" drafted sending a message of unity, of collective responsibility for what had happened, and a joint effort should be launched to manage the current situation. Shujaat's intervention eased the tension. Everyone's body language improved and they relaxed.

The 2 July DCC meeting, which lasted for five hours, had ended inconclusively.[16] There had been a thorough and candid assessment of the overall diplomatic and military situation. The pros and cons of how withdrawal would impact internationally and domestically were also discussed. Yet the prime minister took no decision. The meeting was adjourned. A question mark lingered over the issue of troop withdrawal. The prime minister decided to reconvene another meeting of the DCC to take a final decision on the key question: whether to withdraw or to stay. The prime minister decided that the DCC would reconvene after the weekend. He set July 5the date for the next meeting.

The press reports on this crucial meeting were generally accurate. Most detailed the presentations and the issues that were discussed at the DCC. They reported on the parallel tracks that the participants had explored. One of the papers reported that prime minister had been authorized "to initiate appropriate steps to engage India in peaceful negotiations for dealing with the core issue of Kashmir." [17] Quoting "ministerial sources", another correspondent reported that the participants appreciated the "all time high military preparedness, they favored military-to-military contact and also the need to pursue high level diplomacy in order to tell the world of Pakistan's interest in de-escalating the tensions."[18] According to the reports, the DCC also decided to step up diplomatic efforts by arranging high profile visits, by cabinet members like Chaudhry Nisar Ali as special envoys, to some important capitals.

Detailed debriefs produced reports which stated, "The COAS gave a true assessment of the situation by discussing some vulnerable points and many strong ones of the Pakistan Army and told the meeting that in case India tried to escalate the conflict it would be a big loser." It further added that the army chief informed the participants that "What was humanly possible had been done to meet any challenge and that the Pakistan armed forces were ready to take on the enemy if it tried to widen the conflict to full-fledged war…" [19]

The press reports did indicate that the discussions had veered towards withdrawal. For example one report almost laid down the conditions for a withdrawal, stating that "India should concede something to resolve the issue by pushing back its increasing infantry formations on the LOC."[20] According to the report participants "did not rule out possibility of a meeting between DGMO in a day or so to work out demarcations…"[21] Another report, quoting one of the "participants "of the meeting, indicated, "We have decided not to go for war but if it is imposed Pakistan's armed forces backed by the whole nation will defend every inch of the motherland."[22]

The meeting had been long but not decisive. The press reported, "Lengthy discussions on pros and cons, on policy options, but no final decision was taken. The meeting was informed that any premature step in either way may lead to some drastic developments and before taking a final decision it should be kept in mind."[23] Reflecting perhaps the concerns of some of the DCC participants, one newspaper report suggested, "The so-called withdrawal from Kargil by Mujahideen will have serious repercussions." It went on to argue, "First, the morale of the nation and armed forces personnel, two the political loss and the present government will have to suffer; three its impact on the freedom movement and the Mujahideen inside occupied Kashmir and four does it mean burying the liberation movements for many years to come; five what will happen to the Kashmir cause and who will guarantee that the Kashmir issue will be taken up in future talks with India."[24] The same daily documented the consequences feared by some DCC participants of the continued military and diplomatic stand-off leading to a limited or full-scale war with India: "First neither Pakistan can afford any war with India; two the state of preparedness, three any spillover of the war may result in a disaster for the region; four where was Pakistan in the diplomatic community as international pressure is mounting for withdrawing the so-called infiltrators and the pressure of India to de-escalate.."[25]

According to media reports, the DCC in its meeting held on 2 July also expressed its "regrets that India had failed to respond to the various positive initiatives taken by the PM to de-escalate the situation."[26] Minister for Religious Affairs Zafarul Haq said, "The Back-channel is continuing and there is no question of withdrawal." He briefed the meeting about his visit as a special envoy to Saudi Arabia, Egypt, UAE, and Bahrain." The

DCC had agreed to send some key ministers as "special envoys to various capitals" with the objective of "highlighting Pakistan's position." The Prime Minster also decided to brief the DCC members on the back-channel interlocutor Niaz Naik's mission to Delhi.[27] Only three days earlier, the Foreign Office had insisted that Naik was in Delhi on a private visit.

There were two incontestable facts about the 2 July DCC meeting, held two months into the Kargil crisis. One, no decision on Pakistan's future moves on Kargil was taken. While adjourning the meeting, the prime minister had called another DCC meeting on July 5 to take some "final decisions." This later meeting never took place. Two, at no point during the meeting did the army chief Musharraf recommend a military withdrawal from Kargil.[28]Contrary to the view held by the prime minister, his kitchen cabinet and the navy-air force chiefs that India would expand the war to the international borders, the army leadership believed the Indians would remain bogged down in Kargil. Yet the general thrust of the civilians was that army wanted 'out' of Kargil. This reading flowed from indirect inferences. For example, according to one of the participants, while he did not "remember any specific indication from the Pakistan Army wanting to withdraw from Kargil, but their discomfort at the military setbacks and diplomatic backlash the world over was discernible." The civilians, who had earlier concluded that Pakistan had been led into disaster by its military leadership, now believed that high casualties plus the loss of Tololing and the Tiger Hills had also put the military under pressure.

Interestingly, on the day the DCC met, two other Kargil-related developments also took place. In Washington, the US Congress passed a resolution with overwhelming majority asking Pakistan to vacate Kargil. The House International Relations Sub Committee on Asia passed the resolution by a 20 to 5 vote. The Committee Chairman Benjamin Gilman, a Republican from New York, said in his opening statement, "The government of Pakistan has previously supported terrorism in India. This latest incident, however, is far beyond the murder of innocent civilians on a train or at a wedding party…it is widely reported that Pakistan Army intelligence service and government have moved thousands of men and materials up to the Pakistan side of the LOC and sent hundreds of army regulars across the line. Pakistan is laying down artillery fire in support of the invaders and the leaders of Pakistan should now withdraw its forces."[29] While Gilman acknowledged the need for the US to encourage both India and Pakistan to adhere to the principles of the Lahore Declaration, he insisted that it should be the policy of the US to "oppose Government of Pakistan's support for armed incursion into the Indian side of the LOC...it should be the policy of the US to support the immediate withdrawal of intruding forces supported by Pakistan and urge the re- establishment and future respect for the LOC and encourage all sides to end the fighting and exercise restraint." [30]

And in Delhi the Indian National Security Council Advisor Brajesh Mishra publicly said that the US had the impression that Pakistan wants to withdraw its forces from Kargil. Delhi, aware that the Nawaz Sharif government was by now psychologically ready to unilaterally withdraw from Kargil, was upbeat. Hence, by now clearly in the know of an imminent Pakistani withdrawal, Delhi could afford to be dismissive of Washington's role in successfully bringing Kargil to a close. Referring to Delhi's refusal to receive US CENTCOM chief General Anthony Zinni[31], Mishra had said, "We do not want any general coming to us."[32] The fact remains that, whatever the rhetoric, Delhi had sought and received unstinted US support in getting Kargil vacated. In fact, forcing unconditional Pakistani troop withdrawal from Kargil had become a joint Indo-US objective.

Meanwhile, in Pakistan, as 2 July drew to a close, there was no doubt about where the chips would fall on Kargil. Pakistan's political leadership was more than ready to withdraw. Key foreign office officials were equally clear about the need to withdraw. Only the army chief, at the DCC meeting had insisted his forces had 'staying power' in Kargil. Musharraf had also claimed that the Kargil operation had accrued political and diplomatic advantages to Pakistan.

The prime minister, unbeknown to even his close advisors, had decided on the path Pakistan would take to bring the Operation Koh Paima to a close. As was his usual routine, he flew for the weekend to Lahore, his home-town.

On Saturday morning, from the Governor's House, Sharif spoke to the US President.[33] The closure of Pakistan's fourth military encounter with India had begun.The army chief was likely to go along with the chief executive's decision. He had already stated this categorically at the DCC meeting.

Chapter 14

THE END GAME

The Making of 4 July

After the DCC meeting concluded, Prime Minister Nawaz Sharif flew to his hometown Lahore for the weekend. His concerns were clear. His thinking process was not. He was playing his cards close to his chest. The chief of army staff, ostensibly satisfied with the military situation of his troops, went off with family and friends to a hill resort for the weekend. He believed that his troops had staying power but he was also beginning to note the international pressures that were being applied on Pakistan.[1]

The Foreign Office had begun to focus on the Monday meeting. Mindful of the fact that the final decision on withdrawal was to be taken in the 5 July DCC meeting, they were keen to weigh the pros and cons of the decision of whether to stay or to withdraw. In the Friday meeting, they had witnessed a 'house divided' There was tension evident between the prime minister and the army chief. The service chiefs had also differed. They knew that the political leadership was keen to withdraw, but the Army seemed unclear. They believed, 'The Army's body language conveyed their wanting to withdraw too.' However, Musharraf had made no such statement. The bureaucrats were not there to take decisions but they believed their input influenced decision-making. The Foreign Secretary, Shamshad Ahmad, had already spoken of Pakistan's diplomatic isolation. A section within the core Foreign Office group was unsure of the wisdom of withdrawal.[2]

The Prime Minister's Principal Secretary, Saeed Mehdi, called US Ambassador Milam to convey Sharif's intention to talk to the US President. Milam relayed the request to the State Department. Shortly before this request, Clinton had also received a letter from Sharif asking to meet him. However, the letter, which had been drafted by Sharif's Foreign Office team, had yet again linked the Kargil flare-up with the broader Kashmir problem. In Washington, the tone of this letter conveyed that 'Sharif was wringing his hands … that he was looking for personal cover … he was not a man of great courage'.[3] Sharif had written in response to Clinton's letter, written a few days after Zinni's return to Washington. Clinton had thanked Sharif for receiving Zinni but had wondered why there was no action on Zinni's report that Sharif was willing to withdraw troops from Kargil. By now, the bottom line message of Washington's communication to Islamabad was: 'Get out!' Clinton himself, his envoy General Zinni, and the State Department had repeatedly told Sharif that negotiations over the withdrawal of Pakistani forces from Kargil were out. This was now Washington's and Delhi's shared objective.

On 3 July, Pakistan's PM played his usual weekend sport. In the late afternoon, he arrived at his favorite cricket ground in one of Pakistan's oldest gardens, the Jinnah Bagh. After his cricket game, Sharif, as was his routine, chatted with spectators gathered around. He told them to 'pray for him and for the nation as he was passing through hard times'.[4] Earlier in the day, in a meeting with ruling party activists, he had said, 'You are fully aware that my entire attention is diverted towards the Kashmir issue and Kargil. I am trying my best to fulfill national responsibilities. You should pray for me that I shall perform my duties in accordance with national aspirations.'[5]

Early in the evening, Sharif went to the Governor's House and called the US President at the agreed time. This was the sixth Sharif-Clinton conversation since the Kargil crisis had erupted.[6] It was Saturday morning in Washington. South Asia's Kargil crisis had brought the concerned State Department officials to work on a weekend. When news of the 4 July

Sharif-Clinton meeting travelled from the White House to the State Department, the South Asian team was at work.

The PM telephoned from the Governor's House in Lahore.[7] During the call, Sharif was not assisted by members of either his 'kitchen cabinet' or of the core Foreign Office group. In attendance were Saeed Mehdi and Iftikhar Ali Khan. The prime minister's brother, Shehbaz, was at the family home in Raiwind. Chaudhry Nisar, his close confidante and a member of his 'kitchen cabinet', was two hundred miles away in his home town, Taxila. The Foreign Office team was at work in Islamabad. By contrast, at the White House, Clinton was surrounded by his key aides. He remained, therefore, within the parameters set by Washington's primary objective of forcing an unconditional Pakistani withdrawal. During the telephone conversation, the US President sent no mixed signals to his Pakistani friend.

Sharif, once again, urged Clinton to play a role in defusing the Kargil crisis and in resolving the Kashmir dispute. He asked to see him. Clinton reminded Sharif of the precondition for a meeting. Sharif did not contest Clinton's suggestion of a unilateral, unconditional withdrawal. Clinton told Sharif that he wanted to help him and to help Pakistan but Pakistani forces had to first withdraw. Clinton again rhetorically queried why Pakistan had done this. Sharif said he could give him 'the entire scenario when we meet'. Clinton emphasized that time was of the essence and that they 'are losing time'. According to Pakistan's Ambassador to the United States, Riaz Khokhar, Clinton agreed to receive Sharif because the Americans wanted that the prime minister to personally convey that the Pakistani troops would vacate Kargil. Clinton wanted to hear for himself from Sharif that he was willing to withdraw.[8]

The phone call had made it clear to the Clinton administration that 'Sharif was looking for a political cover for withdrawing Pakistan's forces'.[9] Equally, Clinton made it clear to Nawaz Sharif 'that he could not provide cover and withdrawal had to proceed on its own merit'. Sharif insisted that they talk face-to-face. It was an unusual conversation between two heads of government. Clinton's advisors saw it no differently. They had 'never seen anything quite like that, i.e., you invite yourself, that it was a bizarre time to invite yourself'.[10]

Clinton agreed that the beleaguered Sharif come the following day. It was a national holiday, US Independence Day, but Clinton agreed, sensing that the Pakistani prime minister was likely to concede unconditional withdrawal. In Islamabad, it was read differently. According to one of Sharif's close confidantes, by inviting him on a holiday, Sharif was told by Clinton, 'While we do not work on a national day, but this is a measure of the importance we give to this issue.'[11] The American account of this call also confirms that, detecting from Sharif's conversation the willingness to withdraw troops from Kargil. Clinton conceded to an immediate meeting with the prime minister, who offered to arrive the next day.[12] A Sunday surprise was in the offing.

It was to be a historic meeting. It would signal the end of the first military conflict on the Jammu and Kashmir territory between the two nuclear-armed South Asian neighbors. For the Americans, it would be memorable as the first ever peacetime summit that a US President would hold on the American Independence Day. Soon after the meeting was finalized, preparations at the State Department and the National Security Council were under way to prepare briefing material for the President. From Sharif, Washington needed a withdrawal as well as a commitment to help Washington find Osama Bin Laden.[13] The State Department laid out these demands on the one-page briefing paper it prepared for the US President for the 4 July meeting.[14]

In Pakistan, there was no preparatory work that Nawaz Sharif sought from his core Foreign Office team, the cabinet members, or the Army. The focus was now on getting the logistics done for the Washington dash. Sharif knew that, in getting a meeting with Clinton, he had in fact proceeded ahead with his 'kitchen cabinet's' consensus on involving the US.[15] According to a key member of the 'kitchen cabinet', 'The call was made in line with the inner circle's thinking about the need for an honorable withdrawal.'[16] He explained, 'Since the Americans kept telling Nawaz Sharif there was a peaceful way of settling this issue, the idea was to suck them in to help settle Kargil peacefully.' The 'kitchen cabinet' believed 'it was preferable to talk to the US, not to the Indians, because talking to the Indians was like insulting the honest brokers [US]'.[17]

Sharif's Foreign Minister, Sartaj Aziz, was not in this inner loop. He was not even remotely clued into his PM's decision to explore the withdrawal option with Clinton. Therefore, when on arrival from Burkina Faso, when he was asked to comment on US Ambassador Milam's statement that US 'perceived flexibility' in Pakistan's position on the Kargil issue, Sartaj merely reaffirmed the existing position that the Kargil flare-up was not of Pakistan's doing. He told reporters, 'I think there is no flexibility or new position. Pakistan has always respected the LOC … The question is: What is the LOC? Who is sitting there? It needs verification and these violations on LOC, on either side, Pakistan side or Indian side, should be corrected. As far as Pakistan Army is concerned, it has not violated the LOC … We have invited UN observers that they should come and see where the LOC is. If anybody had violated it, it should be corrected.'[18]

At the prime minister's family home in Raiwind, the prime minister, his father, and his younger brother, vigorously discussed the Sharif's decision to go to Washington. At the DCC, there had been no discussion at all on a possible immediate Washington trip. It seems that major policy matters, which were not even brought up in constitutionally mandated forums, such as the DCC, were to be debated by the members of the 'first family' in their private home. The prime minister's younger brother, a key political player and the chief minister of Punjab, vehemently opposed Nawaz Sharif's visit to Washington. He opposed it 'tooth and nail'. He argued that the PM's attempt at closure would be portrayed by the Army as the squandering of a military victory by the civilians. The prime minister's elderly father, Mian Mohammad Sharif, who often influenced key national decisions taken by his son, disagreed with the younger son. He supported the Nawaz Sharif's decision to fly to Washington. He saw the Washington trip as 'an effort to get Pakistan out of trouble'. Mian Mohammad believed that the developments in Kargil had landed the country, much like a family, in trouble and, therefore, it was required by the chief executive as head of the family to get the family out of trouble. Shehbaz was emphatic that, if the trip to Washington had to be made, it was important that the army chief be taken along for the 4 July meeting, so that the withdrawal agreement would not been seen as a 'sell-out by the civilians'. The prime minister agreed. However, in subsequent conversations with his two close aides, Saeed Mehdi and Chaudhry Nisar, he became convinced otherwise. The prime minister felt that, if he, the elected prime minister, took the army chief along with him to Washington, the Clinton administration would conclude that, since the prime minister moved nowhere without the army chief, it would be better to cut Sharif out and directly deal with Musharraf.[19] Shehbaz's suggestion to take along the army chief was torpedoed. The PM only went along with his brother's decision to take the army chief 'into confidence'. Sharif instructed his military secretary to later put a call through to Musharraf. The army chief was spending the weekend in the hills in Murree.

After the plan was made, phones started ringing. The prime minister was seeking attendance for an unusual meeting at the Islamabad airport. It was scheduled for around midnight between 3 July and 4 July. This airport meeting was to be a pale shadow of the DCC meeting that had been scheduled for 5 July. The participants of the 'airport' meeting were to be informed of the chief executive's meeting with the US President. Actually, the finalization of Pakistan's Kargil strategy was now to take place in Washington at the Sharif-Clinton meeting.

In its 9pm news bulletin, *Pakistan Television* (PTV), the state-run television service, announced Sharif's departure. The Foreign Office also issued a late night press statement. According to the statement in Washington, Sharif would take stock of the 'deteriorating situation and the need for a settlement of the Kashmir dispute, which holds the key to durable peace and security in South Asia'.[20] The Orwellian machine was at work. There was no mention of the word Kargil in the statement. Instead, it stated, 'The main purpose of the visit is to discuss the Kashmir situation.' Earlier in the evening, the Pakistan Foreign Office spokesman had said, 'He [Sharif] would be happy to meet the US President … no dates have been finalized so far.'[21] A day earlier, on 2 July, US Ambassador Milam had categorically said that there was no meeting scheduled between Sharif and Clinton.[22]

It was past dinner time when the prime minister began calling his team. The first call was made to his key confidante Chaudhry Nisar[23], who had advocated American involvement in the crisis. Nisar was told by Nawaz Sharif to prepare for departure. Sharif said that there was no time for discussion and he must get ready and arrive at the airport within two hours. Sharif then called his Foreign Minister, Sartaj Aziz. Only hours before, Sartaj had arrived from Burkina Faso after attending the OIC foreign minister's conference. Exhausted by the endless hours of flying, the minister had just begun settling in for a relaxed evening. The green phone rang. The PM had 'desired' to speak to him. Sharif shocked him with news of his Washington dash.[24] He was to be ready within a few hours for his turn-around trip, this time across the Atlantic. The meeting with Clinton had been set for 4 July.

At the Hotel Scherzade, in the Foreign Secretary's office, it was business as usual. It was past 8pm and the three-man diplomacy team led by the foreign secretary,[25] was reviewing diplomatic developments related to the Kargil crisis. A strong Congressional resolution censuring Pakistan had been passed. From Delhi, the accusations had continued unabated. Suddenly, the green phone rang. It was the prime minister's call for the foreign secretary. He was given instructions to prepare for the Washington trip and arrive at the airport by 11pm. Similarly, the Defense Secretary also received a call around 10pm to arrive at the airport by 2am.

Ambassador Milam was the next one to know about the trip. Late night on a holiday, Milam received a call from an unlikely caller with an unlikely request. The Foreign Office spokesman, Tariq Altaf, wanted US visas. Milam was obliging. 'Sure, send your passport in on Monday,' he told the FO spokesman. But Altaf wanted 30 visas right away so that the delegation could board the PM's plane! That was the first Milam heard of his President's meeting with the Pakistani prime minister. He was not in the loop. That evening, the US embassy issued visas to around 30 people accompanying Nawaz Sharif. But, before doing that, Milam called Karl Inderfurth and 'screamed about not being told of Sharif's visit'. Inderfurth too pleaded ignorance. The State Department too had not been informed in advance by the White House.[26]

Sharif contacted the army chief in the end. He was unsure of his reaction to the prime minister's unilateral decision to leave for Washington. He knew Musharraf was keen to bring the Americans into the fray because he had naively hoped that Clinton would help Pakistan extract a better deal on Kashmir. But Sharif's Washington departure was for a different purpose. Sharif wanted Clinton on his side as he agreed to troop withdrawal. The Clinton meeting, given Pakistan's domestic power realities, was going to be a morale booster for Nawaz Sharif. Otherwise, negotiations and even assurances on Kashmir were out. Also, no diplomatic or strategic benefits could have accrued from the Clinton meeting. The Sunday dash was planned in complete secrecy. Neither his cabinet members, nor the core Foreign Office team, or even all the members of his 'kitchen cabinet' were privy to the planning of the visit. Sharif had planned his 4 July trip with the surprise and speed of a guerrilla operation. He planned the end of the Kargil Operation in the kind of secrecy in which it had been launched. It was past 9pm. At the hill resort of Murree, the army chief, on a weekend break, received a call from his Commander-in-Chief. Musharraf was instructed to arrive at the Islamabad airport immediately for an important meeting. Sharif also informed President Rafiq Tarrar of his departure.

Around 12:30am, the prime minister left Lahore for Islamabad. The Falcon jet carrying him flew into Islamabad around 1am. In the dead of night, while the nation slept, the cars of Pakistan's ruling men had begun rolling into the Islamabad/Chakala airport. The passengers were assembling at the VIP lounge. Clad in a safari suit, the army chief arrived at the airport. He and the ISI chief had driven together from Murree. The Chief of General Staff General, Mohammad Aziz, had also been summoned. Upon meeting the prime minister, a surprised Musharraf had remarked that he had no clue about the trip. Sharif explained it had been suddenly planned. Musharraf supported the idea of including the Americans and, hence, the Sharif trip. Musharraf again reassured his commander-in-chief regarding the military situation. He said, 'There is no pressure on us …we can sustain our position. So, please do not take any pressure.'

The Prime Minster chaired the hurriedly called meeting at the airport before his departure. It lasted for 90 minutes. The Foreign, Minister Sartaj Aziz, defense secretary, Iftikhar Ali Khan, Foreign Secretary, Shamshad Ahmad, DG ISI, Lt General Ziauddin, General Pervez Musharraf, Additional Secretary, Tariq Altaf, and Tariq Fatemi attended the meeting. Sharif explained in the meeting that he had spoken to Clinton three times and that Clinton was keen to resolve the problem. The prime minister also said that the theatre of war would spread and, given that India and Pakistan were nuclear powers, it could be a disaster. The prime minister also told the gathering that he had told Clinton the real issue was Kashmir and that he was going to press that point during his meeting with him. Musharraf said Pakistan wanted to use the Kargil Operation to highlight Kashmir. The army chief urged the prime minister to 'get the best deal'.[27] He was not opposed to Nawaz Sharif's Washington trip. In fact, he supported the move to engage the Americans, whom he believed could help Pakistan leverage its hold over Kargil to extract a favorable commitment from India towards a Kashmir resolution. In fact, Musharraf's 26 June statement that a Sharif-Clinton meeting may be on the cards had been widely reported in the local press.[28] After the PM's plane took off, the army chief and the DG ISI left together for Murree.

The army chief's reading of the military situation completely contrasted with that of the two military men in Nawaz Sharif's inner circle: the defense secretary, a former general, and the DG ISI, a serving Engineers Corps general. These two believed that militarily India was beginning to gain the upper hand and that Tiger Hill had already been lost. Through formal and informal channels, they had begun informing the prime minister and his key cabinet members that the Pakistani forces had been pushed back from at least half the positions they had earlier occupied in the Operation.

In the civilian political camp, there was no doubt left that Pakistan's military operation in Kargil had to end. Withdrawal was the only option. The naval and air force chiefs also shared this view. The cumulative effect of the key developments during the last week of June had contributed to this conclusion. First, the failure of the backchannel; then, the G-8 statement calling for Pakistan's withdrawal; third, the response of the Chinese; four, the United States pressure following the Zinni trip; fifth, France's decision to not allow Pakistan's submarines to enter French waters; and, finally, the clear cut message by the Indians that no dialogue with Pakistan could take place without withdrawal of forces from Kargil.

In Washington, meanwhile, after the Sharif-Clinton telephone conversation, the White House announced the meeting. A White House statement noted, 'All agreed that the situation is dangerous and could escalate if not resolved quickly. At the prime minister's request the President will meet him at the Blair House ... to discuss how to resolve the immediate situation.'[29] What Washington did not state was the extent to which Delhi had sought Clinton's involvement to get Kargil resolved on Delhi's terms.

Public conversation

While there were two kinds of views reflected in the media, the skeptical and the triumphal, it was the latter that had captured the public imagination. The expectation was that Pakistan would successfully pressurize Delhi into working on an early settlement of the Kashmir issue. Given the contradictory and contending assertions constantly made by different institutions, the majority of the reporters and commentators were unable to ascertain the facts of the situation. Most veered towards triumphalism. The average Pakistani mind was in the grip of official propaganda and patriotic zeal. But there were also exceptions.

'Whereas the world community has been calling on Pakistan to end its 'intrusion' across the LOC, the ISPR has again pointed out that the Pakistani posts overlooking the Kargil-Leh road are on the Pakistani side of the LOC, it is now the Indian intention, under the guise of clearing out the infiltrators' to those posts, which would amount to an Indian intrusion across the LOC ... India, therefore, has to escape the noose as soon as possible, while Pakistan has only this opportunity to tighten it. Pakistan's offer of a ceasefire was actually India's best option, for it would have let it off the hook militarily, allowing it a breathing space to complete its supply operation. However, the Indian government which felt confident of its ability to suppress the freedom fighters, refused to talk at all. Unfortunately, the international community encouraged India by pressing unfairly on Pakistan to withdraw from Kargil. Pakistan has stuck to its guns, with the result that the world community is now moving towards the position that talks are more important than humiliating Pakistan. India's internal consensus, essential for a caretaker government's effectiveness, seems to be crumbling; and it is faced with high casualties, just before an election, for a minimal military success. Pakistan's resolve at this point must not weaken, and it should be ready to cut a deal with India, but based on the ground realities, which India must acknowledge.' Editorial, *The Nation,* 1 July 1999.

'It can be confirmed on the basis of sound evidence that not a single Pakistani soldier is present inside Kashmir across the LOC. Such allegations by India are patently absurd and an attempt to cover up her own designs. Pakistan would be insane in sending its soldiery into a highly disputed and disturbed area ... Those opposing the Indian aggression in the Drass-Kargil area are the docile and peace-loving sons of the soil in Kashmir who have been driven to take up arms to defend their rights, honour, and dignity in the face of brutal Indian aggression ... The on-going Indian bellicosity is a matter of deep concern to the world ... India has shut the diplomatic doors the way Hitler did in 1938–39.' General (retd) Khalid Mahmud Arif in 'What Realism Demands', *Dawn*, 3 July 1999.

'Like it or not, what has stood internationalized over the past few weeks is not Kashmir but Kargil. We deceive ourselves if we mistake one for the other, or believe one can easily made to lead to the other. And the internationalization that has occurred is no accession of strength to Islamabad ... But the emphasis, both in the official US position and the G-8 statement, was on the intrusion, the infiltrators' return to the former positions and strict abidance by the LOC. They call for end to the Indo-Pakistan confrontation and resumption of talks was only subsidiary to that which almost echoed the Indian position ... The point was driven home by this mission of the Commander-in-Chief of the US Central Command. He wasn't sent down to urge the adversaries to cool it, as normally happens in explosive situations. He was sent exclusively to Pakistan. It was Pakistan that was seen as requiring to pipe down, Pakistan that was considered primarily responsible for the new development ... The mission was, thus, also in part on behalf of the Indians ... All this had been obvious to many, but not the establishment in Islamabad. It came out even more explicitly into the open when a US spokesman emphasized that the Pakistan-supported forces need to be withdrawn back over LOC and the LOC established ... The Foreign Office here was reduced to pleading that the US was taking a 'narrow view' of the situation. But it was always taking that view. And so were most others abroad ... Those who had planned the

Kargil act had not apparently taken all the possibilities sufficiently into the calculation ... The Kashmir dispute, thus, resists being internationalized even in the face of a major war scare. It does that, not because bilateralism is a sovereign principle … If Kashmir resists internationalization, it is simply because India does not want it … The Kashmir issue will be resolved, whenever and in whatever way, resolved only by mutual agreement … It seems better, therefore, that a way is found rather than forced downhill from the wuthering Kargil heights soon.' Aziz Siddiqui, 'Downhill from Kargil', *Dawn*, Islamabad, 29 June 1999.

'In my view, G-8 and Washington have made a serious error in diplomacy by laying the blame at Pakistan's door. I believe there could have been a much more constructive approach that the G-8 could have backed with its substantial economic and political influence in India and Pakistan … I propose that, since both countries are at a dangerous war-threshold and both must talk, the following modality can meet the requirement of both. The modality I am proposing is proximity talks, under the good offices of UN Secretary, General Kofi Annan, to be held in Geneva or New York. The G-8 must give diplomatic support to this initiative. The proximity talks must have three rounds ... I believe, if the first two rounds are completed to satisfactory solutions, the Third Round of Proximity Talks can engage the two sides in the difficult task of dispute resolution of Kashmir. The three-stage proposal I am putting forward can perhaps be a suitable modality for conflict prevention, leading to dispute resolution. The G-8 countries, especially the White House and 10 Downing Street, must put all their weight behind this proposal, and use their influence both with India and Pakistan to accept it.' Sardar Aseff Ahmad Ali (former Foreign Minister), 'Three Stage Proximity Talks', *The Nation*, 30 June 1999.

Triangular Diplomacy

This Sharif-Clinton engagement was part of a triangular diplomacy, with the Indians as the third party. In deference to this fact, the Americans had the Sharif-Clinton meeting cleared with the Indians.[30] And, after the meeting was firmed up with Sharif, the US president called Vajpayee on the evening of 3 July to personally inform him of the planned meeting with Sharif.[31] The following morning, the US Ambassador in Delhi, Richard Celeste, met with the Indian External Affairs Minister, Jaswant Singh, to brief him on how Washington would proceed with Sharif.[32] The Indians were reassured that Clinton's decision to receive Sharif was conditioned on the Pakistani decision to withdraw from Kargil.[33] Washington had also shared its assessment with Delhi that Sharif was desperate to see Clinton so that he could help him get some face-saving from the Indians which could help to make the withdrawal palatable for the Pakistan Army and for the militants.[34] The last act of the script, jointly prepared by Delhi and Washington on forcing Pakistani withdrawal from the Kargil heights, had begun. The principle objective of this joint scripting was: 'Pakistan must not be allowed to reap political gains from its aggression in Kargil.'[35] The shared Indo-US thinking on this, often articulated by the Indian officials and commentators, was that failing to take a hard line against Pakistan on Kargil would 'encourage military adventurists and religious fundamentalists in Pakistan'.[36]

Yet, despite this level of US engagement on Kargil, there was complete denial of Washington's mediation in the Kargil crisis. Delhi was 'dismissive of any implied suggestion of American mediation either in the current Kargil crisis or in future about the Kashmir question'.[37] It sought to create an optical reality of Delhi wanting to maintain a distance from Washington during Kargil.[38] However, the statement issued by the White House on the evening of 3 July was closer to reality. It highlighted Washington's involvement in defusing the Kargil crisis but not in resolving the perennial Kashmir conflict. In stating that 'as part of the President's ongoing efforts regarding the current conflict in Kashmir, the President spoke again today with both Prime Minister Nawaz Sharif of Pakistan and Prime Minister Atal Bihari Vajpayee of India … all agreed the situation is dangerous and could escalate quickly if not resolved quickly',[39] the statement explicitly acknowledged Clinton's role in defusing the crisis. On its involvement in the broader Kashmir conflict, the statement emphasized that, while the Sharif-Clinton meeting was taking place on 'Prime Minister Nawaz Sharif's request, given that the situation in Kashmir is increasingly tense, we have made our position on the conflict clear … we believe this [Kashmir] has to be resolved through bilateral dialogue'.[40]

The triangular diplomacy, which India had initiated in early June by directly seeking Washington's involvement the Kargil crisis, was now poised to bring Kargil to a close. Washington-Delhi, as willing partners, worked in tandem with each other to put pressure on Islamabad, the third member of this triangular diplomacy. Within the context of the Kargil crisis, this triangular diplomacy was to achieve the ultimate goal Delhi had set for this partnership: withdrawal of Pakistani troops from Kargil. Beyond that, it was expediting the Delhi-Washington strategic convergence that was already under way.

The 4 July Trip

In the early hours of 4 July, at 2:30am, the prime minister took off in the New York bound PIA commercial flight PK 761. The sudden departure had precluded the prime minister traveling in a special aircraft. The flight was to make an unscheduled stop at Washington's Dulles Airport to drop the VIP passengers. Nawaz Sharif was accompanied by his wife, Kulsoom Nawaz, Sartaj Aziz, Chaudhry Nisar, Shamshad Ahmad, Tariq Altaf, and Tariq Fatemi.

Pakistanis were stunned by the news of Sharif's sudden departure for Washington. After all, the next publicly announced move on Kargil had been the much awaited 5 July DCC meeting at which, according to the government's own announcement, 'The next moves on Kargil are to be finalized.' Those who had missed the late night television announcement on the morning of 4 July were confronted with the bold newspaper headlines: 'PM dashes to US to discuss LOC tension' (*The Nation*), 'PM rushes to US for talks with Clinton' (*Dawn*), and 'PM leaves for US amid continuing LOC crisis' (*The News*).

The media was generally upbeat on the purpose of the meeting. According to one paper, 'The visit seems significant against the backdrop of the US House of Representatives Foreign Relations Committee's condemnation of Pakistan's backing of the alleged incursion into Kargil, passing the resolution by 22-5 majority vote. It seems Pakistan's failure at the diplomatic front, which formed the basis of such a resolution, will be an additional issue which the PM might want to address on his visit, to make the actual picture on the Kargil issue clear to the world.'[41]

The only report that was closest to impending developments had been filed by a Pakistani correspondent from Washington. Quoting diplomatic circles, the report claimed, 'The urgent summit between the leaders of the two countries was interpreted in diplomatic circles as indicative of a major breakthrough in which Pakistan would concede some of the pressing demands of the White House in return for a firm pledge by President Clinton that he would pursue the larger Kashmir issue in right earnest.' [42]

The day the prime minister took off for his crucial meeting at the White House, the editorial of a leading daily lamented the confusion on the government's policy on Kargil and advocated taking the public into confidence. The editorial regretted, '... despite a slew of top-level meetings and volumes of statements issued afterwards, where exactly Pakistan stands in the shifting sands of diplomacy remains a matter of conjecture.'[43] Pointing to specific issues the editorial maintained, 'The outcome of General Anthony Zinni's visit to Pakistan, for instance, is still as unclear as the nature of former Foreign Secretary Niaz A. Naik's Delhi sojourn is obscure.'[44]

Advocating transparency, it held, 'While tactical details and technical matters, which may impinge upon the country's national security, may not be for public audience, the direction in which the decision makers intend to take the nation on this issue ought not to be marked by any ambiguity.'[45]

The editorial of another national daily had expressed satisfaction about the DCC's decisions to not vacate Pakistan's Kargil position, to beef up Pakistan's defense, and to not initiate war. Commenting on the DCC's decision, it wrote, 'This is an expression of continued resolve to continue with the present policy of defending Pakistani positions along the LOC in the Kargil sector, while refusing to bring pressure to withdraw on the freedom fighters fighting the Indian Army across the LOC. The DCC must be satisfied that the country's armed forces are capable of defending the country against both Indian incursions across the LOC which are likely, across the international border, which is likely but cannot be ruled out. The mechanical details of the DCC decisions have not been disclosed but there are certain requirements for enhanced preparedness, such as extra funding for defense works and supplies, which the DCC must have approved. That was probably about as far as the DCC can go for preparation, as it has ruled out the possibility of Pakistan initiating or escalating the conflict, which throws the ball in the Indian court.' [46]

Regarding the Indian position the liberal-leaning daily *Dawn* criticised Delhi for 'wanting Pakistan to make all the concessions and do all the withdrawing while it sticks rigidly to its position.'[47] While praising Pakistan's willingness 'to explore all peaceful options to defuse the present crisis', *Dawn*, in its editorial suggested, 'India should match it so that there is a quick de-escalation of the present dangerous tensions ...'[48]

Sharif's Washington departure had even baffled many of his own cabinet members. Reacting, one of the cabinet members said, 'We are neither aware of it, nor we were taken into confidence.'[49] But, supporting the move, he added, 'We have full trust and confidence in our leader that he will do the best in the national interest.'[50] Some members, however, believed the prime minister should have held a cabinet meeting before leaving. Concern was expressed about the political orientation of the cabinet members accompanying the prime minister, specifically that, instead of all 'doves', some 'hawks' too should have been taken. Those worried about the developments in Kargil were supportive of Sharif's decision to take 'peace birds and not eagles',[51] as he landed in Washington to avert what they believed was an impending disaster.

The public was less sanguine. The media was filled with reports of the Pakistan Army's impregnable position in Kargil. The public was sensing a victory of sorts. Hence, the street talk over Kargil was expressed apprehensions that 'what the military has gained in the lingering battle along the LOC may be given a serious jolt by the political leaders and diplomats'.[52] The news of Sharif's departure had hit them hard. They wanted the prime minister to be 'bold' while in Washington. There was no constituency for war with India, only for peace. Nevertheless, they wanted a 'historic lesson' be given to India, in case it opted for aggression towards Pakistan. Kargil was seen as a provocation by India.[53]

As Sharif was flying towards DC to take a U-turn on policy, there were other non-governmental policy critics who were writing in the press.

The former army chief, General (Retd) Aslam Beg wrote, 'The Indians, therefore, are seized with a grave problem, how to oust the Mujahideen, as they, from their strategic positions are controlling the route through which the Indian troops, located in Siachen and against China, are supplied logistics and succour. After initial setback and perplexity, the Indian government, it appears, is well poised to undertake a large scale offensive against the Mujahideen and, from the way they are going about, one is reluctantly inclined to think that they may succeed in turning the table in their favor, not so because of their military might or strength, but because of the wooliness the Pakistan government is gripped with, lacking a clear delineation of objective and emitting confusing signals. In moments of grave crisis, there has to be an orchestrated sense of direction, where the people, the government, the opposition, and the armed forces have to act in unison. Alas, it is surprisingly lacking. Part of the reason could be that the Mujahideen, prior to their action, neither consulted the Army nor apprised the government of their contemplated move.'[54] In taking a contradictory position, the former army chief, while conceding that by using overwhelming force 'India could convert the success of the Mujahideen into failure', criticized the government for 'losing the war on the diplomatic front'.[55]

The former army chief criticized the government for its 'apologetic' position, that its troops had not crossed the LOC, and that it was not supporting the Mujahedeen. Such a position, he argued, enabled India to plan 'an all-pronged decisive encounter' with the Mujahedeen to reverse the situation in its favor. 'What indeed is ironic is that the Mujahedeen's heroic success, which could have been channelized into strategic advantages, has been squandered away.'

Another commentator wrote, 'Whatever the exact reason for the Washington dash by Nawaz Sharif, Pakistanis expect that decisions relating to national interest are made in Pakistan. Nawaz Sharif needs to return from his Washington dash with his credentials intact as a man who stands firm on national security issues and does not cave in to external pressure. This will be possible if Nawaz Sharif manages either; (i) to get a public declaration from President Clinton that a settlement is only possible if India makes an American underwritten public commitment to resolving the Kashmir problem within a specific time frame and agree on increased UNMOGIP presence in Indian-occupied Jammu and Kashmir, or (ii) to publicly declare before leaving Washington that as a country committed to abiding by UN laws, resolutions and international treaties, Pakistan and the Mujahideen seek a solution to Kashmir issue, the basis for the Kargil eruption. In case India is not prepared, Pakistan and the Mujahideen are willing and capable of holding on to their positions in the Kargil-Drass area until it hurts the Indians enough to want to talk provided the military situation is not reversed.[56]

Insulated from the clamour of these opinions and headed towards Washington, the prime minister was keen that the 'last act' on Kargil should be exactly as he had wanted it. He was preoccupied with just one question. As soon as flight PK 761 made its usual refuelling stop at Shannon, the prime minister called his trusted ambassador, Riaz Khokhar, to Washington. He wanted to know from his ambassador if a one-on-one meeting with Clinton had been fixed.[57] The answer was negative. Clearly, there were more than just policy matters that a worried Sharif was keen to discuss with Clinton, matters that he only wanted to discuss in complete confidentiality. Nawaz Sharif was seeking 'political cover' to deal with what he feared may be the domestic fallout of what he was about to agree to. Within the domestic context, it was the Army's reaction that he was most concerned about. He realized that the Army was not keen to leave Kargil and felt that his decision to withdraw troops from there could threaten his survival as prime minister. He hoped Clinton would bail him out on the domestic front.

Meanwhile, the Foreign Office team was busy preparing talking points for the prime minister. They knew Sharif was to face a tough interlocutor and had to convince Clinton that without some move by India on Kashmir the Kargil crisis could not be drawn to a close. The US President had to be told of the numerous diplomatic attempts Pakistan had made to engage Delhi in talks to end the Kargil crisis. A statement for release after the Sharif-Clinton meeting was also drafted.

Around 11am, flight PK 761 touched down at Dulles International Airport to drop off the VIP passengers. The Saudi Ambassador to the United States, Prince Bandar, received the prime minister at the airport.

Washington had sought Saudi 'help' to bring Kargil to a close. The Americans had found Nawaz Sharif trying till the end to extract some commitment, some concession, from the Americans on Kashmir as the quid pro quo for vacating Kargil. Washington's response to this was to engineer compound pressure on the Pakistani prime minister to vacate Kargil immediately and unconditionally.[58] Pakistan's key strategic ally Beijing had already been contacted. Beijing and Washington were in agreement that Pakistan had to withdraw unilaterally. However, it was Saudi Arabia, the provider 'of usually discounted oil to Pakistan,' which Washington believed would be most effective in 'pushing Pakistan in the right direction'.[59]

The United States government was represented by the US Chief of Protocol. The prime minister travelled to Blair House with Prince Bandar. In Washington, before delivering Nawaz Sharif to Blair House, Prince Bandar briefed Sharif on the mood in Washington and stressed that nothing less than an agreement to withdraw from Kargil was expected.[60]

Sharif-Clinton Meeting

Despite the expectation from the Pakistani prime minister of agreeing to unilaterally withdraw troops from the Kargil heights, the Americans were still not sure of the actual outcome of the Sharif-Clinton summit when Nawaz Sharif arrived at Blair House.[61] The Clinton administration was, however, fully prepared for this unusual summit. The Americans had prepared two draft statements, one of which they shared with the Pakistanis upon arrival. It was a draft statement, to be signed by Clinton and Sharif at the end of the summit, which categorically stated that Pakistan would uphold the sanctity of the LOC. The foreign secretary told the United States National Security advisor that the term 'sanctity' was unacceptable for Pakistan. The LOC was not an international border. It was a temporary dividing line which had been accepted by Pakistan, India, the United Nations, and by the entire international community, as a temporary arrangement. This was reflected in both the Tashkent and the Simla agreements. The other draft statement, which the Americans did not share with the visitors from Pakistan, was to have been unilaterally issued by them in case of Sharif's refusal to agree to a unilateral withdrawal of Pakistani troops. Predictably, such a statement from the White House would have stated that the President urged the prime minister to withdraw the Pakistani forces to behind the LOC, Pakistan had not agreed, and, therefore, the responsibility for the crisis lay on Pakistan's shoulders.

Clinton's South Asia team knew that more than just the future of US-Pakistan relations hinged on the outcome of this meeting. It would also determine whether it was war or peace in South Asia, with the risk of a war turning into nuclear holocaust. Clinton's high profile involvement meant that the personal prestige of the US President was at stake. Washington's extraordinary engagement in the Kargil conflict brought US stature and diplomatic skills into the global limelight. All this notwithstanding, what occupied the minds of the Clinton Administration's regional specialists at the State Department and the NSC was that the success of one of their most important foreign policy initiative also rested on the outcome of this summit. The breakthrough in US-Indo relations was to be the crowning glory of the Clinton era. The US now had the chance of a life time to show the Indians that they meant business as friends of India. All Indian eyes were on this unusual summit. And the Americans realized that 'Indians were extremely skeptical that we will succeed and suspicious about what we were doing'. Only a success would have convinced the Indians of what the Americans kept telling Delhi they were doing 'to get Pakistan to back down'.

Sharif's delegation arrived at Blair House in the morning and waited for Clinton. There was palpable apprehension in the Pakistan camp as they waited for Clinton to arrive. During the wait, one of Nawaz Sharif's ministers held on to his hand and said, 'prime minister, why should you worry when the world's most powerful man considers you his friend?' The Foreign Office team, which included Shamshad Ahmad, Tariq Altaf, and Tariq Fatemi, was amongst the more nervous at this point.

This was the third Sharif-Clinton meeting since Sharif became prime minister in 1997. First the two met with their aides. Nawaz Sharif was joined by the Foreign Minister Sartaj Aziz and Foreign Secretary Shamshad Ahmed. Clinton was assisted by National Security advisor Sandy Burger, assistant Secretary of State for South Asia Karl F. Inderfurth and a senior

National security council official handling South Asian affairs Bruce Riedel. This meeting with aides lasted for barely five to seven minutes. It was followed by an almost two-hour long meeting between Clinton and Nawaz. While Clinton was joined by Bruce Riedel as a note taker, Nawaz Sharif went in without one. He did not want one.[62] Unknowing of this fact the Pakistan Foreign Office team insisted that their prime minister be treated on an equal basis with the host and also be accompanied by his aide to the meeting. It lasted approximately two hours. Clinton began by telling Sharif why Kargil was a blunder and how two nuclear powers were almost at the brink of war. Clinton told Sharif that he had information that the Pakistan Army had begun preparation to use nuclear weapons. Sharif said he was unaware of any such move. As a nuclear power, Clinton said, the international community expected Pakistan to behave more responsibly. Sharif's refrain was that Kashmir was very volatile and required immediate resolution. The thrust of the talking points that the Foreign office team had prepared for Nawaz was: 'Kargil has to be seen as the outcome of the frustration of many people, flowing from the unresolved Kashmir problem.' Clinton said he recognized that and admitted that the United States should take more interest. He also said that he could visit the region for this purpose by the end of the year.

In the plain talking during his meeting with the Pakistani prime minister, the US President also demanded his government's full cooperation in capturing OBL. Clinton in his memoirs recalls, 'On 4 July, I also told Sharif that unless he did more to help I would have to announce Pakistan was in effect supporting terrorism in Afghanistan.'[63] Clinton was basing his assertions on the information and analysis provided by CIA's Counter-terrorist Center. Pakistan was identified as the principal supporter of the Taliban, the principal protectors of OBL. Significantly, on the very day of his meeting with the Pakistani prime minister, Clinton announced sanctions against the Taliban. He subsequently wrote, 'On the day I met Sharif, I also signed an executive order placing economic sanctions on the Taliban, freezing its assets, and prohibiting commercial exchanges.'

Significantly, there was no discussion between Nawaz Sharif and the Foreign Office team before the Clinton meeting regarding the formulation of the statement that he and Clinton would sign. The Foreign Office team had prepared a Pakistani version of a draft agreement. The Americans were determined to stay with their own version.

During the meeting, the Americans found the 'super-nationalist' Sharif pressing Pakistan's case on Kashmir vis-à-vis India. However, from the tone and tenor of his words, it seemed that there were key domestic issues that bothered him at that juncture. Kashmir was important but not 'a top issue on his agenda'. According to the only outsider in the meeting, 'It was not a top issue on his agenda but still it was pretty hard to withdraw your forces under fire without appearing to be a loser. He knew the right answer. He knew what to do and looked around desperately for an answer. But the latitude the US had to provide cover was limited.'[64] Sharif carefully chose his words so as not to directly implicate anyone but kept saying that it was an operation that 'got out of control'. He did, however, distance himself from the Operation. The striking contrast in the self-confidence of the two interlocutors could not have been lost. While one was backed by a unified and competently functioning government, the other was pretty much on a solo flight.

Nawaz Sharif was insisting that Clinton help him to get out of the crisis. An anxious Sharif's long rambling on diplomacy with China and with Indian intermediaries was to establish his bona fides as a man in search of a solution. He was like a man who 'wanted out' off a train wreck approaching him. At one point, Sharif asked Clinton for a one-on-one meeting. Clinton declined. The Pakistani prime minister was told that the note-taker, Bruce Riedel, would not leave his President. US government rules made it obligatory upon Clinton to have this historic meeting documented. The President of the USA was not free to have his way. He could not act upon his whims.

During the break between the two sessions of the Sharif-Clinton meeting, Sharif's team found him to be a 'drained man'. He has been badgered by Clinton's queries and hard talk on Kargil, OBL, etc. No less was the tension of what he was doing: giving a commitment for a Pakistani retreat from what the military was still publicly projecting as a successful occupation. In fact, during the meeting, the TV in the room was telecasting news of the fall of a strategically important peak, the Tiger Hill. During the break, the prime minister called his army chief to confirm news of the fall of the Tiger Hill.[65]

In their private session, the Foreign Office team vehemently criticized the substance and language of the American draft. Recalling the draft and the internal discussion on it, one of Sharif's key team members says, 'The draft from the other side was awful, it was stinking. In our private discussions we raised hell.'[66] Recalling Nawaz Sharif's condition after the Clinton meeting, he said, 'The big man appeared drained, he had been badgered in the one to one session. From his reaction to our words I realized that there was little fight left in him.' The Foreign Office team still 'offered' a few amendments to the draft. Sharif was extremely reluctant to take them to Clinton. He said he had been told it was a take it or leave it situation. His team still urged Sharif to 'not give in'. They were all aware that their internal discussions were being monitored. The Americans knew what they were trying to convince Sharif to do, since the room they were sitting in was 'not only bugged but also had cameras in it'. Sharif promised his team to make one last effort.

The 4 July meeting was turned into a battle of nerves. Clinton was well prepared for this battle while the Pakistani prime minister had arrived in Washington having already lost his nerve, owing to what he believed were the Kargil reversals. Sharif had left Islamabad in panic and entered the Clinton meeting with a major psychological handicap. Clinton saw sitting before him a needy and desperate man, not a negotiator. The Americans too found Sharif nervous. In fact, they believed his decision to 'invite himself at short notice and bringing the family along opened the possibility of his staying back in Washington in case the Army took over in his absence'.[67] This was a drastic and incorrect conclusion. The Americans were unable to comprehend Sharif's ability to mix matters of policy and of recreation.

Tough times test leadership mettle and a state's collective institutional competence. Sharif's mettle was being severely tested. He had opted to do mostly a lone act, nearly a personal operation, on the entire 4 July summit, from planning to execution. He had drawn on external wisdom and an external platform. He seemed to have banked on a major external power even for the political strength required for his 4 July decision. This bail-out operation, as Sharif saw it, of a medium-sized power by the major global power, was a page out of Wallerstein's classic center-periphery relationship. The 'comprador' politician was at play, exposing so starkly the heavy interconnectedness between Pakistan's internal power game and the global center, with the levers of control heavily tilted in the latter's favor. Nothing could more acutely demonstrate Pakistan's systemic weakness as a state run by those with scarce appreciation of institutional decision-making.

The meeting ended with the decision that Pakistan would withdraw its troops behind the LOC to the pre-Operation position. He had left his army chief with the understanding that he would negotiate gains for Pakistan and the Kashmiris in Washington. The withdrawal had not been factored in as a possibility. Pakistan and India would vouch for troop movement as planned.[68] There would be no third party monitoring the withdrawal.

The withdrawal discussion had not included any talk about safe passage for the withdrawing Pakistani forces. Earlier, in meetings with US officials, the Pakistani Ambassador, Riaz Khokhar, was told that, in case of a withdrawal, Washington would get Pakistan a 'bargain',' especially regarding the withdrawal. The US Under Secretary of State, Thomas Pickering, had told Khokhar that the Americans would 'talk to the Indians regarding no attacks on withdrawing Pakistani soldiers.'[69] However, during the 4 July meeting, Sharif did not raise any question about safe passage for withdrawing troops.[70] Evidently, it was not an issue that had occupied his mind, nor was it part of the talking points that his Foreign Office team had prepared. This issue escaped their respective radars because the premise from which it would logically flow, the Pakistani forces actually battling in Kargil and now their withdrawal, did not exist in their articulated consciousness. This kind of denial meant major lapses in policy-making. The costs were to be horrendous. Also, psychologically, the Pakistani prime minister did not appear to be in negotiating mode. Self-invited, he had arrived in Washington as a man in need. At best, he sought political cover for an unconditional withdrawal from Kargil. While the Americans could not have themselves guaranteed safe passage, Clinton was in a position to extract at least some commitment from the Indians as he was delivering what they desperately needed and were not managing militarily: eviction of the Pakistani troops.

Clinton then waved the nuclear card at Sharif, as if a referee were shouting 'foul play' to a player. Reprimanding the Pakistani prime minister, the irate US President declared, 'Pakistan is messing with nuclear war.'[71] Rhetorically, he queried Sharif whether he had ordered Pakistani nuclear missile forces to get ready for action and if he realized how crazy that was.[72] A baffled Sharif responded in the negative. There was never any mention of such a move. After all, in Pakistan, a nuclear missile force did not exist. Clinton had purposefully been primed on this issue. His advisors had judged the threat of a nuclear war as a sound casus belli for their President's involvement in Kargil.[73] A limited battle on the world's highest peak, involving around 500 Pakistani troops alone would not have justified the personal engagement of the US President. The key men tutoring Clinton on the Kargil crisis had built the nuclear case. Accordingly, Clinton had shot off half a dozen letters and made numerous phone calls to Sharif during the Kargil crisis. In Clinton's mind, he was avoiding a nuclear cataclysm.

Clinton, as part of a premeditated strategy, used this moment of Sharif's utter vulnerability to aggressively raise the issue of the Osama bin Laden and the alleged ISI connection.[74] Before Sharif sat the man who had been told that Pakistan was at the center of supporting the Taliban and by extension the OBL network. This network, according to the CIA, was functioning in 60 different countries and was directly responsible for attacks on American embassies. Clinton reminded Nawaz Sharif that he had 'asked repeatedly for Pakistani help to bring Osama bin Laden to justice from Afghanistan' and that Sharif had 'promised often to do so, but had done nothing. Instead, the ISI worked with OBL and the Taliban to foment terrorism'. Sharif had made a personal commitment to Clinton in December 1998 to help the United States in capturing OBL, but had not followed through on it.[75] A clearly agitated Clinton threatened to tell the world of Pakistan's support to bin Laden if Pakistan's help in capturing him was not forthcoming.[76] The Pakistani prime minister reassured the US President that he would now follow through on his earlier commitment. The only quid pro quo that Clinton could offer to Sharif was a mere intention to try and visit the region at the end of the year to help push forward the Lahore process.

At the conclusion of the meeting, Nawaz Sharif told his team that all he had got was a verbal assurance that 'the American interest in Jammu and Kashmir would be far more intense and sustained than reflected in the joint statement'. Clinton, he said, had given his 'solemn assurance'. These were not reassuring words. The Foreign Office team believed the 'die had been cast'. There was no feeling of elation or satisfaction. The outcome of the 4 July summit was more like a 'wake-up call' for Pakistan, signalling Washington's policy shift in South Asia.

The last attempt made by Pakistan's Foreign Secretary to make the 4 July statement more acceptable for Pakistan was also unsuccessful. Shamshad Ahmad asked National Security Advisor,Sandy Berger, to make two changes in the "" two, include Clinton's commitment to visit the region by the end of the year.

Around 3pm, the Sharif-Clinton meeting concluded. The Pakistani prime minister had agreed to sign a statement which amounted to a global broadcast and an irrevocable documentation by the government of Pakistan that the Kargil Operation had been a mistake.

The Washington Statement [A heading]

The text of the Washington Statement was as follows:

'President Clinton and Prime Minister Sharif share the view that the current fighting in the Kargil region of Kashmir is dangerous and contains the seeds of a wider conflict.

They also agreed that it was vital for the peace of South Asia that the Line of Control in Kashmir be respected by both parties, in accordance with their 1972 Simla Accord.

It was agreed between the president and the prime minister that concrete steps will be taken for the restoration of the Line of Control, in accordance with the Simla Agreement.

> The President urged an immediate cessation of the hostilities once these steps are taken. The prime minister and the President agreed that the bilateral dialogue begun in Lahore in February provides the best forum for resolving all issues dividing India and Pakistan, including Kashmir.
>
> The President said he would take a personal interest in encouraging an expeditious resumption and intensification of those bilateral efforts, once the sanctity of the Line of Control has been fully restored.
>
> The President reaffirmed his intent to pay an early visit to South Asia.'[77]

The Washington Statement had no legal value but it reflected the personal commitment, binding on the State of Pakistan, made by the prime minister to the global community. It was not a bilateral statement between two interlocutors directly engaged in conflict which would have made the undertaking in the agreement binding. Instead, it was a one-sided statement binding only one interlocutor to take action, committing itself to the actionable portion of the agreement. While Pakistan committed itself to unconditional withdrawal from Kargil, the other interlocutor, Bill Clinton, made a statement of non-statist personal intent regarding his involvement in trying to resolve the Kashmir dispute.

The statement called for 'restoration of the LOC in accordance with the Simla Agreement'. Call for the 'sanctity of the LOC' was also a reminder of Washington's preferred solution for the Kashmir dispute. Thirty seven years earlier, during the 1962, Washington-brokered Bhutto-Swaran Singh talks, the US had advised Pakistan to accept the LOC as a border. Significantly, there were two opposing thrusts of this agreement. If one sought withdrawal of Pakistani troops to the pre-Kargil position, the other sought restoration of LOC in accordance with Simla Agreement in which:

Article 1 (ii) explicitly states, 'Pending the final settlement of any of the problems between the two countries, neither side shall unilaterally alter the situation and both shall prevent the organization, assistance or encouragement of any acts detrimental to the maintenance of peaceful and harmonious results.'[78]

Under this clause, which categorically rules out any change to the LOC without mutual consent, India's 1983 occupation of Siachen was a clear violation of a bilateral agreement. Since India was not a party to, only a beneficiary of this statement, it was not obliged to take any action on Siachen, the territory it had illegally occupied.

The Washington statement brought to a close the fourth Pakistan-India military encounter. This encounter, in which Pakistani troops had occupied territory across the LOC in the disputed state of Jammu and Kashmir, was indeed ending with a difference. As if giving up on their 'gains' the Pakistani troops were to withdraw from the territory they had occupied -territory that India had in fact occupied during the 1971 war. The irony of India seeking the 'sanctity of the LOC', after having violated it in 1984, 1991 and in 1992, was not lost on the Pakistanis. So it was a 'triple withdrawal' since this was a disputed area, taken by India by force, and, after all, India had a track record of LOC violations.

The contentious nature of Pakistan-India relations ensured that Delhi and Islamabad would interpret the Statement differently. Yet two facts regarding the Statement were incontrovertible. First, it was limited in its scope and was only seeking Pakistani troop withdrawal from Kargil. It was not linked to political upheaval in the Kashmir Valley. Secondly, this Statement would not substantively alter the dynamics of the ongoing Kashmir dispute.

Reflecting the global community's concerns[79] regarding the dangers arising from the unresolved dispute, a *New York Times* editorial urged India to 'pledge to reopen talks on Kashmir and other issues.'[80] It argued that 'Kashmir is a seemingly intractable dispute of religion, ethnicity and borders. But as the world learned in Kosovo, these disputes can spin out of control. India and Pakistan, now armed with nuclear weapons, have no choice but resolve their agreements peacefully.' [81] Tracing the recent history of the dispute, the editorial wrote, 'Since independence and partition in 1947 India and Pakistan have fought two wars over Kashmir, a coveted region of lakes, lush valleys, and snowy mountains. The Kashmiris themselves seem to want outright independence, A guerrilla uprising has raged for most of the last decade, killing thousands as Indian troops have been sent to put it down.'[82]

It was not a matter of chance that Washington became Pakistan's key interlocutor in bringing Kargil to a close. In Pakistan, the US had been a key factor throughout Pakistan's history and therefore inevitably in the Kargil episode. Various policy-making groups – the politicians, the army, the bureaucrats – had held different opinions of the role Washington was would play during Kargil, based on their own locational realities as perceived from their varying vantage points. However, the prime minister did not get all the differing 'locational realities' onto a common platform to produce a common reality.

For Washington, Kargil became the justification for Washington's first ever overt mediatory role in any Pakistan-India conflict. Unlike Washington's earlier engagements, which ended without inconclusively, in 1999, Washington was able to play an important role in bringing an end to an active conflict between two nuclear states.

Kargil had presented both opportunities and risks for a power that was seeking to expand its engagement in South Asia. Washington's first response to Kargil was marked with a lack of clarity. It then rapidly moved towards the Indian MEA position, which had evolved under the leadership of its Minister Jaswant Singh. Four specific factors made this evolution of a common Washington-Delhi policy viable: Pakistan's blatant violation of the LOC, Delhi's diplomatic strategy, Washington's own strategic interests, and the nuclear environment.

Behind the scenes, US officials were making two supplementary points. The first was that, although the statement did not mention Pakistani troops, the Americans believed 'Pakistani soldiers are directly involved in the conflict'. The second point was the need for quick action on Pakistan's part. US officials publicly stated, 'Our understanding is that there will be a withdrawal of the forces now … we want to see steps taken very quickly.'[83] The Pakistan Foreign Office spokesman, meanwhile, took the position that Pakistan had not agreed to call back anyone from Kargil. He had told the press corps in Washington, 'There is neither mention of people, nor return of anything in the Joint Statement.'[84]

When the prime minister returned to the hotel, Shehbaz Sharif called. Quite agitated, he told the prime minister that Punjab would just not take it and the people would be out on the streets. The elder brother had little to say in response except that the Americans wanted disengagement at any cost. Pakistan, he said could not continue on the present course. Sharif said there was no option left for him but to do what he had done. Shortly after Shehbaz's call, the Information Minister, Mushahid Hussain, spoke to the prime minister and asked him what he should tell the people. He was told that he had no option but 'he would tell him of the advantages'. Subsequently, in Pakistan, the supporters of this statement would see it as a 'face-saver'.[85] Experienced diplomats held that 'Pakistan had been cornered and Nawaz Sharif had moved with alacrity'.[86] Its critics labelled it as a 'political cover'[87] sought by the prime minister for regime survival.

For the Pakistani prime minister visiting the US, 5 July was just a touristy day. He got involved in a family photo op at the White House and did some computer shopping. At the conclusion of the 4 July meeting, Sharif had expressed his interest in organizing a White House tour for his family. They all also wanted to be photographed with the Clintons. On the morning of 5 July, Sharif, his wife, and children toured the White House and had a photo op with the Clintons.

Later in the day, the prime minister travelled to New York. Known for his penchant for gadgets, he first went window shopping at the Sony Centre in midtown Manhattan. Later, he held a meeting with PML members. This display of temperamental nonchalance was reminiscent of the burger-imbibing Nawaz Sharif in London's Marble Arch MacDonald's while at home the Establishment was busy engineering his ouster by organizing desertions from his party. By the evening, Nawaz Sharif and his family, accompanied by the Saudi Ambassador, Prince Bandar, left for London in the Saudi Ambassador's airplane.

The homeward-bound Sharif sought a meeting with the British prime minister. The meeting was to help him set the optics right at home. Like many before him, this beleaguered Prime Minster too may have thought that the chorus of criticism maybe blunted by high profile Clinton and Blair meetings. On the evening of 6 July, the pleased British prime minister received his Pakistani counterpart for a brief meeting at 10 Downing Street.

During the London stopover, the real newsmaker was Pakistan's articulate Foreign Minister, Sartaj Aziz. In a *BBC Hard Talk* interview, Sartaj declared that the reference in the 4 July statement to 'upholding the sanctity of the LOC' also implied that India must vacate the Siachen Glacier it had illegally occupied in 1984. A rapid rebuttal from Washington stated that the 4 July Statement was only about Kargil, that the US believed in the sanctity of the entire LOC but of immediate interest was the resolution of the Kargil conflict.

Meanwhile, some from among Pakistan's brave sons, still engaged in battle with the Indian troops, were dying for the Motherland at the Tiger Hill. Occupying posts along the steep ridges and the mountain-top at Tiger Hill, these Pakistani soldiers were facing India's well-planned and well-executed three dimensional land, air, and artillery attacks.[88]

Delhi's response and some myth-making

The Indian government's reaction to the statement was quick and pointed. Delhi was declaring victory from what continued to be a difficult military situation. Although India had managed to re-claim strategic peaks in the Batalik Sector of Kargil, Indian officials acknowledged that they continued to 'face stiff resistance'.[89] While air force pounding helped to soften targets, the fight-back from Pakistani troops perched at high altitude still posed a difficult military situation. Yet, India would frame the US-aided Pakistani force withdrawal as a victory. From Delhi, the following statement was issued:

> 'We have seen the US-Pakistan joint statement issued in Washington yesterday. Our US interlocutors have informed us that 'concrete steps' referred to in the statement mean withdrawal by Pakistan of their forces from our side of the Line of Control in the Kargil sector.
>
> We have also noted the sequencing of steps agreed to in the statement, that only after withdrawal is completed will other contemplated steps be initiated. We hope Pakistan will heed

> this call immediately. We will be watching developments on the ground.
>
> We reaffirm that Pakistan's armed intrusion and aggression has to be vacated. Our military aggression in the Kargil Sector, which has been initiated for this purpose, is making steady progress. It will continue with full force until the aggressors are cleared out, and the status quo ante on the Line of Control fully restored.
>
> One word about the Lahore process. It is direct and bilateral. In this process, there is no place whatsoever for any third party involvement. The same is true for any other aspect of India-Pakistan relations.'[90]

If Pakistan was continuing with its myths, India too was generating its fables. Smarting from the capture of around 700 kilometers of territory and 139 peaks by Pakistani forces, India promoted a few half-truths. The Indian spin to Pakistan's decision to unconditionally withdraw from the peaks was that Indian troops had successfully beaten back Pakistani troops.[91] Admittedly, the overwhelming deployment of Indian artillery and air power could not have allowed Pakistani troops to hold the peaks for much longer; however, Delhi's claims of an Indian military victory were inaccurate. Secondly, when there was no third party mediation involved, the allegation regarding this was merely self-serving. Thirdly, the contention that the army-civilian divide in Pakistan would make the withdrawal impossible was not true. And, finally, it was suggested that Osama bin Laden was somehow connected to the Kashmir struggle. Delhi also intermittently claimed that Pakistan was continuing its military campaign.

Coinciding with the 4 July statement, New Delhi announced a change in its military fortunes. The retaking of the strategically significant 16,500 foot peak, the Tiger Hill, was announced.[92] Key members of the Vajpayee-led government, including Vajpayee himself, his National Security Adviser, Brajesh Mishra, Foreign Minister, Jaswant Singh, and the Indian ambassador in Washington worked closely with the Clinton team to jointly formulate policy on Kargil. US officials acknowledged that especially the Jaswant-Talbott connection established during the nuclear dialogue proved extremely helpful. Delhi had proactively sought 'third party mediation' (Washington's involvement) in ensuring the unconditional withdrawal of Pakistani troops from Kargil. In fact, the format of the 4 July Sharif-Clinton Blair House meeting also had a 'proximity talks' dimension to it, with Clinton talking to Indian prime minister Vajpayee before, during, and after the talks with Sharif. Yet, senior Indian officials insisted that none of this amounted to foreign mediation. India's eloquent foreign minister spoke an untruth as he insisted, 'I do not accept this as mediation or even as playing the role of an intermediary, we have consistently said no mediation is necessary. We don't need interpreters, because we speak the same language.'[93]

For the Vajpayee-led government, this Agreement was a major electoral plus point. His government converted the Washington-engineered withdrawal of Pakistani troops from Kargil as the Indian Army's victory. Moreover, the Agreement helped Vajpayee deflect the Indian Opposition's criticism that his Lahore bus ride was a miscalculation of Pakistan's intentions. After Pakistan's withdrawal announcement, Vajpayee team's diplomatic acumen was widely applauded at home and abroad.

Meanwhile, in Pakistan, there was widespread surprise over the 4 July statement. Kashmiri guerrilla fighters and Sharif's political opponents, including the religious parties, accused him of a 'sell-out' and 'treason.' In Muzaffarabad, capital of Pakistan-controlled Azad Kashmir, Sharif and Clinton effigies were burnt.

In IOK, too, the Washington statement was unanimously criticized by most anti-Delhi Kashmiri groups. According to the statement issued by Hizbul Mujahideen, a key guerrilla group fighting for Kashmiri independence, 'No country has the right to suggest the withdrawal of Mujahideen (holy warriors) who have launched an armed struggle against Indian forces to liberate Kashmir. The withdrawal of Mujahideen from Kargil is impossible ... America is trying to impose its will on every country, but we are not slaves of America and we will not accept American slavery.'[94]

Addressing a political gathering in Srinangar, the chairman of the pro-Pakistan and anti-India All Parties Hurriyat (Freedom) Conference coalition group said, 'The US considers India as a business center and does not want to annoy it.' This indeed was generally true but in this case it was not possible for Washington to extricate Pakistan unscathed from the trap of a military and diplomatic siege that its own three senior military generals has set for Pakistan.

Chapter 15

IN THE EYE OF STORM

On July 8, after spending around a hundred hours overseas, Pakistan's prime minister returned to Pakistan. He knew, as was reinforced in his telephone conversations[1] with his principal aides in Pakistan, that the Washington Agreement would not be an easy sell. Its criticism in Pakistan had already begun. Sharif's Washington dash had earned him a statement with no face-saver for Pakistan. Sharif, in his pre-departure telephone conversation, had been clearly told by Clinton to expect no more and had seemed OK with that. In fact, he had cancelled the crucial meeting of the Defense Committee of the Cabinet (DCC) scheduled for July 5, whose agenda had been the Kargil Operation. With input of all stakeholders, the prime minister was to decide on how to draw curtains on Operation Koh Paima. However, at this crucial juncture in Pakistan's history, Sharif had walked away from collective institutional decision-making. Instead, he headed to Washington.

The Costly Cancellation

The cancellation of the DCC[2] had meant abandoning engagement with the army command and all other stakeholders, including the Foreign Minister, Foreign Office bureaucrats, the naval chief, the air force chief, the Information Minister, and others on serious policy questions. No DCC meeting essentially meant there would be no serious discussion on the military situation, such as the strategic significance of holding on to even 70 percent peaks if Pakistani forces had been evicted from the most strategically located peaks closest to NH-1A, including Tololing and Tiger.

There would be no questioning of the Kargil clique about the casualties, about the problems of logistics faced by Pakistanis occupying the post across the LOC, on how was the army proposing a draw-down of the soldiers still across the LOC. Given that it was clear that no diplomatic advantage could be gained for Pakistan or for Kashmir, could the army command propose ways in which the draw-down of soldiers could reduce casualties? Was engagement with the Indian command a viable option, one that would help reduce casualties at the withdrawal stage? Also, there was no discussion on the only vital policy platform, the DCC, on how Pakistan, with depleting military leverage, expected the US President to exert pressure on India to settle the Kashmir issue. The prime minister had instead opted to scamper off to Washington.[3]

Meanwhile, as the prime minister departed for Washington, most media reports on Kargil were upbeat. Kashmiri Mujahedeen were fighting the Indian Army bravely and Delhi was under great pressure to negotiate on ending Indian occupation of Kashmir. Only in private conversations did the army chief and others of the Kargil clique concede rising Pakistani casualties and logistical difficulties. Beginning mid-June, there was guarded conversation within the army command of the crisis of logistics, high casualties, and India's very heavy force deployment. Reports about this alarming situation were trickling in from the front. Nevertheless, at the 2 July meeting the army chief had insisted that, despite rising Pakistani casualties, compromised logistical supplies, and India's re-taking of the strategically located Tololing and Tiger Hill posts, it was not a militarily unsustainable position. No hard questioning or holistic discussion had followed. While moments of acrimony between the prime minister and the army chief did occur, the amiable Chaudhry Shujaat had intervened to cool off matters. Thus, policy matters had remained unsettled.

Without A Real Face-Saver

Interestingly after his London stopover, the prime minister decided to land in his hometown Lahore instead of his seat of power. Heavy security and his trusted Information Minister Mushahid Hussain awaited him at the airport. His brother, the Chief Minister of Punjab Shehbaz

Sharif, bound even by protocol rules to receive the prime minister, was absent. There was an air of uncertainty and some fear. The PM changed planes and flew back to Islamabad in his falcon aircraft. He Nawaz Sharif had obtained no face-saver, Clinton only conceding a "promise that he would take personal interest in solving the 52-year dispute over Kashmir."[4] Foreign Minister Sartaj Aziz had, however, tried to establish a linkage between withdrawal and progress on Kashmir. In his July 6 BBC interview, Aziz warned, "It would be difficult for Pakistan to persuade the Mujahedeen to pull out of Indian-held Kashmir unless the status of Kashmir was put back on the international agenda..." Nevertheless, with these mere verbal commitments in exchange for his own promise to take "concrete steps"[5] to end the Kargil crisis, disturbing questions may have crossed Sharif's mind: what fate awaited him on his return to Pakistan? Would he be able to implement the 4 July statement? How would the army command respond to the 4 July statement? In a country in whose sixty-five year history the military had subverted the Constitution three times to remove an elected civilian ruler, these would have been valid apprehensions. In the White House, Clinton's aide Bruce Riedel had made the dramatic deduction that the Pakistani prime minister had arrived in Washington with his family because, after agreeing on troop withdrawal from Kargil, he was hesitant to return to Pakistan because of fear of the army command.

Within hours of his return to Islamabad, Sharif moved to construct a pro-withdrawal constituency. He planned engagement with the army, the Kashmiri guerrillas, the Opposition parties, and the public at large through the media. The prime minister held four meetings: a senior aides meeting, the Defense Committee of the Cabinet (DCC) meeting, a Cabinet meeting, and a meeting with the Kashmiri guerrilla fighters of the United Jihad Council. To bring the army chief on board and to publicly signal his support for the withdrawal agreement, Sharif ensured the army chief's presence in all these key meetings. To cover the political turf, Sharif planned addressing workers of the ruling Pakistan Muslim League party, and finally made a televised speech.

The general assumption was that the army command would resist unconditional withdrawal. All attention was riveted on the response of the individual and of the institution: the army chief, and the army. Without their support Sharif could not fulfill his commitment of an unconditional withdrawal from the Kargil heights.

In Pakistan, however, matters unfolded in many shades of grey. Even before the prime minister arrived in Islamabad, his army chief had publicly supported the prime minister's Washington decision. Mindful of the untenable situation at the front, Musharraf had told the press, "There is complete harmony between the government and the armed forces."[6] He asserted a complete understanding between the government and army about the prime minister's Washington mission.[7] He knew of the pressures that the government was facing, the embarrassment arising from the operation he as chief had cleared. Musharraf was perhaps wary of what he said as the prime minister had earlier confronted him on the reported military reversals. After all, only ten months earlier, his predecessor General Jehangir Karamat had been removed for what Sharif saw as operating outside of his professional parameters.

Alongside the planned withdrawal, an official narrative, originating from the policy-makers and policy-making institutions, including the DCC, fully supported the withdrawal decision. The Washington Agreement was projected as Sharif's "peace initiative" that had helped to internationalize the Kashmir issue in an unprecedented manner, while simultaneously preserving peace in the region.[8] Pakistan's policy of "moral, diplomatic, and political support to the freedom struggle of the people of Jammu and Kashmir" was also emphasized. The "heroic contribution of the Kashmir freedom fighters was praised, particularly that of the martyrs of Kargil, who had laid down their lives for a just and legitimate cause."[9] According to this official narrative the withdrawal mechanics involved the Cabinet requesting the supposed Kashmiri guerrillas who had occupied the Kargil heights to withdraw and the guerillas acceding to the withdrawal.[10] Also to emphasize civil-military unity, the Chairman of the National Assembly's Standing Committee on Foreign Affairs, Mian Abdul Waheed, rejected differences between the prime minister and the army chief on issues of "vital national interest." He insisted that "the military and political leadership of the country has complete unanimity of perceptions over the issues of vital national interest."[11] As if to establish the political leadership's commitment to national defense, the Chairman said that the political government had done its best to bolster the defense by equipping the army with modern weapons."

With the Vajpayee government busy in preparation for the forthcoming elections, and publicly taking credit for inflicting a defeat on Pakistani forces, Pakistan's Foreign Minister Aziz made the surprising announcement: " Today a consensus has emerged that immediately after the de-escalation in Kargil the focus must shift to the expeditious solution of the Kashmir dispute, so that one billion people, who inhabit South Asia can lead a life of peace and engage in the endeavors of economic prosperity and development."[12]

On the question of safe withdrawal, the ISPR brigadier claimed incorrectly, "During the last 12 hours there has been no aerial activity and artillery fighting in the Kargil sector."[13] And then came the inexplicable claim, "They are fully capable of looking after themselves."

The Clique Explains

A meeting was held at the Joint Services headquarters. All the service chiefs, along with the DG MO, DG ISI and MI, were present. The first briefing for the military commanders took place at the 10 Corps headquarters in Rawalpindi. The corps commander, General Mahmud, also an architect of Operation Koh Paima, urged those present, "Gentlemen, let's honour the brave." The army chief then came to the dais and explained why the withdrawal was necessary. Musharraf made brief comments, "It's all over. Our troops are at their original locations but we are still sitting on some dominating heights astride the LOC." In the somewhat sullen silence that followed, one general did point out, "Sir, they (the Indians) are celebrating." Many present in the room must have recalled the army chief's 16 May assurance that Pakistan was in a "win-win" situation in Kargil as its positions were "unassailable." Words did not matter. The original and vocal critics of Kargil, including commanders 1 Corps General Saleem Haider, Quetta corps general Tariq Pervez and other had been proven right. Also, with restive troops and reports of low morale, especially of those who had participated in the Operation, the army chief had a huge task before him.

The prime minister too was facing a barrage of criticism targeting him for agreeing to the withdrawal.

Sharif Bashing: "Traitor and treacherous…"

It was going to be a hard sell, since government rhetoric had built a public perception since end May of victories for the Mujahedeen fighting Indian troops in the Kargil-Drass area. The ISPR, which led the information campaign at home, had convinced the media of the Mujahedeen's staying power despite India's overwhelming force. The public had begun to believe that the liberation of Kashmir was now possible, if not imminent. According to media reports based on official sources, Delhi was in a very difficult position since its troops were facing the danger of starvation in Siachen if the blockade of the Drass-Kargil Road continued. In fact, after the Washington agreement, the army spokesman said, "There is no change in ground realities as Drass-Kargil Road is still in range of Pakistani artillery fire…"

Based on these claims, the Washington agreement was seen as a sell out. People drew a parallel with the 1965 events, when Pakistan was about to "liberate the whole of Kashmir...when Pakistani leaders succumbed to world pressure and stopped the military operation and we are facing a similar situation now..."[14] Against the expectation of a victory in Kargil, phrases like suffering "humiliation at India's hand"[15] typified the widespread reaction to the Washington agreement. The agreement was viewed as Pakistan losing to India and was "hard to bear in any circumstance; it is the worst sin a government can commit," wrote a leading columnist and added that such a defeat "shocks the people even more when they have been made to expect the opposite."[16]

Politicians fully capitalized on this anti-Nawaz mood. Pakistan Peoples' Party (PPP), Pakistan's leading opposition party, was critical of the prime minister for carrying out secret negotiations with Clinton. The MQM also opposed the Washington agreement as a 'sell out of Kashmir.'[17] It demanded details of the Sharif-Clinton talks and said that an agreement on withdrawal "without a quid pro quo" would be a "a serious disappointment for the nation."[18] The Jamaat-i-Islami, a right-wing party, who had protested in Lahore against the Lahore summit, was predictably critical of the prime minister. Its leader Munawar Hassan said the Washington statement was "treachery." The prime minister, he claimed, had "betrayed the national interest…just as the freedom fighters were winning the war and the Indian forces were demoralized." [19]

PTI, an emerging national party, led by former cricketing icon Imran Khan, also rejected the Washington agreement. PTI leader Abdus Sattar,[20] with forty years as Pakistan's top diplomat behind him, predicted that Sharif "will be ousted from power like former rulers who compromised Kashmir's interest." Sattar's recall of history was faulty. Of the assassinated prime minister Liaquat Ali Khan the seasoned diplomat claimed "in 1949 Liaquat Ali Khan was involved in a sell-out and he had to leave in 1951…" ![21] Military ruler Ayub Khan's exit he singularly linked to the 1965 ceasefire. Ayub Khan, he said "sold out with a ceasefire in 1965 and he also had to go in 1968."[22] Regarding the 4 July agreement Sattar said while the army would carry out out orders of the political government in the given environment, the agreement applied to the Mujahideen, not to the Pakistan Army. Sattar merely repeated Pakistan's official position as he claimed "they (the army) are on the LOC and you cannot ask them to vacate."[23]

The opposition unrelentingly went for the prime minister. It refused to attend a Foreign Office briefing session on the Washington statement. In the first National Assembly session, the combined opposition created uproar against the lack of protocol extended to its leaders by the Foreign Office. It demanded that Nawaz Sharif should have personally addressed the parliament to take them into confidence on such a critical matter, the way Zulfikar Ali Bhuto did after the Simla Agreement and Mohammad Khan Junejo did after the Geneva Accords.[24] For the already agitated Opposition, the Washington Agreement presented another opportunity to attack the government. The spokesperson of the country's largest Opposition party, the Pakistan Peoples' Party, had already warned that "without a quid pro quo" any agreement on withdrawal would be "a serious disappointment" for the nation.[25]

Retired generals too joined the fray. "They simply succumbed and surrendered to the US and to India and deprived the Mujahideen of whatever advantage they had hitherto gained,"[26] Former army chief General Mirza Aslam Beg and former ISI chief General Hameed Gul labelled it a " total sell-out" and warned Sharif that he "scuttled his own mandate by going against the wishes of the nation."[27] Gul warned the lawyers at the Lahore High Court Bar that the Washington agreement was a "Nawaz-Clinton-Vajpayee trio against the Mujahedeen who had been holding a better position at Kargil."[28] Sharif, he said, had misused democracy and heavy mandate by personally deciding to sign the agreement dictated by the US. "We are not an American state…we should not follow American instructions blindly…"[29] He warned of a clash in case the Mujahedeen refused to withdraw from their positions in Kargil. Azad Kashmir, the former ISI chief said, must declare Kargil as part of the state. The refrain was that Washington had imposed all conditions on Pakistan. But only lone voices like former DG ISI General Asad Durrani were clear that he did not see the Americans putting any conditions on the Indians in the present agreement and all conditions had to be fulfilled by Pakistan. In fact, he queried," What possibly could they ask the Indians at this stage?[30]

Sharif found no sympathizers in the press. The widely read independent columnist Ayaz Amir lashed out "That the Kargil adventure was ill-conceived, if not downright foolish, is becoming clear, albeit slowly, even to the congenitally blind and benighted." Of the Washington statement, he wrote, "A more complete negation of Pakistan's stand and a more complete vindication of India's position is hard to envisage."[31] In its editorial, the pro-army daily *The Observer* wrote, "The national press presents the nation as totally divided on the issue with conflicting versions attributing divergent political and military motives to the government's undertakings in accordance with the Washington accord...The nation was not prepared for the prime minister's commitment with president Clinton to withdraw the Mujahideen from Kargil heights..."[32] The elderly chief editor of the *Nawa-i-Waqt,* Majid Nizami, another media voice and convener of the government-funded Nazaria-i-Pakistan Foundation, was confident that the Washington agreement "won't be implemented because it would be political suicide for Nawaz Sharif."[33]

All the talk of Mujahideen disengaging or not was all fiction. The Mujahideen, were not involved. Op KP had no support by Hurriyat , ISI or the ongoing struggle in Kashmir creating rear area insecurity; a repeat of a Operation Gibraltar.

Prime Minister Fights Back

In response to this harsh criticism by politicians and commentators, Islamabad consistently declared the pluses of the Agreement. In his July 12 address to the nation, the prime minister emphasized that a nuclear war had been averted and that "there would be no winners and losers in a nuclear war; the result would only be dreadful destruction and devastation." [34] The government also took credit for "internationalizing the Kashmir issue" in an unprecedented manner. Its constant refrain was that without the settlement of Kashmir issue sustained peace was not possible - "Kargil is an eruption while Kashmir is a volcano."[35]

A day later, in his July 13 address to the PML joint parliamentary party, the prime minister explained that the decision for disengagement was a "step to avert a wider conflict in South Asia between two nuclear powers."[36] This meeting and the resolutions were effectively rejoinders to the barrage of criticism from the opposition, the militants, and sections of the press.

Predictably, his own party extended vigorous support to him. There were resolutions galore. Five were unanimously passed, reposing full confidence in Sharif's leadership and supporting the "courageous steps" he took to save South Asia from the horror of a nuclear war. Another resolution was adopted, emphasizing that "Nawaz Sharif's bold decisions have proved to the international community that Pakistan was a peace-loving nation and wants settlement of Kashmir issue through amicable and peaceful dialogue."[37] This resolution reiterated the approach that had culminated in the Lahore Sharif-Vajpayee summit. The parliamentarians also praised their leader for his patriotism and for his commitment to the Kashmir cause. "We have no reservations on our decisions; we have taken correct and realistic decisions in the larger interest of the country." Another resolution was passed appreciating the Mujahedeen for the Kargil battle.

They had "braved the persistent carpet bombings and artillery fire from India but refused to budge an inch from their positions." And, most importantly, the Mujahedeen were thanked for their positive response to the PM's request that they vacate the Kargil-Drass posts. Pakistan's armed forces were praised for the reason that they "always remain prepared for the defense of the country."

While the main thrust of all criticism targeting the Prime Minster was that he was responsible for Pakistan's humiliation, some of Sharif's cabinet members also rose to his defense. His close confidante, the Minister for Provincial Coordination and Political Affairs, was quick to retort to the critics, "The record of these generals is self-evident." He reminded them that "in their period of leadership, the enemy occupied Siachen glacier. And so where was their military capability and patriotism then?" [38] The beginnings of a civil-military confrontation were discernable. A Sharif loyalist, General Javed Nasir, who had been appointed by Sharif as ISI chief, also supported the withdrawal. He wrote in Pakistan's most widely read Urdu daily *Jang*, praising Sharif's withdrawal decision, even though this former spy chief had equally vehemently supported the Kargil operation. In his *Jang* piece, he praised Sharif's India policy and wrote that the prime minister had "spared no effort for the peace offensive, which he had launched on 21 February 1999 in the form of the Lahore Declaration. Privately, he has also been expressing the desire that we should enter the new millennium with pride and that Allah has ordained the Muslims to serve as an example worth following for the world."[39] The spin did not work.

Nevertheless, troubling question were raised in public spaces. In the chatter of cabinet members, of military men, of the outsider-insiders, including journalists, questions from the planners of Kargil, of the Operation's objectives and now its outcome. The million-dollar question, raised in subdued tones since mid-June, was: "With whose permission was Kargil initiated?"

Reality Unchecked

With ISPR the only source of all Kargil-related information their version of Kargil was the only reality the press knew. Hence, pressmen had not been privy to the ground situation, which had tilted in India's favor. Having lost Tololing posts by the middle of June, Pakistani troops had also lost posts on the strategically located Tiger Hill. The Adjutant General branch at the GHQ had been getting reports of increasing casualties. Even the worried Kargil clique was deeply concerned over mounting deaths of senior colleagues.[40] Supply lines had come under enemy attack, making it difficult to maintain supplies to the posts. A catch-22 situation has been created. Neither was troop pullout possible nor was managing critical logistical supplies.

The shortage of food had meant that some soldiers even had to resort to eating grass.[41] Ill-equipped, underfed, and frost-bitten, many soldiers had been surrounded by Indian infantry and come under artillery and aerial attacks. The inevitable question was: Where would this continued battle on the world's highest and most vicious battleground have led? In the face of overwhelming force deployment by the Indians, the troops across the LOC would have either been killed or captured by the Indians.

The news of the prime minister's effort to end the battle evoked a mixed response among those in the battle-zone. When the news of withdrawal blared from their wireless sets, it was received by many with a sense of relief. Most field commanders were not surprised. Some even prayed for Nawaz Sharif's long life when they heard of the 4 July agreement.[42] They were losing their colleagues while India was beginning to succeed in reclaiming the peaks and ridges. They knew the balance of forces and numbers was heavily tilted in India's favor.

Nevertheless, fighting in the inhospitable terrain under terrible conditions, the question uppermost in the minds of many soldiers was: What had been the purpose of the Operation and of the battle that followed? If a unilateral withdrawal was the final outcome, why the sacrifices? At posts where the young and courageous soldiers had not experienced reversals, many were unable to understand the compulsion to withdraw. There was frustration. Having been commanded to the battle on behalf of their country and having fought bravely, having sacrificed their colleagues, many could not understand why their country did not own them. Why were the dead bodies of their martyred colleagues not being received and honoured? Many also wondered why a seeming victory was being squandered and was turning into a surrender, and that too a globally broadcast surrender?

Withdrawal

Upon his return, the prime minister immediately passed withdrawal orders. On July 8, Sharif's key aide Tariq Fatemi called the Indian Director-General military Operations (DGMO) to convey the coded message for withdrawal, "We have started rolling our beds." While through the withdrawal phase there was communication began between the Pakistani and Indian DGMOs, Fatemi was the PM's point-person for any trouble-shooting.[43] Pakistan's DGMO even formally sought and was given a couple of days extension to complete the 'disengagement' process.[44] Interestingly, Delhi kept Washington in the loop throughout the withdrawal phase to ensure Pakistan would not delay the withdrawal.

To execute the withdrawal, the message was transmitted down the line. The corps commander 10 Corps, Lieutenant General Mahmud, called the operational point man FCNA Commander Javed Hasan and informed him of the decision to withdraw.[45] Although GHQ instructions were to abandon posts and fall back to original positions, disengaging from the enemy too would take time.

After receiving withdrawal orders, a series of meetings were held at the GHQ and in the FCNA headquarters to decide how, when, and the sequence of vacating the posts. Elements of security, mobility, distance, and enemy response were factored in. Extra planning was required since Pakistan's retreating troops were vulnerable to enemy fire. Implementing these orders was going to take time. The dynamics of a battle being fought in the ridges, nullahs, and mountaintops, along with an elaborate battle spread consisting of communications, food supplies, ammunition, weapon systems, artillery, etc. could not be instantly arrested. In fact, in some areas the withdrawal declaration changed little on the ground immediately. The overall withdrawal process, the de-inducting of troops, which involved withdrawal of ammunition, artillery pieces, air defense systems, communications systems, mules and man-packed or mule-packed rations, etc. took about two months. Only some troop movement began as soon as withdrawal orders were received. Positions in the forward areas overlooking the NH-1A began to be vacated.

In some areas commander FCNA did not pass on the instructions immediately and there the troops did not leave their posts and returned weeks after the withdrawal date. For example, on 4 July the commanding officer in the Batalik sector was asked to consolidate.[46] By the third week of July the forward positions had been vacated.[47] The Indians were reporting that "national highway 1A was now totally safe and there was no danger to convoys moving along it. The intruders had lost all positions from which they were earlier keeping a watch on the highway."[48] These posts had, however, been vacated...not lost!

For Delhi, beneath the contrived casualness about the Washington statement was the reality that Pakistan's withdrawal was a morale boost for its troops. On the heels of the MEA spokesperson's July 5 statement, "Yes there is a time frame, which is immediately," came many statements acknowledging that Indian forces faced "fierce resistance" as its air and ground attacks continued.[49] Although the military tide had begun to turn in India's favor, the claim by some in India immediately after the Washington agreement that "they had already driven out 95 percent of the intruders"[50] was rather disingenuous!

In the tough battle terrain, the 4 July agreement had limited relevance as Indian troops sought to settle scores with their 'enemy.' The Indian troops attacked the withdrawing Pakistani troops almost right up to the LOC. Exiting Pakistani troops confronted fierce artillery shelling. In some areas, avalanches caused casualties and blocked exit routes. In some instances, Indian troops also attempted to thwart the withdrawal by blocking the exit routes. Indian troops having suffered heavy casualties in the early stages of the battle, saw this withdrawal as payback time. There was scant hope of India showing consideration, as the *New York Times* advocated. In its editorial of July 7, the *NYT* wrote, "India can make the withdrawal easier by not firing on militants if they leave." Equally, the

Indian intentions of allowing Pakistani soldiers 'safe passage' or, as NSA Brajesh Mishra claimed, "The Indian Army has no tradition of shooting at the backs of people,"[51] the issue of whether retreating troops would be given a safe passage had become contentious issue within India.[52] Yet India's military men were against providing "safe passage."[53] The Indians took advantage, of Pakistani forces withdrawing haphazardly under pressure, by inflicting maximum casualties on them. Pakistan lost approximately 300-400 troops in the retrograde action. The complaints ended only when the troop withdrawal had completed by late August. And India's last attack on Pakistan's withdrawing troops was inflicted on 30 August.

By end-July, Pakistan had pulled back from the bulk of the Indian-held territory. Artillery shelling from the Pakistani side had also stopped.[54] While it took around two weeks for Pakistani troops to pull back from critical areas, in others it took almost two months.[55]

Casualties and Martyrs

Predictably when the Kargil battle came to a close no official casualty figures were issued. The pretence of no Pakistani troop involvement also meant that accepting bodies of martyred soldiers would be difficult. Even during the withdrawal, the Indians claimed that they buried "army soldiers of 12 Northern Light Infantry, who had been killed at Point 4875" in the battle to reclaim posts in Drass sector.[56] Also, while several guesstimates were made, the government issued no official casualty figures. For example, in Pakistan, the military quoted the figure of around 500 deaths, while there was talk of an estimated one thousand Pakistani casualties. The prime minister claimed there were more than thousand casualties.[57] Senior military officers claimed the worried army chief had shared a figure of one thousand casualties.[58] The war martyrs issue and their number came up when the army chief sought a rehabilitation budget for families of martyrs and veterans.

The official policy of not accepting dead bodies of martyred Pakistani soldiers meant that not more than 300 dead bodies were recovered. These were bodies that the Pakistanis themselves recovered from the battle zone, often flying them from the frontline in the MI-17 helicopters. Towards end-July, however, the army command changed its policy on receiving bodies of their fallen men because of Colonel Sher Khan. The high commission in Delhi was instructed through the Defense Attaché to receive the bodies. The Ministry of External Affairs handed over around 12 bodies and a number of injured soldiers captured in the Operation area, to the Pakistan High Commission. Colonel Sher Khan was the hero in whose memory a well-deserved tomb was built in his hometown. Although many martyred sons were honoured but their bodies were not recovered. Families of the martyrs, while proud of their sons' sacrifices, yearned for the bodies of their loved ones. In Talagang Chakwal, the parents of Captain Haseeb Ahmad Malik waited for their son's remains. Similarly Captain Ammar's family longed to get his remain. When an army officer informed Ammar's father, himself a former army officer, about his son's death, crying he said, "I wanted my son to be martyred but at least I should have been given his remains." As an acknowledgement of Captain Ammar's bravery, a round-about on the main road in Rawalpindi[59] was named after him.

India, meanwhile, claimed a low casualty figure. Delhi claimed that 265 Indians were killed and 451 were wounded, while 486 Pakistanis were killed.[60]

Throughout July, the US Administration also continued to put pressure on Pakistan to expedite its troop withdrawal from Kargil. The Indians kept saying the Pakistani forces were not moving fast enough. Later, a senior US official would accept that the Americans were clearly unaware of the difficult terrain from which the Pakistani forces had to retreat. "Maybe we thought there was a broad highway from where troops would have been brought back," he conceded.

The Myth of the Mujahedeen

Pakistan continued with its disingenuous approach of claiming that the Mujahedeen, not its army, were present in the mountains. The army chief was the first to link the withdrawal to the Mujahedeen. Immediately after the announcement, he told the press, "About 1500 to 2000 Mujahedeen are fighting courageously in Drass and Kargil. Pakistan will ask them to change their position and wait for their response. Final decision on how to call back the Mujahedeen will be taken on the prime minister's return."[61] With free play of words and logic, Musharraf also praised the Pakistan Army for having "written a bright chapter of their history by foiling Indian aggression and planned attacks…that Pakistan Army's performance against Indian aggression in Drass and Kargil has proven their highly professional expertise."[62] Meanwhile, at the July 11 joint presser, while giving an update on the withdrawal along with the ISPR's Brigadier Rashid, foreign minister Aziz claimed, "In the past few weeks the Mujahedeen action has been gloriously successful as the just and legitimate cause of Kashmir has engaged the international community's undivided attention throughout the period."[63] The brigadier also recounted the Mujahedeen's military victories over the Indians, who, he claimed, were suffering from "sagging morale." If the Indian morale was "sagging" and the Mujahiedeen were "gloriously successful, then why the 4 July agreement?

What questions would the repeatedly and publicly held official position bring up in peoples' minds? Why then the withdrawal? What guarantee did the prime minister have that the Mujahedeen pull back from this "gloriously successful" feat in Kargil, would help to further the Kashmir cause? Given these inevitable questions, would then the prime minister's Washington withdrawal agreement and his request to the 'Mujahedeen' to withdraw, appear to be a correct move?

No less confused were the conflicting responses of the 'Mujahideen' to the prime minister's request that they withdraw from the mountains. For example, Sartaj Aziz said, during his July 12 presser, that Pakistan "had received positive response from Mujahedeen to withdraw," while the ISPR announced that the "Mujahedeen may stay there since they belonged to IOK." At the same presser, while Aziz repeatedly announced that Pakistan had requested the Mujahedeen to withdraw, the ISPR spokesperson Tariq Altaf said, "Mujahedeen have taken a voluntary decision to disperse."[64]

There were contesting voices from Mujahedeen groups. The al-Badar announced, "We will come down when it is too cold, will stay there till September and until then we will send reinforcements." The umbrella organization of Kashmiri freedom fighters, the Hizb-ul Mujahideen (HUM)[65], also rejected the withdrawal call. "The withdrawal of the

Mujahedeen from Kargil is impossible," they declared. The HUM, extremely critical of the United States, accused it of "trying to impose its will on every country." They declared, "We are not slaves of America and we will not accept American slavery."[66] These groups also had links with Pakistan's security agencies and the Kashmiri guerrilla movements operating in Indian-Controlled Kashmir.. For example, as late as 22 July, the chief of Markaz-ud-Daawa al-Irshad, Hafiz Mohammad Saeed, said the Mujahedeen were still fighting the Indian Army. "Shariah does not allow any withdrawal and we have told the same to the government and the world," announced Saeed.[67] Kashmir, he insisted, would only be solved through Jehad.[68] He claimed that the Mujahedeen would continue to occupy mountaintops since the onset of rains had made it difficult for the Indian Army to move heavy weapons in the mountainous battle areas. Also, he claimed, "The Indian Army is not advancing seeing that the area is infested with land mines planted by the Mujahedeen."[69] In an attempt to distance himself from the army, he said that, while the army "took steps for the betterment" of the country, "The army had its own objectives and the Mujahedeen had their own aims."

Statements from the Srinagar-based Hizb ul Mujahideen (HUM) also joined in. "No country," it argued, "Has a right to suggest the withdrawal of Mujahedeen who have launched an armed struggle against Indian forces to liberate Kashmir." While announcing "the withdrawal of Mujahideen from Kargil is impossible," HUM criticized Washington for "trying to impose its will on every country, but we are not slaves of America and we will not accept American slavery."[70] From Srinagar, the chairman of the umbrella body of Kashmiri freedom fighters, the All Parties Hurriyat Conference (APHC), Syed Ali Geelani also opposed Washington's "conciliatory " approach. "The US considers India as a business center and does not want to annoy it,"[71] Geelani concluded.

These endless statements claiming Mujahedeen presence also clashed with the widely known facts about Pakistani soldiers fighting in Kargil. Pakistan continued to spin this bizarre narrative. While the prime minister's trusted bureaucrat Tariq Fatemi told the Indians we are "rolling our beds" and the Pakistan and Indian DGMOs were in contact coordinating Pakistani troops withdrawal and the international community was also commenting on Pakistani troop withdrawal, Islamabad was making a parallel stream of statements claiming that Pakistan had in fact requested the Mujahedeen groups fighting in Kargil-Drass, to withdraw!

The army chief meanwhile also sprang another surprise. By 16 July, he finally did concede the crossing of the LOC by Pakistani troops. "Aggressive patrolling done by our troops had put them across the LOC. It was done to make sure that we have our eyes and ears open before any action takes place on LOC,"[72] the army chief explained. He justified the crossing because of the "offensive action by Indians and aircraft bombing across the LOC. That is what got us involved on the LOC." To pre-empt any attacks by Indian troops, his own troops crossed the LOC and carried out aggressive patrolling on the Indian side.[73] Finally, when he himself was President, Musharraf opted for full disclosure. He acknowledged in his book that "as few as five battalions in support of freedom fighter groups, were able to compel the Indians to employ more than four divisions…"[74] In fact, adding a new dimension, the former army chief also claimed it was the "Pakistani freedom fighters"[75] who had occupied the front-line positions.

Engineering Dismissal

Politicians, militant groups, and opinion-makers argued that the political government's decision to withdraw had compromised the army's winning position. The army's information arm remained engaged with most among these parties and groups.

They insisted that the 4 July withdrawal decision was a betrayal of the Kashmiri cause by the Pakistanis and an American betrayal of Pakistan. Among the front-line critics were men from Sharif's own party, who also criticized Sharif's decision-making style. The most comprehensive critique in the counter narrative came from a senior Vice President of the ruling party Ejaz-ul-Haq. At a public meeting, Haq declared, "the Pak-India war was not over but suspended." He argued that the government could not solve the Kashmir issue without use of force. He criticized the US State Department for giving priority to the Indians and for betraying the

Pakistani leadership and criticized the government that "despite several past political dodges, Pakistani leaders have given another chance to the US." Son of the former military dictator General Zial ul Haq, Ejaz ul Haq had close ties with the Pakistan Army.[76] In a meeting with military representative first, and subsequently with the army chief, Haq was tasked to mobilize various individuals within the ruling party and the right-wing parties, especially the Jamaat-i-Islami. The former military ruler's son also targeted Pakistan's Foreign Office bureaucrats. He lamented that, because of Pakistan's slack diplomacy, "Pakistan's international position is so low that it is held responsible for anything wrong in occupied Kashmir." Haq eulogized the Mujahedeen who, he claimed, "had occupied every peak in held Kashmir" and that "even if they may be resource less they are continuing the fight."[77] Recalling their Kargil feat, he said, "They have captured India's life-line, Kargil, which it could not re-capture despite 65 days of continued aggression." Interestingly, in direct contrast with what his prime minister noted as an achievement, the avoidance of a nuclear catastrophe, Haq commended the Mujahedeen for making "a nuclear India eat dust." About Kargil, Haq said, "Our army fought with spirit…India would have surrendered if 50,000 people had died in Kargil. It was unfortunate that Pakistan failed to reply to the Indian propaganda."[78] The contradictions in his assertions were obvious. He rejected the Simla Accord and the Lahore Declaration as being "valueless" and insisted that without the use of force the Kashmir dispute could not be resolved. [79] Simultaneously he insisted that "the government should hold talks with India on a one-point agenda - Kashmir."[80] He opted to overlook the advice that the Chinese gave during the Kargil crisis, first to the foreign minister on June 11 and later to the prime minister on June 30. The Pakistani leadership was advised that patient bilateral diplomacy was the only way if the Kashmir dispute had to be peacefully resolved. This notwithstanding, the PML leader still advocated that "instead of looking towards America, we should seek China and other Islamic countries' help to settle the issue."[81] Through this kind of counter-factual rhetoric, phony patriotism proliferated.

Sharif was criticized for his "emperor-like" decision-making style. There was an increasing demand to set up a National Security Council so as to institutionalize coordination between various ministries and departments dealing with matters of national security. Sharif's critics argued that after Pakistan became a nuclear power it was necessary to establish a body for coordinated and institutionalized decision-making. Haq said the government should take into confidence the nation and opposition parties on every issue.

The government was also under attack from former generals. Men with links to Pakistan's Security Establishment were also very critical of Nawaz Sharif. The former chief of Inter Services Intelligence (ISI) Lieutenant General Hameed Gul, who had been directly involved in organizing the Mujahedeen groups during the Afghan resistance, believed that "The Islamic groups now have a very powerful rallying point after the Washington agreement."[82] He was sure that "the reaction may take time to build up, it may be a week or ten days or more, but the resistance will build up."[83] Woven into the criticism was also the demand that Pakistan should not allow its territory to be used for action against the Taliban and bin Laden. Men privy to ISI's under-takings knew there was a plan to train Pakistani ex-commandoes to launch a get-Osama operation across the border in Afghanistan.

Musharraf Challenged

Musharraf was confronted with an unprecedented two-pronged challenge: managing his relations with the army, as well as with the civilian leadership.

The conduct and the conclusion of Kargil had generated pressures internal to the army. The army chief's public support for withdrawal notwithstanding, the army was against the manner of withdrawal which many in the army believed amounted to advertising the army's capitulation. Critical of the manner of the withdrawal, one analyst wrote, "The original political blunder of approving a strategically flawed and unsustainable plan of guerrilla action was compounded first by diplomatic and domestic mishandling and then by a sudden and inadequately explained policy volte face."[84]

The Kargil clique also owed explanations to its soldiers on multiple counts: Why the military withdrawal from Kargil when media reports were that there were no reversals? Why was a military victory reduced to a unilateral and dishonorable withdrawal? Why was the identity of the soldiers participating in the Kargil Operation concealed which led to not acknowledging the valor and the sacrifices of the Pakistani soldiers? How could Pakistan keep denying involvement of its troops when the martyred NLI soldiers from Kargil were being buried with honours? Why the refusal by Pakistan to not accept the dead bodies of their own soldiers? Did the civilian government support Kargil? Was the nation not grateful for the sacrifices made by the soldiers?

To allay the anguish and the concerns of men within his own institution, Musharraf moved on two tracks. For one, the army chief began touring military garrisons explaining the Army leadership's position on the Kargil Operation. Restive soldiers sought explanations for partially the conduct and mainly the withdrawal from Kargil.[85] In his first address to young officers at the Lahore cantonment garrison, only within two days of the withdrawal announcement, the army chief declared that Pakistan's desire for and peace and not war "should not be considered our weakness." Recalling that India had to pay heavily for casting " an evil eye on Pakistan," the chief informed them that according to one estimate the Indian Army had received at least 600 dead and over 1000 wounded and the material loses have been equally bad, including loss of jet fighters, helicopters and artillery guns.[86] Critical of Indian war hysteria for petty political objectives, Musharraf warned his officers that "we are facing a clever and conniving enemy, who has been extremely unpredictable due to internal stability and low morale of its troops." He nevertheless urged them to "draw strength from our faith in Allah, have firm resolve and avoid paying any heed to the malicious distortion of facts, rumour-mongering and propaganda."[87] Internal whispering had also begun.

Secondly, the army leadership decided, "The highest services of all those who participated in the conflict must be recognized at the highest level." The Northern Light Infantry was given the status of a regular regiment of the Pakistan Army. Plans were made to honour the martyred and the injured soldiers who fought in Kargil. Programmes honouring the soldiers were broadcast on PTV, the official channel. The army chief repeatedly and publicly expressed his support for the withdrawal; yet he repeatedly refuted any accusation of the army 'going it alone' in the Operation.

Musharraf was also in a difficult situation vis-a-vis the civilian leadership. While the prime minister believed he had, through the Washington Statement, pulled the 'chestnuts out of fire,' the weaknesses of the Kargil Operation and the consequent strategic, diplomatic, and institutional costs to the State of Pakistan were evident. As noted earlier, at the 2 July DCC meeting, the prime minister had criticized the Operation. Within the domestic context too Sharif wanted civilian leadership to formulate and project his government's public policy on the Kargil and post-Kargil developments. On the external front, the civilian government had begun to determine ways to deal with the diplomatic and strategic fallout of Kargil. In the minds of the authors of Kargil, who were grudgingly cognizant of Sharif's intentions while also being sensitive to the simmering resentment within their own institution, civil-military tension was inevitable. The army leadership was nervous about Sharif's next move. There was apprehension that the army chief may be dismissed, as newspaper columnists close to the government were demanding.

Framing Sharif

The Kargil crisis was a spin-off of personalized, unstructured, and whimsical decision-making plus Pakistan's chronic civil-military divide. Interestingly, as the end of the Kargil encounter with India, popular debate within Pakistan had little to do with the facts of either the Kargil Operation or its diplomatic fallout. The principal focus was on internal shortcomings, ranging from the functioning of the state to the process of decision-making.[88]

The blame game had started in earnest. Sharif believed he had tried to save Pakistan from a disaster. Yet the post-decision dissonance had sparked off severe criticism of the Sharif government. The government was critiqued by the press for bad planning and faulty execution of the Kargil Operation and attacked for "selling out the Kashmir cause at the behest of Washington."

While the reasons for the Kargil withdrawal were plenty and valid, there was no doubt that political danger lay ahead for Sharif. Despite the Sharif-Musharraf publicly stated common positions, the subtext of the khaki narrative was that Kargil, a great military victory was turned into a defeat. The Sharif government saw it as a khaki-authored disaster that Sharif's 4 July Washington visit had helped to curtail.

Within days of the Washington agreement, the prime minister, who believed he had pulled the army's chestnuts out of the fire, stood politically cornered. The Opposition, hostile to the prime minister, was now focused on the outcome of the prime minister's Washington dash. They wanted Sharif's ouster. For the quietly nervous Kargil clique, this political opposition was a welcome development. Although the blunders of Op Koh Paima continued to lie outside the public view, there was audible whispering over who cleared the Op, why did the army cross the LOC, did the army go it alone, etc. These questions did not go unanswered. The prime minister's supporters and the Kargil clique offered conflicting responses.

While Musharraf publicly obeyed the prime minister's orders on matters ranging from the withdrawal to creating a new institution for national security, there was tension brewing in the subtext of the relationship. Significantly, the prime minister convened the DCC and cabinet meetings to engage with the army chief on policy matters; yet there was a clear trust deficit between the two. The beginnings of the Sharif-Musharraf trust breakdown lay in the near-showdown that took place at the 2 July DCC meeting. Although Sharif had exercised his constitutionally sanctioned executive authority to organize the 4 July Clinton meeting, in doing so he had discontinued the practice of collective decision-making he had adopted since the 17 May Ojhri Camp meeting. Subsequently, although the formal policy-making platform the DCC was not regularly convened, through continuous interaction with all stake-holders, collectively and in groups, the prime minister ensured there was relative transparency and disclosure for all key stake-holders on most Kargil-related key decisions - the Foreign Minister's 12 June Delhi trip, the Zinni meeting, the back-channel with India, the China meetings, engaging Clinton, etc. However, this pattern changed after the 2 July

Sharif-Musharraf near showdown. After this, the two key men in Pakistan's power construct were left second-guessing each other's next move. The obvious question must have bothered Musharraf: How would the prime minister deal with the army chief under whose watch the Kargil blunder had occurred?

Finally, in the closing days of Kargil, a creeping instability had entered Pakistan's power scene. Showdown between the civil and military power centers was not inevitable, although in the dynamic of distrust was the potential for a clash. Given the widespread political antagonism, the Kargil clique had likely allies, in case the tensions translated into a clash.

Someone had to be made the scapegoat

Chapter 16

THE AUGUST QUADRANGLE

By August, the tentacles of the Kargil debacle had begun to spread through Pakistan's power structure, within the Army itself, and across the political divide. It significantly impacted Pakistan's civil-military relations, its foreign policy, and its domestic politics. While Washington's pressure on the Sharif-led government was the immediate stimulus in the aftermath of Kargil, it was, in fact, a return to his government's own preferred policy. But Sharif had a 'repairing job' to do on the domestic and the foreign policy fronts. The end of Pakistan's ill-conceived Kargil adventure marked the beginning of new pressures for his government. The formidable environment that Pakistan's elected prime minister faced in the post-Kargil phase posed five specific, yet overlapping, challenges for him: One, to manage civil-military relations; two, to fix the distortions and push back the increasing political pressure; three, to bring back on track the de-railed India policy; four, to modify Pakistan's Afghanistan policy; and, five, to aid the Clinton administration to go after al-Qaeda and specifically to capture OBL.

Civil-military relations

The Kargil blunder proved that there could be exceptions to the maxim 'failure is an orphan'. As the country's chief executive, it was Sharif who was left to deal with the fallout of the Kargil blunder. He publicly adopted the failed Operation KP as his own, while its actual architects were not only refusing to accept exclusive responsibility but were surreptitiously feeding the myth that it was a success and that, hence, the 4 July withdrawal decision was a wrong one. Against the backdrop of the multiple critiques of the Operation, its architects went into a veiled offensive defense mode. By August, they had replaced their seemingly cooperative post-Kargil stance towards the government, with a pro-active survival strategy. As architects of the concluding chapter of the flawed and failed Kargil Operation, they felt insecure. They feared possible retribution from within their own institution as well as from the civilian prime minister. The almost surreal elements of the Operation itself included the government insistence that the Mujahideen had carried out the Operation, to Pakistan's refusal to accept dead bodies of martyred soldiers, to the post-4 July announcement by the Pakistanis that the Mujahideen have been requested to climb down from the Kargil heights and then publicly complaining that India was attacking the withdrawing Pakistani soldiers. There were too many contradictions to be resolved. Amidst these vacillating positions, gallantry awards were announced for Pakistani soldiers who had fought in Kargil.

Pakistan's prime minister had a major 'repairing job' to do, both on the domestic and the foreign fronts. By contrast, for his Indian counterpart Vajpayee, the initial debacle had been converted into an election-winning strategy.

For the elected prime minister, by August at the core of domestic troubles that confronted him were his relations with the army chief. The Sharif-Musharraf tension had begun building up in the closing days of Kargil. His public endorsement in May of Musharraf's misadventure, which gave the impression that the PM seemed willing to share the glory of Kargil's potential success, had begun evaporating by-mid June as the Indian military launched its counter offensive and the international community began to exert concerted pressure on Islamabad to withdraw from Kargil. However, by early August, with the outcome of Operation KP bearing heavy on their minds, the Kargil planners found themselves in the midst of a blame game that threatened their survival. Sharif's

Washington dash, in the very early hours of 4 July, with no preparation, had its own fallout. Specifically, it created the dynamic of the prime minister versus the army chief. While Sharif had bailed out the Army and had shown no inclination to hold the generals accountable for the disaster, the army leadership had decided to launch a systematic propaganda offensive against the prime minister.[1]

While, in the subtext of Sharif-Musharraf interaction, tension was writ large, there were pockets of business as usual. In early August, the army chief held a meeting in the GHQ, where Sharif was presented a proposal for a Higher Defense Council, to be headed by the PM. Sharif handed over the proposal document to Sartaj Aziz and asked him to review it.

Meanwhile, multiple factors had prompted the army high command to work on an anti-Sharif campaign: their chronic distrust of the civilians; the barracks, drawing room, and media chatter of the Kargil failure; the discontent within the Army; and the 'rogue army' advertisement that appeared in the US press. It was in this environment of distrust that the army leadership was convinced that the Sharif-led government was behind the placement of the 'rogue army':[2] advertisement[3]. Reiterating this belief, Musharraf wrote in his book, *In the Line of Fire*, 'All kinds of carefully placed articles appeared including one page advertisement in the United States, maligning the army and creating a divide between it and the government.'[4] But, as was subsequently revealed, with documented evidence, the Indian government had been behind authoring and financing the publication of the advertisement.[5]

The August tensions were a carry forward from end-June, when news of increasing Pakistani casualties trickled in, and the question arose of India opening other fronts, international pressure began to mount on Islamabad to withdraw from Kargil. The prime minister had begun to lose his patience. As the talk of Operation KP turning into a fiasco trickled into the prime minister's House, Sharif in closed meetings began questioning the calculations regarding the Operation by Musharraf and the Army planners. The prime minister recalled in a subsequent interview, 'I kept asking General Musharraf: After all what did you have in mind when you planned such an Operation?'[6]

The tensions of an Operation gone sour and having become a textbook casualty of the Clausewitzian 'fog of war'[7], had unraveled whatever bonhomie had existed through May between Nawaz Sharif and his military commander. Specifically, at the 17 May briefing on the Operation, the prime minister had lock, stock, and barrel bought into the military command's suggestion that, through the KP Operation, India could be forced to vacate Jammu and Kashmir. Such an achievement would have made him Pakistan's most popular national leader, second only to Jinnah.

In the post-Kargil period, clearly Pakistan's power construct, with civilian and military leaderships distrustful of each other, had begun functioning in a heightened instability zone with Washington too as a relevant player. Nevertheless, according to one of Nawaz Sharif's right-hand men, his Defense Secretary, the PM had no intention of taking any action against the army leadership. He never once mentioned the need to set up a Kargil Inquiry Commission targeting the army chief. In fact, according to him, 'Sharif's inner coterie of advisors was keen to settle matters. The discarded politicians and journalists played a role in drumming up tension after the withdrawal.' Inherent in this situation was the possibility of an overt political clash between the two. Would the military leadership strike through a coup d'état or would the elected prime minister use his constitutional authority to do the unprecedented: fire the second army chief within a one year period. This was the million dollar question doing the rounds.

Energile drink, grass, and an Ibex

After the 4 July decision to withdraw the jolted morale of sections of the Army began to become apparent. In ways unknown to Pakistan's highly disciplined Army, many began asking their seniors harsh and angry questions. Bottled up resentment across all ranks began to surface in senior command meetings and, in open forums, younger officers were raising uncomfortable questions. Trained in the elite training institutions to inquire and question, some among the inquisitive and now agitated minds were daring to ask uncomfortable questions.

For many who participated in this Operation, which was launched secretively and never acknowledged publicly, it was one in which many nameless soldiers were also killed[8] and which had been ended in indecent haste. Many Pakistanis, both civilians and military men, who had not been privy to the facts at the time Nawaz Sharif left for Washington, believed that a military victory had been bartered away at the Washington meeting. The fact that the Indians had already reclaimed at least 50 per cent of the Pakistani occupied posts was not known to many. 'Why did we go in?' asked resentful younger soldiers, who were initially getting news of their colleagues occupying unchallenged hundreds of posts deep inside the Indian-held territory. Those who were yearning to go to the front, whose friends had fought and lost their lives, and who were told by their seniors that Operation KP had brought the Indians to their knees, wondered why the political leadership had crafted an ignominious end to the brave and bold winning efforts of their colleagues.

By August, from within the cracks in the leaden walls of secrecy shrouding the Kargil Operation, sagas of suffering soldiers had started slipping through. Men sent in with backpacks bearing three-day supplies had gone hungry for days as there was minimal or no logistical support for them. Soldiers from NLI 5 had been sent hurriedly from the plains in June straight onto the deadly heights without getting themselves acclimatized and only with backpacks. Indian interdiction of Pakistan's supply lines through air attacks had succeeded and insufficient logistical supplies had hampered these brave men throughout the Operation. And yet Operation KP had extended beyond the original blue print, with men who had been given the green signal to press ahead beyond Koh Paima's original blueprint to occupy the unprotected heights of Kargil. They faced major food shortages. Kargil veterans talked of surviving on stocks of *Energile* drink, clumps of grass, and by killing the odd ibex. 'We were living under survival conditions,' was how one major recalled their plight. 'At times, there was even no food to eat. Some even had to eat grass. A rare ibex use to be a treat,' recalled a young captain who had fought in Kargil, whose brother too was a captain at the Pakistan Military Academy, Kakul.[9] The cumulative blame for the appalling subsistence conditions, most among the troops believed, lay with the High Command, which was oblivious tp their miserable plight and was found wanting in its professional responsibilities.

Returning veterans talked subsequently of how 'there was no war gaming involving logistics base, time requirement, operations, time factor for preparation to face the entire range of the enemy reactions'.[10] The concept of Kargil, another complained, was 'made in the staff posts and hence not linked to the ground reality'.

The architects of Kargil were reacting to widespread reservations among the soldiers. While visiting garrisons and hospitals, they were grilled by soldiers about the objectives of Operation KP, about the wasted sacrifices of the brave young men and about the decision to withdraw. General Musharraf decided to tour the corps and personally explain the Kargil situation to his restive soldiers. Upon his arrival at the different stations, he realized that explaining the situation was a tall order. He mostly received cold, if not aggressive, receptions from the officers. For example, in the Quetta Garrison 41 Division auditorium, a captain asked the visiting army chief, 'If you had to pull-out in exchange for a Nawaz Sharif and Clinton breakfast meeting, why did you go in?' Another wanted to know why prime minister Nawaz Sharif had let them down. The Corps Commander Quetta, accompanying the army chief, had to intervene to ask his officers to take it easy. This resentment among the officers sprang from the widely held belief that, by calling off Operation KP when it was virtually impossible for the Indians to militarily dislodge Pakistani troops from their posts, the prime minister had committed a blunder.[11]

In the emerging season of discontent, according to eye witness accounts, when the Commander 10 Corps Mahmud and Commander FCNA Javed Hassan visited Gilgit at the end of June, the 'gestures of the junior officers and the troops could have been equated to mutiny'. Angrily, they said to each other of the NLI commander that 'he bites'.[12] Similarly, at the Artillery and Armour School meeting in Nowshera at the end of July, the Q&A was filled with aggressive emotions. The chief was asked by a young captain, 'Did you visualize the enemy's reaction?' The answer was, 'No!' Resentment reeked from every word that young officers fired at their chief. These young warriors had many hard questions. 'Why did we conduct the Kargil Operation?' asked one. 'This one operation and so many casualties?' lamented another. 'The nation spends so much money on us and what have we done?' was a taunting query from another. The chief refrain was: 'Who is responsible for this fiasco?' And the young soldiers wanted to know.

In rare cases, soldiers lying in delirious conditions on hospital beds even cursed at the commanders visiting the injured. According to one Kargil veteran who, after fighting at the Tiger Hill, lay injured in a hospital in Gilgit, another veteran on the bed next to his shouted and in abusive language cursed the military commanders as they came to visit the injured. Similar accounts of highly resentful NLI jawans were widely discussed. Injured soldiers at the army hospital in Gamba, Skardu[13] interacted very aggressively with the FCNA commander. Another injured brigadier, who had commanded an NLI brigade, was evacuated to Rawalpindi because it was not safe for him to be around the injured and extremely angry troops.[14]

By such public expression of their angry emotions, the young officers and jawans of NLI had broken rigid institutional codes. This was particularly evident at the traditional Darbar gatherings convened by the NLI commander who had led the Kargil operation.

The soldiers who returned home after almost being trapped in the world's most inhospitable and treacherous battle field and having a close brush with death had expected heroes' welcomes. Instead, they felt hurt and unappreciated. Many complained that the media 'mistreated' them and the people did not give them 'the credit' they deserved. And the withdrawal phase made matters even worse. Failure to ensure a proper scheme of withdrawal, to prevent the unnecessary loss of life to Indian artillery fire, had caused soldiers to feel badly let down. Not only were there no rules of disengagement agreed upon but the withdrawal process dragged over several months with the returning soldiers narrating unrelenting attacks by the Indians.

In August, angrily weeping families had received Prime Minister Nawaz Sharif and the army chief in Gilgit with the demand that their sons, brothers, or husbands be brought back, dead or alive. Their anguish stemmed from the extraordinary circumstances. There was no declared war and their men had not announced they were going to the front, and there were dead bodies arriving and, worse, there were highly disturbing Indian media reports that the Pakistani authorities were refusing to accept many of the bodies of their soldiers.

In July, Pakistan's Political Counsellor in Delhi, Jalil Abbas Jillani, had received a call from his Indian counterpart asking him to receive the bodies of fallen Pakistani soldiers. Under instructions to refuse, Jillani told Vivek Katju, Additional Secretary in the Indian Ministry of External Affairs, that there were no Pakistani soldiers fighting in Kargil. The bodies Indian authorities wanted to handover included the body of Colonel Sher Khan who had been awarded the Nishan-i-Haider, the highest military award. By the end of July, these instructions to the Pakistan High Commission were changed and they had begun accepting the bodies. As Islamabad accused Delhi of torturing Pakistani soldiers, the Indian Ministry of External Affairs spokesman offered to handover several Pakistani soldiers, captured in Kargil, to the International Committee of the Red Cross (ICRC).[15]

The increasing resentment among the officers and the jawans was no secret. The army chief, keen to rebuild the troop morale and their esprit du corps, chose unique ways to do so. Musharraf ordered that a camp fire be organized for the troops where, sitting around the fire, they recounted their battle stories and sang songs. The chief also danced to some songs. At the conclusion of the campfire, Walkmans were distributed among about 450 soldiers.[16]

The army chief decided to be with the troops. As a special morale-boosting gesture in July, Musharraf spent a night with the SSG battalion. In three MI-17s helicopters, the battalion was flown to Chota Deosai. A campfire was arranged with music and food and the chief spent the night with soldiers from 12-NLI and 5-NLI. The commander 10 Corps and commander FCNA were also present as the army chief delivered his pep talk to the despondent troops. 'I too am from the SSG,' he told those present, 'You must please be mindful of my respect.'[17]

In the mini-mutiny that was being exhibited by the young soldiers, the commanders on the defensive had to compromise on matters of discipline. For example, while Commander FCNA Javed Hassan was keen to punish the soldiers who left their posts, his Corps Commander, General

Mahmud, advised relieving them instead of court-martialling them. He feared punishing them would open up a Pandora's Box.[18]

Political Pressure

On the political front, the Opposition was already busy demanding that the elected prime minister, with a terrible governance record, be sent home. Earlier in April 1998, Benazir and her husband were convicted on corruption charges. Deeply drawn battle lines all targeted Sharif's corruption—his refusing to return billion of rupees of loans, his seeking to control the parliament by becoming *Ameerul Momineen*, his party workers' attack on the Supreme Court, the controversy around the 4 July decision to withdraw: all these gave the Opposition another stick to seek government's early removal. The ruling family's loan scandals were snowballing into a major crisis. Interestingly, the Army, despite its huge and dangerous blunder in Kargil, was in a secure spot.

Opposition parties attacked the government for different reasons. The PPP insisted that the government, and specifically the prime minister, had cleared the Kargil Operation. The religious parties criticized the withdrawal and the Sharif-led government's re-engagement with India, as well as his decision to pull back support to the Taliban and enter into dialogue with the Northern Alliance. They consistently attacked the government for allowing US Special Forces to come to Pakistan to train Pakistanis involved in the 'Capture bin Laden' Operation. Through August, these protesting parties and sections of the media, who dominated popular discourse as well as public space, reiteratively popularized the narrative that Washington had stepped in to save India from a certain military defeat that the Mujahedeen had almost inflicted on India. The Washington Accord, for them, was a sell-out of the Kashmiri cause.

Political pressures emanated also from non-political sources. Buoyed by the increasing political pandemonium, the army command felt confident to raise issues of governance. They sought improved governance. The army chief in his meeting with the prime minister's younger brother and Chief Minister of Punjab, Shehbaz Sharif, suggested that he must consider becoming the deputy prime minister in order to streamline the federal government's performance![19] The younger Sharif, while having heard the army chief attentively, was clear that neither would his brother fancy such a suggestion coming from him and nor was his vacating Punjab, the fortress of Pakistan's politics, a wise move. Meanwhile, the authors of the country's biggest military debacle would call out the elected government on governance matters. The blundering group in khaki would hold the weak civilians accountable while they launched a campaign to discredit the elected government.

'Worst Debacle in Pakistan's History'

In addition to the resentment within the rank and file, the army chief had to deal with internal rifts between his top military commanders, as their criticism of the Kargil Operation began to surface. They believed the ill-conceived Operation had caused embarrassment to the entire institution. Even the military's own top spymasters and senior commanders were actively kept out of the loop. When they had picked up indicators of unusual troop movement, the existence of the Operation was denied. Others, who had questioned the viability of the Kargil plan during the early May Corp Commanders meeting but had their concerns dismissed by the architects of Kargil, were also talking. This, after 4 Jul many a hitherto tight-lipped and resentful commander was now more vocal in his indictment of the Operation.

The professional credibility of the architects of Kargil was under fire within their own institution. Of the retired generals, the former ISI chief Lt. General Asad Durrani, was quick to criticize the 'self-serving hopes and hypes' based planning. He wrote, 'We had chinks in our armor, but as the events unfolded it was the Indian external pincer that forced us to agree to restore the LOC ... Pakistan was pressured to restore the status quo ante, not only because the West desired to prevent turmoil in the region, but also due to our comparative vulnerability to coercion ... It [Kargil] has not only brought home the realities of international politics... It has also taught us to regard events in their correct perspective, rather than getting carried away by self-serving hopes and hypes.'[20]

The public critique later by one of Pakistan's most professional generals, Lt. General Ali Quli Khan,[21] best captured the views of Pakistan's top commanders. Commenting on General Musharraf's own conclusion on the Kargil Operations, 'Considered in purely military terms, the Kargil Operations were a landmark in the history of the Pakistan Army,'[22] Khan, the former Chief of General Staff wrote, 'I am totally amazed at such ostrich-like behavior when the whole world considers Kargil to be the worst debacle in Pakistan's history and where countless innocent young lives were lost for nothing. Absolutely nothing!'[23] He further added, 'I regret to say that the conception and planning at the highest level had been poor—in fact, so poor that the only word which can adequately describe is it unprofessional. We all know that the main duty of the high command is to ensure that with their meticulous planning they create conditions whereby their junior combatants can fight easily. This was certainly not done at Kargil. It is also fairly obvious that the Kargil Operations was not conceived in its totality, with the result that apart from bringing ignominy to Pakistan it also caused unnecessary misery to a lot of innocent people.'[24]

Internally, within the institution, there was disquiet after the withdrawal. Instructions were that Kargil would not be discussed in any school of instruction, neither in any class nor in any study period. No courses would be taught at the NDC etc. The subject of Kargil was a 'banned item'.

'Rogue Army' and *Kargil Kay Heroes*

Criticism from beyond the borders also hit hard, especially when it floated in world capitals in form of the vicious, scathing criticism in the 'Rogue Army' advertisements campaign that targeted the Pakistan Army and multiplied the woes of the Kargil clique. Within days of the 4 July Sharif-Clinton Statement, the advertisement ran in leading US newspapers, including the *New York Times*. Musharraf wanted an official and very prominent rebuttal issued in the very papers in which the advertisement appeared. It was a matter of the troop morale, he asked a common friend to convey to the prime minister. The army chief also sent an offer of army funds to pay for the rebuttal in case the government had funding problems.[25] The prime minister disagreed. Despite the intervention of his father and brother, Sharif was unrelenting. Only one article could be commissioned to counter the advertisement.

Thus, the pressure from within the Army, the vocal criticism by the navy and the air force, and the general political chatter prompted the architects of Kargil to adopt an offensive defense posture. In August, deeper fault lines emerged between the civilian and military leadership's approach to handling the post-Kargil period.

The most public manifestation of this difference was over the question of decorating the Kargil heroes, martyrs and the living, with national awards for valor. Why this issue became a controversial one between the government and the Army was principally because the Army had publicly taken the position that it was not Pakistani soldiers but freedom fighters who had fought in Kargil. The prime minister had sustained this charade, begun initially by the Army during the Kargil Operation, even after the 4 July withdrawal. The army leadership now wanted the government to approve national awards for the 'Kargil heroes.'

The GHQ also wanted nationally broadcast television programmes honouring the heroes of Kargil. There was a reason why the Kargil clique now wanted to acknowledge and honour the brave and the best of the Army, earlier having opted to let them be projected as Mujahideen. The clique now detected the increasing anger and agitation of the troops caused towards their commanders, not only because of the debacle-like end of Kargil, but also in their role and sacrifices not having been acknowledged.

Sitting in their secure garrisons, these were men of command and authority who must have silently been haunted by the calamitous Operation they had designed. More blood, their critics argued, of Pakistan's brave soldiers had flowed in this calamity called Kargil, than put together in the two wars Pakistan fought in 1965 and 1971.

On 13 August, at the GHQ, the army leadership decided, 'The highest services of all those who participated in the conflict must be recognized at the highest level.' Soon after, the men who had conceived and led the Kargil debacle sat in the Ops Room at Gilgit to decide on the honours and awards to be given out to the soldiers who had fought the battle. This well-attended Honours and Awards meeting decided to award 80 citations.[26] Interestingly, although Pakistan's public position was that Kashmiri Mujahideen, not Pakistani soldiers, were fighting the Indian Army in Kargil, yet, that night the Kargil clique, identified the recipients for the highest gallantry award, Nishan-i-Haider. Additionally, approximately 80 soldiers were given various other awards on General Javed Hassan's recommendations. He insisted awards were necessary to raise the morale of the soldiers.

The Awards ceremony, called *Kargil kay Hero*, was televised by *PTV*, but the Sharif-led government was keen to call off its broadcasting. The prime minister was trying to re-engage with the Indians. Thus, Nawaz Sharif and Shehbaz Sharif did not participate in the programme. While all the chief ministers participated, the Punjab chief minister avoided it.

This civil-military divide over awarding the NLI men who had participated in the Opèration further increased the existing trust deficit.

Foreign Policy

Beyond the personal angle involving insecurity and assertion of the key architects of Operation KP and the resentment of the soldiers who participated in the Operation, there was an institutional resistance to Nawaz Sharif's decisions in key foreign policy areas, including strategy relating to India, the United States, and Afghanistan. From Washington, the triple push was to honour the 4 July withdrawal agreement, provide help in capturing OBL, and to return to the spirit of the Lahore Declaration in engaging with India. Within Washington, the consensus was that only a civilian government could deliver on these and, hence, Sharif's survival as prime minister was of interest to the Clinton administration.

With India, Nawaz Sharif reverted almost instantly to the policy of dialogue that had been sabotaged by the Operation In August Nawaz Sharif sent Tariq Fatimi to Geneva to meet with the Indian National Security Advisor Brajesh Mishra. Vajpayee's message was that while he was keen that the countries return to the Lahore process, he needed time.

In Pakistan, the political leadership and bureaucracy wanted to bring the relationship back on track and make a determined effort to move ahead with the Lahore process. Nawaz Sharif was keen on rapprochement, not only because after Operation KP the onus of fence-mending was on Pakistan, but also because the Washington-Delhi strategic engagement meant the bilateral route was the primary route available to Islamabad for engagement with Delhi. Washington was keen, as expressed by the US Secretary of State, Madeleine Albright, during her September visit to the UN session[27] that the Pakistan-India dialogue be resumed, Islamabad was also seeking direct bilateral engagement.

The political will in Islamabad and Delhi to revive bilateral relations led to a meeting of senior diplomats in Europe. Within weeks of the 4 July withdrawal decision, Nawaz Sharif sent Additional Secretary Tariq Fatemi, his point-man on foreign policy and his trusted aide, to Geneva to meet with the Indian National Security Advisor, Brajesh Mishra. Vajpayee's message to Nawaz Sharif was that he too was keen to come back to the Lahore process but he needed time. With Indian general elections scheduled for October, Vajpayee wanted to go to the October election having turned the liability of Pakistan's Kargil Operation into a vote-rewarding election asset.

The Sharif-led government had consistently demonstrated that its preferred route of engagement with Delhi was the bilateral route. Significantly, following the May 1998 nuclear tests, bilateral engagement had acquired new energy. A set of summit-level and senior officials' meetings had resulted in some revision of Pakistan's India policy. By the end of 1998, using institutional mechanisms, including the DCC, the Foreign Office, and the ISI, Sharif had practically begun policy reorientation. Bilateral engagement had also delivered the landmark Lahore Agreement. Moving onwards from Lahore, at Norelia, Sri Lanka, Foreign Ministers Sartaj Aziz and Jaswant Singh opened a dialogue on the intractable Kashmir dispute. They agreed to explore middle-of-the-road solutions.

In Islamabad, the Foreign Office was convinced of the advantage of bilateral engagement between Pakistan and India. Pakistan's Foreign Office actively opposed any US involvement during the Kargil crisis.

Throughout the crisis, Pakistan's Foreign Office and the prime minister's office had been keen to keep the Americans out of the negotiations. They even discouraged top-level Pakistan-US telephone contacts, such as when Secretary of State, Madeleine Albright, and US President Bill Clinton tried to call Nawaz Sharif. They preferred bilateralism over Washington's third party interlocutor role. There was now also a growing Washington-Delhi nexus, with India making a concerted effort in the post-Kargil period to project Pakistan's regional policy as one marked by promoting terrorism and extremism. Pakistan's reckless behavior in Kargil was contrasted with what was viewed as Indian restraint.

On a parallel track, belligerence remained alive. Indian media accused Pakistan of a major troop build-up along the LOC,[28] of heightened militant activity in IOK, including attacks on Indian occupation forces,[29] and infiltrating and shelling across the LOC.[30] Alongside the quiet, high-level efforts at re-engagement, ran the perennial tensions flowing from chronic distrusts, old patterns and unresolved issues. Delhi's return to bilateral dialogue was accompanied by the framing of Pakistan as a country supporting terrorism. In the post-Kargil period, Indian efforts to project Pakistan's regional policy as supportive of terrorism and extremism increased. Pakistan's reckless behavior was contrasted with what was viewed as Indian restraint. Old ways, from a mindset of unresolved issues, of habitual intelligence hawks on both sides, remained, the thrust towards notwithstanding. The broader policy thus retained its usual duality.

Alongside this mutual agreement to re-engage, an India buoyant from its diplomatic victory, playing on the twin post-Cold War global threats of proliferation and extremism, advocated that Washington're-examine' its relations with Pakistan. Indian diplomacy highlighted the 'dangers Pakistan had courted during Kargil'. During their visits to Washington and to the Association of Southeast Asian Nations (ASEAN) meetings, senior Indian diplomats, including the Indian foreign minister and special envoys, invoked the Taliban-Mujahideen and the 'Islamic terrorist' mantra against Pakistan.

Delhi brushed aside all reports of Indian military build-up as 'ill-conceived and unfounded' and justified it because of Pakistan's 'aggressive posture'.[31] Pakistan-India leadership's efforts, through the backchannel, to return to the negotiating table, remained wobbly. Caught between electioneering compulsions and the heightened Kashmiri Mujahideen militant activity, the message from India's man of peace was, 'Attempts are on to create trouble in parts of Jammu and Kashmir, violence cannot be the road to talks.'[32] From Pakistan, between the Fatemi talks and the determination to keep the pressure on the Indian forces who had scored an ostensible victory, however costly for India, in Kargil, the message was inevitably a mixed one.

Kargil was winding down to the ratcheting up of global concerns on the unresolved issue of Kashmir. Pakistan's misadventure was coming to an ignominious closure, but not without flagging the centrality of the resolution of the Kashmir issue as a necessary prerequisite for ensuring peace between the two nuclear South Asian states. On the ground, meanwhile, it was not over for all the NLI jawans who were traveling through Indian-held territory to cross back into Azad Kashmir. Retreating, they were confronted with the jubilant and angry Indian soldiers, still in battle mode against the NLI intruders.

As August drew to a close, the withdrawal from Kargil had yet to be completed, Atlantique 2 had been shot down and it was business as usual on the spy front with continuing sagas of accusations and abduction of embassy staff members on both sides of the divide. Competing complaints of staff being seized, 'seriously injured', 'badly beaten', 'bruised', and 'severely tortured' were emanating from the two capitals and there inside Indian-held Kashmir there was a resurgence of guerrilla activity and grenade, rocket, and bomb attacks against military targets. The official line was that Kargil had reinvigorated and internationalized the forgotten Kashmir cause and the official defense for Kargil was that it was only a fair response to India's 1984 occupation of Siachen.

Whatever the Sharif and Vajpayee intent, the 9 August , 1999 Atlantique incident reflected the unchanged texture of the post-Kargil operational-level interaction. India's MIG fighters had shot down a Breguet Atlantic patrol airplane of the Pakistan Navy's Air Arm, with 16 people on board. India claimed it had violated Indian airspace. Washington attributed the manslaughter shoot-down to both India and Pakistan having violated a 1991 agreement related to parameters set for military aircrafts along the border. Days later, Pakistan fired a missile at an Indian helicopter it claimed had violated laid down parameters for flying too close to the border. While, on Delhi's demand, Washington had been actively involved in Kargil-related withdrawal issues, on the expectation of engagement over the Atlantique shoot down, National Security Council spokesman, David Leavy, said that Washington would not be a 'referee between India and Pakistan'. Reinforcing the point, State Department spokesman, James Rubin, said that, even on Kashmir, the US could mediate only if Pakistan and India both sought mediation. Away from 4 July, Pakistan had to manage its own relationship with India.

But drawing upon his 4 July encounter with the US president, Pakistan's prime minister could still reach out to Washington but not to get policy direction. Sharif's battle at home was brewing.

Taliban, OBL, and Sharif

While Pakistan had its own problems with the Taliban, including providing refuge in Afghanistan to sectarian killers, Sharif had a commitment to fulfill, which he had made in the 4 July meeting with Clinton. It included helping Washington capture OBL and reorienting Pakistan's Afghan policy. In Pakistan, civilian intelligence agencies had reports of sectarian killers finding safe havens in neighboring Afghanistan. By the middle of August, Islamabad had begun to publicly criticize the Taliban. Senior Pakistani officials handed over a list of killers to the Taliban government. Regrettably, there was weak internal coordination between Pakistan's military intelligence agencies and the civilian institutions.

The actual implementation of the 'Capture Osama' plan also began in August. The Taliban remained committed to protecting the 41-year-old Saudi millionaire. They kept him 'under the protection of a special security commission'.[33] The US President's most unusual threat of 4 July that, unless Pakistan did more, he 'would have to announce Pakistan was in effect supporting terrorism in Afghanistan' had worked.[34] The plan to capture OBL was first proposed by the Pakistani prime minister himself in his 2 December 1998, Washington meeting. Economic sanctions on the Taliban were already in place. Around this time, with Sharif's support, US officials also began to train 60 Pakistani troops as commandoes to go into Afghanistan to get bin Laden. 'I was sckptical about the project; even if Sharif wanted to help, the Pakistan military was full of Taliban and al-Qaeda sympathizers. But I thought we had nothing to lose by exploring every option.'[35]

In Washington, a major chunk of the counter-terrorism policy thrust was, 'Go after bin Laden' and the mode of operation was expanding. To capture this international terrorist, the US President had approved a more proactive approach for the CIA, clearing the way for this Agency to adopt a more penetrating approach. The CIA planned a 'ring of kidnapping squads around Afghanistan to move in to capture OBL when required'.[36]

After his commitment with Clinton, Sharif personally led the effort to convince the Taliban government to handover OBL. In July, he met, along with the visiting the Saudi Defense Minister, Prince Sultan, the Afghan Foreign Minister Mulla Mutawakil at the Punjab House in Islamabad. With the help of an interpreter, the Saudi Prince reminded Muttawakil, 'We had helped you, we had recognized you, but you are ungrateful.' The Taliban leader was reprimanded in 'strong and humiliating term'. Muttawakil said they were grateful, that they wanted Saudi assistance to continue, but handing over OBL or 'extraditing him' was 'impossible'. This blanket refusal annoyed the prime minister and his Saudi guest.[37] Clinton's 'Get OBL' policy included use of force at multiple levels. The Taliban leader Mullah Omar was under attack. At the end of August, a saboteur's bomb exploded near his home in Kandahar.

With Pakistani cooperation, the Americans were pursuing a two-track strategy to get OBL, combining negotiations with a military operation. The 'Capture Osama' Operation was being launched. The Americans were funding the construction of barracks, three miles south of Rawalpindi, for SSG commandoes. According to the plan, Pakistani commandoes, on intelligence information, would be infiltrated into Afghanistan to kidnap bin Laden. While the ISI chief, now reporting to the prime minister and following his instructions, went along with the plan, the top operational tier opposed it. Senior generals believed that 'nothing could be more foolish'. OBL, they believed, was an 'ellusive target' and looking for him was tantamount 'to searching for a needle in a haystack'. The DG ISI believed Pakistan needed a trained force that could look for the Saudi billionaire. The CIA's role was also agreed upon. While the US sent FBI officials to train the commandoes and to monitor the operation, senior officials were skeptical of the scheme. 'We said to ourselves: Why do they need searchers for someone they are already aware of? Well, we played along,' recalled one US official.[38]

At the political level, in late August the prime minister personally tried to bring in other stakeholders in Kabul.[39] In an effort to move forward along UN's unsuccessful attempt, Pakistan began its shuttle diplomacy between Kandahar and the Tajik capital, Dushanbe, trying to get talks restarted between Ahmed Shah Masood and the Taliban.[40] While the Northern Alliance blamed Pakistani officials for, in reality, siding with the Taliban, Pakistani officials repeatedly spoke of their 'peace agenda' and for initiating the shuttle diplomacy in response to President Burhanuddin Rabbani's request.[41] At the end of August, Pakistan invited a high level Taliban delegation led by Foreign Minister Mulla Akhund to get the Taliban fully on board with the prime minister's intra-Afghan peace initiative.

There were no signs that Pakistan's main Taliban interlocutor, the Army, was not fully on board with this initiative.

Following the Kargil disaster, unlike the 1971 war, neither were its architects openly indicted and nor was the disaster acknowledged. Instead the army's propaganda wing plus distraught anti-Sharif politicians were able to project the 4 July Washington Declaration as a move that denied the Pakistanis victory in Kargil! But it was this myth-making, combined with Nawaz Sharif's political troubles, that provided space and confidence to the army leadership to conceive a battle plan to stage a fight back against the even the muted criticism of Kargil by civilian government.

Conclusion

In the post Kargil period, the divergent views of Pakistan's elected leadership and the military generals on key foreign policy issues, including India, Kashmir, Afghanistan, and the US, became particularly pronounced. This divergence had an impact at two levels. One, Pakistan's policy-making and policy implementation mechanisms became dysfunctional against this backdrop of dual leadership and conflicting policy objectives. Often the civilian institutions under the elected government's control and those under the security establishment's control worked at cross-purposes thereby undercutting each other's effectiveness.

Two, the two main, yet, contesting pillars of Pakistan's power construct, elected leadership and military command, entered a pronounced phase of distrust of each other. The military leadership, at least privately cognizant of the blunder it had committed in the Kargil Operation, feared reprisals by the civilian leadership, including removal of the army chief. By invoking his constitutional authority as commander-in-chief and firing his earlier army chief, General Jehangir Karamat, in October 1998, Sharif had already demonstrated the political guts to do so. He had charged Karamat with stepping beyond his Constitutional mandate to comment on problems of governance and recommending the setting up of a National Security Council.

The elected leadership, meanwhile, was taking steps to ensure the constitutional subservience of the Army to elected civilian authority. Sharif in the late 90s, like Zulfikar Ali Bhutto in the early 70s, was dealing with an army leadership which was smarting from its Kargil blunder and, perhaps professionally, did not feel much stronger than the military leadership which had lost half the country in 1971 and surrendered to the Indian Army in Dhaka. Similar to the steps taken by the end of 1998, using institutional mechanisms including the Defense Committee of the Cabinet, the Foreign Office, and the ISI, Sharif had practically begun policy reorientation, even after the Kargil debacle.

Pakistan's elected government and the military leadership's divergent views on foreign policy issues meant the two adopting differing policies on key issues. Policy differences between institutions was indeed not unique to Pakistan, the ability of one institution to actually have the ability to pursue its own preferred policy autonomously of the civilian government was. On foreign policy matters, the Foreign office, the armed forces, and intelligence institutions within every government would normally make their varied policy recommendations to the country's chief executive. The policy submissions would be made through constitutionally laid out policy-making mechanisms, with the chief executive leading the decision-making process. However, in Pakistan, the ability of one institution, the army, to pursue its policy preferences independent of the elected chief executive points to the asymmetrical and unconstitutional power enjoyed by the army.

From the end of August onwards, although there was palpable tension between the civil and military leaderships, yet, the PM had no intention of taking any action against the army chief. As August drew to a close, while the ghost of Kargil haunted both the civil and military leaderships, neither were making any rash moves. There were no knee-jerk reactions.

As August came to a close, there was no indication that Pakistan's civilian leadership, while dealing with the political and diplomatic fallout of Operation KP, was planning to hold the architects of Kargil accountable. Only 'disgruntled journalists talked about a Kargil Inquiry Commission'.[42] Whatever his concerns or complaints regarding the debacle, publicly the prime minister stood by the Army. Sharif was primarily engaged in dealing with the credibility crisis that Pakistan, the year-old nuclear State, was facing on the external front.

But the Kargil architects thought differently. Triggered by the muted indictment streaming throughout the subtext of the post-Kargil debate within sections of the Army and the civilians, the architects were struck by insecurity and resentment. Given the Army's ascendancy in Pakistan's power structure and the recurrence of Army takeovers, this pall of insecurity and resentment set the stage for an Army pushback. Whatever were coup-maker Musharraf's justifications at the time of the coup, years later, he was more truthful as he wrote in his book, 'It was in dealing with Kargil that the prime minister exposed his mediocrity and set himself on a collision course with the Army and me.'[43]

This reflected the state of political affairs, of inter-institutional imbalance and of the quality of leadership. By the end of August, the Kargil clique found itself in a relatively more comfortable zone than the government. Caught between trying to pull Pakistan out of the Kargil debacle, reviving the dialogue process with India, containing the fallout in the military and political circles, and also dealing with the political pressures generated from his government's incompetence, no inquiry was instituted against the army chief and other architects of Kargil. Instead, a campaign was launched against the civilians, the army leadership feeling ironically confident enough to hold the civilian leadership over issues of governance.

Chapter 17

A BRIDGE TOO FAR

Mounting Contestations

The bonhomie of the Prime Minister and the army chief's early September trip to the NLI headquarters in Skardu was short-lived. Although on Kashmiri rights, Sharif was unrelenting, calling for a UN-supervised plebiscite in Kashmir similar to East Timor[1], the ghost of Kargil had sown distrust between Sharif and the military command. Behind closed doors, in the corridors of power, and in the homes of the powerful, subdued games were on. Some played for survival, others for reprimand and retribution. Tool bags for menacing games were thrown open. All was fair play: wiretapping, inspired media reports, surveillance, interpreting intercepts, spy men on the prowl, instigating anger, manufacturing street protests. The ghost of the Kargil debacle was haunting Pakistan's corridors of power. The members of the Kargil clique, architects of the debacle, were fearful of being fired. Armed with institutional resources and experience at surreptitiously fighting civilian authority, they were all set to fight back.

Sharif was in a difficult position. Unlike Sharif's unbridled October 1998 reaction to a speech by Musharraf's predecessor army chief general Jahangir Karamat, which led to latter's dismissal, the post-Kargil situation was a very complex one. Pakistan had lost in martyrdom many of its brave young men yet internationally the country was being criticized. Pakistan's credibility as a responsible nuclear State had received a serious setback. Yet the prime minister could not hold the army chief accountable for the debacle at Kargil. He was constrained by issues around his own public ownership of the Operation and of "national honor." [2]

Nevertheless the inevitable blame game had begun. As expected it was a sinister one involving high stakes for the two principals…the prime minister and the army chief.

Soon after the 4 July statement Sharif had re-engaged with India. With the Indians at least he had to disown the Kargil Operation. His Washington interlocutors were already aware of the real architects of Kargil. But, under siege from domestic troubles, with political opponents multiplying and unifying under the 19-party Grand Democratic Alliance[3] banner, the prime minister seemed to have concluded that he was going to work silently on tackling the Kargil clique. Ouster of the army chief was unlikely. However, some form of reprimand was inevitable. The cumulative impact of all this was the rise of distrust and suspicion among Pakistan's power players.

The play-off had started.

Headstrong men, who in cavalier moments had made blustering offers, such as putting their 'necks on the line'[4], were now anxious about their professional survival. At when it was launched, they had billed Operation KP, now a visible debacle, as a guaranteed success. In a heady moment during the landmark 17 May briefing, General Aziz, the Kargil kingpin, had prodded Pakistan's prime minister to dream about being second only to Jinnah. Operation KP, he claimed, would liberate Kashmir! The PM, now confronting a nightmare, had actually begun to dream the dream. Sharif suffered from the common ailment of having a weakness for praise. So Thus, Kargil had then continued with ownership from by the elected prime minister. As Chaudhry Nisar, his key aide, later argued, once the ball was set rolling, the Kargil Operation was 'irreversible', even if the Prime Minister had wanted to reverse it.[5]

In the media, a plethora of accusations surfaced, targeting the prime minister: that he had sold Kashmir, surrendered in Washington the victory won at Kargil; he had wasted the sacrifices of the brave soldiers at Kargil, had appeased the Americans, bowed before the Indians etc. With facts of the beginnings, the conduct, and the military outcome of this Operation little known, these accusations seemed plausible. Sharif's dash to Washington had been widely publicized.

'Chatter' picks and the Spiraling Blame Game

With rising levels of distrust between the elected government and the military high command, Pakistan's chief executive was now under an extraordinary level of intelligence watch. The intelligence under the army's high command maintained a close tab on the prime minister and his cabinet. The army intelligence picked up the Prime Minister House chatter. The army chief complained to a confidante that the PM's intercepts had revealed that he would make Musharraf apologize publicly,[6] claiming that the PM had promised this to the Indian Prime Minister! Considering that, ever since the cover was blown from the Kargil Operation plan, the PM had taken ownership of it and tried to extricate, in his calculation, Pakistan and its Army with honour, self-respect, and minimal diplomatic damage, such an undertaking seemed highly unlikely. The PM, however, was determined to proceed with normalizing ties with India. In early August, Sharif's trusted foreign policy man, Tariq Fatemi, had met Vajpayee's National Security Advisor, Brajesh Mishra, in Geneva.

The army chief's anger and nervousness persisted. The blame talk would just not end. There were complaints from within the army high command, chatter in Army messes, insinuations from the government's men, and a few voices even within the media. He had requested the government several times to respond to news reports blaming the army chief for the debacle–indeed, even of conducting it unconstitutionally, i.e., without the chief executive's permission.

Beginning in early September, Islamabad and Rawalpindi were intermittently abuzz with the possibility of the army chief's removal. The July saga of the 'Rogue Army' advertisement targeting the Pakistan Army had lingered. The prime minister's refusal to issue a prominently displayed rebuttal to the damning advertisement added grist to the rumour mill. In this heightened atmosphere of suspicion, the usual suspect that the intelligence authorities would inevitably turn to, i.e., India, they chose to ignore.

Behind the bravado and the ostensible overconfidence of the Top Guns lay fear of their 'necks on the line situation'. Nervous and jumpy, the Kargil clique arranged to target its principal adversary, the prime minister himself, by weaving a two-front siege around him. They reached out to journalists to gauge the mood in the civilian quarters. Others were tasked to gauge the mood and reach out to the distraught Opposition parties and estranged politicians within the ruling party.

The 14 September interview splashed by Pakistan's most widely read Urdu daily, in which Sharif's backchannel point-man Niaz A. Naik held the army responsible for sabotaging, what he claimed was, a time-bound plan that the two prime ministers had agreed upon for resolving the Kashmir dispute, deepened suspicion in the barracks. Naik had also asserted that Sharif had not been informed of the Kargil operation, first hearing of it around 25 April. This contradicted Musharraf's public statement of 16 July that 'everyone was on board'.[7] On 15 September, a prestigious English daily published 'military source's expectation that "some responsible functionary would remove the impression created by the former foreign secretary that the Army did not want resolution of the Kashmir dispute"'.[8] The same day, Foreign Minister Sartaj Aziz stepped in to more than clarify. In his Senate speech, he said that the armed forces had acted in the interests of Pakistan and it was 'totally untrue' that through the Kargil crisis the armed forces had undermined the Pakistan-India peace process.[9] Nevertheless, the foreign minister seconded Naik's claim that a time-bound approach to resolving Kashmir had been agreed upon. Sartaj's speech also addressed the signing of the CTBT, a red herring issue in the hands of the political opposition. He was categorical that Pakistan 'will not consider signing it till the time sanctions imposed by the US were removed'.[10]

Matters were in a flux. On 15 September, the Foreign Office spokesperson formally announced that the Prime minister had 'no plans' to attend the United Nations General Assembly (UNGA) session. The cancellation was unexpected. The reason that circulated in the press was that, because Pakistan had decided against signing the CTBT, the PM wanted to avoid the pressure he was likely to face at the UNGA, especially from the Clinton administration. However, less known was the fact that a close confidante of the army chief, who was also an intimate friend of the Sharif family with easy access to the prime minister's father, contributed to the PM's decision to miss the UNGA session. Musharraf, wary of what the PM might say about the Kargil clique, and especially about him, was keen that he not attend the UNGA.[11] The confidante was therefore sent to Mian Sharif to convince him to dissuade his son from traveling to New York. Mian Sharif was convinced that, with trouble brewing at home, it was unwise for his son to travel. The PM did not travel.

Signs of growing distrust were evidenced elsewhere too. The army chief on a visit to the naval chief's residence had expressed his 'unhappiness' with the PM and would have 'preferred that the PM not be in that slot'.[12] On 17 September, the army chief had personally complained to the Secretary Defense, a former general and the army chief's senior in the army, which he had been talking against the army. 'It was the Operation I talked against, not the Army,' was the Defense Secretary's response.[13] The army chief had reports of the Quetta Corps Commander, Tariq Pervez, also publicly criticizing the recently concluded Operation.

The angry chief's words were interpreted by many as signalling a possible coup looming around the corner.

Wanted: a Special Envoy

On 4 July, when Sharif had urged Clinton to take a position on Kashmir, in order to give Pakistan political cover while withdrawing from Kargil, Clinton had refused. Instead, he had promised that he would help to restart the Lahore process. He had asked the Pakistani prime minister to send his envoy to Washington to discuss ways in which to go back to the Lahore process. However, by August, the Sharif government had bilaterally engaged with India anyhow. Sending an envoy to Washington was therefore no priority.

Nevertheless, in Washington, receiving Sharif's envoy was a priority. Since the end of July, the Clinton administration had been sending messages through US Ambassador Milam, to send his envoy, so that Clinton could follow up with his 4 July promise of helping restart the Pakistan-India dialogue on Kashmir. 'Do not send someone from the Foreign Office,' was the message. In Islamabad, it was expected that the US would help Pakistan to continue with the Lahore process. Nawaz Sharif had opted send, for this foreign policy matter, someone who was not a member of his foreign policy team. Neither the political man, Foreign Minister Sartaj Aziz, nor the bureaucrat, Foreign Secretary Shamshad Ahmad, was to be sent. 'Trust' was the key consideration for the prime minister. So, in the midst of raging political troubles, Nawaz Sharif sent off his brother Shehbaz Sharif as his special envoy to Washington.

In Washington, however, from mid-July onwards Sharif's envoy had been awaited with a more elaborate agenda. The State Department's South Asia men had gauged Sharif's political troubles. The Islamabad whispers of a possible coup or a likely Musharraf sacking were loud enough to reach Washington. They wanted to hear from Sharif's emissary how deep the civil-military divide was. They were keen for facts on the follow-through on Pakistani troop withdrawal from Kargil and Islamabad's re-engagement with India. Away from the India question, Islamabad and Washington were active partners in a 'Get Osama' Operation. This included both Islamabad directly persuading Mullah Omar to give up OBL and also the launch of a joint operation with the CIA to physically capture the al-Qaeda chief.

Washington was also responsive to India's unrelenting criticism of Pakistan's support for the Mujahideen and the Taliban. Delhi had continued to counter Pakistan's advocacy of Kashmir with the accusation that Pakistan was encouraging terrorism in the region. The Clinton administration was keen to see the Sharif government re-trace its steps to the pre-Kargil days, to put its regional policy back on track. There were sufficient signals from Islamabad that the Sharif government had in fact begun the process of retracing its steps.

The Clinton administration was also hoping that, through Sharif's special envoy, they could also get some movement from Pakistan on Washington non-proliferation agenda, especially on CTBT. From the American perspective, the Talbott-Shamshad negotiations on the nuclear issue had reached a dead end. The interlocutors seemed almost to hate each other. While Talbott expected compliance, especially on the CTBT, Shamshad was unrelenting. In the US, the question was: When would the Pakistanis pick up how badly the negotiations were going?[14] Talbott had, by contrast, exercised great patience and indulgence with India's equally blunt and unrelenting Foreign Minister Jaswant Singh—a fact that Talbott had proudly documented in his book, *Engaging India: Diplomacy, Democracy, and the Bomb*.[15]

The Clinton administration was ready to extend public support to Nawaz Sharif. Given a history of troubled Pakistan governments, both civilian and military, frequently turning to Washington for help, the Clinton administration believed their support give a fillip to the Sharif government.

Before his departure, Shehbaz Sharif sought a briefing from a Washington insider on the mood in Washington regarding Pakistan. He called his friend, the former US Ambassador to Pakistan, Robert Oakley's blunt and brash ways in his heyday as Ambassador in Pakistan had earned him the disparaging title of 'Viceroy'. But now, a consultant with UNOCAL, he was an aging, mellowed man. Oakley had cheered on the ISI for its role in putting together the Afghan Interim Government (AIG). He had never hesitated in criticizing the Pakistan Foreign Office for being weak and indecisive. Now Shehbaz's friend, he was flown in for a day to the provincial capital, Lahore. The Corps Commander Lahore, Lt. General Khalid Maqbool, also hosted a dinner for Shehbaz's guest. Oakley's message to Shehbaz was that Clinton was interested in Kashmir but not committed. This was no different from the assessment of the Pakistan Foreign Office team engaged with Washington.

'Extra Constitutional Pressures' and Musharraf Invite

On 15 September, First Brother Shehbaz, 'Smart Sharif'[16] to some in Washington, arrived as the special envoy of the man in the midst of crisis. He was joined by elder brother's trusted bureaucrat in Washington,

Ambassador Tariq Fatemi. Fatemi had after all handled the Kargil crisis from the PM secretariat.

Shehbaz held detailed meetings with Clinton's South Asia men, including Strobe Talbott, Karl Inderfurth, Thomas Pickering, and officials from the State Department's intelligence wing. In most meetings, Pakistan's Ambassador Fatemi accompanied Shehbaz.

At a one-on-one dinner meeting with Talbott on the day Shehbaz arrived, there was some discussion on Kashmir. But the bulk of the discussion was on extra-constitutional pressures on the government. Talbott also raised the CTBT matter. Feeling stonewalled by Shamshad Ahmad, he was seeking some 'give' on CTBT from the prime minister's younger brother. Shehbaz repeated Pakistan's policy of linking its signing the CTBT with a coercion-free environment, and the lifting of arbitrary restrictions and discriminatory sanctions against Pakistan by multilateral institutions and Washington.[17]

Shehbaz held a six-hour-long marathon session with Karl Inderfurth and Walter Anderson. The meeting took place at Washington's historical Willard Hotel, where Shehbaz was staying. The Willard was where Abraham Lincoln had spent the night before his first inauguration as President in 1861. Before the Inderfurth-Shehbaz marathon session began, as an ice-breaker gesture, the otherwise frugal Inderfurth had spent $80 to buy his Pakistani guest *The History of the Willard Hotel.*

In Washington, Shehbaz Sharif's concern about the possibility of a coup was apparent. Although he 'never said he feared a coup but was beating around the bush'. There was very little discussion on how to advance the Lahore process. Some among the US side found that 'the dialogue was sterile on Kashmir'.[18]

The US was keen to get a first-hand account of the follow through by the Pakistanis on the 4 July process. On Kargil, Shehbaz Sharif informed them that troop movement was going according to plan. However, throughout the meeting, Shehbaz repeatedly expressed concern about 'extra constitutional' developments. He, in fact, referred to it 15 times. Yet, he did not once mention the word 'military' nor asked for US help in dealing with the military. His focus on 'extra constitutional pressures on an elected government', combined with what Washington was picking up from Islamabad, left no doubt among the Americans that trouble was brewing for the elected government that the Clinton administration would have rather seen in office. However, Sharif's special envoy never said he feared a coup. He gave mixed signals and the Americans did not get candid answers on facts.

Washington's interlocutors had a common concern and that was Musharraf. Washington wondered if Musharraf was abiding by the 4 July agreement. In whispers, State Department officials asked, 'What is the army chief up to?' Shehbaz, without ever mentioning Musharraf, spoke about the 'extra-constitutional pressures' on the elected government. Shehbaz, always the more pragmatic of the two brothers and, hence, more cautious on political matters, remained deferential towards the Army, the traditional power center, and was unlikely to make any deals against it in Washington. In fact, as Talbott would later recall, 'Shehbaz would not quite confirm, even in response to direct questions, that a military coup was brewing.'[19] However, he added, 'Shehbaz's mannerisms, his mirthless smiles, long silences, and abrupt changes of subject when we asked about the situation at home, left us in no doubt that something was afoot.'[20]

Seeking Washington's engagement with Musharraf, Shehbaz wanted an official American invite for a Musharraf visit to Washington.[21] He believed it would work to the Pakistan government's advantage. When Inderfurth pulled him to the side and asked him if Musharraf was alright, Shehbaz told him he was implementing the 4 July agreement and asked if he knew Musharraf.[22] Inderfurth replied in the negative. 'Why don't you invite Musharraf?' Shehbaz advised him.

There was some discussion on the Kashmir issue as well. The State Department people gave Shehbaz a briefing with a historical overview. They repeated their concerns: Pakistan supported cross-border activity, undermined the sanctity of the LOC, supported terrorism, and prevented the solution of Kashmir. Pakistan, they felt, was on the slippery slope of tension and war[23] and complained of Pakistan's non-cooperation on the CTBT. Shehbaz stressed that an unresolved Kashmir issue was harmful for Pakistan on both the economic and security fronts. He reiterated Pakistan's position that the solution needed to be a win-win one and the US must play a role in finding it. Good on optics only, it was an unrealistic expectation.[24]

Within a week of their meetings with Shehbaz Sharif, the US officials were announcing at the New York UNGA that the 'only appropriate role' for Washington was 'to support bilateral engagement between Delhi and Islamabad'.[25] Pakistan's request for a special envoy on Kashmir was opposed by Inderfurth since, 'Washington saw no purpose to be served by a special envoy'.[26] Secretary Of State Albright had also categorically said, 'No US involvement.'[27] This was exactly how Washington's new-found strategic partner wanted it.

The meeting ended with the promise that the Pakistani government would prevent cross-border terrorism, respect the LOC, and pick up the threads of the Lahore process. The Americans did not make any commitment to intercede with India on finding a resolution of Kashmir. Instead, American officials wanted to ease the political pressure exerted on Delhi by Kashmiri freedom fighters and Kashmiri political parties including the Jammu and Kashmir Democratic Party.

The main focus of the Shehbaz visit ended up being the Sharif government's political difficulties. On the other side were Washington's keenness to see resumption of Pakistan-India dialogue, the end of cross-LOC activities by militants, the end of all Pakistani support to Kashmiri freedom fighters and the Taliban, and the arrest of Osama bin Laden, there was an overlap in Washington's objectives and in Nawaz Sharif's survival in office. Sharif was tipped in Washington as the Clinton administration's partner in these endeavors. Hence, a pro-Sharif statement was effectively in Washington's own interest. Shehbaz welcomed such support, thinking as all Pakistani politicians had believed that it would prove an enabling factor for a civilian government attempting to assert its control.

Shehbaz left the US armed with an invite for Musharraf and the trust of Clinton administration, believing perhaps that these would help stabilise the Sharif-led government.

The Unusual Statement

A major American takeaway from the Shehbaz visit was that the Sharif-led government was in trouble at home. Senior US administration people like the Under Secretary of State for Political Affairs, Thomas Pickering, saw Shehbaz as being 'worried that they would have to pay for what they did (troop withdrawal)'.[28] The US Administration then took an unusual step. From New York, where the Clinton team was attending the UNGA session, Karl Inderfurth issued a statement that called on the Pakistan Army not to try any 'extra-constitutional method' to remove the Nawaz Sharif-led government.[29]

Senior US officials believed that the United States statement of 20 September was issued to reaffirm that things would stay stable. Washington was keen to extend support to Nawaz Sharif, the man Clinton trusted, the man who had already become a high-value friend after consenting to Washington's Pak-US collaborative 'Capture OBL' Operation. US officials had hoped this statement would alter the prevailing power dynamics in Pakistan to Sharif's advantage. Such an expectation suggested two problems. One, Washington was delusional about the power its mere word carried. Two, Washington was ignorant of the local dynamics at work in Pakistan.

This became the most publicised outcome of Shehbaz's visit. The 20 September US statement[30] supported democracy and warned that any 'unconstitutional steps' would adversely affect bilateral relations. It unleashed a wave of criticism from politicians, the media, and the Army. Washington's lectures were never welcomed. Yet, a desperate government, under political near-siege, welcomed the statement. Its spokesperson claimed it was a 'slap on those Pakistani politicians who are seeking to destabilize our elected government'.[31]

At home, the political knives were out. The PPP accused the Sharifs 'of beseeching Americans' to save their collapsing government and that the US statement confirmed that perception.[32] When asked by a journalist to comment on the State Department functionary's statement, Musharraf's public position unsurprisingly was, 'It is an old story ... I don't want to comment on it.'[33] For the Jamaat-i-Islami leader, the statement proved that the government was a 'US lackey … yet, in the end, the decision will rest with the people of Pakistan'.[34]

Meanwhile, in Pakistan, the stories spun in abundance: the prime minister would be arriving in Washington to sign the CTBT (that, in fact, a cameraman had arrived in DC for coverage of the event!); Shehbaz was there to get Washington's clearance for removing Musharraf and appointing a new army chief; Director ISI Lt. General Ziauddin Butt was there to be interviewed and cleared by Washington for his new appointment as the army chief. No one was keen to know the facts but only to play out their own insecurities and fight imagined ghosts. Sharif and the army chief, the latter backed fully by the Kargil clique and his institution, were in the boxing ring, each contesting for survival.

It was the annual season of international diplomacy. The two foreign policy principals, US Secretary of State, Madeleine Albright, and Indian Foreign Minister, Jaswant Singh, had arrived in New York for the UNGA session. The ice-breaker for this meeting, that held much promise after Washington had facilitated the drawing to a close of what for Delhi was an embarrassing battle, was a gift exchange. Jaswant Singh's gift to Albright was *United States and India, 1777 to 1996: Bridge over River Time* with Albright reciprocating with *Engaging India: U. S. Strategic Relations with the World's Largest Democracy*, a collection of essays on America's strategic relations with India.[35] In a sign of growing cordiality between the two capitals, there were unprecedented 'long, intensive discussions on Afghan developments', on Clinton's Delhi trip, the first in 21 years, and on possible counter-terrorism cooperation[36].

In New York generally, the Indians found themselves in a comfortable situation, with global focus being on terrorism and counter-terrorism, the very issues for which Delhi sought support. After decades of Washington-Delhi strategic dissonance, signs of strategic convergence were emerging. In fact, the US, Russia, and even Pakistan's staunchest ally, China, all converged on sanctions against Kabul's Taliban regime—hosts of the terrorist mastermind OBL, who planned terrorist attacks against both American and Russian targets.[37]

Status Quo Kashmir

For India, the troubles inside IOK were persisting. Sabotage and targeting of individuals by Kashmiri freedom fighters was on the increase,[38] as were the Indian military operations against the freedom fighters.[39] Delhi's complaints and claims multiplied. There was talk of Pakistan allegedly deploying Chinese-supplied M-11 short-range ballistic missiles and surface-to-air missiles across from Ladakh,[40] and allegations of cross-LOC infiltration were on the increase.[41] Delhi rejected Sharif's call for a plebiscite in Jammu and Kashmir since 'the state's accession to the India Union'. India's Home Minister, L. K. Advani, reiterated Delhi's stance that the demand for a plebiscite had lost relevance following the 1972 Simla Agreement.'[42] Meanwhile, from Azad Kashmir, the Jammu and Kashmir Liberation Front took to a novel way of protesting the reported Indian plan of converting the LOC into an international border. Thousands of Kashmiris threatened to cross the LOC on 4 October. Delhi threatened to open fire on those crossing the LOC while Islamabad urged them to call off their march.[43] While Islamabad, already reeling from the Kargil debacle, decided to let them go and cross over at Chhakoti, the Indian forces were to prevent the crossing in stages through a graduated application of forces.[44]

The international media focused on the heightened militant activity in IOK. The press recalled the decade-old freedom movement that had originated as an *Azaadi*—shouting revolt had meandered towards becoming guerrilla campaign committed to 'send India packing with a few well-placed bombs and high-profile kidnappings'. In support, 'Shopkeepers gave them cash and mothers made them sandwiches.'[45]

For Kashmiris, distraught from the world's lack of attention to their struggle, the Kargil battle had offered a ray of hope. They pinned 'considerable hope' on the pledge the US President had made during the Sharif meeting that he would take 'personal interest' in Pakistan-India peace talks. They believed that the international community would now be more attentive to resolving problems between the two nuclear-armed adversaries.

These expectations were ill founded. Global attention, including Clinton's personal involvement in ending the Kargil battle, was fundamentally linked to establishing the status quo along the LOC. The limited Pakistan-India war in Kargil had prompted no capital, nor the UN, to be any more concerned about the Kashmiris exercising their right to self-determination than they were before the Kargil Operation. UN Secretary-General Kofi Annan in his annual Report [46] emphasized 'the recent upsurge of fighting along and across the line of control in Kashmir, especially in the Kargil area, is a reminder of the fragility of the situation in this region'.[47] He too recommended, 'The process initiated in Lahore needs to be put back on track as there are serious grounds for concern, not least because of the dangers of an unintended escalation in a subcontinent in which nuclear devices have been tested.'[48]

Beyond this routine flagging by the UN, the unstated consensus among the permanent members of the UN Security Council including Pakistan's 'all-weather friend' and strategic partner China, was that Kargil was a diplomatic and political blunder that derailed the promising Lahore process. There was also a buy-in by the international community into framing the Kashmir issue the Indian way: Pakistan was behind the ten-year-old Kashmiri Uprising and, hence, the attention-worthy problem really was of ending cross-border terrorism. From Delhi, the September spin on the Kashmir freedom struggle was the Osama spin. India's Home and foreign ministers both claimed they had evidence of OBL's active involvement in the Kashmiri uprising. They promised to show evidence at 'an appropriate time'.[49]

Meanwhile, the Alliance Ways …

Meanwhile in Pakistan, GDA, the 19-party anti-Sharif alliance, was in full cry.[50] Nearly coinciding with the controversial US statement, the formal launch of the *Nawaz Hatao, Mulk Bachao* [remove Nawaz, save the Country] movement was launched.[51] Sharif was criticized for 'the Kargil retreat', for 'overnight change in the Kashmir stance', and for being against democracy and the Constitution.[52] The alliance also announced its nine-point, virtually a do-it-all national agenda,[53] to be implemented after the removal of the Sharif-led government. All the familiar politicians figured in this alliance as did the familiar *ehtesab* call. The ever-present Dr Tahirul Qadri announced that a new caretaker government would set up an independent authority to conduct accountability under 'a new Ehtesab (Accountability) Act'.[54]

The Kargil Operation and the subsequent Washington Statement became primary political point-scorers and dictated the alignment of forces. Both energized, an Opposition already seeking ouster of the Sharif government. The security agencies supported, even encouraged, this programme. It seemed that all the political forces in the country, across the entire ideological spectrum, were seeking Sharif's ouster. The Opposition's street strength was on display, with the Muttahida Qaumi Mahaz, PPP, and Jamaat actively protesting. The Sharif-led government was resorting to arrests, albeit for short periods.[55] For the religio-political parties and the various groups fighting in Kashmir, the conclusion to Kargil was the *casus belli* for Sharif's removal. This included the religio-political parties and groups conducting operations in IOK. The anti-Sharif's forces, which included many within the media, had amplified. Significantly, most anti-Sharif forces sought military intervention to remove the Sharif-led government.

The other Visitor in Washington

Meanwhile, even before Shehbaz Sharif had landed back, DG ISI Ziauddin, had arrived in Washington, primarily to meet his Langley colleagues in order to review progress of the 'Capture Osama' plan. It was a plan that Ziauddin's team was not keen on. It also had no supporters in the GHQ. With Washington impatient for progress on tracking and nabbing bin Laden, the CIA's counter-terrorism cell saw the ISI as a partner of last resort. In fact, the ISI was viewed as a Taliban and OBL sympathizer, but Ziauddin was not viewed as hard core ISI. Also, Clinton's South Asia men were against getting directly involved in the Afghan battlefield or directly confronting Pakistan over Afghanistan. Instead, the policy decision was to use Pakistan's influence with the Taliban to track OBL. During his Washington trip, Pickering sought a meeting with

Pakistan's top spy. Pickering urged Ziauddin to actively nudge Taliban head Mullah Omar to hand over bin Laden to the Americans. And Ziauddin did.

The ISI chief responded quickly to Washington's concerns. Soon after his return from Washington, General Ziauddin arrived in Kandahar on 5 October. The head of the Afghanistan-Kashmir desk, Major General Jamshed Gulzar, accompanied him. They arrived in a special plane and met Mullah Omar at his abode, a small mosque in Kandahar. At this meeting, the Pakistani intelligence officials offered condolences over the death of his wife and child.[56] The ISI officials then informed Omar of the reason for their trip. An agitated Omar's response was, 'Osama bin Laden is like a bone in my throat. Neither can I digest it nor can I cough him out ... My problem is that I have given him a commitment as an Afghan and I cannot get out.' Omar continued, 'I pray that I die or he dies.' Omar was clear that he 'will not extradite him but if he goes on his own he should go'. Omar then asked his guests, 'Can you tell me a country where he could be given protection?' His guests could not. Omar then told the Pakistanis, 'You are under pressure so you can stop supporting us. We will bank on Allah.' Omar's parting shot was, 'I don't want to be called Mullah the Traitor.' Somewhat enamoured by their personal interaction with the Taliban leader, Pakistani officials insisted that Omar 'never said kill the Americans'. The Taliban leadership also did not ask for military support from the US.[57] Omar lived 'in one room with wild grass growing around it and always talked bluntly with sincerity oozing out'.[58]

The CIA, in their effort to get OBL extradited, were in direct contact with their Pakistani counterpart, the ISI. Recalling the extent of the US desperation to get OBL, a senior ISI official said, 'If I would have asked him to lick my feet, he would have.'[59] The ISI, meanwhile, maintained a distance from CIA officials. For example, meetings with the CIA regional chief were held in ISI-run 'safe houses' instead of the ISI headquarters.

Meanwhile, in Pakistan, the DG ISI's Washington visit widely criticized.[60] The Opposition demanded that the general 'must inform the nation that on what assignment he had gone to the United States'.[61] The media also speculated that Ziauddin was there to get Washington's nod before taking over as the new army chief!

The Shehbaz-Ziauddin trips added grist to the already active rumour mills. The New York statement and the ISI chief's trip had the expected effect. The whispering campaigns became louder. The one that greatly amplified existing distrust between the prime minister and the army chief was that the prime minister's brother was in Washington to get clearance from the Americans to appoint the ISI chief as Pakistan's new army chief. For Musharraf and the Kargil clique, there was plausibility in this story; they knew that Musharraf had no presence in Washington while Ziauddin was now in partnership with Washington on Washington's top priority issue. Yet, the reality was different.

In Washington, while Shehbaz talked of 'extra-constitutional' moves, he had, in fact, proposed that Washington engage with Musharraf. If Shehbaz planned a Musharraf-related event in his meetings with the US officials, it was the army chief's Washington trip, not his removal.[62]

The Survival Strategy

Nevertheless, the growing insecurity of the army chief and his circle led them to practically work out an Operation Self-Survival. With the GHQ under the administrative control of the key Kargil man, CGS General Aziz, he along with his chief Musharraf worked on ways to counter any attempt by the prime minister to remove Musharraf. The entire lower tier of the ISI was clued into the GHQ's thinking, while the institution's head was bound by the constitution and personal interest to report to the prime minister. Ziauddin, Musharraf's three-decade old friend, was perhaps secretly eyeing his worried friend's position.

The political turbulence also kept growing. Nawaz Sharif, increasingly under political siege, could clutch at no straw. By contrast, Musharraf, fully backed by the military's high command, was positioned to work on a survival strategy. After the 20 September US Statement, concern grew within the Army. By 22 September, the climax of the statement's fallout was reached. Islamabad was buzzing with rumours about a change in the military command, about an imminent coup, about the decision of the army command to hold the following morning the fourth meeting of the top army command in one week, about the Prime

Minister's orders for the army chief's removal. Following a cabinet meeting, in which purportedly the decision to remove Musharraf had been taken, Information Minister Mushahid Hussain categorically rejected the rumour. After the cabinet meeting he said, 'There was complete harmony and complete coordination between all sections of government of Pakistan, between civilian and non-civilian components.'[63]

Essentially, the self-survival strategy that seemed to be at work was five-fold. One: Use the media to spread disinformation about Kargil. Hold back the facts of the military fiasco, the discontent within the Army, and instead train the guns on the prime minister. Paint him as pro-India, pro-US, and anti-Pakistan.

Two: Encourage and, if needed, facilitate all the anti-government parties to work together on a common platform and demand the ouster of the government. Sections within the Jamaat-i-Islami were already against the Nawaz-led government and had led the Lahore agitations during the Sharif-Vajpayee Lahore Summit. It worked to the Army's great advantage that the opposition was hitting out at Nawaz Sharif for the Washington Statement. It gave strength to the Opposition's existing call for the government's ouster. Similarly, the religopolitical parties and several of the guerrilla groups fighting in Kashmir, severely criticized the Washington statement and called for Sharif's removal. The upcoming leader, cricket hero Imran Khan, had launched a major offensive against Nawaz Sharif. Sharif was friendless. The security agencies encouraged this situation. Significantly, all the anti-Sharif forces advocated military intervention. Numerous analysts also supported this position.

Three: Widen the existing cracks within the PML leadership by working on those already alienated from the central leadership. Individuals like MNA Ejazul Haq were ready partners for Sharif's ouster.

Four: Be in a readiness mode to launch a *coup d'état* at short notice. This required the army chief to post his most trusted commanders in key posts and corps and finally also conduct actual drills of forces likely to be involved in staging a coup. Accordingly, through September, Musharraf posted his trusted men in key positions critical to successfully launching a coup. He assigned command of the traditional coup-maker brigade, the 111 Brigade, to his most trusted man, Brigadier Salauddin Satti. He had been a Brigadier Major with Musharraf when he was commanding 25 Brigade. During Kargil, Satti had commanded Brigade 323 at Siachen. His performance at Kargil had raised questions of disciplinary action against him. Instead, he was given command of the Army's coup-maker brigade. Lt. General Shahid Aziz from ISI research and analysis, a distant relative of Musharraf, replaced Lt. General Tauqir Zia as DGMO. Zia was appointed Commander I Corps (Mangla). The chief of general staff (CGS) was part of the Kargil clique, as was Commander 10 Corp, Lt. General Mahmud Ahmad. Musharraf had ensured that Lt. General Muzaffar Usmani was Corps Commander 5 Corps, and Major General Tariq Majeed Lahore GOC 11 Corps, were all on board.

Five: Develop special SOPs to deal with unusual developments, especially involving the removal of the army chief. The army chief feared that he could be called to the prime minister's House and informed of his dismissal. Hence, any delay in the army chief's return from a meeting with the prime minister would be interpreted as a danger signal.

By the end of September, the deployment of soldiers around the Prime Minister's House had been increased beyond the normal one unit. Extra commando units were brought in and stationed in Rawalpindi. More sophisticated intelligence gadgets for transmitting information were also being used by the security. The prime minister was under full army intelligence watch. All incoming and outgoing communication from the Prime Minister's House was monitored.

Truce Efforts

The tables had been turned on the civilian leadership. In the face of mounting political pressures, the somewhat worried Kargil clique began regaining confidence. The political fallout of Shehbaz Sharif's Washington trip, and especially the statement by a State Department official, further queered the anti-Sharif pitch. Finding the Sharif-led government politically isolated and cornered, the PM's key advisors planned a pushback. To create space for the government to maneuver, two key men of his 'kitchen cabinet', the fire-fighting pair of brother, Shehbaz Sharif, and Chaudhry Nisar, made the pragmatic decision to engage with the army chief. Musharraf was comfortable with and trusted both men. In fact, in August Musharraf had suggested to Shehbaz that he move to the Centre as deputy prime minister, to help his brother govern better. Both felt that Musharraf was the only individual who, backed by his institution, had the capacity to subvert the current ruling setup. It was through Musharraf they believed that this gathering political storm in the streets, mosques, seminar halls, and the media could be contained. Pakistan's political landscape was marked by the central role that the army chief played.

In this highly volatile political situation, coupled with growing distrust between Nawaz Sharif and the Army, Shehbaz and Nisar became active to salvage the situation in late September. Their primary objective was building trust. Rumors about Musharraf's removal were to be dispelled. Three related issues had sped up the rumor mill: the matter of the appointment of the chairman Joint Chief of Staff Committee (CJCSC), the rumors regarding appointment of DG ISI General Ziauddin as the new army chief, and the removal of Corps Commander Quetta, Tariq Pervez. Musharraf's removal was linked to all three.

The prime minister's decision to not appoint the senior-most services chief, Admiral Fasih Bokhari, as the CJCSC had worried Musharraf, who believed that the PM had decided against appointing the admiral because he had decided to 'kick the army chief upstairs'. Musharraf did not want to be appointed as the CJCSC, a largely ceremonial position. He was, therefore, keen to see the CJCSC slot filled. The PM, in fact, was against appointing Admiral Bokhari.[64] Interestingly, the ISI chief, Lt. General Ziauddin Butt, was only four months away from retirement; with the rumours regarding his appointment as the new army chief that spread during his Washington trip with Shehbaz, Musharraf feared that the PM had made definite plans for a new army chief as well. Musharraf raised these questions in his meeting with Shehbaz Sharif and wanted to specifically know if the PM was going to appoint an air force man in the chairman's slot. A perturbed Musharraf told Shehbaz, and later the Defense Secretary as well, that his father had called from the US asking him if he was being fired. Twice, Musharraf had tried to reach the Defense Secretary, who was in Turkey.[65] Musharraf also complained to Shehbaz that he felt that his and his commanders' phones were being bugged.

Shehbaz Sharif assured him to the contrary. Shehbaz was also mindful of the parallel advice that his brother was receiving from his friend, the Chairman of the notorious Ehestab Commission, Saifur Rehman. In a subsequent meeting, Shehbaz raised these concerns during a meeting between the prime minister, Musharraf, and Shehbaz.[66] At that meeting, the prime minister took the decision to give Musharraf the additional charge of Chairman JCSC. Sharif's father, with whom a Musharraf confidante had lobbied regarding Musharraf continuing as army chief, had also advised his son to retain him. That ended the uncertainty about Musharraf's retention as army chief.

Similarly, on the issue of the Quetta Corps commander, whom Musharraf wanted out because of his public criticism of the Kargil Operation, the reluctant prime minister gave in to the advice of his brother and key aide Chaudhry Nisar ... On 4 October, the army chief handed over to the Defense secretary the early retirement orders of the Quetta Corps Commander, Lt, General Tariq Pervez. He said he took the decision because Tariq Pervez was trying to 'destabilize' him.[67]The Corps commander having close connections in the PML-N leadership ranks, the defense secretary advised Musharraf that he should be 'sent out somewhere'. The chief declined. By 6 October, the PM signed the retirement orders of Tariq Pervez (popularly known as TP). Sharif queried the implications on the Army of the retirement and was told there were none. The Defense Secretary did, however, advise the PM to inform his minister Raja Nadir Pervez of this decision, since the latter's sister was married to the Corps commander. GHQ received the signed orders on 7 October.

The day before Musharraf was to leave for Sri Lanka, Shehbaz received a call from Bob Oakley.[68] The invitation for Musharraf was on its way. Shehbaz was in Islamabad and he immediately called Musharraf and asked him when he was planning his trip to the US. Musharraf asked, 'Which trip?' Shehbaz told him the invitation from the Americans was on the way. Light heartedly, he also told the army chief, 'Do take me along as well'.

The same day the PM hosted a farewell lunch for Admiral Fasih Bokhari in the PM House. The naval chief had resigned. As he later claimed, he had resigned because he had learnt there was likelihood that Musharraf was planning a coup.[69] At the lunch it was a small group comprising the army chief, the air chief, the defense secretary, and the PM's private secretary. With conspiracies and sentiments camouflaged, the atmosphere was pleasant and relaxed. Musharraf mentioned about his evening trip to Karachi en route to Sri Lanka. After his good-byes the army chief flew to Karachi.

He was confidante that all was 'under control'.

Dynamics of Distrust

All was not well on the Islamabad front. Despite steps taken by the end of September, a Zero-sum game between the PM and the army institution had begun. It was not about civil-military tussle. In fact, for his critical decision-making, Nawaz Sharif was almost isolated from not only his cabinet but also from his two-man trouble-shooter, the Shehbaz-Nisar pair.

A blunder had been committed, the institutional, State Constitutional framework was to review and restrain such a move in the future. But seemed the chronic distrusts, Sharif's own person seemed to trigger the process in a different direction. There was institutional approach that was being developed. From the November 1998 meeting to now 10 months later, the PM decided to develop an institutional platform for decision-making. It was to be led by civilian authority with top-level representation from the armed forces. The prime minister asked his trusted and experienced Foreign Minister Sartaj Aziz to work on the mechanics of National Security Committee.

Soon after Musharraf left for Sri Lanka his confidante learnt of Nawaz Sharif's plans for his removal. He called Musharraf who was in Karachi en route to Colombo. Upon being told of his planned removal, Musharraf reassured his worried confidante that all was 'under control'.

In the prime minister's camp, it seemed that distrust was receding. The blame game was over and there was no longer any talk of a Kargil Inquiry Committee. The PM's chief advisors, Shehbaz and Nisar, had proactively worked to remove two key reasons for a potential Sharif-Musharraf showdown: Musharraf had been given the additional charge of Chairman Joint Chief of Staff Committee (CJCSC) and, on Musharraf's request the prime minister had removed the Corps Commander, Quetta Lt. General Tariq Pervez, even though this had caused a political problem for Sharif as the dismissed general was the brother-in-law of a leader from Sharif's party.

The Sharif camp's decision to agree to Musharraf's demands was an effort to alter the post-Kargil dynamic of distrust. However, much more than Musharraf's own personal concerns were at play and had generated a dynamic of distrust between the Army and the government. Multiple influences were at work. In addition to the prime minister's brother and his closest political confidante, Chaudhry Nisar, these influences included the DG ISI, among others. General Ziauddin overseeing the 'Capture OBL' Operation, had long been eyeing the army chief's position. The historical civil-military distrust was anyway there. The bravado of the Kargil clique notwithstanding, they were still fearful of possible ouster. There were enough critics of Kargil within the senior army generals to support a prime minister seeking the Kargil clique's ouster. Suspicion and insecurity defined the times and everyone seemed to be treading on eggshells ... The prime minister's pragmatic partners, keen on damage limitation, had zeroed in on the one man they feared would pull the trigger on the system and were engaging that man,

Yet toxic undertones were rampant.

Despite this attempt at damage limitation, the steps being taken at the GHQ had the toxic undertones of a coup-in-the-making. Rumours were floated and claims on 'known facts' by many close to the coup-makers' clique maintained that the date of 25 October had been set for the coup.[70] A civilian façade for the military coup was also being engineered. The Jamaat-i-Islami, Muttahida Qaumi Mahaz, and Ejazul Haq-led angry men of the PML-N were mobilized for anti-Sharif street protests.[71] There was talk that the crescendo of these partially engineered street protests would be reached at the 25 October sit-in in front of the Parliament, to be staged by all these groups. To create a supportive context, especially within the Army, Musharraf wanted loyal and sympathetic officers in important positions. For example, a specially deputed confidante brought the Karachi Corps commander and the ISI sector commander on board.[72]

Pakistan was positioned to witness, yet again, the playing out of a very basic and straightforward power contest. Law, constitution, and policy were to again become irrelevant. From the uncovering of Kargil to the curtains on it, the elected prime minister had been cooperative towards the blundering Kargil clique. Even if it was for national interest, honour, and dignity, the approach was largely personalized, featuring side meetings, side conversations, and personal assurances. That was a relatively pressure-free period. When the diplomatic and military pressures began building, the Sharif and Musharraf camps fought for survival. Musharraf's camp made alliances while Sharif became isolated. At the end, seemingly stripped of all moral authority and political clout, Pakistan's elected PM had fallen very low on legitimacy in the public eye. The legitimacy that helps to counter the force equation that a military commander enjoys was very asymmetrically poised in Pakistan's power context. Pakistan's elected prime minister was in such a weak position that the coup strikers may have assured themselves of their success by comparing the unpopular Nawaz Sharif to the Pope about whom Stalin in 1935 had disparagingly remarked, 'The Pope? How many divisions has he got?'[73]

Criticism was muted and veiled. No talk of blunders or mishaps figured in public conversations. Pakistan's position was not be undermined externally; so, the Kargil Operation was projected as a Kashmiri freedom fighter's activity. Importantly, by the end of September, the space for a Sharif narrative was in any case shrinking. Anti-Sharif mass mobilization of the Opposition, facilitated by the agencies, was initiated. From moral authority to political clout to street power, the architecture of protest, with a willing opposition and with sections of the obliging press, was being engineered by the Musharraf camp.

Whatever the size of Opposition rallies, it appeared unlikely that street power would remove the Sharif-led government. The most vociferous and repeated cries from the Opposition were: 'Sharifs Trying to Destroy Army'[74] and 'The government is putting the responsibility for all its misdeeds on the Pakistan Army and undermining this institution'.[75] Meanwhile, the public response to the official Kargil withdrawal story, the

Washington visits, and the 20 September pro-Sharif Washington statement was best reflected in an article titled 'Pakistan's Survival Depends on Army'. The writer argued, 'Almost every institution in the country appears to be on the verge of collapse or has already broken down … few would disagree with me at this juncture in our country's history that Pakistan's survival literally depends on this institution …'[76]

All this gave the much-needed psychological and political boast to the Kargil clique.

Hard Facts

To recap, while Sharif's inner coterie of advisors was keen to iron out differences between the civil and military leaderships, the distraught politicians, insecure and suspicious generals, sensationalistic journalists, and Sharif's own reactive nature contributed to the tension. In September, the Washington factor also significantly influenced the state of Pakistan's internal affairs. Against the backdrop of Indian focus on Pakistan's role in supporting the Mujahideen and the Taliban in the region and Washington's own push to capture OBL, the Clinton administration sought a strategic reorientation in Pakistan's regional policies. Washington hoped to achieve this by extending political support to Nawaz Sharif, the man who they saw under siege from the military.

Clinton trusted the man, who had already become a high value friend after acquiescing to Washington's 'Capture OBL' Operation. Washington and Islamabad drew closer to each other. Both had an interest in activating the Pakistan-US connection though they were working at cross purposes. In Washington, the prime minister's special envoy had cordial talks with senior US officials, but on diverse agendas. Interestingly, although the common denominator was reining in of the Pakistan Army, both sides ascribed low priority to Kashmir. In Pakistan, as tensions ran high, Shehbaz Sharif saw American backing as an enabling factor for the civilian government attempting to assert its control. The most publicized outcome of this meeting proved the point. On 21 September 1999, a US statement supported democracy and warned that any 'unconstitutional steps' would adversely affect bilateral relations. However, staying with his theme of rapport-building with the Pakistan Army chief, Shehbaz also sought an official American invite for a Musharraf visit to Washington. Meanwhile, within the Army and media circles in Pakistan, the other high profile Pakistan visitor to Washington had set tongues wagging along with audible clatter of pre-emptive guns. Rumour was more powerful that reality. While Shehbaz and the ISI chief's trips did not overlap, rumour had it that the prime minister's brother was in Washington to get clearance from the Americans to appoint the ISI chief as Pakistan's new army chief. Civil-military distrust did not abate.

The army leadership's post-Kargil recoil expanded space for civilian assertion. It presented Nawaz Sharif the opportunity to assert the constitutionally-mandated hold of the government over Pakistan's state institutions—the only time since 1972, when Zulfikar Ali Bhutto had been presented a similar opportunity. Significantly, early October seemed to signal a Nawaz-Musharraf détente. The blame game was over and the question of a Kargil Inquiry Committee had completely evaporated. Sharif's two key aides, his brother Shehbaz and Chaudhry Nisar, had proactively ensured that all reasons for potential Sharif-Musharraf conflicts were removed. Musharraf had been given the dual charge of Chairman Joint Chief of Staff Committee and, on his request the Corps Commander from Quetta, Lt. General Tariq Pervez, had also been removed.

However, the détente was short-lived. Influences stronger than the prime minister's brother and his closest political confidante, including the US-befriended ISI chief Ziauddin, propelled the prime minister into a reactive mode. Ziauddin, overseeing the 'Capture OBL' Operation, had long been eyeing the army chief's position. The historical civil-military distrust had also kicked in to prompt Nawaz Sharif to fire his army chief, the second time within a year. Meanwhile, given the civil-military divide over Kargil and the subsequent misgivingswithin the army regarding prime minister's moves against its leadership, the Army had become prepared with countermoves to prevent their chief's ouster.

Chapter 18

THE COUP

Prime Minister Nawaz Sharif was an agitated man.[1] He believed he was not responsible for Kargil yet it was he who was taking the flak. He neither publicly blamed the army chief General Musharraf nor instituted an inquiry against him. Instead, goaded by his key advisors Shehbaz Sharif and Chaudhary Nisar and instructed by his authoritarian father, he had accommodated the army chief's wishes on several scores. The family patriarch Mian Mohammad Sharif had also received the Musharrafs at the Sharif family home and had tried to defuse the palpable Nawaz-Musharraf tension. In the hope that it would bring about a ceasefire between the two, the senior Sharif had purposefully told Musharraf, Shehbaz, and Nawaz, "You three are my sons."

By 10 October, however, this September sentiment had been overtaken by severely contrasting events. On the morning of the 8th the day after the the removal of corps commander Quetta general Tariq Pervez, commonly known as TP, a national daily carried the story. According to the news story, TP had been removed for meeting the PM without seeking clearance from the army chief. His removal was one of the CBMs brokered by the Shehbaz-Nisar team and extended by the PM to the uneasy army chief.[2] However, on being informed of the news report, the PM instructed his Principal Secretary to call the Defense Secretary to find out who provided the 'facts' for the story and who had it published. The PM instructed that GHQ should be asked to issue a rebuttal. The Defense

Secretary asked the Chief of General Staff (CGS) Lt. General Aziz Khan and the director-general Inter Services Press Relation (ISPR) Brigadier Rashid Qureshi to issue a rebuttal. Both responded, "Not without the army chief's permission." The PM House was adamant about getting a rebuttal out. The Defense Secretary then had his own ministry issue a rebuttal. An agitated Sharif, also encouraged by a few cabinet ministers and family members, had concluded that the news item was a direct challenge to his authority.

Interestingly, the newsmaker in the controversial story, the Quetta corps commander, also arrived in the capital the same day. He was en route to Murree to collect his family. The agitated ex-commander met with the Defense Secretary to protest against his dismissal. Unsuccessfully, the Defense Secretary tried to pacify him, promising an ambassadorial posting. Having just been forced to retire, the heavy built, loud-voiced TP, angry at Musharraf as the man who had demanded his dismissal, was challenging his retirement. . TP's man, his brother-in-law Minister Nadir Pervez, was part of Sharif's inner circle and the PM was fully aware of his interpretation of what TP's dismissal and the controversial news report signaled.

The following morning, 9 October, the newspapers carried the rebuttal. The PM had wanted the rebuttal to come from an army institution. On that Saturday morning, around the time he left for his weekend visit to Lahore, in an interview to an Urdu daily, Tariq Pervez strongly criticized the decision to retire him. His tone was threatening. The same day, Raja Nadir Pervez, Minister for Communications, returned to Pakistan from a foreign tour and met with the PM in Lahore.

The next forty-eight hours proved to be critical in influencing the course of Pakistan's history. Away from the policy-making venues of Pakistan's capital Islamabad, the setting was Jati Umra, the PM's private family estate. Mian Muhammad Sharif, the PM's father and the family's patriarch, presided over these history-making events. By that evening, he had ordered his younger son, the chief minister of Punjab, to be present there on Saturday. The PM's older son Hussain had called his uncle to say, "Grandfather is calling you right away." Shehbaz arrived at the family gathering, only to receive hell from his father. He was reprimanded for advising the PM to dismiss Nadir Pervez's brother in law, the Quetta corps commander. The 8 October controversial news report and the subsequent refusals from the CGS and the DG ISPR to issue a clarification had earned Shehbaz this ire. TP was considered the government's 'own man.' Not only was he related to their Minister but he was also the only corps commander who had publicly criticized Op KP. Meanwhile, faced with this paternal anger, Shehbaz still insisted that there must have been some misunderstanding. Musharraf could not have had anything to do with the news report. The PM recalled that General Majeed Malik had said that, after this, no corps commander will listen to us. The agitated PM shared his decision to fire the army chief. The family patriarch listened as his younger son shot back to advise his older brother against such a move. "It will end in a coup," was the Punjab chief minister's refrain. Musharraf's post-Kargil story, spread in the barracks, had targeted the PM: the Kargil Op had got India by the neck, but for the 4 July Washington statement, Kashmir had been on the brink of freedom. Shehbaz argued that the time to remove Musharraf was early June when the naval and air chiefs were critical of the Operation. The PM had no doubt that Musharraf had to go. However, he announced no final decision.

On Sunday, he summoned his Military Secretary Brigadier Javed Iqbal to the Jatti Umra estate at Raiwind. The Brigadier's family was politically aligned with the PMLN and he had developed a fondness for his boss, who clearly found him trustworthy. When the PM met the brigadier in his garden, he first instructed him to switch off his cell phone. After switching off his own phone too, both phones were handed over to the PM's valet Shakeel. "I have decided to remove Musharraf," Nawaz let his MS know. The brigadier warned him of serious consequences. "Remember, Zia took Bhutto to the gallows," he said. In this one-on-one interaction, he was emphatic about what Musharraf's removal would lead to. Nawaz was curious, if not uniquely naïve, about why trouble would follow his rightful exercise of Constitutional authority to change an army chief. His MS had a soft corner for General Ziauddin – the man tipped as Musharraf's replacement – billing him as "docile and stable"[3]. However, he did remind Sharif that Musharraf had the Kargil debacle in his closet, and would wrest power from Sharif rather than be charged with the blunder after being dismissed. The brigadier made it clear to the PM that the commander 10 Corps was bound to "hit back" in case of his chief's removal. Nevertheless, as the half-hour garden chat ended, the PM had been assured that under all circumstances his MS would remain loyal to him.

That afternoon at the Sharif household there was a reading of the Holy Quran,[4] followed by a special prayer. The journalist Brigadier Nazir Naji was also there. The PM's decision to remove the army chief was final. He even gave his son Hussain Nawaz the task of writing the speech he planned to deliver while announcing Musharraf's retirement. Hussain also penned down some of the speech ideas his father shared with him. However, it was a closely guarded secret, one he was unwilling to share with even his younger brother Shehbaz.

The following morning, October 11th, the PM returned to Islamabad and government resumed its business; albeit in some unusual ways. The PM accompanied by no foreign office official left for Abu Dhabi. It was ostensibly a call on the ailing Sheikh Zayd Bin Sultan. Instead, the ISI chief, his military secretary, Nazir Naji, and his son Hussain accompanied him.[5] During the flight, the PM discussed his plans with the ISI chief, the man Nawaz would appoint as the next chief. Shehbaz was still not in the loop. When he called to talk to his brother, to his surprise he was told that the PM had flown to Abu Dhabi. Meanwhile, upon landing at Abu Dhabi, in an unusual move, the military secretary and the Chief of Protocol Colonel Farrukh were kept away from the PM and driven to the Pearl Continental hotel. Only the PM's core entourage, comprising General Ziauddin, Hussain, Naji, and ambassador Khayyam Qaiser, accompanied him to the palace. After the entourage's collective call on the UAE ruler, the PM stayed on to have a detailed one-on-one conversation with him. Naji and Hussain continued working on the PM's speech.

Meanwhile, back in Islamabad-Rawalpindi, the matter of the corps commander's removal, which seemed to have precipitated the impending PM-Army showdown, still remained. The corps commander's brother-in-law minister Nadir Pervez met General Iftikhar, the Defense Secretary to seek an interview with the PM on behalf of the abruptly retired corps commander. Iftikhar was unrelenting. Military men must seek interviews with the PM only "through proper channels"; the meeting request had to come through the GHQ.

Away from what had become the prolonged sage of the corps commander, there was the world of the Foreign office. At the foothills of the Margallas, the foreign Secretary was happily watching the Foreign Office team playing cricket. Meanwhile, in the former Hotel Scherzade building, which now houses the Foreign Office, Foreign Minister Sartaj Aziz was finalizing the draft on the Cabinet Committee on Defense and National Security (CCDNS).[6] He had worked for weeks on fine-tuning this constitutionally mandated decision-making structure. He sent the finalized draft for approval to the air chief Pervez Mehdi. Significantly, two otherwise contesting stakeholders in the national security formulation, the Army and the Foreign Office arrived at a consensus. An idea that in 1998 had sent the former army chief packing for home, now had buy-in from both stakeholders.[7] The foreign minister was relieved that army chief Musharraf and his team had "very actively cooperated"[8] with him to work out a consensus document. This elaborate policy-making structure[9] was being finalized, paradoxically, at a time of acute tensions between the PM and the army chief. Perhaps the post-Kargil sense of vulnerability had led to the army command's receptivity to the changes Sartaj Aziz had proposed rather than to the army command's own original plan.

It was a long day for the PM. In the security of the private quarters of the PM House, until late into the night, he worked with his son on finalizing the speech. He had decided to tell the people that the army chief had kept him in the dark about Kargil, about Operation KP. That, in doing so, Musharraf had violated official trust and rules of business. Sharif would also share how he had tried, in the national interest, to work with Musharraf, but simply could not.

Sharif's Solo Flight[10]

Although the prime minister's key aides, Shehbaz Sharif and Chaudhary Nisar, were a partially satisfied that bridges, however rickety, between the government and the army had been built, subsequent events were to prove how wrong they were. The bridges they had built could not bear the weight of the controversial news story about the Quetta corps commander's removal. Inching towards a total confidence breakdown, the moment of collapse came on 12 October.

The day began with the PM's hour-long air journey from the national capital to the Central Punjab district of Shujabad. Accompanied by politician Javed Hashmi, Chairman PTV and Pakistan Broadcasting Corporation (PBC) Pervez Rasheed, his son Hussain, speechwriter Nazir Naji, and Military Secretary Brigadier Javed Iqbal, he was to speak at a political rally organized by parliamentarian Javed Shah.[11] A condolence stopover at a party worker's residence was also planned. During the flight, the PM discussed his seniority with the ISI chief General Ziauddin.[12]

On arrival at Shujabad, Pervez Rasheed, Nazir Naji, and Hussain remained in the aircraft. They were preparing the PM's speech. All present had handed over their cell phones, as was the PM's instructions. The PM arrived on the podium to address the rally and, while on the dais, received a phone call. The call left him tense and he barely spoke a few words at the rally. He skipped the planned condolence call and promptly flew back to Islamabad. Before boarding the plane, he instructed that the army Sepoy with the metal/weapons detector, a normal part of the PM's permanent security squad, be sent to Islamabad separately on a PIA flight. Sharif did, however, trust his Military Secretary Brigadier Javed Iqbal, the only other army person, to travel in his plane. Before the plane took off for the roughly hour-long flight to Islamabad, the PM sent out instructions that his two key aides, Principal Secretary Saeed Mehdi and Defense Secretary Lieutenant-General Iftikhar, receive him on arrival at Chaklala air base.

The defenses secretary, who was resting at home, received the PM's message. He had gone in for an early morning endoscopy and the effects of the anaesthesia were still wearing off. At sharp 3:00 pm, the DS was at the tarmac to receive the PM when came out of the plane. The PM instructed him to sit with him in the car. The PM's Military Secretary sat in the front seat. The DS opened the conversation by saying,"So, sir, you went to Shujabad." The PM responded that he had fixed the cotton price at Rs. 850 per maund. The DS then mentioned that, in case he wanted to discuss TP's case, the matter was closed and the retirement orders have already been issued. Nawaz Sharif asked him to forget that case and said that he was taking him to PM House for something else. He told the DS that he had decided to retire Musharraf and to appoint Ziauddin as the new army chief. Taken aback, the DS said, "Sir, this is too serious a decision." The PM's response was, "General Sahib, I have already decided." The unrelenting DS again asked, "Sir, have you consulted your cabinet.?" The cabinet, he was told, "had nothing to do with the decision." The DS insisted, "You should at least consult your key ministers." The PM said, 'General Sahib, the time for consultation is over." The DS still did not give in, "You should discuss this with Nisar and Shehbaz. You have always consulted them in the past."

But this was to be the PM's solo flight. He said Nisar and Shehbaz must not know of this move. Frustrated, the DS asked why he had taken the decision to remove Musharraf. "He has been giving statements against me," was the response.[13] General Iftikhar tried to pacify Sharif. He explained that all that the army chief had said at an embassy function was that the economy was in bad shape and that law and order was not in good shape either. The DS, desperate to prevent the PM from making a suicidal move, added that the army chief had also made the qualifying statement, "The government is trying its best." The PM was undeterred. His constant refrain was that the DS should issue Musharraf's retirement order immediately. The DS said he could not issue retirement orders of the army chief unless he got "written orders from the PM." The PM tauntingly said, "You are scared of the chief; you are a supporter of the chief."

Upon arrival, the PM also reprimanded his Principal Secretary Saeed Mehdi. "Didn't you get my orders?" asked the PM. Orders had been given by the PM almost 90 minutes ago. Mehdi held that he had received instructions only 15 minutes ago. "Order an inquiry immediately," the PM shot back. The PM was tense and in a tearing hurry. He indicated to his PS that he would implement the plan discussed earlier. The Chief Security Officer of PM House, Pervez Rathore, was also present.

The Prime Minister then directed his Principal Secretary, the Defense Secretary, and the Military Secretary to the side room opposite his main office. Upon entering, the PM himself locked the door and yanked the telephone lines from the phone sets. "Each one of you must take a Quranic oath that, whatever is said in this room, none of you will talk about it until it is announced on TV," he instructed those present. He also added, "You will not even tell your wives." Mehdi had not yet heard of the plan. Early elections maybe, he wondered. After all, the PM's loyalists would often assure the PM that he would win an early election hands down. Then came the bombshell, "I have told the MS and the Defense Secretary that I have decided to retire Pervez Musharraf and promote and appoint General Ziauddin." "When?" asked his shell-shocked Principal Secretary. "Today... and just now. It's very urgent," the PM shot-back. Mehdi not quite privy to the entire plan queried, "So, he remains Chairman of the JCSC?"[14] Irritated, the PM quipped, "We are removing him and you are planning to elevate him!" Mehdi inquired, "Since Shehbaz Sharif and Chaudhary Nisar are here, will you consult them?" But the decision had been taken and "Consultation time was over," the PM was clear. The three men were then sent out of the room. The PM summoned Commander Zahid[15] to type his orders and his MS to prepare the PM's order for the President's approval.[16] He announced that he would personally take the typed order to President Rafiq Tarrar. Tarrar wrote 'seen' not 'approved', alongside his signature.[17] The PM was weary of his plan being sabotaged until before the army chief's dismissal orders were formalized. For example until thenThus, he wanted his Defense Secretary be kept in a room separate from Shehbaz and Nisar. He told his Principal Secretary, "Take general sahib and keep him in a separate room." He turned to the Defense Secretary and said, "You cannot meet your brother there."

Throughout 12 October, while pulling off his undisclosed plan to fire the army chief, the PM did not engage with his two otherwise trusted aides, Shehbaz Sharif and Chaudhary Nisar. His brother, who had arrived from Lahore, sent a message informing the PM that he was at the PM House But the PM did not call for him. When Sharif was informed by his PS that Chaudhary Nisar and Shehbaz Sharif were waiting to meet him, he said, his response was, "I have no time to meet them, keep them away for now." Nevertheless, after his lunch meeting with the Japanese ambassador, Shehbaz sat with Nisar in one of the PM House's guest rooms. Still oblivious to the real time execution of the Musharraf ouster plan, the two were concerned about what the PM's anger against Musharraf would likely produce. Suddenly, Nisar spotted something unusual outside the guest room window. Pervez Rasheed, Nazir Naji, and Hussain were peering at a paper.[18] Unknown to Nisar and Shebaz, they were finalizing the speech the PM was to deliver shortly; perhaps not different in tone from the 1993 speech he had made about palace intrigues.

The PM, meanwhile, after getting the order signed by the President, handed over a signed copy of the typed order and instructed the Defense Secretary to issue the formal notification announcing the change in the army's top slot.[19]

The new chief was summoned to the PM house. Ziauddin, the ISI chief, arrived with an unusually large contingent of armed men. He was surrounded by eighty to ninety former SSG troops trained by the army for the Get Osama force. These former SSG troops, carrying Uzi machine guns, periodically resorted to dramatic gun cocking gestures as a show of strength by the ISI chief.

For the PM, the moment had arrived to make public his decision to "retire" the army chief. Only he was doing it differently. Twelve months earlier, on his Principal Secretary's advice, Sharif had called in Musharraf's predecessor General Jehangir Karamat and asked him to resign. He had also hosted a lunch to bid him farewell. Karamat had himself informed his institution of his decision to retire. By contrast, Musharraf and his institution were to hear of his "retirement" from the airwaves. The PM was exercising his Constitutional authority. The official notification read, "It has been decided to retire General Pervez Musharraf, Acting Chairman Joint Chiefs of Staff Committee and Chief of Army Staff, with immediate effect. Lt. General, Ziauddin has been appointed as the Chief of Army Staff with immediate effect and promoted to the rank of General. Before orders to this effect are issued, President may kindly see." Sharif had personally taken the draft to the president for his signature.

The PM instructed PTV chairman Rashid to organize the broadcast of this very significant news. Rashid, with the PM's son and speech-writer, was still busy giving final touches to the PM's speech. He called a PTV team to the PM House to film the PM decorating the newly appointed army chief with the pips; as the chief, he had to be decorated with an additional star. The Military Secretary, a two star-general, removed a pair of his own stars, which the PM and the brigadier himself pinned them on the new chief. Interestingly, this was the exact manner in which the PM a year ago had formalized the appointment of General Pervez Musharraf - the putting of pips. However, then the time had been about 10pm.

This very significant news had now to be broadcast on television. The PM was also keen to give a speech about the reasons for removing Musharraf. This speech by now, based on Naji's input, also included a historical trajectory outlining the impact, ranging from the breakup of Pakistan to the hanging of an elected Prime Minister, Zulfikar Ali Bhutto, that successive military interventions had had on Pakistan. However, his aides stopped him from delivering a speech that would necessarily involve a discussion of Kargil. They feared that discussion on Kargil would turn the Army, as an institution, against the PM and his government. Sharif followed their advice. Instead, he handed over the signed copy of the orders to Chairman PTV Pervez Rashid. There was instant compliance. The PTV Managing Director, Mirza Yusuf Beg, who was in a board meeting, received a chit from his boss Chairman instructing him to air the news immediately that the current army chief had been "retired" and a new chief had been appointed. He was instructed to air this news every five minutes. Footage of the PM putting on the pips on the new chief had already been sent to the PTV MD for immediate airing. Around 5pm the Kashmiri news bulletin was interrupted and the news of Musharraf removal and Ziauddin's appointment was announced.

Thereafter, the newly appointed army chief communicated with several generals. Ziauddin informed the PM he had given orders to the Military Secretary[20] at the GHQ for several key appointments. General Akram was to be appointed chief of General Staff, replacing General Aziz, and General Saleem Haider as Commander 10 Corps in place of General Mahmud. The new chief had summoned these two new appointees and two senior officers from the ISI, Generals Ghulam Ahmad and Ashfaq Kayani, to the PM House. He also informed the Military Secretary at the GHQ that he would go to the GHQ the following morning to take over. When the PM asked Ziauddin the response of the Military Secretary, a satisfied Ziauddin said the response was "most welcome." There were only two key generals, the principal confidantes of army chief Musharraf, whom the new chief was unable to access. They were playing tennis.

The PM had also instructed the new chief that, on arrival at Karachi, Musharraf was to be given the protocol due to a retired army chief. General Ziauddin called Corps commander 5 Corps, Lt. General Usmani, and informed him of his appointment. He asked Usmani to take Musharraf to the Corps Guest House. Usmani's chief of staff also informed him that the army chief had been removed.

The Defense Secretary, still waiting for the formal announcement, stepped out for a smoke. Finding the Deputy Military Secretary's room empty, he proceeded to the Military Secretary's office where he found Raja Nadir Pervez. By now, it was around 4.45pm. Nadir Pervez again complained about Nawaz Sharif retiring his brother-in-law Tariq Pervez despite his many "sacrifices". Iftikhar advised him to remain calm. The two heard footsteps. Men were gathering. Apprehension filled the air. A group of seven or eight, including Ziauddin, the man tipped to replace the COAS, Saeed Mehdi, the Deputy Military Secretary, and the Military Secretary arrived. The television was switched on. Around 5pm, a TV newsreader announced that the prime minister had retired General Musharraf and appointed General Ziauddin as the new chief. The newly appointed chief got up and started shaking hands with everyone as they congratulated him. The PM's Principal Secretary asked the Defense Secretary to go to his ministry and issue the orders regarding the new appointment.

As the Defense Secretary walked out of the office, he heard someone shouting, "General Sahib, General Sahib, wait, wait." The prime minister's distraught brother was hysterically asking, "What has happened? What is all this? I won't serve. I will resign..." The equally shocked Defense Secretary suggested that he could get all the answers to these questions from his brother. When Shehbaz got upset with Iftikhar for keeping Musharraf's removal a secret from him, Iftikhar said he had to keep his promise to his boss. Inside the Military Secretary's office, the very anxious chief minister turned to the newly appointed army chief to wryly congratulate him. "It's all because of you," was the response from the half-appointed chief, who had yet to take effective command at GHQ. Ziauddin was clearly oblivious to the fact that in 1998 Shehbaz had opposed Ziauddin appointment as a replacement to then army chief Jahangir Karamat.[21] In this theatre of the absurd, a close confidante of the PM also stepped forward to take credit for the unfolding spectacle. "I told the PM to end this here. How can you let someone who is challenging your authority carry on?" After congratulating the PM's younger brother, this person asked for a job for his son in the FIA!

The Defense Secretary left for his office in Rawalpindi. There was an ominous foreboding in the air and he knew that Sharif had crossed a red line. Iftikhar called his wife and asked her to leave their house. He then rang his two senior-most officers, the Additional Secretary and the Joint Secretary, to get to the office. At this sombre and potentially explosive time, he wanted his team to be there with him.

The First Response

Meanwhile the news broadcast triggered the inevitable. A limited and localized response came from the GHQ. The newsroom at Pakistan Television (PTV) Islamabad, where the report of Musharraf's "retirement" was prepared for broadcast, turned into the first scene, and perhaps the only venue, of a semblance of struggle between the prime minister's men and the Pakistan Army. Around 5.30, the newsroom informed MD Beg that a dozen soldiers led by a major had entered the newsroom. The major had given instructions not to run the news of the army chief's removal while continuing with the normal transmission. The MD made successive calls to the PM House to apprise the PM of the happenings inside the PTV studios. The PM was unavailable and his Principal Secretary urged the MD to run the news as instructed. The PM's son Hussain was emphatic that the crisis was manageable. "It's a colonel-level coup," he assured the MD. "Do not worry. We have the army chief sitting with us and he will sort it all out."

Meanwhile, the Director News at PTV also called to inform the PM's team of the troops' arrival. The soldiers were physically preventing repeat broadcast of the news.

The Military Secretary assured sharif that he would "control the situation." As he held his weapon and prepared to leave for the PTV, he turned to the PM and half jested, "Sorry, sir, I am not allowed to hold a naked weapon in front of my PM." Armed with his weapon, the confident brigadier left for the television station.

Meanwhile, with this stalemate continuing at PTV, MD Beg again conveyed the gravity of the situation to the PM's son Hussain and expressed his inability to follow the PM's instructions. A riled up Hussain almost thundered, "Is this why we appointed you? You better follow instructions and if, in doing so, you lose your life, you will be called a shaheed (martyr)." Beg urged Hussain to take the coup seriously while Hussain instructed Beg to move from his headquarters office and go to the newsroom. The PM instructed his military secretary to "control the situation." Armed with his weapon the confident brigadier left for the television station. He reassured Sharif that all would be ok.

When PTV MD Beg arrived at the newsroom, he saw the army major standing in the middle of the newsroom with his twelve accompanying soldiers surrounding him. Brigadier Javed was standing close to the major and ordered him to disarm. "Sir, I am under the command of the 111 Brigade, not under your command. And I am doing what I was ordered," was the major's response. The Brigadier pushed his pistol against the major's side and in seconds the troops loaded their guns and pointed them towards the brigadier. There was pin drop silence as the petrified PTV staff looked on. The major ordered his troops to put down their guns. The troops were ordered by the major to disarm and a group of around 15 commando-trained Elite force militia collected the guns and locked the soldiers in a side room.

Immediately thereafter, Chairman Rashid went from the newsroom to the news studio. Musharraf's dismissal news had to be repeated. Rashid decided to read it himself in case by now the newscaster was too uneasy. He entered the news studio, where veteran news caster Shaista Zaid was present. Immediately after the weather bulletin, at around 6.20 pm, PTV in its English bulletin again flashed the news of the chief's shuffle.

There was a show of thumbs…she had read the news! PTV was now ostensibly set to resume its normal transmission. The PM's instruction was to re-telecast the news of the chief's dismissal at regular intervals.

But the fight-back from the GHQ had only just begun. Additional troops were despatched. To tell their story some journalists were contacted. For example an intelligence officer had reached out to Hamid Mir a leading Urdu columnist. Mir was on his way to the airport to take the Dubai flight.

His column on ISI and Afghanistan had ruffled feathers. Prime minister's most trusted aide Saifur Rehman's men and then Rehman himself demanded Mir issue a corrigendum backing off from the criticism penned in his column. Rehman had threatened him with an FIR. Mir had been advised by a senior PML-N politician to leave the country. Now he was being asked by an intelligence man to arrive with a camera man in front of PTV to witness essentially the military take-over.

PK805 Must Not Land In Karachi

The Army's initial push-back at PTV after the announcement of Musharraf's removal had surprised the PM. "But I am legally competent to change the army chief… Why is the army doing this?" a perplexed Sharif had queried. In response to these counter-moves by what seemed to be a few army soldiers, the agitated yet determined PM decided the plane carrying the army chief should not be allowed to land in Karachi and ordered the flight be diverted elsewhere. He suggested Muscat. The army chief, traveling from Colombo to Karachi with 198 other passengers, was aboard the Airbus flight PK 805. The prime minister personally called the Director General Civil Aviation Authority (DGCAA) Aminullah and ordered him not to let the plane land at any airport in Pakistan. The PM's instruction was that PK 805 had to proceed to Muscat. Sharif made another call and repeated his instruction to the chairman PIA Shahid Khaqan Abbasi was also brought into the loop. To ensure removal of Musharraf successfully, he wanted all his flanks covered; above all he wanted to render Musharraf, the man whose removal he had ordered, professionally ineffective.[22] Accordingly he changed his earlier instructions that Musharraf be received at the Karachi airport and be given protocol due to a former army chief. As prime minister and Defense Minister Section 6 of the Civil Aviation Ordinance, 1960 gave him the legal authority to order such a diversion[23] however only in the "event of war or other emergency, or in the interests of public safety or tranquillity…"[24]

At the PM House, meanwhile Nisar and Shehbaz had no access to the PM, the defense secretary had left for his office, Pervez Rashid was at the PTV headquarters, only the PM's son Hussain and Minister Saifur

Rehman were present in the PM's vicinity when the mind-boggling decision regarding diverting PK805 was taken. In this unfolding Pakistani version of Game of Thrones, it seemed no one in the PM's close circle realized the ability of the Army to retaliate. The PM also drew confidence from squashing of the Army's response at PTV and his unchallenged 1998 removal of the former army chief.

The action now moved to the Air Traffic Control complex[25] at Karachi airport. Down from the chain of command, following the PM's orders, men from CAA, PIA, and the police force were busy preparing the environment within which to implement the PM's order. The Secretary to the DG CAA, a Wing Commander, was working on closing down the Karachi airfield.[26] The Inspector General Police for Sindh was gathering the police force at the airport to physically block the runways. By 6.29 pm, the airfield had been closed.

From the Air Traffic Control (ATC) room, the ATCO passed the prime minister's orders via intercom to the highly guarded radar room, one of the few locations with a communication link to all airborne flights.Accordingly, at 6.22pm, the radar room passed the orders to the flight Captain Sarwat Hussain, "Do not land at Karachi or at any other airport in Pakistan." There were only around 20 minutes to PK 805's touchdown.

Baffled by the orders, the Captain however was clear that the authorities had no reason to deny him landing rights. The plane, the crew, the passengers, the airspace, were all Pakistani. It was not an alien spacecraft, nor an Israeli aircraft. He realized there was only one man aboard who was different from the rest, the army chief. His presence alone could have triggered the unusual messages from the ground. Captain Sarwat then called for someone from the army chief's staff. Musharraf's trusted ADC, Brigadier Nadeem Taj, came to the cockpit and was told that they had no permission to land at Karachi. He wanted to know the options. "In front of us, we have Rahimyar Khan. Behind us is the Arabian Sea. On our left is the Iranian city of Bandar Abbas and on the right is the Indian city of Ahmadabad," was the Captain's response. "India is out," was Taj's expected response. Who to contact to find what on earth was happening – and literally that, from an altitude of 10,000 feet (It's 10,000)

- may have crossed his mind. He asked the Captain if he could use his mobile phone. He left the cockpit to report the incredible and potentially horrifying developments to his army chief, who by now had 'technically' been retired. Taj tried to use his mobile phone. There was no signal. The army chief and his ADC both entered the cockpit. They hoped that, using the cockpit's special communication equipment, they would be able to communicate with people on the ground. Flight Engineer Amir, present in the cockpit, offered to help. Using the PIA frequency, he was unsuccessful in connecting their number. On the ground, the PIA Chairman's men had taken charge of the PIA communications center at the airport. Following direct orders from Islamabad, they did not allow any non-flight related communication from the cockpit.[27]

In implementing the PM's orders DGCAA Aminullah Chaudhary[28] and Khaqan Abbasi adopted different routes. Abbasi checked with PIA Director Flight Operations Captain Shah Nawaz Dara if the plane could continue on to Muscat. Dara said the plane would not have sufficient fuel. DGCAA, meanwhile, took steps to physically block the Karachi run way to prevent PK 805 from landing in Karachi

At Dumbell and to Muscat

Abbasi reported back to the PM that the plane did not have sufficient fuel to fly to Muscat. The PM cleared PK 805 to land in Nawabshah for refuelling and onward flight to Muscat. Abbasi instructed his special assistant Nasir Haider to convey the PM's instructions to Director flight Operations Captain Dara walked over to the control room at the Karachi airport and Captain Sarwat was informed that he could land at Nawabshah airport…"the airport was open and the weather clear. Around the same time the DGCAA was trying to reach the PM. He managed to reach the PM's Military Secretary. "What do we do about the plane.It doesn't have fuel to go to Muscat," he asked the brigadier. He was not privy to the earlier instructions, given directly by the PM to the CAA head. "Make the plane land at Karachi. I am giving you clear instructions," the brigadier responded, then rushed to inform the PM. "The captain of PK 805 is reporting shortage of fuel and saying that the plane cannot fly to Muscat."

The prime minister told his MS to let the plane land at Karachi airport but ensure that it was parked in a remote and unlit corner of the airport. "No one," instructed the PM, "should be allowed to leave the airplane." [29]After refuelling, he instructed, the plane should take off for Muscat. In a resigned tone, his Military Secretary muttered, "The army may have got to the airport by then."

Meanwhile, in the cockpit of PK 805, theCaptain was the decision-maker, both by physical control of the plane and by law. Yet he was receiving instructions from the general in the cockpit, from the chief pilot on the ground and finally also from the military men who took control of the airport. The Captain, while taking his own decision based primarily on the safety of the "198 souls" aboard his flight. Instead, factoring in his fuel position and the alternate airport nominated, in case of closure of Karachi airport, in his flight plan at take-off from Colombo, Captain Hussain made his own decision.[30] At 6.43 the (pg 26) he was informed from ATC that the Nawabshah airfield is closed. However a subsequent message from that control room at the airport informed him the Nawabshah airport was open. Captain Sarwat was on his way decided to fly to Nawabshah. He couldn't guarantee what awaited his plane at touchdown on the Nawabshah runway. Nevertheless the aircraft only had enough fuel to fly to Nawabshah. The plane would have touched the Nawabshah runaway in less than 20 minutes overcoming all concerns regarding fuel shortage.

Yet, halfway to Nawabshah, by around 7:30 pm, the tremors from the unfolding drama 20,000 feet below were being felt in the cockpit. Instructions came from the ATC. Flight PK 805 could turn back to Karachi. The Captain turned around. Touch down was at 7.47pm.[31] When PK 805 parked, it had only about 12 minutes of fuel left. The safe-fuel level of this flight at landing should have been half hour,[32] even if there was a diversion.

PK 805 had been in holding position for about fifty minutes. with no one from the radar room monitoring it for safety. Instead, those at the ATC were seeking to have the PM's order implemented. [33]

Announcement 2 and D-Day

On the ground, with this second broadcast of the Musharraf news at around 6.20pm, the army's institutional response had been triggered; albeit partial. As soon as the news got to Mahmud and to Aziz of Musharraf's removal, they rushed to the counter-strike. There was no communication between Musharraf and commander 10 Corps or CGS Aziz asking them to take over. Through the past month, there had been an understanding among Musharraf's trusted men in the top brass on the mode of launching a counter-strike in case of the chief's removal.

Around 6:40pm, the MD was informed by the PTV World team that two truckloads of soldiers had arrived and closed down the transmission. The Army instructed them to only play national/patriotic songs. Again, the MD called the PM. His PS, who came on line, was informed. Minutes later, Saeed Mehdi returned and said, "The PM says he has sent the local SHO police to look into the matter." By this time, the Army had come and taken over the PTV Headquarters. The transmission was shut down from 8 pm to 11pm. For the first time in PTV's history, there was no news bulletin at 9pm.

Before Musharraf's flight was to land the Corps reserve commander, Major General Iftikhar, received reports of unusual activity at the airport. Chief Minister Ghaus Ali Shah and Inspector-General (IG) Sindh Police Rana Maqbool were there. The airport had been closed. Delay in PK 805 was being reported. He communicated with corps commander Usmani. Corps commander 10 Corps Mahmud and CGS Aziz had already both contacted Usmani. General Mahmud called Usmani to move his troops immediately. Musharraf's plane had been diverted to Nawabshah. Usmani ordered the local Rangers in Nawabshah to take charge of the airport, clear the runway and to protect the chief.

By 6:38pm Major General Iftikhar directly contacted the ATC, ordering them not to divert the PK 805. He received a negative response from the ATC, "Wing Commander Farooq Sahib will do it, he has given us instructions. Right now he is in complete authority." In Karachi, Usmani ordered Brigadier Jabbar Bhatti to move in with troops to open the airport and end the blockade of the runway.

The brigadier ordered his troops, including units from Malir, to the airport. A few hundred troops arrived and surrounded the airport. They took control of the ATC complex and finally gained access to the secured radar room.

All this was in contrast to the earlier, relatively localized response. For the army high command this was an entirely unprecedented situation. With the chief airborne, his retirement orders were issued. However surprising or alarming, the order was constitutional.[34] Also, while the "retired" chief was airborne, the new chief had engaged with several corps commanders and major generals. Several had responded positively. Initially, therefore, there was no unified resistance from the army's high command. Unified resistance came coinciding with PTV's announcement of Musharraf's removal in the English news bulletin. Key generals close to the airborne chief, and part of the Kargil clique, led the institutional response.

Across the country, the army was on high alert. In Rawalpindi-Islamabad, troops had begun to move.

Alarm bells rang within the PM House too. Past 6:30 pm, the Defense Secretary was only minutes from his office when his phone rang. It was the prime minister's brother. The army troops had arrived at the television station and a panicked Shehbaz wanted him to find out "what was happening" and let him know. There was nothing left to find out. The die had been cast. Nawaz Sharif's coup against the army chief had earned the country a counter coup. This was a real coup, the one which with all its destructive consequences has been visited upon the country time and again. By now, the Defense Secretary had also been informed that his home had been surrounded by troops.

All the major stakeholders in Pakistan's power construct were active.

Defense Secretary at his office

At his office, the defense secretary and his officers sat in front of the television set to witness the unfolding events. Around 9 pm, a major from the GHQ Military Intelligence Directorate (MI) arrived. The chief of general staff (CGS) had sent his Salaams; in military parlance, this was a polite summons. Along with one of his officers, Iftikhar arrived at the GHQ. The CGS was in the office of the Director-General Military Operations. With numerous military officers talking on their telephones, the office was a happening place. The coup was being executed from here.

The CGS suggested they move to his office. There, the CGS said, "Sir, I would like to tell you two things: first, that the action was inescapable and, two, that we are very clear that you and your brother are not involved in it." The ministry official accompanying him asked the CGS why troops had been sent to Iftikhar's house. The Director General MI General Ehsan ul Haq was summoned and queried. Orders were issued for withdrawal of these troops. As Iftikhar got up to leave, the CGS said, "No, Sir, you cannot go. You have not had lunch. Please eat with us first." Obviously, the movements of Nawaz Sharif's team had been closely monitored; Iftikhar had indeed had nothing to eat since his endoscopy test in the morning. They ate lunch at around 9.30pm and then left the GHQ.[35]

Meanwhile unaware of these developments yet fully aware that his boss would be ousted, the defense secretary was on his way to his ministry in Rawalpindi. There was an ominous foreboding in the air, he knew Sharif had crossed the red line. Iftikhar called his wife and asked her to leave the residence. He then rang up his two senior-most officers, the additional Secretary and the joint secretary, to get to office. He had wanted his team to be there with him. It was past 6pm and he was just a short distance away from his office when his phone rang. It was the prime minister's brother. The army troops had arrived at the television station and a panicked Shehbaz wanted him to find out "what was happening" and let him know. There was nothing left to find out. The dye had been cast. Nawaz Sharif's ouster of the army chief had resulted in a military coup. This was a real coup, the one which with all its destructive characteristics had visited upon the country time and again. By now the defense secretary had also been informed that his residence had been surrounded by troops.

Somewhere, Business As Usual

Totally oblivious to all this was the government's Finance Minister Ishaq Dar, going about conducting business as usual. Dar was busy with follow-up work related to the annual IMF meeting he had just attended. He was preparing a letter committing the government to WAPDA reforms and the letter had to be signed by Chairman WAPDA General Zulfiqar. Later, around 5.30, he had convened a major meeting with about thirty cotton growers in the Q block, of the Pakistan Secretariat, home to the unpopular Finance Minister. The chief minister Punjab, on whose recommendation the meeting had been organized, was also meant to participate.

Around 4pm, the Finance Minister got a call from the Chairman WAPDA telling him that the army chief had been sacked. Dar checked a couple of channels but didn't pick up any news. The cotton growers had started arriving. The meeting started at 5:30. The Punjab CM's chair lay vacant. Around 6:15, the FM asked his PS to check on him. The PS informed him that the CM was "busy with Sahib (the prime minister)". It was around 7:15, when a panicked official of the Ministry informed the FM of the army takeover. Dar swallowed the information, calmed the official, and continued with the meeting. He announced the steps they all had agreed on and then just, before concluding the meeting he announced, "Gentlemen, maybe the army has taken over." Pandemonium broke loose. The participants, burly landlords and weighty politicians, ran for the elevators. Goodbyes and niceties were abandoned. They knew too well that, when the coup came, little else mattered. It was the ultimate game changer in Pakistan's power tussles.

After the participants exited, the FM tended to the IMF business. He wanted to follow up the letter with a phone call to the relevant IMF officials. But it was all over for him too. The Gateway recording said, "We are sorry, no calls can be put through at this time." The men in uniform has covered all flanks. All external information from government offices was blocked.

By now, there was army at the main gates of Q Block. The Minister and two of his officials, Tariq Bokhari and Ghafoor Mirza, used the rear gate of the ministry to exit. While the secretariat was getting vacated and ministers were leaving their ministries, the defense secretary was at his office.[36]

Enter the Coup Makers

At the PM House, Colonel Shahid from the 111 Brigade, with some troops, had entered the room where the bigwigs had gathered. "Look here. don't you know there is a sanctity of the PM House? You lay off," he was reprimanded by the newly appointed CGS Akram. "Sir, I have orders from my commander, you kindly talk to him," came the confident response from the colonel of the coup-making brigade.

General Akram asked the colonel to use his Defcom network to put him through to his commander. "I am CGS General Akram. The army chief will take a guard of honour tomorrow morning but he will not review the parade," Akram instructed the 111 Brigade commander Satti. "Yes, sir," was the only response Satti was trained to give. The next morning was a million unpredictable moments away. Satti passed on General Akram's message to his commander, General Mahmud. "Tell him, forget it!" was Mahmud's response. Meanwhile, for any other instruction related to troop movements and the PM House, Satti was clear that only Commander 10 Corps, General Mahmud, could issue instructions.

In the now tension-ridden, heavy as lead atmosphere, the PM's Military Secretary suggested that there be no civilians there since a shoot-out was likely. The three military men present were the new chief General Ziauddin, the new CGS, and the PM's military secretary. The PM was surrounded by his brother Shehbaz Sharif, his most trusted friend Saifur Rehman, and the latter's brother Mujeebur Rehman. Seeing the writing on the wall, Chaudhary Nisar had earlier left the PM House. Suddenly, the door was flung open and in walked General Mahmud and the Vice-chief of General Staff, MajorGeneral Mohammad Jan Orakzai. About two dozen soldiers followed. Shehbaz Sharif was the first to speak. "Why so many people, general? This is a private lounge of the PM." Mahmud asked the troops to leave. He then turned to the PM, "Sir, why did you have to do this?" The PM repeated what he had said a couple of hours earlier on hearing that army troops had arrived at the television station,"I was legally and constitutionally competent to do this." The Commander 10 Corps, whose troops had executed the coup plans, sardonically replied to the all-but deposed PM, "What was constitutional and legal, we will now find out." He further added, "I had always prayed I would never have to see this day.."

Mahmud asked his men to take Ziauddin and Brigadier Javed Iqbal to a separate room and Saeed Mehdi to another room. Mahmud and Orakzai escorted the PM and his brother Shehbaz Sharif to a Mercedes car parked outside. Mahmud accompanied them to the 10 Corps Annexe, essentially a VIP Mess. Saeed Mehdi was kept in the annexe of the PM House, Saif ur Rehman, and Mujeeb ur Rehman, accompanied by Orakzai, were taken to the corps headquarters in Chaklala. The PTV Chairman, Parvaiz Rasheed, was held in the PTV Headquarters till 1:30 am, then taken to his Parliamentary Lodge and kept under detention there.[37]

Away from the PM's initial order of banning the landing of PK805 on Pakistani soil and the subsequent GHQ trashing of the Constitution, the theatre of the absurd continued. After the army take over was confirmed, the Governor Sindh Mamnoon Hussain called President Tarrar to inquire about the fate of the dinner he had invited him to. "The dinner must go on," the President told his guest. And it did.

Epilogue

It was curtains for the Sharif government.

Pakistan had gone through its third military coup d'état.

The next day belonged to the Coup maker. There was talk of Musharraf's "sincerity" in attempting to carry out the reforms he had claimed to conduct in his first national address. There was also talk of the inevitability of the coup after the "conspiratorial" manner in which PM Nawaz Sharif sought to remove the army chief. According to the majority of media reports, the public welcomed the military takeover.[38]

Pakistan's main opposition leader, Benazir Bhutto, had no sympathies for the coup struck Sharif. In an interview with CNN, Bhutto said, "Nawaz is a fascist. The people of Pakistan don't want him."[39] The coup, she argued was a consequence "of a general feeling of frustration in Pakistan that Nawaz was dismantling all democratic institutions."[40] While she acknowledged that Sharif had lost public support, she urged the coup makers to respect peoples' desire for democracy.

The General's justification was all too familiar. Musharraf justified the coup in his nationally televised address. "I wish to inform you that the armed forces have moved in as a last resort to prevent further destabilization," he said. He further asserted, "Despite all my advice, they tried to interfere with the armed forces, the last remaining viable institution in which all of you take so much pride..."

Foreign media also reported in the same vein. Global chatter had again begun. It fell on deaf ears. A case in point was the only three-week-old Sept 21 statement issued by the US State Department strongly opposing any attempt to change the government through "any extra constitutional moves," which was now obviously being ignored. Fundamentally, Pakistan's domestic power players would always determine domestic power dynamics. Pakistan's power players and analysts have often opportunistically exaggerated the limited leverage of the US and global opinion.

US media reported Washington's rapid U-turn on SHARIF. 'There are few tears being shed in Washington for Sharif who was widely considered autocratic and inept," reported *USA Today*.[41] It was "not a White Hat Black Hat Situation,"[42] a State department official had explained. While US officials called it a "setback for democracy" and "a political crisis," they also blamed Nawaz Sharif "for provoking' what they considered 'a needless confrontation with the military." Sharif was blamed for dumping Musharraf two weeks later when he was out of the country, after first granting him the ceremonial title of Chairman Joint Chiefs of Staff, which was interpreted as a peacemaking gesture.[43]

Meanwhile, in the theatre of the absurd, the Pakistan Embassy in Washington, many hours after the coup, sketched an imaginary wishful scenario for the local media. According to Embassy spokesman Ahmad

Malik Zahoor, " You cannot say it is a coup…we are not very clear what is happening…naturally we are waiting for things to settle down…" [44]

The angry prime minister had freed himself of his kitchen cabinet and the pragmatic advice of Nisar and Shehbaz. Instead, his own temperament had hijacked him. His actions and decisions were in some ways reminiscent of Nawaz Sharif during the closing days of his previous government. He was then touring Germany and England when his ministers began abandoning him as new political factions were being scripted. On his way home, he began thinking of his response. To the last journalist he talked to before his plane landed at Islamabad airport, the agitated PM had said, "Enough is enough, I cannot continue this *naukari*. I must be allowed to exercise my authority as an elected PM. I would have resigned long ago, but my father keeps instructing me to carry on for the sake of Pakistan. But now I will tell him this cannot continue."

Nawaz believed the intel agencies and the sitting President had been conspiring for his ouster. Within two days of arriving home, on 17 April 1993, the prime minister strongly attacked those "hatching palace intrigues." He claimed the President was behind these intrigues. Defiant, the PM had concluded, "I will not resign; I will not dissolve the National Assembly, and I will not be dictated." Army chief Kakkar intervened in July 1993 and forced Sharif and the President both to resign.

Now, six years later, on 10 October 1999, Prime Minister Sharif again found himself in a complex and frustrating situation. He was convinced that his removal through a coup d'etat was imminent. The outraged PM fought back.[45] He exercised his constitutional authority to advise the President to remove the army chief. In thirteen months this was a second change in the army command that Sharif had sought. The modus operandi of the two removals were vastly different. In September 1998, the PM had called in the Army chief general Jehangir Karamat and asked him for his resignation. Karamat had preferred resignation to a dismissal. Now in October 1999, unmindful of the army's Rawalpindi-based high command's readiness to hit back in case the PM took action against their chief and of the hostile country-wide anti-Sharif political environment, Sharif fired the army chief. Led by the key men of the irrationally planned Kargil operation, the army hit back. Musharraf survived as the chief and

Sharif was removed and imprisoned. The prevailing power dynamics had trumped constitutional clauses.

Ironically, the Kargil clique's misadventure, the original trigger that created a coup- enabling environment, receded into the background. Pakistani analysts and politicians mostly focused on the blunders that Nawaz Sharif had committed during his years in office. The Kargil clique had hoped for just such an outcome. Sharif's orders that PK 805 must not land anywhere in Pakistan, created the perfect setting for the dramatic entry of the coup maker Musharraf. The word that the PM had tried to "hijack" PK 805, had ordered that the plane carrying the army chief not land in Pakistan, had spread like wild fire.[46] Accordingly Sharif's removal was widely accepted as the inevitable outcome of the 12 October gripping Sharif-Musharraf power tussle.

The army had seized power. Not a bullet had been fired. Not a word had been exchanged between the coup makers and their technically "retired" chief. The Kargil clique won out. Musharraf became King. The SC ruled that his word was to become law. He rewarded the Kargil clique by making the following appointments; Corps commander 10 Corps Mahmud the ISI chief, FCNA commander Javed Hasan was made president of NDU, and Aziz retained the critical position of CGS.

Meanwhile, after the coup, military men were heard saying that the Kargil documents had been burnt. Yet the man with the operational command claimed in 2006 that all the Kargil decisions and reports were fully documented.

Yet the some facts remain indestructible.

Anatomy of the Kargil blunder was now on no one's agenda. A new round of power play had begun.

Folklore

In Yasin and other villages of district Khizer, in the valleys of Waadi-i-Shuhada from where Pakistan's countless sons went to fight for their Motherland, where countless mothers of countless martyred Lalik Jans now live, Nawaz Sharif was the villain. The story was that he had sent off their precious sons to fight, even without uniforms. Yet their sons went, fought fearlessly and even got the Indians by the jugular. Had Nawaz Sharif not ordered their return, these Lalik Jans would have defeated India. This folklore lives on in the villages of Waad-i-Shuhada. Even beyond.

Such folklore would have been inevitable. Through centuries, ordinary folk have woven together simple stories about complex human existence. In times of acute anguish, people in pain grasp at the facts and fiction that blow in the wind. Never tested for facts, often from the 'truth' the wind carries, healing stories are woven to dull the pain. Often silver linings are also created. The abiding power of folklore to bring contesting realities of pain and joy together amicably in a common space, remains undeniable.[47]

But when the State explains costly policy blunders through fiction and folklore, it almost inevitably guarantees repeated policy failures.

Chapter 19

READING KARGIL

Much of Pakistan's political and security debate has veered towards the binary: civilian versus military. With military rule spanning more than 50 per cent of its history, Pakistan's political journey lends itself to such thinking. Amongst our social intelligentsia, this promotes a flawed reading of decision-making, policies, and policy impact. The most sensitive of topics in this dialogue are Pakistan-India, relations in which too the intellectual discourse has tended to tread the civil-military binary path. As a result, achieving consensus on Pakistan's India policy has been exceptionally difficult. Acquiring consensus from a deeply divided narrative is often challenging, if not impossible. For example, on wars, the narratives in the two countries are sharply contradictory as to who started the wars, in which political and diplomatic environments they were initiated, what was achieved or lost etc. In the history of Pakistan, narratives have always been influenced by this civil-military binary, but never more so than in the case of the Indo-Pak wars. The appraisal of the original text on some of these wars has been carried out in hindsight. For example, the wars in 1948 and 1965 now have revisionist histories, written even by military generals. But this has yet to be the case with Operation KP, the most recent—albeit limited Pakistan-India military encounter.

The foregoing chapters have endeavored to document a non-binary, comprehensive account of Operation KP, from its planning, through the implementation and finally to its impact. Operation KP can be divided broadly into the following six, somewhat overlapping phases:

- First, the Euphoria phase, in which the Kargil clique, with an ominously euphoric mindset, planned Operation KP in complete secrecy. This euphoria of the Kargil clique emanated from several factors: First was the belief that Pakistan's nuclear leverage has driven a full-scale confrontation out of the realm of possibilities. This thought—combined with the unfathomable miscalculation that blocking NH-1, India's lifeline to Indian troops in Leh, would result in the Indian armed forces withdrawing from the disputed territory of Siachen that Delhi's forces had occupied in 1984—was the primary ingredient of the mix. The secondary ingredients were that, with their buddy General Pervez Musharraf as COAS, they could plan a surreptitious operation across the LOC and the Indians would never fight back. Based on these 'supposedly irrefutable facts', it was concluded that the military and diplomatic success of Operation KP was guaranteed.

- Second, the Excitement phase, when its planners and participants initiated the Operation with no significant resistance from the Indians. The theatre of the Operation was almost empty and the only 'adversary' the NLI troops encountered was the combination of inhospitable terrain and harsh weather. Yet, as they trudged ahead with great physical difficulty, they found these uncontested vacant spaces very alluring. In fact, Pakistan's courageous men on a daredevil mission interpreted the winter drawdown of Indian troops as a virtual walkover opportunity. Weak aerial surveillance of the Drass-Kargil area was an added advantage. Back at the GHQ meetings, the Kargil clique, led by Operational Commander Javed Hassan, boasted of complete success.

- Third, the Expansion phase, in which, due to the absence of Indian resistance, the COs and their troops went beyond the original lines drawn for setting up of posts. In fact, for the first eight months at the prowl, Pakistani troops did not encounter a single Indian soldier despite the audacious setting up of 116 posts.

- Fourth, the Encounter phase, which began in early May with limited and indirect hostilities between Pakistani and surprised Indian troops. These initial encounters had left both sides confused. Kargil planners were unclear about the type and scale of the Indian military response to be expected. Meanwhile, within Pakistan, the secret of the Kargil Operation, hitherto confined to the clique of four generals, was revealed to the wider military command and also to Pakistan's prime minister and his cabinet. In India, the military command was divided about the scale and intent of the Pakistani presence and did not consider it significant enough to inform Delhi. By early June, however, the Pakistan-India encounter had snowballed into a battle in the mountains. Operation KP, planned as a smooth, unhindered military Operation in IOK, had turned into a Pakistan-India mountain battle of attrition. The die had been cast: Operation Kargil had turned into Battle Kargil.

Once there was clarity in Delhi of the scale and depth of the Pakistani intrusion across the LOC, the Vajpayee-led government decided to hit back with overwhelming military and diplomatic might and political resolve. Combined with its aggressive military retaliation, that included heavy artillery and aerial attacks, Delhi stonewalled every Pakistani effort to extract strategic advantage from Operation KP. By early June, although still holding on the heights, Pakistani troops had come under tremendous physical and psychological pressure from both the Indian military offensive and from the disruption of supply routes. These iconic combatants on hostile peaks, enduring vicious weather, depleting supplies, deafening sorties, and unending mortar fire, were lodged in imperilled zones but with no victory formula. As stories from the war theatre trickled into the hallowed corridors of the Kargil planners, they responded with concern, confusion, and even some bravado. The Euphoria and Excitement were no more. The military encounter had extended to the diplomatic and political levels. Delhi overruled every Pakistani effort for a bilateral political dialogue. On 12 June, the Indian foreign minister categorically told his Pakistani counterpart, Sartaj Aziz, that India was willing to sit on a negotiating table only after Pakistani troop withdrawal to pre-Operation KP positions. The message for the prime minister from Beijing and Washington was no different. The reality slowly sank in that Operation KP could accrue no gains for Islamabad.

- Fifth, the Exit phase, which began around mid-June, by when it had become clear to the prime minister and his key advisors that, with the depletion of supplies to Pakistani troops, mounting Indian attacks, and a unified global demand that Pakistan immediately and unconditionally withdraw its troops from Kargil, Islamabad had to make some hard decisions. Pakistan's valiant soldiers remained under a determined and deadly Indian attack, ruling out all chances of any further operational success. At the 12 June meeting in Lahore, attended by all the DCC members, the PM asked his FM to explore ways towards an honorable exit. These included engaging the Chinese and even working on a backchannel settlement attempt with Delhi. Finally, the PM opted to fly to Washington, seeking withdrawal under a futile and controversial US cover.

- Six, the Effect phase that began once the 4 July Washington Statement formally announced Pakistan's exit from Kargil. The effect of the withdrawal statement in a battleground dotted with peaks, ravines, and waterways was complex and staggered. Skirmishes between Pakistani-Indian troops continued beyond 4 July and retreating Pakistani troops under Indian attack suffered heavy casualties. Within Pakistan's power structure, throughout its duration, Operation KP infused deep distrust, resentment, and latent antagonism between the elected leadership and the Kargil clique, thereby shaking the foundations of the Sharif-led government. On the political front, the Opposition used the Operation to further bulldoze the reckless Sharif-led government. Given Pakistan's asymmetrical power structure, it was no surprise that the blundering military clique of Kargil staged a coup against the elected prime minister.

Assessment of Operation Kargil

The remaining chapter focuses on the assessment of the Operation from five prisms: one, the military plan and its execution; two, decision-making and coordination between national security institutions; three, effects on national, regional and international environment: four, response to critical questions; and five, the major impact of the Operation.

1) Military Plan and its Execution:

Leading military thinkers throughout history have written about both the distinctiveness of each war and the commonality of all wars, hence handing us down general principles that have been extrapolated to help generals plan and execute wars. Since Sun Tzu in prehistoric times, war has been a mystery to man to which answers have constantly been sought by both military commanders and thinkers. In the corpus of military literature, while Carl von Clausewitz led the study of the infinite variety of war situations, it was the Swiss soldier-thinker, Antoine-Henri, Baron de Jomini who led the study of the commonality of rules and correct techniques in war-like situations. The work of these leading war theorists helps us subject the reality of Operation Kargil to logical and systematic analysis.

For an objective assessment of the Kargil Operation, while factoring in its specific particularities, we will examine the Operation from six specific angles; all critical for assessing the quality of planning and execution of wars: the planning principle, strategy and tactics, von Clausewitz's 'friction', logistics, Mission Creep Versus Napoleon's 'rapid march', and evaluating the objective.

2) The Planning Principle:

In underscoring the significance of planning, Sun Tzu directly links the success of a battle to the extent a general has made 'calculations for victory'. A victorious general according to Tzu, widely acknowledged as one of the wisest generals ever, is the one who 'makes many calculations in his temples (before) the battle is fought'. Conversely, he maintains that a defeated general, the one who loses a battle is the one who 'makes but few calculations beforehand'. Summing up the criticality of comprehensive planning and of scenario-building before battle, Tzu wrote, 'Thus do many calculations lead to victory, and few calculations to defeat; how much more no calculation at all!'[1]

Similarly, Clausewitz, another military genius, maintains that going into battle means entering into a space in which myriads of factors and events flowing from politics and from inter-state relations are at play. He maintains that entering into such a space in battle is akin to entering a 'vortex' and, hence, it requires thorough planning, anticipating the multiple chain of events a battle will inevitably trigger. No battle can be successfully planned unless its planner is able to factor into his planning the entire chain of events that would follow after he takes the first step. The planner must, therefore, be aware of the effects that his action would trigger and the subsequent chain of events, which in Clausewitz words would generate a vortex-like context demanding multiple level responses from the battle planner and initiator.[2]

For the French general, Napoleon Bonaparte, whom Clausewitz called the 'very god of war'[3], the centrality of the planning principle for any military campaign meant looking at the 'worst-case scenario'. This necessarily required that the campaign planner, irrespective of his record of battle successes, not operate from a point of confidence. Instead, as a critical aspect of the planning principle, Napoleon explained how the planner's personal mindset is central in applying the 'worst-case scenario'. According to Napoleon, while planning any military campaign, 'There is no man more pusillanimous than I when I am planning a campaign. I purposely exaggerate all the dangers and all the calamities that the circumstances make possible. I am in a thoroughly painful state of agitation.'[4] Rarely have world class generals uttered such words of caution and humility, as did Napoleon, thus, emphasizing the criticality of thoroughness of planning for any success in military campaigns.

Bravado or overconfidence was, thus, unknown to this military genius who, at the age of 26, had commanded the armies of the French Republic against Lombardy (in present-day Italy) and demonstrated near-invincibility in battle.[5]

Clearly, most military theorists have not only emphasized the centrality of planning in war but have warned against letting a general's personality traits and biases undermine his own planning. For example, Clausewitz[6] especially underscores personality traits like vanity, ambition, and vindictiveness that can move a general from the very planning course that alone is critical to his success and the success of the battle he has planned.

In contrast to the above mentioned approach of the world's leading military theorists and military commanders, the Kargil planners were overtaken by enthusiasm and a sense of payback. They were so obsessed with settling historical scores that it never crossed their minds to factor in the worst-case scenario. When the junior officers at 10 Corps heard of the operation, some had muttered their concerns. A confidential document moved through GHQ pointed out, 'Indians won't be stupid enough to humiliate themselves by politicizing the conflict.' On this, an intelligence officer had written, 'What if they are?' The officer got rebuked but the question was never answered. Finally, the army chief General Pervez Musharraf raised the question of the Indian response at the January meeting convened for final clearance. However, the Operation had already been launched two months earlier, in November.

Thus, the foremost planning blunder committed by the Kargil clique was their absolute failure to even factor in, leave alone follow the Napoleonic principle of 'exaggerating', possible dangers and calamities that may have arisen during Operation KP. Some 150 years after Napoleon, even the Viet Minh Commander, General Vo Nguyen Giap, who led and won the guerrilla war against the US, was categorical in stating, 'In a time of war, you have to take your lead from the enemy. You have to know your enemy well. When your enemy changes his strategy or tactics, you have to do the same.'[7] In the case of Operation KP's planners, they made no discernible effort to 'know' the enemy. Their personal opinions and sense of mission, the desire to punish India for 1971 and for the 1984 occupation of Siachen, their respective command experiences along the LOC, and the opportunity of revenge for the protracted injustice of Kashmir, substituted for sound analysis. The planners only factored in the local war theatre environment, i.e., the Drass-Kargil region, at the time of launching Operation KP. Implicit in the planning was the faulty notion that by the time India discovered Pakistani troops across the LOC and controlling India's lifeline to its troops in Leh, Delhi would find itself locked in a virtual surrender mode with no option but to settle on terms dictated by Pakistan. In such an all-victorious projection for Operation KP, the Kargil planners had turned on its head the cardinal war planning principle of exaggerating your adversary's response.

Another planning principle missing during Operation KP was clarity of orders/instructions. Clear and precise instructions to junior commanders on posts/detachment, required for successful planning and execution of the Operation, were never given by the senior commanders. Hence, the post commanders were unaware of their roles, the duration of resistance, or the eventual timeline for the expected success of the Operation. Also, they were not provided with adequate air cover, artillery support, engineering expertise, or logistical supply lines for the execution of a long battle of attrition, which is what it eventually turned into.

3) Strategy & Tactics:

According to the Swiss army general and military theorist Antoine-Henri, Baron de Jomini, strategy encompasses the entire theatre of operations and is defined as 'the art of making war upon the map, and comprehends the whole theatre of operations'.[8] Strategy outlines deployment and movement of troops to achieve war objectives. It goes beyond the simple relations between material and static factors like weapons, terrain, and predictable weather. Hence, strategy is the determining framework from which operational planning, tactics, and execution must flow.

Clausewitz underscores the demands of the strategy formulation in military campaigns by introducing the element of the intellect. He explains, 'It is only in the highest realm of strategy that intellectual complications and extreme diversity of factors and relationships occur. At that level there is little or no difference between strategy, policy, and statesmanship.'[9]

Clearly, as the preceding account of Operation KP explains, its planners had faulted at the strategic level. By not factoring in the 'worst-case scenario', i.e. the range of possible Indian responses, the Kargil planners bungled at the foundational level. Their appreciation of a critical factor in the ecosystem, of the entire war theatre of the Operation was missing. The planners had seemingly opted to remain blindfolded at the strategic level. Built upon the faulty foundations of Operation KP, the structure of strategy and tactics had to inevitably be faulty. And so it was.

Beyond strategy and closer to the actual war theatre is the domain of tactics. Tactics detail troop positioning, logistics spread, communication coverage, medical, and engineering back-up, etc. Tactics, according to classic military philosophers, are described as 'the use of military forces in combat'[10] and 'the art of posting troops upon the battlefield according to the accidents of the ground, of bringing them into action, and the art of fighting upon the ground, in contradiction to planning upon a map'.[11] Operation KP was a tricky tactical problem as it involved making potentially complex tactical moves and maneuvres in a hostile geographical environment. As de Jomini explained, 'There are other operations of a mixed nature, such as passages of streams, retreats, surprises, disembarkations, convoys, winter quarters, the execution of which belong to tactics.'[12]

At the tactical level, the planning of Operation KP was relatively detailed, but weak in some areas. For example, the operational plans were comprehensive insofar as they factored in the existing Indian troop position in the local Drass-Kargil theatre. Mapped battle plans, therefore, covered Pakistani troop deployment, movement, and concealment. A de Jomini-style geometrical campaign was planned. To safeguard the flanks of advancing Pakistani troops and to divide retaliating Indian troops, the plan followed the 'lines' approach. The availability of space for maneuvre warfare was exploited. This included positioning of own troops at several points, dividing the base and the front into at least three parts: 'a center and two flanks'. Planning, however, remained weak on the logistical front. Only to a limited extent, therefore, was Operation KP—a textbook example of fighting the de Jomini way.

The commander FCNA, Major General Javed Hassan, who ventured into occupation of uncontested posts, utilized the factors of speed, surprise, and secrecy in deploying his troops. Yet, discreetly, he had raised the backup architecture, bringing engineering and medical corps into forward positions.

But there was a foreboding for Operation KP in the Clausewitz observation: 'The difficulty is not that erudition and great talent are needed … there is no art to devising a good plan of operations.'[13] According to him, it was the actual waging of war that was difficult since the major challenge lay in the necessity 'to remain faithful in action to the principles we have laid down for ourselves'.[14] In action, principles can crumble when confronted with unanticipated realities.

For Operation KP, in taking the battle across the LOC into IOK, the planners, according to established guerrilla warfare logic,[15] had to ensure an environment where the troops were both going to disperse and occupy Kargil heights but also, upon being discovered by Indian troops, be ready for staggered offensive actions. This exactly was the plan. The Pakistani troops, having scaled undetected the dizzying Kargil heights, would initiate offensive action upon being discovered by Indian troops. Yet, things did not go according to plan. The massive artillery-fronted Indian response—proactive, aggressive, and unprovided for by the Kargil planners—made it impossible for the Pakistani troops to conduct a protracted offensive action against the Indian troops.

The tactical level planning had been premised on a virtually non-responsive war theatre with no significant force application considered from the Indians. Accordingly, the planners did not provide for any substantive response variations for tackling Indian retaliation to the Pakistani soldiers, who displayed legendary bravery while advancing through the bitter cold and extremely harsh Drass-Kargil terrain. For example, in the face of an overwhelming and decisive aerial assault, there was no option of retaliatory air power being available to the troops. The planners had built a response deficiency into the plan. Similarly, as Indian airpower bombed out Pakistan's original supply routes, there were no alternative routes available. As the classical Napoleon quote goes, 'An Army marches on its bellies'; however, these troops had been left exposed, vulnerable, and unfed.

Therefore, the strategic level miscalculation by the Kargil planners of not factoring in the worst-case scenario around the Indian response, squandered the tactical advantage that the courage of the Pakistani troops gained in the war theatre. Despite the thorough mapping and clerical micro management of Kargil Operation, it was the launching of the Operation in a blindfolded strategic context that was a fatal blunder committed right at the planning stage. Operation KP's overall module, at the strategic and tactical level, was fundamentally faulty. The failure lay at the doorsteps of the planners who blundered while formulating strategy. Hence, they faltered at the all-encompassing level, at which 'there is little or no difference between strategy, policy and statesmanship'.[16] While tactical level planning and ground maneuvres were exceptional, Operation KP, with its flawed strategic plan, was doomed to failure. Perhaps nowhere else has Sun Tzu's declaration that 'wars are decided before even the first soldier steps on the battlefield' been more relevant. It was in the cosy conference rooms of GHQ that the battle was lost, rather than the rocky crags of Kargil.

While the principle of incorporating the 'worst-case scenario' as a factor sets the context within which a military operation is planned, it is strategy and tactics that constitute its structure.

4) Clausewitz's 'friction':

The Kargil clique, influenced by their respective experiences of being posted along the LOC and their shared belief in Pakistan's nuclear leverage as a negotiating tool, were confident of the success of a battle plan prepared using the de Jomini rules of battle. The planners had ignored the question that the military philosopher Carl von Clausewitz had posed as among the most critical: the question of how to 'to remain faithful in action to the principles we have laid down for ourselves'.[17] The planners' approach instead anticipated uncomplicated execution of Operation KP as if in a void and, hence, their battle plans were premised on their own one-sided advocacy and wishful thinking. To counter such susceptibility, Clausewitz introduced the concept of 'friction'.[18] This comprises all elements that cause friction and resist smooth implementation of a battle campaign. Factoring in the concept of friction, Clausewitz believed, could guard against the dangers of exaggeration, of being blinded by contemporary conditions and one-sided advocacy. In the case of Operation KP, these friction elements included both physical factors, including bad weather, hunger, and psychological factors, such as confusion, fatigue, and observational errors.

Clausewitz emphasized that the intricate war planning or, in this case, battle planning—done on the map would always face tremendous friction. Hence 'combinations which are easily planned on paper can be executed only with great effort, since the commander's free will and intelligence find themselves hampered at every turn'. To overcome this, Clausewitz observes that, for the commander, 'remarkable strength of mind and spirit are needed ...'. In Operation KP, it was at the encounter stage that massive military retaliation by India caused this Clausewitzian 'friction'. However, since the Kargil planners had completely overlooked any possible 'friction', the commander was operationally unable to effectively deal with this friction and, thereby, failed to achieve any battle objectives.

5) Logistics:

The significance of logistics in a battle plan is hard to overemphasize. Logistics is to war what oxygen is to the human body. Just as without oxygen every human body is dead, without logistics every battle plan is stillborn. According to Clausewitz, logistics comprises the means and arrangements necessary to implement plans of strategy and tactics. Strategy decides where to act; logistics brings the troops to this point and provides them with munitions and supplies; 'grand tactics decides the manner of execution and the employment of the troops'.[19] De Jomini presents an 18-point list required to 'embrace every duty and detail' relating to the movement of armies 'and, therefore, all logistical requirements'.[20] It presents an elaborate and extended architecture of logistics in all stages of war and in all scenarios.

Before launching Operation Kargil, the Operation commander had, with unusual rapidity, overseen the movement of engineering, artillery, medical, and other supplies units to the forward lines. These units were positioned to efficiently service troops involved in the Operation. In the early phases, this forward positioning did adequately serve the troops in the war theatre. In fact, even in the earlier part of the expansion phase, there was expanded demand for logistics, which was easily met, given that the supply lines were established under the personal supervision of the Operation Commander Major General Javed Hassan. However, in the encounter phase, there was severe pressure on logistics. The first major Indian attack on the supplies targeted a key forward ammunition dump. Subsequent aerial bombing and heavy artillery attacks in the encounter and exit phases almost entirely disrupted the supply lines. The Indian counter-attack had effectively cut-off what the Kargil planners and, subsequently, the field commanders had established as the Pakistani perimeter within which Operation KP was to be conducted. This made it virtually impossible for men and mules to ply on the supply routes. The Kargil clique had anticipated secure supply routes. Instead, in the encounter phase, Pakistan's brave young soldiers occupying the cold and barren Kargil heights, suffered deeply from acute shortage of supplies.

6) Mission Creep versus Napoleon's 'rapid march':

When in winning zones, foot soldiers are often tempted to expand their battlegrounds .However, since expansion has multiple implications, it is the battle commander not the foot soldiers who must make the decision concerning expansion. Expansion of the war theatre, a classic mission creep phenomenon, has serious implications for logistics, supply lines, and manpower. In Operation KP, the situation for the Pakistani foot soldiers was no different. Within two months of the Operation, they were lured by the vacant spaces and strategic heights in the Kargil area. They had calculated that deeper spread of Pakistani posts on the dominating heights meant greater strategic positioning to tackle Indian retaliation. For example, a platoon in a dominating position could destroy a battalion.

The field commanders after communicating this ground scenario to the Commander FCNA were granted permission to increase the number of posts to be established across the LOC in Indian-held territory. Hence, instead of the initial seven to eight posts, around 196 posts (including defensive centers and outposts) were established. These covered five sectors instead of the planned single sector. This mission creep had led Pakistani troops almost 10 to 15 km into IOK, positioned across 500–600 km of Indian territory. Beyond strategic reasons, there was also the element of competitiveness and adventure among the soldiers that contributed to what had presented itself as classic mission creep.

'Rapid march … press on!' Napoleon counselled men at war. In his seminal work on military operations, Napoleon explains, 'The strength of an army is like the power in mechanics estimated by multiplying mass by rapidity; a rapid march augments the morale of an army and increases its means of victory.' This obsession of Napoleon with rapid marches was the major pitfall in his flawed Russian campaign. Almost 200 years later, a similar lesson was manifested again at Kargil.

7) Evaluating the Objective:

According to Clausewitz, 'War is nothing but a duel ... Each strives by physical force to compel the other to submit to his will. Each endeavors to throw his adversary and, thus, render him incapable of further resistance. War, therefore, is an act of violence intended to compel our opponent to fulfill our will.'[21]

The Kargil planners launched Operation Kargil to exploit Indian vulnerability along the Srinagar-Leh Highway and to sufficiently weaken India so that Pakistan could literally, as Clausewitz would argue, 'Impose conditions ... at the peace conference.'[22] These conditions, which the Kargil clique had initially hoped to impose, related to getting Siachen vacated. Subsequently, they changed to seeking freedom for Kashmir, and then to 'internationalizing' the issue of Jammu and Kashmir.

The planners' version was that, taken by surprise, the Indian government would respond like Pakistan did under military ruler General Ziaul Haq in 1984 to the occupation of Siachen, i.e. to not fight back. It was assumed that, with their Leh-based troops facing the prospect of receiving no supplies after Pakistan virtually blocked the Srinagar-Leh Highway, Delhi would be accommodating. The Kargil clique also believed that the global community would promptly intervene diplomatically to defuse a potentially war-like tension between the two new nuclear states.

At several points, the planning clique's half-baked and ill-conceived approach was exposed. There was talk that the planning and analysis wing of the ISI wrote a detailed report on the proposed operation when the plan reached its office but the COAS personally intervened with DG ISI to close down the study. In March, when a young team proposed opening new fronts in Kargil to increase the pressure on the Indians, they were warned that Pakistan could not risk destabilizing the relationship with India. Subsequently, the responses of the Kargil planners when, from May onwards they were in the dock, were muddled and confused. For example, in May, General Aziz, a key planner, had boasted of the Kargil Operation as providing an opportunity to the PM of becoming the Pakistani leader responsible for liberating Kashmiris. At the FO meeting that month, when asked by the deputy air chief what they wanted, the response was unclear.

Similarly, at the 2 July DCC meeting, when Ishaq Dar asked what they wanted, the response was again ambiguous. Clarity of purpose, which is the first principle of all military planners, had vanished in a haze of euphoria and wishful thinking.

According to Napoleon, 'Never interrupt your enemy when he is making a mistake.'

Operation KP, as a military episode, revolved around the enthusiasm and passion of an undisciplined planning clique comprising four senior commanders and the dauntless military spirit of several thousand foot soldiers. What began as an operation against no significant Indian response escalated into a battle—a battle not foreseen by the planning clique and for which the field troops had not been logistically equipped. Yet, courageously, the young troops went through the ordeal that Operation Kargil had become with heads held high.

The Kargil clique's flawed planning caused the deaths of hundreds of young Pakistani soldiers, wasted national resources, and deepened existing distrust between Pakistan's elected Parliament and government, and the army generals. Abroad, this military adventure helped to reinforce the hostile image of Pakistan as an irresponsible nuclear state whose military generals could easily undermine the elected leadership and call the shots on Pakistan's India policy.

8) Decision-Making and Coordination

From Operation KP to the Kargil battle, leading to the 4 July exit, and culminating in withdrawal of troops from the Drass-Kargil area and finally dealing with the domestic political upheaval, Pakistan's decision-making gave a revealing account of itself. The Kargil clique covertly and surreptitiously planned Operation KP by cherry-picking some battle principles while recklessly ignoring others. Above all, the decision-making clique factored in no substantial reaction from the Indians.

By May, the cover had been blown off Operation KP and it had transformed into a mountain battle for which neither the Sharif-led government, nor the Foreign Office, nor the armed forces—particularly the air force, navy, and intelligence agencies—were prepared. However, to deal with the unfolding military and diplomatic challenges that followed the Kargil battle, the Sharif-led government became active. The first critical requirement for decision-making was information. Sporadic information was brought by the army chief and other members of the Kargil clique to meetings convened by the PM. However, it was in individual non-institutional meetings between COAS Musharraf and members of the PM's 'kitchen cabinet', including Chief Minister Punjab Shehbaz Sharif, Chaudhry Nisar, and the Defense Secretary, that the army chief shared more candid battle information.

From mid-May onwards, in meetings at the PM House, Foreign Office, and GHQ, the PM and relevant cabinet members were briefed on the ground situation. Once Pakistani troops began to lose posts, the flow of information from the battleground became irregular and inaccurate. For example, after the battle of Tololing, there were several versions of when exactly they had lost the post they had earlier occupied. However, the PM and his team had other sources providing them a ground count of Operation KP. These included the network within the Army of the Defense Secretary, a retired general, the grapevine running through friends and families of the vast number of troops involved in Operation KP, and even the DG ISI. There was, however, no formal system of information flow from the battle zone to Sharif, the country's chief executive and the final decision-maker. On occasion, revealing information on the Kargil clique's thinking came from the Indians, who produced in their national newspapers the entire text of a discussion on Operation KP between the army chief and the CGS, the two senior-most members of the Kargil clique.

Meanwhile, there was a flow of reliable information about the diplomatic front that had inevitably opened along with the Kargil battle. Pakistan's diplomatic missions were keeping the Foreign Office informed of the rising diplomatic temperatures. Senior US officials, including the US President, were in contact through phone calls and letters with the PM and his foreign policy team. Similarly, through direct contact and subsequent meetings with senior Chinese officials, Islamabad was also aware of the Chinese policy view throughout the Operation.

From May onwards, the Prime Minister did activate several decision-making forums.These forums, however, had to function below the public radar because, even after the operation became public and the world community knew that Pakistani troops had conducted it, the Kargil clique still insisted that only the Kashmiri Mujahedeen were fighting in Kargil. Moreover, at home also, the ISPR was briefing the media about Kashmiri Mujahedeen presence across the LOC in IOK. Accordingly, the prime minister avoided convening full cabinet meetings and sessions ofParliament, to either discuss Kargil or to get support for Pakistani troops fighting in Kargil. Instead, the government opted for a secretive decision-making approach through informal huddles.

Through the approximately fifty-day period, the PM convened meetings of the Defense Committee of the Cabinet (DCC), chaired special meetings in the PM House and Governor's House, Lahore, attended by armed forces chiefs, his relevant cabinet members, and senior bureaucrats. The army chief also convened Corps commanders and PSO meetings, to brief the top military command regarding the military situation. However, the most candid discussions on the military situation took place within the Kargil clique.

Key individuals in Pakistan's decision-making hierarchy took uncoordinated and inexplicable steps. For example, the Kargil clique decided to expand the operation when the prime minister had conveyed his decision to assign primacy to diplomatic engagement with Delhi and to provide only diplomatic and moral support to the Kashmiris. The army chief held a telephone discussion from Beijing with the CGS on Operation KP using an open unsecured line. Other uncoordinated steps taken by individuals and institutions included: opening, at a critical juncture during Operation KP, multiple tracks of engagement with Washington over the visit of CENTCOM Chief General Zinni and Under Secretary Lanpher; Musharraf offering the PM that he could withdraw his troops from across the LOC and the PM declining the offer; the MI acknowledging Pakistan troop presence in Drass-Kargil in briefings to defense attaches while the Pakistan government publicly denied Pakistani troop presence; the PM's decision to keep the policy-making hub during Kargil, i.e. his Foreign Office team, outside his decision-making loop at the most critical point of terminating the Operation and withdrawing from the battle. These bizarre events demonstrated individual naiveté, which in the affairs of a state can amount to criminality because of the high costs such confused decision-making and action can incur. In the case of Kargil, there was loss of valuable lives, waste of resources, and frittering away of the diplomatic advantage accrued to Pakistan globally in its conduct of policy after the nuclear tests.

Pakistan's key decision-makers and critical institutions were not positioned for responsible and clearheaded decision-making. There was distrust between decision-makers and fear of the other, as if there were an ongoing battle within. During the Operation's planning stage, it was a complete secret. In the battle stage, reliable and regular information required for informed decision-making did not flow in. Equally, the institutional linkages were dysfunctional. No SOPs for information sharing and coordination existed. Even within the one critical institution, relevant commanders were not aware of Operation KP.

In the last stages of Kargil, power politics within institutions and among individuals dominated decision-making. Although there was a reluctant acknowledgment that the Kargil Operation was no longer militarily or diplomatically tenable, yet, stealth was applied in taking and executing the final decision of withdrawal. The prime minister's manner of exit from Kargil was dictated by internal power politics. He walked away from the institutional consultative decision-making that he had earlier opted for because he feared his political survival was at risk. Once the PM realized that the India and China exit routes were not available and was faced with the army chief's aggressive denial in policy platforms of the difficulties faced by the Operation, the PM withdrew into his 'kitchen cabinet' to engineer the termination phase in absolute secrecy. In engineering this termination, Sharif sought his own political survival, the exit of the Pakistan Army from Drass-Kargil, return to the negotiating table with India, and a demonstrable contribution to the Kashmir issue. He chose to exit secretly via a Washington dash.

Decision-making in this climate of divisions, denials, and divergences was at best going to be erratic. Ironically, if the beginnings of Operation KP were crafted in the huddle of a clique, so was its termination.

9) Impact on national, regional, and global environment

Any cross-border operation or offensive operates simultaneously in a contextual triad of three spheres: the military, political, and diplomatic. So was the case with Operation KP. Beyond its exclusively military theatre, which comprised planners, commanders, soldiers, logistics, supply lines, terrain, etc, Operation KP was to be implemented in the broader national, regional, and international contexts. The Kargil clique generally understood this fact but, as with the military aspects of the Operation, it depended on its own understanding of the political and diplomatic situations. The Operation was subjected to a war game in which the commander of the opposing army (Foxland) showed only token resistance and it was concluded that such a plan could be implemented. That 'Foxland' commander was General Aziz. There is ample evidence that the Kargil planners ignored, if not outright rejected, all questions raised by their junior officers regarding the domestic, Indian, and US responses to the Operation. Operation KP's timeline spread across a spectrum of 90 days to nine months. The planners began its implementation as early as October, ending after nine months on 4 July. The first signs of Operation KP were uncovered, both by the Indians and the Pakistanis, in early May, which ended, after around 90 days, in July. In terms of its response to Operation KP, the national, regional, and global environments did change over the nine-month period essentially because as an Operation, it remained a secret but became public after turning into a battle.

National

At the national level, the Kargil clique was almost unconcerned about the political and institutional fallout from mounting this level of cross-LOC operation. The newly appointed army chief, General Musharraf, and his key group had calculated, that, as always, the elected leadership would neither notice nor hinder an operation along the LOC. They feared no disapproval, largely because they seem to have ingenuously calculated that handing down to the elected government the blockade of NH-1 as leverage in forcing the Indians to give up Siachen would silence all political and institutional criticism about the secrecy of their undertaking. In the 17

May presentation made to the prime minister and his team, the PM seems to have bought into the planners' logic, including General Aziz's delusionary fantasy that Sharif would go down in Pakistan's history as the liberator of the Kashmiris.

Throughout the Kargil battle, the Sharif-led government stood by the Army. There was no public criticism, despite mounting Indian retaliation and global censure. Historically, Pakistanis had largely learnt to stand united against India. Kargil was to present no exception. The actual developments around the Kargil battle were kept away from the public view, although internally, Kargil-related developments had triggered concern, criticism, and confusion of members of the Sharif cabinet, some military commanders, and the air force and naval chiefs. The Sharif-led government worked to lead the Army out of the Kargil quagmire.

Also at the national level, the elected government's Lahore Summit initiative was in direct contrast with the Kargil track. However, with Operation KP still under wraps and the political and institutional proclivity of Pakistan's religio-political parties to display their street power in criticizing Indian occupation of IOK, political protests erupted in the streets of Lahore, especially when the visiting Indian prime minister and his entourage were hosted at the Lahore Fort. The angry shrillness of the street protests, funnelled into public space primarily through the media,[23] emerged to counter the official view that the Lahore Summit was a historic and constructive Pakistan-India diplomatic engagement. Also, the deliberate and widely noticed absence of the Pakistani army chief from the official reception line for the visiting Indian prime minister, was, in fact, the Kargil clique's public signalling of its active divergence from the elected government's India policy.

Similar to 1965, when Pakistan's Foreign Minister Zulfikar Ali Bhutto had used the Tashkent Agreement to discredit his political mentor, Field Marshal Ayub Khan, and launch his own political career, in 1999 the Kargil clique led by Musharraf used the Washington Agreement to discredit the elected prime minister. Sharif's political battles with his opponents also helped the Kargil clique to discredit him. His opponents became willing allies of the Kargil clique and supported the Army's view that, at Blair House, the prime minister had squandered the hard-earned military victory.

The generals, having blundered in the military battle at Kargil, won the political war in Islamabad. The government's silence over whatever they knew about the Kargil Operation, including the military situation after heavy Indian artillery and aerial attack, had enabled the Kargil clique to craft and broadcast, virtually uncontested, its own version of 'facts'. According to their version, the Mujahideen were militarily strangulating the Indians. It was no surprise, therefore, that in public perception, Sharif's trip was interpreted as the prime minister arriving in Washington to barter away a Mujahideen victory in exchange for his own survival. The few voices in the media that pointed to the facts of the Kargil battle and raised valid questions remained buried under the dominant story of a sell-out in Washington.

Regional:

Within the regional context, for their impact on Operation KP, China's response as Pakistan's strategic ally was important and India's was critical, as the target of and subsequent respondent to the Operation. China, under its post-Deng Xiaoping leadership, was busy building its economic power and had opted for peaceful engagement with all its neighbors, including India. Accordingly, it had welcomed the Lahore Summit and advised its strategic ally Pakistan to resolve its disputes with India through dialogue. It was no surprise that Beijing virtually read the Riot Act to Pakistan's foreign minister when he arrived in China for an SOS trip on 11 June. Pakistan, he was told, had to vacate Kargil, Kashmir had to be resolved bilaterally, and Beijing had no influence on Indian dealings with Pakistan. Within three days of Aziz's departure, the Indian foreign minister arrived in Beijing to a rousing welcome.

For the Kargil planners, when they initiated the Operation around early November, Siachen talks had yet again ended in a deadlock. Accusations were flying across the border at each other's armies for 'unprovoked cross-LOC firing'. With the army chief among the clique, they were dismissive of the decisions taken at the November DCC to pursue a primarily political track with India on Kashmir. Equally, they had no connection with or respect for the prime minister's initiative in engaging Vajpayee.

This Vajpayee-Sharif initiative, soon after the nuclear tests, had held promise. Sharif was banking on the expertise of Pakistan's best India 'hand diplomats' to work out ways to engage with them. Equally, both governments were drawing upon the policy options being explored in the Track-II dialogues.

Global:

By August, the post-May cantankerous engagement between the two new nuclear states had been replaced by sustained dialogue at the highest level. To Pakistan's satisfaction, the international community, in adopting UNSC Resolution 1172, had itself upheld Pakistan's consistent position that, for sustainable peace in South Asia, resolution of the Kashmir dispute was vital. But the Kargil clique was being propelled by a different mindset: diplomatic engagement with Delhi had not yielded results; hence, military force should be tried. In dealings with the Indian political leadership, Pakistani authorities were naïve and incapable of getting outstanding disputes settled. With the new army chief and a nuclearized South Asia, plus a Washington sympathetic to Pakistan's complaints against India, this was the time to take action and force the world to intervene in Pakistan's favor. Their thinking was that Washington wanted Pakistan to go for India. In the mode of the Saddam Hussain-US Ambassador Glaspie exchange in Iraq, Javed Hassan's exchanges as defense attaché in Washington had left him believing, though utterly unfounded,[24] that in case of a Pakistan-initiated military exchange with India, Washington would support Pakistan against India.

The past occasions, when perception of movement of some kind of nuclear weapons from Kahuta, had rung alarm bells in Washington, the Kargil clique saw a potential for nuclear blackmail working to Pakistan's advantage. They believed that a panicked world community, led by Washington, would instantly intervene after the impact of a successfully executed Operation KP was publicized and the newly nuclearized neighbors would be seen as being on the brink of war. India checkmated this calculation primarily by Delhi's decision to restrict Indian military response restricted to the Kargil region and by not opening new fronts. Hence, a consensus emerged within the global community, especially in the US and the EU, that a nuclear Pakistan's rash behavior, which involved forsaking of diplomatic engagement and opting for military engagement with traces of nuclear blackmail, would not be rewarded.

In conclusion, it seems that the complexity and fluidity of the world of power politics and diplomacy had escaped the Kargil planners. They were unmindful of the current strategic context. The first trip in ten years by an Indian foreign minister to China was in the works. Pakistan, by contrast, was in a difficult strategic situation. Its Afghanistan policy was under criticism and it was blamed for facilitating 'terrorism' and 'Islamic militancy'. Following the nuclear tests, it had also come under economic pressures. Perhaps the only silver lining was the beginnings of détente with its eastern neighbour. But now Pakistan had undone the détente, while India appeared to have been salvaging it.

The Kargil clique was singularly India-focused. It was passionate about settling scores with the Indians, was deeply influenced by the old hostility towards India, and also by its training, to think in linear and binary terms. They were also driven by their passion to settle scores with the Indians, their belief that Kashmir, the unfinished agenda of partition, had to be settled, and also their chronic distrust of the country's elected leadership. Cumulatively, these factors, combined with the professional experience, the personal proclivities of the Kargil clique, and their overconfidence, enabled them to launch unhindered Operation KP. The military's historic dominance in Pakistan's power structure had given its top command near autonomy of action. This reality of Pakistan's power structure, however, could not trump the logic and the dynamic of military strategy. There is always a synthesized aspect to the strategy; political, diplomatic, and economic considerations are dominant which, in effect, create space for military action. The outcome of Operation KP for Pakistan demonstrated this reality.

10) Answers to Critical and Abiding Questions About Operation Koh Paima:

Did the military inform the Prime Minister about the Kargil Operation?

There is no evidence that the Kargil clique kept the prime minister in the loop on its plan to cross over the LOC to set up dozens of posts and pickets on the Kargil heights to finally choke the Drass-Kargil Highway, essentially the lifeline to the Indian troops based in Leh. The Kargil clique's extent of secrecy for the Operation was so great that even top army commanders, including the intelligence chiefs, were kept outside the Operation KP loop. The Kargil clique did, however, keep the prime minister apprised of steps they took to respond to three specific challenges. The first was the construction of an alternate route to avoid Indian shelling in the Khel area, flying the prime minister to Khel to see the construction of the alternate route. The second was the provision of support to the Kashmiri Mujahideen in the Valley. The third was that, in March 1999, the concerned agencies gave detailed briefings to the prime minister on the ground situation of the Kashmir struggle in IOK. Beyond these briefings, there is no evidence, direct or indirect, of anyone in the Kargil clique making a presentation on Operation KP. Only in March, General Aziz had asked one of his staff officers to hand him a map that he would use to brief the PM. Such a briefing pre-17 May did not, however, take place. Subsequently, the May Musharraf-Aziz telephone recordings left no doubt that the Kargil clique had undertaken Operation KP without specific clearance from the prime minister.[25]

Beginning with the November 1998 DCC meeting[26], when the prime minister had taken the decision to provide mostly political and diplomatic support to the Kashmiri freedom fighters, it was unlikely that the Kargil clique would have reached out to the same prime minister to get his support and clearance for Operation KP. Equally, the clique would have known that getting the prime minister's support for a major operation in contested territory, just when arrangements for the Lahore Summit were under way, was unlikely. The prime minister was viewed by a section of the army high command and hard line analysts as being overly committed to peace with India, to the extent of a failing. Nawaz Sharif was, therefore, the most unlikely candidate to play a double game with India.

Did Pakistan's Intelligence Agencies Fail over Kargil?

The two agencies mandated to pick up intelligence are the Military Intelligence and the ISI. In the case of Kargil, while individuals from within the ISI and the MI both appear to have attempted to investigate, both these agencies failed to pick up anything indicating unusual troop movements as leads to the covert yet unfolding Kargil Operation. The ISI's failure meant that this cross-service agency, reporting directly to the PM, was unable to report the moves and the implications of the Kargil Operation to the government. Similarly, the MI's failure ensured that, except for the gang of four, no one within the army top brass knew of the Operation. This dual institutional failure also raised broader questions regarding the effectiveness of Pakistan's intelligence in monitoring stray and subversive Pakistani elements within the country's own defense institutions. If the remoteness of the theatre of operations prevented the ISI and MI from monitoring the crossing of the LOC, the failure to pick up unusual military and paramilitary troop movements, either of the NLI troops or the 19 Division or of the SSG, was symptomatic of a deficient intelligence setup. The ISI's defense was that it does not follow any movements, including internal troop movements; therefore, unless the army informs them about its operational plans, the ISIwill not know. Meanwhile, with ISI and MI both outside of the planning and execution loop of Operation KP, they also failed to report Indian preparations for force deployment, including troops and weapon systems, in the zone of conflict. Significantly, among other factors, this complete 'intel blindness' also ruled out all possibility of any early and pre-emptive course correction during Operation KP.

Was Pakistan militarily on a winning curve when the July fourth withdrawal decision was made?

Pakistan remained on a winning curve only until the Encounter Phase, when in early May Indian troops first discovered Pakistani troops across the LOC. That initial encounter was marked by artillery exchanges and with Indian induction of aerial power. From early June onwards, after the Indian Army command began discovering the extent to which Pakistani troops had penetrated deep into IOK, there began a graduated Indian military retaliation. Operation KP had turned into a battle. For the Indian government, Kargil had become an election period war and it had to win it at all costs. As the Indians deployed massive air power, disrupting Pakistan's supply lines, hitting logistic dumps, targeting soldiers, and generating severe psychological pressure on the Pakistani troops, the original advantage to the Pakistani troops, of being positioned at heights and enjoying lethal strategic advantage over the Indian troops climbing to attack them, began to erode. On 4 June, Pakistan lost Tololing, the first peak, to the Indians. Thereon, as they came under severe artillery and aerial attacks and faced deployment of the Bofors guns, Pakistani troops began to lose posts and pickets. Pakistani troop casualties were also on the rise. While news of Pakistan's reversals were coming through the grapevine to the Secretary Defense, the ISI chief, and even to several members of Sharif's cabinet, the Kargil clique was unwilling to acknowledge this reversal in the war theatre. Troops on the ground, while bravely battling the Indian troops, felt greatly relieved after the 4 July statement was made public. An army major fighting on Tiger Hill said that, upon hearing about it on their radio transmitter, 'We said a two *rakaat* prayer of gratitude to Allah.' Contrary to the allegations made against the prime minister that he had bartered away in Washington the military victory that the troops were winning in Kargil, the PM brought to a rapid close costly military, diplomatic, and political losses in Kargil.

Did the Kashmir cause get a fillip after Kargil?

Neither in the Valley, nor in Delhi, nor at the international level, did the Kargil Operation help to take the Kashmir issue any closer to a solution. In fact, the Operation undermined the Pakistan-India diplomatic initiative that followed the Lahore Summit. Sartaj Aziz and Jaswant Singh had earnestly begun to explore possible ways to resolve the Kashmir dispute. And it was this bilateral engagement route to resolving the dispute that the international community had always supported. In fact, ever since the passage of the UNSC resolutions, the international community has opposed the use of force by Pakistan to resolve the dispute. At the same time, the international community has also remained hesitant to push a recalcitrant and pro-status quo India, to engage in dialogue.

Kargil reinforced the already known fact that an unresolved Kashmir dispute remains the main cause of instability in South Asia. It moved the focus from the UNSC Resolution 1172, calling for resolution of unresolved issues like Kashmir, to highlighting the inviolability of the LOC.[27] For example, the Kargil crisis prompted the US to adopt as an objective, reflected in the 4 July statement, the 'sanctity' of the LOC in Kashmir.

Could the international community have forced India to buckle under Kargil pressure?

There were neither individual nor collective compulsions for key members of the international community to have even advised Delhi to enter into negotiations on any outstanding bilateral dispute. The question of any member, including Pakistan's strategic ally China, to have even advised, leave aside forced, India to buckle under the pressure from Operation KP and enter into negotiations over Siachen etc. with Pakistan, did not arise. In fact, any move likely to culminate in a military confrontation between Pakistan and India, the two hostile neighbors who had recently acquired nuclear weapons, would make the international community panic. And Pakistan had made the move—which was also being interpreted as nuclear blackmail by Pakistan. Further, Washington had already initiated its strategic relationship with India and would tend to use this opportunity to cultivate its own ties with Delhi. The State Department lobby, led by Under Secretary Karl Inderfurth, did just that. There was complete consensus within the key members of the international community, including the US, EU states, the UN, and also Pakistan's closest strategic ally, China, that Pakistan should not be rewarded for Operation Kargil. Under the Simla Accord of 1972, Pakistan and India had agreed that the LOC would not be changed by force. Accordingly, barring small and occasional cross-LOC operations that remained below the national and international radars, there had been no precedent where a cross-LOC operation by either side was acceptable to the international community. The only exception to this was the 1984 Indian occupation of the Siachen Glacier. Since Pakistan's military ruler General Ziaul Haq chose not to raise the Siachen issue at the international level, the international community was not tested on that one occasion.

Did Pakistan plan to deploy nuclear weapons in an all-out war?

Throughout the Kargil conflict, there was no active signalling by Pakistan's military command that Pakistan would deploy nuclear weapons. During Kargil, the only reference, and that too indirect, to nuclear weapons made by any Pakistani official was by Foreign Secretary Shamshad Ahmad. On 26 May, in an unguarded moment immediately after two Indian war jets flew into Pakistani territory, Shamshad had said that Pakistan would be willing to go to any extent to protect its territory. His statement was made from a fundamental principle of self-defense. Its thrust simply was that, if within the asymmetrical military power context Pakistan faced the threat of all-out war, then no option available to Pakistan for its own defense could be ruled out. In Washington, this statement was used to accuse Pakistan of intending to use nuclear weapons. From Washington, the loudest warnings and subsequent assertions of Pakistan's intended deployment of nuclear weapons came from the Clinton administration's South Asia and non-proliferation specialists, but was not backed by substantive evidence. The intense gaze of nuclear specialists on nuclear developments was liable to fanciful interpretations of sketchy information available to them; hence their illusion of Pakistan's plan to deploy nuclear weapons.

Meanwhile, for South Asian specialists already engaged in developing an Indio-US strategic relationship, this nuclear factor during Operation KP had presented Washington with a unique opportunity to bolster ties with India. On the seventh floor of the State Department sat 'Indophiles' like Strobe Talbott, Karl Inderfuth, and Bruce Reidel, reading the Kargil reports that kept pouring in. These were men who were convinced that the Pakistan military's high command had sabotaged the Lahore Summit and should not be rewarded. Pakistan had to be made to retreat unconditionally. There was, however, a realization among the 'Indophiles' that Operation Kargil provided an opportunity to Washington whose ties with Delhi were now graduating to a strategic level. If President Clinton could be instrumental in resolving for India an awkward and costly military setback in Kargil, Washington could earn credibility among those in Delhi who viewed the Clinton Administration as having pro-Pakistan leanings. Indeed, the US engagement was elevated from Under Secretary of State-level to the US President's level. While Pakistan too sought Clinton's involvement, without the nuclear bogey this may not have happened. Washington's men on the ground in Pakistan, familiar with the inside policy track during Operation Kargil, saw no evidence that signaled Pakistan's plan to deploy nuclear weapons.[28] In Washington, men like John Laughlin, Deputy Chief of the CIA looking after global affairs, confirmed that during Operation Kargil, there was no mention in Langley of any intelligence that pointed to Pakistan preparing to use nuclear weapons. Yet, the flagging in subsequent writings by US policy-makers and analysts of Pakistan's decision to use nuclear weapons seemed based less on sober analysis and more on framing Pakistan as a negative force in the regional and global context. The Kargil clique had also made Pakistan vulnerable to this negative framing.

Kargil illustratedthe paradox of nuclear weapons. While the Kargil clique's military adventure in Kargil was based on the assumption that the international community would rush to tackle a crisis between two nuclear-armed states, it was these very nuclear weapons that had a restraining impact on India. Despite pressure from retired military officers that India must take its military operations across the LOC, the existence of nuclear weapons restrained decision-makers in Delhi who decided against crossing the LOC.[29]

Washington's strategic community acknowledged 'the danger of escalation of the conflict and nuclear weapons use was one of the driving factors, probably ultimately the pivotal one, in the US diplomatic intervention that culminated at Blair House on 4 July'.[30]

Was there any nuclear blackmail during Kargil?

In the subsequent 2001 Pakistan-India military stand-off, leading Indian strategists believed that successful nuclear blackmail need not involve use or even brandishing of nuclear weapons. If the likelihood of use of weapons is established, thereby evoking the required response from an opponent, then nuclear blackmail has been successful.[31] At Kargil, there was a two-way nuclear blackmail that worked without using or indeed threatening to use nuclear weapons. The Kargil clique, while planning the Operation, had calculated that in a recently nuclearized South Asia, now on the radar of the major powers, the move of upsetting the existing LOC-specific status quo by blocking NH-1 would draw global attention. In Washington, the architects of the budding US-India strategic ties also projected as most unlikely the possibility of Pakistan opting to use nuclear weapons during Kargil. In addition to some minimal genuine fear, Washington's 'Indophiles' were keen to engage their President in the Kargil diplomacy and Clinton would have been a willing recruit if there was a clear and present danger of a nuclear war.

The Kargil clique had calculated that crisis-creation between two nuclear powers would kick in nuclear deterrence involving a third party. They believed that, six months after the launch of Operation KP, when it would be discovered, a shocked India would be faced with a fait accompli. Such a development, for fear of an Armageddon would immediately suck in Washington diplomatically. Hence, the clique had calculated that Washington's intervention would prevent direct military conflict. The Kargil planners' nuclear deterrence calculation was third-party dependent, with coercive diplomacy at its core. Without Washington's intervention, this deterrence was unworkable. As a key member of the clique later recalled, they conveyed to the country's elected leadership, 'We are holding this. Now you take advantage, whatever you can, at military and political level.'[32] However, the unfolding Kargil crisis proved the clique's nuclear deterrence calculation flawed on two counts: Operation KP did turn into a military conflict and, while Washington and other Security Council members did exercise forceful diplomacy, it was to force Pakistan to retreat from Kargil, not to reward Pakistan's operation. The spin-off of this clique's brinkmanship (read nuclear blackmail) was immensely negative. It undid the diplomatic gains accrued to Pakistan for its mature diplomatic and political moves after the nuclear tests.

Meanwhile, in Washington, Clinton's key policy men read in the unfolding crisis of nuclear South Asia an opportunity of another kind. In opting for an alarmist nuclear scenario, the South Asia and non-proliferation specialists in the White House and the State Department were able to substantively further the Clinton Administration's goal of cultivating a strategic relationship with India. In the US setup, compared to other equally qualified men, who could interpret the intelligence data available on Pakistan's readiness on the nuclear front, these 'Clintonian Indophiles' exercised license to embellish what the intelligence data actually conveyed. Harking back to the 1990 Gates Mission, they saw an opening for highest level engagement by Washington. The extended Talbott-Jaswant Singh non-proliferation dialogue had significantly contributed to Washington's conceptualization of this strategic relationship. With individuals like Talbott and Inderfuth in the lead, these men believed that inducting the US President into effectively a pro-India role would be an invaluable investment into the future of a US-India strategic relationship.

Thus, apart from the Kargil clique, it was the 'Indophiles' in Clinton's Administration who veered towards nuclear blackmail. Many observers believe that they manipulated the situation by exaggerating the likelihood of Pakistan readying nuclear weapons for use during Kargil. For example, former ambassador to Pakistan, Robert Oakley, also a close advisor of Clinton, later maintained, 'Most certainly, there was exaggeration about nuclear threat. There was nothing there…'[33]

Three factors point to deliberate manipulation. First, Pakistan was not in such a desperate military situation that it would have needed to opt for nuclear weapons. Secondly, and most importantly, Pakistan did not then have the capability to the deploy nuclear weapons[34], nor had the Indians picked any intelligence on Pakistan readying nuclear weapons. Thirdly, the Americans deliberately chose an attitude of benign neglect and ignored Indian moves to ready its nuclear missiles for use.[35] Most importantly, they achieved their objective of nuclear blackmail, which was to accelerate Delhi's slow yet ongoing move towards entering into a strategic embrace with Washington. Ironically, it was the Kargil clique that initially handed down this opportunity to Washington's 'Indophiles'; later, it was Prime Minister Nawaz Sharif who in the final phase, by seeking Clinton's cover for Pakistan's exit from Kargil, enabled Washington to build its credentials in Delhi as a reliable and trustworthy strategic partner.

Was there a pro-India tilt in Washington during Kargil?

With the Kargil blunder, Pakistan provided the Clinton Administration a priceless opportunity to invest in strategic trust-building with India. Throughout the crisis, Washington's key policy men opened multiple lines of communication with their Indian counterparts. It began with the 27 May call by Inderfurth, who called the India ambassador, Naresh Chandra, to inform him about what Pickering had told the Pakistanis. Subsequently, on 16 June, Inderfurth met with Brajesh Mishra in Cologne. After the 23 June Islamabad meetings between US CENTCOM Chief General Zinni and Prime Minister Nawaz Sharif and army chief General Musharraf, State Department official Lanpher went to brief Delhi on the Islamabad meetings. Similarly, during the crucial Sharif-Clinton summit on 4 July, in a manner unprecedented in summit diplomacy, Clinton would call Vajpayee to brief him of the summit talks. Similarly, the Indian NSA and External Affairs Minister were also updated on Sharif-Clinton talks by their counterparts, NSA Sandy Berger and Acting Secretary of State Strobe Talbott. The sole purpose was to share with the Indians every aspect of their communications with Pakistan.

Was there a role for the backchannel?

Washington's decision to maintain complete transparency with Delhi on its diplomatic and political exchanges with Islamabad had left Islamabad with no negotiating space. Guaranteed for itself a bailout by Washington and for Islamabad an embarrassing retreat, Delhi was left with no motive to engage with Islamabad. The backchannel initiative was, thus, squeezed of any possibility of success.

Was the Prime Minister's Washington dash necessary?

As the country's chief executive, Prime Minister Nawaz Sharif could have ordered withdrawal of Pakistani troops, bringing an end to Operation KP. In keeping with Islamabad's public position that the Kashmiri Mujahideen and not the Pakistani troops had seized the heights, Sharif could have announced that Islamabad would use its goodwill to urge the Kashmiri Mujahideen to return from IOK. This would have been consistent with the farcical 'Mujahideen' position Pakistan had illogically and clumsily maintained since the beginning of Operation KP. The international community would have been relieved that the battle between two nuclear powers had drawn to a close. The prime minister, however, chose to engage the Clinton Administration because he had hoped that Washington would make a public statement of support for the Kashmiris and of facilitating a political resolution of the Kashmir dispute. Sharif and his close political aides also believed that American involvement at this withdrawal stage would make it more palatable for the army high command since the army chief had himself had sought Washington's engagement. However, as subsequent developments showed, neither did the Clinton administration make any public statements supporting the Kashmir struggle, nor did the Sharif-Clinton 4 July encounter influence the post-Kargil tensions that surfaced between the elected prime minister and the army chief.

Could the Prime Minister have Ordered an Inquiry Against The Kargil Planners, Especially the Army Chief?

Immediately after 4 July, tensions began developing between Sharif and Musharraf, with each worried about his survival. Investigating the why, who, and how of Operation KP, to establish responsibility and to take action against those who had launched an operation that had ended in such a fiasco, was, however, far removed from the prime minister's mind. Civil-military coordination remained generally smooth almost throughout the Kargil period. Some briefings for the PM were held at the 10 Corps Headquarters. Most, however, were held in the PM House, where the army brass would bring its maps, etc. Often, meetings would almost take the form of the DCC but hardly any decision-making took place in these. The prime minister had, in fact, left the decision-making process during Kargil in military hands. Although Sharif had the constitutional authority to directly lead decision-making, he did not 'interfere'[36] and had simply supported the army.

The thought of holding an inquiry against Musharraf is unlikely to have occurred to a PM who had supported Operation KP. It is true that the PM was first briefed of the Operation only after it was a done deed. The PM had also declined Musharraf's rhetorical mid-stream offer to withdraw his troops from Kargil. In fact, there was written evidence of the Parliament's bipartisan Defense Committee's positive support for Operation Kargil in a letter written by the Committee chairman in praise of the army chief's presentation.

In the overall asymmetric civil-military relations in Pakistan's power structure, there have been only two incidences when elected prime ministers sought to hold army commanders to account. One was when, after the 1971 surrender at Dhaka and the breakup of Pakistan, Prime Minister Zulfikar Ali Bhutto formed the Hamoodur Rehman Commission to conduct an inquiry into the military debacle. His army chief, Zia ul-Haq overthrew him in a military coup and hanged him following legally dubious court proceedings. The second was in 1984, when Prime Minister Junejo ordered an inquiry into the deadly Ojri Camp ammunition disaster. No sooner had he announced the inquiry, the military President Zia ul-Haq sacked him.

In the absence of a political culture of holding the military accountable, the reactions of military men when held accountable, the complexities of the initiation and, indeed, of the termination of Operation KP, the fiercely anti-Nawaz mood of the political opposition, and the dominant claim of the time that Kashmiri Mujahideen had fought the Indians across the LOC while Pakistani troops fought mostly along the LOC: all these militated against Sharif conducting a Kargil inquiry. By contrast, in India, the Vajpayee-led government immediately instituted an inquiry.

Was the coup d'état inevitable?

Soon after the 4 July statement, anxiety surfaced in the prime minister's mind as well as that of the army chief—the fear of one striking a knock-out blow against the other. Despite their show of confidence, the Musharraf camp was mindful of the embarrassment Operation Kargil had caused to the institution and to the country. Sharif knew the withdrawal option was the only option, yet, his camp feared the Army's reaction. Both camps' apprehensions found expression in the local press. This further intensified the prevailing distrust.

Beyond fear, the contradictions of the Operation, Kargil produced serious frictions even in the post-Kargil phase. For example, while maintain its insistence that Mujahideen had been fighting in Kargil, how could the army receive the bodies of the martyred soldiers? Similarly, while insisting that only Mujahideen fought in Kargil, how could major programmes honouring the martyrs of Kargil be organized by the Sharif government? Most importantly, immediately after Kargil, the two camps pursued opposing agendas on India. Sharif re-engaged with Vajpayee to continue with the Lahore process. The army sought widely publicized honouring of the Kargil martyrs and of those having returned alive from across the LOC.

The US factor also figured in the power play between the two camps. Public American support of democracy and censure of extra constitutional forces (read Sharif and Musharraf) acutely deepened civil-military distrust without providing Sharif the security he hoped for. In such an environment, Sharif-Musharraf co-existence was becoming untenable.

Both sides read conspiracy in every move. That it was finally a news item regarding the removal of the Corps commander of Quetta that unraveled all the efforts Shehbaz Sharif and Chaudhry Nisar had made at peace-making between Sharif and Musharraf, demonstrated how deeply the dynamic of distrust had permeated through the relationship. After Operation Kargil, a military coup had become inevitable because the barrel of the gun, not a politically besieged prime minister, exercised the power to call the shots.

Finally, this internal power play became the proverbial last straw that brought about the coup.

Kargil and a General's Acid Test

Throughout history, the acid test of generals at war or in military operations has been the victories they have piled up. No general is more successful than the outcome of the war he leads. In more complex situations, like South Asia in the second half of the twentieth century, the yardstick for assessment has to be what have the wars have achieved. History has examples of individual brilliance leading armies to victories and steering nations away from disaster. Outstanding military commanders, such as Alexander, Khalid bin Walid, Genghis Khan, Julius Caesar, Salahuddin Ayyubi, Napoleon Bonaparte, and Vo Nguyen Giap, were men who wrested victory from situations where deep imprints of defeat were written. Bin Walid became the legendary general who, despite the numerical superiority of battle-hardened adversaries like the Romans and the Sassanids, piled up victories for the Rashiddun Caliphate. Napoleon 'inspired a ragged, mutinous, half-starved army and made it fight'[37] like a winning combination that few would fight before or after. Salahuddin, with his less experienced army, reversed the Crusaders' winning streak with his grand victory in the decisive Battle of Hattin in 1187. Julius Caesar, personally brave in battle, was creative in tactics and engineering. There was Alexander, another general facing most armies who outnumbered his own, but always remaining undefeated. Genghis Khan, a masterful general who, through excellent military intelligence and tactics and by uniting nomadic tribes and confederation and his strategic raids, became the founder of the Mongol Empire, the largest contiguous empire in history, which included most of Eurasia and substantial parts of Eastern Europe. In more recent times, the Viet Minh Commander, General Vo Nguyen Giap, who led his men to defeat a technologically superior adversary by perfecting and applying a unique war technique, which was the most important dimension of the Vietcong's overall political, economic, and diplomatic strategy for defeating the Americans.

In the Kargil operation, the performance the clique of commanders, the quality of their strategic planning, and their command, tell a different story. Yet the power equation, absence of any accountability, the absence of censure when it mattered, and bravado minus logic or sound analysis, have ruled the day. Despite repeated blunders, the commanders in charge escaped accountability.

The Indian threat and sense of having been wronged had catapulted the army of the new-born state into adopting a missionary mindset. Uppermost in their minds was the conviction that the wrong done by India in Kashmir and elsewhere had to be undone. Major General Akbar Khan, the lead military man in Pakistan's first attempt to regain Kashmir, had readily accepted Indian Prime Minister Jawaharlal Nehru's label of 'raiders' for the Pakistani forces involved in the 1947–48 'Acquire Kashmir' Operation. The former general, eulogising the Pakistani 'raiders', suggested, 'We may perhaps also qualify for sitting in that distinguished gallery of personalities like Genghis Khan, Timur Lang, Mahmud of Ghazni, and even Alexander.' Interestingly, Pakistan's senior-most general equated his own men with history's prized military leaders, who had raided, ravaged, and even reigned over foreign lands in the pre-Westphalian world. This voluntary characterization of a state's army as 'raiders', in the context especially of the Kashmir operation, flowed from the juxtaposition in this Pakistani soldier's mind, of the Pakistan Army as a force for right, dedicated to undoing the wrong committed at the time of Pakistan's creation. Subsequent moves, mostly led by Pakistan's military generals, to 'undo this wrong' through guerrilla moves and covert operations in Kashmir, reveal that this mindset remained dominant within the military's high command. Multiple factors gave sustenance to this mindset: their own Kashmir-centerd security paradigm, India's mostly recalcitrant mindset (other than at the exception of the post-1999 Lahore Summit Sartaj-Jaswant dialogue) on taking the dialogue route to resolving Kashmir, the series of covert operations conducted against each other by the two neighbors, India's systematic role in being a mid-wife to the 1971 breakup of Pakistan, and the dynamics of distrust dominating the civil-military relations within Pakistan. It has been within this overall context that the Pakistan's military leadership has planned its operations, mostly with faulty calculations or a pre-Westphalian calculus, disregarding inter-state, regional, and international implications.

The narrative passed down through the generations—the words of the father of the nation, the stories written by those who were generals at Partition, the grave faults of the Maharaja, the betrayals by the Radcliffe Commission, the Muslim killings in the Kashmir state by the Maharaja's troops, great undermining of Pakistan's security, Delhi's positioning of the Indian troops along western Kashmir—has largely stayed alive. So has the passion for undoing the wrong.

The first pushback by Pakistan, on the Kashmiri state's non-accession to Pakistan, was the provision of weapons to the first group of Kashmiris seeking help. Then onwards, in contradistinction to the Indian outreach to the United Nations to pushback Pakistan's military advances in Jammu and Kashmir, Pakistan concluded that force, not law or diplomacy, is what works.

Pakistan's battle legacy, as old as the country itself, has been India-focused. The 1947 military raid was launched within a month of Pakistan's birth, jointly by Pakistani soldiers, tribesmen, and the World War II-hardened veterans from Poonch. The 1947 raid ended in the 1948 Kashmir War. Later, the 1965 Operation Gibraltar ended, as had the 1948 war, merely leaving the Pakistani soldiers more battle-hardened.

A war comprises a plethora of components. Planning for their complexities and interrelationships requires an exceptional mind. This calculus of an exceptional mind with the capacity and the mental discipline to attend to complexity and detail is indispensable to war planning. Such competence was missing in the Kargil planners but the asymmetry within Pakistan's power structure, tilted in the army's favor, provided the space and authority to the generals with the bravado and vigour to undertake

Kargil. The planners of Operation KP gravely mishandled the strategic and logistical aspects of the military situation and entirely misread the geopolitical context in which they launched the Operation. Hence, Operation Kargil was doomed to end as in disaster. The high point of Operation KP was its opening phase but, as Clausewitz argues, 'Since in every victory there is a culminating point beyond which lies the realm of losses and defeats ... in view of all these intrinsic characteristics of war we say there is only one result that counts: final victory...'[38] Operation KP resulted in final retreat.

The Kargil planners punched beyond their weight. The key men, used to conducting operations along the LOC, having won some and lost some, were confident that they could pull off this one too. But the ill-planned Operation snowballed into a mountain battle. Neither the planners nor the soldiers were prepared for this. The Kargil clique bears much of the responsibility for its launching.

Nor did this blunder translate into a major military or political advantage around the issue for which Operation Kargil had been launched: to make gains in Kashmir or, at least, in Siachen. On Siachen, the status quo has remained intact. On the question of Jammu and Kashmir, Delhi still faces political and military challenges. Pakistan's successive battle-based attempts to settle the Jammu and Kashmir issue, the unsettled issue of the 1947 Partition, may have been foiled by India but the 'final victory' for India on Kashmir remains elusive. Nevertheless, for Pakistan, these half-planned battles have cost excessively in managing and governing the affairs of the state, politics, and society.

Repeating Mistakes

From a historical perspective, one of the most striking features of Operation Kargil was how it was a repeat of the key faulty premise on which the earlier Operation Gibraltar and Operation Grand Slam had been planned, that is, that India would not strike back heavily. In all three cases, the planners were overcome by desires and sentiments that prevented them from fully appreciating the realities. False foundations for war planning are often outcomes of well-meaning motives and objectives but are drained of the discipline of objectivity, of wholesome appreciation of the context. It is, as Clausewitz states, the taking over of the commander's mind by the 'unruly goddess' of the imagination, which strips the general of his ability to appreciate reality and, thus, ends in disaster.[39] What ends in disaster or in less than victory is only failure. In Clausewitz's words, 'The effects of genius show not so much in novel forms of action as in the ultimate success of the whole...'[40]

History is indeed our abiding teacher. It broadens understanding and strengthens critical judgment. But do we let ourselves learn from history?

Chapter 20

CONCLUSION

Repeating Mistakes

From a historical perspective, one of the most striking feature of Op Kargil was how it was a repeat of the key faulty premise on which the earlier Operation Gibraltar and Operation Grand Slam had been planned, that is, that India would not strike back heavily. In all three cases, the planners were overcome by desires and sentiments that prevented them from fully appreciating the realities. False foundations for war planning are often outcomes of well-meaning motives and objectives but are drained of the discipline of objectivity, of wholesome appreciation of the context. It is as von Clausewitz states, the taking over of the commander's mind by the "unruly goddess" of imagination that denudes the general of his ability to appreciate reality and ends in disaster.[1] What ends in disaster or in less than victory is only failure. In von Clausewitz words, "The effects of genius show not so much in novel forms of action as in the ultimate success of the whole…"[2]History is indeed our abiding teacher. It broadens understanding and strengthens critical judgment.

But in Pakistan Have We learned from History ?

The Abiding Structural Hindrance

The period from Kargil to the Coup epitomizes the inherent and continuing problems that Pakistan faces in three specific areas. These include two policy areas Pakistan-US relations, relations with India including Kashmir. There is also the third structural issue of thorny civil-military relations. While on the two policy areas of India and Kashmir, there are external players that influence the nature of the challenges that Pakistan faces, Pakistan too as an interlocutor contributes to the dynamic of the relationship. Meanwhile the structural problem of civil-military relations, rooted in the process of State formation, and the unequal stature and authority of the political and the garrison entities, evolved into asymmetrical strengths of both. Within the ensuing power chemistry of Pakistan, the army acquired a dominant role, paving the way to military coups.

This further weakened Pakistan's political class, rendering it weak and insecure. This asymmetrical relationship, within the context of Pakistan's security dilemmas including the troubled relations with India, the ongoing Kashmiri struggle for self-determination, the growing instability on its Western border with Afghanistan and the perennial distrust with the US, has acquired an overarching significance in Pakistan's decision-making structure.

The asymmetry of authority in the army's favor has continued because of the inability of most elected governments, except for Zulfiqar Ali Bhutto, to bolster its Constitutional authority through institutional decision-making. There is also the acrimony within the political class often even at the cost of undermining the democratic system. This combined with the linearity of the army's outlook and the generating of a US-backed India's increasing security pressures on Pakistan, have not strengthened the authority of Pakistan's elected governments.

During Kargil these fundamental realities were played out. Kargil crystalized the contradictions in Pakistan's decision-making process. The Kargil clique took advantage of 4 July and turned the tables on the elected Prime Minister. The inherent tensions in civil-military relations that marked the Kargil episode continue to bedevil the power structure in Pakistan; and by extension its decision-making process.

Epilogue: Lighting Matchstick in the Wind

It is impossible to escape the logic of interdependency and interconnectedness. Regardless of the games we play, no phenomenon, living or otherwise, can exist in isolation.

As a child I was told if you have matches you can light a fire. And I always believed it to be true.

Now, many years later, I find it proven wrong.

As I sit at the side of my Mother's grave I take my matches to light the incense stick but time after time the flame flickers and dies. I saw what I believed as a child to be true, proven wrong.. The wind would rise to douse the struggling flicker almost instantly.

The matchstick, like life, like politics, is also governed by the same phenomena of interdependency and interconnectedness. Inside away from the wind, supported and sheltered from the wind, the matchstick could ignite and burn bright.. But outside without the support and protection of the shelter the matchstick succumbed to the wind, flickered and died.

The lesson: Even the non-living object cannot escape the logic of interdependency, of interconnectedness.

Pakistan's political history testifies to the inescapable interconnectedness in life. Constitutional authority without a supportive context is akin to lighting matchstick in the wind.

To what degree can constitutional power be exercised is dependent on how the elected leadership determines the context in which it operates.

END NOTES

Introduction

1 Z. H. Zaidi, *Jinnah Papers*, First Series, Volume VIII, Quaid-i- Azam Papers Project, Government of Pakistan, distr. Oxford University Press, Karachi, 14.

2 Chaudhry Muhammad Ali, *The Emergence of Pakistan*, Columbia University Press, 1968, 297.

3 A. G. Noorani, 'Bilateral Negotiation on Kashmir: Unlearnt Lesson', *Criterion Quarterly*, 27 September 2013. Accessed at <http://www.criterion-quarterly.com/bilateral-negotiation-on-kaskmir-unlearnt-lesson/> .

4 ibid

5 Sardar Patel's Correspondence, Vol, 1, "New Light on Kashmir," p.32, edited by Durga Das.

6 *Selected Works of Jawaharlal Nehru,* vol. 4, pp. 346-7 quoted in A. G. Noorani, 'Bilateral Negotiation on Kashmir: Unlearnt Lesson', *Criterion Quarterly*, 27 September 2013. Accessed at <http://www.criterion-quarterly.com/bilateral-negotiation-on-kaskmir-unlearnt-lesson/>

7 *Selected Works of Jawaharlal Nehru,* Vol. 4, p.337 quoted in A. G. Noorani, 'Bilateral Negotiation on Kashmir: Unlearnt Lesson', *Criterion Quarterly*, 27 September 2013. Accessed at <http://www.criterion-quarterly.com/bilateral-negotiation-on-kaskmir-unlearnt-lesson/>

8 *Selected Works of Jawaharlal Nehru, vol. 15, part II, p.281 , quoted in* A. G. Noorani, 'Bilateral Negotiation on Kashmir: Unlearnt Lesson', *Criterion Quarterly*, 27 September 2013. Accessed at <http://www.criterion-quarterly.com/bilateral-negotiation-on-kaskmir-unlearnt-lesson/>

9 Dealt with in detail in A.G.Noorani, The Kashmir Dispute 1947-2012, pp 437 & pp 442 (Oxford University Press,2014)

10 Nehru writes that while in Karachi for talks with Prime Minister Mohammed Ali Bogra from 25–27 July 1953, he conveyed this to Bogra. (*Selected Works of Jawaharlal Nehru* vol. 23 pp 300-303) .

11 *Selected Works of Jawaharlal Nehru,* Vol. 24, 341.

12 Ibid. 347.

13 Kargil clique includes the four principal planners of Operation KP

Chapter 1

1 The first armed encounter between the Maharaja's troops and the rebel forces occurred in August 1947. Faced with a rebellion from his people, who were joined by few hundred civilian volunteers from Pakistan, the Maharaja fled to Jammu on 25th of October 1947.

2 This is taken from the Maharaja's 26 October 1947 letter to the Governor-General of India Lord Mountbatten with which he had attached the Instrument of Accession for Mountbatten's acceptance.

3 Under the Treaty of Amritsar of 19 March 1846, the British Colonial Government of India had transferred "forever, independent possession" of the Muslim majority Jammu and Kashmir state to Maharaja Gulab Singh. This territory was ceded to the British government by the Lahore state, according to the provisions of Article 4 of the Treaty of Lahore, dated 9 March 1846. Gulab Singh was to pay seventy-five lakh rupees to the British Government. In addition as an acknowledgment of "the supremacy of the British government" he would present annually to the British Government one horse, twelve perfect shawl goats of approved breed (six male and six female), and three pairs of Kashmir shawls.

4 In 1931, the people of Kashmir made their first organized protest against Maharaja Hari Singh's cruelty. This led to the "Quit Kashmir" campaign against the Maharaja in 1946, and eventually to the Azad (free) Kashmir Movement.

5 Mountbatten's acceptance letter of 27 October 1947 written to Hari Singh.

6 In *India's Commitment to Kashmir,* edited by Dhirendra Sharma, (1994), there are several statements made by Jawaharlal Nehru to the effect that the question of Kashmir's accession to India must finally be decided in accordance with the wishes of the people. These cover a period between 27 October 1947 and 7 August 1952. In one of these statements, Nehru made reference to a "referendum" and in another to a "plebiscite." (The source of all these statements is not mentioned in the publication available in Centre for Education and Documentation, Bombay).

7 Since both parties desired that the question of accession should be decided through an impartial plebiscite, the Council developed proposals based on the common ground between them. These were combined in the U.N. Security Council resolution 47 adopted on 21 April 1948, which called for a cease-fire, the withdrawal of all outside forces from the state and a plebiscite under the control of an administrator, who would be nominated by the Secretary General. For negotiating the detail of the plan, the Council established a five member commission known as "United Nations Commission for India and Pakistan" (UNCIP) to implement the resolution.

8 Following the letters of 1 January and 15 January of the governments of India and of Pakistan respectively, the UNSC adopted UNSC Resolution 39 on 20 January 1948 setting up the UNCIP to function as the operational arm of the UN dedicated to facilitating the resolution of the Jammu and Kashmir problem in line with the numerous UNSC resolutions calling for a plebiscite in the State. See resolution text for the detailed mandate.

9 When the Indian subcontinent was partitioned in 1947, the Nizam elected to resume independent status rather than join India. On Nov. 29, 1947, he signed a standstill agreement with India to last one year, and Indian troops were withdrawn. Difficulties persisted, however; the Nizam continued his efforts to assert his autonomy; India insisted that Hyderabad join India; and the Nizam appealed to King George VI of Great Britain. On Sept. 13, 1948, Hyderabad was invaded by India, and within four days Hyderabad's accession to India was achieved.

10 Sir Owen Dixon wrote "Without going into the causes or reasons why it happened. I was prepared to adopt the view that when the frontier of the state of Jammu and Kashmir was crossed by hostile elements, it was contrary to international law, and when in May 1948, units of regular forces moved into the territory of the state that too was inconsistent with international law." Dixon Report to the Security Council. UN Document General S/1791 p.8

11 Official Records(S.C.O.R): 3rd Year Supplement for November 1948, Doc. 2 pp.68-75

12 The UNSC directed the UNCIP "to study and report to the Security Council when it considers it appropriate on the matters raised in the letter of the foreign minister of Pakistan, dated 15 January 1948." S.C.O.R., 3rd Year 312th Mtg., 3 June 1948, p.21.

13 During the May 7, 1948 meeting Pakistan's representative Sir Zafaraullah Khan declared, "Pakistan would welcome reciprocal investigation, arrangements, and settlements for achieving the objectives that we have set out here." S.C.O.R., 3rd Year, No.64, 289th and 290th Meetings., 7 May 1948, p.32

14 Kashmir Dispute: US Charge' in Pakistan to the US Secretary of State, 24 September 1948. US Department of State. Foreign Relations of the United States, 1948. Volume V, part 1. Washington DC: Government Printing Office, 1975, 405-410

15 Ibid

16 Ibid

17 Ibid

18 It brought to a conclusion the 1971 military conflict which led to the breakup of Pakistan. As a consequence of the clauses pertaining to the withdrawal of forces, Indian troops withdrew from the 5,139 sq. miles of Pakistani territory in Punjab and Sindh it had occupied during the war. Similarly, Pakistani troops withdrew from 69 sq. miles of territory in Punjab and Rajasthan. In Kashmir, India retained 480 sq. miles and Pakistan 52 sq. miles. Pakistan ratified the Simla Agreement on 15 July and India on 3 August after which the agreement came into effect on August 4, 1972.

20 Point made by Professor Iqbal Cheema in P R Chari, Director of the Indian Institute of Peace and Conflict Studies, and P I Cheema, President of the Islamabad Policy Research Institute, have written a monograph entitled "The Simla Agreement 1972: Its Wasted Promise" for the Regional Centre for Strategic Studies, Colombo. 2001

20 The latest unilateral cease-fire initiated by Pakistan in November 2003 has held till now.

21 The word "hegemony" was used originally to describe the relationship of Athens to the other Greek city-states that joined it in an alliance against the Persian Empire. "Hegemony" in this case "mean[t] that [Athens] organized and directed their combined efforts without securing permanent political power over the other[s]. Gramsci used the term hegemony to denote the predominance of one social class over others (e.g. bourgeois hegemony). This represents not only political and economic control, but also the ability of the dominant class to project its own way of seeing the world so that those who are subordinated by it accept it as 'common sense' and 'natural'.

22 For example, Indian scholar Sumit Ganguly in *India-Pakistan Tensions since 1947 (New Delhi: Oxford University Press, 2002)* argues that "Congress and the League had markedly divergent organizational strategies and also

espoused different ideological goals. The organizational and ideological base of the two parties was diametrically opposed and thereby embodied competing visions of nationalism and state-building. Consequently, the two emergent states were already locked into a potential collision course after the demise of the British empire."

23 In 1999, the former Indian Director General Military Operations Lieutenant General V.R. Raghavan argued in his Frontline Web service column (5-18June 1999) that Indian capture of heights around Kargil in 1965 was necessary to prevent Pakistan from making the Kargil-Leh road unusable for long periods through incessant artillery firing.

24 Among others acknowledged by Robert Wirsing in India, Pakistan and the Kashmir Dispute (New York: St. Martin's Press, 1994), pp 150-52

25 See Indian General Jack.Farj.R Rafael Jacob's book Surrender at Dacca.(Manohar Publishers & Distributors , New Delhi-1997) Jacob was a major general in 1971 and served as COS of the Indian Army's Eastern Command.

26 Sumit Ganguly acknowledges this in his book *India-Pakistan Tensions since 1947 (New Delhi: Oxford University Press, 2002)*, pg 84.

27 For detailed and well documented account of the Indian position on the Boundary Agreement expressed by Nehru publicly and in meetings with Ayub Khan read A.G. Noorani's article Facing the Truth , Frontline Issue 20: 7-20 October 2006,
(http://www.frontline.in/static/html/fl2320/stories/20061020001608500.htm) On 5 March 1963 the Indian Prime Minister Pandit Jawaharlal Nehru while criticizing the Agreement acknowledged Pakistan's control of the Siachen area as he stated "In fact the Pakistan line of actual control ran along no definite natural features, but cut across the tributaries of the Shaksgam River and sometimes lay half way up the slopes. It then reached the Karakoram Pass." Infact as the Pakistan-India negotiations began Nehru's statement in the parliament acknowledged Pakistan's control over the Siachen area. He said "On May 3rd and 4th May that three days ago simultaneous announcements were made by the government of Pakistan and China to the following effect. They said that the former boundary between China's Sinkiang and the continuous areas the defense of which is under the control of Pakistan had never been delimited and demarcated in history….I do not know-sounds rather an opportunistic attempt to take advantage of a particular position, even though this might involve changes in the well-known boundary which has been known to exist for a long time...we have made it perfectly clear even in the past, both to the Pakistan government and the Chinese government about those parts of the frontier now in possession of Pakistan that we would not recognize any arrangements arrived at between them and Pakistan." (Pakistan government records) On 10 May 1962 Indian government protested through a written note dated May 1962 which specifically acknowledged Pakistan's area up to Karakoram Pass. It read "the Ministry of External Affairs present their compliments to the High Commission of Pakistan in India and have the honor to state that according to a communiqué issued by the government of Pakistan on 3rd May 1962, the Governments of Pakistan and China have agreed to enter into negotiations to locate and align that part of the boundary between India and China West of the Karakoram Pass, which is presently under Pakistan's unlawful occupation."

28 Fedarko, Kevin, in The Coldest War (Outside Magazine February 2003) writes that between 1974 and 1981, Pakistan issued permits to about 16 major expeditions from Japan Austria, UK and US," for climbing up to Siachen. https://www.outsideonline.com/1912811/coldest-war

29 General Raghavan in *Siachen: Conflict without end(2002) recalls this.* Also according to Pramila N. Phatarphekar in The Colonel Who Got Us Siachen,(in the magazine Open) it was in 1978 that Colonel Narinder Kumar as commandant of the High Altitude Warfare School in Gulmarg, saw a US map that placed Siachen in Pakistan. http://www.openthemagazine.com/article/india/the-colonel-who-got-us-siachen

30 Colonel Narinder Kumar..recalls for Fedarko, Kevin, in The Coldest War , Outside Magazine February 2003. https://www.outsideonline.com/1912811/coldest-war

31 Fedarko, Kevin. The Coldest War, Outside Magazine February 2003. https://www.outsideonline.com/1912811/coldest-war

32 ibid

33 6 May 2000, the Dawn correspondent in *Former Indian General seeks peace with Pakistan* reports that "While replying to a question on the Siachen glacier, he says the world must recognize the truth behind the issue. Lt-Gen Jehan Dad Khan (retired) of Pakistan has mentioned many hidden truths of the issue in his book published in 1999. The general claims that Siachen was an un-demarcated area and India came to know in 1978 that some enterprising agent in Pakistan was pursuing mountaineering expeditions there. He alleges that many

developments that followed indicated a Pakistani desire to occupy the area in May 1984. And India occupied the place on 13 April 1948, in order to prevent the alleged occupation of Siachen by Pakistan.

34 For the Indian version of what led to India's 1984 Operation Mehgdoot read Lt genral M.L. Chibber in Siachen, The Untold Story : A Personal Account , India Defense Review 29 July 2017, (http://www.indiandefensereview.com/spotlights/siachen-the-untold-story-a-personal-account/)
and Maninder Dabas Siachen Glacier was going to Pakistan, then Came this Bull Who Saved it for India in India Times, 13 December 2016 https://www.indiatimes.com/news/siachen-glacier-was-going-to-pakistan-then-came-this-bull-who-saved-it-for-india-267352.html

35 Siachen Issue (Internal Document) July 2004 , General Head Quarters , Pakistan Army, Rawalpindi.

36 In his interview to *Defense Journal* Lt Gen (Retd)Imtiaz Warraich who was Deputy Chief of Army Staff (from early 1989 to July 1991)and FCNA commander from 1982 to 1984, acknowledged,"No intelligence report ever mentioned of any enemy activity at Zing-Rulma which on the map we thought belongs to us…Unfortunately, due to comprehensive planning by the Indian Army at an exceedingly high cost, both of logistics and manpower, succeeded. Our higher Intelligence agencies failed to provide early warning of the impending debacle." (Pakistan Defense Journal, October 2001).

37 Lt. General Chibber's arguments that he "was alarmed to learn that the Pakistanis were accompanying mountaineers to the glacier. Just as troubling were maps printed in the West. They showed Siachen as part of Pakistan. By the early 80's, both armies were sending expeditions into the area, and suspicions accumulated like fresh snow. In late 1983, the Indians became convinced the Pakistanis were about to seize the glacier, General Chibber said. This was inferred from intercepted communiqués. If further evidence was needed, he said, it came when India sent procurers to Europe to buy cold-weather gear. They ran into Pakistanis doing the same shopping."

38In a detailed account of the Indian view read Lt genral M.L. Chibber in Siachen, The Untold Story : A Personal Account , India Defense Review 29 July 2017,
http://www.indiandefensereview.com/spotlights/siachen-the-untold-story-a-personal-account/

39 In the same interview, Lt Gen (Retd) Imtiaz Waraich acknowledged, "Beyond this point it was difficult to go because of excessive snow and so we returned." (Pakistan Defense Journal, October 2001).

40 The Ladakh scouts are trained mountain warriors with experience in high-altitude and white-out operations. Their primary role is to guard Indian borders in the high altitude areas of the Ladakh region and Jammu and Kashmir as well. The Ladakh scouts,a 4000 strong paramilitary unit of local Bhuddhists and Tibetans commandoes, have participated in all wars fought in India since independence.

41 Siachen Issue, MO Branch GHQ, July 2004

42 Lt. Gen Jahan Dad Khan, Pakistan Leadership Challenges,pg 224, Oxford University Press(OUP), Karachi. 1999

43Ejaz Haider, Siachen the Facts, Express Tribune 13 April 2012,
https://tribune.com.pk/story/364237/siachen--the-facts/

44 As told by one of the two pilots who flew the helicopters, Colonel Muhammad Farooq Altaf to Kevin Fedarko field editor of *Outside* Magazine. See 'The Coldest War' by Fedarko in *Outside* Magazine, February 2003

45 Named after the divine cloud messenger in a Sanskrit play

46 In interviews conducted by the author with former military officers, it became clear that sections within the Pakistan Army leadership believed the Indian occupation of Siachen was also encouraged by the Russians. They argued that the Soviet Union wanted Pakistan 'punished' for the trouble its Afghan policy was causing to the Soviet Occupation forces in Afghanistan.

47 Explained by Feryal Gauhar in her article Wild Roses Dawn, 22 April 2012
https://www.dawn.com/news/1141375

48 This included the navy and air force leadership. Earlier only the army leadership was involved in the developments related to Siachen. Confirmed by participants of the two meetings.

49 Interestingly, many references made to earlier Kargil plans notwithstanding, no written plan documenting a Kargil operation exists either at the FCNA or in the Military Operations Directorate. All references also are restricted to conversations and suggestion but point to no detailed written plan. The former prime minister Benazir Bhutto had talked of such a plan being presented to her by General Pervez Musharraf when he was Corp Commander 1 Corps. Also former COAS Jehangir Karamat had publicly referred to such a plan.. The Kargil opportunity was first conceived in the late seventies during General Ziaul Haq's time. Benazir Bhutto said that,

as Prime Minister, she too was given a briefing by General Pervez Musharraf, who was than Corps Commander Mangla with Javed Hasan was his CO of 19 Brigade.

50 Every winter, the few Pakistani posts at the glacier were vacated by the Pakistan Army.

51 The assumption was that the Indians would leave their posts in winter and return in the summer months

52 Foreign minister and General Sahibzada Yaqub Khan to the author

53 Indian scholars too acknowledge this. See Summit Ganguly, *India-Pakistan Tensions since 1947 (New Delhi: Oxford University Press, 2002)*

54 For attempts made by Pakistan after 1984 to militarily occupy positions in area beyond point NJ9842 & India's reaction see Brigadier Javed Hussain's informative article of 22 April 2012 'The Fight for Siachen' published in the daily Express Tribune. https://tribune.com.pk/story/368394/the-fight-for-siachen/ For Pakistan's official position on the trajectory of Siachen conflict read retired brigadier Mahmud's article The Madness of Siachen appeared in Dawn 13 April 2012 https://www.dawn.com/news/710074

55 For details, see A.G Noorani's Review Article, *The Siachen Impasse Frontline(Volume 19-Issue 23) 9-22November 2002*

56 For an incisive first-hand account from the glacier zones read environmentalist and peacenik Faryal Gauhar's brilliant article Siachen, the place of Wild Roses." Gauhar wrote this article after the April 2012 Gayari catastrophic avalanche which left 124 soldiers, including 5 civilians, dead.
https://www.dawn.com/news/1141375

57 Former Commander 10 Corps General Jamshed Gulzar, during an interview to the author on 28 March 2008 at his residence in Rawalpindi

58 Ibid

59 Interesting since, as per rules, there exists a National Military Operation Center, where in war time the Supreme Commander i.e. the President sits with the CJSC and the three services chiefs. Practically all plans should come to the Joint Staff headquarters but now they come only when forces other than the army are required in an operation.

60Major Tariq Khan (who later retired as Commander 5 corps) shared this with the author in a conversation on 6 January 2018. According to Lt. General Tariq he recalled his 1990 assessment not because it necessarily influenced any military thinking but merely illustrates how even a young officer could see the flaws of a only-Kargil operation.

61 Former army chief confirms to the author.

Chapter 2

1 In his 2 April letters to the world leaders, including President Clinton, the Pakistani prime minister warned that he had "every reason to believe that Indian policy pronouncement connotes a giant step towards fully operationalizing Indian nuclear capability." Sharif warned them, "Pakistan will be obliged to take cognizance of these alarming developments, and it cannot but exercise its sovereign right to adopt appropriate measures to safeguard its security." Pakistan's ambassadors in all the major countries were asked to issue a demarche to their hosts that India would conduct a nuclear test.

2 Office of the Press Secretary, May 13, 1998

3 USIA Washington File, May 11, 1998

4 Office of the Press Secretary, May 13, 1998

5 Reuters, May 13 1998

6 Steve Coll, *Ghost Wars*, p. 394. Penguin Press, New York 2004

7 Ibid, p.386

8 http://news.bbc.co.uk/2/hi/world/west_asia/37021.stm

9 Coll, Steve *The Ghost Wars* Penguin Press, pg 380 New York 2004

10 Al-Zawahiri, *Knights Under the Prophet's Banner* (quoted in Coll, Steve *The Ghost Wars* Penguin Press, pg 383 New York 2004)

11 For details on the attack plan and why it was aborted, Steve Coll, *Ghost Wars, (Penguin Press, New York 2004)* p. 394-396.

12 A British defense expert Bristo has already pointed out on BBC the impossibility of Washington not being pre-warned about India's nuclear explosion.

13 Weiner and Risen, *"Policy Makers, Diplomats, Intelligence Officers All Missed India's Intentions,"* New York Times, May 25, 1998

14 Ibid
15 ECO summit on May 10-12, 1998
16 https://www.youtube.com/watch?v=hcu6-EGCtGA
17 ibid
18 John F. Burns, *NUCLEAR ANXIETY: THE OVERVIEW; PAKISTAN, ANSWERING INDIA, CARRIES OUT NUCLEAR TESTS; CLINTON'S APPEAL REJECTED, The New York Times, May 29, 1998*
http://www.nytimes.com/1998/05/29/world/nuclear-anxiety-overview-pakistan-answering-india-carries-nuclear-tests-clinton.html
19 IRNA, May 28 1998; Reuters, May 28, 1998
20 Pakistan's nuclear tests. Statement made by H.E. Prime Minister Muhammad Nawaz Sharif at the Press Conference held in Islamabad on 28 May, 1998 in
nuclearweaponarchive.org/Pakistan/SharifAnnounce.txt
21 ibid
22 See http://news.bbc.co.uk/2/hi/world/monitoring/103085.stm. Yet, at varying degrees, two issues concerned the Israelis; one was Pakistan's status as a Muslim country; two, as Israeli government spokesman David Bar-Ilan told Voice of Israel radio, Pakistani nuclear tests "might encourage Baghdad and Tehran to acquire nuclear weapons". Israel feared the transfer of Pakistan's nuclear technology to Tehran was possible was possible given Iran's "greater proximity" to Pakistan and hence "more threatening accessibility" to the latter's nuclear technology.
23 Adil Najam, *"American Reaction to Pakistan's Nuclear Weapons Tests"*
24 Bhutto, Zulfiqar Ali. *The Myth of Independence , 1967*
25 See account of the meeting in Steve Wiessman, Herbert Krosney, *The Islamic Bomb (NewYork:NewYork Times Books Co. 1981)* pp 42-48.
26 Aga Shahi to the author in March 2002.
27 For detailed discussion read A.G.Noorani Bilateral Negotiation on Kashmir: Unlearnt Lesson in Criterion Quarterly Articles, Vol 1 No 1 http://www.criterion-quarterly.com/bilateral-negotiation-on-kaskmir-unlearnt-lesson/
28 Japan offers to host Indo-Pak talks, Reuters, 7 August 1998.
http://www.tribuneindia.com/1998/98aug08/world.htm#1.
29 ibid
30 ibid
31 ibid
32 *Permanent-5 Joint Communique on the Indian-Pakistani Nuclear Crisis*, Geneva June 4, 1998
33 ibid
34 Judy Aita, UN MEMBERS DEPLORE PAKISTAN'S NUCLEAR TESTS, May 28, 1998
http://archive.li/AlAcc
35 There were four NS-Gujral meetings. After the meeting, the indication of continuing dialogue was clear. In an interview with the author in August 9 2002 at his Delhi residence, the former prime minister recalled the couplet he had read to the press after their meeting, "*Guftago bund na ho, baat sai baat chalay...*"
36 Sartaj Aziz in an interview with the author. Also see, A. G.Noorani *Truth About the Lahore Summit,* in Frontline Volume 19 - Issue 04, Feb. 16 - Mar. 1, 2002
37 Ibid. Also interview with India Today
38 According to Sartaj Aziz, after Wisner left, Sharif said to him that as a Punjabi, no one would doubt his (Nawaz) commitment to Pakistan
39 Significantly this suggestion was not part of the original draft response put together by the Foreign Office. Instead the lines regarding revival of talks were added on his Finance Minister Sartai Aziz's suggestion.
40 Foreign secretary level talks broke down in January 1994 as Pakistan claimed India refused to engage on the K-issue.
41 Taking note of this in the Congressional Committee Hearings, Under Secretary of State Robin Raphel said "We were encouraged by Pakistani and Indian moves toward dialog, starting with the upcoming Marchforeign secretaries meeting. We and many other well-wishers hope both countries will take full advantage of this opportunity to resume a serious high-level dialog."
http://commdocs.house.gov/committees/intlrel/hfa43264.000/hfa43264_0.htm

42 The defense secretary decided to go on leave starting 13 October. On 14 October his resignation letter was delivered to the Chief Martial Law Administrator General Pervez Musharraf. On 21 October (Pl REMOVE IFTIKHAR WRITTEN HERE) Musharraf accepted his resignation and heard of his retirement over the television

43 A.G.Noorani, *The Siachen Impasse* Review Article, *Frontline* http://www.hindu.com/thehindu/thscrip/print.pl?file=20021122000207000.htm&date=fl1923/&prd=fline&

44 For details on Pakistan-India talks on Siachen, see A.G.Noorani's review article which appeared in Frontline http://www.hindu.com/thehindu/thscrip/print.pl?file=20021122000207000.htm&date=fl1923/&prd=fline&

45 Talbott, Strobe. *Engaging India*,. Washington,D.C., 2004. 114-115.

46 The Press Statement on Pakistan-India Relations by Pakistan at the end of the talks on July 13 summed up Pakistan's version of the foreign secretary level talks. It stated: "Pursuant to the directive of their prime ministers, the Foreign Secretaries of Pakistan and India have met twice on 29 and 30 July, 1998 to overcome the procedural as well as substantive impediments to the resumption of Pakistan-India talks. It has not been possible for them to reach an agreement. As such the Pakistan-India dialogue remains stalemated and no progress has been made in Colombo." http://www.fas.org/news/pakistan/1998/07/980731-pak-press.htm

47 Text of Prime Minister Nawaz Sharif's Speech, *The Nation*, Lahore. 30 July 1998

48 Ibid

49 With Additional Secretaries Tariq Altaf and VivakKatju as note-takers

50 Vajpayee was joined by Principal Secretary Brajesh Mishra and Nawaz Sharif by Foreign Minister GoharAyub and Foreign Secretary Shamshad Ahmad.

51 Sharif's aides advised him that no joint statement which does not acknowledge the centrality of Kashmir and which does not support the composite dialogue framework could be acceptable.

52 The bureaucrats were clear that given the international community's advocacy for a Kashmir dialogue Pakistan had to remain firm on no dialogue without a working group on Kashmir.

53 The statement issued by Pakistan at the conclusion of the talks acknowledged that "it is expected that the prime ministers will have their next meeting at the sidelines of the NAM Summit in Durban, South Africa." http://www.fas.org/news/pakistan/1998/07/980731-pak-press.htm

54 John F Burns, India and Pakistan Fail to Narrow Differences, The New York Times , Augusts 1, 1998, http://partners.nytimes.com/library/world/asia/080198india-pakistan.html

55 By Los Angeles Times, Pakistan, India halt attempt at ending feud Three days of talks fail to bridge difference over Kashmir border dispute, 1 August 1998 http://articles.baltimoresun.com/1998-08-01/news/1998213013_1_kashmir-india-pakistan. Also see CRS Report for Congress India-Pakistan Nuclear Tests and U.S. Response
Updated 24 November 1998 http://congressionalresearch.com/98-570/document.php/

56 Rifaat Hussain, Pakistan's Relations With Azad Kashmir & Impact on Indo-Pakistani Relations, in Prospects for Peace in South Asia (Stanford University Press, 2005) pg 130; Editors Rafiq Dossani, Henry S Rowen.

57 PAKISTAN WARNS INDIA AFTER KASHMIR SHELLING, The Washington Post, August 3, 1998, https://www.washingtonpost.com/archive/politics/1998/08/03/pakistan-warns-india-after-kashmir-shelling/d507307f-d571-406e-8b95-aafd21377251/?utm_term=.071447d96745
http://articles.baltimoresun.com/1998-08-01/news/1998213013_1_kashmir-india-pakistan

58 Asia Watch & Physicians for Human Rights , Rape in Kashmir, A Crime of War, https://www.hrw.org/sites/default/files/reports/INDIA935.PDF ; Global Press Institute,Mass Rape Survivors Still Wait for Justice in Kashmir, 7 March 2012 http://news.trust.org//item/20120307023000-i7m26/

59 Served as Deputy Secretary of State from 1994 to 2001.

60 Talbot, Strobe. *Engaging India*. Washington, D.C., 2004. 108

61 Ibid

62 Ibid

63 http://www.aljazeera.com/indepth/interactive/2013/09/201391014244467318 4.html

64 Vajpayee's reproach was direct and hard. He said, "Let me say this loud and clear that there is no place for any third-party involvement in this process, howsoever well-intentioned." PTI, 3 September 1998 http://www.tribuneindia.com/1998/98sep04/head.htm

65 Hasan, Khalid. *Kashmir Chronology*. 48.
http://www.infopak.gov.pk/public/kashmir/kashmir-chronology.htm

66 Sumita Kumar, Trends in Indo-Pakistan Relations https://www.idsa-india.org/an-may-02.html

67 For an Indian critique of BJP policy, see Murlidharan, Sukumar. *Nuclear Issues: The aftershocks.* Frontline magazine, June 20-July 03,1998

68 The MEA thinking on the Dhaka formula versus the Composite Dialogue Framework was accurately reflected in Indian journalist Amit Baruah's article *Raising the Stakes,Frontline* magazine, 20 June to 3 July 1998. He wrote, "Kashmir may be a priority for Pakistan (as it has always been), but it cannot be put on a par with peace and security in South Asia."

69 *Vajpayee rebuffs Mandela, Says no to mediation on Kashmir*, Press Trust of India, 3 September 1998 http://www.tribuneindia.com/1998/98sep04/head.htm

70 Ibid

71 Ibid

72 Sartaj Aziz in an interview with the author. He was present in the meetings.

73 Clinton's meetings in New York with Nawaz Sharif and Vajpayee. See Talbott, Strobe. *Engaging India* and Shamsha-Talbot talks.

74 Misra had started as an editor of *Patriot*, a left wing paper. Significantly his back-channel engagement with Pakistan dated back to 1969 when the Indian Prime Minister Indira Gandhi had set up an Apex group consisting of P. N. Dhar, Haksar and Mani Dixit. Misra was possibly the most well-informed person on the Indian polity. India's top leadership ranging from the Congress, BJP and individuals like I. K. Gujral and Narasimha Rao all sought his advice. In the nineties Mishra was the editor of the *Business and Political Observer*. He was particularly close to Vajpaee and a political advisor of the business tycoons the Ambaanis.

75 Shahryar Khan and Niaz A Niak were also considered

76 He had brain cancer.

77 *Pakistan tables nuclear offer*, 24 September 1998. http://news.bbc.co.uk/1/hi/events/asia_nuclear_crisis/latest_news/179088.stm

78 Ibid

79 *And then Mullah Omar screamed at me.* http://www.spiegel.de/international/spiegel/spiegel-interview-and-then-mullah-omar-screamed-at-me-a-289592.html, 8 March 2004

80 Two different accounts of the meeting given by the Saudi Intel chief himself. *And then Mullah Omar screamed at me.* http://www.spiegel.de/international/spiegel/spiegel-interview-and-then-mullah-omar-screamed-at-me-a-289592.html, 8 March 2004 Katz, Mark N. *Prince Turki on Osama Bin Ladin.* http://katzeyeview.wordpress.com/2011/12/26/prince-turki-on-osama-bin-laden/

81 However, on 27 May fierce street battles broke out between the Taliban and Malik's forces. The Taliban, unused to urban warfare, were soundly defeated, with thousands losing their lives either in battle or in mass executions afterward. On 8 August 1998, the Taliban re-captured Mazar-i-Sharif.

82 Saudi Arabia's recognition came the following day.

83 *And then Mullah Omar screamed at me.*http://www.spiegel.de/international/spiegel/spiegel-interview-and-then-mullah-omar-screamed-at-me-a-289592.html, 8 March 2004

84 Conversation with the author in October 1998

85 Lt Gen (Retd) F.S.Lodhi, in *General JehangirKaramat* recounts what General Karamat said at the Naval War College and how a section of the media covered it. http://www.defensejournal.com/nov98/genjehangir.htm

86 *Shut up, or else.*TFT, Dec 12-18, 1997, Vol-IX No.41 — Editorial. http://www.thefridaytimes.com/editorials/Book4%20(1997-99).htm

87 In 1989, the elected Prime Minister Benazir Bhutto had awarded the medal of democracy to the army chief General Aslam Beg. He had succeeded military dictator and army chief General Ziaul Haq. Beg had conducted elections and seen the return of democracy. However two years after Benazir's election, Beg supported dismissal of Benazir on corruption charges.

88 *The stuff of history.* TFT, 31 July 6 Aug, 1998 Vol-X No.22 — Editorial. http://www.thefridaytimes.com/editorials/Book4%20(1997-99).htm

89 'Accountability is here to stay'. *TFT*, May 02-08, 1997 Vol-IX No.9 — Editorial. http://www.thefridaytimes.com/editorials/Book4%20(1997-99).htm

90 This section on the Siachen talks has largely been informed by A. G. Noorani's Review Article on *Siachen: Conflict* Without End,by Lt.-Gen. V.R. Raghavan, The Siachen Impasse The Frontline, 22 November (Vol:19

Iss:23). See for the most comprehensive review of the seven rounds of Pakistan-India Siachen talks from 1989 to 1998, http://www.frontline.in/static/html/fl1923/stories/20021122000207000.htm

91 Indian journalist A.G.Noorani quotes these statements in his column based on the Voice of America recording of the joint presser.

92 Following Indian press reports, the COAS General Karamat called the FCNA Commander Brigadier Javed Hasan to ask him if in fact the FCNA forces were actually launching such attacks. Subsequently in October, the new COAS asked the Commander 10 Corps Lt. General Aziz if Musharraf also asked the CGS (Aziz) Aziz.

93 Ibid.

Chapter 3

1 During the Kargil War in 1999, General Aziz Khan was serving as the CGS under General Pervez Musharraf. Secret recordings of alleged conversations between General Musharraf and General Aziz were apparently "intercepted" by the Indian intelligence during the Kargil Campaign. Said recordings proved that Pakistan Army had secretly invaded Kashmir.

2 Mahmud was promoted to Lieutenant General in June 1998, and posted by GeneralJehangir Karamat, then COAS, as Commandant, National Defense College. On taking over as the COAS in October, 1998, General Musharraf brought him as Commander 10 Corps replacing Lieutenant GeneralSalim Haider who proceeded as Corps Commander Mangla. Mahmud was posted, after the coup, as DGISI, in place of Lieutenant GeneralZiauddin Butt.

3 There were 13 NLI battalions in 1999., a 14th battalion was raised after the Kargil operation. Each battalion had 700 persons.

4 Second line forces like the rangers and scouts

5 Technically loaned to the NLI

6 . This includes all other ranks uptil junior commissioned officers (JCOs). Raised from the local population of the Northern Areas, their inclusive composition draws in troops from all castes/sects. For eg includes i.e. Shia, Sunni, Ismailis, Noorbakhsi,.etc.

7 Brigadier Javed Hassan was the Defense Attaché from 1 February 1995 till October 24, 1997

8 Ibid

9 In an interview to the author

10 10 Major General Javed Hassan in an interview with the author

11 To the author during May 10, 2003

12 Ibid

13 As recalled by several senior officers during their interviews with the author. Also publicly admitted on the floor of the Senate by Senator retired general Javed Qazi headed the Inter-Services Intelligence from 1993 to 1995 and Military Intelligence from 1990 to 1991

14 Thrust of several officers who were his juniors or others who were under his command during the Kargil Operation

15 A named given to this Indian post by the Pakistani troops deployed on the LOC.

16 According to his core staff in an interview with the author

17 In the 16 SP (Self-Propelled) Regiment.

18 Former army Chief Jehangir Karamat in an interview to the author

19 Shuja, Nawaz. *Crossed Swords.* Karachi, 2008. 511.

20 Ibid

21 Praveen, Swami. *Skeletons in the Cupboards.* August 19, 2009 http://www.thehindu.com/todays-paper/tp-opinion/Skeletons-in-the-Generalsrsquo-cupboards/article16530736.ece

22 Pakistan's army comprises a total of ten corps. Corps are divided into the offensive corps and defensive corps. The offensive corps is not deployed in the area of their responsibility but are stationed in the cantonments. They are typically static, in peacetime are used for other tasks, have reserves for offensives, their own contingencies and their own routes etc. 1 Corps headquartered in Mangla is an offensive corps meant to provide offensive covers to the Ravi-Chenab Corridor. Similarly, 31 Corps located in Bahawalpur is also offensive. The defensive corps, meanwhile, are deployed along their areas of responsibility. The seven defensive corps in the Pakistan Army are the 2 Corps, the 4 Corps, the 10 Corps, the 11 Corps, the 12 Corps and the 30 Corps that looks after the Sutlej Ravi corridor.

23 This essentially meant that the NLI budget came from the Interior Ministry

24 Hasan, Brigadier Javed. *The fight for Siachen*. 22 April 2012. http://tribune.com.pk/story/368394/the-fight-for-siachen/

25 GSO I Operations Colonel Nisar Ahmad had been an instructor at the Command & Staff College Quetta and has served as Military Observer in Bosnia in 1993-1994. In Bosnia, he was in an unfortunate car accident in which a woman died. He was sent back as PNG but Nisar wrote to the UN authorities asking that he be punished more severely since sending him back as PNG was not sufficient given that a woman had died at his hands.

26 Grade 1 referred to as G-1 and is a Lt Colonel rank officer.

27 Explained to the author by an officer directly involved in the planning.

28 A Note for Consideration for the chief was prepared. The standard NFC has analysis, options and recommendations. The MO Directorate prepared it, sent it to the chief of general staff (CGS), who endorsed it and went to the chief. The input for the NFC came from the MI, ISI and the 10Corps. Subsequently MO conferences reviewed the situation and gave the 'green signal'. MO also recommended that the prime minister be informed.

29 As recalled by several military officers, this explanation was given by members of the Kargil clique to those who noticed some unusual troop movement.

30 These were confirmed by the two reports given by the Indian 'rebel' officers to their COs.

31 Ziaul Haq grabbed power from the elected Prime Minister Zulfikar Ali Bhutto through a coup d'état.

32 NH1 also supplies Ladakh, where India has its own separate territorial/border dispute with China. Cutting off resupply for Ladakh would be a serious matter given the need to replenish food and other supplies over the brief summer season.

33 The other alternative track the Indian Army had begun constructing was the Drass-Sanko-Kargil track.

34 The core team comprised of Chief Staff (COS) Brigadier Imtiaz, Colonel General Services/Operations Colonel Azhar Hussain and Col Administration/logistics Colonel Mahmud Ali.

35 Recalled to the author by a GSO based at the 10 Corps headquarters during the planning phase of Op KP.

36 Author's interviews with key men overlooking the operational aspect of Kargil

37 Author's interviews with senior army official present in these discussions

38 FCNA commander to the author on May 10, 2003

39 FCNA commander to the author on May 10 2003

40 Confirmed by the then FCNA commander in 2003, by the brother of the former Prime Minster in July 1999 and by a civilian minister of the Nawaz government in September 2004. The Operation commander confirmed to the author that after his troops had crossed the LOC and saw "open points in the LOC I ordered plug the gaps. I said go across if we can go, we can come back, but I said you should go."

41 The later version of a few in Pakistan that the Operation KP was launched because of the unusual Indian move to not withdraw its forces from the area during winter was factually incorrect.

42 The FCNA Commander to the author on May 10, 2003

43 Sartaj Aziz, Pakistan's Foreign Minister (1997-99), in an interview with the author.

44 Talbott, Strobe. *Engaging India*,. Washington,D.C., 2004. 109

45 http://www.washingtonpost.com/wp-dyn/articles/A17798-2004Mar23.html

46 Among the Taliban

47 Indians saw this as a Helsinki-Oslo kind of interaction. The groups would also discuss the forbidden questions, primarily Kashmir as well as nuclear stabilization)

48 Member of Vajpayee government National Security Advisory Board and until 1986 the Vice Chief of Naval Staff - Commander-in-Chief South.

49 According to Admiral Nayyar in the 14 August 2002 interview with the author , Vajpayee was not hopeful that Nawaz Sharif would accept this offer. Nevertheless he agreed that it be made. Not clear whose idea was this. Tariq Fatimi also confirmed this offer to the author.

50 Nayyar said that Pakistan was already in default to the World Bank and to Pakistan had taken loan from IDB ("…25million dollars at 15%")

51 Admiral Nayyar to the author

52 Admiral Nayyar and Tariq Fatimi to the author

53 World Bank, Report and Recommendation of the President of the International Bank For Reconstruction and Development to the Executive Directors on A Proposed Structural Adjustment Loan, 28 December 1998. Report No. P-7284 Pak

54 ibid

55 http://www.gpo.gov/fdsys/pkg/WCPD-1998-12-07/pdf/WCPD-1998-12-07.pdf

56 In implying responsibility for "all the misperceptions that existed in Pakistan-US relationship, Nawaz Sharif entered the league of his predecessors and successors, including military ruler general Musharraf and the elected President Asif Zardari, who all seemed comfortable placing themselves virtually in culpable modes.

57 Bhutto was widely criticized for his policy of nationalizing private industries. It proved damaging for growth of industry, discouraged private investment and also failed to benefit the labor class.

58 ibid

59 ibid

60 Chaudhary Nisar to the author on Sept 11, 2004

61 Confirmed by senior Pakistani diplomats in attendance during the trip.

62 President Clinton briefed Pakistani Prime Minister Nawaz Sharif on US efforts to compensate Pakistan for the $658 million it paid for the 28 F-16s. US officials said the United States has already paid $157 million of this back to Islamabad, raising the money by selling aircraft components to other countries. At the end of 1998, the United States announced it would pay Pakistan $326.9 million in cash and up to $140 million in grains, to settle the eight-year dispute.

63 Based on discussions with Pakistani officials including Ambassador Riaz Khokhar

64 The White House Washington: Memorandum of Telephone Conversation between President and Prime Minister Nawaz Sharif, 18 December 1998 Declassified Clinton Library Photocopy

65 Passed on 8 December 1998. UNSC Resolution 1214:
http://www.un.org/en/ga/search/view_doc.asp?symbol=S/PV.3952

66 UNSC Resolution 1214: http://www.un.org/en/ga/search/view_doc.asp?symbol=S/PV.3952

67 Saddam's Iraq: Key Events: Iraq Under Sanctions 1991-2002: Desert Fox 16-19 December 1998 http://news.bbc.co.uk/2/shared/spl/hi/middle_east/02/iraq_events/html/desert_fox.stm

68 The White House Washington: Memorandum of Telephone Conversation between President and Prime Minister Nawaz Sharif, 18 December 1998 Declassified Clinton Library Photocopy

69 ibid

70 Shamshad Ahmad, Tariq Fatimi and Tariq Altaf

71 The drafting team from Pakistan comprised of the Foreign Secretary Shamshad Ahmad. Additional Secretaries Riaz Mohammad Khan and Iftikhar Murshid and Director-General Salman Bashir. The Indian drafting team from the Ministry of External Affairs, consisted of Joint Secretaries Rakesh Saood and Vivak Katju

72 Confirmed by two members of Pakistan's drafting team, to the author in separate interviews. First the idea of working out a non-aggression pact was verbally proposed by the Indians and the Pakistanis asked for details. The following morning Rakesh Saood handed over a hand written draft to the Pakistanis. The Pakistanis had the document typed with their own amendments. Pakistanis specifically mentioned that a non-aggression pact would be premised on peaceful settlement of all bilateral issues especially Kashmir. The Indians after seeing the Pakistani-amended draft asked the Pakistanis to first sell it in Islamabad before the Indians could sell it in India. The Indian team was clearly testing the waters.

73 Rakesh Saood in the drafting team, who was very close to his Foreign Minister Jaswant Singh, had initiated this with Jaswant Singh's blessings. More importantly Indian policy moves on Pakistan have always flowed from well-coordinated and fully thought-through planning. There is no evidence to the contrary in the history of India-Pakistan relations.

74 The former ISI chief general Ashraf Qazi as a Senator publicly stated this on the floor of the Senate.

75 Documented in Zahid Hussain's FrontLine Pakistan The Struggle With Militant Islam, Columbia University Press , August 2008.

76*Sharif's sectarian nemesis.* TFT, Jan 23-29 1998, Vol-IX No.47 — Editorial

Chapter 4

1 Abbas, Hasan. *Pakistan's Drift Into Extremism.* London, 2005. 171

2 The account of this meeting is based on an eye witness account shared with the author by a middle-rank army officer who was part of the Commander FCNA's core team.

3This unit set up after the 1971 military debacle, was mandated to monitor the forces and conduct specially assigned operations. Although effectively a network of counter and counter-counter intelligence was spread across the entire agency, within its different sects secretariats3 this particular unit was meant to be the eyes and ears for the Supreme Commander. It was originally authorized to prepare classified reports on unusual developments within the forces and, bypassing the DG ISI and the army chief, directly send them to the prime minister. However after the 1977 coup led by Ziaul-Haq, the coup-maker inserted the army chief as the channel through which the COD would send reports to the President or the prime minister3.

In a set up where every officer's movement and communication was closely monitored through the corps, the GHQ and the intelligence network of the armed forces, it was unlikely that the extraordinary movement of units and troops would not be picked up. According to one source, who claimed to be a key man in the special unit and also the co-author of the report, it was around early November, that this special unjt's field network flagged information about the movement of troops and about an unusual level of interaction between members of the Kargil clique.Since the author was unable to confirm the veracity of this information , the account of this report has only been foot-noted.

This lead man in the special unit feared repeat of a Zaheer ul Islam Abbasi type episode. Brigadier Abbasi had conceived a Siachen operation with his own brigade and without clearance of the higher command. So, to get a clearer picture, with his colleagues, the head of the unit arrived in Skardu on a plausible pretext (to evaluate land to be purchased for a ski training center).

At Skardu, there was unusually heavy air traffic and movement of men and weapons. They came across formations of out of area regiments, the Sindh Regiment and the Frontier Forces Regiment. Transit camps had been put up, those normally put up for a major exercise, but no exercise was planned. Men from the spy agency visited Gilgit, Chilas, Kalam, and Naltar and picked up enough evidence and chatter to observe that an unusual operation was underway. Information was gathered from the FCNA headquarters as well.

For the unsuspecting, it all added up. Soldiers of various formations were told by their senior command that this was an exercise within Pakistan's own area. An exercise was underway and the usual information was being gathered to be passed on after evaluation and analysis to the GHQ or to the chief.

Back at the headquarters at the end of November, unit's lead man, in complete secrecy and hidden from all his colleagues, began compiling a report. Armed with information on troop movement, deployments, surveys, and his unit's reconnaissance, the lead man discovered that an operation that involved crossing the LOC was under way. He had personally been involved in the evaluation of an earlier incarnation of the operation across the LOC into Kargil. In December, he sat down to prepare a detailed report on the operation, now surreptitiously under way. He divided the 104 page document in two sections, the strategic and the tactical. With sufficient data on the current operation and his awareness of the critique of the earlier Kargil plan, he completed his solitary undertaking by the end of December. The report outlined the strategic reservations.

Following standard operating procedure, the author sealed the report in a white envelope using red tape. He met the army chief at the golf course to hand him the report to be passed on to the prime minister. Musharraf accepted the white envelope without asking any questions. But, within two days, the author received a coded message summoning him to meet with Musharraf immediately. They met at a neutral venue. The chief told him that he had read the report but was surprised that the author was familiar with the earlier Kargil plan. Musharraf nevertheless said he was pleased that the report was written. He also indicated that the prime minister had seen the report and had appreciated it. The overall takeaway for the special unit was that those conducting the operation would remain mindful of the suggestions given in his 104 page report. Later, the author was asked by the GHQ to come and observe the operation. He politely declined, citing a conflict of interest since he had already detailed the strategic risks involved in undertaking the Operation.

4 For reliable and detailed account, see Gauhar, Altaf. *Ayub Khan Pakistan's First Military Ruler*. Lahore, 1994.

5 In interviews with the author as late as 2004 some senior army officers still insisted there was no mention of Kashmir in the Lahore Declaration; others said it was included after the military leadership insisted it be included. General Pervez Musharraf claimed that the first draft of the Declaration prepared by the Foreign Office did not mention Kashmir and he personally got the word Kashmir included. All FO officials involved in the drafting of the Lahore Declaration deny this. Also a section within the establishment felt that the '"bus diplomacy would induct dormancy within the civilian political scene" regarding the Kashmir cause.

6 Confirmed by military sources in interview with the author that there was no discussion of gaining any direct negotiating leverage over Kashmir. They maintained that the operation was not designed with these objectives because such an objective was never discussed during the planning meetings held at the Military Operations wing of the GHQ. The thinking that accompanied the expanded operation, which was prompted by the opportunity that stared them in the face, was not necessarily discussed beyond the top key planners is quite possible.

7 According to key individuals within Pakistan's top military hierarchy in their interviews with the author during and after the Kargil operation.

8 A senior commander to the author "I did not want a repeat of Siachen."

9 The local forces could include 70 and 114 brigades or the 6 and 8 brigades of the Northern Command located inside Kashmir.

10 12 Div commander General Ashfaq Pervez Kayani and Chhamb Jaurian 23 Div commander General Taj ul Haq…

11 Based on interviews with participants of the meeting & with General Pervez Kayani

12 In 1989 when Indian Prime Minister Rajiv Gandhi was asked the same question at the Benazir-Rajiv press conference in Islamabad by the Editor of The Nation Arif Nizami, Rajiv had responded in the negative.

13 The notion of a pre-Pakistan united India.

14 Governor's House reception, Feb 21

15 It organized major and violent demonstrations in Lahore and attacked cars carrying diplomats to the State banquet. Hundreds of policemen ordered out by the chief Minister of Punjab handled them very firmly. The author's car was also attacked.

16 I was among the journalists covering the banquet. There were roadblocks in major areas and some of us ended up traveling with diplomats to the venue. Sitting in the Turkish ambassador's car, we were attacked with sticks and rods. When the front screen of the car was smashed, we stopped the car to reprimand these young men.

17 For example, the army leadership believed that the original drafts of the Lahore documents did not mention Kashmir. Senior army command insisted that Kashmir as an issue figured at the Lahore summit only because they promplted the foreign office that it be raised at the summit. This was repeated to the author in interviews conducted with the top military brass .\ This was factually incorrect. Clearly there was miscommunication within the army ranks itself. The army chief said to the author in an interview on May 9, 2003 that far from initiating a process to resolve Kashmir at the Lahore, the original Lahore Declaration did not even have the word Kashmir there. He insisted that Foreign Secretary Shamshad Ahmed knew this and he would conform it..

18 Parthasarthy, G. *Memories of Pakistan in David Page Diplomatic Divide.* New Delhi 2004. 109

19 Told by Shehbaz Sharif, Nawaz Sharif's brother and Chief Minister Punjab(1997-1999) and Foreign Minister Sartaj Aziz to the author.

20 Ibid

21 Nawaz Sharif told Vajpayee that if he did not move to resolve the dispute within 12-18 months, he would have to go for elections and Vajpayee's "would have lost a chance to resolve Kashmir."

22 As recalled during interviews with the author by Prime Minister Nawaz Sharif, the foreign minister and senior Pakistani officials as well as by the Indian PM's close confidantes including Vajpayee's media advisor/speech writer Sudheendra Kulkarni, former Vice Vhief of the Indian navy Naval KK, Nayyar, National Security Advisor Brajesh Mishra

23"Fiscal Year 2000 Budget," Secretary of State Madeleine Albright, Testimony before the Senate Foreign Relations Committee, 24 February 1999, US Department of State, <http://www.state.gov>.

24 The other four were Bomb (national security), Bus to Pakistan (peace with neighbors), Bihar (protection to Dalits and ending the politics of criminalisation), Budget (sound pro-people and pro-India economic policy) and Betrayal (the Congress-led Opposition's disregard for the 1998 mandate). Advani said speaking to the media at the conclusion of the party's National Executive meeting in New Delhi on May 2,1999. See Venkatesan, V. *The BJP's trauma.* Frontline Volume 16 - Issue 10, May. 08 - 21, 1999 http://www.frontline.in/static/html/fl1610/16100080.htm

25 *PTI Report: PM defends bus trip to Lahore*, The Tribune, Sunday 18 April 1999. http://www.tribuneindia.com/1999/99apr18/nation.htm#3

26 According to senior military officers, the operation began with 200 and by the end the number occupying all the posts was between 2000 to 2400

27 Interviews with key planners and some officers involved indicated that pressures of logistical operational stretch did emerge from these secondary sector movements. The NLI chief recalled that he had raised the need to reinforce presence in the "primary gain area" of Drass-Kargil and also in the secondary sector. According to him the field unit commander and the brigade commander both were confident that they could manage an expanded operation in the secondary sectors. That even if the stretch occurred, it would be in the South and that it could be managed. Instead operational stretch did surface. The Pakistani unit commander and the brigade commander knew these were auxiliary movements in the secondary sector. The NLI chief said he had told the unit and brigade commanders to reinforce there but they said they were fine-even if stretched it's the South from where Indian were unlikely to deploy troops.,

28 On completion of this Leh-Manalee road, Indian troops would have an alternative route available to Leh reducing both Indian dependence on NH1 and Indian vulnerability to Pakistani interdiction. For Pakistan, a functioning Leh-Manalee road would have decreased the strategic advantage they had over India because of the access they had over India's sole communication channel to Leh.

29Military Police

30 A figure quoted in interviews with the author by several military officers involved in either planning or participating the operation. This figure was also quoted by ministers and senior Pakistani diplomats

31 First engagement with the enemy was projected 5-6 months after the troops had begun to move in the extremely hostile terrain and weather. In May the Indians first discovered the troops.

32 Plans and arrangements for a defensive battle were always there, with defensive formations of 323 Brigade, also called the Siachen Brigade defending the LOC, 62 Brigade headquartered at Skardu deployed in Olding Sector covering Shyok and Pune areas, 12 Division deployed opposite Drass, Kargil and Pune

33 Colonel to the author

34 Most details on cross-LOC transportation of supplies based on author's interviews with troops involved in the Operation. Also see Gill, John H. *Military Operations in Kargil* pp 98-99 in Lavoy, John. *Asymmetric Warfare in South Asia.* Cambridge University Press, 2009.

35 Based on interviews with FCNA HQ staff, Directorate Military Operations, troops in posts across the LOC

36 According to military officer-eye witness account.

37 Aziz, Sartaj, *The Kargil Crisis in Between Dream & Realities*. Oxford University Press (2009), 253.

38 Aziz, Sartaj, *The Kargil Crisis in Between Dream & Realities*. Oxford University Press (2009), 253-4

39 ibid

40 Jaswant told his counterpart clearly said that he would deny having had this conversation if any thing of this becomes public.

41 Sartaj Aziz believed this would help to narrow down to problem the valley and the two three districts of Jammu.

Chapter 5

1This Corps was raised by the British in 1916 with headquarters in Port Said in Egypt. After independence, the Corps was re-raised in 1955 at Udhampur and made responsible for the security of complete state of J&K. Subsequently on raising of HQ Northern Command the Corps shifted to its present location at BadamiBagh, Cantt Srinagar in 1972.15 Corps also known as "Chinar Corps", derives its name from the formation sign of a Chinar leaf with a battle axe on it. It is responsible for the securing the Line of Control from infiltration.

2 The most comprehensive and credibly sourced account of these reports and the Indian high command's response is Praveen Swami's'Skeletons in the Generals' Cupboards', *The Hindu*, Aug 10th, 2009 http://blogs.thehindu.com/delhi/?p=27639

3 Praveen Swami, 'Resolving the Kargil Conundrum', The Hindu , 6 May 2006

4 ibid

5 Praveen Swami, 'Resolving the Kargil Conundrum', The Hindu , 6 May 2006

6 Praveen Swami's'Skeletons in the Generals' Cupboards', *The Hindu*, Aug 10th, 2009 http://blogs.thehindu.com/delhi/?p=27639

7 ibid

8 Based on interviews with Pakistani military officers closely associated with the Operation. Also see accounts in Gill John H, "Military Operations in Kargil" in Lavoy, John.*Asymmetric Warfare in South Asia* (Cambridge University Press, 2009), 102-3

9 Dinesh Kumar, 'Kargil War 15 Years On', *Tribune*, Sunday, 20 July 2014, Chandigarh, India, http://www.tribuneindia.com/2014/20140720/pers.htm#1

10 Gaurav Sawant & Muzamil Jaleel,' Pakistan pounds Srinagar-Leh Highway', *Indian Express* June 1, 1999.

11 As narrated by participant in the meeting.

12 Statesman News Service. Army Braces to Pounce on Kargil Raiders *The Statesman* May 15,1999

13 Special Correspondent, *The Hindu* May 14, 1999

14 Statesman News Service. Army Braces to Pounce on Kargil Raiders *The Statesman* May 15,1999

15 Statesman News Service. Army Pushes Out Raiders From Kargil *The Statesman* May 17,1999

16 Dateline Jammu, Drass Population Evacuated, Tribune News Service , *The Tribune* (Chandigarh) May 16, 1999

17 Dateline Jammu, Tribune News Service Drass Population Evacuated, *The Tribune* (Chandigarh) May 16, 1999

18 Rain damper on army push', *Daily Telegraph,* June 1, 1999

19 Army beats back Pak Infiltrators, HTC , New Delhi, *Hindustan Times* May 17, 1999; Statesman News Service. Army Pushes Out Raiders from Kargil, *The Statesman* May 17, 1999

20 Statesman News Service. *The Statesman* May 15, 1999

21 Special Correspondent, *The Hindu* May 14, 1999

22 Dateline Jammu, Tribune News Service , Drass Population Evacuated *The Tribune* (Chandigarh) May 16, 1999

23 Dateline Jammu, Tribune News Service , Drass Population Evacuated *The Tribune* (Chandigarh) May 16, 1999

24 Kumar,Dinesh, Kargil War 15 Years On , *The Tribune*, Sunday, 20 July 2014, Chandigarh, India,
http://www.tribuneindia.com/2014/20140720/pers.htm#1

25 Ibid

26 Praveen Swami, The Bungle in Kargil , *Frontline*, Issue 13, June 19 -July 02, 1999
http://www.frontline.in/static/html/fl1613/16130040.htm

27 Kumar, Dinesh, 'The air was rare, but the IAF's feat rarer' *Tribune*,
http://www.tribuneindia.com/2014/20140720/pers.htm#2

28 According to press reports the minister began tour of the area on May 11.

29 *The Hindu* May 15, 1999 [Please elaborate]

30 Praveen Swami, The Bungle in Kargil, *Frontline*, Issue 13, June 19 -July 02, 1999
http://www.frontline.in/static/html/fl1613/16130040.htm

31 Parthasarthy was speaking at the Pakistan Institute of International Relations in Karachi. The daily *Dawn* of May 18,1999 carried a report entitled "Indian Envoy Rules Out Full Scale War"

32 Pakistan Army Captures Held Kashmir Village', *The Nation*, May 15,1999

33 India Moves Heavy Weapons to Pak Border'[please provide link and article/news story title]

34 Parthasarthy was speaking at the Pakistan Institute of International Relations in Karachi. The daily *Dawn* of May 18 carried a report entitled "Indian Envoy Rules Out Full Scale War"

35 Discussion on the surprise factor in chapter 8 'Surprise at the top of the world: India's systemic and intelligence failure' of Peter Lavoy's edited book Asymmetric Warfare in South Asia(Cambridge University Press 2009) while being insightful on India, is a bit removed from reality where the utility of surprise for Pakistan is concerned

36 In his May 31, 1999 Comment "No Need for New Pressure Points" in the Indian daily *The Pioneer* India's former Vice Chief of Army Staff Lt. General V.K.Sood reflected the army's reading. Spelt out the likely military dimensions of the 'intrusion' plus the Indian military response which should include the army and air force.

37 Ibid

38 Ibid

39 In his May 31, 1999 Comment "No Need for New Pressure Points" in the Indian daily *The Pioneer* India's former Vice Chief of Army Staff Lt. General V.K.Sood reflected the army's reading. Spelt out the likely military dimensions of the 'intrusion' plus the Indian military response which should include the army and air force.

40 Key member of the Operational team at the FCNA Headquarter

41 The author's own writings throughout the Kargil operation were premised on the assumption that the mujahideen, supported by the Pakistan Army, had conducted the Operation.

42 India Launches Major Offensive In Kargil'. (Associated Press report)*The News* May 17, 1999.

43 India's Kargil Crisis. Published by Directorate General of Films and Publications, Ministry of Information & Media Development, Government of Pakistan (early June 1999), pg. 1.

44 India Moves Heavy Weapons to Pak Border', *The News*. May 16 1999
45 LOC Firing Violation of Lahore Declaration, *Dawn* May 16,1999
46 Pakistan first proposed the Strategic Restraint Regime for South Asia to India in October 1998.It composed of three main elements: stable deterrence, proportionate reduction in the armed forces and a peaceful resolution of all lingering disputes.
47 According to Niaz Naik, Pakistan's lead man in the dialogue
48 The ambassador met with Karl Inderfurth and Thomas Pickering.
49 Recalled by the Ambassador in an interview with the author.
50 Singh, Jaswant, *India At Risk: Mistakes, Misconceptions and Misadventures of Security Policy*. Faridabad, 2013. 185
51 Ibid

Chapter 6

1 According to an MO army officer
2 Told to the author by the military planners.
3 *In the Line of Fire*, General Pervaiz Musharraf
4 The defense secretary to the author on 27 May 2007.
5 The accounts of these meetings were confirmed by the participants of these meetings, civil and military. It includes the prime minister, the defense minister, army and ISI officials.
6 Recalled by the intelligence chief to the author in September 2007
7 Pointed out to the author by senior officer within the DMO and the R & Analysis wing of the GHQ
8 Former army chief Jahangir Karamat, during whose tenure this cell was set up, explained to the author that the cell was first headed by brigadier Khalid Kidwaiand it later evolved into Strategic Plans division. Interestingly, another Lt Colonel Ashfaque Pervez Kayani posted in the cell later rose to become army chief.
9 Recalled by the Lt Colonel himself on 29 November 2006. He subsequently retired as a brigadier from the SPD.
10 Subsequently appointed the deputy chief
11 He narrated this during in 1978 in a lecture he delivered at the Quetta Staff and Command College.
12 It included corps commanders, formation commanders, principal staff officers, Inspector General Frontier Corps(Baluchistan)
13 The account of this meeting is based on interviews with several participants including Generals RafiAziz Khan, Qadir Baluch, and Brigadier Nadeem Ahmad.
14 The Generals who specially raised questions were Lt. General Jamshed Gulzar Kayani, Lt. General Abdul Qadir Baluch, Lt. General Niazi and Major General Akram.
15 As recalled by Lt. General Jamshed Gulzar(20 March 2008) and several others who participated in the meeting .
16 Significantly a leading Pakistan daily *The Nation* wrote in its May 17 editorial that Pakistan's own forces were fighting in Kargil.
17 Details of this meeting are based on author's interviews with several ministers, bureaucrats, and generals who attended the meeting. These included foreign minister Sartaj Aziz, Foreign Secretary Shamshad Ahamd, Defense Secretary Lt. General Iftikhar Ali Khan, army chief General Musharraf, CGS Aziz Khan, CO NLI Major General Javed Hasan, NLI General Aziz Khan, Director ISI Lt. General Jamshed Gulzar)
18 Lt. General Jamshed Gulzar, who was a Director in the ISI, in an interview with the author on 26 April 2008.
19 Lt. General Jamshed Gulzar, who was a Director in the ISI, in an interview with the author on 26 April 2008.
20 As told by a participant to the author.
21 ibid

23 Recalled by numerous participants of the meeting in their interviews with the author.
24 General Gulzar to the author in an interview on 20 March 2008
25 ibid
26 Genera Shahid Aziz, Putting our children in line of fire Published in The Nation, 6 January 2012
27 Several participants of the meeting recalled to the author.
28 Confirmed by three different participants of the meeting.
29 Confirmed by military and civilian sources who attended the meeting and also those close to Nawaz Sharif.
30 The CGS said this to Nawaz Sharif during the meeting.
31 Recalled by numerous participants of the meeting in their interviews with the author.

32 Recounted by several participants in the meeting including Ministers, generals and senior bureaucrats,
33 Confirmed by the civilian ministers and bureaucrats who attended this meeting.
34 ibid
35 Some of the participants were unclear if Nawaz had earlier given a green signal for Koh Paima. However many present, including the military men, the ISI and even the Defense Secretary had heard about the operation only on that very day.
36 Recalled by the Defense Secretary.
37 The meeting details, as recalled by the Secretary of Defense. I tried to cross-check this account with the PM and the army chief , who neither denied nor confirmed it. However, the circumstantial evidence, especially how the PM went along until mid June, diplomatically and politically supporting the operation and linking it to the Kashmir issue, would confirm this exchange.
38 Chaudhary Shujaat to the author
39The deputy chief of the Air Force was one of those who questioned.
40 According to several participants present in the meeting.
41 Recalled by several participants including Minister for Religious Affairs Raja Zafarul Haq, Foreign Minister Sartaj Aziz, Foreign Secretary Shamshad, and Addl Secretary Riaz Mohammad Khan.
42 ibid
43 It was a point that had been discussed institutionally with the Foreign Office before the 23 May meeting.
44 Recalled by several participants of the meeting.
45 Recalled to the author by an additional foreign secretary who attended the meeting.
46 A point made in a meeting with the author by the Minister Raja Zafar ul Haq.
47 Several participants in the meeting who recalled in meetings with the author that this concern had been flagged after the meeting.
48 Significantly a leading Pakistan daily *The Nation* also wrote in its 17 May editorial that Pakistan's own forces were fighting in Kargil. The editorial coincided with the comprehensive 16 May military briefing given to the prime minister and his team at the ISI by the army leadership.
49 Confirmed by US ambassador Milam and some senior Pakistani military generals
50 Briefing to the author by DG ISPR Rashid Qureshi
51 US ambassador William Milam in an interview with the author on 21 October in Washington
52 US ambassador William Milam in an interview with the author on 21 October in Washington
53 In his interview with the author the former MI chief [Lt. General Ehsan ul Haq denied having acknowledged Pakistani presence. To the contrary he recounted that when the British defense attaché pointedly asked him during the Q & A of the number of Pakistani troops present cross the LOC, MI chief's response was none. Nevertheless the stories of defense attaches who had been briefed by the MI chief , regarding Pakistani troop presence remained in circulation.
54 Confirmed by several participants of the meeting.
55Served as foreign minister from 1997 till August 1998
56 Account shared by several participants of the meeting including ministers and bureaucrats. Also see account in Urdu Digest August 1999
57 Recruits in the Northern Light Infantry came from Bajaur agencies
58 Lt. General Jamshed Gulzar, who was a Director in the ISI, in an interview with the author on 26 April 2008.
59 ibid
60 FCNA commander claimed credit for "setting up the network to misguide and for deception. Indians were therefore kept in the dark on who they were attacking." Referring to the formal decision to publicly call the NLI as mujahideen he said he "was disturbed when the order was passed in May."
61 FCNA Commander General Javed Hasan to the author on 10 May 2003. He said "I got orders from the GHQ that our troops should go in civvies". He found the decision questionable but did not know who issued the orders. He said despite being upset with the decision "how could I resign or leave my troops."
62 By late-May or early-June, the India media had begun publishing these stories. See Mody, Anjali. *UK Mujahideen join Kashmir Jihad: Mercenaries getting hefty amounts for duty in Kashmir.* Indian Express June 1, 1999; Burke, Jason. *More Than 40 Camps sponsored by ISI on Pakistan side of the LOC have turned out militants recruited from Kashmir and middle east countries-Thousands trained in ISA camps were paid 5200 for 3 month stint'*, Indian Express June 1, 1999
63 The key ISI interlocutor in an interview to the author.

64 Told by the US ambassador Milam during an interview in October 2003 with the author. Subsequently confirmed by a senior foreign office official dealing with the Kargil crisis.
65 As witnessed by the author this was the official position consistently adopted by the DG ISPR, Pakistan foreign officials and also by the Foreign Minister Sartaj Aziz. At the Delhi presser on 12 June 1999 he adopted this position in the face of aggressive questioning by the Indian media on why had Pakistan Army crossed the LOC
66 Told to the author by senior military and foreign office officials present at the briefings.
67 This Cell was set up in September 1996 with major general Ahsan Saleem Hyat as its first Director General with a staff of two brigadiers and a Lt colonel.
68 A junior officer from the Cell recalled while in conversation with the author on 29 November 2006.
69As recalled by the Lt colonel to the author.
70 Text of 26 May and 29 May telephone conversations between the army chief Musharraf and the CGS gen Aziz http://watandost.blogspot.com/2006/09/jaswant-singh-on-kargil-conflict.html
71 Pakistani military base virtually on the LOC
72 FCNA Commander Javed Hasan at the January Skardu briefing. Told to the author by the FCNA commander.
73 ibid
74 Head of Kashmir & Afghan affairs in ISI
75 The FCNA commander Major General Javed Hasan to the Head of Kashmir & Afghan affairs in the ISI
76 Various Indian writers have written about the Indian Army's failure. For example India's leading defense reporter & analyst Praveen Swami illustrates the point using example in his articles 'Skeletons in the Generals' Cupboards', *The Hindu*, Aug 10th, 2009 http://blogs.thehindu.com/delhi/?p=27639 ; Praveen Swami, It is time for the truth about command failures during the Kargil war to be made public http://blogs.thehindu.com/delhi/?p=27639 ; Praveen Swami, 'Resolving the Kargil Conundrum', The Hindu , 6 May 2006
77 Violation of this ban, Mahajan said, would be severely punished by the governments in the State and the Center.
78 Nawaz Sharif to the author at the PM House in mid June 1999
79 Wilson John, India Launches Air Strikes; Operation Vijay in Kargil: 200 Mercenaries, Pak Troops Perish, *The Pioneer*, 27 May 1999
80 Special Correspondent, Atal dials keep-off Kargil message to Sharif, *Telegraph* 26 May 1999
81 Express News Service, Kargil may be cleared by airpower: Vajpayee, *Indian Express* 26 May 1999
82 ibid
83 ibid
84 ibid
85The *Watershed* is a ridge, like that formed by a chain of mountains, which sends water to two different rivers on either side.
86 The Indian press reports reflected this fact. For example Shishir Gupta in his 20 May 1999 Hindustan Times story 'Pakistan Army had crossed LOC' wrote "Although Defense Minister George Fernandes sought to platy down the Kargil situation by saying that the was more than equipped to tackle the scenario, it is apparent that it would take quite some time for the Army to evict the intruders." Vikram Jit Singh in his 28 May 1999 Indian Express report '4 captured Armymen likely in PoK' wrote "An officer and three soldiers of the 4 Jat are believed captured and taken across by the infiltrators to POK while two more officers and soldiers are missing in action in the Drass sector…toll on the Army's side mounted to 121 dead, wounded and missing." ; HT Correspondent in his 24 May 1999 Hindustan Times story 'Malik in Kargil for spot assessment: High ridges still under control of intruders, exchange of fire continues' wrote " The sources believe that given the difficult terrain , the eviction operation could take some time as the Indian troops will have to literally wrench the Pakistani intruders from the heights they occupy….the Army (Indian) will have to counter heavy artillery fire from a geographically and logistically advantageous position held by the other side."
87 This thinking was articulated by the prime minister and his foreign minister. For Vajpayee's thinking see Editorials 'Talking Terms' Times of India June 1, 1999 and 'Cool Indica,' *Indian Express* 1 June 1999 . For the FM see Jyoti Malhotra, 'Aziz Visit on, gloves are off,' *Indian Express* 1 June 1999
88 Statesman News Service, 'India Agrees to Sartaj Visit for Dialogue' *Times of India* 1 June 1999
89 According to Clause of the Simla Accord, neither side could change the status quo unilaterally.
90 For example, the articulate Information Minister Mushahid Hussain declared that "If the UN can act in Kosovo it can act in Kashmir" and that to diffuse the crisis "the onus was on the bigger power." The Foreign Office

spokesman Tariq Altaf said "Kashmir is at the heart of the matter" and "the international community should meaningfully engage."

91 ibid

92 Pakistan's continuous refrain that Kashmir is a nuclear flash point.

Chapter 7

1 Recounted by participants of the meeting, including the foreign minister, interior minister, foreign secretary, etc. Also reflected in the 26 May telephone conversation between the army chief who was visiting Beijing and the chief of general staff who had called him from Rawalpindi. Reservations by senior civilian and armed forces personnel were recalled by CGS Lt. General Aziz as he reported back to the army chief in their telephone conversation. Musharraf on a visit to Beijing was speaking to Aziz on an unsecured line - see Appendix I Transcript of Musharraf-Aziz Conversation

2 Statements made by Pakistani officials and reported in the local press between 27 and 29 May. Islamabad maintained that hawks [Please clarify] were filling the Indian political space, that Indian Army brigades had begun moving along the LOC since September and that India was using human shields in Kashmir to protect its gun placements.

3 No Objection Certificates (NOC)

4 Discussed in Chapter 4

5 Alluding to the bus trip that Indian Prime Minister Vajpayee made by bus from Amritsar to Lahore. According to the FCNA Commander, and other senior military generals at another operational briefing at the GHQ the prime minister also remarked that "*Mazaay kee baat keh aap Srinagar chalaey ja'ain.*" The FCNA commander claimed he said that "the force ratio was in India's favor." In early May, at another briefing in Rawalpindi, military men recalled the PM saying, "This won't be resolved through a bus. You just go to Srinagar."(*'Bus say nahin hul ho ga. Ab aap bus Srinagar ja'ain.*") None of the civilians confirmed this.

6 Recalled to the author by the army chief general Musharraf and the FCNA commander Major General Javed Hassan.

7 Raja Mohan, 'Onus on Islamabad' *The Hindu*, 29 May 1999. Mohan argued that the Indian attempt was to blame the leadership of the Pakistani armed forces for seeking to undermine the peace process initiated at Lahore by the two prime ministers. He maintained that the statement followed the meeting of the Cabinet Committee on Security. He held, "It was a carefully calculated move to sharpen the differences between civilian and military elements in Pakistan."

8 ibid

9 For a detailed account: Strobe Talbot's *Engaging India; Diplomacy, Democracy & the Bomb*, Brookings Institution Press, Washington DC, August 5, 2004

10 Quiet diplomacy had earned Indian government press criticism. See 'MEA Plays the Proverbial Ostrich', *Statesman* 26 May 1999

11 On 24 May when Vajpayee perhaps got the complete details of the Operation, he first established telephone contact with his Pakistani counterpart.

12 Reiterating the significance of the declaration, at a joint press conference, the Russian foreign minister said, "Tthe principles of that declaration, expected to be signed at a Russian-Indian summit later this year, will become the 'foundation for cooperation in the 21st century.''. Russia and India also called for an immediate stop to NATO bombing of Kosovo, called for a political solution to the crisis, emphasizing the significance of their bilateral relations within the context of regional stability, and for the creation of a "multi-polar world". For details see 'Moscow, Delhi to sign cooperation declaration' web edition of *Asia Times On-Line 28* May, www.atimes.com/c-asia/AE28Ag02.html

Yeltsin talks to Jaswant Singh- *The Tribune* Wednesday 26 May 1999 www.tribuneindia.com/1999/99may26/world.htm -

14 Express News Service 'George meets Opposition Leaders, Heads of US, UK missions in *Indian Express*,' 27 May 1999

15 Jyoti Malhotra, 'Aziz Visit on, 15gloves are off,' *Indian Express* June 1, 1999

16 The ambassador met with Karl Inderfurth and Thomas Pickering.

17 Thomas Pickering Under Secretary of State for Political Affairs (1997-1999December) to the author in October 2003

18 The United States Central Command (USCENTCOM or CENTCOM) is a theatre-level Unified Combatant Command of the U.S. Department of Defense. Established in 1983 its area of responsibility (AOR) includes countries in the Middle East, North Africa, and Central Asia, Pakistan Afghanistan, and Iraq.
19 General Zinni to the author at his office in Reston, Virginia. July 8, 2003.
20 General Zinni to the author at his office in Reston, Virginia. July 8, 2003.
21 For more information on IMET see www.dsca.mil/programs-international-military-education-training-imet
22 General Zinni's assessment of Musharraf shared with the author in his October 2003 meeting with the author.
23 General Musharraf shared his account of his meeting with Zinni and his assessment of Zinni with the author.
24 James Rubin State Department's spokesman's remarks at the State Department Noon briefing June 3, 1999
25 ibid
26 Philip Shenon, Risks High in Kashmir Clash, even Huge, US Experts Warn, The New York Times , May 30, 1999
27 US ambassador William Milam to the author
28 Under-Secretary Karl Inderfurth to the author
29 Recalled in conversations with the author by both Pakistan's ambassador in Washington Ambassador Riaz Khokhar and US ambassador William Milam in Islamabad .
30 Statesman News Service , 'PM Accepts talks offer, says situation war-like: PM,' *Statesman* June 1, 1999
31 Pakistan-India composite dialogue began in 1993 was suspended in May 1999..
32 HT Correspondent, 'Minister Aziz is welcome but situation is war-like,' *Hindustan Times* June 1, 1999
33 ibid
34 Kathy Ganon, 'Will use any weapon,' threatens Shamshad, *Indian Express* June 1, 1999. The following day the Pakistan Foreign Office denied that such a statement was made. It maintained he had been misquoted
35 'Crying Nuclear Wolf', Special Correspondent *The Times of India*, June 2, 1999.
36 A term repeatedly used by former US State department officials.
37 In 2002 during Operation Parakram the Indian Prime Minster would issue a much more direct threat to use nuclear weapons as he declared in Lucknow on 3 January 2002 that "...no weapon would be spared in self-defense. Whatever weapon was available it would be used no matter how it wounded the enemy."(quoted in T. Jayaraman, "Nuclear Crisis in South Asia", *Frontline* (Chennai), 21 June 2002)
38 ibid
39 See discussion in chapter two for steps taken by the international community.
40 To the author in Washington on December 17, 2006
41 The transcripts of the Aziz-Musharraf conversation also illustrate the intimate working and common outlook of the army and the Foreign Office over Kargil.
42 For example, at the June 10 meeting of former foreign secretaries convened by the foreign Minister on the eve of his departure to Beijing, the Foreign Secretary Shamshad Ahmad gave a presentation, which was upbeat. The general thrust was that Pakistan can sustain and bring positive results. Former Foreign Minister Yaqub Khan, present at the meeting, had said, "India would go tier by tier and layer by layer and will not rest content until they recover every inch." Shamshad had said that the stretch was very large and the Indians would not be able to recover militarily. The former Secretary Tanveer Ahmed Khan had said that the Indians will not fight shy of paying the price and will not allow the Pakistan Army to alter the LOC even an inch. At the same meeting, Sartaj Aziz said that he had been told that if the Indians will try to recapture the territory they will merely reinforce their failure. Tanvir had said if the Indians fail in one sector they will open fronts at other sectors. He also asked if Pakistan would provide air cover.
43 Since only the Defense Secretary was present in the 16 May 1999] briefing, he must have flagged the concerns regarding the operation to the other two.
44 That the 17 May 1999 editorial of the *Nation*, a paper closely linked to the Nawaz Sharif government, had mentioned that Pakistan's own army was in Kargil, indicated that there had been some sensitive leaks in the press on the classified briefing.
45 Phrase used by Chaudhary Nisar in an interview with the author on 7 September 2004.
46
47 In end June 1999 meeting with the author in the Prime Minister's House Shehbaz Sharif said that the army chief acknowledged that unwittingly the Operation was pressed into over-kill, that vacant spaces prompted the army to occupy more than the originally planned territory. Subsequently in September 2004, Chaudhary Nisar also made the same point.

Chapter 8

1 The US assistant Secretary of State Gib Lampher in an interview to the author on October 23, 2003.

2 Ramesh Chandran, 'United States Views Kargil With Serious Concern' *The Times of India* June 1, 1999

3 'Declare Pakistan a Rogue State: Ackerman' in The *Pioneer* June 11, 1999

4 ibid

5 Indian press spelled out the advantages of the US-India relationship. Sunanda K. Datta-Ray Being Friends of Bill " India-US ties are the key to beating Pakistan in the international arena…Engaging the US means opening up the economy, economics being the solvent for most political challenges" *The Telegraph* June 26, 1999

6 V.P.Singh said to the author during an interview with the author on 7 August 2002 at the Delhi hospital while having his dialysis treatment.

7 In a conversation with the author in his Ministry of Defense office in Delhi on 2 Sept 2002 Interesting after the minister alluded to Pakistan .." someone decided to cheat against the ground rules" when I reminded him that India had done the same and first in 1984 when occupying Siachen, he laughed and said "I cannot contradict you."

8 National Assembly of Pakistan. Standing Committee on Defense. Personal/Confidential Document No.01/SCOD/99

9 Amitabh Mattoo, Kargil's Blunders, *India Today* April, 2000
http://www.india-today.com/itoday/20000424/books.html

10 Indian version of the success: Battle-winning role of the gunners in Kargil
http://www.indiandefensereview.com/spotlights/battle-winning-role-of-the-gunners-in-kargil-war/
How Artillery Changed the Tide of the Kargil War :
http://economictimes.indiatimes.com/articleshow/48216559.cms?utm_source=contentofinterest&utm_medium=text&utm_campaign=cppst Importantly Pakistani field commanders also supported this view. Infact when asked by a former general and friend the former army chief Musharraf also conceded that Bofors amd a great difference

11 http://economictimes.indiatimes.com/articleshow/48216559.cms?utm_source=contentofinterest&utm_medium=text&utm_campaign=cppst

12 Conversation with commander officers and brigade commanders, military officers

13 Military Director Military Operations Brigadier Nadeem Ahmad in conversation with the author

14 Brigadier M.P.S. Bajwa, YSM – Commander ,192 Mountain Brigade quoted in Battle-Winning Role of the Gunners in Kargil War http://www.indiandefensereview.com/spotlights/battle-winning-role-of-the-gunners-in-kargil-war/

15 Maj Gen Jagjit Singh: Artillery: The Battle-Winning Arm reproduced in Battle-Winning Role of the Gunners in Kargil War http://www.indiandefensereview.com/spotlights/battle-winning-role-of-the-gunners-in-kargil-war/

16 ibid

17 Recalled by mid-level officers based in the FCNA and 10 Corps headquarters and other NLI officers who fought in the Op KP.

18 ibid

19 Based on accounts of several NLI officers who participated in Op KP

20 According to officers in his staff and those who interacted with him during Op KP.

21 In interviews with the author, recalled by several military men who were present in the meeting where general Javed Hasan made this comment.

22 Recalled by a Skardu-based officer in his interview with the author and confirmed in interviews with officers based at the 10 Corps HQ.

23 Recalled by several Pakistani officers in their interview with the author, and also supported by books written on the Operation including Blood on the Snow and A Ridge Too Far.

24 Based on battle accounts shared by officers in interviews with the author.

25 Minutes of Meetings 12 June between the Pakistan foreign minister and the Indian foreign minister.

26 What follows is a first hand account since the author was one of the four journalists who flew with the visiting foreign minister in a special jet.

27 The key question of who recorded this conversation remains unanswered. Speculations ranged from the Nawaz Sharif government, to the Americans and the Indian government. Interestingly perhaps the only news report

that addressed this question appeared in the Indian daily *Telegraph* of 4 July 1999. In his story 'Delhi hits Sharif with Army Tape talk' correspondent Pranay Sharma claimed that the MEA joint secretary Vivek Katju was sent by the Indian government to "play before Sharif a purported taped conversation between the two senior most Pakistani generals…" He explained that the "government's decision to send Katju to Islamabad was based on its reading of the situation in Pakistan. New Delhi feels the Pakistani military establishment had kept Sharif in the dark on the Kargil operations. He therefore, will be more amenable to look for a quick solution."

28 A city barely 10 kilometers from the capital, where the army headquarters are located.

29 Ruling out the host country China's interest in recording and releasing the conversation, CIA would have likely recorded the conversation and subsequently shared it with Delhi.

30 Following the October 1999 coup in an interview to Indian television channel (with M.J. Akbar) general Pervez Musharraf as the President of Pakistan acknowledged the authenticity of this taped conversation. However the million dollar question of who taped the conversation remains unanswered, Three possibilities were discussed: one, ISI believed Indians recorded it; two,senior Pakistan military officers believed it was the Americans who recorded the conversation and gave it to the Indians and three, the ISI chief Ziauddin taped and handed it to the Indians.

31 Indian media reports and conversation with Indian Foreign Minister Jaswant Singh and Indian Defense Minister George Fernandz

32 In a conversation with the author in his Ministry of Defense office in Delhi on Sept 2, 2002

33 The Pakistan foreign minister had expressed his reservations over the Kargil operation during the 17 May meeting. However he went along with the game-plan put together by the military and subsequently supported by the Foreign office.

508 Minutes of the Meeting Between Mr. Sartaj Aziz, Foreign Minister of Pakistan and Mr. Jaswant Singh, Minister of External Affairs of India on Saturday, 12 June (12.30pm to 1.40pm) at the Hyderabad House, New Delhi) Copy of the Minutes of the Meeting with the author

35 Para 31 Minutes of the Meeting Between Foreign Minister Sartaj Aziz and Prime Minister Atal Behari Vajpayee on 12 June at 1630 hours

36 The foreign minister listed the following Indian violations: in 1972 occupied areas in Chorbat La, in 1984 India captured Siachen, it took occupied strategic positions in the Qamar area, in 1994 and 1996 heavy shelling to disrupt Pakistan's supply routes in the Neelum Valley. Which resulting in large scale civilian casualties and in 1998 Indian troops marched into Shyok.. The Pakistan Army maintained a record of these LOC violations by the Indians. During Kargil the government, the press and the politicians were briefed given comprehensive briefings by senior army generals and the ISPR spokesman on these violations.

(NOTE : I have the minutes of the meeting. More than what is given here is not needed.

37 Para 17, Minutes of the Meeting Between Mr. Sartaj Aziz, Foreign Minister of Pakistan and Mr. Jaswant Singh, Minister of External Affairs of India on Saturday, 12 June (12.30pm to 1.40pm) at the Hyderabad House, New Delhi) A copy of the Minutes is with the author

38 para 22, ibid

39 Para 6, Minutes of the Meeting Between Mr. Sartaj Aziz, Foreign Minister of Pakistan and Mr. Jaswant Singh, Minister of External Affairs of India on Saturday, 12 June (12.30pm to 1.40pm) at the Hyderabad House, New Delhi)

40 para 17, ibid

41 Para 7, Minutes of the Meeting Between Foreign Minister Sartaj Aziz and Prime Minister Atal Behari Vajpayee on 12 June at 1630 hours

42 Para 21, Minutes of the Meeting Between Foreign Minister Sartaj Aziz and Prime Minister Atal Behari Vajpayee on 12 June at 1630 hours

43 Para 30, ibid (Copy of the Minutes of the Meeting with the Author)

44 Para 24, Minutes of the Meeting Between Foreign Minister Sartaj Aziz and Prime Minister Atal Behari Vajpayee on 12 June at 1630 hours

45 Minutes of the Meeting Between Foreign Minister Sartaj Aziz and Prime Minister Atal Behari Vajpayee on June 12 at 1630Hours

46 Para 26, Minutes of the Meeting Between Mr. Sartaj Aziz, Foreign Minister of Pakistan and Mr. Jaswant Singh, Minister of External Affairs of India on Saturday, 12 June (12.30pm to 1.40pm) at the Hyderabad House, New Delhi)

47 Para 18, ibid

48 Minutes of the Meeting Between Mr. Sartaj Aziz, Foreign Minister of Pakistan and Mr. Jaswant Singh, Minister of External Affairs of India on Saturday, 12 June (12.30pm to 1.40pm) at the Hyderabad House, New Delhi)
49 para 39 Minutes of the Meeting Between Foreign Minister Sartaj Aziz and Prime Minister Atal Behari Vajpayee on 12 June at 1630 hours

Chapter 9

1 K.K.Katyal, "Stalemate in Indo-Pak Talks," *The Hindu*, June13, 1999
2 As reflected in the 26 May telephone conversation between the army chief who was visiting Beijing and the chief of general staff who had called him from Rawalpindi. Confirmed during and after Kargil in author's interviews with senior army personnel, Pakistani diplomats and the political leadership.
3 Pakistan's official line of argument reflected in public statements, in meetings and in briefings to the media. For example in briefings by ISPR in which the author was present. Also in Delhi points repeatedly made by the Pakistani foreign minister Sartaj Aziz in the
June 12 joint presser with the Indian Foreign minister Jaswant Singh.in which the author was present.
4 Significantly it was Pakistan's response to Siachen that defined the international community's response to Indian occupation of Siachen. Pakistan lost Siachen to India when Pakistan was under the rule of the military dictator General Ziaul-Haq. At a press conference when he was asked about Siachen the dismissive Zia had said, "Not a blade of grass grows there so what is the big deal?" Clearly it was a loss that had occurred due to the Pakistan's army failure to defend Siachen. Its threat assessment had been flawed. Consequently, for the military ruler General Ziaul Haq to acknowledge the loss of Siachen domestically would have meant acknowledging his institution's failure as well. He opted for silence 4 thereby helping India to get away with its violation of the Simla Accord and its illegal occupation of Siachen.. Of the various justifications put forward by various army officers for Zia ul Haq not publicizing Indian occupation of Siachen , three are significant. One that since, in 1984, there was still no media revolution, Zia could not have gained international support to censure India over its occupation of Siachen as India had now gotten support. Two that they believed US support would not have been forthcoming for Pakistan as it was now for India. Three,that Zia genuinely concluded Siachen was "a minor tactical loss" so decided to "not to make a big deal." This is contradicted by the subsequent, failed yet costly attempts, made by Pakistan to regain control of Siachen.
5 Interview with the defense minister held on 2 September 2002 in his Ministry of Defense office
6 ibid
7 ibid
8 Sartaj Aziz to the author during July 2002 interview.
9 Confirmed in interviews to the author by Pakistan's key diplomats based in Beijing during Kargil.
10 Told to the author by the Foreign Minister while flying to Delhi on 12 June. The FM and his Additional Secretary Tariq Altaf both remarked on the serious Chinese reservations regarding Pakistan's Kargil action.
11 Statement made by the Chinese Foreign Ministry spokesperson Zhang Qiyue a day before Pakistan foreign minister's trip reported in 'Beijing Silent on LOC' *Times of India* 11 June 1999
12 ibid
13 Arrival Statement distributed by the Ministry of Foreign Affairs on 11 June 1999
14 As recalled by Pakistan's ambassador to France ShaharyarKhan in an interview with the author.
15 US ambassador Milam to the author during an interview
16 Two senior generals present in the meeting recalled in an interview with the author.
17 The induction of air power issue had also been raised earlier. The army believed that entry of the air force would have lifted the morale of the Pakistani army. The army gave a detailed briefing to the air force chief on the military situation. Two Squadron Leaders, F-16 pilots, were also briefed and according to the army they were willing to go to bust. However, since the air chief himself was vacillating, the COAS chose to not raise it with the Prime Minister. The air chief was clear that the air force would not be deployed without the Prime Minister's clearance. After the Indian air force was inducted in the theatre on 27 May the Pakistan air force deployed aircraft radar and flew missions of combat air patrols in the area, mainly on the Pakistan side of the LOC. There was no air to air combat. Pakistan's surface- to-air missiles were used to shoot down two Indian aircrafts that intruded into Pakistani airspace.
18 Arguments favoring deployment of air power were made by several of the Kargil planners and by senior military officers in interviews with the author. The disagreements between the army and the air force on deployment of air power were recounted to the author by civilians attending DCC meetings.

19 Foreign minister, a participant in the meeting, confirmed this to the author during 23 May 2002 interview.

20 The army remained committed to its original calculation of a 'no all-out war scenario'. Interviews with India's army chief General Ved Malik and other military strategists, including General Satish Nambiar, K. Subramaniam, and Commodore Jasjit Singh, as well as seasoned diplomats like J.N.Dixit ,all supported the Kargil planners original 'no all-out war' calculation. The reasons however were more complex than the army had accounted for.

21 According to one of the kitchen cabinet members this presentation contrasted with an early June presentation in a meeting chaired by the prime minister in which the DG ISI was very critical of the operation.

22 Based on accounts narrated to the author by participants of the meetings

23 See discussion in major Indian dailies on effectiveness of air power Air Strikes Continue Times of India Nw Delhi , May 31, 1999"IAF Hits Enemy Supply Base " the Hindu, June 18, 1999; IAF Jets Pound Tiger Hills" The Hindu June 25, 1999 ; IAF Punding of Enemy on Top of Tiger Hill Continues" Hindustan Times June 26, 1999

24 Battle-Winning Role of the Gunners in Kargil War
http://www.indiandefensereview.com/spotlights/battle-winning-role-of-the-gunners-in-kargil-war/
By Maj Gen Jagjit Singh . Interestingly several Pakistani troops on the peaks and ridges also recalled to the author how they could clearly watch the Bofors and other artillery from their posts.

25 Accounts of Pakistani soldiers corroborated by Indian press reports. See Indian reports Key peak taken, noose around Tiger Hill Tightens, Gaurav C Sawant, *Indian Express*, 29 June,1999

26 Told to the author by a Pakistani officer who fought at Tololing through June. The map from the captured post around June 6 ,1999 showed Pak deployments in the area.

27 A term used by Pakistani troops to describe the extent of damage inflicted through artillery fire.

28 Winning Role of the Gunners in Kargil War http://www.indiandefensereview.com/spotlights/battle-winning-role-of-the-gunners-in-kargil-war

29 Officers fighting on Tololing and Tiger Hills including those volunteered to go to Kargil-Drass early June.

30 ibid

31 Winning Role of the Gunners in Kargil War http://www.indiandefensereview.com/spotlights/battle-winning-role-of-the-gunners-in-kargil-war

32 ibid

33 Indian reports Key peak taken, noose around Tiger Hill Tightens, Gaurav C Sawant, *Indian Express*, 29 June,1999 These have been corroborated by battle accounts shared with the author by Pakistani soldiers fighting in these areas.

34 Author's interviews with individuals from core staff at the FCNA and Corps HQ overseeing the operations.

35 To get an Indian readout of the situation read the media reports of the period: Fighting Every Inch Of the Way, Murali Krishnan &Nitin A Gokhale , *Outlook India*, June 28, 1999 ;

36 Gen Malik Warns Troops May Cross LOC, Press Trust of India, June 23 , 1999 http://www.jammu-kashmir.com/archives/archives1999/99june23d.html

37 Recalled by soldiers fighting at the FDL posts to the author.

38 Each NLI battalion had approximately 800 soldiers, adding to 4800 people.

39 According to soldiers fighting in the initial casualties went upto even 50 percent of the 750 troops fighting in the Tololing complex where Pakistanis had taken several posts including Tashfeen, Amjadetc

40 In interviews with the author, as recalled by those who fought at Tiger Hill, Tololing and Mushkoh many jawans and officers opted to fight and embrace shahadat rather than vacate the posts.

41 A brigadier in an interview with the author

42 Eye-witness accounts from HQ 10 corps

43 As recalled in author's interviews with officers who were and directly involved in the unfolding Op KP at FCNA headquarters, Corps 10 headquarters and at the GHQ.

44 One of the key Kargil objectives put by the planners of the Kargil operation.

45 This was confirmed to the author by the foreign minister and the Minister of Petroleum Chaudhary Nisar Ali Khan According to a bureaucrat who participated in all the Kargil related meetings "the middle of June was the threshold time when everybody knew that an exit strategy was inevitable. We started thinking of "using our influence with the freedom fighters to persuade them to withdraw."

46 Sartaj Aziz said had he been sent to Delhi with the position taken at the Lahore meeting he would have brought back Jaswant with him to Islamabad.

Chapter 10

1 In fact, the bureaucrats were zealously guarding the secrecy of this channel, especially during the last week of June that a key bureaucrat told the author that that we needed to keep it a secret from the foreign minister lest he mentions it to the Americans who would sabotage it.

2 All the key political, military and civilian actors that the author met during Kargil indicated that they knew of the back-channel developments. Subsequently in his May 9 2003 interview with the author General Pervez Musharraf confirmed knowledge of the Naik channel and said " I even then thought it was good something could be worked out."

3 Told to the author by the official Riaz Mohammad Khan on October 23, 2005

4 "Honourable exit" was the official term

5 As told to the author by one of the key members of the back-channel strategists.

6 Based on the impression the author got in her direct interaction with some of these officials.

7 Based on the Foreign Office chat, the author directly heard suspicions that Qazi was "too thick with the Pakistan Army." 7

8 As recalled by an additional secretary to the author in interviews during and after Kargil

9 Pakistan's foreign minister was not kept in the loop "fearing he would tell the Americans".

10 US ambassador to the author in August 2003.

11 Milam to the author on 21 October 2003

12 The US ambassador informed the State department of the back-channel diplomacy.

13 Milam to the author on 21 October 2003.

14 Bruce Riedel to the author that they had been informed of "very little".

15 Milam to the author on 21 October 2003. Clearly Delhi was moving on both tracks-the back channel plus the US-pressure track to get the Pakistanis out. but could not afford to let the diplomatic pressure off the Americans regarding the possibility of an all-out war if the Pakistanis do not vacate the Kargil heights.

16 Riedel interview with the author. Nov 2, 2006

17 According to one member, "In the civilian cabinet the thinking was to talk to the US not to the Indians because talking to the Indians like insulting the honest brokers."

18 'As Kashmir fight continues, meeting reportedly sought with President Clinton',CNN , June 27, 1999. According to one of the members of his kitchen cabinet Nawaz Sharif had also had a personal link with President Clinton. At the height of Monica Lewinsky scandal Nawaz Sharif, on the advice of a member of his kitchen cabinet, had made a special gesture of support to Clinton. Sharif had called Bill Richardson, a man Clinton had said was the quickest channel to him, to send his special wishes and support to Clinton at this time of personal crisis.

19 Four letters were exchanged between Sharif and Clinton during June 14 and June 22. After the June 13 meeting Nawaz Sharif did call Clinton asking him to send his emissary so he could take him in confidence.

20 Recalled in a 23 May 2003 meeting to the author by a member of Nawaz Sharif's kitchen cabinet to whom Musharraf had said this.

21 He had made a statement in Karachi before Zinni's arrival indicating that Pakistan would welcome US intervention. He believed that the Americans would intervention to defuse the Kargil crisis would also help to further negotiations on Kashmir.

22 The belief that Washington, sensitive to the possibility of an all-out war between two nuclear states, would curtail India's military response and by highlighting the linkage between the Kargil flare-up and the unresolved Kashmir dispute Islmabad would prompting Washington, and other countries, to urge India to the negotiating table to resolve the "core issue" with Pakistan.

23 Confirmed to the author by the US Ambassador to Pakistan and also by Pakistan Foreign Office officials.

24 Upon hearing of the cancellation of his meeting with Clinton the Pakistani prime minister got angry and blamed the US bureaucrats for not letting the US and Pakistani leadership make headway on Kargil. Sharif believed that Clinton sincerely wanted to help.

25 According to US State officials the 'Indo-philes' at the State department believed such a meeting should only follow after Pakistan vacated Kargil.25

26 Bruce Riedel to the author. Riedel acknowledged that "there was an occasional talk of meeting somewhere in Europe either the Foreign Secretary or Nawaz Sharif. Issue was a pretty clear exit. So a meeting that would guarantee that outcome wouldn't be productive."

27 Bruce Riedel to the author.

28 According to Pakistani officials the State Department was also opposed the meeting because of Pakistan's failure to deliver on Nawaz Sharif November 1998 commitment to Clinton that Pakistan would support a United States executed OBL operation in the areas bordering Afghanistan

29 Nawaz Sharif had indicated to Clinton during his 1998 Washington trip that Pakistan would help on getting OBL.

30 Comment made to the author by a member of Nawaz Sharif's kitchen cabinet. A perception shared by all the important policy players in Pakistan and also confirmed by some State department officials also. Only privately general Musharraf indicated preference for Clinton to have visited Pakistan.

31 Murali Krishnan 'Cold Facts' in *Outlook* June 21, 1999;

32 ibid

33 Manoj Joshi and Raj Cengapa 'The Marathon War' pg 25 in *India Today* June 21, 1999]

34 Pamela Constable, 'India's Mountaineering Warriors: Heights of Kashmir As Hostile as Enemy'. *The Washington Post* June 29,1999

35 C.Raja Mohan 'Will the US Match Words With deeds?' *The Hindu* June 26, 1999

36 ibid

37 ibid

38 Indian press reports on India's fight-back highlighting particularly the great difficulty with which the Indian Army was able to re-take the areas occupied by Pakistani troops: Murali Krishan Nitin Gokhale,'Fighting Every Inch of the Way', *Outlook India*, June 28, 1999, Manoj Joshi and Raj Chengappa, 'The Marathon War', *India Today*, June 21, 1999 Also reported by the US press Pamela Constable, 'India's Mountaineering Warriors: Heights of Kashmir As Hostile as Enemy', *The Washington Post* June 29,1999

39 On this general Javed Hasan, a key man from among the Kargil planners shared his thinking with the author, "the more the troops the better for me to tie Indian troops and then less at LOC and at the international border. They will bring 5 brigades at the Northern Command based in Jammu and Kashmir (J&K). These brigades would be replaced by mainland brigades…" Hence these Kargil planners focused on Indian troop movements in the conflict zone and their implications on the overall military situation effecting Pakistan. However the planners had miscalculated how hard India would hit back in the Kargil operation area.

40 A fact generally acknowledged by Pakistan's senior military and mid-level officers including those who fought in Kargil. The army chief Musharraf conceded to a retired major-general Mahmud Durrani that Pakistani troops were hit the hardest by the Indian deployment of the bofors guns.

41 The army believed the induction of air force would have lifted the morale of Pakistani forces. "In the absence of extensive air-cover and artillery cover the will to stay was a little less," a senior military officer had explained to the author. Pakistani troops in the posts were completely exposed to the Indian air and artillery pounding. The army resented the non-induction of air power. It believed the induction of airforce would have lifted the morale of Pakistani forces. In the absence of extensive air-cover and artillery cover the will to stay was a little less. There was so much pounding that made the people in the posts completely exposed to Indian air and artillery pounding.

42 Reflecting the thoughts on Indian airpower of the battling Pakistani soldiers a young soldier said to the author that "We should have our airpower deployed. Indian airpower use to unnerve our soldiers.- infact terrorized by the sound in that bitter cold weather and those mountains and ungodly heights…"

43 Reports on Indian use of airpower see IAF Hits Enemy Supply Base, *The Hindu*, June 18 1999; IAF Strikes Supply Base in Batalik , *The Hindu*, June 27,1999; IAF Jets Pound Tiger Hills , *The Hindu* June 25,1999

44 A soldiers recall of how he and others fighting in Kargil experienced Indian airpower.

45 In an interview to the author.

46 When in a military operation the spread of forces is not backed by an equivalent spread of logistical support. Including food supplies medical supplies, weapons, communication support etc

47 Often occurs in battles, when troops on the ground decide to go beyond the set geographical parameters for the war; there csn be sverl reasons ranging from bravado, enemvt tioo

48 A young captain explained the impact of this unplanned increase in demand for food etc in the operation areas, In a 5 January 2005 interview with the author he said "At times there was even no food to eat. Some even had to eat grass. There were times that they shot Ibex and ate it. That use to be a treat…On logistics we were very weak. There wasn't enough to feed people on…"

49 In Sohail Warraich's book *Ghaddar Kaun Hai*, the former prime minister and in interviews with the author key aides to the PM Chaudhary Nisar and Shehbaz Sharif all maintained that the army chief shared with them his concern over growing casualties.

50 The messenger shared with the author

Chapter 11

1 Emma Henderson, "Kargil war: Pakistan planned to drop nuclear bomb on India during conflict," former CIA officer claims, *Independent*, London, 3 December 2015

http://www.independent.co.uk/news/world/asia/pakistan-india-nuclear-bomb-kargil-war-former-cia-officer-sandy-berger-bruce-riedel-a6758501.html

Bruce Riedel, "Farewell, Sandy Berger, the Clinton Man Who Stopped Armageddon". *The Daily Beast*, 2 December 2015

http://www.thedailybeast.com/articles/2015/12/02/farewell-sandy-berger-the-clinton-man-who-stopped-armageddon.html

2 Bruce Riedel, "Farewell, Sandy Berger, the Clinton Man Who Stopped Armageddon". *The Daily Beast*, 2 December 2015

http://www.thedailybeast.com/articles/2015/12/02/farewell-sandy-berger-the-clinton-man-who-stopped-armageddon.html

3 Shahhaz interview with the author on 27 May 2003

4 Muchkund Dubey, "Kargil& the limits of diplomacy", daily *The Hindu* July 05, 1999

5 State department officials to the author.

6 According to the drafter of the letter

7 Known as Gib Lanpher his complete name was Edward Gibson Lanpher

8 Shahhaz interview with the author on 27 May 2003

9 The general impression among all officials at the Pakistan foreign office dealing with the Kargil crisis including foreign secretary Shamshad Ahmad, additional secretaries Tariq Fatemi and Tariq Altaf.

10According to the foreign minister, the Foreign Office team, and Shehbaz Sharif, Clinton had proposed this meeting during a telephone conversation with Nawaz Sharif. The Americans claim otherwise. The former Assistant Secretary of State Thomas Pickering said to the author in an interview on 3 July 2003, that "Clinton was not willing to do that…the Europe meeting was only up in the air."

11 Confirmed to the author by key members of Nawaz Sharif's political team, Foreign Office team and by former US ambassador to Pakistan William Milam..

12 See 'Nawaz Visits Forward Artillery Position' in daily *Dawn* June 25, 1999

13 See 'Nawaz Visits Forward Artillery Position' in daily *Dawn* June 25, 1999

14 The participation of the Foreign Office would be necessary for inter-institutional coordination on policy-making. Especially in the case of Kargil the growing difficulties for Pakistan internationally meant that the major task was now of a diplomatic nature. The US military general had come on political mission and required the presence of those who were directly involved in policy-making on Kargil. Additionally absence of an FO representative also meant that meeting would not be minuted for the official records.

15 Gib Lanpher to the author in his October 23, 2003 interview. Also confirmed to the author by General Zinni and US ambassador Bill Milam

16 Underscored in an interview to the author by General Musharraf within hours of the Zinni meeting. Subsequently also mentioned by Gib Lanpher. The Zinni and Musharraf friendship did not influence their respective stands during the meeting. However, it did influence their respective 'read outs' of the meeting. Musharraf believed Zinni had appreciated his position while Zinni believed Musharraf was sympathetic to Zinni's position..

17 A fact confirmed to the author by American participants and Pakistani participants of the meeting. This included General Zinni and Ambassador Milam, General Aziz and the Army chief General Pervez Musharraf. In fact, Pakistan's prestigious daily *Dawn* carried the story *Peace Linked to Kashmir Solution Zinni Told* in it June 26 1999 issue. About the June 24 Zinni-Musharraf meeting it stated that "the two could not reportedly arrive at any agreement…"

18 For example the US ambassador present in the meeting believed Musharraf's "body language indicated that Musharraf was looking for a way to get out from Kargil."

19 Zinni had announced at the end of the meeting that, in case confirmation of the Sharif meeting did not come through, he would leave in his plane the same night.

20 A message that the Foreign Office participants of the meeting conceded that Washington had been conveying to Pakistan at all levels ever since the Kargil crisis erupted. In his various letters Clinton himself had been calling for Pakistan to take remedial measures and return to the Lahore process.

21 Zinni claims in his book *Battle Ready*(co-authored by Toma Clancy and Tony Koltz that Nawaz Sharif agreed to the withdrawal of troops from Kargil.

22 Reported in the press and confirmed by the participants to the author.

23 According to a senior Foreign Office official, "No commitment whatsoever was given to Zinni for withdrawal.".

24 US Ambassador Milam to the author

25 ibid. The American camp ascribed this Pakistani decision also partially to a deal that Nawaz Sharif had struck with the Indians through the Niaz-Misra back-channel negotiations.

26 The Zinni team's observations notwithstanding, what followed Zinni's departure was not a Pakistani withdrawal. Instead Pakistan still explored other options for striking a better deal linking withdrawal with some progress on the Kashmir issue.. The options explored included the back-channel diplomacy, the China trip, and finally the Washington rendezvous. All this activity would obviously not have followed had the Pakistani prime minister agreed to a withdrawal. The Zinni team had come on a specifically defined mission. Therefore they tended to read more than was valid intothe situation.

27 US Assistant Under Secretary of State Gib Lanpher to the author

28 Milam and Zinni to the author

29 Pakistan Army chief Admits Troops are in Kargil, Kamal Siddiqi, *Indian Express*, June, 1999.
http://www.jammu-kashmir.com/archives1999/99june26b.html

30 ibid

31 ibid

32 US Under Secretary of State Gib Lanpher to the author

33 Zinni writes this in *Battle Ready*

34 Vajpayee turns down Clinton Invitation, *Statesman* News Service July 5,1999

35 Told by the prime minister to the author who travelled with him to Lahore shortly after the Zinni visit. Thjs was also confirmed by all Pakistani foreign office officials who were involved in the Zinni-Lanpher meetings.

36 In an interview with the author on August 2004 a senior Pakistani official who participated in the meeting called the Zinni visit "a watershed point in the Kargil episode as it was during his meetings in Islamabad that we came face to face with a strong US demand for de-escalation by unconditional withdrawal from across the LOC of the forces that were occupying the Kargil heights with our support."

37 Nawaz Sharif's conversation with the author on June 26 flying from Islamabad to Lahore in the prime minister's special plane. In response to the author's request for a one-on-one meeting the prime minister offered that the author talk to him during the Islamabad-Lahore flight. In response to the author's query regarding the PM not taking the public into confidence and not preparing them for a possible fall-out of the tense military situation in Kargil, the PM said this would be a dangerous game bound to take an ugly and destructive turn. The author said Pakistan's nuclear weapons would act as a deterrent preventing the Indians from taking any extreme military step. The PM was dismissive of the nuclear deterrent in the current situation and said that India had the capacity to jam all our radars. It would initiate an electronic warfare and also neutralize our nuclear assets. He said this had to be stopped. And he was working on trying to resolve the matter with India. According to Lanpher, "We had told the Pakistanis that we believe the Kargil caper was very stupid plus dangerous given the two were nuclear capable countries."

38 Riedel to the author in an interview on 2 November 2006

39 ibid

40 Inderfurth to the author in July 2003,

41 This overstates the matter- Zinni's graphic description of what the continued military engagement in Kargil could lead to may have worried the Pakistani prime minister but the reports from the operation area of Pakistani casualties and international pressure that Pakistan withdraw , were also major contributing factor.

42 There was an expectation that Clinton, who was visiting Europe, would agree to meet Sharif there to discuss ways to end the Kargil crisis.

43 Documented in Sohail Warraich's book *Ghadaar Koun*, (Saghar Publishers, Lahore, 2006) see pages 142-166. The book is based on the author's interviews with former Prime Minister Nawaz Sharif.

44 See "India Intensifies Diplomatic Barrage to Down Pakistan": George Lype in New Delhi June 22,1999-Rediff On the Net. http://www.rediff.com/news/1999/jun/22iype.htm

45 ibid

46 ibid

47 Details of the Lanpher meetings in Delhi provided to the author in an interview with Lanpher on October 23, 2003

48 Lanpher to the author on October 23, 2003

49 Details of the Lanpher meetings in Delhi provided to the author in an interview with Lanpher on October 23, 2003

50 Mishra himself, in subsequent media interviews, confirms this Lanpher account. For example in the newspaper story Lanpher Felt Pakistan Wants to Withdraw: Brajesh (UNI Report, *The Pioneer* New Delhi, 3 July 1999) Mishra is reported to have acknowledged that "Lanpher had told the Indian officials about his impression that Pakistan wanted to withdraw. "

51 Lanpher to the author on October 23,2003

52 As explained by former Under Secretary of State for Political Affairs Thomas Pickering (May 1997 to January 2001) in an interview with the author on 3 July 2003

53 Most US officials involved in Kargil while talking to the author subscribed to this view.

54 Musharraf to the author on the evening of Zinni's departure

55 Recalled by Tariq Fatemi to the author during an interview.

56 Zinni in his interview with the author was clear that he had demanded Pakistani troops be withdrawn immediately and unconditionally.

57 A. G. Noorani: Kargil Diplomacy, *Front Line*Volume 16 - Issue 16, Jul. 31 - Aug. 13, 1999
http://www.frontline.in/static/html/fl1616/16161000.htmKargil diplomacy

58 *The Nation*, May 31, 1999

59 Recalled by Foreign Minister Aga Shahi in an interview to the author.

60 Bruce Riedel to author during March 17, 2012 interview

61 ibid

62 ibid

63 In an interview with the author Karl Inderfuth, the State Department's point-man during Kargil, unable to explain how the veracity of the data regarding nuclear weapons was established, almost yanked a photograph from the shelf, with Presdent Clinton and his core team poring over a document. "This," said Inderfuth, pointing to the document, "Is the evidence."

64 This was Bruce Riedel's response to my question of how do you really verify this. He said, "Intelligence information cannot be more specific.'

65 Walter Anderson said to the author

66 Walter Anderson (Aug 5, 2005)

67As recalled by John Mclaughlin Deputy Director for Intelligence, in CIA from 1997 to 2000,to the author in Washington in 2006 In 2000 McLaughlin became deputy director CIA.

68 8 August 2005 Larry Robinson Deputy Director South Asia-INS

69 Milam to the author in an interview 21 October 2003

70 Milam to the author, "I did not think so and my Embassy kept saying no nuclear but no one paid attention."

71 Bruce Riedel in interview to the author on 2 November 2006, in Washington.

72 Quoted in Brigadier A R Siddiqui's article *The Military Dilemma* August 1999, website of Pakistan Institute of Air Defense Studies (PIADS)

73 Mahdi Masud,*Dawn* July 10, 1999

74 Kamran Khan, *The News* June 24, 1999

75 The *Nation*, June 25, 1999 quoted in John H Gill, Military Operations in the Kargil Sector, chapter 4 pg 112, in Peter Lavoy, Asymmetric Was in South Asia.

76 *Jang* 29 June, 1999 quoted in John H Gill, Military Operations in the Kargil Sector, chapter 4 pg 112, in Peter Lavoy, Asymmetric War in South Asia.

77 Thinking reflected by V N Sharma General (Retired) in the Overview to Lt. General Y M Bammi's*Kargil The Impregnable Conquered*; Gorkha Publishers, Noida India 2002 pgiX

78 Bruce Riedel, "Farewell, Sandy Berger, the Clinton Man Who Stopped Armageddon" *Daily Beast*, 2 December 2015
http://www.thedailybeast.com/articles/2015/12/02/farewell-sandy-berger-the-clinton-man-who-stopped-armageddon.html

79 General V. P. Malik, army chief during Kargil made a public statement at a conference in Monterey that India ahd no evidence that Pakistan was preparing nuclear weapons for deployment of use.

80 To the author in an interview in his office in Delhi on 2 September 2002

81 K Subramanian, "Crying Nuclear Wolf: Nothing New in Riedel's Revelations" *Times of India* 20 May 2002

82 Ibid

Chapter 12

1 The contents of this chapter are based primarily on the author's detailed interviews with several primary sources, and several secondary sources including Pakistan's point-man and former Foreign Secretary Niaz Naik, Foreign Secretary Shamshad Ahmad, Additional Secretary Tariq Fatemi, army chief General Pervez Musharraf, Pakistan High Commissioner to India Ashraf Jahangir Qazi, Indian National Security Advisor Brajesh Mishra, Indian Foreign Minister Jaswant Singh., Member National Security Advisory Board Admiral Nayyar, , and US Ambassador to Pakistan Bill Milam. Significantly, as a columnist writing on the Kargil operation when it was under way, the author had access to the key Pakistani people directly involved in this process, especially Niaz Naik and Tariq Fatemi. For an Indian view of the back-channel, read A G Noorani 'An Aborted Deal' in *Outlook* of 28 August 28-10 September 1999.

2 R.K.Mishra was an old hand at back-channel with Pakistan.

3 Recalled by Admiral Nayyar, a close friend and colleague of R.K. Mishra and member National Security Advisory Board, in an interview with the author on 14 August 2002

4 Mishra declined to be interviewed by the Kargil Committee panel. The only known documented public statement Mishra made was in an interview to Rediff .He did not divulge the substance of the negotiations but was instead critical of his Pakistani counterpart, "He said many incorrect things were said out of fear of the army."

5 New Delhi Rejects Talks Offer, in the daily *Dawn* 3 July 1999

6 ibid.

7 For example see A 'sell out' and some hard-sell, AmitBaruah, *The Outlook*, July 1999 "Facing mounting reverses on the battlefield and under international pressure, Nawaz Sharif agrees to a pull-out from Kargil, and angers hawks at home". Amit Baruah in Islamabad

8 Pakistan Reinforces Retreating, 30 June 1999, Press Trust of India http://www.jammu-kashmir.com/archives/archives1999/99june30b.html

9 See *The diplomatic battle for Kashmir*, Tuesday 29 June 1999
http://news.bbc.co.uk/2/hi/ south_asia/380927.stm

10 Pakistan Reinforces Retreating, 30 June 1999, PTI

11 ibid

12 Pakistan claimed the invitation indicated "China's continuing friendship at a critical time." See India Confirms Kashmir Diplomacy, *BBC News*, Monday June 28, 1999
http://news.bbc.co.uk/1/hi/ world/south_asia/379853.stm

13 China Cautions Against Nuclear Race in South Asia, *The Hindu*, June 30, 1999

14 Confirmed to the author by the participants of the Nawaz-Zhu meeting.

15 Acknowledging this Chinese position as one that was at a tangent from an otherwise very close Pakistan-China strategic, the well-known US South Asian expert Robert Wirsing writes "Pakistan's satisfaction with China's friendship, we must add, does not extend to Beijing's position on the Kashmir dispute, which has for many years displaced a reticence barely distinguishable from the rest of the world community." (Kashmir in the Shadow of War: Regional Rivalries in a NuclearAge(New York M.E. Sharpep.92). As Wirsing explains, among the many factors that compel China to distance itself from the Kashmir cause, religion is an important one. While Kashmir is defined by the UN as a self-determination issue, he explains "religious identity is bound to figure in the working definition assigned to the dispute by interested foreign powers." Hence, for the Chinese government, its anxieties over the chronic separatist problem in Western China's sprawling and lightly populated,Muslim-majority Xinjiang Uighur Autonomous Region, a would make it even more circumspect about supporting

Pakistan's position on the Kashmir dispute. After all, not only does the Xinjiang share a common border but also a religious identity with Kashmir. (ibid.,p.910).

16 "Other" meant the western block and especially the US. According to Pakistani officials, the Chinese would never directly refer to the US but the 'other' always referred to the US led western bloc.

17 The impression that China supported Pakistan fully on Kargil is therefore not correct.

18 China refuses to Bite the Sharif Bait, urges Talks, HarveyStockwin and Agencies, *Times of India* June 30, 1999

19 Talks with Chinese Leaders 'totally satisfactory': FO, HasanAkhtar, *Dawn*, 2 July 1999

20 ibid

21 ibid

22 ibid

23 ibid

24 Confirmed to the author by Pakistan's then ambassador to China Inam ul Haq who participated in the two premiers meetings.

25Pakistan Ready to Meet Any Eventuality, HasanAkhtar, *Dawn*, 1 July 1999

26 Efforts to get Clinton's approval for a meeting were being made since June 27th-28th. The discussion was on the terms and conditions for a meeting, and specifically on Pakistan's agreement on an unconditional withdrawal. Apparently only Pakistan's ambassador Riaz Khokhar was only in the loop. No one in the Foreign Office knew about it. Khokhar was in the loop because from the Washington end he was keeping the prime minister informed and was also managing the logistics.

27 Not surprising that to put up a brave face the Foreign Office spokesman said the "consultations with the Chinese leadership-had been completely successful to the entire satisfaction of both sides.." (HasanAkhtar, "Pakistan ready to meet any eventuality, *Dawn*, Islamabad, 1 July 1999)

28 APC Demands OIC Summit at Islamabad, Bureau Report, *Dawn*, 1 July 1999

29 ibid

30 APC Demands OIC Summit at Islamabad, Bureau Report, *Dawn*, 1 July 1999

31 Ibid

32 APC Demands OIC Summit at Islamabad, Bureau Report, *Dawn*, 1 July 1999

33 Pakistan Forces Retreating, 30 June 1999, PTI
http://www.jammu-kashmir.com/archives/archives1999/99june30b.html

34 ShakilShiekh, DCC to approve final strategy today, The News, Islamabad, 2 July 1999

35 This included supporting the Kashmiri right of self-determination, condemnation of the violations of human rights and call for an early resolution of the dispute in accordance to the UN resolutions.

36 OIC Endorses Pakistan Stand On Kashmir, Bureau Report, *Dawn* 2 July 1999

37 ibid

38 DCC to Approve Final Strategy Today, Shakil Sheikh, *The News*, Islamabad, 2 July 1999

39 Nawaz Reiterates Call for Dialogue, Bureau Report, *Dawn* July 2, 1999

40 DCC to Approve Final Strategy Today, Shakil Sheikh, *The News*, Islamabad, 2 July 1999

41 ibid

42 ibid

43 Nawaz Reiterates Call for Dialogue, Bureau Report, *Dawn* 2 July 1999

44 It is a policy-making body which is presided over by the prime minister while chairman joint staff, chiefs of the three armed services, DG I (Director General Intelligence) ministers of defense, foreign and internal affairs, information minister and finance minister are its members. If required, the DCC can elect some other member too. Every member of the committee gives his opinion about a given problem with regards to his field after thorough analysis.Eventually the prime minister accepts or rejects the plan or proposes necessary changes in it.

45 I DCC to Approve Final Strategy Today, Shakil Sheikh, *The News*, Islamabad, 2 July 1999

Chapter 13

1 Ihtasham ul Haq , 'DCC okays 3-pronged strategy to tackle issue', *Dawn* 3 July 1999, A senior cabinet minister in an interview to the author

2 Owen Bennet Jones, *Pakistan: Eye of the Storm*, Yale University Press, New Haven and London, 2002, p.94

3 To the author on 11 September 2004.

4 Recalled to the author by several participants including Ministers in the 2 July DCC meeting.

5 Siddiq Khan Kanju sat in for Foreign Minister Sartaj Aziz, who was on his way back from Burkina Faso after attending the ICFM meeting.
6 According to the foreign secretary, he had also stated, "If the deteriorating ground situation remained as it was, no diplomacy could prevent war."
7 Shehbaz Sharif recalled this conversation during an interview with the author.
8 Based on conversations with several who were present including former Finance Minister Dar, (1 Jan 2013)
9 Claims made by the military planners of Kargil during their May presentation to the elected prime minister and senior ministers and shared in interviews with the author by some of the senior ministers, bureaucrats and military officers present.
10 ibid
11 General Pervez Musharraf to the author in an interview on May 4, 2003
12 ibid
13 Back-channel blues, *The Nation*, Islamabad July 1, 1999
14 'Back-Channel Blues', *The Nation*, Islamabad, July 1, 1999.
15 Earlier Musharraf had told a television interviewer that 'everyone was on board' the Kargil operation. See Jones *Pakistan: Eye of the Storm*, p.101
16 For various versions of what happened in the meeting see Ihtashamul Haq , 'DCC okays 3-pronged strategy to tackle issue', *Dawn* July 3, 1999; Shakil Shiekh, 'India warned against wider conflict', *The News* Islamabad, July 3,1999
17 'India Warned Against Wider Conflict: DCC Authorizes PM to Take Steps for Talks With Delhi', Bureau Report ,*The News*, July 3, 1999
18 'DCC okays 3 Pronged Strategy to Tackle Issue', Bureau Report, *The Dawn*, July 3, 1999
19 ibid
20 ibid
21 ibid
22 India Warned Against Wider Conflict: DCC Authorizes PM to Take Steps for Talks With Delhi, Bureau Report ,*The News*, July 3, 1999
23 India Warned Against Wider Conflict: DCC Authorizes PM to Take Steps for Talks With Delhi, Bureau Report ,*The News*, July 3, 1999
24 'India Warned Against Wider Conflict: DCC Authorizes PM to Take Steps for Talks With Delhi', Bureau Report ,*The News*, July 3, 1999 . According to this report the various problems included lack of military preparedness of Pakistan's army to deal with an all-out war which in any event would be disastrous. By early July the international pressure through diplomatic channels had reached a crescendo and the consensus voice was that Pakistan withdraw infiltrators/troops.
25 'India Warned Against Wider Conflict: DCC Authorizes PM to Take Steps for Talks With Delhi', Bureau Report ,*The News*, July 3, 1999
26 'India Warned Against Wider Conflict: DCC Authorizes PM to Take Steps for Talks With Delhi', Bureau Report ,*The News*, July 3, 1999
24 ibid
28 This was supported by observations made in interviews with the by civilian participants of the DCC including cabinet members and core team of the Foreign Office.
29 'US asks Pakistan to withdraw Mujahideen', Bureau Report, *The News*, July 3, 1999.
30 'US Congress asks Pakistan to pull out', Shaheen Sehbai, *Dawn*, July 3, 1999
31 Jaswant Singh, 'In Service of Emergent India', *Call to Honour* (Indiana Press 2006*)*, also makes the same point.
32 'US Has Impression Pakistan Wants to Withdraw Forces', *The News* July 3, 1999
33 Different unconfirmed versions of who was present when he called the US president Clinton include his principal secretary Saeed Mehdi, his military secretary Brigadier Javed and his Defense Secretary Lt. general retired Iftikhar Ali Khan.

Chapter 14

1 On the evening of 2 July 1999 the army chief told the author, a final decision had yet to be made. However, on being told that the newspapers were reporting that, because of the security environment resulting from the Kargil Operation, the French authorities had decided not to release a refurbished submarine to the Pakistan navy, general Musharraf did express surprise and said, 'If this was the case, it was not good.'

2 One of the core members said this to the author after the 2 July DCC meeting. In fact, he seemed concerned that some of the 'cowards' wanted to withdraw. He was keen to be clear about the advantages and disadvantages of staying on and withdrawing.
3 Deputy Assistant Secretary of State, Gib Lanpher, told the author on October 23, 2003
4 Amit Baruah, 'Sharif's US visit may be a turning point', *The Hindu*, Calcutta, 5 July 1999.
5 Ibid.
6 According to Tariq Butt,'Nisar, Majeed air dash to US to assist Nawaz', *The Nation*, 5 July 1999, this was the sixth Sharif-Clinton conversation in the last 20 days i.e., between 4 June and 4 July.
7 Shakeel Shaikh, 'Sharif, Clinton To Hold Strategic Dialogue', *The News*, Islamabad, 4 July 1999; Raja Zulfiqar, 'PM Leaves for US amid continuing LOC crisis', *The News*, Islamabad, 4 July 1999.
8 Ambassador Riaz Khokhar to the author on 15 October 2006.
9 Bruce Riedel to the author in an interview on 2 November 2006 in Washington. Riedel, senior advisor on South Asia and the Middle East to Clinton and in the National Security Council at the White House, was present in the Sharif-Clinton 4 July meeting.
10 Bruce Riedel interview to the author on 2 November 2006
11 Told to the author by Nawaz Sharif's close confidantes.
12 See Bruce Riedel's account in his paper "American Diplomacy and the 1999 Kargil Summit at the Blair House (2002 by the Center for the Advanced Study of India All rights reserved. Published 2002.
http://citeseerx.ist.psu.edu/viewdoc/download?doi=10.1.1.473.251&rep=rep1&type=pdf
13 Confirmed to the author by Pakistan's key Foreign Office officials and later confirmed by the fact that, after the 4 July meeting, US paratroopers arrived in a Pakistani town, Parachinar, to work with local security forces on a plan to capture OBL. Significantly, Nawaz Sharif had made a commitment to Clinton during the 199 Washington Summit that Pakistan would help in the capture of OBL. Sharif was unable to keep that commitment. The Americans kept reminding Pakistan's Ambassador of this commitment, a reminder that he kept transmitting to the Foreign Office in Islamabad.
14 Deputy Assistant Secretary of State, Gib Lanpher, told the author on 23 October 2003.
15 While his brother Shehbaz Sharif also supported the US involvement, he did not agree with the modality of involving the US.
16 Told to the author by a member of the Sharif 'kitchen cabinet', Chaudhry Nisar, on 7 September 2004.
17 Told by a key member of the 'kitchen cabinet' to the author on 11 September 2004.
18 Bureau Report, 'No Change in LOC, says Sartaj', *Dawn*, 4 July 1999.
19 Shehbaz Sharif to the author 27 May 2003
20 Raja Zulfiqar, 'PM Leaves for US Amid Continuing LOC Crisis', *The News*, Islamabad, 4 July 1999.
21 'PM Dashes to US to discuss LOC tension', *The Nation*, Islamabad, 4 July 1999.
22 Raja Zulfiqar, 'PM Leaves for US Amid Continuing LOC Crisis', *The News*, Islamabad, 4 July 1999. In his 1 July 1999 report, 'US perceives flexibility in Pakistan's policy on Kargil', *The Nation*, Islamabad, senior journalist, Arif Nizami, also reported the US ambassador's remarks that the US had decided to 'engage in quiet diplomacy'. Nizami wrote that Ambassador Milam had 'hoped that one outcome of Kargil de-escalation would be revival of Lahore Declaration'. There was no indication of any immediate Sharif-Clinton meeting.
23 According to Chaudhry Nisar, he was not comfortable about the Washington trip. In an interview with the author Nisar recounted on 11 September 2004 that the PM was advised by his brother Shehbaz Sharif that he must go since Clinton had invited him. This was contrary to what Shehbaz Sharif had recalled in his interview with the author.
24 The foreign minister sounded every bit flustered when, on hearing the news of the Washington trip on *PTV*'s 9pm news bulletin, the author called the Minister. He said he was completely ignorant of how and why the trip had been planned.
25 The three men were Shamshad Ahmad, Tariq Altaf, and Tariq Fatemi.
26 Narrated to the author by ambassador Milam and confirmed by the Foreign Office.
27 Those present in the meeting, including the Foreign Minister, Chaudhry Nisar, Tariq Fatemi, and Sartaj Aziz, confirmed this in interviews with the author. Earlier, around the end of June (documented in earlier chapter), the army chief had himself mentioned the possibility of a Sharif-Clinton meeting.
28 'PM Dashes to US to discuss LOC Tension', *The Nation*, Islamabad, 4 July 1999.
29 Shaheen Sehbai, 'PM Rushes to US for Talks With Clinton', *Dawn*, 4 July 1999.

30 According to the well-informed correspondent of *The Hindu*, C. Raja Mohan, 'Before accepting the desperate offer of Mr Sharif to visit Washington, Mr Clinton called Mr Vajpayee on Saturday to inform India of the proposed meeting.' Also see, 'Vajpayee turns down Clinton Invitation', *Statesman* News Service, 5 July 1999, which claims a White House official saying, 'Clinton agreed to receive Mr Nawaz Sharif after Mr Vajpayee said he had no objection.'

31 Tribune News Service, 'Clinton Invites Vajpayee', *Tribune*, 5 July 1999.

32 C. Raja Mohan, 'Vajpayee not to meet Clinton', *TheHindu*, 5 July 1999.

33 Ibid.

34 Ibid.

35 Ibid.

36 Initially—when Delhi and Washington believed, and in fact, Islamabad promoted the notion that the Mujahideen had occupied the Kargil heights—Delhi projected the Kargil Operation as a part of what India was arguing within the context of the Kashmir Uprising which was the dangerous and destabilizing troika of terrorism, religious fundamentalism, and Pakistani military adventurism. Barring the Defense Department, most of Washington's policy institutions, including the State Department, the White House staff, and the influential Senate and House Committee members, also subscribed to this Indian view. This view was reflected in most of the Indian and US officials' statements, strategic experts' analyses, and media reports. For example, C. Raja Mohan quoting 'highly placed sources in Delhi', writes, 'Condoning and rewarding Kargil aggression in any form, the Clinton Administration might have come to the assessment, will only encourage military adventurists and religious fundamentalists in Pakistan.' ('Vajpayee not to meet Clinton', *The Hindu*, 5 July 1999.)

37 Ibid.

38 A plethora of news reports appeared in the local press that made this point. For example, see 'Vajpayee turns down Clinton Invitation', *Statesman News Service*, 5 July1999; Tribune News Service and agencies, 'Clinton Invites Vajpayee', *Tribune*, 5 July 1999; Sridhar Krishnaswami, 'Clinton Talks to Sharif, Vajpayee', *The Hindu*, 5 July 1999; C. Raja Mohan, 'Vajpayee not to meet Clinton', *TheHindu*, 5 July 1999.

39 Sridhar Krishnaswami, 'Clinton Talks to Sharif, Vajpayee', *TheHindu*, 5 July 1999.

40 Ibid.

41 'PM Dashes to US to discuss LOC Tension', *The Nation*, Islamabad, 4 July 1999.

42 Shaheen Sehbai, 'PM Rushes to US for talks with Clinton', *Dawn*, 4 July 1999.

43 Editorial, 'No Room For Ambiguity', *The News*, 4 July 1999.

44 Ibid.

45 Ibid.

46 Editorial, 'The DCC Meeting', *The Nation*, 4 July 1999.

47 Editorial, 'Unlocking a bad situation', *Dawn*, Islamabad, 3 July 1999.

48 Ibid.

49 'People, Ruling Elite Surprised at PM's US Visit', *The News*, 5 July 1999.

50 Ibid.

51 Ibid.

52 Ibid.

53 Ibid.

54 General Mirza Aslam Beg, 'Response Modalities on Kargil', *The Nation*, Islamabad, 4 July 1999.

55 General Mirza Aslam Beg, 'Pakistan has lost war on diplomatic fronts', *The News*, Islamabad, 4 July 1999.

56 Nasim Zehra, 'Prime Minister's Sunday Surprise', *The News*, 5 July 1999.

57 Riaz Khokhar to the author on 15 October 2006.

58 As confirmed by a key US policy maker during Kargil, Bruce Riedel, to the author in an interview: 'The Americans, therefore believed that the more players pushed Nawaz Sharif in the right direction, the better.'

59 Several sources including Pakistani and the Americans confirmed to the author the role Prince Bandar played. It included Bruce Riedel, the Pakistani ambassador to Washington Ambassador Riaz Khokhar. Also Prince Bandar himself confirmed his role in setting up the Sharif-Clinton meeting to two Pakistani ambassadors based in the US, Ambassador Riaz Khokhar and Ambassador Maliha Lodhi.

60 According to US officials coordinating with the Saudis.

61 Bruce Riedel to author "When Sharif came to the Blair House we did not know of the outcome" meaning Clinto administration was not clear how the meeting would end, especially with reference to Nawaz Sharif's

own future. Riedel made the bizarre disclosure that the Clinto administration even wondered if Sharif was going to actually quit his position as PM and settle down in the US !

62 Nawaz called RiazKhokhar from Ireland—the PIA stopover point and asked if the one-on-one meeting with Clinton had been fixed. Nawaz was extremely keen that a one-on-one meeting be organized. Interestingly till today the Pak officials believed that the Americans were unfair because they refused any other officer accompany NS in his meeting with Clinton. Infact Nawaz had himself asked for a one-on-one meeting

63 Bill Clinton, *My Life*, New York: Knopf 2004, 866.

64 Bruce Riedel to the author

65 Recalled by the prime minister during his informal talk with a group of journalists at the Punjab House (Islamabad), on 30 November 2008.

66 Tariq Fatemi to the author July,1999.

67 Bruce Riedel to author. Also Riedel writes this in his paper on Kargil. "American Diplomacy and the 1999 Kargil Summit at the Blair House (2002 by the Center for the Advanced Study of India All rights reserved. Published 2002.

http://citeseerx.ist.psu.edu/viewdoc/download?doi=10.1.1.473.251&rep=rep1&type=pdf

68 Riedel interview with the author 2, November 2006

69 Riaz Khokhar to the author in October 2006.

70 Ibid.

71 Ibid.

72 Coll, Steve, *The Ghost Wars*, The Penguin Press, 2004, 477.

73 See earlier discussion on the Nuclear Factor.

74 A point emphasized by both Bruce Riedel who sat through the Sharif-Clinton meeting and by the US ambassador Bill Milam, during their interviews with the author. Also subsequent developments including CIA-ISI joint August-September, plan to capture OBL.

75 Told to the author by Pakistani Foreign Office officials who were privy to the confidential fax messages received from the Pakistan Embassy in the US. These fax messages urged the officials at the head office in Islamabad to remind the Prime Minster of the promise he had made to the US President.

76 Riedel, Bruce, *American Diplomacy and the 1999 Kargil Summit at Blair House*, Center for Advanced Study of India, University of Pennsylvania, Policy Paper Series, 2002.

77 'Clinton Sharif Statement on Kashmir', *Reuters*, 4 July 1999, Accessed at: http://www.jammu-kashmir.com/archives/archives1999/99july4b.html.

78 Agreement on Bilateral Relations Between the Governments of India and Pakistan Signed at Simla on 2 July 1972; FPI Case Studies Number 11, 'The 1972 Simla Agreement: An Asymmetrical Negotiation', 41, Foreign Policy Institute, School of Advanced International Studies, The Johns Hopkins University, Washington, D. C. 1988.

79 Staff Report, 'Pakistan Bears Burden to End the Confrontation', *The Houston Chronicle*, 7 July 1999.

80 Editorial, *The New York Times*, 7 July 1999.

81 Ibid.

82 Editorial, *The New York Times*, 7 July 1999.

83 Bradley Graham; Nathan Abse, `U. S. Says Pakistan Will Withdraw, *The Washington Post*, 5 July 1999, Accessed at:
https://www.washingtonpost.com/archive/politics/1999/07/05/us-says-pakistan-will-withdraw/0e9bc37a-b5d9-400f-900c-d77b69a7d843/?utm_term=.fd176869a69e.

84 PPI Report, 'Withdrawal Not in Pakistan-US Statement', *The News*, 7 July 1999.

85 Nawaz Sharif's political supporters, including his brother Shehbaz Sharif and the Foreign Office team, saw the Washington statement as a 'face-saver' for Pakistan. They believed it prevented Pakistan from having to make a dishonorable exit from Kargil.

86 Diplomats, in background discussions to the author.

87 Nawaz Sharif's critics, and those who understand the power dynamics of the civil-military relations in Pakistan, saw the 4 July agreement as a political cover that would ensure Sharif's ability to sell the Washington Agreement to the army as well as to his political opponents.

88 Bammi, Y.M., *Kargil 1999, impregnable conquered*, Gorkha Publishers, 2002, 251–62.

89 'World: South Asia: Pakistan plea to Kashmir militants', *BBC News*, 9 July 1999, Accessed at: http://news.bbc.co.uk/2/hi/south_asia/389714.stm.

90 India's statement on Nawaz-Clinton Joint Statement, *Reuters*, 4 July 1999, Accessed at: http://www.jammu-kashmir.com/archives/archives1999/99july4c.html.

91 See claims by Indian officials in: Pamela Constable, 'Domestic Pressures Imperil Kashmir Peace Deal', *The Washington Post*, 5 July 1999.

92 Bradley Graham; Nathan Abse, 'U. S. Says Pakistan Will Withdraw, *The Washington Post*, 5 July 1999, Accessed at: https://www.washingtonpost.com/archive/politics/1999/07/05/us-says-pakistan-will-withdraw/0e9bc37a-b5d9-400f-900c-d77b69a7d843/?utm_term=.fd176869a69e.

93 Pamela Constable, Domestic Pressures Imperil Kashmir Peace Deal, *The Washington Post*, 5 July 1999.

94 'Kashmiri separatists tell US to back out of row', *Reuters*, 6 July 1999, Accessed at: http://www.jammu-kashmir.com/archives/archives1999/99july6a.html

Chapter 15

1 The prime minister had spoken to his brother and Punjab Chief Minister Shehbaz Sharif and Information Minister Mushahid Hussain.

2 "The terms of the charter of the DCC imply that the Committee will be responsible, inter alia, to evaluate the total threat and to lay down the minimum force requirements to meet it, to define the task of the armed forces in accordance with the national strategy and the overall policy of the government, to determine the future force goals and to review from time to time the preparedness of each service to execute the approved plans." However the DCC has no support of an independent think tank to provide facts and analysis to its principals especially the prime minister to ensure that there are informed discussions and informed decision-making on security-related national issues.. Only the military wing of the Cabinet Division serves as the secretariat of the DCC.

3 Army chief general Pervez Musharraf confirms this on pp 96-97 of his *In the Line of Fire*, Pg 93 (Free Press, New York, 2006)

4 Barry Beark, (Islamabad) Foes Report Plan to Begin Pullout in Kashmir In Kashmir Region, *The NewYork Times*, July 12, 1999

5 Barry Beark, (Islamabad) Foes Report Plan to Begin Pullout in Kashmir In Kashmir Region, *The NewYork Times*, July 12, 1999

6 PTV Report, July 6, 1999. BBC Monitoring South Asia-Political, Supplied by BBC Worldwide Monitoring (Lexis-Nexis)

7 Daily *Jang*, pp 1 and 7, July 6, 1999

8 After the July 9 meeting of the Defense Committee of the Cabinet (DCC), presided over by the prime minister, the official statement issued noted that said that the DCC expressed "satisfaction" that the Clinton-Sharif joint statement had incorporated the "main elements" of Pakistan's position; that the DCC had "decided that Pakistan should appeal to the mujahideen to help resolve the Kargil situation."

9 Statement issued after the July 9 Cabinet meeting.

10 An official statement issued after the July 9 Cabinet meeting noted that the mujahideen have responded positively to the appeal of the Government of Pakistan to help resolve the Kargil situation

11 Official Denies Differences Between Sharif, Army Chief, *The News* (Islamabad) July 7, 1999

12 Anwar Iqbal, India,Pakistan Agree to Disengagement, Ceasefire, *The News*, July 12, 1999

13 Anwar Iqbal, India,Pakistan Agree to Disengagement, Ceasefire, *The News*, July 12, 1999

14 Umer Farooq, Islamabad's Haphazard Decisions Viewed, pp 1 & 15, *The Nation*, July 7, 1999.

15 Aziz Siddiqui, a former editor of The Frontier Post, wrote in *Dawn* on July 11, 1999

16 ibid

17 Javed Jaidi, Opposition Leaders Warn Sharif on Fallout from Accord, *The News*, July 7, 1999

18 US Points finger at Pakistan, Correspondents in Islamabad and Kargil, The Australian, July 6, 1999

19 Celia Dugger, Pakistan's Pullout Vow: A Very Hard Sell at Home, *The New York Times*, July 6, 1999

20 After the coup of 12 October 1999 General Pervez Musharraf appointed Sattar foreign minister.

21Nasir Iqbal, PTI Leader Criticizes Sharif for Kashmir Sell, The News, July 7, 1999

22 Nasir Iqbal, PTI Leader Criticizes Sharif for Kashmir Sell, The News, July 7, 1999

23 ibid

24 Opposition Refuses to Attend Foreign Office Briefing, *The News*, July 13 (FBIS Transcribed Text-Dialog Results)

25 US Points fingers at Pakistan, *The Australian* July 6, 1999

26 Celia Dugger, Pakistan's Pullout Vow: A Very Hard Sell at Home, *The New Yor Times*, July 6, 1999

27 Nirmal Gosh, India correspondent, Sharif's daunting task: Sell Kashmir Accord, *The Straits Times* (Singapore), July 7, 1999

28 Waqar Mustafa, Pakistan Wants Peace, Army Chief, *Gulf News*, July 8, 1999

29 Waqar Mustafa, Pakistan Wants Peace, Army Chief, *Gulf News*, July 8, 1999

30 Mariana Babar, Ex-Generals: Pak-US Pact Implementation 'Very Difficult' , The News, July 7, 1997

31 Ayaz Amir, Dawn, July , 1999

32 Editorial, *The Pakistan Observer*, July 9, 1999

33 Celia Dugger, Pakistan's Pullout Vow: A Very Hard Sell at Home, *The New Yor Times*, July 6, 1999

34 Minister Says Islamabad Policy averted Nuclear War, *The News*, July 12, 1999

35 Official Denies Differences Between Sharif, Army Chief, *The News* (Islamabad) July 7, 1999

36 Shakil Shaikh , Sharif Aziz Speak at Ruling Party Meeting, *The News*, July 14, 1999

37 Shakil Shaikh , Sharif Aziz Speak at Ruling Party Meeting, *The News*, July 14, 1999

38 Minister Says Islamabad Policy averted Nuclear War, *The News*, July 12, 1999

39Article Praises Sharif's Peace Initiative, *Rawalpindi Jang in Urdu 17 Jul 99 p11,JANG*Journal Code: 2296 Language: ENGLISH Record Type: FULLTEXT Document Type: Daily Report; *The News*

40 Based on interviews with serving general in the Adjutant–general branch, military officers in FCNA headquarters, 10 Corps HQ and soldiers in the battle zones.

41 Based on interviews of soldiers had who fought in Kargil According to one interviewee "At times there was even no food to eat. Some even had to eat grass, There were times they shot ibex and ate it. That use to be a treat."

42 Based on a series of interviews conducted by the author with soldiers who actually led the assault on Tiger Hill and were on Tiger Hill on 4 July.

43 He was coordinating the movement of two forces from Kargil. Often he would get calls from Delhi or from Rawalpindi saying that the agreed ceasefire by a specific unit at a given time was not being kept.

44 Pakistan Army chief admits his troops crossed LOC, *Indian Express*, 16 July 1999

45 The FCNA Commander in an interview to the author

46 General Javed Hasan Commander FCNA to the author on 13 August 2004 at MI conference room, GHQ

47 Acknowledged by the Indian military spoksman Col Bikram Singh India Reports Pakistan Army chief's remarks, Kargil Pullout , All India Radio , New Delhi, July 16, BBC Summary of World Broadcasts , 19 July 1999.

48 Tribune News Service, Intruders' posts pounded, *The Tribune*, Thursday, 22 July 1999
http://www.tribuneindia.com/1999/99jul22/head5.htm

49 Pakistan plea to Kashmir Militants , World: South Asia, BBC News, 9 July 1999

50 Barry Beark, (Islamabad) Foes Report Plan to Begin Pullout in Kashmir In Kashmir Region, *The NewYork Times*, 12 July 1999

51 Barry Beark, (Islamabad) Foes Report Plan to Begin Pullout in Kashmir In Kashmir Region, The NewYork Times, 12 July 1999

52 ibid

53 Indian Army chief's candid account of this discussion

54 Gaurav C Sawant, Army Blasts its way for a permanent stay at LOC. *Indian Express* 27 July 1999

55 FCNA Commander Brigadier Javed Hasan to the author

56 Pakistani Soldiers buried by Indian Army, 16 July 1999

57Prime Minister Nawaz Sharif to journalist Sohail Warraich quoted in Ghaddar Kaun, Tariq Fatimi to the author in the 11 September 2004 interview.

58 According to a senior general who had served in the GHQ during the Musharaf period, the army chief had confided and told him, "how should I say 1000, I told the prime minister there will hardly be any casualties."

59 Lives in the Askari 3 residential plot

60 Domestic Pressures Imperil Kashmir Peace Deal, Pamela Constable, *The Washington Post*, July 6 Tuesday, 1999

61 Saleh Zafir, Special correspondent, *Daily Jang*, pp 1 and 7,6 July 1999

62 Saleh Zafir Daily *Jang*, pp 1 and 7, July 6, 1999

63 Barry Bearak, Foes Report Plan To Begin Pullout in Kashmir Region, *New York Times*, 12 July 1999

64 Anwar Iqbal, India,Pakistan Agree to Disengagement, Ceasefire, *The News*, 12 July 1999

65 One of nearly a dozen groups fighting for Kashmiri independence or union with Pakistan

66 Kashmiri separatists tell US to back out of row, *Reuters*, 6 July 1999. http://www.jammu-kashmir.com/archives/archives1999/99july6a.html
67 Correspondent Report, *The News* (Islamabad), 22 July 1999
68 ibid
69 Correspondent Report, *The News* (Islamabad), 22 July 1999
70 Reuters, (Srinagar) Kashmiri separatists tell US to back out of row," 6 July 1999.
71 Reuters, (Srinagar) Kashmiri separatists tell US to back out of row," 6 July 1999.
72 Pakistan Army chief admits his troops crossed LOC, BBC World News, 16 July 1999.
73 India Reports Pakistan Army chief's remarks, Kargil Pullout , All India Radio , New Delhi, 16 July BBC Summary of World Broadcasts , 19 July 1999.
74 Pervez Musharraf, *In the Line of Fire*, Pg 93 (Free Press, New York, 2006)
75 Pervez Musharraf, *In The Line of Fire: A Memoir* pg 90 (London:Simon and Schuster, 2006)
76 He had resented Sharif's decision to not appoint him a cabinet minister.
77 For example addressing a gathering on 25 July the Vice President of the Pakistan Muslim League Ejazul Haq criticized them, declared them valueless and said "we have to avenge the 15,000 women, who were raped and seven million people who were killed in held Kashmir." (Pakistan-India war Delayed Not Over, News Correspondent *The News, 26 July 1999)*
78 Pakistan-India war Delayed Not Over, News Correspondent *The News, 26 July 1999*
79 For example addressing a gathering on 25 July the Vice President of the Pakistan Muslim League Ejazul Haq criticized them, declared them valueless and said "we have to avenge the 15,000 women, who were raped and seven million people who were killed in held Kashmir." (Pakistan-India war Delayed Not Over, News Correspondent *The News, 26 July 1999)*
80 Office holder of the Zia FoundationPakistan-India war Delayed Not Over, News Correspondent *The News, 26 July 1999*
81 Ibid
82 Militants in Pakistan Protests Against Agreement on Kashmir, Farhan Bokhari, *Financial Times* (London, England) 7 July 1999
83 ibid
84 Maleeha Lodhi, "Anatomy of a Disaster "*Newsline*, Karachi, July 1999.
85 See Kamran Khan, *The News* 5 September 1999
86 Waqar Mustafa, Pakistan Wants Peace, Army Chief, *Gulf News*, 8 July 1999
87 Waqar Mustafa, Pakistan Wants Peace, Army Chief, *Gul f News*, 8 July 1999
88 Altaf Gauhar former Minister of Information under military ruler President General Ayub Khan(1962-1966) also discusses this issue in his column Four Wars, One Assumption, *Nation* 5 September 1999

Chapter 16

1 A campaign was launched using some politicians from the ruling party, who linked up with parties like Jamaat-i-Islami, a party which opposed the Lahore Summit and the prime minister's India policy, and was also against the withdrawal. In fact, in some cases, the army chief personally met with some PML leaders including Ejazul Haq, who were garnering anti-Sharif support.
2 Pakistan A Rogue Army', *USA Today*, Accessed at: http://www.panditrv.com/roguearmy/paper3.jpg
3 Ibid.
4 Musharraf, Pervez, *In The Line of Fire: A Memoir*, London: Simon and Schuster, 2006, 137.
5 Accessed at: http://www.panditrv.com/roguearmy/a_private_note.htm
6 Warraich, Sohail, *Ghaddar Kaun*, Sagar Publishers, 2006.
7 'War is an area of uncertainty; three-quarters of the things on which all action in war is based are lying in a fog of uncertainty, to a greater or lesser extent. The first thing needed here is a fine, piercing mind, to feel out the truth, with the measure of its judgment.
8 'There was no official count of the number of soldiers who lost their lives in Operation KP. Figures range from 400 to even 2000,' Prime Minister Nawaz Sharif told journalist Sohail Warraich that 2,700 soldiers were killed, This was documented by Warraich in *Ghaddar Kaun*, Sagar Publishers, 2006.
9 To the author on 2 January 2005 at Kakul Military Academy.
10 A Kargil veteran to the author- an observation subsequently made in conversation with the author by many army officers

11 Narrated to author by several army officers who the author interacted with, specially during the early years of researching this book.
12 Recounted to the author by a Kargil veteran – also subsequently many junior and army officers recalled similar gestures of angry veterans targeting the FCNA commander.
13 In the vicinity of the Skardu airport.
14 Details recalled by several injured officers also admitted in the same hospital, details also recalled by senior officers who visited the troops with the senior command.
15 'POWs to be handed over to ICRC', *TheTimes of India,* 17 August 1999.
16 Shared with the author by NLI officers and COs present.
17 According to those present and those who had heard of the event said that the army chief told the troops, 'Meri izaat ka kahayal bhi rakhain.'
18 Shared with the author by their key staff member who witnessed this conversation.
19 The chief minister recalled the Musharraf meeting to the author in August 1999
20 Lt. General (Retd) Asad Durrani, 'Beyond Kargil', *The News,* 9 July 1999.
21 He was also a lead runner for the COAS position.
22 Musharraf, Pervez, *In the Line of Fire*, Free Press, 2006.
23 Lt. General Ali Quli Khan, *The News*, Islamabad, 5 October 2006.
24 Ibid.
25 Shared with the author by a common friend. The unfolding controversy became well known in journalistic circles.
26 Meeting was held in the Ops room in Gilgit. According to two participants, prolonged and somewhat cantankerous discussions were held among senior army officers to decide on the officers to be decorated with awards. Senior army commanders including Commander 10 Corps, commander FCNA and a major general from the GHQ participated in the meeting. Approximately 80 soldiers were given gallantry awards.
27 Ramesh Chandran, 'A Hot Minuet in Sunny New York, *The Times of India*, 29 September 1999.
28 'Pakistan troops launch major build-up along LOC', *Daily Excelsior*, 10 August 1999.
29 'J&K militants raid Army camp, kill five', *The Asia Age*, 6 August 1999.
30 'Infiltration bid foiled in J&K', *The Hindu*, 1 August 1999.
31 'Reports of build-up of Indian troops along border, unfounded', *The Economic Times*, 27 July 1999.
32 'India rejects Kashmir talks as army camp hit', *Reuters,* 8 August 1999.
33 'Taleban supreme commander does not care about US sanctions', *AFP*, 8 July 1999.
34 Bill, Clinton, My Life (NewYork, Knopf 2006) pg 866, Also see Strobe Talbot, The Day a Nuclear Conflict Was Averted, in YaleGlobal OnLine https://yaleglobal.yale.edu/content/day-nuclear-conflict-was-averted
35 Bruce Riedel to the author in a meeting in Washington DC
36 Read detailed account in See Steve Coll's book The Ghost Wars.
37 Eye witness account by an intelligence participant in the meeting
38 Bruce Riedel to the author in Washington 2 November 2006
39 'Sartaj Aziz Discusses Ties With Afghan Counterpart', *The News*, 27 August 1999.
40 'Foreign Staff, Taleban Leader Not US Target', *The Scotsman,* 6 August 1999.
41 'Sartaj Aziz Discusses Ties With Afghan Counterpart', *The News,* 27 August 1999.
42 Secretary Defense to the author. 28 May 2007
43 Musharraf, Pervez, *In The Line of Fire: A Memoir*, London: Simon and Schuster, 2006, 137.

Chapter 17

1 'India rejects Nawaz Sharif's Kashmir plebiscite demand', *Daily Excelsior,* 18 September 1999.
2 In interviews with the author, Sharif's ministers, including Chaudhry Nisar Ali Khan and Raja Zafarul Haq, and the CM Punjab Shehbaz Sharif, all argued that accountability would have been at the cost of national honour, Army's reputation, and Pakistan's international standing, hence, it was not advisable. Also see Rauf Klasra, 'Kargil Debacle: Musharraf's Time Bomb, Waiting to Explode', *South Asia Tribune* (Washington DC), 3 August 2004.
3 Formed in September, the Grand Democratic Alliance consisted of 15 parties, including the main Opposition parties, the Pakistan Peoples' Party, Muttahida Qaumi Mahaz, Awami National Party, Pakistan Tehreek-e-Insaf and others.
4 Refer to chapter three.

5 Rauf Klasra, 'Kargil Debacle: Musharraf's Time Bomb, Waiting to Explode', *South Asia Tribune*, Washington DC, 3 August 2004.
6 Confirmed by a senior general.
7 Discussed in detail in earlier chapters.
8 *Dawn*, 15 September 1999.
9 'Sharif Not Attending UN Assembly Meet', *The Hindu*, 16 September 1999.
10 Ibid. This story also covered Foreign Secretary Shamshad Ahmad's talk at the Islamabad Institute for Strategic Studies in which he clearly stated, 'The first priority for the world must, therefore, be to press India and not Pakistan to sign and ratify the CTBT and to reverse the preparations it had made for further nuclear tests.'
11 According to a trusted confidante of general Musharraf, he was worried because around mid-September, so the story went on: he had received an intercept. According to that intercept, Sharif had assured Vajpayee that he would publicly apologize for Kargil and fire Musharraf. Musharraf then set out to prevent Nawaz Sharif from going to address the UN. Musharraf, who was yet to place his trusted men to cover all strategic places for executing a coup, panicked on getting this intercept. He decided the PM's New York trip for the UN General Assembly Session had to be postponed.
12 Former Naval Chief, Admiral Fasih Bokhari to the author on 7 September 2017.
13 Secretary Defense, former Lt. General Iftikhar, to the author on May 28, 2007
14 A comment repeated by several American diplomats and American experts , to the author during series of discussions and interviews.
15 Talbott, Strobe, *Engaging India: Diplomacy, Democracy, and the Bomb*, Brookings Institution Press, 2004.
16 Ibid. 171.
17 Refer to Nasim Zehra, 'Pakistan puts security before CTBT issue', *Gulf News*, 19 September 1999, for details on Pakistan's position articulated by Prime Minister Nawaz Sharif in his 23 September 1998 UNGA speech and subsequently held as Islamabad's position throughout the Sharif-led government.
18 Bruce Riedel to the author in Washington. 2 November 2006
19 Talbott, Strobe, *Engaging India: Diplomacy, Democracy, and the Bomb*, Brookings Institution Press, 2004, 172.
20 Ibid.
21 Shehbaz Sharif to the author during a 27 May 2003 meeting in New York
22 Based on author's meetings with Karl Inderfurth in Washington and with Shehbaz Sharif.
23 Based on author's meetings with William Milam, Karl Inderfurth, Bruce Riedel, and Walter Anderson on 25 July 2006.
24 In recent decades successive US administrations had engaged Kashmir only in the case of a likely Pakistan-India military flare-up. Their objective had been mere fire-fighting, while effectively supporting Delhi's view that the LOC be converted to a permanent international border.
25 'US opposed to mediation on Kashmir', *The Hindu*, 28 September 1999.
26 Ibid.
27 Ramesh Chandran, 'Hot and Cold Minuet in Sunny New York', *The Times of India*, 29 September 1999.
28 Thomas Pickering to the author in Washington on 3 July 2005.
29 For the contents of the statement and the State Department's response see Amir Mateen, *The News*, 21 September 1999 Statement)US Warns against Unconstitutional removal of govt. Says constitutional means can be used for change; urges govt to respect press freedom Washington:The United States on Monday asked the Pakistan Army not to try any 'extra-constitutional method' to remove the Nawaz Sharif government. The unusual warning came through a State Department official in New York. When the State Department was contacted here in Washington, an official said this did not in any way mean that Nawaz Sharif could stay in power for the rest of his life. 'This warning is based on what we can see what is going on and we thought it would be appropriate to issue this warning,' he said. When asked if the State Department had assured the government its support, the US official said, 'What we said to the government, we gave a two pronged message. We support the constitutional basis of their being in authority but at the same time we remind them they have to obey the democratic rules.'

Reuters quoted the officials as saying that the US was concerned about political ferment in Pakistan and had warned political and military actors there that it would strongly oppose any attempt to overthrow the government. 'We hope there will be no return to the days of interrupted democracy in Pakistan,' a senior official told *Reuters* in an interview. 'We would strongly oppose any attempt to change the government through extra-constitutional means,' the official added.

Reuters said the Administration, acting discreetly through diplomatic channels, had also reminded the Islamabad government that peaceful demonstrations and free speech should be permitted in a democratic system. 'It is a strong message for both the sides. The government should allow legitimate expression and freedom of the press,' the senior official added.

Although there is no sign of any imminent coup against Sharif, *Reuters* quoted a US official as saying that the Pakistani press and the talk in elite circles was full of dissatisfaction with the prime minister. 'This warning does not mean that we oppose proper use of the democratic process in Pakistan. Not at all. If you look at our statement, it says the government should allow legitimate expression and freedom of the press.' 'There is enough speculation out there, both publicly and in the corridors that the administration felt it necessary to issue its warnings,' a US official said. The US statement came shortly after Punjab Chief Minister, Shehbaz Sharif, had detailed talks with topmost US officials in Washington before the weekend during which he had an thorough 'exchange of ideas', as one senior Pakistan embassy official put it.However, the State Department official claimed that if Nawaz Sharif was removed by constitutional mean, the US would have no objections. Asked whether this warning to the army meant that the US was also opposing a constitutional removal of the Nawaz government, the State Department official categorically said, 'No, not at all.'

30 'US Warns Against Unconstitutional Removal of Government', *The News*, 20 July 1999.

31 Nasim Zehra, 'The Americans Statement', *The News*, 24 September 1999

32 'Pakistani Opposition Wants to keep up Campaign to oust Sharif', *Agence France Presse*, 22 September 1999.

33 'Pakistan Army enjoys excellent ties with the government: army chief', *Xinhua News Agency*, 23 September 1999.

34 Refer to Farhan Bokhari, 'Sharif warned of disruption', *The Financial Times*, London, 23 September 1999, for the scenario that prevailed then in Pakistan's twin-cities.

35 Ramesh Chandran, 'Hot and Cold Minuet in Sunny New York', *The Times of India*, 29 September 1999.

36 Ramesh Chandran, 'Jaswant-Ackerman Talks to Focus on Terrorism, Sanctions', *TheTimes of India* , 26 September 1999. See also

Stephen Fidler, 'UN Sanctions against Kabul grow nearer', *Financial Times*, 28 September 1999.

38 Example of Indian press coverage of the Jammu and Kashmir situation, 'Militants attack security forces, politicians in Valley', *Daily Excelsior*, 3 September 1999; '10 Lashkar-e-Toiba militant shot dead in Budhal, Mandi', *Daily Excelsior*, 22 September 1999; Arun Joshi, 'Militants attempt to blast J&K secretariat', *The Hindustan Times*, 29 September 1999.

39 'HUJI chief for J &K among 6 top ultras eliminated in Rajouri', *Daily Excelsior*, 17 September 1999

40 'India rejects Nawaz Sharif's Kashmir plebiscite demand', *Daily Excelsior*, 18 September 1999.

41 'Infiltration in J&K continues despite preventive measures', *Daily Excelsior*, 22 September 1999.

42 'India rejects Nawaz Sharif's Kashmir plebiscite demand', *Daily Excelsior*, 18 September 1999.

43 'Pakistan Not to stop JKLF marchers', *The Indian Express*, 27 September 1999.

44 Pradeep Dutta, 'Violators will be shot at, Army Warns JKLF', *The Indian Express*, 3 October 1993.

45 Barry Bearak, 'Dateline: Srinangar, Kashmir,' *The Gazette*, Montreal, Quebec, 26 September 1999.

46 Report of the Secretary-General on the work of the Organization, General Assembly Official Records, Fifty-fourth Session

Supplement No. 1 (A/54/1), Accessed at: http://www.un.org/documents/ga/docs/54/plenary/a54-1.pdf.

47 Secretary General Kofi Annan, Chapter I: Achieving peace and security, paragraph 84, page 10, Report of the Secretary-General on the work of the Organization General Assembly Official Records Fifty-fourth Session Supplement No. 1 (A/54/1), Accessed at: http://www.un.org/documents/ga/docs/54/plenary/a54-1.pdf.

48 Ibid.

48 For the induction of the Osama factor see 'India to crush Laden's plan to launch jehad against India: Advani', *Daily Excelsior*, 19 September 1999.

50 For the alliance's politics and role in the power-play during the crucial month of September read Aamer Ahmad Khan, 'Desperately Seeking Solutions', in monthly *Herald,* Karachi, October 1999; Ali Dayan Hasan, 'Understanding the Opposition', in monthly *Herald* Karachi, October 1999.

51 'Pakistan's Opposition Alliance Announce Nine Point Agenda,' *The News*, 20 September 1999.

52 Ibid.

53 Independent and financially autonomous election commission, restructuring of the economy, strengthening of the federation by maximum provincial autonomy with the framework of the federation and decentralization and devolution of powers down to local governments, rehabilitation of all national institutions, restoration of

democracy and rule of law, human rights, and freedom of press, effective representation of women in national institutions, special priority to defense, education, health science, and technology.

54 'Pakistan's Opposition Alliance Announce Nine Point Agenda', *The News*, 20 September 1999. Coup-maker General Pervez Musharraf set up this planned Ehetesab Commission soon after the 12 October coup.

55 Farhan Bokhari, 'Police put halt to Karachi rally', *Financial Times*, 27 September 1999; also see 'Pakistan arrests opposition backers', (Dateline Karachi), in *The Gazette*, Montreal, Quebec, 12 September 1999.

56 They had been killed in a house collapse.

57 Ibid.

58 They had been killed in a house collapse.

58 Ibid.

58 The ISI official who was present in this meeting recalled, with admiration, the details of Mullah Omar's abode and of the meeting.

59 Lt. General J. Gulzar Kiyani to the author on 2 April 2008.

60 See 'Opposition Terms Ouster of Sharif "Need of Hour"', *The News*, 27 September 1999; Waqar Mustafa, 'Sharifs Trying to Destroy Army,' *Gulf News*, 27 September 1999.

61 See PPP's Makhdoom Amin Faheem's position in, 'Opposition Terms Ouster of Sharif "Need of Hour"', *The News*, 27 September 1999.

62 Confirmed by Shehbaz Sharif's hosts including Karl Inderfuth, Walter Anderson and also Robert Oakley.

63 Farhan Bokhari, 'Sharif warned of disruption', *Financial Times*, London, 23 September 1999For the scenario that then prevailed in Pakistan's twin-cities see Nasim Zehra, 'The American Statement,' *The News*, 24 September 1999.

64 According to the Defense Secretary, Bokhari's personal file carried some 'adverse comments' about his commitment to democracy and the PM decided against appointing him.

65 Told by the Defense Secretary to the author May 28, 2007. .It was an issue that was echoed in the local media as well.

66 Shehbaz Sharif revealed this in an interview with the author in New York on 27 May 2003. He also made the point that, while remaining loyal to his brother, he did not 'deceive or hoodwink Musharraf'. In fact, Shehbaz emphasized, even when the question of General Jehangir Karamat's successor came up, the then Director General ISI, General Ziaud Din, came to him and said, 'Karamat will be going, I am your Kashmiri brother; so, please keep me in mind.' Shehbaz suspected that Ziaud Din was a mole planted on him by the Establishment. Shehbaz met the prime minister and said, 'Ziauddin wants to be the next COAS, but don't even think of it.'

67 Told to the author by the then defence Secretary.

68 As told by Shehbaz Sharif to the author, and also confirmed by Bob Oakley during the 17 December 2006 interview in Washington.

69 Admiral Bokhari told *TheTribune* correspondent, Muhammad Shahzad, that now he was free to speak because the minimum term to stay quiet after leaving the navy job had been completed. 'I resigned on 5 October 1999, a week before Musharraf's coup of 12 October because I had come to know that he had decided to topple the Sharif government.' Accessed at: http://www.antisystemic.org/satribune/ www.satribune.com/archives/oct7_13_02/DTimes_fasihoct9.htm. In a later conversation with the author on 17 September 2017, the former naval chief said that during a visit to his house Musharraf had talked angrily about the elected prime minister and 'did not want him in the PM's slot'. This made the naval chief conclude, as did many others, that a coup was a strong possibility.

70 Claim made by many then serving senior military officers. A close confidante of army chief Musharraf claimed that 25 October was the anointed date, clearly indicating thatMusharraf planned the coup much before 12 October: Fasih Bokhari, the former naval chief, says the general feared court martial for masterminding Kargil. Accessed at:

http://www.antisystemic.org/satribune/www.satribune.com/archives/oct7_13_02/DTimes_fasihoct9.htm. The Admiral knew about General Musharraf's plans to topple Nawaz Sharif and did not want to be part of these 'dirty games'. According to a report on the web portal, *South Asia Tribune*, the comments by Admiral Bokhari come exactly three years after his resignation. He told *TheTribune* correspondent, Muhammad Shahzad, that now he was free to speak because the minimum term to stay quiet after leaving the navy job had been completed. 'I resigned on 5 October 1999, a week before Musharraf's coup of 12 October because I had come to know that he had decided to topple the Sharif government.'

71

72 The two were easy to convince, especially the Corps Commander who was angered by the performance of Nawaz's Chief Minister, Ghous Ali Shah.
73 As the German threat against Moscow grew around 1935, the weak French government's Foreign Minister Pierre Laval reached out to Stalin for help. He wanted Stalin to observe a more liberal position towards the church in Moscow, as quid pro quo for encouraging the Papacy to be more supportive of the French government's moves. But Stalin, who saw the Pope as a weak, unpopular figure responded by asking, 'The Pope? How many divisions has he got?'
74 See Imran Khan's position in Waqar Mustafa, 'Sharifs Trying to Destroy Army', *Gulf News*, 27 September 1999.
75 See PPP's Makhdoom Amin Faheem's position in, 'Opposition Terms Ouster of Sharif "Need of Hour"', *The News*, 27 September 1999.
76 Anees Jillani, 'Pakistan's Survival Depends on Army', *The News*, 28 September 1999.

Chapter 18

1 This chapter is based on the author's several detailed interviews and conversations with the following key figures on the day of the coup: Defence Secretary Lt. General (Retd) Iftikhar Ali Khan , army chief general Pervez Musharraf, PM's Principal Secretary Saeed Mehdi, commander 111 brigade brigadier Satti, PM's Military Secretary, Corps Commander Quetta Lt. General Tariq Pervez, Chairman PIA Shahid Khaqan Abbasi, Captain flight PK 805, Chief Minister Punjab Shehbaz Sharif, Minister for Petroleum Chaudhary Nisar, Commander, Minister of State for Communication Raja Nadir Pervez Minister of State for Communications, flight Captain Sarwat Hussain, Chief Pilot/Director Operations Captain ShahNawaz Dara, renowned Human Rights activist and lawyer Asma Jehangir, 111 Brigade, Finance Minister Ishaq Dar, Chairman PTV Pervez Rashid, MD PTV Yusuf Baig Mirza, Hamid Mir journalist,
2 Details in the previous Chapter 17
3 Words the brigadier told the author he had used to describe the general when, in 1998, after the removal of army chief Jahangir Karamat, the PM had asked for his assessment of senior generals.
4 Khatam Quran
5 In a subsequent meeting, the ISI chief told the DS that during the trip the PM asked him about his seniority.
6 The idea of the CCDNS had surfaced a few weeks after Kargil and during a GHQ meeting was presented by the top army brass to the visiting PM. The PM tasked the Foreign Minister to work on a consensus structure. After several meetings, including meetings with army chief Musharraf and DGMO Tauqeer Zia, Sartaj Aziz finalized the CCDNS structure.

7 The foreign minister told the author on 19 July, 2002, "As a foreign minister, I had felt that we were not participating in the foreign policy making." Musharraf was happy that this was happening through the civilian government.
8 Foreign Minister Sartaj Aziz to the author.
9 Its members would be the ministers of foreign affairs, finance, defense and interior, the three services chiefs, the chairman of the Joint Chiefs of Staff Committee. A National Security Advisor to the prime minister would be the chairman of the Planning Committee of the National Security Committee. Its members would be the foreign secretary, interior secretary, and director-generals ISI, MI, and IB. The Planning Committee would prepare position paper and recommendations on all security issues.
10 This chapter is based on several detailed sittings with the Defense Secretary, Principal Secretary, Military Secretary, Chief Minister Punjab, Chaudhary Nisar, Commander 111 brigade, MD PTV, Finance Minister Ishaq Dar, and Chairman PTV Pervez Rashid
11 Javed Shah later joined Pervez Musharraf and then returned to the PM's fold
12 According to what the Defense Secretary told the author, the DG ISI Ziauddin told General Iftikhar that, during the trip, the PM asked had queried him about his seniority.

13 The PM was perhaps referring to the statement the army chief had given at an embassy function.
14 Joint Chief of Staff Committee
15 Commander Zahid was a retired naval officer, employed with PIA and appointed on deputation as Director Protocol, PM House.

16 The President's signature is a Constitutional requirement. The order was prepared , the PM signed it and took it to the President Tarrar for his signature.

17 Owen Bennet-Jones, *Pakistan: Eye of the Storm*

18 That was the message about army chief's removal and the new appointment that Minister Pervez Rashid would later read on the television.

1) Under clause 1 of the Constitutional article 243 entitled Command of the Armed Forces "The Federal government shall have command and control of the armed forces." Under clause 4(b) the "President shall on the advice of the prime minister appoint the army chief."

20 GHQ-based Lt. General in charge of postings and transfers.

21 Zia uld Din had approached Shehbaz and said, "I am your Kashmiri brother; please do protect my interests," Shehbaz had reported this to the PM. He had warned the PM that Ziaud Din may be a mole!

22 The justification repeated by the PM's lawyer Khawaja Haris before the SC: The learned counsel for petitioner submitted that the statement of the petitioner made under Section 342 Cr. P.C. before the Trial Court, clearly demonstrated the existence of tension between the petitioner and General Pervaiz Musharraf. That the friction was further aggravated by the replacement of the latter as chief of army staff and that in order to avoid division in the Pakistan Army, on account of the change in its leadership, and to protect the Government established under the Constitution, the petitioner had considered it appropriate, in the interest of public safety and tranquility, to order diversion of the Aircraft carrying General Pervaiz Musharraf. The learned counsel pointed out that as a matter of fact, the instruction of diversion of Aircraft was given after the Army had moved to takeover important government installations. He argued that the decision to be taken by the prime minister was based upon his subjective assessment of the situation.

(Pg 23, http://www.supremecourt.gov.pk/web/user_files/File/Crl.P.200of2009.pdf)

23 As the prime minister as well as the Minister for Defense, he was empowered to exercisethe powers conferred on the Federal Government by Section 6 of theOrdinance. Although the said provision requires notification of the exercise ofsuch powers, however under Rule 5(11-A) of the Rules of Business, the Prime

Crl. P. No. 200 of 2009 25 Also the provision requires notification of the exercise ofsuch powers the Minister was competent to pass verbal orders in case of emergency.

24 Point reproduced on page 23 of the July 2009 judgment of the Supreme Court http://www.supremecourt.gov.pk/web/user_files/File/Crl.P.200of2009.pdf

25 At the Air Traffic Control complex, all communication from the air traffic control room with the cockpit takes place via the radar room. Messages are first communicated via intercom from the traffic control room to the radar room. Radar room then communicates the message to the cockpit.

26 See Idrees Bakhtiar's article "PK 805 100 minutes to Touchdown" in *Herald*, March 2000. Bakhtiar reproduces the conversation that took place between the ATC and PK805 from 6.06 pm till minutes after touchdown at 7.50pm

27 Conversation of the author with the flight Captain on 23 September 2017

28 Aminullah Chaudhary subsequently became an approver in the case. After Nawaz Sharif got acquitted he wrote a detailed apology note to the former prime minister

29 Recalled by Brigadier Javed Malik in interview with the author and also confirmed by the DGCAA Aminullah Chaudhary in his testimony in Court which is reproduced in the SC judgment pages 17 to 21 http://www.supremecourt.gov.pk/web/user_files/File/Crl.P.200of2009.pdf

30 In making his own decision the Captain was going by the book- a fact affirmed by Ground Movement Controller CAA, Nadeem Akbar. He is quoted to have said in the transcript reproduced in Idrees Bakhtiar's article "PK 805 100 minutes to Touchdown" in the *Herald*, March 2000. When asked by Secretary to DG CAA as to who determines flight diversion in case of airfield closure, Nadeem's response was, " If all the airfields are closed, then all aircrafts are informed. Accordingly, it is aircraft's responsibility whether they decide what to do…"

31 For time accuracy, see Idrees Bakhtiar's article "PK 805 100 minutes to Touchdown"..published in the *Herald* of March 2000, Bakhtiar reproduces the conversation that took place between the ATC and PK805 from 6:06 pm till minutes after touchdown at 7:50 pm

32 Generally considered mandatory.

33 Nawaz Sharif was acquitted by the Supreme Court's 5-member bench 17 July 2009 https://www.dawn.com/news/851441 The five-member bench in its Court ruled in its 55-page unanimous order that "Looking at the case from any angle, the charge of hijacking, attempt to hijack or terrorism does not

stand established against the petitioner." The bench headed by Justice Tassaduq Hussain Jillani with Justice Nasirul Mulk, Justice Moosa K. Leghari, Justice Sheikh Hakim Ali and Justice Ghulam Rabbani as its members futher ruled that "In the light of the principles of law of evidence on the burden and standard of proof, we are of the opinion that the Appellate Court had misdirected itself by holding that the petitioner was unable to substantiate the plea taken by him in his statement under Section 342 Cr. P.C." The judgment concluded that "The conviction and sentence of the appellant are set aside and he is acquitted. The Sindh High Court's verdict sentencing Mr Sharif to life term was quashed..

The bench was also sympathetic to Sharif's plea that he had moved the petition after eight years since "the sentence was a "stigma" and "slur" on his character and denied him the right to contest elections, It ruled that "Every citizen is entitled to have his name cleared, if unjustifiably sullied, and it should be of particular importance to the petitioner, who remained prime minister of the country twice and is presently leading a major political party, to remove the stigma of conviction for a crime and that too of hijacking, generally associated with terrorism."

34 Under Army Act 1952 Chapter 3 clause 16-21, especially clause 16 gives the federal government the authority to dismiss any person subject to the Army Act and on whom the Act is applicable.

35 The Defense Secretary decided to go on leave starting 13 October. On yhe 14th, his resignation letter was delivered to the Chief Martial law Administrator General Pervez Musharraf. On 21 October Musharraf accepted his resignation and heard of his retirement over the television

36 The defense secretary decided to go on leave starting 13 October. On 14th his resignation letter was delivered to the Chief Martial Law Administrator General Pervez Musharraf. On 21 October Iftikhar Musharraf accepted his resignation and heard of his retirement over the television

37"My phones were taken away," he told the author, "And I was asked to either bang on the door to communicate a need or slip a piece of paper from under the door. Soldiers were on guard outside his room."

38 Sample of these writings…Zahid Hussain in his article Day of the General wrote "Most Pakistanis have welcomed the military takeoverwith both hope and wariness. The scenes of public jubiliation witnessed on the streets of Karachi and other major cities…" (NewLine October 1999) ; Zaffar Abbas in his Herald (Novem 1999) article Full Circle wrote "Clearly the change was accepted by the Pakistani people in near totality, including most members of the ousted PML(N) government….There is little doubt in the minds of people including many PML(N) stalwarts , thsat Nawaz Sharif is largely to be blamed for the return of military rule." M. Illyas Khan in his article Night of the Coup also reported that "There have been sporadic celebrations and even a sense of relief at the quite coup that turned Pakistan upside down on 12 October but the overall mood was that of indifference.." (Herald, November 1999)

39 Sami Zuberi, "Pakistan Army in control after prime minister ousted in coup", *Agence France Presse* , 13 October 1999

40 ibid

41 Barbara Slavin, "Military Takes over Pakistan Experts fearful of extreme turn," in *USA Today* (13 October 1999)

42 A phrase used by a US official commenting on the 12 October coup- quoted by Barbara Slavin, "Military Takes over Pakistan Experts fearful of extreme turn," in *USA Today* (13 October 1999)

43 John Lancaster & Bradly Graham, "Military Ignored US Warning : Efforts to Shore Up Islamabad's Civilian Government Failed," *The Washington Post* , October 13, 1999

44 James Morrison, No Problem At Embassy, *The Washington Times,* 13 October 1999

45 The July 2009 judgment of the Supreme Court based on a detailed trial validated Sharif's version that the a coup against him had been planned.

46Pakistan's leading human rights activist Asma Jehangir son, was also traveling in PK 805. She would later recall to the author that "12 October was the worst day of her life." For about hour the families of the passengers had no clue of the fate of their loved ones.

47 A point to note ofcourse is that folk tales today are almost interfacing the 'manufacturing' power of the social media. It is not entirely unlikely that social media may gradually prey on folklore like a shredder.

Chapter 19

1 Tzu, Sun, *The Art of War* (Translated from Chinese by Lionel Giles, M. A.), New York: Fall River Press, 2011, 5.

2 According to Clausewitz, 'Theory demands, therefore, that at the commencement of every War, its character and main outline shall be defined according to what the political conditions and relations lead us to anticipate

as probable. The more that, according to this probability, its character approaches the form of absolute War, the more its outline embraces the mass of belligerent States and draws them into the vortex—so much the more complete will be the relation of events to one another and the whole, but so much the more necessary will it also be not to take the first step without thinking what may be the last.'

3 Wilkinson, Spenser, *The French Army Before Napoleon; Lectures Delivered Before The University Of Oxford In Michaelmas Term, 1914*,General Books, 2013. Accessed at:
http://archive.org/stream/frencharmybefore00wilkuoft/frencharmybefore00wilkuoft_djvu.txt.

4 This point made by Napoleon is explained in detail by Wilkinson, Spenser, *The French Army Before Napoleon; Lectures Delivered Before The University Of Oxford In Michaelmas Term, 1914*. Accessed at: //archive.org/stream/frencharmybefore00wilkuoft/frencharmybefore00wilkuoft_djvu.txt.

5 For further explanation of the planning principle see Jomini, Antoine Henri, *The Art of War* (Translated by G. H. Mendell and W. P. Craighill), Arc Manor Publishers, Rockville, Maryland, 2007, 36–37.

6 Clausewitz, von Carl, *On War* (Edited and translated by Michael Howard & Peter Paret), Princeton University Press, 1976, 179.

7 'Interview with Vo Nguyen Giap Viet Minh Commander',*PBS*, Accessed at:
http://www.pbs.org/wgbh/peoplescentury/episodes/guerrillawars/giaptranscript.html.

8 Military philosopher Baron de Jomini's definition of strategy.

9 Clausewitz, Carl von, *On War* (Edited and translated by Michael Howard & Peter Paret), Princeton University Press, 1976, 178.

10 Specifically according to Carl Von Clausewitz

11 Clausewitz's original 1838 writing, *de'l art de la guerre*, and translated in 1862 as *The Art of War* by G. H. Mendell and W. P. Craighill,

12 1862 translation as *The Art of War* by Capt. G.H. Mendell and Lieut. W.P. Craighill, U.S. Army http://l-clausewitz.livejournal.com/190040.html [journal doesn't exist]

13 Von Clausewitz, Carl, *On War* (Edited and translated by Michael Howard & Peter Paret), Princeton University Press, 1976.

14 Ibid.

15 For one view on this approach see Interview with general Vo Nguyen Giap Viet Minh Commander,*PBS*, Accessed at: http://www.pbs.org/wgbh/peoplescentury/episodes/guerrillawars/giaptranscript.html

16 Ibid.

17 Von Clausewitz, Carl, *On War* (Edited and translated by Michael Howard & Peter Paret), Princeton University Press, 1976, 17.

18 Clausewitz first used the term 'friction' during the campaign of 1806 to describe the difficulties Scharnhorst encountered in persuading the high command to reach decisions and the further difficulties in having the decisions implemented. (Von Clausewitz, *On War* (Edited and translated by Michael Howard & Peter Paret), Princeton University Press, 1976.

19 Baron Antoine Henri de Jomini - The Art of War (Arc Manor Publishers, Rockville, Maryland, 2007) pg 51

20 De Jomini, Antoine Henri, *The Art of War* (Translated by G. H. Mendell and W. P. Craighill), Arc Manor Publishers, Rockville, Maryland, 2007, 189–191.

21 Clausewitz, Carl von, *On War* (Translated by Colonel J. J. Graham with Introduction and Notes by Colonel F. N. Maude), Volume III , Routledge and Kegan Paul, London and Boston, Great Britain, 3–4.

22 Clausewitz, Carl von, *On War* (Edited and translated by Michael Howard and Peter Paret), Princeton University Press, Princeton New Jersey, 1976, 17.

23There were also the pulpits of mosques, from where the message of solidarity with the Kashmiris and of extreme anger towards the Indian government and those who engaged with them, was publicized.

24 There is absolutely no evidence that the US at any point since 1947 even contemplated, leave aside made any such proposition to Pakistan. There is enough literature to support that Washington has ever since 1947 sought India's alliance in South Asia and now in Asia.

25 Discussed in chapter 8

26 Discussed in earlier chapters

27 The LOC originated as a ceasefire line in 1948 followed by changes prompted by the 1965 and 1971 Pakistan-India wars.

28 Confirmed to the author by US Ambassador William Milam and by mid-level US officials of the State department, and Defense department and also by a senior CIA official. The Indian Army and intelligence too

made no claims of having any evidence of Pakistan preparing nuclear weapons for use. However, the senior State Department officials' emphasis upon Pakistan's moves to use nuclear weapons is backed by no concrete evidence. Meanwhile, establishing strategic partnership with India was a priority for the Clinton administration. Clinton's senior State Department team led this initiative. For an insider's view of how Clinton was 'guided' by his State Department team read: Strobe Talbott's *The Day A Nuclear Conflict Was Averted*, 13 September 2004. Accessed at: https://yaleglobal.yale.edu/content/day-nuclear-conflict-was-averted.

29 Point made by several Indians including Lt. General Raghavan during interview in Delhi on 22 April 2002.

30 Rodney W. Jones & Joseph McMillan , *The Kargil Crisis: Lessons Learned by the United States*

31 Raghavan, V. R., 'Manipulating Nuclear Deterrence', *The Hindu*, 3 July 2002.

32 General Aziz to the author on 15 January 2002.

33 Oakley to the author in an interview 17 December 2006

34 Brigadier retired Feroz Khan makes the point in his book: *Eating Grass , The Making of the Pakistani Bomb*, Stanford University Press, Redwood City, California, 2012.

35 Washington completely ignored the Indian plan to cross the LOC and also use nuclear weapons if needed, a fact India's leading journalist, Barkha Dutt, wrote in her book: *This Unquiet Land.* In the book, Dutt has quoted former Indian National Security Advisor, Brajesh Mishra, 'Crossing the Line of Control was not ruled out, nor was the use of nuclear weapons.' Mishra tells Dutt in an interview. Accessed at: http://www.business-standard.com/article/current-affairs/india-was-ready-to-cross-loc-use-nuclear-weapons-in-kargil-war-115120300518_1.html.

36 An observation made by the Defense Secretary General Iftikhar in an interview with the author May 28, 2007

37 Sir General Sir Archibald P. Wavell on Napoleon's Strategy and Tactics, Accessed at: http://www.napolun.com/mirror/web2.airmail.net/napoleon/Napoleon_tactics.htm.

38 Clausewitz, Carl von, *On War* (Edited and translated by Michael Howard & Peter Paret), Princeton University Press, 1976, 528.

39 Exhibited for example at Ulm in 1805 by Macks, who premised his planning upon a false foundation and was defeated by Napoleon. The Battle of Ulm on 16–19 October 1805 was a series of skirmishes at the end of the Ulm campaign, which allowed Napoleon to trap an entire Austrian Army under the command of Karl Freiherr Mack von Leiberich with minimal losses and to force its surrender near Ulm in the Electorate of Bavaria. In his proclamation in the *Bulletin de la Grande Armée* of the 21 October 1805, Napoleon said, 'Soldiers of the *Grande Armée*, I announced to you a great battle. But thanks to the bad combinations of the enemy, I obtained the same success with no risk ... In 15 days, we have won a campaign.'

40 Clausewitz, Carl von, *On War* (Edited and translated by Michael Howard & Peter Páret), Princeton University Press, 1976, 17 and 177.

Chapter 20

1 Exhibited for example at Ulm in 1805 by Macks, who premised his planning upon a false foundation and was defeated by Napolean. The Battle of Ulm on 16–19 October 1805 was a series of skirmishes at the end of the Ulm campaign, which allowed Napoleon to trap an entire Austrian army under the command of Karl Freiherr Mack von Leiberich with minimal losses and to force its surrender near Ulm in the Electorate of Bavaria.In his proclamation in the *Bulletin de la Grande Armée* of the 21 October 1805, Napoleon said, "Soldiers of the *Grande Armée*, I announced you a great battle. But thanks to the bad combinations of the enemy, I obtained the same success with no risk... In 15 days we have won a campaign."

2 (Carl von Clausewitz, On War (Edited and translated by Michael Howard & Peter Paret), pg 17 Princeton University Press, Princeton New Jersey (1976) pg 177)

SOURCES OF PRIMARY DATA (INTERVIEWS, CONVERSATIONS AND WRITTEN EXCHANGES)

- AbdusSattar, Former High Commissioner to India, Former Foreign Secretary and Foreign Minister of Pakistan
- Admiral Nayyar, Member National Security Advisory Board, Vice Chief of Naval Staff, Commander in Chief (South) February 1986
- Agha Shahi, Former Foreign Secretary of Pakistan (1973-1977)
- Air Vice Marshal Shahzad Chaudhry
- Ambassador Aziz Khan, Pakistan's High commissioner to India (June 2003-September 2006)
- Ambassador Mufti Abbas, First Secretary in Pakistan High Commission in Delhi (1947)
- Arun Singh Additional Secretary Ministry of External Affairs, New Dehli
- Arun Jethley, Minister of law and Justice
- S. Dulat, Former RAW Chief and Advisor on Kashmir policy in the Prime Minister's Office
- Ashraf Qazi, Pakistan High Commissioner to India (1997-2002)
- Asma Jehangir, Human Rights activist and lawyer

- Brajesh Mishra, Prime Minister's National Security Advisor
- Brigadier Aijaz Ahad, CO NLI 3, Pakistan
- Brigadier Javed Malik Prime Minister Nawaz Sharif's Military Secretary
- Brigadier Khalid Nazir, CO NLI
- Brigadier Masood Aslam, Commander 80 Brigade
- Brigadier Nadeem Ahmad Director Military Operations, FCNA Commander Oct 2001-2003
- Brigadier Naeem Salik, Pakistan Army
- Bruce Riedel, Special Assistant to the President, and Senior Director for Near East Affairs on the National Security Council, USA (1997-2001)
- Captain Sarwat Hussain, captain of flight PK 805 on 12 Octobe, 1999
- Captain Shah Nawaz Dara, Chief Pilot/Director Operations
- Chaudhry Nisar, former Minister for Petroleum and Natural Resources and Special Assistant to the prime minister (1997-1999)
- Chaudhry Shujaat, former Interior Minister (1997-1999)
- Colonel (Territorial Army) Manvendra Singh, Indian Politician and fought at Kargil
- Commander 111 Brigade Salauddin Satti, (retired as Lt. General Chief of General Staff)
- Commodore Jasjit Singh, Head of Institute of Defense and Strategic Studies, Delhi
- Dr. Maliha Lodhi, Permanent Representative of Pakistan to the United Nations, former High Commissioner to the UK & Ambassador to the US
- General (Retd) Anthony Zinni, Commander in Chief, United States Central Command (August 1997-September 2000)
- General Jehangir Karamat, Chief Of Army Staff (COAS).
- General Pervez Musharraf, Chief Of Army Staff (COAS).

- General Ved Malik, former Indian Army chief.
- General V. R. Raghavan, Former Director General Military Operations, India
- George Fernandez, Indian Minister of Defense.
- Gib Lampher, Former US Deputy Assistant Secretary of State for South Asian Affairs
- Hameed Kidwai, Pakistani Diplomat
- Hamid Mir, Journalist
- K. Gujral, former Indian Prime Minister & Indian Foreign Minister
- Inamul Haq, Former Foreign Minister and Foreign Secretary of Pakistan
- Jaswant Singh, former Indian Foreign Minister
- J. N. Dixit, Former Indian High Commissioner to Pakistan (1989-1991), Indian foreign secretary and chief of the IFS (1991-1994)
- Karl Inderfurth, Assistant Secretary of State for South Asian Affairs, USA (August 1997 to January 2001)
- Kashmiri leaders including All Parties Hurriyet Conference, Mir Waiz Umar Farooq, Sajjad Lone and Shabbir Shah
- K. Subramanian, Director Institute of Defense Studies and Analysis and Chairman Kargil Review Committee
- Lt. General(r) Abdul Qadir Baloch, Commander XII Corps, Pakistan Army
- Lt. General (r)Ehsanul Haq Director General Military Intelligence,
- Lt. General (r)Iftikhar Ali Khan, Defense Secretary
- Lt. General (r)Javed Hassan, commander XXX Corps & commander, Force Command Northern Areas (FCNA)
- Lt. General (r)Jamshed Gulzar Kiani, Commander 10 Corps
- Lt. General (r) Tariq Khan, Inspector-General Frontier Constabulary & Commander 1 Corps.

- Lt. General (r) Muhammad Aziz, Chief of General Staff & Chairman Joint Chief of Staff Committee
- Lt. General (r)Salauddin Satti, Chief of the General Staff (CGS) & Commander X Corps
- Lt. General (r) Jacob, Indian Army
- Lt. General (r) Satish Nambiar, Director of the United Service Institution of India from 1st July 1996 to 31 December 2008, New Delhi
- Major Akhtar, NLI 6, Pakistan Army
- Marvin Weinbaum, Intelligence and Research Analyst for Afghanistan and Pakistan, US Department of State (1999-2003) and Scholar-in-Residence, Middle East Institute (2003-Present)
- M Dubey, Indian Foreign Secretary (April 1990 to November 1991)
- Natwar Singh, Former Indian High Commissioner to Pakistan
- Mian Mohammad Nawaz Sharif, Prime Minister of Pakistan
- Niaz Naik, Former Foreign Secretary and Back- Channel Envoy for Pakistan
- Pervez Rashid, Chairman Pakistan Television and later Minister of Information & Broadcasting
- Raja Zafar ul Haq, Federal minister for Religious Affairs (July 1997-October 1999)
- Raminder Jassal, Ministry of External Affairs Spokesperson (1999), later Indian Deputy Chief of Mission in Washington
- Ram Jethalani, Chairman of the Indian Kashmir Committee
- Riaz Khokhar, Pakistan's Ambassador to India (1992-1997), the United States (1997–1999) and China (1999–2002) and former Foreign Secretary of Pakistan (June 2002 to February 2005)
- Riaz Mohammad Khan, former Foreign Secretary, Additional Secretary in charge of international organizations and arms control issues for Pakistan's Ministry of Foreign Affairs (1998-2002) and Spokesman of the Foreign Office (2000-2001)

- Saeed Mehdi, Principal Secretary to Prime Minister Nawaz Sharif
- Salman Bashir, Former Foreign Secretary
- Salman Haider Former Indian Foreign secretary
- Sartaj Aziz, Minister of Foreign Affairs (August 1998 until 1999)
- Shehbaz Sharif, Chief Minister of Punjab
- Shahid Khaqan Abbasi, Chairman PIA, (currently Prime Minister)
- Shahryar Khan, Former Foreign Secretary of Pakistan (1990-1994)
- Shamshad Ahmad, Former Foreign Secretary of Pakistan (1997-2000)
- Sudheendra R. K. Kulkarni, Former Speechwriter for Former Indian Prime Minister A. B. Vajpayee
- Professor Riffat Hussain, Defense Analyst
- Robert Oakley, US Ambassador to Pakistan (August 1988-1991)
- Tanveer Ahmed Khan, Foreign Secretary of Pakistan (1989-90)
- Tariq Fatemi, Special Assistant to the prime minister on Foreign Affairs & former Advisor Additional Secretary, Prime Minister's Office, Pakistan (July 1998 to July 1999)
- Thomas Pickering, US Under Secretary of State for Political Affairs (1997-2000)
- V. P. Singh, former Indian Prime Minister
- Walter Anderson, Former Chief of the US State Department's South Asia Division in the Office of Analysis for the Near East and South Asia
- William Milam, US Ambassador to the Islamic Republic of Pakistan (August 1998-July 2001)
- Zamir Akram, Director General for South Asia, Ministry of Foreign Affairs, Pakistan 1998-2000)

BIBLIOGRAPHY

Books & Articles

Abbas, Hassan. *Pakistan's Drift into Extremism: Allah, the Army and America's War on Terror*. New York: M. E. Sharpe Inc., 2005.

Abbas, Hassan, The Taliban Revival, New Haven and London, Yale University Press, 2014

Abdullah, Sheikh. *Flames of the Chinar*, translated by Singh, Khushwant. New Delhi: Penguin Books India P Ltd., 1993.

Adkin, Mark & Yousaf, Mohammad. *The Bear Trap: Afghanistan's Untold Story*. Lahore: Jang Publishers, 1992.

Ahmad, Shamshad. *Dreams Unfulfilled*. (Pakistan, Jahangir Books, Lahore, XXXX)

Ahmad, Syed Nur, edited by Baxter, Craig. *From the Martial Law to Martial Law, Politics in the Punjab, 1919-1958*. Lahore: Vanguard Books (Pvt.) Ltd., 1985.

Ahmed, Brigadier (Retd.) Gulzar. *Pakistan Meets Indian Challenge*. Rawalpindi: Al Mukhtar Publishers, 1967.

Ahmed, Ishtiaq. *Pakistan – The Garrison State: Origins, Evolution, Consequences 1947-2011*. Karachi: Oxford University Press, 2013.

Aijazuddin, F. S. *The White House & Pakistan: Secret Declassified Documents, 1969-1974*. Karachi: Oxford University Press, 2002.

Ali, Brig. Jamshed. *Defence Horizons*. Karachi: Mas Printers, 2003.

Ali, Lt. Col. Syed Ishfaq. *Fangs of Ice (Story of Siachen)*. Rawalpindi: Pak American Commercial Pvt. Ltd., 1991.

Ali, Sardar Asef Ahmad. "Three Stage Proximity Talks." The Nation, June 30, 1999.

Akbar, M. J. *India: The Siege Within: Challenges to a Nation's Unity*. New Delhi: Roli Books Pvt. Ltd. Lotus Collection, 2003.

Akhtar, Hasan, "Talks with Chinese Leaders 'totally satisfactory': FO," Dawn, July 2, 1999.

Akhtar, Hasan, "Pakistan Ready to Meet Any Eventuality," Dawn, July 1, 1999.

Akhund, Iqbal. *On Revitalizing the International Order, Wye Paper – A Series on Governance.* New York: Aspen Institute for Humanistic Studies, 1983.

"APC Demands OIC Summit at Islamabad," Dawn, July 1, 1999.

Arif, General (Retd.) Khalid Mahmud, "What Realism Demands," Dawn, July 3, 1999.

Arif, General (Retd.) Khalid Mahmud. *Working with Zia, Pakistan's Power Politics 1977-1988.* Karachi: Oxford University Press, 1995.

Associated Press Report, "India Launches Major Offensive in Kargil," The News, May 17, 1999.

Aziz, K. K. *The Murder of History – A critique of history textbooks used in Pakistan.* Lahore: Vanguard Books Pvt. Ltd., 1993.

Aziz, K. K. *World Powers and the 1971 Breakup of Pakistan.* Lahore: Vanguard Books Pvt. Ltd., 2003.

Aziz, Qutbuddin. *Blood and Tears.* Karachi: United Press of Pakistan Ltd., 1974.

Aziz, Sartaj. *Between Dreams and Realities: Some Milestones in Pakistan's History.* Karachi: Oxford University Press, 2011.

Bajwa, Farooq. *From Kutch to Tashkent, the Indo-Pakistan war of 1965.* New Delhi: Pentagon Press, 2014.

Bammi, Lt. Gen. (Retd.) Y. M. *Kargil 1999: The Impregnable Conquered.* Dehra Dun: Natraj Publishers, 2002.

Barnet, Richard J. *Roots of War: The Men and Institutions behind U.S. Foreign Policy.* New York: Penguin Books Ltd., 1973. (1st published by Atheneum Publishers 1972)

Baxter, Craig, ed. *Diaries of Field Marshal Muhammad Ayub Khan 1966-1972.* Karachi: Oxford University Press, 2007.

Bhargava, G. S. *Success or Surrender? The Simla Summit.* New Delhi: Sterling Publishers Pvt. Ltd., 1972.

Bhutto, Zulfikar Ali. *The Myth of Independence.* Oxford University Press, April 15, 1969.

Bhutto, Zulfikar Ali. *The Quest for Peace.* Karachi: Pakistan Institute of International Affairs, 1966.

Bhutto, Zulfikar Ali. *Reshaping Foreign Policy – A collection of articles, statements and speeches.* Lahore: Classic, ??? *purchased by ISSI in 1995*

Bindra, Dr. S. S. *Indo-Pak Relations: Tashkent to Simla Agreement.* New Delhi: Deep & Deep Publications, 1981.

Bolitho, Hector. *Jinnah Creator of Pakistan.* Karachi: Oxford University Press, 1966.

Bose, Sumantra. *Kashmir: Roots of Conflict, Paths to Peace.* New Delhi: Vistaar Publications, 2003.

Brodie, Bernard. *War and Politics: A major statement on the relations between military affairs and statecraft by the dean of American civilian strategists.* New York: Macmillan Publishing Co. Inc., 1973.

Burke, S. M. *Mainsprings of Indian and Pakistani Foreign Policies.* Karachi: Oxford University Press, 1975.

Brodie, Bernard. *War and Politics, A major statement on the relations between military affairs and statecraft by the dean of American civilian strategists.* New York: Macmillan Publishing Co. Inc., 1978.

Burke, S. M. and Ziring, Lawrence. *Pakistan's Foreign Policy, An Historical Analysis*, Second Edition. Karachi: Oxford University Press, 1994.

Burki, Shahid Javed. *Pakistan Fifty Years of Nationhood.* Lahore: Vanguard Books (Pvt.) Ltd., 1999.

Chaliand, Gerard. *Guerrilla Strategies: An Historical Anthology from the Long March to Afghanistan.* London: University of California Press, 1982.

Chandran, Ramesh, "United States Views Kargil with Serious Concern," The Times of India, June 1, 1999.

Cheema, Pervaiz Iqbal. *The Armed Forces of Pakistan.* Karachi: Oxford University Press, 2002.

Clancy, Tom, Zinni, Anthony C. and Koltz, Tony. *Battle Ready.* XXX: Putnam Adult, 2004

Clausewitz, Carl Von. *On War*, edited and translated by Howard, Michael and Paret, Peter. New Jersey: Princeton University Press, 1976.

Clinton, Bill. *My Life.* New York: Knopf Doubleday Publishing Group, 2004.

Cloughley, Brian. *A History of the Pakistan Army: Wars and Insurrections.* Karachi: Oxford University Press, 1999.

Cohen, Stephen P. *Shooting for a Century: Finding Answers to the India-Pakistan Conundrum.* Noida: HarperCollins Publishers, 2013.

Cohen, Stephen P. and others. *The Future of Pakistan.* Washington D.C.: The Brookings Institute Press, 2011.

Coll, Steve. *Ghost Wars, the secret history of the CIA, Afghanistan, and Bin Laden from the Soviet invasion to September 10, 2001.* New York: The Penguin Press, 2004.

Deshpande, Urmilla. *Kashmir Blues.* New Delhi: Tranquebar Press, 2010.

Dixit, J. N. *Anatomy of a Flawed Inheritance, Indo-Pak Relations, 1970-1994.* Delhi: Konark Publishers Pvt. Ltd., 1995.

Durrani, Lt. Gen. (Retd.) M. Asad. *An Un-historic Verdict.* Lahore: Jang Publishers, 2001.

Edited by Klare, Michael T. and Kornbluh, Peter, Low Intensity Warfare: Counterinsurgency, Proinsurgency and Antiterrorism in the Eighties, (USA, Pantheon Books, New York, 1988)

Edited by Pande, Ira, A Tangled Web: Jammu & Kashmir, (India, HarperCollins Publishers, a joint venture with The India Today Group, Noida, 2011)

Edited by Singh, Air Commodore Jasjit, Kargil 1999: Pakistan's Fourth War for Kashmir, (Delhi, Institute for Defence Studies and Analyses, New Dehli, 1999)

The Kargil Review Committee Report, From Surprise to Reckoning, (India, Sage Publications, New Delhi, 1999)

Edited by Jalal, Ayesha, The Oxford Companion to Pakistani History, (Pakistan, OUP, Karachi, 2012)

Edited by Raza, Rafi, Pakistan in Perspective 1947-1997, (Pakistan, OUP, Karachi, 1997)

Edited by Ali, Mehrunnisa, Readings in Pakistan Foreign Policy 1971-1998, (Karachi, OUP, Karachi, 2001)

Edited by Miller, Steven E., Strategy and Nuclear Deterrence: an International Security Reader, (USA, Princeton University Press, New Jersey, 1984)

Gates, Robert M. *Duty, Memoirs of a Secretary at War*. USA: Alfred A. Knopf, 2014.

Gauhar, Altaf. *Ayub Khan Pakistan's First Military Ruler*. Lahore: Sang-e-Meel Publications, 1994.

"George meets Opposition Leaders, Heads of US, UK missions," Indian Express, May 27, 1999.

Gilani, Justice Syed Manzoor Hussain. *The Constitution of Azad Jammu & Kashmir*. Islamabad: National Book Foundation, 2008.

Gill, Azam. *Army Reforms*. Lahore: People's Publishing House, 1979.

Gujral, I.K. *A Foreign Policy for India*. India: External Publicity Division, Ministry of External Affairs, 1998.

Haider, S. Sajad. *Flight of the Falcon: Demolishing myths of the Indo-Pak wars 1965 & 1971*. Lahore: Vanguard Books Pvt. Ltd., 2009.

Haroon, Brig. (Retd.) Asif. *Muhammad Bin Qasim to General Pervez Musharraf: Triumphs, Tribulations, Scars of 1971 Tragedy and Current Challenges*. Rawalpindi: KRL, 2000.

Haroon, Brig. (Retd.) Asif. *Roots of 1971 Tragedy*. Lahore: Sang-e-Meel Publications, 2005.

Hiro, Dilip. *The Longest August: The Unflinching Rivalry Between India and Pakistan*. New York: Nation Books, 2015.

Hussain, Col. (Retd.) Ashfaq. *Witness to Blunder: Kargil's Story Unfolds*. Lahore: Idara Matbuaat-e-Sulemani, 2008.

Hussain, Dr. Riffat, "Securing the system," Herald Dawn, October 8, 2013.

Hussain, Zahid. *Frontline Pakistan, the struggle with militants Islam*. Lahore: Vanguard Books, 2007.

Hussain, Syed Shabbir. *Lengthening Shadows: From Advent of Pakistan to Fall of Ayub*. Rawalpindi: Ferozsons Ltd., 1970.

"IAF Hits Enemy Supply Base," The Hindu, June 18, 1999.

"IAF Strikes Supply Base in Batalik," The Hindu, June 27, 1999.

"IAF Jets Pound Tiger Hills," The Hindu, June 25, 1999.

Ijaz, Mansoor, "Sharif's Tightrope Act in the Heights of Kashmir," New York Times, July 10, 1999.

Imperial Gazetter of India, Provincial Series, Kashmir and Jammu. Lahore: Sang-e-Meel Publications, 1983.

"India Agrees to Sartaj Visit for Dialogue," Times of India, June 1, 1999.

"India Confirms Kashmir Diplomacy," BBC News, June 28, 1999.

"India Moves Heavy Weapons to Pak Border," The News. May 16, 1999.

India's Kargil Crisis. Published by Directorate General of Films and Publications, Ministry of Information & Media Development, Government of Pakistan (early June 1999)

"India's statement on Nawaz-Clinton Joint Statement," Reuters, July 4, 1999.

"India Warned Against Wider Conflict: DCC Authorizes PM to Take Steps for Talks with Delhi," The News, July 3, 1999.

"Indian Envoy Rules Out Full Scale War." Dawn, May 18, 1999.

"Indian Foreign Minister: Resources on India and Pakistan, World Reaction to the Pakistani Nuclear Tests," Infoseek News Channel, May 30, 1998.

"Intruders' posts pounded," Tribune India, July 21, 1999.

Iype, George, "India intensifies diplomatic barrage to down Pakistan," Rediff On The Net, June 22, 1999.

Jacob, Lt. Gen. J. FR. *Surrender at Dacca, Birth of a Nation*. New Delhi: Manohar Publishers, 1997.

Jaffrelot, Christophe. *The Pakistan Paradox: Instability and Resilience*, translated by Schoch, Cynthia. Haryana: Random House India, 2015.

Jalal, Ayesha. *The Sole Spokesman: Jinnah, the Muslim League and the Demand for Pakistan*. Cambridge: Cambridge University Press, 1985.

Javed, Brig. Hasan, "The fight for Siachen," The Express Tribune, April 22, 2012.

Jayaraman, T. "Nuclear Crisis in South Asia." Frontline Volume XXX, Issue XXX, 21 June 2002.

J., General (Retd.) Mohammad Musa H. *My Version: India-Pakistan War 1965*. Lahore: Wajidalis Limited, 1983.

"JI Chief Vows to Oust Nawaz Within 'Few Weeks'," The News, July 17, 1999.

Jomini, Antoine Henri de. *The Art of War*. USA: Arc Manor, 2007.

Jones, Owen Bennett. *Pakistan - Eye of the Storm*. New Haven and London: Yale University Press, 2002.

Joshi, Manoj and Chengapa, Raj, "The Marathon War," India Today, June 21, 1999.

Joshi, Rajesh and Krishnan, Murali. "Time For Big Push." Outlook, June 21, 1999.

Kak, B. L. *The Fall of Gilgit: The Untold Story of Indo-Pak Affairs From Jinnah to Bhutto (1947 to July 1977)*. New Delhi: Light & Life Publishers, 1977.

Kamath, P.M. and Mathur, Krishan D. *Conduct of India's Foreign Policy*. New Delhi: South Asian Publishers, 1996.

"Kargil may be cleared by airpower." The Indian Express, May 26, 1999.

"Kashmiri separatists tell US to back out of row," Reuters, July 6, 1999.

Kasuri, Khurshid Mahmud. *Neither a Hawk Nor a Dove: An Insider's Account of Pakistan's Foreign Relations Including Details of the Kashmir Framework*. Karachi: Oxford University Press, 2015.

Kaul, Gwasha Lal. *Kashmir Through the Ages (5000 BC to 1967 AD)* (8th edition). Srinagar: Chronicle Publishing House, 1967.

Kaul, Lt. Gen. B. M. *The Untold Story*. New Delhi: Allied Publishers Private Limited, 1967.

Khan, Air Marshal Mohammad Asghar. *Pakistan at the Cross-roads*. Lahore: Ferozsons Ltd., 2000.

Khan, Brig. (Retd.) Z. A. *The Way It Was*. Pakistan: Services Book Club, 2000.

Khan, Ex. Maj. Gen. Akbar. *Raiders in Kashmir*. (2nd edition 1975). Islamabad: National Book Foundation, 1970.

Khan, Feroz Hassan. *Eating Grass: Making of the Pakistani Bomb*. New Delhi: Cambridge University Press India Pvt. Ltd., 2013.

Khan, Lt. Gen. Gul Hassan Khan. *Memoirs*. Karachi: Oxford University Press, 2005.

Khan, Major General (Retd.) Fazal Muqeem. *Pakistan's Crisis in Leadership*. Islamabad: National Book Foundation, 1973.

Khan, M. Ashgar. *We've Learnt Nothing from History – Pakistan: Politics and Military Power*. Karachi: Oxford University Press, 2005.

Khan, M. Ilyas. *PK 805 But the Truth*. Karachi: Royal Book Company, 2002.

Khan, Gohar Ayub. *Testing Times as Foreign Minister*. Islamabad: Dost Publications, 2009.

Khan, Roedad, *Pakistan – A Dream Gone Sour*. Karachi: Oxford University Press, 1997.

Khan, Wali. *Facts are Facts: The Untold Story of India's Partition*, translation by Hameed, Dr. Syeda Saiyidain. New Delhi: Vikas Publishing House Pvt. Ltd., 1987.

Khan, Yasmin. *The Great Partition: The Making of India and Pakistan*. New Delhi: Penguin Books India Pvt. Ltd., 2007.

Khasru, B. Z. The *Bangladesh Military Coup and the CIA LINK*. New Delhi: Rupa Publications India, 2014.

Khilani, Sunil. *The Idea of India*. New York: Farrar, Straus and Giroux, 1997.

Korbel, Josef with a foreword by Nimitz, C. W. *Danger in Kashmir*. Karachi: Oxford University Press, 1954.

Krishnan, Murali. "Battle Repor:t Cold Facts." Outlook, June 21, 1999.

Krishnaswami, Sridhar, "Clinton Talks to Sharif, Vajpayee," The Hindu, July 5, 1999.

Krishnaswami, Sridhar. "US Hopes Sharif will keep His Word." The Hindu, July 7, 1999.

Lamb, Alastair. *Kashmir A Disputed Legacy 1846-1990*. Karachi: Oxford University Press, 1992.

Lamb, Alastair. *Birth of a Tragedy Kashmir 1947*. Karachi: Oxford University Press, 2001.

"Lampher Felt Pakistan Wants to Withdraw: Brajesh," The Pioneer, July 3, 1999.

Lavoy, Peter R. *Asymmetric Warfare in South Asia, the Causes and Consequences of the Kargil Conflict*. New York: Cambridge University Press, 2009.

"LOC Firing Violation of Lahore Declaration," Dawn, May 16, 1999.

Lodhi, Maleeha, "Anatomy of a Debacle," Newsline, July 1999

Malhotra, Jyoti, "Aziz visit on, gloves are off," The Indian Express, June 1, 1999.

Malik, General V. P. *From Surprise to Victory*. New Delhi: HarperCollins Publishers, a joint venture with India Today Group, 2007.

Marker, Jamsheed, *Quiet Diplomacy Memoirs of an Ambassador of Pakistan*. Karachi: Oxford University Press, 2010.

Markey, Daniel S. *No Exit from Pakistan: America's Tortured Relationship with Islamabad*. New York: Cambridge University Press, 2013.

Masud, Mahdi, "Kargil Crisis: A Balance Sheet," The Dawn, July 16, 1999.

Mathur, Krishan D. and Kamath, P.M. *Conduct of India's Foreign Policy*. New Delhi: South Asian Publishers: 1996.

Matinuddin, Lt. Gen. (Retd.) Kamal. *Tragedy of Errors (East Pakistan Crisis, 1968-1971)*. Lahore: Wajidalis (Pvt.) Ltd., 1994.

Mattoo, Amitabh, "Kargil's Blunders: Book Review Harinder Baweja's 'A Soldier's Diary'," India Today, April 24, 2000.
McPherson, Kenneth. *'How Best Do We Survive?' A Modern Political History of the Tamil Muslims*. New Delhi: Routledge, 2010.
Menon, V. P. *The Story of the Integration of the Indian States*. Calcutta: Orient Longmans Pvt. Ltd., 1956.
Menon, V. P. *The Transfer of Power in India*. New Delhi: Orient Longmans Pvt. Ltd., 1968.
Munir, Chief Justice of Pakistan (Retd.) Muhammad. *From Jinnah to Zia*. Lahore: Vanguard Books (Pvt) Ltd., 1980.
Murlidharan, Sukumar. "Nuclear Issues: The Aftershocks." Frontline Volume XX, Issue XX, June 20 – July 3, 1998.
Murshed, S. Iftikhar. *Afghanistan: The Taliban Years*. London: Bennet & Bloom, 2006.
Musharraf, Parvez. *In the Line of Fire: A Memoir*. London: Simon and Schuster, 2006.
National Commission on Terrorist Attacks Upon the United States, "Day One Transcript: 9/11 Commission Hearing," The Washington Post, March 23, 2004.
Niazi, Lieutenant-General (R) A. A. K. *The Betrayal of East Pakistan*. Karachi: Oxford University Press, 1998.
Noorani, A. G. *The Kashmir Dispute 1947-2012*. Karachi: Oxford University Press, 2014.
Parthasarthy, Gopalaswami and Khan, Humayun. *Diplomatic Divide: Cross-border Talks*. New Delhi: Lotus Collection Roli Books, 2004.
Raghavan, Lt-Gen. V. R. *Siachen: Conflict Without End*. New Delhi: Penguin Books India, 2002.
Razvi, Dr. S. M. Mujtaba. *Frontiers of Pakistan*. Rawalpindi: Army Education Press, 1971.
Riedel, Bruce. *American Diplomacy and the 1999 Kargil Summit at Blair House*. Center for Advance Study of India, University of Pennsylvania, Policy Paper Series, 2002.
Riedel, Bruce. *Deadly Embrace: Pakistan, America and the Future of the Global Jihad*. Washington D.C.: Brookings Institution Press, 2012.
Riza, Major General (Retd.) Shaukat. *Izzat-o-Iqbal*. Nowshera: School of Artillery, 1980.
Riza, Major General (Retd.) Shaukat. *The Pakistan Army 1966-71*. Dehra Dun: Natraj Publishers, 1977.
Rizvi, Hasan-Askari. *The Military & Politics in Pakistan, 1947-86*. Lahore: Progressive Publishers, 1986.
Rizvi, Hassan-Askari. *NATIONAL SECURITY COUNCIL: A debate on institutions and processes for decision-making on security issues*. Islamabad: PILDAT Discussion Paper, 2012.
Rose, Leo E. and Husain, Noor A. *United States – Pakistan Forum: Relations with the Major Powers*. Lahore: Vanguard Books, 1987.
Salik, Naeem. *The Genesis of South Asian Nuclear Deterrence, Pakistan's Perspective*. Karachi: Oxford University Press, 2009.
Salik, Siddiq. *Witness to Surrender*. Karachi: Oxford University Press, 1977.
Schofield, Victoria. *Kashmir in Conflict: India, Pakistan and the Unfinished War*. London: I. B. Tauris and Co. Ltd., 2000.

Seervai, H. M., *Partition of India Legend and Reality*. Rawalpindi: Services Book Club, 1989.

Shaqat, Saeed. *Civil Military Relations in Pakistan: From Zulfikar Ali Bhutto to Benazir Bhutto*. Colorado: HarperCollins Publisher Inc., 1997.

Shah, Aqil. *The Army and Democracy Military Politics in Pakistan*. India: Harvard University Press, 2014.

Shahi, Agha. *Pakistan's Security and Foreign Policy*. Lahore: Progressive Publishers, 1988.

Sharma, B. L. *The Kashmir Story*. Bombay: Asia Publishing House, 1967.

Sharma, General (Retd.) V. N. *Overview to Lt. General Y. M. Bammi's Kargil The Impregnable Conquered*. Noida: Gorkha Publishers, 2002.

Siddiqi, Brigadier A. R. *The Military in Pakistan: Image and Reality*. Lahore: Pakistan, Vanguard Books Ltd., 1996.

Sattar, Abdul. *Pakistan's Foreign Policy 1947-2005: A Concise History*. Karachi: Oxford University Press, 2007.

Siddiqa, Ayesha. *Military INC., Inside Pakistan's Military Economy, 1947-2007*. Karachi: Oxford University Press, 2007.

Singh, Air Commodore Jasjit. *Kargil 1999, Pakistan's Fourth War for Kashmir*. New Delhi: October 1999.

Singh, Jaswant. *India at Risk: Mistakes, Misconceptions and Misadventures of Security Policy*. New Delhi: Rupa Publication India Pvt. Ltd., 2013.

Singh, Jaswant. *In Service of Emergent India: A Call to Honor*. Indiana University Press, 2007.

Singh, Maj. Gen. V. K. *India's External Intelligence: Secrets of Research and Analysis Wing (RAW)*. New Delhi: Manas Publications, 2007.

Sisson, Richard and Rose, Leo E. *War and Secession, Pakistan, India, and the creation of Bangladesh*. USA: University of California Press, 1990.

Talbot, Ian. *Pakistan: A Modern History*. London: Hurst & Company, 2005.

Talbot, Ian. *Pakistan: A Modern History* (updated edition). New York: Palgrave Macmillan, 2005.

Talbott, Strobe. *Engaging India: Diplomacy, Democracy, and the Bomb*. Washington: The Brookings Institution, 2004.

Wariach, Sohail. *Ghadaar Kaun?* XXX: Saagar Publications, 2006.

Whitehead, Andrew. *A Mission in Kashmir*. New Delhi: Penguin Books India Pvt. Ltd., 2007.

Williams, L. F. Rushbrook. *Pakistan Under Challenge*. London: Stacey International, 1975.

Wirsing, Robert G. *Kashmir in the Shadow of War: Regional Rivalries in a Nuclear Age*, New York: M E Sharpe Inc., 2003.

Wiessman, Steve and Krosney, Herbert. *The Islamic Bomb*. New York: New York Times Books, 1981.

Tamimi, Dr. Muhammad Jahangir. *An Analytical Study of Indian Foreign Policy*. Lahore: Centre for South Asian Studies, 2008.

Toor, Saadia. *The State of Islam: Culture and Cold War Politics in Pakistan*. London: Pluto Press, 2011.
The Kargil Review Committee Report. From Surprise to Reckoning. New Delhi: Saga Publications, 1999.
Wolpert, Stanley. *India and Pakistan: Continued Conflict or Cooperation?* California: University of California Press, 2010.
Wolpert, Stanley. *Shameful Flight: The Last Years of the British Empire in India*. Karachi: Oxford University Press, 2012.
Zafar, S. M. *Through the Crisis*. Lahore: Book Centre, 1970.
Zaheer, Hassan. *The Times and Trial of the Rawalpindi Conspiracy 1951, the First Coup Attempt in Pakistan*. Karachi: Oxford University Press, 1998.
Zaheer, Hasan. *The Separation of East Pakistan, The Rise and Realization of Bengali Muslim Nationalism*. Karachi: Oxford University Press, 1994.

Articles

Baruah, Amit, "Raising the Stakes," Frontline Volume XX, Issue XX, June 20 – July 3, 1998.
Baruah, Amit. "A 'sell-out' and some hard-sell." Frontline, Volume XX, Issue XX, July 30, 1999.
Baruah, Amit, "Sharif's US visit may be a turning point," The Hindu, July 5, 1999.
Beg, General Mirza Aslam, "Response Modalities on Kargil," The Nation, July 4, 1999.
Bokhari, Farhan, "Militants in Pakistan Protests Against Agreement on Kashmir," Financial Times (London, England), July 7, 1999.
Bokhari, Farhan, "Militants in Pakistan Protest against Agreement on Kashmir," Financial Times, July 7, 1999.
Butt, Tariq. "Nisar, Majeed Airdash to US to Assist Nawaz." The Nation, July 5, 1999.
"Musharraf planned coup much before Oct 12: Fasih Bokhari," Daily Times, October 7, 2002.
Najam, Adil, "U.S. Response To Tests," The News, June 3, 1998.
Yusufzai, Rahimullah. "General Ali Kuli refutes Musharraf's narrative." The News, October 5, 2006.
Zehra, Nasim. "Prime Minister's Sunday Surprise." The News, July 5, 1999.
Zulfiqar, Raja. "PM Leaves for US Amid Continuing LOC Crisis." The News, July 4, 1999.
"Accountability is here to stay." The Friday Times, Volume IX, No. 9, May 2 – 8, 1997.
"China Cautions Against Nuclear Race in South Asia," The Hindu, June 30, 1999.
Cleave, Jan, "Moscow, Delhi to sign cooperation declaration," Asia Times On-Line, May 28, 1999.
"Clinton Invites Vajpayee," Tribune, July 5, 1999.
Constable, Pamela. "Domestic Pressures Imperil Kashmir Peace Deal." The Washington Post, July 5, 1999.
"Cool Indica," The Indian Express, June 1, 1999.
"Crying Nuclear Wolf," The Times of India, June 2, 1999.

Datta-Ray, Sunanda K. “Being Friends of Bill.” The Telegraph, June 26, 1999.

“DCC Okays 3 Pronged Strategy to Tackle Issue,” The Dawn, July 3, 1999.

“Declare Pakistan a Rogue State: Ackerman.” The Pioneer, June 11, 1999.

“China Cautions Against Nuclear Race in South Asia,” The Hindu, June 30, 1999.

Cleave, Jan, “Moscow, Delhi to sign cooperation declaration,” Asia Times On-Line, May 28, 1999.

“Clinton Invites Vajpayee,” Tribune, July 5, 1999.

Constable, Pamela. “Domestic Pressures Imperil Kashmir Peace Deal.” The Washington Post, July 5, 1999.

“Cool Indica,” The Indian Express, June 1, 1999.

“Crying Nuclear Wolf,” The Times of India, June 2, 1999.

Datta-Ray, Sunanda K. “Being Friends of Bill.” The Telegraph, June 26, 1999.

“DCC Okays 3 Pronged Strategy to Tackle Issue,” The Dawn, July 3, 1999.

“Declare Pakistan a Rogue State: Ackerman.” The Pioneer, June 11, 1999.

Dubey. Muchkund, “Kargil & the limits of diplomacy,” The Hindu, July 5, 1999.

Dugger, Celia W. and Bearak, Barry, ”Kashmir Thwarts India-Pakistan Attempt at Trust,” New York Times, July 4, 1999.

Dugger, Celia W. “Pakistani's Pullout Vow: A Very Hard Sell at Home,” New York Times, July 6, 1999.

“China Cautions Against Nuclear Race in South Asia,” The Hindu, June 30, 1999.

Cleave, Jan, “Moscow, Delhi to sign cooperation declaration,” Asia Times On-Line, May 28, 1999.

“Clinton Invites Vajpayee,” Tribune, July 5, 1999.

Constable, Pamela. “Domestic Pressures Imperil Kashmir Peace Deal.” The Washington Post, July 5, 1999.

“Cool Indica,” The Indian Express, June 1, 1999.

“Crying Nuclear Wolf,”The Times of India, June 2, 1999.

Datta-Ray, Sunanda K. “Being Friends of Bill.” The Telegraph, June 26, 1999.

“DCC Okays 3 Pronged Strategy to Tackle Issue,” The Dawn, July 3, 1999.

“Declare Pakistan a Rogue State: Ackerman.” The Pioneer, June 11, 1999.

Filkins, Dexter, “Pakistani Admits Troops Are Fighting Indians in Kashmir,” Los Angeles Times, June 17, 1999.

Ganon, Kathy, “Will se any weapon’ threatens Shamshad,” Indian Express, June 1, 1999.

Gauhar, Altaf, “Four Wars, One Assumption,” The Nation, September 5, 1999.

Noorani, A. G. “Truth About the Lahore Summit.” Frontline Volume 19, Issue 4, February 16 – March 1, 2002.

Noorani, A. G., “Review Article on Siachin: Conflict Without End by Lt. Gen. V. R. Raghavan,” Frontline Vol 19, Issue 23

“No Room For Ambiguity.” The News, July 4, 1999.

“Nawaz Reiterates Call for Dialogue,” Dawn, July 2, 1999.

“Nawaz Visits Forward Artillery Position,” Dawn, June 25, 1999.

“No Change in LOC, says Sartaj,” Dawn, July 4, 1999.

Nehru, Jawaharlal. *Toward Freedom: The Autobiography of Jawaharlal Nehru.* USA: The John Day Company, 1941.
"New Delhi Rejects Talks Offer," Dawn, July 3, 1999.
"Official Denies Differences Between Sharif, Army Chief," The News, July 7, 1999.
"OIC Endorses Pakistan Stand on Kashmir," Dawn, July 2, 1999.
"Pakistan Army Captures Held Kashmir Village," The Nation, May 15, 1999.
"Pakistan Bears Burden to End the Confrontation," The Houston Chronicle, July 7, 1999.
"Pakistan's Failure," The Pioneer, June 1, 1999.
"Pakistan-India War Delayed Not Over," The News, July 26, 1999.
"Pakistan Reinforces Retreating," Press Trust India, June 30, 1999.
"Party Leaders Demand Sharif Government Resign," The News, July 17, 1999.
"People, Ruling Elite Surprised at PM's US Visit." The News, July 5, 1999.
"PM Accepts talks offer, says situation war-like: PM," Statesmen, June 1, 1999.
"PM Dashes to US to discuss LOC tension," The Nation, July 4, 1999.
"PM defends bus trip to Lahore," The Tribune India, April 18, 1999.
Reuters, "Japan offers to host Indo-Pak Talks," The Tribune, August 7, 1998.
Sawant, Gaurav C. "Army Blasts its way for a permanent stay at LOC." The Indian Express, July 27, 1999.
Sehbai, Shaheen, "PM Rushes to US for talks with Clinton," Dawn, July 4, 1999.
Sehbai, Shaheen, "US Congress Asks Pakistan to Pull out," Dawn, July 3, 1999.
"Sharif's sectarian nemesis," The Friday Times, Volume IX, No. 47, January 23 – 29, 1998.
Sharma, Pranat, "Dehli hits Sharif with Army Tape Talk," The Telegraph, July 4, 1999.
Sheikh, Shakeel, "Sharif, Clinton to Hold Strategic Dialogue," The News, July 4, 1999.
Sheikh, Shakeel, "DCC to Approve Final Strategy Today," The News, July 2, 1999.
"Shut up or else," The Friday Times Volume IX, No 41, December 12 – 18, 1997
Siddiqui, Aziz. "Downhill from Kargil." Dawn, June 29, 1999.
Siddiqui, Aziz, "In the Aftermath of 'Jihad'," The Dawn, July 11, 1999
Siddiqi, Kamal, "Pakistan Army Chief Admits Troops are in Kargil," Indian Express, June 27, 1999.
Sood, Lt. General V. K. "No Need for New Pressure Points." The Pioneer. May 31, 1993.
Stateman News Service, "Vajpayee turns down Clinton Invitation," Stateman, July 5, 1999.
Stockwin, Harvey (and Agencies), "China refuses to Bite the Sharif Bait, urges Talks," Times of India, June 30, 1999.
"The DCC Meeting," The Nation, July 4, 1999.
"Talking Terms." Times of India, June 1, 1999.
"The Stuff of History," The Friday Times, Volume X, No 22, July 31 – 6 August, 1998.
"US Asks Pakistan to Withdraw Mujahideen," The News, July 3, 1999.
"US Has Impression Pakistan Wants to Withdraw Forces." The News, July 3, 1999.
"US Points fingers at Pakistan." The Australian, July 6, 1999.

"US Says Pakistan Will Withdraw, Bradley Graham, Nathan Abse," The Washington Post, July 5, 1999.

"Vajpayee turns down Clinton Invitation," The Statesman, July 5, 1999.

Venkatesan, V. "The BJP's trauma." Frontline Volume 16, Issue 10, May 8 – 21, 1999.

"Withdrawal Not in Pakistan-US Statement," The News, July 7, 1999.

"Yeltsin talks to Jaswant Singh." The Tribune, May 26, 1999.

"Weiner and Risen: Policy Makers, Diplomats, Intelligence Officers All Missed India's Intentions." New York Times, May 25, 1998.

Newspapers/Periodicals

Pakistani

The Nation

The News

Dawn

Jang

Friday Times

Herald

NewsLine

Urdu Digest

Indian

The Hindu

Hindustan Times

The Indian Express

The Tribune

The Telegraph

The Statesman

Frontline

Others

The New York Times

Washington Post

BBC Website

UN Documents

Declassified Clinton Library.: The White House Washington: Memorandum of Telephone Conversation between President and Prime Minister Nawaz Sharif, December 18, 1998.

INDEX

M

N

O

P

Q

R

S

T

U

V

W

Z